C000138107

OXFORD MONOGRAPHS ON LABOUR LAW

*General Editors*: PAUL DAVIES, KEITH EWING,
MARK FREEDLAND

# The Legal Construction of Personal Work Relations

# OXFORD MONOGRAPHS ON LABOUR LAW

*General Editors*: Paul Davies, Fellow of Jesus College and Allen and Overy Professor of Corporate Law in the University of Oxford; Keith Ewing, Professor of Public Law at King's College, London; and Mark Freedland, Fellow of St John's College, and Professor of Employment Law in the University of Oxford.

This series has come to represent a significant contribution to the literature of British, European, and international labour law. The series recognizes the arrival not only of a renewed interest in labour law generally, but also the need for fresh approaches to the study of labour law following a period of momentous change in the UK and Europe. The series is concerned with all aspects of labour law, including traditional subjects of study such as collective labour law and individual employment law. It also includes works that concentrate on the growing role of human rights and the combating of discrimination in employment, and others that examine the law and economics of the labour market and the impact of social security law and of national and supranational employment policies upon patterns of employment and the employment contract. Two of the contributing authors to the series, Lucy Vickers and Diamond Ashiagbor, have received awards from the Society of Legal Scholars in respect of their books.

Some of the titles already published in this series

*Freedom of Speech and Employment Strategy*
LUCY VICKERS

*Regulating Flexible Work*
DEIRDRE MCCANN

*The Law of the Labour Market*
SIMON DEAKIN AND
FRANK WILKINSON

*The Personal Employment Contract*
MARK FREEDLAND

*The European Employment Strategy*
DIAMOND ASHIAGBOR

*EU Intervention in Domestic Labour Law*
PHIL SYRPIS

*Towards a Flexible Labour Market*
PAUL DAVIES AND MARK
FREEDLAND

*A Right to Care?*
NICOLE BUSBY

# The Legal Construction of Personal Work Relations

MARK FREEDLAND FBA
NICOLA KOUNTOURIS

OXFORD
UNIVERSITY PRESS

# OXFORD
## UNIVERSITY PRESS

Great Clarendon Street, Oxford OX2 6DP

Oxford University Press is a department of the University of Oxford.
It furthers the University's objective of excellence in research, scholarship,
and education by publishing worldwide in

Oxford New York

Auckland Cape Town Dar es Salaam Hong Kong Karachi
Kuala Lumpur Madrid Melbourne Mexico City Nairobi
New Delhi Shanghai Taipei Toronto

With offices in

Argentina Austria Brazil Chile Czech Republic France Greece
Guatemala Hungary Italy Japan Poland Portugal Singapore
South Korea Switzerland Thailand Turkey Ukraine Vietnam

Oxford is a registered trade mark of Oxford University Press
in the UK and in certain other countries

Published in the United States
by Oxford University Press Inc., New York

© M. Freedland and N. Kountouris, 2011

The moral rights of the authors have been asserted
Database right Oxford University Press (maker)

Crown copyright material is reproduced under Class Licence
Number C01P0000148 with the permission of OPSI
and the Queen's Printer for Scotland

First published 2011

British Library Cataloguing in Publication Data

Data available

Library of Congress Cataloging in Publication Data

Library of Congress Control Number : 2011939966

Typeset by SPI Publisher Services, Pondicherry, India
Printed in Great Britain
on acid-free paper by
CPI Group (UK) Ltd, Croydon, CRO 4YY

ISBN 978-0-19-955175-0

1 3 5 7 9 10 8 6 4 2

For Antonio and Taiga
and their families past, present, and future

# *Preface*

The present work has two direct predecessors and one indirect one, and we regard and offer this book as an evolution from those successive works. The two directly preceding books were those of the first author of this work, Mark Freedland, namely his treatise on *The Contract of Employment* (1976), and the re-written and extended version of it, *The Personal Employment Contract* (2003). The third preceding work is that of the second author of this book, Nicola Kountouris, *The Changing Law of the Employment Relationship* (2007). The nature and objectives of this cumulative evolution are described in the Introduction and the first Part of the book itself; the main purpose of this Preface is to identify the practical and institutional arrangements which have enabled this fourth instalment of that writing project to be produced, and to acknowledge the many personal debts which we have incurred along the way.

Two particular aspects of those institutional arrangements have been crucial in providing the resources of research and writing time which have enabled this latest work to be produced. The first of these consisted in the conferring upon the first author by the Leverhulme Trust of a Major Research Fellowship from 2005–8 for the carrying out of this project. The generosity of the Trustees is acknowledged with profound appreciation and gratitude, as is the constantly supportive approach of the Director and staff of the Trust. The other crucial arrangement consisted in the agreement of the second author to participate in the project as co-author, and to contribute insights developing from his own previous and current work, without which the project could not have been brought to fruition in its present form. The second author has also greatly benefited from a generously funded AHRC Research Leave.

Both authors have many further acknowledgements to make. At the outset of the project, we had in common St John's College Oxford as an employing institution. The enlightened approach of the College towards the support of the research and the career development of its Fellows has been of enormous significance to both of us. The same can be said of our two currently respective Law Faculties, those of the University of Oxford and of University College London, as well as the second author's previous employer, the University of Reading.

Moreover, various publishing houses and their respective editors have been more than helpful to us. The publishers and editors of various journals and symposia have graciously accepted that the content of some articles and chapters submitted to them along the way would eventually be embodied in this book; we particularly acknowledge in this respect that generosity on the part of the published lecture series Current Legal Problems, the Industrial Law Journal, and, most especially, the International Labour Review in respect of the first author's article, published there in 2007, on the 'Application of labour and employment law beyond the contract of employment'. Other editors and publishers have facilitated our access to works in the course of publication or immediately upon publication; may we single out in that respect Roger Blanpain and Michele Colucci of the International Encyclopedia for Labour Law and Industrial Relations published by Kluwer Law International, and Richard Hart of Hart Publishing for various such acts of kindness and co-operation. However, first and foremost in this part of our acknowledgements must come the Oxford University Press, as the publishers of the Industrial Law Journal and of this book itself. The commissioning and production editors who have worked with us on this book have been endlessly patient and constructive in their dealings with us, and we especially thank Gwen Booth, Alex Flach, Natasha Flemming, David Lewis, and John Louth, and in another sense Paul Davies and Keith Ewing as the other Series Editors of the Oxford Monographs on Labour Law series in which this book is published and themselves contributors to the sources of intellectual inspiration for this work.

In that latter respect there are many other colleagues to whom our indebtedness is intense for being in various senses the interlocutors and 'critical friends' for our work as it took shape. It is all too likely that the list which follows, long though it is, nevertheless omits some who might have a real claim to be included in it, to whom we apologise; but we wish to name Harry Arthurs, Diamond Ashiagbor, Sue Ashtiany, Lizzie Barmes, Catherine Barnard, Alan Bogg, Alexandra Braun, Douglas Brodie, Giuseppe Casale, Hugh Collins, Sean Cooney, Guy Davidov, Anne Davies, Simon Deakin, Ruth Dukes, Muriel Fabre-Magnan, Matthew Finkin, Sandra Fredman, Judy Fudge, Mario Giovanni Garofalo, François Gaudu, Juan Gorelli-Hernández, Rachel Horton, Guus Heerma van Voss, Bob Hepple, John Howe, Jean-Claude Javillier, Claire Kilpatrick, Robert Knegt, Brian Langille, Julia Lopez, Virginia Mantouvalou, Christopher McCrudden, Luca Nogler, Wanjiru Njoya, Antonio Ojeda Avilés, Jeremias Prassl, Robert Rebhahn, Joellen Riley, Silvana Sciarra, Spiros Simitis, Vanessa Sims (whom we specially thank for the opportunity to consult her Doctoral thesis on 'Good Faith in English and German Contract Law'), Katherine Stone, Alain Supiot, Bruno Veneziani, Evert Verhulp, Lucy Vickers, Christophe Vigneau, Aurora Vimercati, Nicholas Vrousalis, Bernd Waas, Manfred Weiss, and Simon Whittaker. Although these colleagues could between them lay claim to have inspired many of the ideas to be found in this work, they bear no responsibility for its shortcomings. Still less do our families, in particular Geraldine and Isobel, who have had to sacrifice a good deal of our time and attention to this project of research and writing.

We have sought to bring our work up to date to January 2011 but have included some subsequent developments where appropriate. There is one such development which occurred too late for treatment in this work but is of real significance to some of the central arguments of our work, namely the decision of the UK Supreme Court in *Jivraj v Hashwani* [2011] UKSC 40. Arrangements have been made for the publication of an article in the Industrial Law Journal early in 2012 in which we will seek to relate that decision to the arguments advanced in this work.

MARK FREEDLAND
NICOLA KOUNTOURIS

Oxford and London
31 July 2011

# General Editors' Preface

We write this preface on the day that regulations come into force in Great Britain to enhance the rights of temporary agency workers. These controversial regulations – introduced to implement an equally contentious EU Directive – do not, however, address the central question which has vexed English courts and tribunals for some time, this being the legal status of such workers, which will remain to be contested.

The position of agency workers in the United Kingdom is but one of many problems of modern labour law, with its competing demands of the worker for job security and those of the employer for greater flexibility. As such, however, it raises fundamental questions about the purpose, scope, and content of what the authors of this volume encourage us to think of as 'the law of the personal work relationship', questions being asked with growing urgency in a fast-moving global economy.

As editors, we are particularly pleased to introduce this volume to the 'Oxford Monographs on Labour Law' series. The volume builds on the highly acclaimed writings of both authors, and the productive result of this collaboration is work of profound scholarship. In addressing key problems of modern labour law, their study is greatly enriched by its fresh theoretical insights, its comparative methodology, and its infusion by the jurisprudence and literature of other European systems.

More than that, however, the authors provide a fundamental re-analysis of the legal foundations of modern labour law, and in doing so invite law-makers and theorists to reconsider 'the ways in which personal work relations might be legally constructed more rigorously and comprehensively than they at present are' ( p. 76). The book thus offers a most rewarding basis for a reconsideration of the legal construction of personal work relations, at a time when it is sorely needed.

But not only do the authors invite us to think about 'the law of personal work relations': in this rich, profound, and challenging study, they also offer nothing less than a re-conceptualisation of labour law itself. A persuasive new framework is offered as a normative basis for the discipline, focussing upon 'a set of positive claims which workers have to certain kinds of qualities of treatment' (p. 371), these being dignity, capability, and stability at work, all expounded with characteristic lucidity.

In introducing this volume we do so confident in the belief that it will not only be widely admired, but also that it will add greatly to the reputation of the series. This is a quite exceptional book, which sets high standards for labour law scholarship. Just as importantly, it will have long-term implications: not only for how we think about the discipline of labour law, but also for addressing labour law problems in the future, with consequences for all workers.

PLD
KDE

1 October 2011

# Contents

Table of Cases                                                                            xvii
Table of Legislation                                                                        xxi


## PART I.  THE LEGAL ANALYSIS OF
## PERSONAL WORK RELATIONS

Introduction:  Evolution and Reformulation in the Legal
Construction of Personal Work Relations                                                       3

1. The Legal Analysis of Personal Work Relations – Boundaries,
   Paradigms, and Legal Formats                                                              11

   Introduction                                                                              11
   Section 1:  The Relational Scope of Labour Law – An Initial Analysis                      11
   Section 2:  The Personal Work Relation as the Domain of Labour Law                        19
   Section 3:  A Functional Definition of the Personal Work Relation                         28
      A. The Suggested Definition and its Function                                           29
      B. Multiple Interfaces and Contested Areas                                             34
   Section 4:  Aligning the Personal Work Relation with Existing
               Categories                                                                    36
      A. An Emerging Pattern in European Law?                                                37
      B. The Pattern Instantiated in English Law – and in Other
         European Legal Systems                                                              42

2. A European Comparative Approach to the Legal
   Construction of Personal Work Relations                                                   44

   Introduction                                                                              44
   Section 1:  Functions and Perspectives                                                    44
   Section 2:  Methodology                                                                   48
   Section 3:  Sources of Regulation and Hierarchies of Norms                                58
      A. Introduction                                                                        58
      B. Hierarchies of Sources as Identifiers of Labour Law Systems                         62
      C. English Law and its Inherently Non-hierarchical System of Sources                   67
   Section 4:  Programme and Outcome                                                         74


## PART II.  THE PERSONAL WORK RELATION
## AS A CONTRACT

3. The Legal Construction of Personal Work Relations as Contracts                            83
   Introduction                                                                              83

Section 1: Contractuality, Individuality, and Layered Regulation   85
  A. The Law of Personal Work Contracts as Regulatory Modelling   86
  B. Individuality and Contractuality in the Law of Personal
     Work Contracts   89
  C. The Law of Personal Work Contracts as Layered Regulation   96
Section 2: The Personal Work Contract as a Definitional Category
        and the Place of the Contract of Employment within
        that Category   104
  A. The Problems of the Binary Divide   104
  B. A Comparative Assessment of the Binary Divide   112
Section 3: The Contractual Construction of Personal Work
        Relations – Towards a Multidimensional Analysis   120

4. The Formation and Structure of Contracts of Employment   129

Introduction   129
Section 1: The Conditions of Formation of Contracts of Employment   130
  A. The Nature and Functions of Conditions of Formation   130
  B. Employment-Specific Contractual Intention   134
Section 2: Other Factors in the Making of Contracts of Employment   147
  A. Illegality and Other Vitiating Factors   147
  B. Formality and Information   153
Section 3: The Personal and Organizational Structure of
        Contracts of Employment   157
  A. The Bilaterality, Individuality, and Personality of Contracts of
     Employment   158
  B. Organizational Structure   161
Section 4: The Economic Structure of Contracts of Employment   167
  A. A Two-Level Economic Structure?   168
  B. Duration, Continuity, and the Provision of Remunerated Work   171

5. The Content and Performance of Contracts of Employment   177

Introduction   177
Section 1: Implied Terms and Guiding Principles   180
  A. Implied Terms and the Regulation of Content and Performance   180
  B. Fidelity, Obedience, and the Protection of the Interests of the
     Employer or Employing Enterprise   188
  C. Care and the Protection of the Welfare of the Worker   191
  D. Towards a Principle of Mutual Trust, Good Faith, and Fair Dealing?   194
Section 2: Performance   199
  A. Integrated and Dis-integrated Approaches to the Performance of
     Contracts of Employment   199
  B. Performance and the Wage–Work Bargain   201
  C. Performance and the Continuity of Remuneration   203
Section 3: Variation   206
  A. The Contested Approach to Variation in English Employment Law   207
  B. Variation From a Comparative Perspective   208

Section 4: Suspension 213
  A. Approaches to the Regulation of Suspension, and the
    Intersection with Termination 213
  B. The Regulation of Suspension in Specific Circumstances 217

6. The Termination and Transformation of Employment Contracts 222

Introduction 222
Section 1: The Role of Contract Law in the Regulation of
       Termination of Employment 222
  A. Integrated and Dis-integrated Systems of Legal Regulation of
    Termination of Employment 223
  B. Regulation and Integration in the Contractual Construction of the
    Termination of Employment 224
Section 2: The Duration and Termination of Employment
       Contracts – a European Regulatory Spectrum 231
  A. Regulating the Time of Contractual Termination 231
  B. Specifying the Grounds and Procedures for Contractual Termination 239
Section 3: English Law as a Case-Study in the Dual Regulation of
       Termination of Employment 241
  A. The Separation Between Contractually Wrongful Dismissal and
    Unfair Dismissal in English Law 242
  B. The Low Protection of Job Security in the English Law of
    Employment Contracts 245
Section 4: The Construction of Transformations in Contractual
       Employment Relations 251
  A. Transformations in the Identity of the Employer or in the
    Ownership or Control of the Employing Enterprise 251
  B. Other Transformations 259

PART III. THE PERSONAL WORK RELATION
AS A LEGAL NEXUS

7. Personal Work Contracts Other Than the Contract of Employment 267

Introduction 267
Section 1: The Legal Categorization of Personal Work Contracts
       Other Than the Contract of Employment 267
  A. The Category Identified 267
  B. The Traditional View of Other Personal Work Contracts
    as Contracts for Services 269
  C. Other Personal Work Contracts as a Dual Category 276
  D. Other Personal Work Contracts as a Family of Contracts 284
Section 2: Formation and Structure 290
  A. Paradigm and Variety in Structure – the Personal Task
    Contract as a Paradigm for Other Personal Work Contracts? 290
  B. Intention, Formality, and Legality in Formation 296

Section 3:  Performance and Termination                         300
    A.  Performance and Content                                 300
    B.  Termination and Transformation                          302
Section 4:  The Narrowness of the Contractual Perspective       303
    A.  The Individual Independent Worker                       305
    B.  Personal Work in a Joint Enterprise                     306

8.  Contract, Relation, and Nexus in the Legal Construction
    of Personal Work Relations                                  309

    Introduction                                                309
    Section 1:  The Personal Work Relation and the Personal Work
                Nexus as Generic Concepts                       310
        A.  The Shortcomings of the Contractual Analysis of Personal
            Work Relations                                      310
        B.  Concepts for a Different Method of Analysis          313
    Section 2:  The Personal Work Relation as a Complex Network
                or Nexus                                        315
        A.  The Personal Work Nexus as the Internal Structure of the
            Personal Work Relation                              316
        B.  Contract and Relationship Within the Personal Work Nexus  322
    Section 3:  The Legal Connections of Which the Personal
                Work Nexus is Composed                          323
        A.  The Nature of These Legal Connections               324
        B.  Primary and Secondary Legal Connections             327
    Section 4:  The Personal Work Nexus and the Personal Work Relation  330
        A.  A Theoretical Perspective                           330
        B.  A Comparative Perspective                           332

9.  The Personal Work Profile and the Idea of Personality in Work   338

    Introduction                                                338
    Section 1:  The Idea of the Personal Work Profile           340
        A.  The Personal Work Profile and the Personal Work Situation  340
        B.  The Personal Work Profile and the Working Life or Career  342
    Section 2:  A Critical Taxonomy of Personal Work Relations  344
        A.  A Tri-Polar Starting Point                          344
        B.  A Scheme of Empirical Categories                    347
        C.  The Legal Construction of the Empirical Categories  349
    Section 3:  The Personal Work Profile in the Taxonomy and
                Regulation of Personal Work Relations           358
        A.  The Personal Work Profile and the Idea of Normative Characterization  358
        B.  The Personal Work Profile as a Regulatory Framework  364
    Section 4:  The Idea of Personality in Work                 369
        A.  Personality in Work as a Set of Values              370
        B.  The Component Values of Personality in Work: Dignity,
            Capability, and Stability in Work                   371

PART IV. THE PERSONAL WORK RELATION
IN EUROPEAN LAW

10. The Legal Construction of Personal Work Relations and the
       Role of European Law                                                          385

    Introduction                                                                     385
    Section 1:  European Law and the Fragmentation of Personal Work
                Regulation                                                           386
        A. The Denormalization of Personal Work Arrangements                         386
        B. The Fragmentation of EU Employment Law With Regard
           to Taxonomy                                                               390
        C. The Normative Patchiness of EU Employment Law                             396
    Section 2:  A European Legal Framework for Personal
                Work Relations                                                       399
        A. The Objectives and Main Components of a
           European Legal Framework for Personal Work Relations                      400
        B. The Methodology of a European Legal Framework
           for Personal Work Relations                                               404
        C. The Personal Work Relation as the Framing Concept for a
           European Legal Framework for Personal Work Relations                      405
        D. Multilayered Regulation and the Idea of EU Regulatory Layers              410
    Section 3:  EU Regulatory Layers as the Basis of a European
                Legal Framework for Personal Work Relations                          413
        A. The Complex Nature of EU Regulatory Layers                                414
        B. The Relational Aspect of EU Regulatory Layers                             417
        C. EU Regulatory Layers – Some Key Examples                                  421
    Section 4:  A European Legal Framework for Personal Work Relations:
                Prospects and Problems                                               428
        A. Prospects                                                                 428
        B. Problems                                                                  430


Conclusion: Mutualization and Demutualization in the Legal
Construction of Personal Work Relations                                              433

*Bibliography*                                                                       447
*Index*                                                                              461

# Table of Cases

## UNITED KINGDOM

*Addis v. Gramophone Co Ltd* [1909] AC 488(HL) . . . . . . . . . . . . . . . . . . . . .248, 250
*Allen v. Hounga* [2011] UKEAT 0326/10/LA . . . . . . . . . . . . . . . . . . . . . . . . 152
*Autoclenz Limited v. Belcher and others* [2011] UKSC 41 . . . . . . . . . . . . . . . 54, 152, 299
*Berriman v. Delabole Slate Ltd* [1985] ICR 546 . . . . . . . . . . . . . . . . . . . . . . 258
*Blue Chip Trading Ltd v. Helbawi* [2009] IRLR 128 . . . . . . . . . . . . . . . . . . . . 152
*British Telecom v. Ticehurst* [1992] ICR 383. . . . . . . . . . . . . . . . . . . . . . . . 205
*Brown v. Knowsley Borough Council* 1986] IRLR 102 . . . . . . . . . . . . . . . . . . . 240
*Bull v. Nottinghamshire and City of Nottingham Fire and Rescue Authority* [2007]
    ICR 1631 (CA) . . . . . . . . . . . . . . . . . . . . . . . . . . . . . . . . . . .211, 212
*Bunce v. Postworth Ltd* [2005] IRLR 557 . . . . . . . . . . . . . . . . . . . . . . . . . 122
*Byrne Brothers (Formwork) Ltd v. Baird* [2002] ICR 667 . . . . . . . . . . . . . . . . . . 125
*Calder v. H. Kitson Vickers & Sons (Engineers) Ltd* [1988] ICR 232. . . . . . . . . . . . 132
*Callison v. Ford Motor Co Ltd* (1969) 4 ITR 74 (IT) . . . . . . . . . . . . . . . . . . 211
*Carmichael and another v. National Power plc* [2000] IRLR 43 . . . . . . . . . . . . . . 282
*Carmichael v. National Power Plc* [1998] ICR 1167 . . . . . . . . . . . . . . . . . . . . 122
*Carmichael v. National Power plc* [1999] ICR 1226 . . . . . . . . . . . . . . . .124, 299
*Catamaran Cruisers Ltd v. Williams* [1994] IRLR 386 . . . . . . . . . . . . . . . . . . . 211
*Consistent Group Limited v. Kalwak and Others* [2008] EWCA Civ 430. . . . . . . . . . . 54
*Cornwall CC v. Prater* [2006] IRLR 362 . . . . . . . . . . . . . . . . . . . . . . . . . 174
*Cresswell v. Board of Inland Revenue* [1984] ICR 508 (QBD). . . . . . . . . . . . . . . 212
*Daley v. Allied Suppliers Ltd* [1983] IRLR 13 . . . . . . . . . . . . . . . . . . . . . . . 138
*Delaney v. Staples* [1992] 1 AC 687. . . . . . . . . . . . . . . . . . . . . . . . . . . . 234
*Delco Ltd v. Joinson* [1991] ICR 172 (EAT). . . . . . . . . . . . . . . . . . . . . . . . 247
*Devis (W.) & Sons Ltd v. Atkins* [1977] AC 931, ICR 662 (HL) . . . . . . . . . . . . . . 93
*Devonald v. Rosser & Sons Ltd* [1906] 2 KB 728 (CA) . . . . . . . . . . . . . . . . . . 218
*Diocese of Southwark v. Coker* [1998] ICR 140 . . . . . . . . . . . . . . . . . . . . . . 143
*Dunk v. George Waller & Son Ltd* [1970] 2 QB 163 . . . . . . . . . . . . . . . . . . . . 138
*Edmonds v. Lawson* [2000] ICR 567 . . . . . . . . . . . . . . . . . . 123, 138, 295
*Enfield Technical Services Limited v. Ray Payne; BF Components Limited v. Ian Grace*
    [2008] IRLR 500. . . . . . . . . . . . . . . . . . . . . . . . . . . . . . . . . . . . 150
*Express & Echo Publications Ltd v. Tanton* [1999] ICR 693. . . . . . . . . . . 53, 54, 125
*Faccenda Chicken Ltd v. Fowler* [1986] ICR 297 (CA) . . . . . . . . . . . . . . . . . . 189
*Fasuyi v. Compass Contract Services (UK) LTD*, Appeal No. UKEAT/0194/10/MW . . . . . . 318
*Flett v. Matheson* [2006] EWCA Civ 53 . . . . . . . . . . . . . . . . . 138, 139, 295
*Ford Motor Co Ltd v. AUEFW* [1969] 2 All ER 481 . . . . . . . . . . . . . . . . . . . . 70
*Gysda Cyf v. Barratt* [2010] UKSC 41 . . . . . . . . . . . . . . . . . . . . . . . . . . 208
*Hall (Inspector of Taxes) v. Lorrimer* [1994] ICR 218. . . . . . . . . . . . . . . . . . . 122
*Hall v. Woolston Hall Leisure* [2000] IRLR 578 . . . . . . . . . . . . . . . . . . . . . . 150
*Hanley v. Pease & Partners* [1915] 1 KB 698 (KBD). . . . . . . . . . . . . . . . . . . . 218
*Harrods Ltd v. Remick* [1998] 1 All E R 52; [1998] ICR 156 . . . . . . 122, 321, 322, 329–32
*Hawley v. Fieldcastle & Co. Ltd* [1982] IRLR 223 . . . . . . . . . . . . . . . . . . . . . 138
*Hellyer Bros v. McLeod* [1987] ICR 526. . . . . . . . . . . . . . . . . . . . . . . . . . 124
*Henry v. London General Transport Services Ltd* [2002] IRLR 472 (CA) . . . . . . . . . . . 94
*Her Majesty's Commissioners for Revenue & Customs v. Rinaldi-Tranter*
    [2007] WL 3389518 . . . . . . . . . . . . . . . . . . . . . . . . . . . . . . . .138, 139
*Horan v. Hayhoe* [1904] 1 KB 288 . . . . . . . . . . . . . . . . . . . . . . . . . . . . 137

*Instone v. Schroeder Music Publishing Co Ltd* [1974] 1 WLR 1308 (HL). . . . . . . . . . . 152
*IRC v. Post Office Ltd* [2003] IRLR 199 . . . . . . . . . . . . . . . . 124
*Lambden v. Henley Rugby Football Club, Henley Rugby Football Club Ltd*,
    Appeal No. UKEAT/0505/08/DA. . . . . . . . . . . . . . . . . . 275
*James v. London Borough of Greenwich* [2007] IRLR 168; [2008] ICR 545 . . . . . 166
*James v. London Borough of Greenwich* [2008] EWCA Civ 35 . . . . . . . . . . . 294
*James v. Redcats (Brands) Ltd* [2007] IRLR 296 . . . . . . . . . . . 281, 282, 334
*Johnson v. Unisys Ltd* [2001] ICR 480 (HL). . . . . . . . . . . . 199, 249, 250
*Kennaugh v. Lloyd Jones*, Appeal No. UKEAT/0236/09/RN . . . . . . . . . 318
*Lapthorne v. Eurofi Ltd* [2001] EWCA Civ 993 . . . . . . . . . . . . . . 153
*Lincolnshire County Council and Another v. Hopper* [2002] ICR 1301 . . . . . . . . . 143
*Litster v. Forth Dry Dock and Engineering Co* [1989] *IRLR* 161 . . . . . . . . . . . . 257, 258
*Manpower UK Ltd v. Vjestica*, Appeal No. UKEAT/0397/05/DM, [2005]
    All ER (D) 259 (Dec). . . . . . . . . . . . . . . . . 175, 318, 334
*MHC Consulting Services Ltd v. Tansell* [2000] ICR 789 . . . . . . . . . . . . 122
*Mirror Group Newspapers Ltd v. Gunning* [1986] ICR 145. . . . . . . . . . . . 124
*Muschett v. HM Prison Service* [2010] EWCA Civ 25, [2010] IRLR 451 . . . . . . 166, 294
*Nagle v. Feilden* [1966] 2 QB 633 (CA) . . . . . . . . . . . . . . . 152
*Nethermere (St Neots) Ltd v. Gardner* [1984] ICR 612 . . . . . . . . . 122, 124, 282
*New Century Cleaning Co Ltd v. Church* [2000] IRLR 27 . . . . . . . . . . . 122
*New Testament Church of God v. Stewart* [2007] IRLR 178 . . . . . . . . . . 143
*Nokes v. Doncaster Amalgamated Collieries Ltd* [1940] AC 1014 . . . . . . . . . 253
*O'Kelly v. Trusthouse Forte Plc* [1983] ICR 728 [1984] QB 90 . . . . . . . . . . 122, 124
*Pauley v. Kenaldo Ltd* [1953] 1 All ER 226 . . . . . . . . . . . . . . 292
*Percy v. Church of Scotland* [2005] UKHL 73 . . . . . . . . . . . . . . 143
*Protectacoat Firthglow Limited v. Szilagyi* [2009] IRLR 365. . . . . . . . . . . 152, 360
*R v. Derbyshire County Council ex parte Noble* [1990] ICR 810 (CA) . . . . . . . . 143
*Robb v. Green* [1895] 2 QB 315 . . . . . . . . . . . . . . . . . 189
*Robertson v. British Gas Corporation* [1983] ICR 351. . . . . . . . . . . . 243
*Roy v. Kensington and Chelsea Family Practitioner Committee* [1992] 1 AC 624 . . . . . 143
*Sagal (Trading as Bunz UK) v. Atelier Bunz GmbH* [2009] EWCA Civ 700 . . . . . . . 275
*Sandhu v. Jan de Rijk Transport Ltd* [2007] IRLR 519 . . . . . . . . . . . 240
*Sheehan v. Post Office Counters Ltd* [1999] ICR 73. . . . . . . . . . . . . 124
*Sheffield v. Oxford Controls Co Ltd* [1979] IRLR 133 . . . . . . . . . . . 240
*Simmons v. Hoover Ltd* [1977] ICR 61 (EAT). . . . . . . . . . . . . 218
*South East Sheffield Citizens Advice Bureau v. Grayson* [2004] ICR 1138 (EAT) . . . . . . 145
*Stevedoring and Haulage Services Ltd v. Fuller* [2001] IRLR 267 . . . . . . . . . 175
*Sybron Corprn v. Rochem Ltd* [1983] ICR 801. . . . . . . . . . . . . 190
*Thorpe v. Dul* [2003] ICR 1556 . . . . . . . . . . . . . . . . . 139
*Turner v. Mason* (1845) 14. . . . . . . . . . . . . . . . . . . 188
*University of Nottingham v. Eyett* [1999] IRLR 87 . . . . . . . . . . . . . 142
*Usetech Ltd v. Young (Inspector of Taxes)* [2004] All ER . . . . . . . . . . . 298
*Vakante v. Addey and Stanhope School* [2005] ICR 231. . . . . . . . . . . . 152
*Wallace v. CA Roofing Services Ltd* [1996] IRLR 435. . . . . . . . . . . . 138
*Western Excavating (ECC Ltd) v. Sharp* [1978] ICR 221 . . . . . . . . . . . 198
*Wilson t/a Reds v. Lamb* [2007] WL 2817984 . . . . . . . . . . . . . 139
*Wilson v. Racher* [1974] ICR 428. . . . . . . . . . . . . . . . . 188, 247
*Wiltshire County Council v. NATFHE* [1980] ICR 455 . . . . . . . . . . . 124
*Wiltshire Police Authority v. Wynn* [1980] ICR 649 . . . . . . . . . . . . 137
*X v. Mid Sussex Citizens Advice Bureau* [2010] EWCA Civ 28 ICR 429. . . . . . . . 145, 394
*Young & Woods Ltd v. West* [1980] IRLR 201. . . . . . . . . . . . . . 298

## FRANCE

Cass. Soc. 1er mars 1972, D. 1972.540. . . . . . . . . . . . . . . . . . . . . . . 237
Cass. Ass. plén. 81-11647 et 81-15290 du 4 mars 1983 . . . . . . . . . . . . . 133
Cass. Soc. 89-43162 du 2 décembre 1992 . . . . . . . . . . . . . . . . . . . 203
Cass. com. 24 janvier 1995 . . . . . . . . . . . . . . . . . . . . . . . . . . 190
Cass. com. 27 février 1996. . . . . . . . . . . . . . . . . . . . . . . . . . . . 190
Cass. Soc. 98-44292 du 27 mars 2001 . . . . . . . . . . . . . . . . . . . . . . 187
Cass. Soc. 00-41651 du 20 mars 2002 . . . . . . . . . . . . . . . . . . . . . . 258
Cass. Soc. 02-43402 du16 février 2005 . . . . . . . . . . . . . . . . . . . . . . 236
Cass. Soc. 05-40969 du 13 décembre 2006 . . . . . . . . . . . . . . . . . . . . 203
Cass. Soc. 05-42143 du 8 novembre 2006 . . . . . . . . . . . . . . . . . . . . 250
Cass. Soc. 06-41212 du 20 novembre 2007. . . . . . . . . . . . . . . . . . . . 236
Cass. Soc. 1159 du 3 juin 2009 . . . . . . . . . . . . . . . . . . . . . . . . . 54
Cass. Soc. 08-44094 du 16 mars 2010 . . . . . . . . . . . . . . . . . . . . . . 250
Conseil d'État, Avis du 22 mars 1973, Dr. Ouvrier p. 190. . . . . . . . . . . . . 65

## ITALY

Cass. Sez. Un. 7 agosto 1998 n. 7755 . . . . . . . . . . . . . . . . . . . . . . 211
Cass. Sez. Lav. 14 ottobre 1999 n. 11597. . . . . . . . . . . . . . . . . . . . . 238
Cass. Sez. Lav. 15 maggio 2007 n. 11094. . . . . . . . . . . . . . . . . . . . . 234
Cass. Sez. Lav. 20 novembre 2006 n. 24591 . . . . . . . . . . . . . . . . . . . 190
Cass. Sez. Lav. 21 maggio 2007 n. 11740. . . . . . . . . . . . . . . . . . . . . 234
Cass. Sez. Lav. 21 novembre 2001 n. 14646 . . . . . . . . . . . . . . . . . . . 234
Cass. Sez. Lav. 22 agosto 2006 n. 18269 . . . . . . . . . . . . . . . . . . . . . 211
Cass. Sez. Lav. 22 luglio 1987 n. 6375 . . . . . . . . . . . . . . . . . . . . . 250
Cass. Sez. Lav. 4 giugno 2003 n. 8889 . . . . . . . . . . . . . . . . . . . . . . 262
Cass. Sez. Lav. 9 maggio 2007 n. 10547 . . . . . . . . . . . . . . . . . . . . . 211
Cass. Sez. Lav. 9 marzo 2004 n. 4790 . . . . . . . . . . . . . . . . . . . . . . 211
Cass. Sez. Un. Civ. 24 novembre 2006 n. 25033 . . . . . . . . . . . . . . . . 210
Corte Cost. 115/1994. . . . . . . . . . . . . . . . . . . . . . . . . . . . . . . 53
Corte Cost. 121/1993 . . . . . . . . . . . . . . . . . . . . . . . . . . . . . . 53
Corte Cost. 141 and 142/1980. . . . . . . . . . . . . . . . . . . . . . . . . . 64
Corte Cost. 283/2005 . . . . . . . . . . . . . . . . . . . . . . . . . . . . . . 155
Corte Cost. 34/1986 . . . . . . . . . . . . . . . . . . . . . . . . . . . . . . . 64

## GERMANY

BAG of 8.6.1967, BAGE 19, 324, 330 . . . . . . . . . . . . . . . . . . . . . . 133

## EUROPEAN COURT OF JUSTICE

*Adeneler and Others v. Ellinikos Organismos Galaktos* (Case C-212/04) [2006] ECR I-6057. . . . .397
*Allonby v. Accrington & Rossendale College* (Case C-256/01)
    [2004] ECR I-873 . . . . . . . . . . . . . . . . . . . . . . . . . 40, 389, 392, 398
*Andersen v. Kommunernes Landsforening* (Case C-306/07)[2008] ECR I-10279 . . . . . . . . 397
*ASBL Union Belge des Societès de Football Association v. Bosman* ( Case C-415/93)
    [1996] 1 CMLR 645 . . . . . . . . . . . . . . . . . . . . . . . . . . . . . 152
*BECTU v. Secretary of State for Trade and Industry* (Case C-173/99) [2001] ECR I-4881 . . . 393
*Birden v. Stadtgemeinde Bremen* (Case C-1/97) [1998] ECR I-7747 . . . . . . . . . . . . 140

*Bork International A/S, in liquidation v. Foreningen af Arbejdsledere I Danmark*
    (Case 101/87)[1988] ECR 03057 . . . . . . . . . . . . . . . . . . . . . . . . . 258
*Centrum voor gelijkheid van kansen en voor racismebestrijding v. Firma Feryn NV* (C-54/07)
    [2008] ECR I-5187 . . . . . . . . . . . . . . . . . . . . . . . . . . . . 424
*Cipolla v. Fazari* (Case C-94/04) [2006] ECR I-11421 . . . . . . . . . . . . . . . . . . . .95
*Coleman v. Attridge Law* (Case C-303/06)[2008] ECR I-5603 . . . . . . . . . . . . . . . 341
*Collino and Chiappero v. Telecom Italia Spa* (Case C-343/98) [2000] ECR I-6659 . . . . . . . 391
*Commission v. France* (C-255/04) [2006] ECR I-5251 . . . . . . . . . . . . . . . . . . .54
*Commission v. UK* (Case C-127/05) [2007] ECR I-4619 . . . . . . . . . . . . . . . . . 193
*Commissionv. Walter Feilhauer* (Case C-209/90) [1992] ECR I-02613 . . . . . . . . . . . 271
*Del Cerro Alonso v Osakidetza-Servicio Vasco de Salud* (Case C-307/05) [2007] ECR I-7109 . . 397
*Dillenkofer v. Germany* (Cases C-178–9/94) [1996] ECR I-4845 . . . . . . . . . . . . . . 420
*Foreningen af Arbejdsledere i Danmark v. Daddy's Dance Hall A/S* (Case 324/86)
    [1988] ECR 00739 . . . . . . . . . . . . . . . . . . . . . . . . . . . . . . . . 258
*Foreningen af Arbejdsledere i Danmark v. Danmols Inventar* (Case 105/84)[1985]
    ECR 2639 . . . . . . . . . . . . . . . . . . . . . . . . . . . 40, 389, 391–5, 397
*Georgiev v. Tehnicheski universitet – Sofia, filial Plovdiv* (Joined Cases C-250/09 and
    C-268/09) of 18 November 2010 (not yet reported at the time of writing) . . . . . . . 237
*Hütter v. Technische Universität Graz* (Case C-88/08) [2009] ECR I-5325 . . . . . . . . . 393
*ITF v. Viking Line ABP* (Case C-438/05) [2007] ECR I-10779 . . . . . . . . . . . . .388, 427
*Jouini v. Princess Personal Service GmbH (PPS)* (Case C-458/05) [2007] ECR I-07301 . . . . . 416
*Kiiski v. Tampereen kaupunki* (Case C-116/06)[2007] ECR I-7643 . . . . . . . . . . . . . 393
*Kurz (né Yüce) v. Land Baden-Württemberg* (Case C-188/00)[2002] ECR I-10691 . . . . . . 140
*Laval v. Svenska Byggnadsarbetareförbundet* (Case C-341/05) [2007] ECR I-11767 . . . . . .388, 427
*Lawrie-Blum v. Land Baden-Württemberg* (Case 66/85) [1986] ECR 2121 . . . . . . . . . . 389
*Marrosu and Sardino v. Azienda Ospedaliera Ospedale San Martino di Genova*
    (Case C-53/04) [2006] ECR I-7213 . . . . . . . . . . . . . . . . . . . . . . . 397
*Mavrona & Sia OE v. Delta Etairia Symmetochon AE* (Case C-85/03) [2004] OJ C 94/17 . . . 275
*Preston v Wolverhampton Healthcare NHS Trust* (Case C-78/98) [2000] ECR I 3201 . . . . . 392
*Raulin v. Minister van Onderwijs en Wetenschappen* (Case C-357/89) [1992] ECR I-1027 . . . . 40
*Redmond Stichting v. Hendrikus Bartol and others* (Case C-29/91) [1992] ECR I-3189 . . . . . 391
*Roca Álvarez v. Sesa Start España ETT SA* (Case C-104/09) judgment of
    30 September 2010 (unreported at the time of writing) . . . . . . . . . . . . . . . . 398
*Sánchez Hidalgo v. Asociación de Servicios Aser, Sociedad Cooperativa Minerva*
    (Case C-173/96) [1998] ECR I-8237 . . . . . . . . . . . . . . . . . . . . . . . 391
*Temco Service Industries v. Samir Imzilyen and Others* (Case C- 51/00) [2002]
    ECR I-00969 . . . . . . . . . . . . . . . . . . . . . . . . . . . . . . . . . . 256
*Wippel v. Peek & Cloppenburg GmbH & Co KG* ( C-313/02) [2004]
    ECR I-9483 . . . . . . . . . . . . . . . . . . . . . . . . . . . . .40, 318, 392–7

## EUROPEAN COURT OF HUMAN RIGHTS

*Sørensen v. Denmark and Rasmussen v. Denmark* (Applications 52562/99 and
    52620/99) [2008] 46 EHHR 29 . . . . . . . . . . . . . . . . . . . . . . . . . . 69

# Table of Legislation

## UNITED KINGDOM

Agency Workers Regulations 2010,
SI 2010/93. . . . . . . 334, 335, 361
Agency Workers Regulations 2010,
SI 2010/93, reg. 4 . . . . . . . . 334
Commercial Agents (Council Directive)
Regulations 1993, SI 1993/
3053. . . . . . . . . . . . . . 157, 274
Education Reform Act 1988 . . . . . . . 142
Employment Agencies Act 1973,
s. 13(2)–(3) . . . . . . . . . . . 334
Employment Equality (Age) Regulations
2006, SI 2006/1031 . . . . . . . 362
Employment Equality (Repeal of Retirement
Age Provisions) Regulations 2011,
SI 2011/1069 . . . . . . . . . 362, 417
Employment Rights Act 1996, s.1 . . . . 299
Employment Rights Act 1996,
ss. 28–35 . . . . . . . . . . . . 218
Employment Rights Act 1996,
s. 86. . . . . . . . . . . . . . 172, 234
Employment Rights Act 1996,
s. 230(1). . . . . . . . . . . . . 6, 137
Employment Rights Act 1996,
s. 230(3). . . . . . . . . . . 15, 39, 277
Equality Act 2010, s. 29 . . . . . . . . 145
Equality Act 2010, Pt 5, Chap 1 . . . . . 42
Equality Act 2010, s. 41 . . . . . . . . . 42
Equality Act 2010, s. 66 . . . . . . . 68, 72
Equality Act 2010, s. 83 . . . . . . . . . 42
Fixed-term Employees (Prevention
of Less Favourable Treatment)
Regulations 2002, SI 2002/2034,
reg. 8 . . . . . . . . 172, 331, 335, 361
Fixed-term Employees (Prevention of
Less Favourable Treatment)
Regulations 2002, SI 2034/2002,
reg. 9(4) . . . . . . . . . . . . . 154
Gangmasters (Licensing) Act 2004,
s. 4. . . . . . . . . . . . . . . . 335
Health and Safety at Work Act 1974,
s. 1 . . . . . . . . . . . . . . 42, 193
Limited Liability Partnerships Act 2000 . . 307
National Minimum Wage Act 1998,
s. 54. . . . . . . . . . . . . . . 122
Redundancy Payments Act
1965. . . . . . . . . . . 69, 207, 243

Trade Union Reform and Employment
Rights Act (TURERA) 1993, s. 35 . . . 94
Transfer of Undertakings (Protection of
Employment) Regulations 2006
SI 2006/246 . . . . . 256, 302, 335, 361
Working Time Regulations 1998,
SI 1998/1833, reg. 42 . . . . . . . 139

## FRANCE

Code du Travail Article L 781-1 . . . . . . 54
Code du Travail Article L 1211-1 . . . . 154
Code du Travail Article L 1221-19 . . . . 236
Code du Travail Article L 1221-21 . . . . 236
Code du Travail Article L 1222-1 . . . . 236
Code du Travail Article L 1222-5 . . . . 189
Code du Travail Article L 1242-3 . . . . 140
Code du Travail Article L 1232 . . . . 235
Code du Travail Articles L 1233-19
à L1233-20 . . . . . . . . . . . 235
Code du Travail Article L 1235-2 . . . . 236
Code du Travail Articles L 1237-11
to 1237-16. . . . . . . . . . . . 240
Code du Travail Article L 1242-10 . . . . 236
Code du Travail Article L 1242-12 . . . 154, 155
Code du Travail Article L 1251-42 . . . . 402
Code du Travail Article L 3123–31
à 37 . . . . . . . . . . . . . . . 318
Code du Travail Article L 5134-19 . . . . 355
Code du Travail Article L 5134-41 . . . . 140
Code du Travail Article L 5134-69 . . . . 140
Code du Travail Articles L 5134–74
à L 5134–99 . . . . . . . . . . . 296
Code du Travail Article L 6221-1 . . . . 139
Code du Travail Article L 6325-1 . . . . 140
Code du Travail Article L 7313-1 . . . . . 54,
157, 360
Law 596 of 25 June 2008 . . . . . . . 238
*Loi 30 décembre 1986* and
*2 août 1989* . . . . . . . . . . . 236
*Loi de modernisation sociale du
17 janvier 2002* . . . . . . . . . 181
*Loi du 23 mai 2006 relative au volontariat
associatif et à l'engagement
éducatif* . . . . . . . . . . . . . 146
*Loi du 24 novembre 2009* . . . . . . . 296

*Ordonnance no. 2006–433 du 13 avril 2006*
*relative à l'expérimentation du contrat*
*de transition professionnelle* . . . . . 296


## ITALY

Bill 1481 of 2009
Civil Code, Article 1373(2) . . . . . . 205
Civil Code, Article 1655 . . . . . . 110, 269
Civil Code, Article 1678 . . . . . . 110, 269
Civil Code, Article 1776 . . . . . . 110, 269
Civil Code, Article 1703 . . . . . . 110, 269
Civil Code, Article 1731 . . . . . . . 269
Civil Code, Article 1737 . . . . . . . 269
Civil Code, Article 1742 . . . . . . 157, 269
Civil Code, Article 2222 . . . . . . 110, 269
Civil Code, Article 2033 . . . . . . . 205
Civil Code, Article 2087 . . . . . 181, 187, 191, 192
Civil Code, Article 2096 . . . . . . . 236
Civil Procedure Code,
Article 409 . . . . . . . . 39, 122, 278
Constitution of the Italian Republic,
Article 3 . . . . . . . . . . . . . 373
Constitution of the Italian Republic,
Article 32 . . . . . . . . . . . . 187
Constitution of the Italian Republic,
Article 35 . . . . . . . . . . . . 372
Constitution of the Italian Republic,
Article 36 . . . . . . . . . . . . 373
Constitution of the Italian Republic,
Article 41(2) . . . . . . . . . . . 373
Law 108 of 1990, Article 4(1) . . . . 229, 230
Law 1369 of 1960 . . . . . . . . . . 299
Law 219 of 1985 . . . . . . . . . . . 64
Law 223 of 1991, Article 4(11) . . . . 221
Law 247 of 2007 . . . . . . . . . . 319
Law 264 of 1958 . . . . . . . . . 285, 334
Law 300 of 1970 (*Workers Statute*) . . . . 163, 181, 192, 203, 209, 210, 229
Law 533 of 1973 . . . . . . . . . . 122
Law 877 of 1973, Article 1 . . . . . 285, 334
Law 91 of 1981 . . . . . . . . . . . 334
Legislative Decree 1 February 1977,
n.12 converted by Law 31 March
1977, n. 91 . . . . . . . . . . . . 64
Legislative Decree 112 of 2008,
Article 39(11) . . . . . . . . . . 319
Legislative Decree 216 of 2003 . . . . . 289
Legislative Decree 276 of 2003 . . . . . 363
Legislative Decree 276 of 2003,
Article 2 . . . . . . . . . . . . . 155
Legislative Decree 276 of 2003,
Article 8 . . . . . . . . . . . . . 155

Legislative Decree 276 of 2003,
Articles 20–8 . . . . . . . . . . . 155
Legislative Decree 276 of 2003,
Article 33 . . . . . . . . . . . 334
Legislative Decree 276 of 2003,
Article 36 . . . . . . . . . . . 176
Legislative Decree 276 of 2003,
Article 41 . . . . . . . . . . . 160
Legislative Decree 276 of 2003,
Article 61 . . . . . . . . . 39, 122, 278
Legislative Decree 276 of 2003,
Article 69(1) . . . . . . . . . . . 156


## GERMANY

Basic Law of the Federal Republic of
Germany, Article 1 . . . . . . . . . 373
Basic Law of the Federal Republic of
Germany, Article 12(1) . . . . . . . 257
Civil Code (*Bürgerliches Gesetzbuch – BGB*),
Section 613a . . . . . . . . . . . 255
Civil Code (*Bürgerliches Gesetzbuch – BGB*),
Title 8 . . . . . . . . . . . . . 270
Law on Collective Agreements of 1974
(*Tarifsvertragsgesetz*), section 12a . . . 122
Act on Part-time work and fixed-term
employment contracts 2001,
s. 13(1) . . . . . . . . . . . . . 160
Social Code (*Sozialgesetzbuch-SGB*),
§7 s IV, Book IV . . . . . . . . . 289


## SPAIN

Law 7 of 2007 . . . . . . . . . . . 144
Law 20 of 2007 . . . . . . 115, 156, 279, 345
Law 20 of 2007, Article 4 . . . . . . . 289
Law 20 of 2007, Article 6 . . . . . . . 289
Law 20 of 2007, Article 7 . . . . . 155, 157
Law 20 of 2007, Article 11 . . . . . . . 39
Law 20 of 2007, Article 12 . . . . . . 345
Law 20 of 2007, Article 20(2)(a) . . . . . 157
Royal Decree 197 of 2009 . . . . . . . 345


## EUROPEAN UNION

Charter of Fundamental Rights of the
European Union [2010]
OJ C 83/389, Article 30 . . . . 394, 395
Charter of Fundamental Rights of the
European Union [2010] OJ C
83/389, Article 31 . . . . 373, 394, 395
Directive 77/187 EEC on the
approximation of the laws of the

Member States relating to the
safeguard of employees' rights in the
event of transfer of undertakings,
businesses or parts of businesses,
[1977] OJ L 61/26 . . . .   77, 255, 411,
416, 422
Directive 86/653/EEC of 18 December
1986 on the coordination of the laws
of the Member States relating to
self-employed commercial agents,
[1986] OJ L 382/17 . . . . .   157, 274,
288, 408, 410
Directive 91/533/EC of 14 October 1991
on an employer's obligation to inform
employees of the conditions applicable
to the contract or employment
relationship, [1991]
OJ L 288/32 . . . . . 154, 243, 397, 425
Directive 93/104/EEC of 23 November
1993 concerning certain aspects of
the organization of working time,
[1993] OJ L307/18. . . . . . .   77, 423
Directive 94/45 of 22 September 1994
on the establishment of a European
Works Council or a procedure in
Community-scale undertakings
and Community-scale groups of
undertakings for the purposes
of informing and consulting
employees, [1994] OJ L 254/64. . .   427
Directive 96/71/EC of the European
Parliament and of the Council of
16 December 1996 concerning the
posting of workers in the framework
of the provision of services,
[1997] OJ L 18/01 . . . . . . . .   428
Directive 97/81/EC of 15 December
1997 concerning the Framework
Agreement on part-time work
concluded by UNICE, CEEP
and the ETUC as amended by
Directive 98/23/EC (OJ 1998
L131/10), consolidated, [1998]
OJ L131/13, Clause 2(1) . . . .   40, 77,
389, 396, 397, 401, 425
Directive 98/50 of 29 June 1998,
amending Directive 77/187 EEC on the
approximation of the laws of the
Member States relating to the safeguard
of employees' rights in the event of
transfer of undertakings, businesses or
parts of businesses, [1998] OJ
L201/98 . . . . . . . .77, 255, 411, 416

Directive 98/59/EC of 20 July 1998
on the approximation of the laws
of the Member States relating to
collective redundancies, [1998]
OJ L 225/16 . . . . . . . . .236, 420
Directive 99/70/EC of 28 June 1999
concerning the Framework
Agreement on Fixed-term Work
concluded by UNICE, CEEP
and the ETUC [1999] OJ L175/43
corrigendum OJ 1999
L 244/64. . . . . . . . . . .77, 233,
361, 389, 397, 401, 425
Directive 2000/43 implementing the
principle of equal treatment
between persons irrespective of
racial or ethnic origin, [2000]
OJ L 180/22 . . . . . . . . .41, 393
Directive 2000/78 establishing a general
framework for equal treatment in
employment and occupation,
[2000] OJ L 303/16, Article 3 (1)
(a) . . . . . . .   41, 289, 362, 393, 394,
411, 412, 416
Directive 2001/23/EC of 12 March 2001
on the approximation of the laws
of Member States relating to the
safeguard of employees' rights in the
event of transfer of undertakings,
businesses or parts of undertakings
or businesses, [2001] OJ L 82/16,
Article 2(2)   . . . . . 77, 255, 335, 361,
411, 416
Directive 2002/14/EC of the European
Parliament and of the Council of
11 2002 establishing a general
framework for informing and
consulting employees in the
European Community – Joint
declaration of the European Parliament,
the Council and the Commission
on employee representation
[2002] OJ L 80/29 . . . . . . . .   427
Directive 2002/15 EC on the organization
of the working time of persons
performing mobile road transport
activities [2002] OJ L
80/35 . . . . . . . . . . .40, 408, 409
Directive 2003/38 of the European
Parliament and of the Council of
4 November 2003 concerning
certain aspects of the organization
of working time, [2003] OJ L299/9. . .   77

Directive 2003/88/EC of the European
Parliament and of the Council of
4 November 2003 concerning
certain aspects of the organisation
of working time, [2003] OJ L
299/09, Articles 18 and
22 . . . . . . . . . . . . . 66, 93, 215
Directive 2004/38/EC on the right of
citizens of the Union and their family
members to move and reside freely
within the territory of the Member
States, [2004] L 158/77. . . . . . . 427
Directive 2005/36/EC of 7 September
2005 on the recognition of
professional qualifications,
[2005] L 255/22 . . . . . . . . . . 407
Directive 2006/54/EC of 5 July 2006
on the implementation of the
principle of equal opportunities
and equal treatment of men and
women in matters of employment
and occupation (recast), [2006]
OJ L 204/23 . . . . . . . . . 393, 424
Directive 2008/104/EC of the European
Parliament and the Council of
19 November 2008 on temporary
agency work, [2008] OJ L
327/9 . . . . . 77, 165, 335, 361, 398,
401, 425
Directive 2009/38/EC Of The European
Parliament And Of The Council of
6 May 2009 on the establishment
of a European Works Council or
a procedure in Community-scale
undertakings and Community-scale

groups of undertakings for the
purposes of informing and consulting
employees (Recast), [2009]
OJ L 122/28 . . . . . . . . . . . 427
Directive 2009/50/EC of 25 May 2009
on the conditions of entry and
residence of third-country nationals
for the purposes of highly qualified
employment, [2009]
OJ L 155/17 . . . . . . . . . . . 428
Directive 2009/52/EC of 18
June 2009 providing for minimum
standards on sanctions and measures
against employers of illegally staying
third-country nationals, [2009]
OJ L 168/24 . . . . . . . . . . . 428
Directive 2010/41/EU on the application
of the principle of equal treatment
between men and women engaged
in an activity in a self-employed
capacity and repealing Council
Directive 86/613/EEC, [2010]
OJ L 180/1 . . . . . . . . . 40, 410

## INTERNATIONAL LABOUR ORGANISATION

C 111, Discrimination (Employment and
Occupation) Convention, 1958 . . . 394
C 181, Private Employment Agencies
Convention, 1997 . . . . . . . . 334
R 198, Employment Relationship
Recommendation, 2006 . . . . . . . 24, 26,
27, 28

# PART I

# THE LEGAL ANALYSIS OF
# PERSONAL WORK RELATIONS

# Introduction: Evolution and Reformulation in the Legal Construction of Personal Work Relations

This work provides an analysis of the ways in which personal work relations are constructed in English[1] and European[2] law. The two key notions of 'personal work relations' and of the 'legal construction of personal work relations' will be expounded in the course of the work; the purpose of this Introduction is to open an account of the objectives and methodology of the work, and to explain how it will be presented in the succeeding chapters.

The objectives of the work could be identified in various different ways, and at various different levels of ambitiousness. As will have been apparent from the Preface, the objective might be stated, in one sense, as the production of a third and expanded version of the first author's works on *The Contract of Employment*[3] and on *The Personal Employment Contract*,[4] this time placed on a European comparative footing. However, this only really serves to describe the programme of work in which we have engaged, rather than its ultimate goals. We found that the carrying out of that programme of work required us to reflect at length and in depth as to the rationale for the work, and as to the insights which could be derived from European comparative reflection. This was necessary in order to feel confident of the validity or utility of the changes in scope and methodology which have been made as between this work and the previous versions of it.

As the result of those reflections, we have come to identify the objectives of this work in a more ambitious way which is free-standing from the previous versions of the work. Our aim has become that of trying to provide a foundational analysis of the legal construction of personal work relations primarily in English law and secondarily in European law more generally, starting from the English law of personal work contracts, and comparing that with the corresponding bodies of law

---

[1] We use the term 'English law' to refer to the law of England and Wales. The treatment of 'English law' in this work is broadly speaking applicable to the laws of the United Kingdom at large, but we do not assert that this is precisely the case in all respects.

[2] In general in this work, we use the term 'European law' to refer to the laws of Member States of the EU. In Chapter 10, at p 385, we expound upon the relationship which we envisage between 'European law' in that sense and EU law.

[3] M. R. Freedland (1976) *The Contract of Employment*, Oxford: Clarendon Press.

[4] M. R. Freedland (2003) *The Personal Employment Contract*, Oxford: OUP.

in other European jurisdictions and in the fast developing EU legal order. In essence, then, we can declare from the outset that in the course of this writing project our aim has become that of identifying or re-analysing the basic legal paradigm for English labour or employment law by a method of comparison with the corresponding legal paradigms in other European legal systems, both national and supranational.

Although our objective for the work can be stated in that free-standing way, we nevertheless need to refer to the way in which our project developed from the two earlier works in order to explain the way in which that objective identified itself and the way in which we now seek to achieve that objective. The first author's work on *The Contract of Employment* was written in the conviction that the contract of employment had become the central legal category for British labour law but was underanalysed both in the courts and in the secondary literature, so that there was scope for more extensive analysis of it than was then available. The first author's work on *The Personal Employment Contract* was written in the rather different conviction that this analysis, in order to retain any utility in a greatly transformed practical and juridical environment, needed to be extended into a wider legal category, that of the personal work or employment contract.

The further project from which the present work has emerged consisted, at its inception, of pursuing the analysis of the personal work or employment contract on a European comparative basis. At quite an early stage in that project, the first author decided that he should invoke and deploy an analytical category which was still larger in that it extended into personal work relations which were not necessarily contractual ones; this was the origin of the plan to use the 'personal work nexus' as the legal category for this comparative analysis. For this enlarged endeavour, it seemed, and has indeed proved, to be important to tap into an emerging genre of writing which took the notion of the 'employment relationship' as its categorical starting point. Most felicitously for the first author of the present work, the second author had engaged in that genre of work on a European comparative basis, producing his treatise on *The Changing Law of the Employment Relationship – Comparative Analyses in the European Context* in 2007.[5]

This suggested and gave rise to our collaboration in and co-authorship of the present work. We initially believed that, by putting together and working from our respective theoretical positions, we had successfully devised an adequate comparative method and working hypotheses for the project of making a journey 'from the contract of employment to the personal work nexus';[6] and we put that method and those hypotheses on display in a published article.[7] However, we have since become convinced that there was a larger set of epistemic or foundational issues which we had not sufficiently recognized or confronted, and should seek to resolve, with

[5] N. Countouris (2007) *The Changing Law of the Employment Relationship: Comparative Analyses in the European Context*, Aldershot: Ashgate.
[6] M. R. Freedland (2006) 'From the Contract of Employment to the Personal Work Nexus', 35(1), *ILJ*, 1–29.
[7] M. Freedland and N. Kountouris (2008) 'Towards a Comparative Theory of the Contractual Construction of Personal Work Relations in Europe', 37(1), *ILJ*, 49–74.

the result that we needed to reconsider the methods and the conceptual categories which we should use to develop our comparative study.

When we refer to a set of epistemic or foundational issues, we mean that we perceive there to be a set of problems about the ways in which we describe and understand the very nature and definition of the subject matter of our work. This has occasioned long discussions about how to frame and organize and present this book, and indeed as to what title to put on the front page. Those discussions represent an attempt to engage with a large debate, much pursued in recent years, about the 'scope' or 'personal scope' of labour or employment law. That debate has come to assume – in our view understandably and necessarily – the proportions of a kind of existential crisis for labour or employment law, in which theorists and practitioners of labour or employment law become agitated about whether and in what sense their subject 'exists'.[8]

In this situation of epistemic and subject-existential crisis for labour or employment law, the hardest thing about writing a treatise about its foundational analytical concepts is deciding where and how to begin. That difficulty, as we have indicated, becomes all the more severe when one has the project of pursuing the discussion on a comparative basis as between more than one legal system. Should one first try to establish some definitional starting points for a field or topic of study in one legal system or a number of legal systems, and then identify a comparative methodology and some comparative hypotheses as tools of investigation of that particular subject-matter? Or is there a logic of 'Comparative Law' as a legal science which dictates that we should proceed in the opposite direction?

We have no perceived 'right answer' to that set of questions; it has continued to trouble us. We attempt in the first part of our work somewhat to deconstruct the epistemic or foundational debate about 'the scope of labour or employment law' into some component aspects or elements. We seek to use this deconstruction to enable us to take up a starting definitional position and to identify a basis for comparative analysis from within that position. We take a notion of 'the Personal Work Relation' as our definitional starting point, and seek to develop and flesh out that notion in the course of our work. Suffice it at this stage for us to offer a simple outline definition of the notion of the personal work relation as we shall use it in this work, alerting our readers to the fact that a more complete working definition is contained in Chapter 1 of the present work; we use that notion to refer to the relation or set of relations which a person has with another person or other persons (whether human or legal-corporate) by reason of arranging to engage personally in the doing of work for another or others.

In this Introduction, we concentrate on beginning to elaborate our idea of the 'legal construction' of personal work relations, for the understanding of that idea is at the very heart of the enterprise which we have embarked upon in writing this

---

[8] Cf., for instance, A. Hyde (2011) 'The Idea of the Idea of Labour Law: A Parable', in G. Davidov and B. Langille (eds), *The Idea of Labour Law*, Oxford: OUP; A. Ojeda Avilés (2010) *La deconstrucción del derecho del trabajo*, Madrid: La Ley – Wolkers Kluwer; C. Vigneau (2003) 'Labor Law Between Changes and Continuity', 25, *CLLPJ*, 129–41.

book. The idea of the legal construction of personal work relations is, in its essence, that of the shape or analysis, or construct, which a legal system (or a subsystem thereof) assigns to each personal work relation. The relevant archetypal example of the legal construction of personal work relations would be that, to those personal work relations which are regarded as 'dependent' ones, the English legal system in general (and the subsystem of it which we think of as labour law) assigns the character of a 'contract of employment' and attributes many legal incidents and effects to it as such. However, as we shall show at length, there are many personal work relations to which different legal constructs are assigned, so that they are sometimes construed or constructed as being contracts other than employment contracts and sometimes as being only partly contractual in their nature, or as not being contractual at all.

It might appear from this explanation and this example as if our idea of the legal construction of personal work relations amounts to no more than the legal classification, or taxonomy, of those relations. In other words, it might appear as if this were nothing other than the debate about 'the personal scope of labour law' or of particular 'labour laws'. However, such an impression would mean that we had failed to convey a full and complete idea of what we intend. Crucial to our notion of 'the legal construction of personal work relations' is not only the assignment of a certain character to a particular personal work relation but also, as we said almost in passing, the attribution of legal incidents and effects to that personal work relation as such. So we might build on the archetypal example which we gave in the previous paragraph – a piece or act of legal construction of personal work relations might consist of establishing or deciding or holding that a particular personal work relation was to be regarded as taking the legal form of a contract of employment and that as such it was subject to the law of unfair dismissal[9].

This way of defining the notion of legal construction of personal work relations is not particularly controversial; it may indeed seem to be all too obvious. However, we believe that quite striking conclusions follow from it. Our definition or conception of the legal construction of personal work relations serves to assert and emphasise the way in which the classification of personal work relations is essentially and integrally linked to the attribution of legal incidents or effects or consequences to those relations. The legal construction of personal work relations depends on, indeed consists of, the forging of the link between legal character and legal consequences. We suggest the terminology of 'normative characterisation' to express the idea of this integral combination – it is a terminology which seeks to capture the essential connectedness between identifying the legal character of a given personal work relation and making normative propositions about that relation.

We will seek to develop the notion of normative characterization in some perhaps novel directions. We will argue that each act of legal construction or normative characterization of personal work relations involves or consists of the

---

[9] As might occur under English law where s 94(1) of the Employment Rights Act 1996 provides that 'An employee has the right not to be unfairly dismissed by his employer' and s 230(1) provides that 'In this Act "employee" means an individual who has entered into or works under [...] a contract of employment.'

creation of its own micro-system in and by which legal character and legal consequences are interconnected. It follows from this that, in our view, each act of legal construction or normative characterization of personal work relations has to be analysed and understood in its own regulatory context. By this we mean two things – the 'regulatory context' has two aspects. One aspect consists of the character/consequences link itself. The assignment of character to or the classification of personal work relations takes place in the context of and with reference to a particular kind or piece of legal regulation or a set of such – a piece of legal regulation or a set of such pieces. In the example which we have been using, the classification of a particular personal work relation, as to whether it takes the legal form of a contract of employment, takes place in the regulatory context of the law of unfair dismissal, a body of legal regulation for the application of which the existence of a contract of employment is a precondition.

The second aspect of the regulatory context follows from the first one. The act of legal construction of personal work relations, if understood in the way that we have suggested, consists of or forms part of a process of linking legal character to legal consequences. Each such process has its own in-built principles and rules, and operational dynamics. In the example we have been using, the legal construction of a particular personal work relation as being subject to the law of unfair dismissal involves a law-making part of the process by which it is determined that unfair dismissal law applies to contracts of employment in general, and an adjudication part of the process by which it is determined whether that application takes place in any given instance. (The two parts of the process may merge into each other, as where the adjudicator has some part of the law-making function.) Both the law-making and the adjudicatory parts of the process are subject to rules and principles specific to that process. For example, the law-maker may be subject to specific rules of competence, while the adjudicator may be guided by specific presumptions or rules of procedure which are strongly or conclusively determinative of the outcome of the process.

The process of linking legal character to legal consequences in the construction of personal work relations will, moreover, have its own particular political and forensic dynamics (in the broadest senses of those terms), which form part of the regulatory context in question. Important political-contextual questions include issues about the extent to which the legal consequences are in reality determined or affected by the presence or absence of collective bargaining or collective representation of the worker in the personal work relation. Equally important forensic-contextual questions are those concerned with the difference between mandatory linkings of legal character with legal consequences, and linkings which are derogable or in the nature of default positions. Such questions will be explored at length in the course of our work.

A further step follows from this way of understanding the legal construction of personal work relations as consisting of one or more acts of normative characterization each taking place in its own regulatory context. It follows from this that, in a legal system where personal work relations in general or at least some kinds of personal work relations have, over time, been the subject of extensive and multi-faceted regulation, there will have been many different acts of legal construction of those relations – many exercises in linking legal character with legal consequences – each taking place in its own regulatory context and constituting its own micro-system.

Where that situation of extensive and multi-faceted regulation of personal work relations has arisen over time – a condition which is abundantly fulfilled in European legal systems – it therefore further follows that the legal construction of personal work relations will have resulted in the formation of a great multiplicity of micro-systems existing in a great multiplicity of regulatory contexts.

It may be that, even if our preliminary steps in this argument seemed to be uncontroversial, the regulatory-contextual conclusion which we have reached seems to be very controversial indeed. We might be regarded as saying that each and every act of legal construction of personal work relations had to be regarded as being instrumental to its own regulatory context, and confined to its own regulatory context, so that a truly common discourse between the regulatory contexts could not really exist. That is not our view; we think that the legal construction of personal work relations takes place in a way which is highly interactive as between different regulatory contexts, so that a common discourse of and about the legal construction of personal work relations can exist between regulatory contexts.

However, although we disclaim such radical consequences for our argument, we do accept and indeed assert that it nevertheless has highly significant ones. Our argument means that, if we envisage the existence of a body of law which represents 'the legal construction of personal work relations', that body of law is an enormously contextually elaborate one in any given national legal system or national labour law system. This elaboration is multiplied so that it assumes quite frightening proportions if we consider 'the legal construction of personal work relations' on a European comparative basis, and if we focus – even cursorily – our attention on the influence of European Union social regulation. There is, both among theorists, designers, and practitioners of labour law, an understandable tendency to recoil from the prospect of such elaboration, and to assume or assert that a simple and rationalised vision of the legal construction of personal work relations must be possible and attainable. From that perspective, the path of analysis which we intend to pursue in this work may be perceived as an unduly tortuous and winding one. That is a risk which we take not without trepidation, but in the conviction that a simple vision of the legal construction of personal work relations is quickly found to be a mirage, an imagined clearing of theoretical lucidity in a real jungle of luxuriantly tangled conceptual vegetation.

Although, therefore, we have to expect that our analysis of the legal construction of personal work relations on a European comparative basis will present itself as an intensely complex one, we may on the other hand hope that the starting points which we have established – in particular the idea of normative characterization and the idea of the multiplicity of regulatory contexts – will help to provide a way of understanding the complexities which we have identified. For that purpose, we shall suggest that there is one further explanatory step which we can usefully take at this introductory stage of the argument of our book. Thus far, we have shown various senses in which the legal construction of personal work relations is in its nature system-specific – it consists of a great diversity of acts of legal construction producing outcomes which are specific not only to their own respective legal systems but also to their own regulatory contexts within those legal systems and which moreover themselves constitute micro-systems of their own. We proceed to argue that the legal construction of personal work relations is not only *system-specific* in those various senses but also that it is heavily *path-dependent* in ways that follow from our previous arguments and which we shall now sketch out.

It follows from our previous arguments that acts of legal construction of personal work relations, which forge links between the legal character and the legal consequences of a particular personal work relation or set of personal work relations, will therefore not only *classify* personal work relations but also *form or transform* them at the same time. This creates a kind of constructive circle which reinforces the system-specific nature of the legal construction in question. Let us take as an example the act of legal construction which takes place when a court comes to the conclusion that because a given personal work relation has the legal form of a contract of employment, it is to be deemed to give rise to an obligation of mutual trust and confidence between the parties. Where that conclusion is imposed generically upon contracts of employment,[10] it amounts to an act of legal construction which itself forms or transforms (perhaps in the sense of concretising, or perhaps in some more radical sense) the legal incidents of that whole set of personal work relations – it is now clear that this set of personal work relations does give rise to an obligation of mutual trust and confidence, in a way that was not previously clear, so contracts of employment have become distinctive in a new way.

We now go on to make the further point that, where these self-formative or self-transformative acts of legal construction take place in a context of extensive and multi-faceted regulation of personal work relations – a condition which, as we have said, is abundantly fulfilled in European legal systems – it follows that each act of legal construction will build upon the ones that have preceded it or are contemporary with it within the legal system in question. To pursue our example, the legal construction of contracts of employment as giving rise to a mutual obligation of trust and confidence, under English law, took place in a regulatory context which did not impose obligations of mutual good faith upon the parties to contracts in general. In that regulatory context, the imputing of a mutual obligation of trust and confidence to contracts of employment at once identified and significantly transformed that set of personal work relations.

So, to put the same point in a different way, it follows that formative or transformative acts of legal construction of personal work relations are highly *path-dependent* upon the particular path of evolution which has been followed within the regulatory context in question. Furthermore, that path-dependency may be an elaborate one, reflecting historical effects from various intersecting regulatory contexts. To pursue our example further, the legal construction of contracts of employment as giving rise to obligations of mutual trust and confidence was also path-dependent upon a certain set of developments in the concept of 'constructive dismissal' which were occurring in the context of the law of unfair dismissal – so this crucial development in the sub-system of labour law which we think of as 'the law of the contract of employment' was heavily dependent on the contemporaneous

---

[10] As occurs under English law in a way which is explained in full in later chapters.

emergence of a new subsystem of 'the law of unfair dismissal', those two subsystems being considerably but far from completely intersecting ones.

The four ideas or insights which we have briefly outlined, those of *normative characterization, multiplicity of regulatory contexts, system-specificity,* and *path-dependency* in the legal construction of personal work relations, will pervade the work which follows. They are closely bound up with the nature and objectives of the work as an exercise in European comparative law. These ideas or insights can be seen as both deriving from and contributing to the comparative nature and objectives of our study. They are insights which derive from comparison between European national labour law systems: that comparison, by revealing both commonalities and differences between the normative characterizations which are made in those national systems, throws into sharp relief the system-specificity and path-dependency of the legal construction of personal work relations in any one national system. They are also insights which in turn take the process of comparison further and deeper: the ideas of multiplicity of regulatory contexts, path-dependency and system-specificity enable us to understand more fully why normative characterizations take place in particular ways in the legal construction of personal work relations as between national legal systems and within each such system.

These efforts to show how we will address the intricacy of the legal construction of personal work relations may only serve to increase the sense of a mystifying complexity. Our ambitions for this work have become those of, firstly, establishing a large domain within which to develop the relational and structural analysis of labour law, and, secondly, that of confronting and trying to unravel the complexities of legal construction of the relations within that domain, and, thirdly, that of subjecting that legal construction to a functional critique which we have devised for the purpose. That functional critique comes from a particular critical standpoint which we have designated by invoking an overarching notion of 'personality in work'. As we will explain later, that overarching notion of personality in work is concerned with the protection or vindication of the values of dignity, capability, and stability in the legal handling of personal work relations. The initial chapters of this work develop in more detail our design for carrying out that task.

# 1

# The Legal Analysis of Personal Work Relations – Boundaries, Paradigms, and Legal Formats

## Introduction

As we indicated in the Introduction to our book, the scope, objectives, and methodology of the work are all integrally interconnected. The work seeks to achieve its objectives by examining a certain purposively defined area of law according to a certain rationale and a certain methodology. These aspects of the work are intended to be mutually consistent and supportive. This chapter concentrates on the scope and objectives, while the second chapter considers the method which will be used for the analysis. Between them, the two chapters begin to sketch out in detail the analytical moves 'from the contract of employment to the personal work relation' which it is the essential business of this work to attempt to accomplish.

## Section 1: The Relational Scope of Labour Law – An Initial Analysis

We have set ourselves the task, in writing this book, of trying to establish and to analyse a basic or foundational legal category for English and, by extension, European labour law.[1] In other words, we are seeking to identify a domain or sphere of operation for labour law, to establish a legal category which identifies that domain, and to suggest ways of understanding, at a basic level, the manner in which labour law constructs and regulates the relations which exist within that domain. Since there is no clear existing consensus about the breadth of the domain of labour law,[2] or about the identification of a basic legal category to encompass that

---

[1] Generally speaking, the terms 'labour law' and 'employment law' are used synonymously in this work; sometimes we make that interchangeability explicit by referring to 'labour or employment law'; at pp. 13–15 below we touch upon some issues of variation in usage of these terms and their equivalents in other languages, and we explain why at this point in the work we use 'labour law' as the primary or preferred terminology.

[2] Cf. the collection of essays in G. Davidov and B. Langille (eds) (2011) *The Idea of Labour Law*, Oxford: OUP.

domain,[3] those who wish to establish these entities have to begin by staking out some terrain in order to be able to operate effectively within it. Our first steps consist in adopting one particular name and identification for the discipline within which we are working, and explaining and seeking to justify that decision by invoking a model or outline to describe the way in which we see the discipline as having been formulated and as having acquired a certain particular relational scope.

As will have become apparent, we are using the terminology of 'labour law' to identify the discipline within which we regard ourselves as working, (while, however, regarding the terminology of 'employment law' as having become effectively synonymous with it in a way that we consider later in this section).[4] How did this disciplinary identification come about? We venture to put forward an answer which we think applies in the context of English law and in other European legal systems. The disciplinary identification came about, we suggest, by virtue of the gradual establishment of a broad consensus among legal scholars and legal practitioners that there is a distinctive area of study and practice which we can now identify by this name. We should not think of that consensus as being a complete or exact one at any given moment, or within any one legal system; and that consensus becomes even less complete when considered over significant periods of time, and across different national legal systems.

That incompleteness of consensus about 'what labour law is' touches upon a key feature of our work in this book. Inquiry into the contractual and relational dimensions of labour law on a European comparative basis has made us acutely aware that many of its key terminologies refer to institutional phenomena which are deeply embedded in national legal systems and national labour market practices, and that these institutional phenomena are, as such, strongly diversified both between national legal systems and across historical time within each legal system. In the next chapter we shall seek to identify our comparative methodology for analysing those diversities and their normative implications. At this initial stage in our analysis we need to consider for a moment the diversities of meaning which are attached to the terminology of 'labour law' itself.

At this point in our discussion we should introduce a linguistic theme which will also be a recurring one throughout this work. Again, we articulate it more fully in the next chapter as an aspect of our comparative methodology. Our theme is that, because the development of labour law, both in the practical and the theoretical senses, within national legal systems has taken place within a partly internationalized discourse, it has been necessary to assume a broad equivalence of terminologies as between different legal systems even when they are operating in different

---

[3] Cf. B. Caruso (2010) 'Il Contratto di Lavoro come Istituzione Europea', *WP C.S.D.L.E. 'Massimo D'Antona' INT* – 84/2010; J. Kenner (2009), 'New Frontiers in EU Labour Law: from Flexicurity to Flex-Security' in M. Dougan (ed), *Fifty Years of European Treaties*, Oxford: Hart, 279; P. Cahuc et F. Kramarz (2004) *De la précarité à la mobilité: vers une Sécurité sociale professionnelle*, Paris: La Documentation française; A. Perulli (2003) *Economically dependent/quasi-subordinate (parasubordinate) employment: legal, social and economic aspects*, available online at www.ec.europa.eu/employment_social/labour_law/docs/parasubordination_report_en.pdf.
[4] See below, p. 14.

languages; but that this assumed or presumed equivalence may be incomplete and needs constantly to be questioned. At this initial and epistemic stage of our work, we need firstly to question the apparent equivalence of meaning between the usage of the terminology of 'labour law' as between English-speaking legal systems. Then we need to question the presumed equivalence of meaning between the received and habitual translations of 'labour law' in the context of other European legal systems speaking other languages – *'droit du travail'* in French, *'Arbeitsrecht'* in German, *'diritto del lavoro'* in Italian, *'derecho del trabajo'* in Spanish and so on.

A complete inquiry into the convergences and divergences between meanings attached to 'labour law' and the apparent equivalents in other legal systems and languages would be a very elaborate undertaking; for the purposes of the present work we limit that inquiry in two ways. Firstly, we concentrate on identifying, with the aid of some European comparisons (and one North American comparison), a generally accepted meaning for 'labour law' in the English legal system and the writings about that system. Secondly, we focus on one aspect or dimension of those convergences and divergences (admittedly a very large one), namely the kinds of work relations which regarded as being within the meaning of labour law. We can refer to this aspect or dimension as the 'relational defining of labour law'; it forms an essential preliminary part of the subject-matter of our present work.

So we begin by suggesting a generally accepted meaning for 'labour law' in the English legal system and the writings about that system – that is to say, a meaning which encapsulates the broad consensus, to which we referred earlier, among legal scholars and practitioners that there is an area of study and practice which has to do with the legal regulation of the world of work and which has its own distinctive identity. As the bearer of that very heavy epistemic burden, we offer up this definition: that 'labour law', as understood in the context of the English legal system, consists of a body of legal regulation which has as its subject-matter some or all of the relations of working people with those for whom and with whom they work, and of the governance, in the widest sense, of their working environment and working conditions. It will be observed that by deliberately leaving open the question of whether labour law has as its subject-matter *some or all* of those relations, we have deferred for further discussion the relational specification of our definition.

Before developing our account of the 'relational defining of labour law' in English and European law, it will be important to address another definitional issue or dimension which is associated with it in a tangential way; this is the question of the collective and the individual in the defining of labour law. There is a large and still unresolved question as to whether and how far the terminology of 'labour law' as used in relation to English law, or its assumed equivalents in other European legal systems, is confined to those aspects of work relations and their governance which can be regarded as 'collective' ones and how far, on the other hand, it and its assumed equivalents extend to work relations and their governance which can be regarded as 'individual' ones.

There is a significant divergence of usage on this point as between English-speaking national labour law systems and traditions. The terminology of 'labour law' seems itself to have become a widely used one in North America where (spelt as 'labor law') it has been used very much in the 'collective' sense to identify and refer to the body of legal regulation governing work relations, viewed as essentially collective ones, in the unionized sector of the labour market. In the legal systems of the USA and Canada, that body of legal regulation has been, for the most part, regarded as quite distinct from another body of legal regulation governing work relations, viewed as essentially individual ones, in the non-unionized sector of the labour market; and the terminology of 'employment law' has been used to refer to that body of legal regulation.[5]

If that differentiation can be said to have been made at any stage in or in relation to English law, it was not made in such a sharp form; although the terminologies of 'labour law' and 'employment law' may at times have been regarded as referring to different aspects, the one 'collective' and the other 'individual', of the legal regulation of work relations, they would not have been regarded as denoting two clearly separate bodies of legal regulation applying to two fully distinct sectors of the labour market. Moreover, the usage of the two terminologies in or in relation to English law has been increasingly convergent, to the point where they could be regarded as interchangeable or synonymous. Thus when making our own choice to identify the subject-matter of this work as the relational analysis of a body of law denominated as 'labour law', we found it difficult to decide between that terminology and the alternative one of 'employment law'.

We were somewhat influenced in that choice by a perception that the terminology of 'labour law' resonated more closely with the assumed equivalents in other European legal systems and legal traditions. However, this is a good illustration of the need to be sceptical about the degree of equivalence. The French notion of '*droit du travail*' and the German notion of '*Arbeitsrecht*' seem to combine the collective and the individual aspects of the legal regulation of work relations rather in the same way as they are combined in English law, and there is probably more of a habit of regarding those notions as the equivalent of 'labour law' than as the equivalent of 'employment law'. This is not to say that continental European systems are not familiar with sub-categorizations of the discipline of labour law. For instance, the conceptual distinction in Italian law between '*diritto del lavoro*' and '*diritto sindacale*'[6] appears to be rather a sharp and visible one, almost comparable with the North American distinction between 'employment law' and 'labour law' respectively. However, Italian authors would not regard this conceptual distinction as sustaining the more substantive North American 'distinction between the collective bargaining rights for unionized workers and individual employment rights for other workers'.[7] In fact it would be fair to say that – for reasons that will be further discussed in Chapters 2 and 3 – the relatively ample coverage of

---

[5]  On the distinction, and its declining theoretical and practical relevance, in the North American tradition cf. K. V. W. Stone (2008) 'The Future of Labor and Employment Law in the United States', *UCLA School of Law – Law-Econ Research Paper No. 08–11.*

[6]  G. Giugni (2007) *Diritto Sindacale*, Bari: Cacucci.

[7]  K. V. W. Stone (2008), 'The Future of Labor and Employment Law in the United States', *UCLA School of Law – Law-Econ Research Paper No. 08–11*, 19.

collectively agreed standards in Italy would suggest a much higher level of integration between individual and collective labour law than in countries such as the
USA. It is, for example, natural for Gino Giugni to define '*diritto sindacale*' as '*that
part of labour law* that concerns the system of instrumental rules [that] regulate the
dynamics of the conflict of interests deriving from the unequal distribution of
power in the productive processes'.[8]

However, although for those reasons we preferred the terminology of 'labour
law' to that of 'employment law', we nevertheless regarded these terminologies as
effectively synonymous in the English and European legal context, and we will
quite often explicitly make that point by speaking of 'labour or employment law'.
Having sought to deal, in a preliminary way at least, with the defining of labour law
both in its collective and individual dimensions, we should revert to and take some
care to expound the concept, which we have introduced, of 'the relational defining
of labour law', as it is crucial to the epistemology which we are seeking to establish.
When we speak of 'the relational defining of labour law', we refer to a process of
conceptualization which it has become customary to regard as the defining of the
'boundaries' or 'personal scope' of labour or employment law. This is usually
regarded as a single large debate about whether, and if so how far and in what
forms or respects, the definition and application of labour or employment law
should extend beyond employees, that is to say dependent workers, working under
contracts of employment. It is important to try to refine our understanding of what
is involved in this definitional debate, in particular by separating out several
distinguishable elements in it or aspects of it.

We should begin by remarking upon some features of this definitional debate or
process which may seem very obvious but whose importance is apt to be neglected
or understated. The definitional debate which is customarily understood as the
defining of the personal scope of labour or employment law is the process of
thought and discussion which locates labour and employment law within and
connects it to a sphere of social and economic activity which we may refer to, in
a deliberately loose and non-technical way, as 'the world of work'. This process of
defining usually takes the form of, or at least starts by, singling out categories of
persons recognized as particular kinds of workers – categories such as 'servants' or
'workmen' have historically been used, but the worker-typology most frequently
used in recent times has been that of 'employee', though in the context of English
law the wider personal typology of 'worker' is also now often used as a general
category.[9]

This mode of defining and conceptualizing the subject-matter of labour law
brings with it certain problems which are encountered when we describe and typify
people according to their roles in the world of work – when we say, for example,
that a person *is* an employee rather than saying that a person *works as* an employee.
In the historical dimension, this presents troubling analogies with situations in

---

[8]  The foundational text for which is G. Giugni (2007) *Diritto Sindacale*, XXX edn, Bari: Cacucci, at
p. 11. Our translation. Emphasis added.
[9]  Cf. Employment Rights Act (ERA) 1996, s. 230(3). Cf. below p. 277.

which lowly or servile work-based roles come to define various kinds of firmly imposed social, economic, and legal status, such as that of 'labourer' or 'serf'. Moreover, even in societies and legal systems in which the inherent equality of persons is recognized, the use of work-role personal categories to define the subject-matter of labour or employment law runs the risk of diverting attention from our assertion that the real subject-matter of labour law is of an essentially relational nature – consisting, as we suggested earlier, of the relations of working people with those for whom and with whom they work, and of the governance, in the widest sense, of their working environment and working conditions. Hence we prefer to think of the process of defining and conceptualizing the subject-matter of labour law as 'the relational defining of labour law' rather than 'defining the personal scope of labour law'.

That way of thinking about the process makes it easier to understand what is involved in the debates about it. It is useful to distinguish three main elements or kinds of conceptualization which are involved. These represent different ways of making category connections between labour or employment law and the world of work to which it relates. We begin by identifying two relatively obvious elements or kinds of conceptualization, and then continue by suggesting that there is a third less obvious but no less important element. Firstly there is an element in the process which consists of the identification of an outlining or framing concept, this being an encapsulation of all the relations or arrangements which are or should or might be regarded as forming the subject-matter of labour or employment law. We might call this the 'boundary function'. This could consist, for example, of defining the subject-matter of labour law as extending to all 'employment relationships' of all workers, whether those were employment relationships of private law or of public law.

There is a second element in the process, which is an obvious corollary of the first element, and which consists of ascribing a legal format or a set of legal formats to the relations or arrangements which are or should or might be regarded as forming the subject-matter of labour or employment law. We might call this the 'legal format function'. This could consist, for example, of determining that the general category of 'employment relationships' which defined the overall scope or boundary of labour law, was made up and composed of two legal formats, one the private law employment contract, and the other the public law employment relationship.

One might imagine that the relational defining of labour law could consist entirely of those two elements alone. However, it seems that there is often a third element, which we could call the 'central paradigm function'. This consists of identifying an archetypal kind of employment relation or arrangement which is viewed as representing the primary or core subject-matter of labour law. This central paradigm might be identified, for instance, as 'the private law employment relationship'. Various effects might follow from identifying a central paradigm in this way; it might be thought that all relations which were regarded as within the province of labour law should be regulated in the same way as or in a very similar way to the central paradigm; or it might be thought, on the other hand, that relations, the regulation of which was not and could not easily be approximated to that of the central paradigm, had only a very dubious if any claim to be regarded as within the province of labour law. So for example, it might be thought that the central paradigm of labour law was 'the private law employment relationship', and that public law employment relationships should either be regulated in the same way as private law ones, or, if that were not possible or appropriate, regarded as marginal to or even outside the province of labour law.

It can be observed or deduced from what we have said that this third element, the 'central paradigm function', which may be part of the process of the relational defining of labour law, has a more obviously normative aspect to it than the other two functions. Where and to the extent that the relational scope of labour law is determined by reference to a central paradigm, some kind of critical viewpoint is involved which amounts to a normative judgment that the paradigmatic relation ought in some way to be the dominant one in establishing the regulatory pattern or regulatory model for all relations or arrangements falling within the relational scope of labour law. In the example that we have given, the 'private law employment relationship' figures as the dominant one in shaping the regulatory pattern or model for all relations or arrangements regarded as falling within the province of labour law.

We can go on to observe, from an empirical consideration of the ways in which the relational defining of labour law has occurred in particular legal systems, that this third function, the central paradigm function, although not a logically neces-sary element in the process, nevertheless often forms a very important part of the process. Indeed, we can go further and say that the central paradigm function not infrequently takes the leading part in the relational defining of labour law, so that the relational scope of labour law is defined around a central paradigm, and in the extreme case is actually defined by its central paradigm. Again using the same example, the 'private law employment relationship' may serve both as the central paradigm and dominant regulatory pattern for labour law and as the boundary definition of its relational scope. We can further observe, from empirical consider-ation of the ways in which systems of labour law develop, that if a particular system of labour law is strongly defined by its central paradigm, then it is likely to be subjected to great stresses and strains by 'paradigm shifts' in the functioning or behaviour of the labour market and in the patterns of personal work arrangements.

Although we believe that we can demonstrate that this argument is not one which is artificially constructed around a single real example, it is useful to refer at this point to a real example. We suggest that the relational definition of labour law within the English legal system does very well illustrate the process of definition from and by reference to a dominant central paradigm. The central paradigm in question has been that of the contract of employment. In subsequent sections and in later chapters we will consider at length the causes and the very significant consequences of this paradigmatic mode of relational definition of labour law; and we will conduct that inquiry on a comparative basis. Before doing so, we shall attempt to establish a broader and less normatively charged boundary definition for labour law. As a preliminary to that exercise, we shall seek to explain more fully why we think that the relational defining of labour law became a normatively charged one in the first place.

In order to do that, we revert to our starting notion of a consensus, albeit incomplete, which identifies labour law as a distinctive subject of study and practice in English law and as having correspondingly distinctive equivalents in other European legal systems. In what sense should we think of the area of study and practice, which is the subject of that (incomplete) consensus as a 'distinctive' one? There are many possible answers to that question, and the best answer varies as between different contributors to the consensus. A legal practitioner may contribute to that consensus because he or she is in a professional situation in which he or she operates as a specialist in that area, and in which he or she finds it necessary or useful for the knowledge base on which he or she relies to be classified in that way. A legal scholar may think it important for him or her to study and teach and write within an area which is identified in that way. Those perceptions or preferences may be passive and receptive ones, or they may be active and creative ones. We may find it convenient to accept and work according to an established perception that there is a distinctive area of study and practice which we can identify as labour law; or on the other hand we may strive to create, maintain, or shape and enhance such a consensus.

It is useful for us to concentrate on the active or creative contributors to the consensus which identifies labour law as a distinctive area of study and practice, hence the ones who give shape and specificity to the area. In so doing, they will typically be animated by normative perceptions, which provide reasons or motivations for seeking to develop and shape labour law as a distinctive area of study and practice. A normative perception which often animates such contributors is that there is a special importance to ensuring that the legal systems with which they are concerned contain a specialized body of law and regulation devoted to the protection of the welfare of workers in their working lives. But that is by no means the only motivation which may be encountered; a frequently encountered alternative perception is that there is a special importance to identifying and shaping a specialized body of law and regulation which reconciles that objective with ensuring the efficient functioning of the productive economy.

We might expect to find, and we do in various ways in fact find, that these normative perceptions closely and significantly inform the creation and shaping of the consensus which identifies labour law as a distinctive area of study and practice. This kind of normative shaping occurs in all sorts of ways; the reason for drawing attention to it at this point in our discussion is that it crucially affects and determines the relational defining of labour law. In particular, we can observe many points at which the active and creative contributors to the prevailing consensus about the relational definition of labour law within national legal systems have steered that consensus towards a central and dominant paradigm, such as that of 'the contract of employment' or 'the subordinate employment relationship'; and they have done so with some more or less conscious normative objective, which is of a worker-protective character.

While we do not in any way denigrate those normative objectives nor the achievements which have resulted from the pursuing of those objectives, we think it is useful and important that the relational defining of labour law, at least as to its outer relational boundaries, should not be artificially constrained by reference to those normative objectives. We suggest that the three functions of establishing relational boundaries, legal formats, and central paradigms should be maintained as distinct ones in the process of the relational defining of labour law, and that the fulfilling of the first of those functions, the boundary function, should not be overwhelmed by the normative objectives of the third, central paradigm, function. In the next section, we argue for a way of defining the relational domain and outer boundaries of labour law which seeks to achieve that aim.

## Section 2:  The Personal Work Relation as the Domain of Labour Law

In the previous section, we presented arguments for beginning this work with a 'relational defining of labour law'; and we sought to show that this could most satisfactorily be accomplished by distinguishing between three separate functions which often tend to become inter-mixed, namely those of the boundary definition of the sphere of operation of labour law, the ascribing of legal formats to relations deemed to be within that sphere of operation, and the establishing of a central paradigm for those relations. We concluded by suggesting that it would be useful to separate out the first function, that of boundary definition, and to concentrate upon it as an initial step in our 'relational analysis of labour law'. In this section we first present arguments for regarding the task of establishing a 'relational boundary definition' of and for labour law as a feasible and important one, and we put forward an initial outline of our 'relational boundary definition' for English labour law on a European comparative basis, using the terminology of 'the personal work relation' to express that definition.

So we begin our discussion of the relational boundary definition of labour law by considering whether and how far it is on the one hand useful and on the other hand feasible to establish such a definition, either for a particular national legal system or more broadly. In the previous section, we argued that this process of relational definition could best be carried out by separating it from the functions of identifying central paradigms and legal formats; but that still does not demonstrate that the process of relational definition is a useful or feasible one. Refining the question may have helped towards an answer, but does not in and of itself provide the answer.

The question about the relational boundary definition of labour law has, as we have indicated, become one of a set of millennial controversies for theorists of the subject, spoken of as a 'crisis of fundamental concepts',[10] and those controversies

---

[10] Cf. J. Clark and Lord Wedderburn, in Lord Wedderburn, R. Lewis, and J. Clark (eds) (1983) *Labour Law and Industrial Relations: Building on Kahn-Freund*, Oxford: Clarendon, 144 et seq.

have, as we shall seek to show, also affected the decision-making processes of the practical making and applying of labour law. We can use our distinction between the three functions partially at least to deconstruct these controversies. There is grave doubt as to whether we any longer have a clear central paradigm for labour law such as the contract of employment once seemed to provide in the English legal system, and such as its equivalents seemed to provide in other European legal systems. There is similar doubt about how to classify and articulate the legal formats in which to embody the work relations with which labour law is concerned. There seems to be a separate, though of course associated, controversy as to whether we can maintain an overall relational boundary for labour law, and if so where that boundary should be placed.

As we have said, refining the question does not answer it; separating out the boundary-defining question does not reduce it to a merely technical one which has an obvious technical answer. On the contrary: if, as we do, you accept that there is a crucial connection between the purpose of legal regulation and its relational scope, then you have simply distilled down the whole set of epistemic questions about 'labour law' into one foundational problem; what is or should be the essential equation between purpose and scope for labour law? So we should not expect an easy answer for any one national legal system, let alone for a multiplicity of legal systems. Indeed, it could be said that by distilling out this essential problem, we have identified its enormity, perhaps even its insolubility.

It is this doubt about the validity of the essential purpose/scope equation which has produced the sense of the 'crisis of fundamental concepts' in labour law. There is a widespread perception that there was a received or traditional wisdom about the purpose/scope equation at the heart of labour law, and that this equation is no longer valid because of a series of social, economic, and legal evolutions in the world of work and its governance. That traditional purpose/scope equation consists of the proposition that the essential function of labour law is the redressing of the inequality of bargaining power inherent in the subordinate employment relationship as expressed in the legal format of the contract of employment.

Within that widespread consensus that there has been a breakdown, or at least a growing dysfunctionality, in the purpose/scope equation of labour law, there seems to be a divergence of approaches about the possibility of repair. There are divergent tendencies towards two extreme positions; neither of these two extreme positions is openly taken, but argumentation tends in one or other direction. One extreme position, towards which some theorists tend, is that once the traditional purpose/ scope equation is discarded, there is no available alternative which maintains the essential integrity or functionality of labour law. At the opposite extreme of the theoretical tendencies is the view that the traditional purpose/scope equation can be re-worked without losing the essential integrity or functionality of labour law, as long as the adaptation is sufficiently intelligent, and suitably reflexive of social, economic, and legal evolutions in the world of work and its governance.

If we were obliged to locate ourselves in that spectrum of theoretical positions, it would be towards the latter end of it. We think that it is useful and feasible to work towards an adapted purpose/scope equation for labour law. Within that adapted equation, as we shall show more fully in later chapters, an important element would be a notion which we identify as that of 'personality in work'. The essential idea of that notion, as we shall later show, is to maximize the dignity accorded to workers in personal work relations and to optimize their capabilities in and through those relations while recognizing the need to attribute some degree of stability to all personal work relations. Our intuition is that this adaptation of the traditional equation might serve to identify in a useful way a long-term shift in the pre-occupations of labour law, in the context of the English legal system at least, from supporting and providing default substitutes for collective bargaining for workers in 'standard' work relations, to providing basic minimum labour standards, redressing inequalities between groups of workers, and controlling the oppressive or arbitrary treatment of individual workers across a rather wider range of work relations.

Perhaps the most controversial element in that adapted equation, and certainly the element upon which our attention needs to be focused for the purposes of the present work, consists in its assertion of a new and wider scope for labour law: this is the move from the contract of employment to the personal work relation. In other words, the controversy as to whether it is feasible and useful to move to an adapted purpose/scope equation tends to focus upon the scope, that is to say upon the new boundary definition. So in relation to our proposed equation, the controversy would be concentrated on the assertion of the 'personal work relation' as an appropriate new boundary definition.

Here again, we might expect to find a range of opinions. At one extreme, the view might be that once labour law ceases to be anchored in and by the contract of employment, it is bound to drift aimlessly. At the other extreme, the squarely contrary view might be that labour law, having broken free of the definitional constraints of the contract of employment, should not be subjected to a different definitional constraint but should range freely across a 'world of work' which is conceived of in a totally loose or open-ended way. By espousing the notion of the 'personal work relation' as the boundary definition, we seek to take up a middle position between those extremes. We go on to explain why we seek that particular intermediate position, and of what, more precisely, our middle position consists.

We think that a boundary definition, albeit an open-textured one, is necessary in order to create, or at least focus the discussion about, an overall purpose/scope equation for labour law as a whole. We are quite clear that this general purpose/scope equation does not apply and should not necessarily apply to each specific intervention which labour law makes into the regulation of personal work relations: each such intervention has, quite appropriately, its own specific purpose/scope equation. Law-makers impose their own purpose/scope equations upon their specific interventions; theorists may press for different purpose/scope equations either for those specific interventions or on a general basis: we do not envisage our boundary definition as pre-empting those decisions or foreclosing those theoretical debates.

So we put forward 'the personal work relation' as an overarching category, not with the implication that it should denote the relational scope of each and every labour law intervention, but with the idea that it should be a framing and organizing notion which would give a conceptual unity to the process of striking particular purpose/scope equations for particular interventions. Hence we suggest that it is useful and important to identify 'the personal work relation' as a concept which frames a discussion within which we can observe and evaluate the fact that, in English law, there is a rather narrow purpose/scope equation for unfair dismissal law, another rather wider purpose/scope equation for the law of working time regulation, another still wider one for the legal interventions to combat various types of discrimination in employment and so on.

We also suggest that the establishing of a boundary definition for labour law has another and somewhat more prescriptive function. We suggest that a boundary definition is necessary in order to identify a domain or sphere of operation within which labour law, as a distinctive branch of legal science, has a kind of technical task or responsibility. That technical task or responsibility, we suggest, is to ensure that some kind of carefully and suitably designed legal format is assigned or at least is available to be assigned to the work relations or work arrangements which fall within that domain or sphere.

We make that suggestion because we are concerned about the possibility – indeed, as we shall argue in the course of this work, in some instances the actuality – that the body of labour law within a given national legal system may fail to discharge that technical responsibility, allowing certain work relations to remain in a condition of legal 'anomie' or lack of normative structure. That would seem to us to fail to give effect to the general purpose/scope equation which we are putting forward, loose and permissive though that formula is. In other words, the failure to assign a carefully and suitably designed legal format to a work relation or arrangement falling within the broad category of 'personal work relations' would, we suggest, amount to a failure to respect the values of dignity, capability, and stability which ought to shape and inform the regulation which labour law effects within that domain.

We have thus argued that the establishment of a relational boundary definition for labour law does have a significant normative function; and we have put forward the notion of the 'personal work relation' as the one which is in our view best suited to carry that normative burden. However, that normative function cannot be fulfilled merely by choosing that form of words to identify the relational boundary of labour law. To fulfil that normative function, the definition has to be given detailed substance. We might imagine that this could be achieved simply by providing a verbal definition of the concept. If so, our proposed definition would be, in its basic outline form, that the personal work relation consists of an engagement, or arrangement, or set of arrangements for the carrying out of work or the rendering of service or services by the worker personally.

However, we do not believe that such an act of verbal definition, even if carried out at the highest level of legislative power or theoretical authoritativeness, could in itself accomplish the task of providing a useful specification of the relational boundary of labour law within a given legal system. If there is to be a meaningful overarching relational 'category of categories' for a labour law system, such a category has to be established and maintained not by a single determination but by a continuing process of debate, articulation, and argument. We first consider some existing locations or starting points for such a process, and we then suggest how the process of relational boundary definition for labour law might be further developed within the context of the English legal system on a European comparative basis.

Our existing locations or starting points for considering the process of relational boundary definition for labour law are varied in nature; and it is important to observe that such processes may be of several different types, located at different levels of debate. Such processes may vary as to the rigour or exactitude of the relational definition which they seek to establish, from loose definition to tight definition. They may also vary as to the extent to which they are purposive, that is to say consciously seeking an optimal purpose/scope equation for labour law; so there may be a variation as to whether the process is functionalist or formalistic. Finally, there is a spectrum from theoretical processes not directly concerned with detailed law-making to practical processes which are directly concerned with law-making or legal adjudication. We shall look at actual examples of relational boundary defining processes which vary in these dimensions, with a view to understanding the dynamics and problems of those processes and using those conclusions to optimize the design of our own proposal for a process of relational boundary definition of labour law, constructed around the notion of 'the personal work relation'.

The two actual examples of boundary defining exercises which we shall consider, both of which occurred or were initiated in the middle to late 1990s, were driven by a perception internationally shared among law-makers and theorists working in the field of labour law – the very same perception that inspires the arguments of this chapter – that it had become important to enlarge the relational space within which labour law operates if the original goals of labour law were to remain capable of being realized in a world of work whose organizational norms and structures were changing in their social, economic, and legal dimensions. This broad consensus, as we have previously observed, identified the importance of breaking out of the confines of the subordinate employment relationship legally embodied in the contract of employment: but, very understandably in view of the inherent difficulty of the issue, that consensus did not extend to an agreement as to what larger framing concept should be put in its place.

The first such boundary-defining exercise to which we wish to refer was undertaken by the International Labour Organization ('ILO'). It took place in two phases, in the first of which a radical proposal was made but rejected, and in the second of which a more cautious proposal was made and accepted. The radical proposal which was originally advanced in the mid-1990s was for an ILO Convention which would have provided for the extension of the apparatus of ILO labour standard-setting to a specially devised category of 'contract workers'.[11] This additional category was devised in an attempt to ensure the inclusion within the scope of national labour standards of workers in triangular work relations. Its rather unexpected rejection by the ILO Conference was partly attributable to a rearguard

---

[11] ILO (1997) *Contract labour – Fifth item on the agenda Report V (1) to the International Labour Conference 86th Session 1998*, Geneva.

resistance by the representatives of employers to such a radical extension of the protective scope of ILO labour standards, but partly also to an incomprehension and suspicion of the terminology of 'contract workers' which extended right across all three representative sections, governments, and trade unions as well as employers.[12]

The disappointed protagonists of this proposal took some years to regroup. The expression 'contract labour' was abandoned and the discussion centred upon a resolution referring provisionally to 'workers in situations needing protection'.[13] Even this line of enquiry was, however, toned down, wisely in our view, in favour of a new focus on the notion of 'scope of the employment relationship'. Their eventually successful proposal was for the Recommendation on the Employment Relationship,[14] with no reference to the notion of 'scope', possibly to suggest that the instrument was more concerned with clarifying the definitions of employment relationship rather than re-elaborating any particular scope for it. That Recommendation, using the notion of the 'employment relationship' as its overarching category, seeks to open up a line of escape from the constraints of the contract of employment in the contract dimension at least, if not in the employment dimension. The legislators on this occasion, rather than seeking to make this a prescriptively imposed new outline category for ILO labour standard-setting, more cautiously settled for a recommendation to participating states to engage in a comparative process of reconsideration of the scope – in fact of what we have envisaged as the purpose/relational scope equations – of their own national labour law interventions.

Meanwhile, a profoundly important exercise in the reconsideration of the relational scope and definition of labour law was taking place, at the level of policy-making and theoretical development, within the European Union (EU) as a whole. This exercise took the form of the instituting by the European Commission of a group of experts, under the chairmanship of Alain Supiot, to formulate ideas and proposals about the evolution of labour law. Their Report, officially presented in 1998,[15] was published in French in 1999 under the title *Au delà de l'Emploi*[16] and in English translation in 2001 under the title *Beyond Employment* (the 'Supiot Report').[17] Their central objective, as the title of their work implies, was for a reframing of labour law in such a way as to free it from the constraints of

[12] Cf. ILO (2003) *International Labour Conference Report V – The Scope of the Employment Relationship – Fifth Item on the Agenda*, Geneva, p. 6.

[13] For an overview of the debates leading to this shift of emphasis see ILO (2003) *International Labour Conference Report V – The Scope of the Employment Relationship – Fifth Item on the Agenda*, Geneva, pp. 6–16.

[14] R 198, Employment Relationship Recommendation (2006) (95th Conference Session, Geneva, 15 June 2006). The instrument refers to the concept of 'worker in need of protection', though only in its Preamble.

[15] A. Supiot, M. E. Casas, J. De Munck, P. Hanau, A. Johansson, P. Meadows, E. Mingione, R. Salais, P. van der Heijden (1998) *Transformation of labour and future of labour law in Europe – Final Report*.

[16] A. Supiot, et al. (1999) *Au-delà de l'emploi: transformations du travail et devenir du droit du travail en Europe: rapport pour la Commission des Communautés européennes*, Paris: Flammarion.

[17] A. Supiot, et al. (2001) *Beyond Employment – Changes in Work and the Future of Labour Law in Europe*, Oxford: OUP.

the subordinate or dependent employment contract. As that is the very objective of this initial part of our own work, and as they made a very significant and influential theoretical contribution to the achievement of that objective, the construct which they devised deserves our close attention.

The central idea or strategy of the 'Supiot Report' was to recognize, and to promote a consciousness of, an essential continuity of concern to labour law, across a very broad range of situations in which people engage in work, or seek work, or prepare themselves for work, or stand in readiness to work, and so can be recognized as members of the labour force. They also recognized a still more extended continuity of concern between those situations and a further set of situations in which people capable of operating as members of the labour force were in fact engaging in activity beyond the realm of the labour market, for example, because they are engaged on the kinds of work which are regarded as taking place beyond the labour market, of which a very important instance is unpaid domestic work in a person's own household or unpaid caring for a person's own children or other dependents.[18]

Supiot and his colleagues conceived a grand design to give effect, in the framing of labour law, to these continuities of concern. We suggest that they provided the basis for a particular kind of relational boundary definition for labour law, and a re-imagining of the basic purpose/scope equation of labour law, in just the way that we are seeking to do. However, we think that the nature of this design has not always been fully and clearly understood, especially among the English-speaking audience of the Report, because of some difficulties in transposing into an English legal discourse some of its key concepts originally devised in other languages and legal discourses, especially the French one. We go on to suggest that, when those misunderstandings are teased out, it becomes apparent that our own proposal of the 'personal work relation' is very closely similar, though not identical, to the essential defining relational idea of the 'Supiot Report'.

The relational design of the 'Supiot Report' is constructed around two key concepts, which have deservedly become catchwords for theorists and students of labour law. One is the idea of, in the original French, the '*statut professionnel*', translated in the English version as 'labour force membership';[19] and the other is the idea of '*droits de tirage sociaux*', translated as 'social drawing rights'. The notion of 'social drawing rights' identifies the claims to social support which attach to all the work situations, in the broadest sense, which the Supiot Commission identified, both within and beyond the labour market. The 'Supiot Report' has, we think, often been understood as linking together the two notions of '*statut professionnel*' and 'social drawing rights' so that some kind of '*statut professionnel*' is or should be associated with all those situations to which 'social drawing rights' are attached; and

---

[18] Cf. N. Busby (2011) *A Right to Care? – Unpaid Care Work in European Employment Law*, Oxford: OUP, especially Chapter 5, 'European Union Law and Policy: Balancing Paid Employment and Unpaid Care within a Market Order'.
[19] Cf. Chapter 2 and Chapter 8 in both the French original and the English translation.

so between them these two concepts provide a new kind of purpose/scope equation for labour law.

We believe that the 'Supiot Report' in fact envisaged a rather tighter kind of purpose/scope equation for labour law. For the authors of the Report, the continuity of concern across all those situations attracting 'social drawing rights' described a larger sphere than that of 'labour law' alone, namely the wider domain of '*Droit Social*' in French, '*Sozialrecht*' in German, and social law in English – 'labour law' being a subset of 'social law'.[20] The domain of labour law was envisaged as the narrower sphere, albeit one much wider than the traditional one of subordinate or dependent employment, in which people work under some kind of work obligation to another or others which is or can be legally recognized. That is the sphere of the '*statut professionnel*', and so in that particular sense the '*statut professionnel*' becomes the relational boundary concept which defines the domain of labour law (while in a rather different way the concept of 'social drawing rights' defines the wider domain of 'social law').

It is this relational definition which is, we believe, somewhat obscured by the translation of '*statut professionnel*' into 'labour force membership'. That is because the English terminology of 'labour force membership' sounds as if it extends to the situations of those who are capable of work but not in fact working nor in any significant relation with a particular employer or potential employer; whereas, if the original French terminology of '*statut professionnel*' extends at all into that territory, it does so only to a very slight extent. The original French terminology of '*statut professionnel*' is tied to a notion of relational work obligation which is not adequately conveyed by the English terminology of 'labour force membership'.

In fact, we do believe that the intentions and associations which Supiot and his colleagues encapsulated in their original terminology of the '*statut professionnel*', that is to say their allusions to the idea of being in a work situation involving some kind of relational work obligation, are fairly closely replicated in our own notion of the 'personal work relation' as providing a relational boundary definition for labour law, and as providing the basis for a newly extended purpose/scope equation for labour law (though there are some divergences which we consider in Chapters 8 and 9). However, we are dealing in highly nuanced and slippery conceptions, which need to be further elucidated by argumentation which will give them substantial meaning in practical contexts. In the next section we seek to provide that further elucidation, invoking an idea of the 'personal work relation' as multi-faceted and as having a multiplicity of interfaces with other kinds of social, economic, and legal relations or situations.

Before doing so, it will be useful to recapitulate upon the two exercises in normative development which we have identified as having taken place in recent years – that is to say the presentation of the 'Supiot Report' in 1999 and the enactment of ILO Recommendation 198 on the Employment Relationship in 2006 – which have each articulated their own corresponding scoping notion.

---

[20] See for instance p. 54 of the English version, where, in discussing 'The Four Circles of Social Law' 'social law' is described as an amalgam, 'in the broad sense [of] labour law and social security law'.

This will give an indication of the choices which have been seen to present themselves to those engaged in such exercises, and will also enable us to locate our boundary concept in relation to the choices which were made on those other occasions.

Both of these two exercises in normative development appear to have been prompted by concerns – on the part of the European Commission and the ILO respectively – that developments in the labour market had brought about a state of affairs where the relational categories of labour law were no longer adapted to the regulatory tasks which presented themselves. Each of the two exercises in a sense generated its own new foundational category or boundary concept for labour law; these represented two widely divergent strategies for the articulation of such a category or concept, and we shall attempt to locate our own suggested boundary concept in relation to those other two. The relational category which had traditionally been used by labour law systems both as a paradigm and as a boundary concept was that of the contract of employment, and it was the boundary imposed by that concept which both these normative exercises were concerned to enlarge.

The strategies for doing so were, however, very different; and this difference may well be attributable to the divergence in function between the two exercises. The 'Supiot Report' was essentially a normative treatise, and was in no sense legislative in character, nor indeed did it even recommend specific reforming measures. In that mode of discourse, the authors could and did assert an intellectual and practical freedom to break right out of the existing confines of labour law, and the very title of their report – *Au delà de l'emploi*, translated as *Beyond Employment* – proclaimed that intention. Their chosen alternative scoping concept, an exceedingly wide one, was that of '*statut professionel*', translated as 'membership of the labour force'.

The officials and policymakers of the ILO had been, from the mid-1990s onwards, for their part preoccupied with the perceived insufficiencies of the relational categories of national labour laws in the face of labour market evolution, and had embarked upon a long and tortuous exercise in normative reform which culminated, somewhat disappointingly in the eyes of many, in the adoption of Recommendation 198 on the Employment Relationship in 2006. This exercise was essentially one which had the ambition of enacting international legislation, and of which the original hope had been that it might result in an ILO Convention. Therefore, essentially constrained by the difficulties of securing tripartite international consensus to legislative categories, those who framed and conducted this exercise felt that they had to be somewhat cautious as to the extent and manner of their challenge to the existing relational categories of national labour laws.

This was a caution which was very greatly heightened by the unexpectedly abrupt rejection by the International Labour Conference of 1998 of preliminary proposals for such Convention to address a growing set of issues about the classification of triangular employment relations which had been advanced under the conceptual heading of 'contract labour' by a Committee tasked to consider that subject. The officials and policymakers appreciated the sheer difficulty, at the terminological as well as at the political level, of securing agreement to a conceptual fresh start in this area. They widened their focus to include an even broader range of problems about the relational categories of labour law, but found that this only increased their terminological and conceptual difficulties.

Having experimented with the normatively tautological notion of 'workers in need of protection', they adopted a strategy of seeking to set up a framework for the extension or inclusive development of existing categories rather than for the introduction of a new foundational category or set of categories. It was that strategy which, in our suggestion, generated the decision to deploy the notion of the 'employment relationship'; that notion was itself probably intended to represent a kind of internationally inclusive amalgam of evolving national conceptions of the contract of employment.

Our framing of the notion of the personal work relation or personal work nexus, and our working definition of that notion, are aimed at steering a path which lies between those two different strategies and between the formulations which they respectively generated. By comparison with the 'Supiot Report', we have chosen a boundary concept which is, as we have said, a somewhat narrower one – we elaborate the difference in detail in Chapters 8 and 9 – and which is, we suggest, accordingly more capable of delineating a distinctive sphere of operation for labour law. On the other hand, by comparison with ILO Recommendation 198, we have chosen a boundary concept which is a significantly broader one – indeed one operating at a different level and with a different set of normative ambitions – and which therefore poses a stronger challenge to the existing relational category concepts of national labour law systems.

Our underlying aim in pursuing this strategy is to create a pressure for the re-evaluation and rethinking of the existing relational categories of labour law – an aim which we share with those who were engaged in both of those two normative exercises. We have argued that this has to be done within a conceptual space which is, on the one hand, sufficiently large to expose the existing categories to open-minded questioning, but on the other hand sufficiently precisely and narrowly bounded as to maintain its convincingness as a coherent area of legal regulatory activity. We have suggested that the notion of the personal work relation is the most apt one which we can devise to delineate that conceptual space, and we have offered an outline definition of it which seeks to walk that particular tightrope between openness and boundedness. In the next section we elaborate that definition and begin to show how it might function to bring about the re-evaluation of existing categories.

## Section 3:  A Functional Definition of the Personal Work Relation

In the previous sections, we have identified as the epistemic starting point of our work the idea of a reconceived and extended purpose/relational scope equation for labour law, and we have put forward the concept of the personal work relation as our chosen relational boundary concept. The purpose of the succeeding chapters is to show, on a European comparative basis, how the relational framework of labour law is currently constructed in the English legal system on an essentially contractual basis, and how that relational framework might, with advantage, be differently constructed with more direct reference to the idea of the personal work relation. Some further preliminary and preparatory steps are necessary in order to pursue that objective. One such step is to develop and further to define the concept of 'the personal work relation'.

For that purpose, we present in this section a series of assertions or arguments. Firstly, we explain what we mean by 'developing and further defining the concept of the personal work relation'; we suggest that this consists not of immediately regarding the concept of the personal work relation as a legal term of art, but rather of initiating a process of discussion about 'the personal work relation' as a component in a general purpose/scope equation for labour law (Subsection A). Secondly, we suggest that this process of discussion can be developed and advanced by considering 'the personal work relation' as being recognizable from the way in which it interfaces with a number of other relations or personal situations (Subsection B). By this route, we seek to reach a point where, in the following section, a working definition of our concept of the personal work relation can be aligned with existing relational category definitions in English and European labour law.

## A. The Suggested Definition and its Function

So the first in this sequence of assertions or arguments is that the best and most appropriate way for us to develop and more fully articulate the concept of 'the personal work relation', as the relational boundary-defining notion for labour law, is not by seeking to provide a static definition of it as a legal 'term of art', but rather by regarding it as a concept which acquires and maintains its meaning through a process of discussion. That process of discussion, we suggest, should take the following form; it should be regarded as the establishing of a zone or sphere for the working out of the whole set of purpose/scope equations for the whole set of labour law interventions which occur within a given legal system at a given moment in time. As those sets of interventions and those sets of equations change over time, so in consequence does the overall purpose/scope equation for labour law as a whole, and so in turn may the zone or sphere, within which that equation is struck, need to be reconsidered from time to time. Hence we think it is counter-productive immediately to attempt a fixed definition of 'the personal work relation', and that the productive use of the concept consists in refining our understanding of it by means of continuing reflection.

So we suggest that it is useful to think of the notion of 'the personal work relation' as providing, in the first instance, a 'soft boundary' for labour law. That is to say, it provides a loose parameter which identifies a sphere of operation within which labour law interventions may be appropriate, or within which it may be appropriate to regard legal interventions as forming part of labour law. As such, the notion of the personal work relation serves to describe a zone within which precise legal conceptions of the scope of particular labour law interventions may be formulated. So this parameter is a 'soft' one in the senses both that it does not function as a legal term of art technically defining the relational scope of particular legal interventions, and in that it is the subject of continuing discussion or reflection.

However, even if it is 'soft' in those senses, this boundary notion must have some shape and specificity if it is to serve as a way of usefully developing our understanding of the general purpose/scope equation for labour law in a given legal system at a particular time. We suggest that this required minimum of shape and specificity might be provided in two ways. Firstly, we expound somewhat further, but still at a rather general level, upon the formulation of the idea of the personal work relation which we put forward earlier. Secondly, we seek to show how that formulation may be more specifically or concretely understood by regarding it as having a series of interfaces with other and different social or economic relations. Our starting point for those two sets of assertions consists of the outline formulation which we suggested earlier for our notion of the personal work relation, namely that it consists of an engagement, or arrangement, or set of arrangements for the carrying out of work or the rendering of service or services by the worker personally. We now proceed to flesh out that formulation more fully.

So we are at this point seeking to put in place the cornerstone of the conceptual edifice which we have sought to erect in the course of this chapter. We have sought in the preceding sections to demonstrate the need for an expansive and inclusive boundary or framing concept to designate the social and economic relations with which labour law should properly be concerned. That boundary conception, as we have acknowledged, has a normative role; it is a functional or instrumental one in the sense that it is integrally linked to the functions of labour law itself. Our boundary concept will therefore necessarily imply a choice or position as to those functions within a range of possibilities about which theorists disagree. Our choice or position as to those functions is comprised in an idea or ideal of 'personality in work' which we seek to flesh out in later chapters, and especially in Chapter 9. At this stage, we concentrate on defining the boundary concept for labour law which we hope and believe will be normatively sustained and justified in the course of this work as a whole.

That boundary concept, as we have previously indicated, is that of the personal work relation, which, as we shall explain more fully in Chapter 8 of this work, we may alternatively speak of as the personal work nexus. We are using those two terminologies in an effectively synonymous way; as will be explained more fully in due course, we refer to the personal work relation when concentrating on the external or boundary aspect of this foundational concept, and we refer to the personal work nexus when concentrating on the internal or analytical aspect of the same concept. Our suggested definition has a primarily inclusive thrust or emphasis because, as we shall seek to show in the course of the subsequent chapters, we think there is a strong case to be made on functional grounds for drawing our boundary concept in such a way as to transcend some particular restrictions which have traditionally been placed on the framing of the boundaries of labour law. At the same time, our suggested definition is framed in recognition of the contrary need to describe the boundary concept of labour law sufficiently narrowly and clearly, with sufficient separation from other kinds of social and economic relation, as to sustain the essential autonomy or distinctiveness of labour law as a legal discipline and as a policy pursuit.

So our suggested definition of our boundary concept seeks to break the bounds of the contract of employment – both as to the element of 'contract' and as to that of 'employment' – and to extend into a wider realm of 'relation' or 'nexus' rather than of 'contract' and of 'work', and more precisely of 'personal work', rather than 'employment'. In order to give some shape and precision to those two notions of 'relation' and 'personal work' and their conjunction with each other, we propose the following working definition:

The personal work relation is a connection or set of connections, between a person – the worker – and another person or persons or an organization or organizations, arising from an engagement or arrangement or set of arrangements for the carrying out of work or the rendering of service or services by the worker personally, that is to say wholly or primarily by the worker himself or herself.

We proceed to elaborate that suggested or working definition of the personal work relation or nexus. Before doing so, we consider in slightly more detail the purpose or purposes for which we might be defining and using our boundary concept, since that will influence the ways in which this elaboration is carried out. First we suggest the purposes for which we might conceivably be doing so, and then, within those alternatives, the purposes for which we actually propose to do so. Our boundary concept might conceivably be used and defined for one or more of the following purposes:

We might conceivably wish to elaborate the definition of the personal work relation for a very fundamentally prescriptive purpose so that it could be used as the criterion of personal or relational scope for all labour laws or labour rights.

Alternatively, we might wish to elaborate the definition of the personal work relation for a less fundamentally prescriptive purpose so that it could be used as the criterion of personal or relational scope for some labour laws or labour rights rather than for all of them.

As a further alternative, we might wish to elaborate the definition of the personal work relation for a still less fundamentally prescriptive purpose so that it could be used simply as a scoping notion for the normative discussion of the criteria of personal or relational scope for labour laws or labour rights, rather than as a criterion for the relational scope of particular labour laws or labour rights.

This delineation of the possible purposes of defining our boundary concept could itself be further elaborated, for example, by considering it as the basis for presumptions rather than hard rules about the personal or relational scope for labour laws or labour rights. But it is perhaps more useful to indicate our intentions within that relatively straightforward set of alternatives. We do not intend to elaborate our definition of the personal work relation for the first of those three conceivable alternative purposes. That is primarily because we think that such a project would, even if we were convinced of its theoretical desirability, be regarded as representing an aspiration which was wholly remote from the present realities of English labour law and that of other European countries. In addition, this is also because we firmly believe that it would be disingenuous to suggest the first, more practical, purpose as the object of our work, without first elaborating convincingly on the other two, and on the third one in particular.

Paraphrasing the perceptive statement by Gerry Cohen, that 'principles that reflect facts must, in order to reflect facts, reflect principles that don't reflect facts',[21] our initial and main purpose in elaborating our working definition of the personal work relation is to combine the second and third of the three alternatives which we have delineated, in a context of relative abstraction from specific normative proposals. Thus in the remainder of this subsection, we will begin to elaborate our working definition of the personal work relation or nexus simply as a scoping notion for the discussion of the criteria of personal or relational scope for labour laws or labour rights. However in the next subsection, we will further elaborate the definition with the more radically prescriptive purpose of showing how it could be used as the criterion of personal or relational scope for some labour laws or labour rights. At that second stage, we will seek to show how that elaborated definition would be aligned in relation to boundary concepts which are currently used in English labour law and that of other European countries.

The notion of 'the personal work relation' which we are putting forward, and for which we are suggesting that fuller formulation, is a narrower and more specific one than the notion of 'work' itself, and *a fortiori*, narrower than other broad notions such as 'activity'. For the broader notion of 'work' itself, it seems to us satisfactory to adopt and use any chosen dictionary definition. The notion of 'the personal work relation' is a narrower one than that of 'work' itself in that it confines itself to work taking place within a 'relation' and it further confines itself to work relations which are 'personal'. Our fuller formulation seeks to make clear the sense in which it is confined to work taking place within a 'relation', and also touches upon the sense in which it is further confined to 'personal' work relations; but it is useful to bring out those elements somewhat further.

So, as to the first of those two elements, namely the relational one, our formulation confines the broader notion of 'work' to the narrower notion of a 'work relation' by referring to working in the context of an engagement or arrangement or set of arrangements. We are conscious that this is in some respects a normative definition; it is not the only or self-evident way in which we might specify a relational element in our boundary conception for labour law. If pressed to declare the basis for that normativity, we would fall back upon the idea, which we have invoked earlier, of a general purpose/scope equation for labour law as a whole, and upon the idea, also invoked earlier, of respect for dignity, capability, and stability in the context of work as an element in that equation. The combination of those two ideas seems to us to point towards an essentially relational conception of the sphere of operation of labour law. In addition, we suggest that 'work' and 'relation' are mutually reinforcing concepts. Work, as opposed to 'action' or an unqualified notion of 'activity' – which can occur outside a relational framework, or be recreational in character – is, it seems to us, essentially relational. And for this

[21]  G. A. Cohen (2003) 'Facts and Principles', 31, *Philosophy & Public Affairs*, 211–45, at 214.

reason we venture to suggest that work that is not 'relational' falls outside our concept of 'personal work relation'. We shall revert shortly to a further development of our normative reasons for identifying that relational element in the particular way that we have done.

If our conception of the appropriate boundary-defining notion for the sphere of operation of labour law is an essentially relational one, it is also an essentially 'personal' one. There are various senses in which this terminology of 'personal' might be used; we should distinguish between two obviously possible senses, one of which is intended and the other of which is not. The terminology might be used to refer to work which is personal in the sense that it involves working in a physical connection with another person or persons or carrying out work upon, or immediately affecting the mind or body of another person, or persons. We are not using the terminology in that sense; we might describe a work relation as a 'personal' one although it did not involve any of those components, as for example in the case of work on a manufacturing assembly line, or on the programming of a computer. Such a work relation might still be 'personal' in the different sense, which is our intended one, that the understanding is that the worker will, normally at least, do or carry out the work himself or herself in person.

We could distinguish between these two possible senses by saying that the first sense concerns the question of whether the work is personal while the second concerns the question of whether the relation is personal. So we use the terminology to identify a work relation which is personal rather than work which is necessarily personal in and of itself. The distinction may appear more clearly in other languages; for example, in French, as between *'une relation de travail personel'* and *'une relation personelle de travail'*. We intend the latter rather than the former. As with regard to the relational element in our boundary, we think it is important to acknowledge the normative thrust of this definitional element, and to explore the implications of the normative proposition which is involved.

So we are at the point in our discussion where we can identify two crucial elements in our definition, and the normative thrust which each of those two elements exerts. The two crucial elements in the definition are:

1. the idea of a relation arising from engagement or arrangement for work; and
2. the idea that this relation is a personal one in the defined sense.

We can understand the normative thrust which each of those two elements exerts by contrasting each one with a corresponding element in the concept of 'the contract of employment'. So we can contrast the element of 'relation arising from engagement or arrangement' with the element of 'contract'; and we can contrast the element of 'personal work' with the element of 'employment'.

Each of the two elements in our suggested boundary concept is intended to be generically more inclusive than the corresponding element in the concept of the contract of employment. Thus:

1. the idea of a relation arising from engagement or arrangement is generically more inclusive than the idea of a contract, in that it may include engagements

or arrangements which would not be regarded as contracts because they fail to fulfil requirements which particular labour law systems impose upon the contractual element in their conception of contracts of employment, such as requirements of formality, bilaterality, and/or continuing mutual obligation; and

2. the idea of personal work is generically more inclusive than the idea of employment, in that it may include occupation, activity, or services which would not be regarded as employment because they failed to fulfil requirements of dependency or subordination which particular labour law systems impose upon that element in their conception of contracts of employment.

So this analysis identifies the normative thrust which we think that the use of the personal work relation as a boundary concept would bring to bear upon labour law systems. This would exert a pressure upon those systems to be readier than they currently are to think that labour laws might apply to relations based upon arrangements even if those arrangements do not amount to contracts, and to relations of personal work even if they do not amount to subordinate or dependent employment. In short, it would tend to displace the contract of employment as still to some extent a totem for labour law systems, and to dispel what is still something of a taboo about applying labour laws beyond the contract of employment.

Moreover – and this is a crucial point – this normative pressure might be expected to exert itself not just at a single traditional boundary between the contract of employment and the contract for services, but more generally upon the many diverse boundary concepts or levels of inclusion which exist in modern labour law systems. We can develop that point further by identifying the multiple interfaces at which, and the many contested areas within which, labour laws are delimited in those systems. That involves a set of arguments which are presented in the next subsection.

## B. Multiple Interfaces and Contested Areas

In this subsection, we suggest that the normative implications of our boundary concept can best be understood by considering our boundary conception of the personal work relation as one which acquires meaning, and plays its normative role, by providing a series of interfaces with other kinds of legal regulation and the other spheres of social or economic activity to which they respectively apply.

There has been a strong tendency among the theorists and practitioners of labour law to envisage its archetypal boundary concept – the contract of employment – as having a boundary with just one other set of legal and economic relations, that is to say with those commercial relations which form the subject-matter of the private law of contract. Historically speaking, labour law has been imagined as the regulation of an island of dependent employment relations sitting in a sea of commercial activity conducted by independent contractors. The precise mapping of the shoreline of this island has been perceived as difficult, but its basic geography has generally been taken for granted as being of this kind. We suggest that, at least in its most simplified form, this perception is a misleading one. A fully explanatory map of the sphere of operation of labour law would show it as a territory which is defined in relation not to one other area or kind but to a number of other areas or kinds of social and economic activity.

So our suggestion is that a number of discussions in labour law treatises, which tend to be presented as subsidiary or secondary issues once the definitional outlines of the subject have been established, should be regarded as part and parcel of the primary identification of the relational boundary of the subject as a whole. That relational boundary should be regarded as consisting of a number of different interfaces with a large set of areas of social and economic activity which are adjacent to or overlap with the sphere of operation of labour law, in that they involve work in the broad sense of the term. So it is useful to identify a number of kinds of work, described in terminologies which are not necessarily established legal categories, whose place in the firmament of labour law is either denied or contested, and which therefore form interfaces with other legal domains in which labour law is not the primary source or kind of legal regulation.[22]

We suggest that the following such areas can be identified, though we regard the list as a fluctuating one:

1. work as a self-employed person, commercial agent, consultant, freelancer, or independent contractor;
2. work in a public function or office;
3. work as a minister of religion or for a faith organization;
4. charity work, voluntary work, and volunteering;
5. work in a liberal profession;
6. work as a director or senior manger of a company or enterprise;
7. work as or for a labour intermediary, such as a labour-only subcontractor, a gangmaster, or an employment agency or business;
8. occasional, casual, or other work of a temporary nature;
9. work in informal or undocumented work relations;
10. work as a trainee or apprentice;
11. work in placements or schemes to facilitate employment;
12. work for the benefit of a household or by way of care for dependents as a member of a household or family.

If it is accepted that the relational boundary of labour law is a multi-faceted one in this sense, then it becomes clearer why the personal work relation might be regarded as a useful and appropriate conception by which to describe this complex parameter. We have previously suggested reasons why, at the single interface between employment relations and commercial relations upon which almost all attention has traditionally been concentrated (which is identified in the first of the

---

[22] At a later stage in this work, in Chapter 9, Section 2 at pp. 347–57, we suggest and present a somewhat differently organized 'map of the domain of personal work relations'; the purpose of this initial delineation of different kinds of work is to identify, in particular, the principal interfaces with adjacent areas of social and economic activity.

above categories), it is important to have a boundary-defining concept which is on the one hand free of the restrictive confines of 'contract' and of 'employment', but is on the other hand sufficiently specific and concrete to identify a functionally distinctive sphere of operation for labour law. We now suggest that a similar need or necessity presents itself and is replicated at all these different interfaces with all these various other types of social and economic activity which are adjacent to or overlap with the sphere of operation of labour law. At each of these interfaces, there is the need for a loose and expansive yet meaningful outline conception of the sphere of operation of labour law within and around which an evolving discussion of purpose/relational scope equations can take place; and we suggest and will hope to demonstrate in the succeeding chapters that the notion of the personal work relation fulfils that function well.

In particular, we think that the normative utility of our boundary concept is further substantiated by European comparative reflection. There has been quite a lot of comparative discussion of the question of how the boundary of labour law is drawn, as between different legal systems, at the interface between employment relations and commercial relations, and more particularly between relations of 'employment' and of 'self-employment'.[23] The comparisons and contrasts between European legal systems turn out to be just as rich and complex and significant on the various other interfaces which we have identified. This strengthens the case for using a loose and expansive boundary concept to frame the whole discussion. By so saying, however, we identify the next steps which our discussion needs to take. Firstly, we have to locate our boundary concept in relation to the categories which are presently used in English law, in EU law, and in other European legal systems. Secondly, we need to specify as clearly as possible the function and methodology of our comparative discussion of the legal construction of personal work relations. These are the tasks, respectively, of the next section and the next chapter.


## Section 4: Aligning the Personal Work Relation with Existing Categories


In this section, we begin the task of aligning our suggested boundary concept for labour law, that of the personal work relation, with the categories which are currently used in English and European law to define the relational categories or personal scope of particular labour laws or bodies of labour law. While we have

---

[23] Cf. *inter alia*, A. Supiot (2001) *Beyond Employment: Changes in Work and the Future of Labour Law in Europe*, Oxford: OUP; A. Perulli (2003) *Economically dependent/quasi-subordinate (parasubordinate) employment: legal, social and economic aspects*; M. J. Bernier *et al.* (2003) *Les Besoins de Protection Sociale des Personnes en Situation de Travail non Traditionnelle*; P-H Antonmattei and J-C Sciberras (2008) *Le travailleur économiquement dépendant: quelle protection? Rapport à M. le Ministre du Travail, des Relations sociales, de la Famille et de la Solidarité*; N. Countouris (2007) *The Changing Law of the Employment Relationship: Comparative Analyses in the European Context*, Aldershot: Ashgate; Labour Asociados (2008) *The Impact of New Forms of Labour on Industrial Relations and the Evolution of Labour Law in the European Union*, IP/A/EMPL/ST/2007-019 9, Brussels.

presented our conception of the personal work relation as an essentially 'soft' or discursive one designed to stimulate normative development, we have also been concerned to ensure that it has a reasonably concrete definition – indeed, we have asserted that it needs a certain minimum of specificity if it is to fulfil that developmental function. In this concluding section of the chapter we will now argue that our conception of the personal work relation is a sufficiently concrete one to enable that alignment with existing categories to be a meaningful one; and we suggest that the exercise is a revealing one in displaying a very broadly common pattern of development of existing categories in English and European legal systems, but with many local variations. We first suggest what that broadly common pattern might be, and consider the ways in which that pattern is displayed in EU law (subsection A); we then consider in outline the approach of English law to this set of issues, and initiate a comparative discussion with other European national labour law systems (subsection B).

## A. An Emerging Pattern in European Law?

In the previous sections of this chapter, we have sought to develop an argument in favour of the use of the concept of the personal work relation as a normative boundary for labour law. We have also sought to show how each labour law system may simultaneously draw upon several different categories of inclusion for particular labour laws, thus creating several layers of inclusion. We have suggested that the normative pressure of our boundary concept should be seen as exerting itself not only upon the largest category of inclusion of each labour law system, but also upon its smaller or inner categories of exclusion. That is to say, we have argued in favour of the use of the concept of the personal work relation not only to encourage a more inclusive or at least open-minded approach to the overall relational scope of labour law, but also to encourage a corresponding approach to the inner categories which lie within that overall scope.

In order to begin to get a sense of how that normative discussion might proceed, we need to try to sketch a somewhat clearer and fuller picture than we have hitherto presented of the patterns of relational categories, larger and smaller, which actually occur or are actually evolving in existing European labour law systems. In this subsection, we shall now argue that a newly emerging pattern of relational categories can be discerned, and that it is a pattern which is reflected by and manifests itself in EU law. We suggest that this newly emerging pattern, although still somewhat inchoate, is already sufficiently well established and distinctive to be contrasted with the traditional pattern of relational categorization which prevailed in European labour law systems during most of their twentieth-century evolution. This change of pattern can be represented as the move from a binary classification of work contracts to a complex multilevel and multipolar classification of work relations – so from an earlier binary contractual analysis – the old pattern – to a later complex multi-level relational analysis – the emerging new pattern.

We have to be careful of falling into what is often the serious historical and intellectual error of contrasting a crude and unsophisticated analytical past with a more complex and nuanced analytical present and future. Nevertheless, it is reasonably convincing to depict an analytical universe for twentieth-century labour law in which its prevailing category of inclusion was that of the contract of employment involving subordinate or dependent service, and in which that category of inclusion was largely defined by contrast with a category of exclusion composed of other work contracts generally envisaged as contracts for services rendered on an independent or self-employed basis. Labour law systems whose relational categories can be described in that way, let us say at the beginning of the final third of that century, nevertheless still carried the remnants of their own more complex past histories, and there was no one static defining moment when each system was not to some degree in a state of flux with regard to its relational classifications; but the generalization in terms of the binary divide is still, we think, a helpful one.

It is received and genuine wisdom that this state of relative categorical stability fragmented into a 'crisis of fundamental concepts'[24] brought about by evolutions in labour law systems themselves and in the functioning of labour markets, and that this crisis has been a continuing one. It is more controversial to suggest that a new overall pattern can be discerned as emerging from that crisis, but nevertheless we tentatively advance that claim. There is much that is familiar in the way that we develop this claim – it depends partly on an already well-canvassed analysis of the many ways in which the concept of the contract of employment as a relational category is being expanded or softened. But there is also a novel and experimental element in our argument, consisting of a claim that an altogether wider analytical category of a multi-polar kind is also identifying itself outside and beyond even the expanded versions of the contract of employment, and perhaps starting to create a rather different analytical universe for labour law systems from the one in which we have been accustomed to locate ourselves. We proceed to consider in turn the relatively familiar and the unfamiliar aspects of this set of claims.

The relatively familiar aspect of the new emerging pattern of relational categories consists in the observation that there are many and various ways in which the core category of the contract of employment is tending to be expanded and in which its definitional outlines are tending to be softened. There has, of course, been a long history of expansive departure from a restrictive test for subordination or dependency which requires that the worker be subject to the 'control' of the employer.[25] However, in a sense this softening of the core concept starts to go to the further lengths of modifying the notion of subordination itself, transforming it into looser notions such as that of quasi-subordination or merely economic dependency as opposed to a more rigorously hierarchical notion of dependency.[26]

Even within this relatively familiar territory, moreover, we think that a less obvious development has occurred; the variations upon the theme of the dependent

---

[24] See above note 10.

[25] Cf. A. Supiot (2001) *Beyond Employment*, Oxford: OUP, 10–17; N. Countouris (2007) *The Changing Law of the Employment Relationship: Comparative Analyses in the European Context*, Aldershot: Ashgate, 58–71; A. Supiot (2000) 'Les nouveaux visages de la subordination', *Droit Social*, 131; A. Jeammaud (2002) 'L'assimilation de franchisés aux salaries', *Droit Social*, 158.

[26] J. Pélissier, A. Supiot, and A. Jeammaud (2000) *Droit du travail*, Paris: Dalloz, p. 151, noting that: '*La notion de subordination économique est, en effet, trop imprécise.*'

employment contract have come to be divided into two types – in one type, the core notion of the contract of employment is itself analysed as a wider category than before, for example by extending it to the case of merely economic dependency. In another contrasting typology, the originally single conception of the contractual employment relationship opens out into two overtly separate variants, a more exclusive one defined in terms of full subordination or dependency, and a less exclusive one defined in terms of quasi-subordination or partial dependency.[27]

Even more challenging, however, to previously existing understandings of the classification systems of labour law is a further claim which we make, namely that a new pattern is emerging whereby some labour laws have assigned to them a larger category which represents a radical shift right away from the core category of the contract of employment towards other kinds of work relation traditionally regarded not merely as being on the outer edges of the contract of dependent employment but as definitionally distinct from dependent employment or even as definitionally opposed to dependent employment. This radical shift occurs most conspicuously where relations of fully independent work or self-employment are overtly imported into the categories of labour law, thus transforming the domain of labour law into an undeniably multi-polar one which it is decreasingly satisfactory to envisage as merely a set of concentric circles around the contract of employment alone. In this emerging new pattern, the outer boundary of labour law has to be imagined, as we have earlier claimed, not in terms of a single interface between dependent and independent work contracts, but rather as a set of interfaces with a wide variety of social and economic relations, interfaces which cut through many different contested areas of intersection between the relations of labour law and relations regulated in other legal spheres, such as those of commercial law or family law.

We advance the suggestion that this emerging new pattern of relational categorization is discernibly manifested in European labour law systems, and that this can usefully be demonstrated in the principal supranational legal system of the European region, namely EU law – hence in the subset of that system which is regarded as constituting EU employment law or EU labour law. In the course of enacting and applying what is by now a rather extensive body of labour or employment law, the law-making or juridical institutions of the EU have in effect articulated a set of relational category classifications for the various different components of that body of law. They have done this in ways which have been at times relatively or even absolutely independent of the relational category classifications which are used by or in the national legal systems of the Member States, and at other times in ways

---

[27] Of which a very clear example is the 'worker' category in UK employment legislation, where in the Employment Rights Act 1996, s. 230(3) an overt distinction is made between contracts of employment and other personal work contracts, but from which the fully self-employed are still expressly excluded. As functionally equivalent examples from other jurisdictions one may consider the notions of *'parasubordinati'* (Article 409 of the Italian Civil Procedure Code; and in respect of *'lavoro a progetto'* Article 61 of Legislative Decree 276 of 2003), *Trabajadores autónomos económicamente dependientes* (Article 11 of the Spanish Law 20/2007) and *Arbeitnehmerähnliche Personen* (Section 12a of the German Act on Collective Agreements). For a further discussion of these issues cf. pp. 122 and 278–80.

which are reflexive of or even deferential to those national classifications,[28] and we shall find that it is very important to bear in mind the significance of those alternative modes of interaction between EU law and national legal systems.

In the final chapter of this work, we will consider in some detail this set of relational category classifications which is being generated by and within EU law, and European law more broadly, through these modes of interaction with national legal systems. At this point, we suggest in brief outline the sense in which that EU set of relational category classifications manifests the new pattern whose emergence we are asserting. The story is of a 'game in two halves', but of 'halves' which are partly synchronous with each other, if that can be said without straining the metaphor too much. In one half of the game, EU employment law uses a set of relational category classifications which revolves around and stays close to the conception of the contract of employment. This is generally done by using the terminology of the 'employment contract or employment relationship' but deferring the specifications of that terminology to the Member States.[29] On other occasions a slightly wider but still similar effect is achieved by characterizing as 'workers' those who work under a range of personal work relationships, which may extend to what some national courts might see as self-employment, but the ECJ would see as disguised employment.[30] This loose conception is, typically, not regarded as extending to those working in fully independent or self-employed capacities, and where the EU lawmakers have, on occasion, wished to extend measures framed around the conception of the employment contract or relationship to those working in such capacities, they have done so by means of distinct supplementary measures addressed to the self-employed.[31]

There is, however, another 'half of the game' of the relational development of EU employment law in which, exactly manifesting the emerging new pattern which we are seeking to identify, an altogether wider set of classificatory conceptions is deployed which breaks out of the confines of the employment contract or relationship, thus becoming multi-polar and embracing a larger set of work relations which in particular includes those of personal self-employment. There is one key

---

[28] G. Cavalier and R. Upex (2006) 'The Concept of the Employment Contract In European Union Private Law' 55:3, *ICLQ*, 587–608; N. Countouris (2007) *The Changing Law of the Employment Relationship: Comparative Analyses in the European Context* Aldershot: Ashgate, chapter 5; J. Kenner, 'New Frontiers in EU Labour Law: From Flexicurity to Flex-Security', in M. Dougan and S. Currie (2009), *50 Years of the European Treaties: Looking Back and Thinking Forward*, Oxford: Hart, 279–310.

[29] Cf. for instance the interpretation of Clause 2(1) of Directive 97/81 in Case C-313/02, *Wippel v. Peek & Cloppenburg GmbH & Co. KG* [2004] ECR I-9483, para. 40, as well as the more classic approach in Case 105/84, *Danmols Inventar* [1985] ECR 2639, para. 26.

[30] Thus in Case C-256/01, *Allonby v. Accrington & Rossendale College* [2004] ECR I-873, the ECJ employed this interpretative approach to the concept of worker, as used in what was then Article 141 EC, applying it to include a work relationship characterized as one of self-employment but constituting a relationship of disguised employment in the view of the Court (para 71). The ECJ there cited a similar interpretative approach in cases concerning the free movement of workers such as Case C-357/89, *Raulin*.

[31] Cf. Directive 2002/15 EC on the organization of the working time of persons performing mobile road transport [2002] OJ L 80/35; Directive 2010/41/EU on the application of the principle of equal treatment between men and women engaged in an activity in a self-employed capacity and repealing Council Directive 86/613/EEC, [2010] OJ L 180/1.

manifestation of this kind of deployment of such wider conceptions; it consists of the application of new kinds of protection against discrimination, in particular on the grounds of disability, sexual orientation, religion or belief, and age, to a set of work relations identified as those of employment, self-employment, and/or occupation.[32] We suggest that, at this crucial point, EU employment law is establishing large zones of application bounded by categories closely approximating to our own suggested boundary conception of the personal work relation; and that EU employment law is therefore starting to operate at two complex levels just as our suggested pattern of development predicts.

If that analysis is accepted so far as EU employment law is concerned, it becomes very important to consider whether, in manifesting that pattern of development, EU employment law is replicating – or departing from – patterns of development which are being pursued in the national labour law systems of the Member States. There is, of course, quite a high degree of convergence between EU employment law and the national labour law systems of the Member States, if only because the Member States are obliged to implement or give effect to EU employment law. But there are various senses in which the relational categories of EU employment law and those of the labour law systems of the Member States do not exactly mirror each other. For example, the law concerning the freedom of movement of workers within the EU is an area in which EU law has articulated its own category of 'worker' in a way which is overtly independent of any particular national legal system.[33]

Moreover, even where EU employment law implicitly reflects or expressly defers to the relational categories of national labour law systems – as, for example, frequently occurs when the concept of the 'employment contract or employment relationship' is deployed in EU legislation[34] – it is still very hard to know whether and how far this brings about an exact match or fit between the relational categories of EU employment law and those of national labour law systems. That is because there are deep-seated ambiguities in the definition of those relational categories within national labour law systems, which are compounded by complex divergences of pattern as between the different national labour systems. Sometimes we are obliged to conclude that EU employment law purports to have established a kind of shared vocabulary of relational categories where there is in truth no underlying conceptual common language. That observation suggests that we need to turn our attention to the relational classification of the national labour law systems themselves, which we do in the following subsection.

---

[32] Cf. Article 3(1)(a) of Directive 2000/43 implementing the principle of equal treatment between persons irrespective of racial or ethnic origin, [2000] OJ L 180/22, explicitly referring to 'employment, to self-employment and to occupation'; Article 3(1)(a) of Directive 2000/78 establishing a general framework for equal treatment in employment and occupation, [2000] OJ L 303/16.

[33] See further below at pp. 390–9.

[34] See further below at pp. 391–2.

## B. The Pattern Instantiated in English Law – and in Other European Legal Systems

This concluding subsection considers in outline the approach of English law to conceptualizing its internal boundary concepts, and how our normative boundary concept might provide a critique for the relational approach adopted domestically in a number of other European national labour law systems. We conclude our analysis by initiating a discussion about the need to construct a comparative methodology on the legal construction of boundary concepts, and of personal work relations in particular, a discussion that we go on to develop more fully in the following Chapter 2.

English law does instantiate the emerging pattern of relational categorization which we have suggested for European labour law systems generally and have started developing in relation to EU law. At one level, English law has evolved a dual or split-level approach to the scope of the contract of employment – splitting between a relatively rigorous 'contract of employment' concept and a rather more inclusive 'worker's contract' concept. The latter concept, we have argued elsewhere,[35] seeks to extend some labour rights to semi-dependent workers. But it remains quite closely linked or penumbral to the idea of the contract of employment, is still irrevocably committed to contractual reasoning, and still seeks to exclude the 'genuinely self-employed', from which it remains – or seeks to remain – conceptually distinct.

At another level, in the sphere of employment equality legislation, English law has sought to transcend the binary divide much more fundamentally, with its idea of all contracts for personal performance of work or labour, and has extended itself to multilateral relations consisting of chains of contracts, an extension embodied in the notion of 'contract workers'.[36] Recent equality legislation has sought to restate and reinforce this approach, with the Equality Act 2010 seeking to extend anti-discrimination law in the spheres of 'work' and 'employment' beyond employees, to include 'contract[s] personally to do work',[37] contract workers,[38] as well as a large number of nominated categories of persons in employment, including police officers, partners, barristers and advocates, and personal and public office holders.[39] Beyond these internal boundary concepts we find a further one adopted for the purposes of health and safety legislation, casting a duty for employers to ensure the health and safety and welfare of 'persons at work'.[40]

In abstract terms, this conceptual and normative panorama instantiates quite closely some of the normative ambitions of EU employment law, for instance to the extent that the latter envisages extending employment equality law to employment,

---

[35] M. Freedland (2003) *The Personal Employment Contract*, Oxford: OUP, at 30–3.
[36] See below p. 320.
[37] Equality Act 2010, s. 83.
[38] Equality Act 2010, s. 41.
[39] Cf. Equality Act 2010, Pt 5, Chap 1.
[40] Health and Safety at Work Act 1974, s. 1.

self-employment, and occupation. In practice, as we will discuss in Chapters 3, 4, and 10, both English law and EU law fail, in many ways and for different reasons, to deliver on their respective normative ambitions and potential. But these considerations arguably fall beyond the scope of the present chapter, and certainly beyond that of the present subsection. Here we simply seek to highlight how our normative idea of the personal work relation as a boundary concept might provide a critique of this complex dual-level approach of English law. On the positive side, we would suggest that it highlights and identifies the way in which English law has embraced the notion of 'personal work' as an outer defining category, and it can be used to encourage greater open-mindedness in thinking about 'personal work' as a critical notion which challenges the binary divide. We might even venture to argue that it helps to give a clear conceptual identity to a notion of 'personal work' which is already present in English law, albeit with the limitations that we will discuss in Part II of the present work.

On the negative side, it can be used to show that the English law approach is still very restricted by the notion of contract, which permeates all domestic normative characterizations sustaining the various areas of English labour law. The chapters forming Part III of the present work have the specific purpose of contrasting this national approach with the more open-minded one underpinning our own normative notion, based on relation, engagement, and arrangement. But as we will further highlight in the following chapter, the normative notion of the personal work relation can also be used to open up a comparative inquiry – and so to ask in a critical way how far other national relational classification systems are bounded by employment and by contract or how far they have moved into broader, probably multi-level, approaches.

We can already suggest that as soon as we embark upon this kind of journey, we are straight away confronted by deep-level divergences in the way that different European labour law systems would think not only about 'employment' and 'personal work' but also about 'contract' and 'relation' as boundary notions. We can see those divergences, and the uncertainties generated by them, surfacing in many of the contested areas and at many of the interfaces with other relations which we have identified in this first chapter. The next chapter starts to develop a methodology for tackling those problems.

# 2

# A European Comparative Approach to the Legal Construction of Personal Work Relations

## Introduction

In this chapter, a further step is taken in the development of our work: we set out the European comparative approach to the legal construction of personal work relations which will be tested and explored in the subsequent Parts of the book. In successive sections we consider: firstly, the function of our European comparative analysis; secondly, the perspective from which the analysis is conducted; thirdly, the comparative method which will be followed; fourthly, the theory of institutional embeddedness which we pursue, and our view that personal work contracts in general, and the contract of employment in particular, form the essential starting point though not the endpoint of our comparative analysis; and finally our aspiration that our comparative approach might ultimately give rise to an outcome consisting in the formulation of a common framework for the legal construction of personal work relations in European law.

## Section 1: Functions and Perspectives

In the previous chapter, we sought to establish the starting points for our European comparative analysis of the legal construction of those work relations which form or might be regarded as forming the subject matter of labour law. For this purpose we introduced the notion that it is useful to imagine a long series of purpose/relational scope equations for the many diverse kinds of regulatory intervention of which labour law is made up. Moreover, we argued that one could and should envisage an overarching purpose/relational scope equation for labour law as a whole; and we suggested that most suitable relational framing concept for labour law as a whole was that of the 'personal work relation'. The aim of that exercise, therefore, was to sketch out a conceptual space within which to attempt a European comparative analysis of the legal construction of a set of work relations identified as 'personal work relations'. In this section we consider more fully the function of that analysis, and the perspective, or normative standpoint, from which it should be conducted.

To recapitulate further upon the previous chapter, we there put forward a broad notion of what we would regard as the appropriate overarching statement of purpose for the legal construction of 'the personal work relation'. That stated purpose is to maximize the dignity accorded to workers in personal work relations and to optimize their capabilities in and through those relations while recognizing the importance of stability in the relations between workers and those for whom they work. Within that broad statement of purpose for the theoretical development of labour law to which we seek to make a contribution, it is useful to reflect upon the function of the particular exercise in which we are engaged, namely the comparative analysis of the legal construction of personal work relations.

Our suggestion in this respect is that the function of this comparative analysis is to provide as firm as possible a foundation of knowledge and understanding of the legal construction of personal work relations, upon which the purpose/relational scope equations for particular labour law interventions may be based. Suppose for example that we are considering what is the appropriate relational scope for minimum wage legislation, or for legislation controlling working time. It is crucial, for that purpose, to understand what the practical application of any given relational category – such as that of 'employee' or 'worker' – will be, and that can only be accurately assessed on the basis of a clear analysis of the legal construction of those personal work relations which come within the 'employee' category or the 'worker' category.

We think that this kind of clarity can best be achieved by comparative analysis, and we will turn in the next section to the articulation of our proposed comparative method of analysis; but we must first say something about the perspective, or critical standpoint, from which it will be conducted. In this respect it will be useful to follow in the first instance a path of discussion which has been established by Anne Davies, and to distinguish between the alternative perspectives of 'human rights', 'social justice for workers' and 'law and economics' – and more especially between the 'rights' perspective and the 'economics' perspective.[1] Those contrasts indicate the respective priorities or special preoccupations of those taking each of those perspectives; in the case of those taking an 'economics' perspective, the priority is for labour law interventions to ensure or at least not to undermine the competitiveness of the employing enterprises which are subject to those interventions.

It will be apparent that we have identified the underlying purpose of the legal construction of personal work relations in such a way – especially in the reference that we make to the notions of dignity and capability – as to show that our primary perspective, if categorized in that way, is from 'rights' or 'social justice', although the contrasting, economic, perspective partially figures in our reference to stability in work relations. We shall have more to say in later chapters about the relevance to our work of the choice between those perspectives; it will be relevant to draw attention to the essentially *contractual* vision of personal work relations which is derived from the 'economic efficiency' perspective. However, we approach the particular exercise of comparative analysis of the legal construction of personal

---

[1] A. C. L. Davies (2009) *Perspectives on Labour Law*, 2nd ed., Cambridge: CUP; Chapters 2 and 3.

work relations from a perspective which is rather different from any of the above-mentioned ones. We can best describe this as an 'institutional' perspective, a notion which we now proceed to expound more fully.

Our 'institutional perspective' is one from which, when thinking about labour law in general and about the legal construction of personal work relations in particular, special importance and special explanatory significance is accorded to the institutions and institutional arrangements by which the labour market is governed and regulated. Crouch (2005) has offered a definition of institutions and a gloss upon that definition, stressing the process by which an institution is constituted:

Institutions will be defined here as: patterns of human action and relationships that persist and reproduce themselves over time, independently of the identity of the biological individuals performing within them. Sociologists have long understood such a concept, but much of this earlier history has been ignored by recent political scientists and others who have come autonomously to the idea of the institution as they have sought to convey the idea of behaviour being shaped and routinized, fitting into patterns, which are not necessarily those that would be freely chosen by a rational actor needing to decide what to do.[2]

Although we accept and assert the importance of a wide range of institutions in the governance of and regulation of the labour market, our particular focus is upon what we single out as 'legal institutions', by which we mean institutions forming part of a legal system. That is not a precise distinction, but legal theorists offer various pointers towards the main defining characteristics of the concept of a legal institution. Thus, for instance, Ruiter observes that:

Legal institutions can be roughly characterised as distinct legal systems governing specific forms of social conduct within the overall legal system. The hallmark of legal institutions is that they can be dealt with as independent social phenomena.[3]

Our perspective upon the legal analysis of personal work relations is an 'institutional' one in two particular senses. Firstly, our perspective is institutional in that it takes a specially inclusive view of what counts as an 'institution' within this sphere of legal activity and legal thought. Secondly, our perspective is institutional in that it regards 'legal institutions', identified in that inclusive way, as often having normative impacts which have not been as fully perceived as they should be. So we believe that the legal analysis of personal work relations in a given legal system will tend to have been shaped and determined, to a greater extent than is generally understood to be the case, by the operation of practices or ways of thinking which have institutional standing and are embedded in labour market structures and in the legal system itself. Moreover, we are convinced that those embedded institutional practices may have major normative effects which are wholly or partly concealed behind an appearance of technical neutrality.

---

[2] C. Crouch (2005) *Capitalist Diversity and Change – Recombinant Governance and Institutional Entrepreneurs*, Oxford: OUP, at p. 10.
[3] D. W. P. Ruiter (2001) *Legal Institutions*, Dordrecht: Kluwer, at p. 71.

We can illustrate this set of propositions about our 'institutional perspective' with a relatively obvious example, and we will then go on to apply them to the legal analysis of personal work relations more generally, indeed as a whole. Our relatively obvious example is that of specialized labour courts or tribunals. It is not controversial to assert that specialized labour courts or tribunals are to be regarded as legal institutions, indeed institutions of labour law, and that they give rise to their own institutional practices which become embedded in the labour law system in which those courts or tribunals function. It is scarcely more controversial to assert that the institutional practices of specialized labour courts or tribunals may have significant normative effects. So we might and quite often do find that in a given labour law system, the outcomes of adjudication by specialized labour law courts or tribunals are different from the outcomes which do or would result from adjudication of the same issues by non-specialized courts or tribunals. Such differences represent the normative impact of that institution.

From that uncontroversial example, we can develop our institutional perspective further by using it as a critical standpoint from which to revisit the notion of the relational defining of labour law which we articulated in the previous chapter. It will be recalled that we distinguished between three distinct elements of the relational defining of labour law, consisting of, firstly, the identification of a relational framing or boundary, and, secondly, the ascribing of legal formats to work relations within that boundary, and, thirdly and less obviously, the establishing of one central paradigm or a small number of dominant paradigms for those work relations. We could certainly think of those central or dominant paradigms as assuming an institutional character. We shall argue at length that the contract of employment has done precisely that, in English labour law and in the labour law of many other European states; and we shall suggest that there have been profound but concealed normative effects from this institutional configuration. For example – and it is one of many – we shall suggest that the institutionalization of the contract of employment as the central paradigm for the personal work relation has, in the particular form that it has taken, contributed very significantly to an essentially individualistic understanding of that relation in English labour law.

We can take this argument from the institutional perspective one crucial stage further. We could take a deeper view of what constitutes the institutional framework of the legal analysis of personal work relations. On this deeper view, we could regard as institutional, not only the central or dominant paradigms which legal systems identify for personal work relations, but the whole of the process or mechanism which each legal system provides for the legal construction of personal work relations. By this we mean the set of arrangements which locates the powers of legal construction of personal work relations and which lays down the ground rules for that process of legal construction. Our argument is that this set of arrangements should be regarded as itself constituting an institution which is embedded in the legal system and which has a highly significant normative impact upon the role and functioning of labour law within the legal system in question.

We advance this argument as a challenge to an almost unquestioned assumption that this set of arrangements for the legal analysis or legal construction of personal work relations is, in and of itself, more in the nature of neutral technical apparatus than in the nature of an institution with its own normative impact and significance. For example, we do not habitually consider the normative significance and impact of the set of arrangements under which much of the legal construction of personal work relations in the English legal system takes place within the sphere of tax and social security law, according to rules laid down by the tax and social security authorities which are applied by the adjudicative system for tax and social security issues. Yet this in fact has considerable normative significance and impact, if only because workers have conflicting interests according to whether the legal construction of their personal work relations takes place for tax and social security contribution purposes – in which case they usually wish to be regarded as self-employed, or for labour law purposes – in which case they typically wish to be classified as employees.

Moreover, we suggest that this argument becomes much stronger and more significant when the perspective which is taken upon the legal construction of personal work relations is not only an institutional one in the above sense, but also a comparative institutional one. From a comparative institutional perspective, the normative impact of each national institutional set of arrangements for the legal construction of personal work relations is thrown into heightened relief by the fact that these sets of arrangements vary considerably between legal systems. Thus, for example, there appears to be considerable divergence between European legal systems, as to whether or how far uniformity of legal construction of personal work relations is maintained as between the sphere of labour law and that of tax and social security law. So the normative impact of that particular kind of uniformity might be revealed more clearly by comparison with arrangements which do not maintain that uniformity.

This brings our set of arguments to the point where we have set out an account of the functions of our comparative analysis of the legal construction of personal work relations, and have identified the perspectives from which we are viewing that analysis, so that we now need to specify our comparative methodology, that being the task of the next section.

## Section 2:  Methodology

In this section, we locate the methodology of our comparative analysis of the legal construction of personal work relations within the area of debate about comparative law methodology. This involves firstly considering the extent to which and the sense in which our methodology is a 'functional' one, and secondly considering the sense in which our methodology is an 'institutional' one.

Comparative lawyers frequently debate that first question of the extent to which and the sense in which their methodology is a functional one; that can be a way of articulating the virtues of their own exercises in comparative law and contrasting them with the vices which they attribute to those of others. The virtues in question are those of clarity and transparency of purpose, while the vices are those of subverting impartial and scientific inquiry by reason of over-commitment to preconceived policy objectives or policy perceptions. In the spirit of trying to maximize the clarity and transparency of purpose of the exercise in comparative law of which this book consists, we seek to identify its methodology as a 'functional' one at several levels.

At the most general level, we have declared our view of the function of labour law as a whole, in the form of the purpose/relational scope equation which we envisage for a labour law system which takes 'the personal work relation' as its relational boundary concept. That overarching purpose or function we conceive to be that of maximizing the dignity accorded to workers in personal work relations and optimizing their capabilities in and through those relations while recognizing the importance of stability in the relations between workers and those for whom they work.

At a second and more specific level, we have also delineated the specific task or function of the present work as being that of analysing the legal construction or architecture of the personal work relation; and we see the purpose of that task as being that of revealing the extent to which this ostensibly technical and policy-neutral aspect of labour law has normative or regulatory impact and effects. So at this second level our approach and methodology is a functional one in that dual sense. As we have previously indicated, our principal focus in the carrying out of that analytical task will be upon the enormous normative or regulatory impact of the legal construction of personal work relations in a contractual frame and especially around the central paradigm of the contract of employment.

So that represents a second sense or dimension in which our analysis and our methodology are functional ones. There is, however, a third sense or dimension in which it is useful to consider whether and how far our analysis and methodology are functional ones. That is to say, we need to consider whether and to what extent our method of comparison between legal systems is itself a functional one. This involves the defining of what we hope and intend might be the outcome or product of the various comparisons which we shall make. That brings us to the heart of the debates which legal comparatists conduct under the heading of functionality.

Under the heading of 'functionality', legal comparatists seem to envisage a wide range of possibilities as to how strongly normative the outcomes of the process of comparison between legal systems can and should be.[4] In fact there seems to be a spectrum of possibilities, from non-normative outcomes to very strongly normative outcomes. At the former end of this spectrum there are exercises in comparison which seek no more prescriptive outcomes than the kind of increase in the understanding of particular systems which can be derived by comparison with other systems. At the latter end of this spectrum are highly normative exercises in comparison which seek to arrive at various kinds of 'upward harmonization' between legal systems, in the sense that they seek to distil out a unified set of

---

[4] Cf. R. Michaels (2006) 'The Functional Method of Comparative Law', ch. 10 of M. Reimann and R. Zimmermann (eds.), *The Oxford Handbook of Comparative Law*, Oxford: OUP especially section II, 'Concepts of Functionalism'.

principles, and even rules, which in some way amounts to the 'best' common version of the products of the several legal systems, assessed by reference to some notion of 'coherence' or systemic integrity.

In between those two extremes, there is an area of discussion in which legal comparatists put forward various specific choices between different kinds of techniques and outcomes of legal comparison. Thus they consider whether to be more concerned with similarities or with differences between legal systems, the similarity-seeking alternatives tending to be somewhat more prescriptive than the difference-focused ones.[5] Thus also they discuss the difficulties which arise when the outcomes of comparison amount to 'legal transplants', that is to say transpositions of particular legal phenomena from one system to another in an acontextual fashion.[6] Some comparatists who are sceptical about the viability of 'legal transplants' urge the preferability of 'legal irritants', that is to say the deployment of contrast between legal systems to provoke normative reflection within those systems, but of a less directly prescriptive kind than is involved in processes of legal 'transplantation'.[7]

We hope to have devised a methodology of comparison which avoids the two extremes which we have depicted and which engages in a meaningful way with the more specific discussions about comparative method which we have mentioned. Our methodology is on the whole more difference-focused than similarity-seeking, because our observation has been that the differences in the basic architecture, that is to say the construction of the basic legal formats of personal work relations, are more fundamental than we had initially realised. Many of the comparative points which we make are presented as having the function of 'legal irritants', though they could also be seen as pointing towards a certain 'soft' and reflexive form of harmonization between European labour law systems at this basic architectural level. The nature of these methodological choices or tendencies will become clearer if we develop our notion of 'institutional' analysis, and also if we introduce our aspiration that this work might contribute to an eventual outcome of European comparative labour law studies consisting in the articulation of a European common framework for the legal construction of personal work relations.

In the previous section, we set forth our 'institutional' perspective upon the comparative analysis of the legal construction of personal work relations: we explained that this consisted of attributing very great importance to the ways in which dominant paradigms had established themselves, and had assumed institutional significance, in the processes of legal construction of personal work relations which had taken place within European legal systems. This, we suggested, was

---

[5] Cf. G. Dannemann (2006) 'Comparative Law; Study of Similarities or Differences?', ch 11 of M. Reimann and R. Zimmermann (eds.), *The Oxford Handbook of Comparative Law*, Oxford: OUP.

[6] Cf. M. Graziadei (2006) 'Comparative Law as the Study of Transplants and Receptions', ch. 11 of M. Reimann and R. Zimmermann (eds.), *The Oxford Handbook of Comparative Law*, Oxford: OUP.

[7] The *locus classicus* for this notion can be found in the writings of G. Teubner; see G. Teubner (2000) 'Legal Irritants: Good Faith in British Law, or How Unifying Law Ends Up in New Differences' in F. Snyder (ed.) *The Europeanisation of Law: The Legal Effects of European Integration*, Oxford: Hart Publishing, pp. 243–68.

especially well instantiated by the emergence of the contract of employment as an institution which, in varying degrees, dominates the legal construction of personal work relations in most if not all European legal systems. It could also, we believe, be said that a category of or corresponding to 'self-employment' exists and has assumed institutional significance in those systems, though not necessarily in a specifically contractual form.

We also indicated that it follows from the embeddedness of these institutions in the particularities of their respective legal systems and labour market systems, that they might be expected to differ significantly as between those national systems. And indeed we have found and will explain that there are significant differences in the case, for instance, of the contract of employment. Although, as we have said, the contract of employment can be regarded as an institution which is found in a more or less common fashion within European labour law systems, that appearance of commonality should not mask the very great differences as between such systems in the role which that institution plays, and in the degree of centrality which is accorded to it in the legal construction of personal work relations. Thus, as we shall see, there are, for instance, wide variations in the degrees of worker-protectiveness to which the contract of employment is legally constructed in different European legal systems, in the relationships which are envisaged between the contract of employment and legislation and collective bargaining, and in the different extent to which contracts of employment are standardized in their legal construction.

The existence of these dimensions of variety, between apparently similar or parallel institutions embedded in their respective national systems, presents us with a major analytical issue, and requires us to consider our comparative institutional methodology more closely. The question here is how far we can or should regard these significantly heterogeneous institutions, which exert shaping influences upon the legal construction of personal work relations, as being able to be grouped into families by reference to characteristics or tendencies which might unify some of them and divide them from others. Two possible forms of grouping present themselves; one is a grouping of legal systems as between common law ones and Civilian ones; the other is a grouping of labour market systems according to notions of 'varieties of capitalism'. We proceed to consider how far such groupings might be informative and helpful.

It is quite tempting, when engaging in intra-European comparative analysis of the legal construction of personal work relations, to regard the distinction between common law systems and Civil law systems as a powerful mechanism of explanation and understanding. This is an especial temptation so far as the central or dominant paradigm of the contract of employment is concerned. As we shall see in more detail in later chapters, there are differences in approach to the legal construction of personal work relations as contracts which seem to correspond rather well to the idea of a generic common law/Civil law divide.

Thus English labour law, as the representative within the European context of a common law tradition, does seem on the face of it to display a preference for a casuistic and fluid approach to the legal construction of personal work relations which apparently stands in generic contrast to preferences for more systematic, codificatory and taxonomical approaches which seems to be manifested by the principal Civil law-based continental European counterparts. More specifically, as we shall explain in more detail in a later chapter, the legal construction of personal work relations in many continental jurisdictions does seem to be strongly influenced by the historical development of, and antithesis between, the two essentially contractual categories of the *locatio conductio operarum* and *locatio conductio operis*; that duality could be regarded as a truly Civilian legal phenomenon,[8] a notable example of a kind of continuity of discourse with classical Roman law itself.

However, there are several reasons for being cautious about overuse of a supposed common law/Civil law contrast to explain or account for divergences between European legal systems as to the legal construction of personal work relations. Firstly, it tends to contrast English law with the legal systems of other European states. Secondly, and by the same token, it tends to group the legal systems of other European states together in a way which might easily understate differences between them as to the legal construction of personal work relations. Thirdly, and perhaps most importantly given the focus of the present work, it might easily overstate the influence of general private law – as the domain within which the common law/Civil law contrast has primarily developed – upon the legal construction of personal work relations: in other words this might easily understate the role of an autonomous body of labour law in the legal construction of personal work relations.

This latter consideration provides us with an opportunity for introducing a methodological point that will be further elucidated upon in the following chapters, that is to say the idea that contractually constructed personal work relations are subject to a number of 'layers of regulation', to use a terminology very usefully developed and deployed by Mückenberger and Deakin (1989)[9] and that it is methodologically appropriate, and indeed necessary, to assess the impact of each relevant layer for a correct understanding of the regulation of personal work relations. For most systems, the foundational layer of regulation, in which is embedded the main body of *legal principles*, is that of the common or private law of contract as it has developed and been applied in the sphere of individual personal work relations.[10] In English law, that body of common law principles has developed in such a way as to be loosely rather than tightly specific to a certain general type of personal work contract, so that we can discern the outlines of 'the common law of the contract of employment', though it is often not fully clear how

---

[8] Cf. R. Zimmermann (1990), *The Law of Obligations: Roman Foundations of the Civilian Tradition*, Johannesburg: Juta & Co, 1990; reissued (1996) Oxford: Clarendon Press, Chapter 12 'Locatio Conductio II'.

[9] U. Mückenberger and S. Deakin (1989) *From Deregulation to a European Floor of Rights: Law, Flexibilisation and the European Single Market*, Zeitschrift für Ausländisches und Internationales Arbeits und Sozialrecht, at p. 153.

[10] Cf. S. Deakin and F. Wilkinson (2005) *The Law of the Labour Market – Industrialization, Employment and Legal Evolution*, Oxford: OUP at pp. 100–105; S. Vettori, *The Employment Contract and the Changed World of Work*, Aldershot: Ashgate.

universally those principles apply to all contracts of employment, or how far they may extend beyond contracts of employment to other personal work contracts.

By contrast, in the continental and Civil law systems covered by the present work, this foundational layer of regulation – while present – tends to be compressed within other, statutory and collective, layers of regulation and the contracts in question are formed within the framework of quite highly organized and systematic legal taxonomies, which firmly identify types and sub-types of personal work contracts, especially in the context of dependent personal work relations. The parties' freedom to decide what type or sub-type of personal work contract should be used to characterize a specific employment or work relationship is severely restrained and restricted by statute and case-law. The Italian Civil Code, for instance, contains article 2239, 'according to which the subordinate work relationships "that are not inherent to the exercise of an enterprise" are regulated by the provisions of Title I [of the Civil Code] on subordinate work in the enterprise, "to the extent that they are compatible with the speciality of the relationship"'.[11]

A good example of this approach is provided by the Italian doctrine of the 'inderogability of the characterisation of the contract',[12] applying to the contractual type of subordinate employment which is the subject of Article 2094 of the Italian Civil Code. The principle acts as a limit both upon any arbitrary classification by the parties to the contract and upon any undue interference by statutes purporting to exclude the application of employment protection legislation by labelling the contract as one of self-employment. The high watermark of this doctrine is visible in a number of decisions of the Italian Constitutional Court in which the court was adamant that even the Parliament 'could not authorise the parties to exclude by contractual provision, directly or indirectly, the applicability of the mandatory regime, provided as a protection for workers, from relationships having the content and modalities of execution typical of the subordinate work relationship'.[13]

The French *doctrine* and jurisprudence are, for their part, insistent upon the fact that 'the existence of an employment relationship depends neither on the expressed intention of the parties nor on the denomination which they have given to their agreement but on the factual conditions in which the activity of the workers in question takes place'.[14] This can usefully be contrasted with the typically British approach taken in cases such as *Express & Echo Publications v. Tanton* [1999], where it was asserted that 'to concentrate on what actually occurred may not elucidate the full terms of the contract. If a term is not enforced that does not justify a conclusion that such a term is not part of the agreement ( . . . )' and that one would be 'wrong ( . . . )

---

[11] V. Speziale (2007) 'Il Lavoro Subordinato tra Rapporti Speciali, Contratti "Atipici" e Possibili Riforme' (D'Antona Working Paper No 51, 2007), at p. 8 (our translation).

[12] *'indisponibilità della qualificazione del contratto'*.

[13] *Corte Cost. 23–31 Marzo 1994, n. 115* (our translation). In a similar vein see *Corte Cost. 121/ 1993*.

[14] J. Péllissier, A. Supiot, A. Jeammaud (2006) *Droit du Travail*, Paris: Dalloz, at p. 330 (our translation from the original French).

in concentrating on what occurred rather than seeking to determine what were the mutual obligations spelled out in the contract'.[15]

We are, of course, keenly aware that even in continental systems, as Bruno Caruso has put it, 'standard employment [is] no longer the great sun that attracted all the planets in the system (as it had done during the Fordist era), but just one of many stars of equal rank (if anything, it was diminishing in size)'.[16] Clearly if there ever was an implicit general presumption that work relationships had to be constructed as subordinate ones unless they were clearly autonomous, that presumption no longer operates as a general rule but, at best, as an exception.[17] Nevertheless, the overall effect seems to be that the choice of design accorded to individual contracting parties is strongly shaped by a set of legally defined moulds or matrices,[18] whether 'sun shaped' or 'star shaped' to borrow Caruso's analogy, into which individual personal work relations have to be slotted, and that judicial interpreters feel entitled, and indeed compelled, to look beyond the contractual dimension of the relationship and to reshape it according to these moulds.

We believe that that this methodological hypothesis, which will be further explained in the remainder of this work, can partly explain why, for instance, the Court of Appeal in *Consistent Group* v *Kalwak* (2008) could assert that: 'It is not the function of the court or an employment tribunal to re-cast the parties' bargain',[19] whereas the French *Court de Cassation* judged it appropriate to reconfigure into a fixed-term contract of employment the contractual relationship between the participants in a French 'reality' television programme '*l'Ile de la tentation*' and the broadcasting company in question, again asserting that: 'the existence of an employment relationship depends neither on the expressed intention of the parties nor on the denomination which they have given to their agreement'.[20]

However, although we shall find that the contrasting of common law and Civil law approaches will at some points be a useful method of improving our understanding of certain divergences in the legal construction of personal work relations as between European legal systems, we need to be sceptical about its use as a pervasive and all-explanatory theme. This may be a pointer against any groupings of legal systems with regard to the legal construction of personal work relations, or it may simply be a contra-indication for this particular one, so implying a need to look elsewhere for more effectively explanatory ones. Another avenue down which that

---

[15] *Express & Echo Publications Ltd. v. Tanton* [1999] ICR, 697–8.

[16] B. Caruso (2004) 'The Concept Of Flexibility In Labour Law. The Italian Case in the European Context' *WP C.S.D.L.E. 'Massimo D'Antona'* N. 39/2004, pp. 13–14 (our translation).

[17] See for instance the legal presumptions of employment status provided by the French Labour Code in articles such as, for instance, what used to be L. 781.1, now L. 7313–1. But cf. also C-255/04, *Commission v. France* [2006] ECR I-5251.

[18] Or 'new contractual models' as E. Ghera (2006) termed it in 'Subordinazione, Statuto Protettivo e Qualificazione del Rapporto di Lavoro', 109, *Giornale di Diritto del Lavoro e Relazioni Industriali*, 29.

[19] *Consistent Group Limited v. Kalwak* [2008] EWCA Civ 430, Rimer LJ at para. 40. Contrast, however, a possibly emergent new approach in *Autoclenz v Belcher* [2011] UKSC 41.

[20] Cour de Cassation (Soc.), Arrêt no. 1159 du 3 juin 2009 (our translation).

search might be pursued is one which leads away from generic contrasting between groups of legal cultures towards forms of generic contrasting between groups of labour market structures and traditions, and ultimately towards generic contrasting between groups of national market systems in an even more general sense.

One of the major lines of thought which has been pursued in recent years by proponents of institutional theory has consisted in the idea that the ideology and the practice of market capitalism are not homogeneous or even necessarily convergent as between the many countries whose systems can be regarded as market capitalist ones. There has been much interest in the possibilities of demonstrating how divergences of style and method as between national normative and regulatory institutions in the European region give rise to distinctive 'varieties of capitalism', a notion now especially associated with the work of Peter Hall and David Soskice and their colleagues.[21] Their writings gave rise to the conception that the different European institutional forms of market capitalism can usefully be regarded as falling into two generic groupings, those of liberal market economies and co-ordinated market economies.[22] There is much debate and discussion about how to classify particular national systems, and about what sub-categories or cross-cutting categories can be identified in relation to that broad dichotomy; but there is nevertheless a broad consensus in favour of regarding the UK as representing the leading European example of, or paradigm for, the liberal market economy, and in regarding countries such as France or even more especially Germany as providing major illustrative models of the co-ordinated market economy.

The 'varieties of capitalism' discussion, and the contrast between co-ordinated and liberal market economies, provide valuable insights for our comparative study; in the course of this work, we shall see that they help to understand some deep-seated differences in the construction of personal work relations as contractual ones as between different European legal systems. However, like the legal cultures discussion and the common law/Civil law contrast, their utility can easily be overstated. Here, two major caveats need to be emphasized. Firstly, we should remind ourselves that, however informative and sustainable we may regard the general taxonomy of national market institutions as being, we have to be careful not to overuse it in the analysis of something as specific and technical as the legal construction of personal work relations.

A second caveat comes from within the very sphere of political economy in which the 'varieties of capitalism' thesis is itself located. Crouch has recently levelled some serious criticisms against the way in which some of his colleagues have presented the 'varieties of capitalism' thesis.[23] Without taking up a position in that particular debate,[24] we should recognize the relevance of those criticisms to our

---

[21] As embodied in P. A. Hall and D. Soskice (eds.) (2001) *Varieties of Capitalism – The Institutional Foundations of Comparative Advantage* Oxford: OUP.

[22] The dichotomy is introduced ibid., at p. 8.

[23] Colin Crouch (2006) *Capitalist Diversity and Change – Recombinant Governance and Institutional Entrepreneurs*, Oxford: OUP.

[24] It is a debate which is taken further by a number of the papers in the symposium B. Hancké (ed.) (2009) *Debating Varieties of Capitalism – A Reader*, Oxford: OUP; reference should especially be made

own more specialized attempt at institutional analysis. He points out the dangers of being over-ready to impose a dichotomized view upon a variety of national institutional styles and practices which is in reality a very complex and intricate one.[25] He is also concerned that such a dichotomy might represent an over-extrapolation from some particular national examples, and furthermore that it, indeed along with the whole 'varieties of capitalism' analysis itself, might be over-deterministic, tending irrevocably to characterize particular national systems in particular ways.

However, Crouch also suggests a way of dealing with those difficulties, with regard to the 'varieties of capitalism' analysis, which we might with advantage regard as helpful in relation to our more specific institutional analysis. Crouch introduces[26] an argument about institutional adaptability or mutability, the alleged absence of which he regards as a serious flaw in or limitation upon the 'varieties of capitalism' thesis. Disclaiming, as we have said, any intention to enter into that debate in respect of the general 'varieties of capitalism' thesis, we can nevertheless accept that Crouch thereby offers a very useful refinement to that kind of institutional analysis, which we should seek to deploy in the context of our own more specific institutional questions.

Crouch's suggested adaptation of the 'varieties of capitalism' analysis consists of invoking the two notions of 'recombinant governance' and 'institutional entrepreneurs'. The notion of 'recombinant governance' is, in effect, the idea that institutional governance systems may be subject to profound reconstitutions of themselves or remixing of themselves with different institutional governance systems, in a way which is analogous to the genetic 're-combination' of natural physical organisms. 'Institutional entrepreneurs' are 'social actors' (such as political leaders) who bring about or catalyze such 're-combinations', just as business entrepreneurs bring about corresponding changes in economic enterprises. Crouch's idea, with which we agree, is that this capacity of 'institutional entrepreneurs' to bring about 're-combinations' in governance arrangements endows the institutions of market capitalism with a significant degree of mutability. This means that we can give an account of those institutions which is free of the most deterministic constraints of 'path dependency': the institutions in question need not be seen as locked into patterns of behaviour which are typical of their respective 'varieties of capitalism'.

We shall suggest that it is possible to identify many examples both of 'recombinant governance' and of 'institutional entrepreneurs' in our comparative analysis of the legal construction of personal work relations. In fact we can use Crouch's analysis to sustain and validate the particular methodology of comparative analysis which we intend to apply to the legal construction of personal work relations. His theoretical approach to the understanding of diversity and change in the general

---

to the first chapter by P. Hall and D. Soskice and the second by C. Crouch. Cf. also G. Menz (2005), *Varieties of Capitalism and Europeanization – National Response Strategies to the Single European Market*, Oxford: OUP, especially Chapter 1 'European Liberalization, National Varieties of Capitalism and Re-regulation'.

[25] The critique is developed in Crouch (2006), from p. 2 onwards.
[26] Ibid., from p. 3.

development of market capitalism in European countries supports a particular approach to the comparative analysis of the legal construction of personal work relations. This is an approach or methodology according to which there is a high expectation or strong hypothesis that the legal construction of personal work relations will be significantly diverse between European national legal systems, but in patterns which are quite mutable ones. Those patterns will be institutionally embedded in national legal traditions and national labour market structures, but will be susceptible to quite rapid and significant shifts effected by changes in legislative and public policy on the part of legal and political actors, and by changes in the behaviour and practice of labour market actors. We could identify this idea as our 'mutable diversity' hypothesis.

We suggest that this mutable diversity hypothesis has one further implication for our methodological approach to the comparative analysis of the legal construction of personal work relations. This concerns the legal language and legal terminologies in and through which the legal construction of personal work relations is expressed. We venture into a problematical area for legal comparatists which can be identified as that of 'legal translation', or, at a deeper level, as that of the role of language in comparative law. Problems about 'legal translation' and about the role of language are necessarily at the heart of comparative law.[27] That is true, in one sense, even where the comparison is between legal systems which share a common spoken and written language – so between legal systems which share the language of English, or French, or German, or Spanish, and so on. Even where that is the case, the meaning attached to a particular terminology may be diverse as between the systems. For example, the term 'employee' might well be differently understood as between two Anglophone legal systems both of which use that terminology, shall we say those of the UK and the USA.

This is a potential diversity which is essentially and intensely compounded where the comparison is between legal systems that are cast in different written and spoken languages. That is because, although it is evident that linguistic translation or interpretation is needed in such situations, it is all too easy in practice to assume that linguistic translation or interpretation produces exact equivalents – that the French '*contrat de travail*' finds its equivalent in the English 'contract of employment' and so on. It is hard to maintain the constant scepticism and vigilance which is needed in this regard, and there are few greater dangers for comparative law than those which are caused by lowering one's guard in this respect. We could think about this as the problem of the unreliability of apparent linguistic counterparts – in brief, the 'linguistic unreliability problem'.

An important aspect of our methodology will consist of identifying the scope and extent of the 'linguistic unreliability problem' in the comparative analysis of the legal construction of personal work relations. We believe that the unreliability problem is a very significant one in this area: that is for two distinct, indeed almost opposite,

---

[27] A useful survey of this aspect of comparative law studies is provided in M. Reimann and R. Zimmermann (eds.) (2006) *Oxford Handbook of Comparative Law*, Oxford: OUP, Chapter 20 by V. G. Curran, 'Comparative Law and Language'.

reasons. On the one hand, as we have indicated, the legal construction of personal work relations in European legal systems is dominated by certain central paradigms – pre-eminently that of the contract of employment – which have become deeply embedded institutions in their respective legal systems, and have, in the course of so doing, developed in very diverse ways as between systems. This creates great risks that apparent equivalences between legal systems with regard to those long-established dominant paradigms may turn out to be false or unreliable ones.

On the other hand, in the sphere of legal construction of personal work relations which lies beyond or outside the dominant paradigm of the contract of employment, we find that there is a good deal of innovation, both by law-makers and other labour market actors, and of experimentation with novel and 'atypical' work arrangements and legal formats for those work arrangements. As analysts and policymakers strive to understand these innovations, and to relate the innovations of one legal system with those of another, they experience new instances of the 'linguistic unreliability problem' which are different in character from, but may be no less severe than, those which are thrown up by the functioning of longer-established and more deeply embedded legal institutions. So for these various reasons we think of the investigation of the 'linguistic unreliability problem' as an important plank in our methodological platform.

We have therefore now elaborated the methodology of our comparative analysis in its principal dimensions. We have considered the sense in which it can be viewed as a functional one, and have identified it as in a particular sense an institutional one. This discussion was followed by a brief introduction to the notion of 'layers of regulation' and the system-specific relevance of each particular layer. We are now in a position to develop it further in one specific way, namely by considering some comparisons and contrasts between European labour law systems in their treatment of the relationship between the different sources of regulation of personal work relations.

## Section 3: Sources of Regulation and Hierarchies of Norms

### A. Introduction

In this section, we further develop our institutional comparative methodology by applying it to one particular aspect of the law of personal work relations. That aspect consists of the way in which European national labour law systems identify and interrelate the sources of regulation of personal work relations. There is a highly significant set of comparisons and contrasts between the ways in which that is done in different systems. In particular, some systems envisage and construct carefully and consciously articulated hierarchies of sources or norms in ways that others do not. We shall argue that the differences of approach to the hierarchical ordering of sources profoundly affect the whole understanding within each legal system of the way in which personal work relations are legally constructed.

We shall also hope to show in the course of this section that these differences of approach as between European labour law systems, with regard to the hierarchical ordering of sources of regulation, provide very good instances of the insights which can be gained from deploying our institutional methodology. We could regard hierarchies of sources as institutions of labour law in and of themselves, or as important elements in the formation of those larger institutions which between them amount to the legal regulation and legal construction of personal work relations in any given national legal system.

We shall argue that the degree of development of these institutional hierarchies of sources differs as between legal systems in a way which corresponds, at a basic level, to the broad distinction between common law and civil law approaches. On the other hand, we shall also argue that these differences are part and parcel of the distinctive development of the regulation of personal work relations in each European legal system. Each legal system has produced its own approach to the recognition and hierarchical ordering of the sources of regulation of personal work relations: that distinctive approach forms an identifying characteristic and forma-tive part of its system of labour law, and an expression of the autonomy of that labour law system within the national legal system as a whole.

So with that introduction we revert to one of the methodological suggestions which underlies our analysis, namely that the legal systems we are focusing on can be broadly subdivided into two fairly distinct models, or types, which we refer to as common-law-based and Civilian. We are very much aware, and have already pointed out in the previous section, that this simple dichotomy can easily lead to simplistic generalizations. On the other hand, we are also conscious of the fact that merely comparing legal institutions without seeking to tease out systemic simila-rities and differences, inevitably leads to heuristically weak and analytically frag-mented results which prevent the observer from appreciating more structural phenomena and dynamics.

We seek to navigate between these two extremes by advancing a methodological middle-ground where the dichotomy between common-law-based and Civilian systems is introduced with a series of clarifications that consolidate the existence of the two models, while recognizing more discrete and precise dimensions of variation within them than has been hitherto suggested. Taking as our starting point our institutional hypothesis, we go on to argue that, in the various systems under examination, the contract of employment is regulated by reference to various sets of regulatory sources which are interrelated in different ways and according to doctrines which may differ from one legal tradition to the other. As already pointed out in the previous section, collectively agreed norms play an important role in the regulation of the employment relationship. And, of course, statutes and other instruments of a legislative nature, such as labour codes and consolidated employ-ment relations Acts, have been a key element in regulating contracts of employment. Norms of a constitutional character similarly play a central role in the regulation of this important institution in most continental systems and, through the influence of EU law and human rights legislation, they are increasingly emerging as key factors in the regulation of the contract of employment in English law too.

However, merely stating that the personal work relation, or the contract of employment, is regulated and shaped by reference to different sources of regulation in different legal systems, does not advance in any particular way our methodological hypothesis based on the existence of two broadly discernible models of regulation, an English common-law-based one and a continental European Civilian one. It does serve to highlight the fact that constitutional norms play a more active part in regulating personal work relations in systems with a written and 'codified' constitution, or that collective agreements are more relevant in some systems than in others, but this is not *per se* a very revealing conclusion.

On the other hand, we do not seek to suggest that the main difference between common-law-based and Civilian systems is the existence, in one but not in the other, of a variety of external, and internal, sources of regulation of the contract of employment and other personal work contracts. Our suggestion is that, generally speaking, Civilian systems, in contrast with English law, structure all these sources of regulation according to a vertically integrated approach which gives rise to a more or less rigid hierarchy of norms or sources of regulation. These are sources of labour law in general, but for the purposes of our present work we focus on their role in the regulation of personal work contracts and relations. In legal systems such as those of Germany, Italy, France, and Spain, the regulation of the contract of employment is defined by an orderly cascade of collectively agreed norms, statutory rules, and constitutional principles, on the basis of the general principle that every level of regulation below is only able to derogate *in melius* – that is to say, broadly speaking, in a more worker-protective fashion – from the level above.

While even within the various continental systems this general rule has a number of exceptions – which have markedly increased in recent years – we advance the proposition that the presence and operation of a fairly rigid hierarchy of norms system acts both as a unifying element for the Civilian legal regimes the present work focuses on, and as an element of differentiation of these legal regimes from the less hierarchical system of sources shaping the regulation of contracts of employment, and even more markedly of other personal work contracts, in English law. In fact we suggest that the hierarchy of norms factor is the single most important unifying element in approximating continental systems of regulation and, at the same time, one of the most important elements in distinguishing Civilian systems from the English one. It is mainly, though not exclusively, on the basis of this systemic element that we advance the proposition that it is descriptively and analytically accurate and enriching to refer to the existence of common-law-based and Civilian models.

At the same time, however, we emphasize that this unifying element, establishing systemic commonalities between Civilian legal orders, coexists with a number of 'diversifying elements', whose presence points firmly against viewing the Civilian category as a uniform one. There are several such diversifying elements, or sets of elements. Firstly, even within the Civilian cluster, there are a number of significant nuances of difference in constructing the hierarchical relationship between the various sources of regulation. Some continental systems are readier than others to accept statutory regulation as being invested with some sort of '*jus cogens*' status, or as the French would say, as having the character of '*ordre public absolu*' (strictly applicable public policy). Moreover, there is no denying that the original rationality of the 'hierarchical' constructs has been diluted by a series of creeping exceptions allowing lower levels of regulation to derogate *in pejus* from statutory provisions, usually under the control of the social partners. These are important distinctions that should at the very least suggest caution in attributing uniformity to the Civilian category.

There are, of course, other diversifying elements that are less directly connected to the 'hierarchy of norms' discourse. Thus we should emphasize from the outset the different approach that each national system takes in classifying the *varieties* of personal work contracts and personal work relations. A very visible example would be the readiness of systems such as those of Germany, Italy, and Spain to identify intermediate categories of 'quasi-dependant labour', and the relative resistance hitherto shown to that by the French system, which seeks instead to rationalize the variety of personal work relations by relying on legal 'presumptions' of status. Having said that, one should not be drawn into hastily concluding that, solely because some continental systems – as indeed to some extent does English labour law – accept the existence of 'quasi-dependant workers' as a category of personal work contracts, the German *arbeitnehmerähnliche Personen* (employee-like persons) category can be seen as synonymous with the Spanish category of *trabajadores autónomos económicamente dependientes* (economically dependent autonomous workers), a point that we shall further explore in Chapter 3. Less obvious, but no less significant examples, can be derived from considering the rules shaping the provision of personal work services through an intermediary, and whether these rules tend to classify these work relationships by reference to the standard contract of employment, to autonomous work, or by configuring *sui generis* contractual constructs. To give a tangible example of how differentiated and fragmented these taxonomies can be, in recent times two Italian labour economists, Boeri and Garibaldi, suggested that the various contractual typologies for the provision of personal work in the Italian labour market may amount to forty-four.[28]

Moreover, we should not forget that even within Civil law systems which take similar approaches to the hierarchy of sources, and to the classifying of personal work contracts and relations, there are considerable differences between the ways that important aspects of the formation, content, performance, and termination of personal work contracts, are regulated. Very often the presence of minor distinctions in the treatment of a given area of regulation can effectively result in that area bearing a significance in the overall architecture of that labour law system, that sets it apart from the treatment of other comparable aspects in different jurisdictions. For instance, the emphasis placed on reinstatement as a remedy against the unfair termination of an individual contract of employment in Italian labour law clearly sets this system apart, almost in a league of its own, in its protectiveness of

---

[28] T. Boeri and P. Garibaldi (2008) *Un Nuovo Contratto per Tutti*, Milano: Chiarelettere, 54.

contractual job security, even by comparison with other worker-protective systems such as the Spanish or the French ones.

Very often the differences in the regulation of specific areas of personal work contracts will be the result of a different approach to the classifying of particular work relations, so in practice there is considerable conceptual overlap between these 'diversifying elements'. For instance, the differences in the regulation of the formation, or the termination, of the personal work contracts of public servants could be the consequence of their having a nationally distinctive public law employment status – and as such of a different taxonomy – as well as the result of specific collective agreements, or other regulatory arrangements, applying to them. So while we feel confident in suggesting that it is possible to draw broad contrasts between an English law model for the regulation of personal work relations and a distinct continental and Civil law model based on the different ways in which the sources of regulation are envisaged, we also stress the differences existing within the Civilian cluster.

While these elements of diversity will be analysed in the remaining chapters of the present work, the remainder of this section is devoted to exploring in more detail the operation and functioning of the idea of a hierarchy of norms, which so significantly shapes the legal construction of personal work relations in general and of the contract of employment in particular in many European labour law systems. We shall proceed in two stages, first considering the way in which, for those Civilian systems which do envisage a hierarchy of sources of regulation of personal work relations, that hierarchical approach is intimately associated with the 'autonomy of labour law'. Secondly we consider the way in which English law stands in broad contrast to those systems by pursuing a largely non-hierarchical, or at least a much less systematically hierarchical, approach to the sources of regulation of personal work contracts and relations.

## B. Hierarchies of Sources as Identifiers of Labour Law Systems

Labour law is a composite legal discipline, and throughout its development it has had to balance a quest for autonomy from other disciplines, and in particular from general contract law, with active borrowing from other legal domains, while co-ordinating these external rules with regulatory and normative standards deriving from *sui generis* sources such as collective agreements. Lord Wedderburn stressed the fact that 'no branch of law can be "completely autonomous, within the body of the juridical order as a whole". Fortress labour law, like Fortress Wapping, cannot survive in total isolation.'[29] As Collins (1989) has put it: '[a]lthough some fields of law such as contract and crime are marked by the quest of coherence according to a small set of principles, Labour Law, like other contextual fields such as Family Law, has never aspired to such conceptual unity'.[30] Nevertheless, in many continental European legal systems there has been a tendency for labour law to evolve as a

---

[29] Lord Wedderburn (1987) 'Labour Law: From Here to Autonomy?', *ILJ*, 1–2.
[30] H. Collins (1989) 'Labour Law as a Vocation', *LQR*, 473.

distinctive and autonomous legal discipline, and the pursuit of autonomy of labour law has been greatly intertwined with a quest for the rationalization of the various sources of regulation shaping and affecting its institutions in general, and the employment relationship in particular. Barassi's 1949 treatise on *Diritto del Lavoro* discussed '*il concetto del diritto del lavoro*' (the concept of labour law) alongside the concept of '*le fonti*', (the sources)[31] and he noted that: 'while having as a focus the regulation of the employment relationship...it is evident that this [enquiry] of mine will necessarily lead me to recollect those other norms that more or less directly react on the employment relationship: that is to say protective laws, social security institutions and the organization of trade unions'.[32]

Barassi's analysis covered various sources of regulation, ranging from statutory regulation ('*La legge*'), to collective regulation (which he referred to as the '*regolamento concordatario*') in its various configurations and levels, 'enterprise level work rules', and 'custom and equity'.[33] His enquiry extended to the role of supranational regulation in the forms of '*la disciplina internazionale del lavoro*',[34] and, perhaps most importantly for the purposes of our present analysis, the question of 'the various forms of the regulation of labour and their hierarchy'.[35] There is no mention of constitutional norms, but this can possibly be explained by the circumstance that the new Constitution of the Italian Republic had only been adopted a year before, and that the earlier *Statuto Albertino* had clearly not contributed to the development of fundamental social rights as a juridical concept. Santoro-Passarelli's 1952 edition of *Nozioni di Diritto del Lavoro* recognized both the importance of constitutional principles as sources of regulation,[36] and their dominant position in the '*sistema delle fonti*' (system of sources).[37]

For contemporary French labour lawyers the issue of autonomy of labour law was even more tightly linked to the preservation of an equally autonomous set of regulatory sources, which arguably had been fairly distinct at least since the, rather laborious, creation of a labour code between 1910 and 1922. In 1945 Paul Durand's notion of autonomy, or rather '*particularisme*' (particularism), of labour law was inextricably connected to a crusade for the establishment of an even more comprehensive Labour Code and against any temptation of following 'the example of Italian law' and splitting the regulation of the employment relationship between different statutory sources and various codes, in particular the Civil Code and the Code of Civil Procedure.[38] 'If labour law is an autonomous body of law ' he

---

[31] L. Barassi (1949) *Diritto del Lavoro – Vol. I*, Milano: Giuffrè, 1.

[32] Ibid., 5–6.

[33] Ibid., Chapter 1, 'Le Fonti', 1–190.

[34] Ibid., 51.

[35] Ibid., 47.

[36] F. Santoro-Passarelli (1952) *Nozioni di Diritto del Lavoro*, 6th ed., Napoli: Jovene, 16.

[37] Ibid., 17.

[38] P. Durand (1945) 'Le Particularisme du Droit du Travail' *Droit Social*, 301. Our translation from the French original.

wrote 'it would appear that . . . neither the legislative expression of this discipline, nor the jurisdictions in charge of its application, nor the general system of interpretation can be any longer conceived according to the traditional mode.'[39]

In such ways, continental employment lawyers became very familiar with both the notion of 'sources of regulation' of labour law – a notion that they kept enriching and refining – and with the more specific concept of a 'hierarchy of norms'. Ludovico Barassi had already developed a fairly articulate description of the relationship between the various sources of regulation of the employment relation. In discussing the '*gerarchia delle fonti*' (hierarchy of sources) he placed at the top of the chain 'the expression of a general command contained in *leggi* (legislation)', followed by 'the collective inter-union will (in collective agreements), and the enterprise regulation that in a way constitutes a bridge between the pure collective will and the exclusively individual one expressed in the contract of employment', and 'finally . . . usage and equity'.[40]

The '*leggi*' were further broken down into '*leggi categoriche*' (non-derogable legislation) and '*leggi dispositive*' (derogable legislation), but he readily acknowledged his discomfort with the idea that some laws may not be subject to improvement by way of collective agreements,[41] and only reached a 'by and large rather perplexed conclusion' that if in some cases the legislator believes that the protection deriving to the worker from the inderogable statutory provision is 'absolutely the best . . . we must obey and really believe him'.[42] This prudent assessment by Barassi eventually turned out to be correct since, between 1977 and 1992, the law on the indexation of wage increases[43] provided, initially in Article 4, that collective agreements seeking to ameliorate the salary increases determined by means of the legal mechanisms of the inflation wage-adjustment arrangement called *scala mobile* were 'null by law', and in doing that it eventually received the support of the Constitutional Court jurisprudence.[44]

This already sophisticated construct was further refined through the years, in Italy as in other continental systems, as the applications of social provisions of national constitutions of the post-World War II era were proliferated through the activity of national constitutional courts, and collective bargaining, and as social legislation flourished with a crescendo during the 1960s and 1970s. Camerlynck's 1968 *Traité du Droit du Travail*, the first volume of which was dedicated to the regulation of the contract of employment, provides one of the most sophisticated descriptions of the 'sources of the juridical regime of the contract of employment' covering legislation, jurisprudence, collective bargaining, customs, and work rules.[45]

[39] P. Durand (1945) 'Le Particularisme du Droit du Travail', *Droit Social*, 301. Our translation.

[40] L. Barassi (1949) *Diritto del Lavoro – Vol.I*, Milano: Giuffrè, 50–1 (our translation).

[41] Ibid., 76–7.

[42] '*assolutamente la migliore . . . bisogna obbedire e crederlo davvero*'. Ibid., 77.

[43] Decreto Legge 1 February 1977, n.12, converted by Law 31 March 1977, n. 91.

[44] See *Sentenze 141 e 142 del 30 luglio 1980*. Cf. also *Sentenza n.34 del 7 febbraio 1986* on the far more controversial law n. 219 of 12 July 1985. See more in general G. Giugni (2007) *Diritto Sindacale*, Bari: Cacucci, 179–81.

[45] G.H. Camerlynck (1968) *Traité du Droit du Travail – Vol 1 Contrat de Travail*, Paris: Dalloz, 27–35.

But it is his analysis of the 'hierarchy of sources' and of the concept of *'ordre public social'* (social public policy) that deserves our greatest attention as it provides a set of fairly definitive clarifications of the relationship between sources, and in particular between the various levels of collective bargaining, and between these sources and the individual contract of employment.

The key to his analysis is that the top of the chain, that is to say *'la loi'* (legislation), provides what he defines as, 'the worker's floor of rights'.[46] On this 'floor of rights', collective bargaining has the 'essential mission of obtaining… further advantages for the sake of the worker in his profession', so that in the presence of a 'national level collective agreement', regional and local agreements can then 'provide new dispositions and clauses that are more favourable to the workers'.[47] The 'establishment level agreement' can further improve on these terms, and 'finally, by a last adaptation to the worker considered as an individual, the contract of employment will confer upon him his definitive regime of terms and conditions'.[48]

Moreover, Camerlynck opined, 'This "progressive" character of labour law, its uniquely social orientation, serves to instantiate the notion of *ordre public social.'*[49] Under the notion of *'ordre public social'*, statutory provisions having as an object that of guaranteeing or ameliorating the working conditions of the salaried worker *'revêtent un caractère imperatif'*, that is to say are mandatory in character. Each and every 'contrary term of the individual contract of employment is null, and significantly the corresponding provision of the collective agreement is over-ridden'.[50] By contrast, the author continues, it is always possible to derogate in a more worker-favourable sense, 'from a legal or professional norm that is in the nature of a minimum provision'.[51]

Furthermore, French law, perhaps even more markedly than Italian law, is very familiar with the concept of *'ordre public absolu'*, that is to say with norms, often 'social law' norms, that are laid down by legislation as a matter of 'public policy' and that collective or individual agreements cannot modify either *in melius* (for the better) or *in pejus* (for the worse), though we endeavour further to analyse this point in the next section of this chapter. To quote the words of the *Conseil d'État*:

A collective agreement cannot validly derogate from dispositions which, in their own terms, manifest an imperative character, nor from the fundamental principles enounced in the Constitution, nor from the rules of national or, as the case may be, international law, whenever these principles or rules extend beyond the domain of labour law or concern the benefits or guarantees which, in their nature, are not the subject of collective bargaining.[52]

---

[46] *'la condition plancher du travailleur'*, Ibid., 35.
[47] Ibid.
[48] Ibid., Our translation from the original French *'va lui conférer son statut définitif'*.
[49] Ibid., 36. Our translation.
[50] Idem. Our translation.
[51] Idem. Our translation.
[52] *Conseil d'État, Avis du 22mars 1973, Dr. Ouvrier p. 190.* Our translation of the original: *'Une convention collective ne saurait légalement déroger ni aux dispositions qui, par leurs termes mêmes, présentent un caractère impératif ni aux principes fondamentaux énoncés dans la Constitution ou aux règles du droit*

These complex hierarchical structures rely on a series of complex legal and doctrinal devices that retained a discrete space for private contract law. Undoubtedly, when confronted with the dominant role attributed to the various extra-contractual sources of regulation one may almost be excused for 'having doubts about the contractual nature of the work relationship whose content (...) is largely determined by (...) external and superimposed sources'.[53] However, we can be reassured that the contractual analysis still prevails:

[we] are not confronted with a suppression of contractual freedom, but rather with its narrowing by reference to inderogable norms that, by restricting the self-regulatory powers of the stronger party in favour of the weaker party, have the function of supporting individual autonomy on the workers' side.[54]

In practice Italian labour law reaches this high degree of integration by means of important legal mechanisms such as the so-called '*sostituzione legale*' (legal substitution) and '*inserzione automatica*' (automatic insertion) of the '*norme inderogabili*' (inderogable norms) which prevail over attempts to displace those norms '*in pejus*', that is to say to the detriment of the worker.

This hierarchical nature of the systems of sources of continental and European legal orders needs to be qualified by reference to the occasional exception to the rule, for instance in those cases where a collective agreement is exceptionally permitted to derogate *in pejus* from a statutory provision. This is a feature most commonly associated with Scandinavian systems, where: '[e]ven important statutory rules may be overridden by collective agreements. One example of such semi-mandatory rules can be found in the [Swedish] Employment Protection Act'.[55] A further qualification to a strict hierarchy of sources is also introduced by the collective and individual derogations or opt-outs to the otherwise 'supreme' EU rules in the area of labour and social regulation, which are occasionally permitted by the EU social directives themselves.[56] But by and large, it remains the case that European systems, especially when contrasted to the British one, remain characterized by a high level of vertical integration of the various sources of regulation, and by the location of the individual contract of employment at the very bottom of this regulatory pyramid.

---

*interne ou, le cas échéant, international, lorsque ces principes ou règles débordent le domaine du droit du travail ou intéressent des avantages ou garanties échappant, par leur nature, aux rapports conventionnels'.*

[53] E. Ghera (2007) *Diritto del Lavoro*, Bari: Cacucci, at. p. 62.

[54] Ibid (our translation).

[55] M. Bogdan (ed.) (2000) *Swedish Law in the New Millennium*, Stockholm: Norstedts Juridik, Chapter 13, A. Numhauser-Henning 'Labour Law', 346.

[56] The most obvious example in that sense being contained in provisions such as Articles 18 and 22 of Directive 2003/88/EC of the European Parliament and of the Council of 4 November 2003 concerning certain aspects of the organisation of working time, [2003] OJ L 299/09.

## C. English Law and its Inherently Non-Hierarchical System of Sources

The contemporary analysis of English labour law in the 1950s and 1960s was markedly different to the legal and theoretical panorama described so far. Otto Kahn-Freund's 'collective *laissez-faire*' provided a captivating and compelling analytical key for the understanding of labour law, or industrial law as it was often called, as a legal discipline, and for the proper conceptualization of the relationship between the regulatory and normative sources and institutions presiding over its evolution during the twentieth century. Collective *laissez-faire* suggested a regulatory environment based on voluntarism and minimal legislative interference. Even in 1977, the date of publication of his second edition of *Labour and the Law*, Kahn-Freund unequivocally stated that 'statutes are not the primary factor in filling the blank of the empty "contract of employment". The primary factor is of course the collective agreement.'[57] Kahn-Freund delineated a clear role for collective bargaining, as well as for statutory intervention, in relation to what he famously depicted as 'Blackstone's neglected child', the contract of employment.[58] Most importantly, he traced the terms of the relationship between the three in a way that had not hitherto been attempted by many of his contemporaries, and already in his first edition of *Labour and the Law* explored what, at that time, was the concept – rather unfamiliar to English law and perhaps slightly continental – of 'Sources of Regulation'.[59]

Kahn-Freund's description of the English labour law 'sources of regulation' in the 1970s was based on three fundamental insights, which immediately set the system apart from the rest of Europe. Firstly, the key relevant sources are collective bargaining, regulatory legislation, and the common law, with the concept of the contract of employment falling predominantly within the latter. The notable absentees here were, for obvious reasons and in stark contrast with the continental experiences, sources of a constitutional character. Similarly he noticed the comparatively minor influence of supranational legal sources, although a careful observer like Kahn-Freund already appreciated the importance of Community law, noting that while 'in the past the reluctance to legislate has been an obstacle to the acceptance of international standards, we have seen more recently how international and foreign standards have in their turn helped to promote a more positive attitude to regulatory labour legislation in this country'.[60]

Of course, the relationship between these sources was, and still is, affected both by doctrines of general public law, such as that of Parliamentary supremacy and the supremacy of statute over the common law, and by doctrines and principles which are more closely related to industrial relations, labour law, and – as convincingly

---

[57] O. Kahn-Freund, *Labour and the Law*, 2nd ed., London: Stevens & Sons, at 20.

[58] O. Kahn-Freund (1977) 'Blackstone's Neglected Child: The Contract of Employment', *LQR*, 508.

[59] O. Kahn-Freund (1972) *Labour and the Law*, Stevens & Sons: London, 21–50. It should be noted that other equally authoritative monographs on the subject did not specifically refer to this concept. Cf. for instance R. Rideout (1976) *Principles of Labour Law*, London: Sweet & Maxwell.

[60] O. Kahn-Freund (1977) *Labour and the Law*, 2nd ed., London: Stevens & Sons, 42–3.

argued by Deakin and Wilkinson (2005) – by the regulation of the welfare state.[61] As such, he noted, 'the parties to the contract of employment are, by a statutory fiction, deemed to make a contract on the basis of the statutory terms',[62] and that 'a promise to work at a wage lower than the collectively agreed or imposed minimum...is displaced by the collective norm'.[63] These two considerations in respect of statute and collective bargaining, may suggest some similarities with the continental notions of *in pejus* inderogability, and '*sostitutzione automatica*', since in Britain 'the terms of the statute can be contracted out only for the benefit of the worker, and if the parties purport to agree on terms less favourable...they are nevertheless deemed to have contracted for the minimum'.[64]

However, we should be careful with comparisons here, as there are in practice very few statutes that provide for the automatic insertion of statutory provisions directly into the contract of employment,[65] with the traditional method in English law being that of attaching to the contractual relation obligations that simply override any contrary agreement. Kahn-Freund also stigmatized the ambition of recently produced British regulatory legislation to act as a floor of rights, since: 'in different ways the statutory norms on redundancy payments and on unfair dismissal can be supplemented in the employee's favour or even (with the consent of the Secretary of State) be replaced by collective agreements',[66] though by the 1977 edition of his book he noted that while 'autonomous regulation was hoped to predominate, in practice [this] did not happen'.[67]

The second perceptive insight of Kahn-Freund as to the dominant, albeit at that point progressively declining, role of collective bargaining vis-à-vis the other sources. The dominance of collective agreement over statutory regulation is well known and much commented upon, but it is worthwhile stressing some points that are particularly important in the context of a comparative perspective. We have pointed out that English law readily recognizes the idea of supremacy of the law to the rules deriving from collective and individual agreements. However, the law had traditionally set minimum standards exclusively in respect of a restricted number of categories of workers, leaving collective bargaining as the exclusive source of regulation for much of the workforce. For instance 'minimum remuneration is fixed only for workers in need of a statutory "floor of wages"',[68] and in respect of other workers the exact working of the hierarchical relationship between statute and collective agreement was a moot point.

---

[61] S. Deakin and F. Wilkinson (2005) *The Law of the Labour Market*, Oxford: OUP, 86–95.
[62] O. Kahn-Freund (1972) *Labour and the Law*, London: Stevens & Sons, 34.
[63] O. Kahn-Freund (1972) *Labour and the Law*, London: Stevens & Sons, 34–5.
[64] O. Kahn-Freund (1977) *Labour and the Law*, 2nd ed., London: Stevens & Sons, 31.
[65] Cf. for instance the 'equality clause' in the Equal Pay Act 1970, s. 1(1), providing that: 'if the terms of a contract under which a woman is employed...do not include...an equality clause they shall be deemed to include one'. An equivalent provision is now contained in the Equality Act 2010, s. 66.
[66] O. Kahn-Freund (1972) *Labour and the Law*, London: Stevens & Sons, 30–1.
[67] O. Kahn-Freund (1977) *Labour and the Law*, 2nd ed., London: Stevens & Sons, 26–7.
[68] O. Kahn-Freund (1977) *Labour and the Law*, 2nd ed., London: Stevens & Sons, 34.

Of course, at the time Kahn-Freund was writing, this type of selective legislation was already in the process of being marginalized by a series of significant new developments. Important statutes such as the Contracts of Employment Act 1963, the Redundancy Payments Act 1965, and the various pieces of equal treatment legislation visibly distanced themselves from the earlier norm-setting mode since: 'none [was] restricted to particular branches of the economy'.[69] Unsurprisingly, Kahn-Freund was developing a theoretical apparatus analogous to the continental ideas of *'ordre public social'* or 'inderogability *in pejus'* whereby 'the terms of the statute can be contracted out only for the benefit of the worker, and if the parties purport to agree on terms less favourable to him or her . . . or terms less favourable than those applied to a member of the other sex doing . . . equivalent work, they are nevertheless deemed to have contracted for the minimum or for equal treatment'.[70]

However, even in this increasingly statute-based environment there were some marked differences in terms of the limits that the law sought to impose upon the worker-protective effects of collective bargaining. English legal reasoning, as opposed to French and to some extent Italian reasoning, was far less keen to accept that in some circumstances statutory 'floors of rights' could also act as 'ceilings' for collectively set terms and conditions. For example, while closed-shop arrangements played a pivotal role in the development of English labour law in the twentieth century, and in the establishment of collective bargaining as the dominant source of regulation, they were prohibited in most European systems: for instance in France, by being contrary to measures currently contained in Articles L. 2141–5 and L. 2134–2 and originally introduced by *Loi 27 avril 1956*, the *Loi Moisant*, and by reason of their conflict with the constitutionally protected and *'ordre public'* non-discrimination principle or,[71] as would be the case in other systems, with the notion of 'negative freedom of association'.[72]

In its heyday in the United Kingdom, not only did collective bargaining, as was widely acknowledged, overshadow statutory legislation as a source of regulation, but it also marginalized the common law and, indirectly, the contract of employment. '[C]ourts have had a share, but only a small share in [the] evolution [of the rules regulating the relations between employers and workers]',[73] since '[t]he great success of collective bargaining has greatly reduced the need for the intervention of the courts'.[74] Moreover, as Kahn-Freund (1977) puts it, '[the] atrophy of the contract of employment had consequences which were quite extraordinary. The mutual rights and duties of

[69]  O. Kahn-Freund (1977) *Labour and the Law*, 2nd ed., London: Stevens & Sons, 35.

[70]  O. Kahn-Freund (1977) *Labour and the Law*, 2nd ed., London: Stevens & Sons, 31.

[71]  Cf. G. Lyon-Caen (1973) 'Négociation Collective et Légilsation d'Ordre Public' *Droit Social*, 89; G. Borenfreund (2001) 'Les syndicats bénéficiaires d'un accord collectif' *Droit Social*, 821. More in general see M.-A. Souriac-Rotschild (1996) 'Le Contrôle de la Légalité Interne des Conventions et Accords Collectifs' *Droit Social*, 395 and Court de Cassation, *Les Discriminations dans la Jurisprudence de la Cour de Cassation – Rapport Annuel 2008* (La Documentation française, Paris, 2009), particularly section 1.1.1.3. Les discriminations syndicales.

[72]  Cf. G. Giugni (2007) *Dritto Sindacale*, Bari: Cacucci, 34–5. Cf. *Sørensen v Denmark* and *Rasmussen v Denmark* (Applications 52562/99 and 52620/99) [2008] 46 EHHR 29.

[73]  O. Kahn-Freund (1977) *Labour and the Law*, 2nd ed., London: Stevens & Sons, 18.

[74]  Ibid., 22.

employers, and employees are mainly determined by collective agreements and by statutes. Collective agreements shaped the individual contractual relation because their terms are tacitly or expressly incorporated in the contract of employment.[75]

However by comparison to Civilian systems, English law does not offer the same sort of conceptually clear-cut solutions in respect of the normative relationship between collective agreements and individual contracts of employment. Firstly, and in contrast with most continental systems, English law offers a rather ambiguous answer to the question of the legal effects of collectively agreed standards. While it is certainly not the only system in Europe that does not attribute to collective agreements any universal, *erga omnes*, effects, it undeniably stands out for its paucity of rules clarifying what normative effects collective agreements have over individual contracts. Those continental systems that expressly include collective bargaining in the formal sources of regulation in the labour sphere clearly have an edge in this respect. France for instance has long incorporated collective agreements among the sources listed by its *Code du Travail*. The '*effet normatif* of French collective agreement: 'extends to all employment contracts concluded with employers that belong to one of the employers' organizations that have signed the agreement... regardless of the fact that the workers are members of the signatory trade unions'.[76]

Somewhat similarly, Germany, while not having a labour code as such, laid down the fundamental principles regulating the effects of collective agreements in the *Tarifvertragsverordnung* (Collective Bargaining Decree) of 1918. The contemporary *Tarifvertragsgesetz* (Collective Bargaining Law) of 1949 effectively provides that: 'the parties to collective agreements in Germany are entitled to act as if they were legislators, namely to set norms to be respected by the parties to an individual employment contract as if they were contained in a statute. Therefore, in setting such norms they are bound by the collective agreements as if they were legislators, which means that they are directly bound.'[77] This is notoriously not the case in English law, where both scholarly analyses and jurisprudence have overwhelmingly suggested that: 'no legally enforceable contracts resulted from... collective agreements'.[78] Thus the legal effects of collective agreements under English law effectively depend on the presence of a specific 'bridging term' in the individual contract of employment, or in the statutorily required written statement of particulars of terms and conditions of employment.

Moreover, there has been a historical inadequacy of the common law in clarifying and resolving conflicts between different levels of collective agreements.[79]

[75] O. Kahn-Freund (1977) 'Blackstone's Neglected Child: The Contract of Employment', *LQR*, 526.
[76] J. Pélissier, A. Supiot, A. Jeammaud (2006) *Droit du Travail* (23rd ed., Paris: Dalloz), 120. The relevant provisions are contained Part II of the French Labour Code, regulating 'Collective Employment Relations'.
[77] M. Weiss (2005) 'The Interface between Constitution and Labor Law in Germany' *Comp. Labor Law & Pol'y Journal*, 182.
[78] *Ford Motor Co Ltd v. AUEFW* [1969] 2 All ER 481.
[79] S. Deakin and G. Morris (2009) *Labour Law*, 5th ed., Hart: Oxford, 243.

Continental systems seem to display a considerably clearer set of arrangements for clarifying the relationship between the various levels, and the different geographical scopes of application of collective bargaining, although this an area where, over the past few decades, successive reforms inspired by a deregulatory rationale have somewhat reduced the clarity originally provided by the concept of hierarchy of norms and by the application, in this context, of the principles of *inderogabilità in pejus*, *Günstigkeitsprinzip*, (inderogability for the worse) and the like. In France for instance: 'as a consequence of the principle of *faveur* [presumption in favour of the worker] the law would oblige the parties to an agreement of lower level to adapt its text whenever a more favourable term was adopted by an agreement of higher level'.[80] This, however, was modified by the adoption of the *Loi Fillon* of May 2004 which, after some thirty-three years of general inderogability, has maintained this principle only when the collective agreement concluded at the higher level has expressly stated that lower levels can only improve upon the floor of rights it establishes.

While this is not the only case in which hierarchically lower sources of regulation can in effect reduce the level of protection provided by a superior source, it needs to be pointed out that this is a far cry from the general *anomie* that pervades the relationship between different levels of collective bargaining in English law. Once more, any device which might resolve possible conflicts between levels of bargaining is to be found neither in legislation, nor in collectively agreed standards. Following the repeal in 1980 of Schedule 11 of the EPA 1975, the common law has sought to solve the problems arising, by reference to the scope of any express or implied bridging term clarifying the relationship, and possible conflicts, between different levels. In the absence of such terms, however, the only clear point is that: 'the courts have evidently not been guided by the argument that sectoral agreements should be viewed, at least presumptively, as providing a non-derogable floor of rights'.[81] This can be contrasted, for instance, with the way German law deals with the potentially divisive issue of the relationship between collective agreements and works councils agreements in Germany. As a general rule: 'Collective bargaining agreements are protected against similar rules entered into by works councils. The legislature regarded collective bargaining as more important than the jurisdiction of works councils.'[82]

In all these instances, under English law the burden of rationalizing the various sources and levels of regulation falls on the terms of the individual contract of employment; there is in effect a reversal of what occurs in most Civil law systems. Whereas in countries like Germany and France collective agreements, with the support of statutory regulation, shape the terms and conditions and normative effects of the individual contract of employment, in English law the burden of

---

[80] J. Pélissier, A. Supiot, A. Jeammaud (2006) *Droit du Travail*, 23rd ed., Paris: Dalloz. Our translation from the original French.
[81] S. Deakin and G. Morris (2009) *Labour Law*, 5th ed., Hart: Oxford, 243.
[82] B. Zwanziger (2005) 'Collective Labour Law in a Changing Environment: Aspects of the German Experience', *Comp. Labor Law & Pol'y Journal*, 309.

clarifying the legal effects of the collective agreement falls on the terms and conditions of the individual contract. The results of this inversion of roles can be quite dramatic. Far from being invariably bound by the terms of a collective agreement, an employer can – at least in theory, but often also in practice – displace these terms simply by forcing upon the employee a unilateral variation of, for instance, the bridging term contained in his contract or, more realistically, by recurring to the practice of terminating the contract and re-engaging the employee under new terms and conditions of work. While neither strategy is a risk-free one, as it subjects the employer to a series of potential constructive and unfair dismissal claims – as we will further discuss in Chapters 5 and 6, the fact remains that English law, as opposed to the law of continental Civil law jurisdictions, fails to provide a solid normative framework clarifying and establishing a hierarchy between collective agreements and individual contracts.

The third insight is possibly the most relevant for the purposes of a twenty-first-century analysis of the sources of regulation of labour law in general, and of the contract of employment in particular. In 1977 Kahn-Freund noted that: 'even in the most recent legislation we can see that the Blackstonian severance of statutory and contractual rights has not entirely disappeared'.[83] This is an important and peculiar feature of the English labour law system, which is still present to date and which is reinforced by the procedural rules on the determination of labour law disputes and on the *ratione materiae* judicial competencies of employment tribunals and the common law courts respectively, with the former having jurisdiction, broadly speaking, for disputes over statutory employment rights and the latter, again broadly speaking, being responsible for matters of contract and tort. There are a few statutes that expressly provide for a tighter integration between legislative provisions and contract, for instance, by providing an automatic incorporation into contracts of specific statutory clauses.[84] However, it is still correct to assert that there is a strong separation between contract and statute, and an absence of systematic interrelation between the two.

Summarizing, English labour law has traditionally displayed the features of an inherently unhierarchical system of rules, in which statute, collective bargaining, and the contract of employment as shaped by common law reasoning have traditionally been far less integrated than in continental European systems. Undoubtedly the role of collective agreement had the effect of rendering the other sources of regulation comparatively 'atrophic'. In the heyday of 'collective laissez-faire', the relative dominance of collective agreements partly obscured this lack of integration between the various sources of regulation, and particularly between statute and contract, though this peculiarity of English labour law did not escape the attention of a careful observer such as Kahn-Freund. These three insights, jointly, provide us with a toolbox for the understanding of the role

---

[83]  O. Kahn-Freund (1977) 'Blackstone's Neglected Child: The Contract of Employment', *LQR*, 526.

[84]  The best example of this is the sex equality clause which is implied into contracts of employment (and 'terms of work' more generally) by the Equality Act 2010, s. 66.

of the contract of employment in twenty-first-century English labour law. This is a role that we can only begin sketching in this chapter but that will be more fully explored in the reminder of the present work. The normative vacuum left by the rapid decline of collective bargaining was progressively filled by statutory intervention and by an increasingly central role for an emboldened, and still predominantly common law-based, contract of employment.

This is a distinctive feature that sets English law quite apart from the other European systems in which, as we pointed out in the previous subsection, the various layers of regulation shaping personal work relations are far more integrated and hierarchically organized. Admittedly, continental European labour law regimes have not remained impermeable to change and reforms inspired by the logic of deregulation, flexibilization, and individualization of labour law, and industrial relations.[85] We have already referred to the adoption of the *Loi Fillon* of May 2004, and to its inherently counter-hierarchical effects. Italian law maintained a very robust hierarchical approach to the relationship between different levels of collective bargaining till the mid-1980s, when the Court of Cassation allowed for pejorative changes carried out by successive collective agreements concluded by the same trade unions.[86] However, neither these changes, nor subsequent reforms adopted in the 1990s, altered the substantially hierarchical philosophy of collective bargaining structures in Italian industrial relations. Giugni, commenting on the reform known as the 'Protocol of 23 July 1993', would still argue that 'on the basis of [these] new principles . . . the relationship between the various levels [of collective bargaining] presents itself [as] *hierarchical*, in that it is the national sectoral collective agreement that determines the areas of competence of decentralised bargaining'.[87]

The trend towards decentralization is of course a constant one, as demonstrated by recent reforms such as the Italian Framework Agreement on collective bargaining of January 2009.[88] But this does not substantially alter the fact that, when compared to the British one, most continental systems remain visibly committed to a substantial level of hierarchical integration between statutory, collective, and contractual sources of regulation and, ultimately, to a different approach in construction and regulating personal work relationships. We thus introduce the idea of variation between national labour law systems in the extent to which sources of regulation, which may be of similar substantive content, are viewed as integrated into contracts of employment or other personal work contracts. We regard this kind of variation – which we might style as an 'integration variable' – as being of

[85] Cf. in general, B. Hepple and B. Veneziani (eds.) (2009), *The Transformation of Labour Law in Europe: A Comparative Study of 15 Countries 1945–2004*, Oxford: Hart; S. Sciarra (2005) *The Evolution of Labour Law 1992–2003 – Vol.1 General Report* (Office for Official Publications of the European Communities, Luxembourg).
[86] Cass. 4 October 1985 n. 4819. Cf. G. Giugni (2007) *Diritto Sindacale*, Bari: Cacucci, 174.
[87] Ibid., 166. Emphasis original.
[88] Cf. F. Carinci (2009) 'Una Dichiarazione d'Intenti: l'Accordo Quadro 22 Gennaio 2009 sulla Riforma degli Assetti Contrattuali' (D'Antona Working Paper No 86).

crucial comparative significance, so that its occurrence and its importance will be a recurrent theme in later chapters.

We hope that this set of arguments has begun to demonstrate the uses to which our comparative methodology may lend itself, and in particular the way in which it may disclose differences in approach to the legal construction of personal work relations which are deeply embedded in European labour law systems. The identification of this methodological approach places us in a position to formulate a programme for the succeeding parts and chapters of this work, and to specify the outcomes which we might hope to achieve and will be aiming at. That is the task of the next and concluding section of this chapter.

## Section 4:  Programme and Outcome

The intended outcome of this work is the provision of a critical analysis of the legal construction of personal work relations in English and European law. We have reached the point at which the broad outline of that 'critical analysis' has been sketched out, at least in a general and abstract sense. In the previous chapter we sought to establish the notion of 'the personal work relation' as the one which would denote the relational scope and boundary of our study, and to identify the purpose/relational scope equation upon which we base that choice. The normative purpose, upon which that equation is based, was loosely specified by reference to the values of 'dignity, capability, and stability', a set of normative purposes upon which, under the umbrella concept of 'personality in work' we will further elaborate in Chapter 9.

Our next set of arguments, in the earlier sections of this chapter, has presented a methodology for the critical analysis of the legal construction of personal work relations. This consists firstly in viewing that legal construction from an institutional perspective, secondly, in concentrating upon the significance and impact of dominant institutional paradigms, thirdly, in considering the ways in which dominant paradigms might on the one hand be grouped into families but were on the other hand mutable and recombinant, and fourthly, in investigating the problem of unreliability in the translation of conceptions between apparently equivalent paradigms in different legal systems. Between them, these specifications of the scope, underlying purpose, and methodology of our analysis indicate the sense in which it is intended to be a 'critical' one, aiming to challenge hitherto received analyses of the legal construction of personal work relations at various points.

In this section, we set forth the programme, that is to say we specify the series of steps according to or by which we shall seek to carry out this critical analysis. This involves a set of moves from a traditional analysis essentially constructed around the contract of employment towards an analysis which is constructed around broader suggested notions of the personal work relation and the personal work nexus. That leads on to a further elaboration of the outcome of the work: in the course of moving from contractual analysis towards analysis based upon relation and nexus, we thereby move from an analysis which is strongly focused upon national legal systems and in particular upon English law to one which is more supranational in character.

Our first move, therefore, is to explain the purpose and intention of the proposed move from the contract of employment to the personal work relation and the personal work nexus as the organizing paradigms for our analysis of the legal construction of personal work relations. Our argument will be that the legal construction of personal work relations in a way which is centrally focused upon a contractual understanding of those relations, and particularly in a way which accepts the contract of employment as the supremely dominant paradigm, lacks something in rigour and comprehensiveness. This is a deficiency which can be discerned and has been discerned within particular national systems of labour law: but we think this shortcoming is more clearly revealed by comparative analysis, which exposes the unreliability of the apparent equivalence between the ways in which personal work contracts in general and the contract of employment in particular are identified and articulated in different European legal systems: and we hope that trying to make good that kind of deficiency might in principle serve the normative purpose which we have identified for our own analysis.

So our programme is to make out our argument about the deficiencies of rigour and comprehensiveness in the legal construction of personal work relations as contracts in general and predominantly as contracts of employment in particular. It will become clear that we identify and locate those deficiencies in various different dimensions of the legal construction of personal work relations as contracts. For instance, we will suggest that the legal construction of personal work relations as contracts and especially as contracts of employment may lead to a significantly restricted view of how 'the employer' is constituted. In another dimension, we shall suggest that contractual construction may produce a narrow understanding of what amounts to a continuing personal work relationship. Many such dimensions will be evoked.

In order to obtain a clear picture, in those various dimensions, of the legal construction of personal work relations in general, and in particular of the effects of construing them primarily as contractual ones, we begin by an analysis which follows the contours of that existing primarily contractual construction. Indeed, we go with the grain of the existing primarily contractual legal construction of personal work relations in one further respect. We accept for the purposes of efficient exposition the fact that the domain of personal work contracts is conventionally divided into two contract types, that of the contract of employment and that of the contract for services. We adopt that mode of exposition despite the fact that we are critical of that binary division, regarding it as one of the ways in which the primarily contractual legal construction of personal work relations may be deficient in rigour and comprehensiveness.

So the lengthy second part of this book follows that pattern. We begin by considering what it means to construct personal work relations as primarily contractual ones and predominantly as contracts of employment. We continue by examining the legal architecture which different systems have created for contracts of employment with regard to their formation and structure, their content and performance, and their termination and transformation. We then repeat that sequence of discussion for personal work contracts beyond the contract of employment, that is to say for that part of the domain of personal work contracts normally considered as the sphere of the contract for services.

Our programme of analysis of the legal construction of personal work relations then continues in a different mode. Having in the manner specified above followed the existing contractual contours, we then re-analyse the legal construction of personal work relations in a way which cuts across those contours. This re-analysis proceeds from a starting point which differs from the existing primarily contractual one. This different starting point consists in the idea that personal work relations can be legally constructed as having at their core a 'personal work nexus' between the worker and whatever person, enterprise, or assemblage of persons or enterprises has the employing role or function in the relation in question. That 'personal work nexus' may be wholly or partly contractual in nature; but, crucially, it may be wholly or partly of a different nature – that is to say, it may be relational rather than contractual in character. The third part of this book is devoted to a re-analysis of the legal construction of personal work relations which is based on this notion of the personal work nexus.

It will be evident that this 're-analysis' will be quite consciously innovative in character, deliberately invoking an organizing concept which is not found to any significant extent in existing law. This implies some degree of normative intention, in the sense that this 're-analysis' is put forward as one which might lead to reconsideration by law-makers and theorists of the ways in which personal work relations might be legally constructed more rigorously and comprehensively than they at present are. So the outcome of the work will consist of an attempt to provide a basis for that kind of reconsideration of the legal construction of personal work relations.

In order both to identify that hoped-for outcome more precisely, and to complete our account of our programme for achieving it, we need to describe one more methodological step. This involves specifying slightly more precisely than we have done the way in which our analysis focuses on particular national legal systems within Europe. It also involves bringing into play a further set of legal institutions and institutional actors, namely those of European Union or European Community law as they affect personal work relations and their legal construction in European legal systems. Although we do not regard EU Law as 'the elephant in the room' in our discussion of the legal construction of personal work relations, it nevertheless has a significant part to play, and may in a certain sense provide a platform on which to mount the further pursuit of some of the objectives of the present work. We proceed to explain this suggestion slightly more fully.

As we have indicated previously, our programme of analysis of the legal construction of personal work relations consists primarily of a study of how this is done in and by English law, in comparison with the way that this is done in other European legal systems. In this process of comparison, those other systems are not considered on the same basis or footing as English law because the resources of time and expertise which are available to us do not permit that. So we proceed by means of episodic comparison with those systems with which we are most familiar. Even if a more systematic and exhaustive comparison between national systems were feasible, it would still be important to draw upon any sources from which or locations in which the comparison could be lifted above this interstate level by reference to any supranational discourse which might provide an overview or at least some insights from a higher denationalised plane. That is even more important when the interstate comparison is episodic in character.

We take the view that the intervention or involvement of EU law in the regulation of personal work relations has been sufficiently extensive to identify it as just such a source of supranational discourse with regard to the legal construction of those relations. Although those relations have not been the subject of anything amounting to systematic regulation at EU level, there have nevertheless been many interactions between national labour law systems and the EU legal system itself which have impacted upon personal work relations at a structural level. Prominent among the EU interventions at that structural level have been the Acquired Rights Directives,[89] the Working Time Directives,[90] and the relatively recent series of Directives on 'atypical' forms of work;[91] but various other EU legal instruments could be viewed as also having that significance.

Indeed we could go so far as to say that the law-making institutions of the EU should figure in an account of the legal construction of personal work relations in the Member States not merely as institutional actors but also on occasion as 'institutional entrepreneurs' in the sense that Crouch has given to that terminology[92] – that is to say as agents of mutation and recombination of that institution of governance with which we are concerned. This role of institutional entrepreneur with regard to the legal construction of personal work relations may be instantiated at a very specific and technical level, as where EU law identifies what counts as the 'transfer of an undertaking' or what comes within its definition and conception of 'working time'. Examples may also be found at a higher level of generality and abstraction, such as where the conception of 'flexicurity' has been articulated as a basis for regulation and structuration of personal work relations.

---

[89] Council Directive 98/50 of 29 June 1998, amending Directive 77/187 EEC on the approximation of the laws of the Member States relating to the safeguard of employees' rights in the event of transfer of undertakings, businesses or parts of businesses, [1998] OJ L201/98. The two now consolidated with Council Directive 2001/23/EC of 12 March 2001, [2001] OJ L82/16.

[90] Council Directive 93/104/EEC of 23 November 1993 concerning certain aspects of the organization of working time. [1993] OJ L307/18. The Directive has been consolidated with the adoption of Directive 2003/38 of the European Parliament and of the Council of 4 November 2003 concerning certain aspects of the organization of working time [2003] OJ L299/9.

[91] Council Directive 97/81/EC of 15 December 1997 concerning the Framework Agreement on part-time work concluded by UNICE, CEEP and the ETUC as amended by Directive 98/23/EC (OJ 1998 L131/10), consolidated [1998] OJ L131/13; Council Directive 99/70/EC of 28 June 1999 Concerning the Framework Agreement on Fixed-term Work Concluded by UNICE, CEEP and the ETUC [1999] OJ L175/43, corrigendum [1999] OJ L244/64; Directive 2008/104/EC of the European Parliament and of the Council of 19 November 2008 on temporary agency work, [2008] OJ L 327/9.

[92] C. Crouch (2006) *Capitalist Diversity and Change: Recombinant Governance and Institutional Entrepreneurs*, Oxford: OUP – see above, p. 56.

However, if EU law can be regarded as providing a dynamic element in the development of a comparative discourse about the legal construction of personal work relations in European national legal systems, it also serves to highlight the problems and deficiencies which still attend that discourse. Thus, at a detailed technical level, the incursions of EU law into the regulation of personal work relations often presuppose a common and shared conceptual vocabulary of legal construction as between national legal systems where no such common shared vocabulary in fact exists. The problem, which we have identified, of unreliability of apparent linguistic equivalents looms very large in this sphere of law-making and legal adjudication.

Moreover, even more fundamental problems present themselves at the general level of high policy development of EU law. While in the sphere of collective labour action a great threat presents itself that such protections as are afforded by national legal systems will be increasingly eroded by the EU law of free movement of enterprise and service provision, a more subtle threat presents itself with regard to the legal construction of personal work relations. Here, we suggest, there is a particular problem arising from the development towards a common private law of contract for the EU, currently represented by the articulation of a 'Draft Common Frame of Reference' for European contract law.[93]

For a striking feature of the Draft Common Frame of Reference, which permeates both the draft itself and its *travaux preparatoires*, consists in the way that, while it treats the law of the contract of employment as being outside and beyond its sphere of concern,[94] it on the other hand subjects all other personal work contracts to its essentially private law regime. While other authors have already started deconstructing this fundamental misconception of the Draft Common Frame of Reference,[95] our concern is that this may renew and deepen the binary divide between two supposedly quite distinct kinds of personal work contracts and personal work relations, a division which arguably no longer accurately describes the reality of European work relations, and that it is one of the purposes of this work to question. If the autonomy of labour law is being denied by EU law in the sphere of the regulation of collective action, it seems on the other hand to be exaggerated by EU law in the sphere of the legal construction of individual work relations.

Thus we feel that the development of EU law with regard to the legal construction of personal work relations presents significant challenges to our analytical enterprise, heightening the functionality and importance of its critical task. This

---

[93] C. Von Bar, E. Clive, and H. Schulte-Nölke (eds.) (2009) *Principles, Definitions and Model Rules of European Private Law – Draft Common Frame of Reference (DCFR) Outline Edition*, München: Sellier. See further below, Chapter 10, p. 386.

[94] Article 1:101 of the DCFR states that the rules are: 'not intended to be used, or used without modification or supplementation, in relation to rights and obligations of a public law nature, or in relation to [the] employment relationship'.

[95] L. Nogler and U. Reifner (2010) 'Social Contracts in the Light of the Draft Common Frame of Reference for a Future EU Contract Law', *WP C.S.D.L.E. 'Massimo D'Antona' INT* – 80/2010.

enables us to round off the specification of the hoped-for outcome of our work. In its fourth and concluding part, we will pursue further the set of issues which we have now raised about the role of EU law in the legal construction of personal work relations in European national legal systems, and we will suggest ways in which our analysis might offer some starting points for the articulation of a common framework for the legal construction of personal work relations in European law.

# PART II

# THE PERSONAL WORK RELATION
# AS A CONTRACT

# 3

# The Legal Construction of Personal Work Relations as Contracts

## Introduction

In the first Part of this work, we set out the scope, objectives, and methodology of our study. We explained that the work is designed to improve our understanding of the law of personal work relations by sketching out the treatment of that topic in English law and subjecting that depiction to an analytical and a normative critique based upon comparison with the corresponding experience of other European legal systems. To those ends, we presented a methodology which relies upon the idea of the personal work relation as a conception which we might use to tackle some analytical problems or shortcomings in existing accounts of labour or employment law which are framed around and heavily concentrated upon the law of the contract of employment. We also advanced some comparative hypotheses for subsequent exploration in the course of the book, and outlined the basis for the normative critique which we would eventually apply to our analysis.

The first big step in that analysis consists in creating an account of the law of personal work relations which is framed around and on the basis of personal work contracts – that is to say, in other words, we have to frame and describe 'the law of personal work contracts'. This is a necessary precursor to the more ambitious study, which then follows, of the law of personal work relations constructed around the conception of the personal work nexus, because the latter is best understood as an extension or elaboration of the former. But the role of this Part of our book is not one of purely preparatory description of the law of personal work relations in its already well-recognized contractual guise, as a mere preliminary to re-presenting it in the novel clothing of 'the personal work relationship', or nexus. This Part of the work itself has a creative task or objective; for, even if the casting of an account of this body of law in a contractual mould is a familiar strategy, the attempt to extend it to the full range of personal work relations beyond the dependent or semi-dependent ones is certainly not so conventional. As we have argued in the first Part of this book, whereas 'the law of the contract of employment' is so well-established a category of legal discourse as to have assumed an institutional character, 'the law of personal work contracts' has no such acquired standing, and we shall need actively to contend for it in the ensuing chapters.

So in order to begin to carry out that creative objective, we shall need first to articulate, more fully than we did in the first Part of the book, our conception of 'the law of personal work contracts'. Our initial or working definition, which concentrates on the notion of 'personal work contracts', has it as 'the law concerning contracts for the personal performance of work', 'personal' in the sense of 'by the worker himself or herself' – this is in contradistinction, therefore, to contracts for the provision of work by the work-provider either personally or through others. That definition is not without its difficulties with regard to the idea of 'personal work contracts', and we shall have to return to those difficulties later.

But no less elusive is the conception of 'the law of' in relation to personal work contracts. We need to reflect quite carefully as to how this particular body of law relates to employment or labour law at large – and also, more fundamentally, as to the sense in which we claim for it the status of a 'body of law' in the first place. In one dimension, 'the law of personal work contracts' breaks and exceeds the traditional boundaries of labour or employment law, in that it extends to 'independent' personal work relations or contracts in a way that traditional labour or employment law does not. But in another dimension, 'the law of personal work contracts' is differentiated in an equally important way from labour or employment law at large, even within the sphere of 'dependent' personal work relations. For, whereas labour or employment law, as a body of law, is not committed to any one particular analysis of, or way of understanding, employment relations or personal work relations, 'the law of personal work contracts' is strongly committed to viewing personal work relations as essentially individual and contractual ones; less so 'the law of personal work *relations*' as we shall in due course show.

In fact we could be even more specific and say that 'the law of personal work contracts' is essentially concerned with the construction or modelling of personal work relations as individual contractual ones. In the first section of this chapter, we elaborate this notion of the construction or modelling of personal work relations as individual contractual ones; and we draw attention to what we regard as the essential link between the contractual and the individual nature of the models of personal work relations which are so constructed. More particularly, we show how this notion of individual contractual modelling can be better understood by reference to the idea of 'layers of regulation', by and through which this process of the individual contractual modelling or construction of personal work relations takes place. A comparative analysis will take up the starting point established in the previous chapter and show how each legal system has its own set of these layers of regulation, arranged in its own distinctive way, and that the modelling or construction of personal work relations accordingly varies in very significant respects as between European national legal systems. It will emerge that 'the law of personal work contracts', and its subset 'the law of contracts of employment' differ in character between those legal systems not only, as we might expect, at the level of practical detail, but also at a profoundly conceptual level.

The first section of this chapter will therefore concern itself with what we might call the 'individual contractuality' of the law of personal work contracts – by which we mean the extent to which and the sense in which that body of law regards personal work relations as individual and contractual ones. Our anticipatory summary in the foregoing paragraph indicates how, in the course of that section, we shall embark upon discussion of the relationship, at a basic level, between 'the law of personal work contracts' as a whole and its subset 'the law of contracts of employment'. We shall thus have initiated the discussion of a set of issues about the taxonomy of the law of personal work contracts which will, in one way or another, permeate this part of our book. That discussion will be centrally (though not solely) concerned with the division, or 'binary divide', between contracts of employment and other personal work contracts. In the second section of the chapter, we shall consider the centrality of that basic division to the contractual framing of personal work relations, and we shall suggest that the issues of contractuality and taxonomy are crucially interlinked. Our argument will be that the whole construction of personal work relations as contractual ones has been crucially dependent upon the delineation of 'the contract of employment' as a distinctive legal sphere – in other words, no contractuality without taxonomy.

However, if the 'binary divide' between contracts of employment and other personal work contracts is central to the whole contractual construction of personal work relations, that does not mean that it is necessarily an analytically satisfactory distinction or the basis for a sustainable legal taxonomy of personal work relations as currently practised in European countries. In the second section of this chapter, we shall also advance arguments which cast doubt upon the viability of the binary divide. We shall suggest that there are a sufficiently large number of dimensions of variation between the contractual arrangements which may be made for the conduct of personal work relations as to defy the drawing of a single 'bright line' which will divide them into just two distinct subsets. In the third and concluding section of the chapter, the identification of those dimensions of variation will be used as a way of organizing the more detailed analysis of the law of personal work contracts in the ensuing chapters.

## Section 1: Contractuality, Individuality, and Layered Regulation

In this section, we start to develop in detail the ideas: (A) that it is (in degrees varying between legal systems) meaningful to envisage a body of law identified as 'the law of personal work contracts' which gives rise to a set of legal models or paradigms which represent the legal accounts of personal work relations; (B) that this body of law imposes (again in degrees varying between legal systems) an essentially contractual and individual vision of those legal models or paradigms and of personal work relations themselves; (C) that we can best understand this contractual and individual legal construction of personal work relations by reference to a particular notion of layered regulation which will be articulated in the course of the section, and that the composition and arrangement of those layers of regulation itself varies between legal systems in ways which are highly significant.

## A. The Law of Personal Work Contracts as Regulatory Modelling

We begin our detailed substantive analysis of 'the law of personal work contracts' with some discussion of whether it is meaningful to assert the existence of such a body of law, and of how, if it is meaningful to do so, we should regard that body of law as functioning. We shall consider these questions firstly in a general and theoretical way, and then comparatively as between some actual legal systems.

At the general or theoretical level, we suggest that it is meaningful to envisage European legal systems as containing a body of law which is identifiable as 'the law of personal work contracts'. That is because, or in the sense that, those legal systems can be regarded as concerning themselves in a more or less systematic way with the set of personal work relations which exist as socio-economic phenomena in each European country, and as according a contractual analysis to some at least of those personal work relations. Explaining that assertion more fully, we can go on to say that European legal systems generally engage in a number of regulatory activities or operations with regard to personal work relations.[1] By focusing upon those regulatory activities which are in the nature of law-making or legal adjudication, we arrive at the idea of a body of law which concerns itself with personal work relations.

We further suggest that such a body of law evolves or gives rise to legal models or paradigms of or for personal work relations. This may occur in various ways; legal regulation may seek to require that personal work relations shall be conducted in certain legal guises or forms, and legal regulation may in a looser sense recognize or interpret personal work relations as taking certain legal forms or having certain legal incidents. If and to the extent that the legal forms and incidents which are thus assigned to personal work relations are contractual ones, we regard the body of legal regulation which characterizes personal work relations in that way as 'the law of personal work contracts'. We proceed to consider concretely whether it is satisfactory to think of particular European legal systems as containing bodies of law of that kind.

The European legal systems which we have examined all make some use of a contractual frame of reference to provide a part at least of their basis for analysis or characterization of personal work relations. In the words of Pélissier, Supiot, and Jeammaud: 'the contract of employment constitutes the first of all mechanisms ordaining work relations'.[2] But they vary in the extent to which the contractual frame of reference is their pre-eminent one, to the point that Italian academics can assert with confidence that 'the relational profile prevails over the contractual one'.[3] There is an alternative set of possibilities in which personal work relations are legally constructed – and recognized as such by domestic legal systems – primarily at a

---

[1] In so saying, we are using the idea of regulation of personal work relations in the widest sense of normative or rule-based actions impacting upon the conduct of those relations.

[2] J. Pélissier, A. Supiot, and A. Jeammaud (2008) *Droit du Travail*, 24th ed., Paris: Dalloz, p. 702. Our translation from the original French.

[3] E. Ghera (2007) *Diritto del Lavoro*, 16th ed., Bari: Cacucci, at 61. Our translation of the original '*il profilo del rapporto prevale su quello del contratto*'.

relational level, or in relational terms, so that their characterization as contracts is a more partial or secondary one. According to Bercusson (1996) it is precisely because of the existence of those alternative possibilities that EU law, as we will further discuss in Chapter 10, sometimes uses the terminology of the 'employment relationship' when specifying the scope of application of measures concerning personal work relations, so as 'to take cognisance of a multitude of forms of work which never acquire contractual status, but are nonetheless carried out in the expectation of some form of reciprocal benefit, which may fall short of the common law concept of contractual consideration'.[4]

In the construction of personal work relations by and within English law, the contractual frame of reference does seem to be the very firmly pre-eminent one. The famous characterization by Otto Kahn-Freund of the contract of employment as the 'cornerstone' of employment law was an observation about English law,[5] and it has continued to reflect the tendency of English employment law at a number of levels. In legislation and in case-law, personal work relations are primarily identified and defined as contractual ones.[6] Legal textbooks and doctrinal writings generally replicate this approach even if they are sometimes critical of it.[7] The normal way of legally characterizing the self-employed person is as an 'independent *contractor*'.

Other European legal systems, as noted above, are slightly more ambivalent in this respect. In French law, the *Code du Travail*, although it has a great deal to say about various types of personal work contracts, does not seem to construct, in the narrow sense of the word, personal work relations as pre-eminently contractual ones, although it does rely on contractual constructs for the purposes of attributing legal effects to those relations. This attitude is majestically explained in the following quotation from a leading treatise:

to the extent that the employment relationship is fundamentally contractual, this is less because it is born of an equal exercise of the contractual freedom of the two parties, than because it lends itself to a *contractual analysis* to fix its effects. In other terms, the consequences of the binding force of the contract are more tangible than those of contractual freedom.[8]

---

[4]  B. Bercusson (1996) *European Labour Law*, London: Butterworths, p. 431.
[5]  O. Kahn-Freund (1954) 'Legal Framework', in A. Flanders and H. Clegg (eds.), *The System of Industrial Relations in Great Britain*, Oxford: Blackwell, 45.
[6]  This is the case with the central consolidation of legislation concerning individual employment relations, the ERA 1996 as subsequently amended and expanded.
[7]  As for example H. Collins (2010) *Employment Law*, 2nd ed., Oxford: OUP at p. 5: 'The primary focus of [employment law] always concerns the contractual relation of employment, which is the legal expression of the economic and social relationship through which work is performed.' An exception which proves the rule is the treatise of J. Gaymer (2001) *The Employment Relationship*, London: Sweet & Maxwell, a conscious attempt to break the contractual mould of analysis of personal work relations in English employment law. Contrast this with one of the most mainstream textbooks of Italian labour law, E. Ghera (2007) *Diritto del Lavoro – il rapporto di lavoro*, Bari: Cacucci.
[8]  J. Pélissier, A. Supiot, and A. Jeammaud (2008) *Droit du Travail*, 24th ed., Paris: Dalloz, p. 703; our translation of the original: '*Mais si le rapport de travail est fondamentalment contractuel, c'est moins en ce qu'il naît d'un égal exercice de leur liberté contractuelle par les deux parties qu'en ce qu'il se prête à une*

Doctrinalists of Italian and French labour law similarly tend to take as their starting points for analysis the notions of *rapporto di lavoro* (employment or work relation) or *relations professionelles* (professional relations) before moving on to discussion of personal work contracts. This is hardly a coincidence since, as in his work aptly entitled '*Diritto del Lavoro – Il rapporto di lavoro*' ('Labour Law – the employment relation') Ghera explains that: 'in respect of... the relationship, one must highlight that... the execution of the contract and the actual performance of the obligations arising from it, are normally to be understood as an exercise of the parties' contractual freedom, since statute concerns itself with imposing directly, or indirectly by reference to collective agreements, a series of precise *limitations* upon the contents of the contract and, moreover, to the parties' conduct during its performance'.[9] The normal way of legally characterizing the self-employed person in France is as a '*travailleur indépendent*' (independent worker) – a personal relational description rather than a contractual one.

Doctrinal accounts of German employment law will often identify the *Arbeitnehmer* (employee) primarily by describing him or her as *persönlich abhängig* (personally dependent) in relation to the *Arbeitgeber* (employer), but will go on to make the point that this relationship is embodied in the *Arbeitsvertrag* (employment agreement or contract of employment).[10] As noted by Weiss and Schmidt: 'an employee is a person who is obliged to work for somebody else on the basis of a private contract in a relationship of personal subordination. The key element of this formula is personal subordination. Another important element is the private contract.'[11] The normal way of legally characterising the self-employed person is as a '*Selbständiger*' (free-standing person) or '*Freier Mitarbeiter*' (freelance worker) – again, a personal relational description rather than a contractual one, and the statutory definition of 'self-employed person', contained in section 84(1)(2) of the *Handelsgesetzbuch* (Commercial Code), further restates this relational dimension: 'Anybody who essentially is free in organizing his work and in determining his working time is presumed to be self-employed.'[12]

There is, of course, no doubt that, as discussed in Chapter 2, all systems recognize the contract of employment as a source of law shaping the regulation of the employment relationship. However, the foregoing assertions about the primacy of the contractual frame of reference in the law concerning personal work relations are still somewhat imprecise ones. In the next subsection we consider

*analyse contractuelle pour fixer ses effets. En d'autres termes, les conséquences de la force obligatoires du contrat sont plus tangibles que celles de la liberté contractuelle*.' Emphasis original.

[9] E. Ghera (2007) *Diritto del Lavoro*, 16th ed., Bari: Cacucci, at 61. Our translation. Emphasis original.

[10] Cf. S. Lingemann, R. von Steinau-Steinrück, and A. Mengel (2008) *Employment & Labour Law in Germany*, 2nd ed., Munich: C. H. Beck, at p. 2: 'An employee is a person who performs "dependent work" for the benefit of another person on the basis of a civil law contract.'

[11] M. Weiss and M. Schmidt (2008) *Labour Law and Industrial Relations in Germany*, Alphen aan den Rijn: Kluwer Law International, p. 45. Footnotes omitted.

[12] M. Weiss and M. Schmidt (2008) *Labour Law and Industrial Relations in Germany*, Alphen aan den Rijn: Kluwer Law International, 2008, p. 45.

how we might make use of the notions of individuality and contractuality in order to try to endow those assertions with more substantial content and clearer meaning.

## B. Individuality and Contractuality in the Law of Personal Work Contracts

In the previous subsection we embarked upon the discussion of whether it is meaningful to envisage a body of law consisting of 'the law of personal work contracts', and we began to consider the degree to which, in different European legal systems, the contractual frame of reference is the primary or predominant one for the legal analysis and treatment of personal work relations. In this subsection we begin to refine that discussion by considering what notions and degrees of individuality and contractuality may be involved in the adoption of predominantly contractual frames of reference for the law applying to personal work relations.

We should begin by defining or explaining our conceptual categories somewhat more fully, and by considering the ideological charge or baggage which they carry with them. We use the notions of individuality and contractuality, in the context of the legal analysis of personal work relations, to mean, respectively, the understanding of personal work relations as essentially individual ones and essentially contractual ones. We advance these as primarily descriptive notions, as such to be contrasted with the more prescriptive notions of individualism and contractualism, which in this context consist of perceptions that personal work relations *ought to be* viewed as essentially individual and contractual ones.

Having said that, we recognize that the distinction between descriptive and prescriptive notions is not a straightforward one in this context. The understandings of personal work relations as essentially individual and essentially contractual ones for the purposes of legal analysis readily and quickly become bound up with ideological and prescriptive perceptions of how those relations should be analysed and treated by and within legal systems. It is quite arguable, indeed, that we travel some distance down a particular normative and ideological path by the mere act of envisaging a body of law consisting of 'the law of personal work contracts', or by thinking about the law of dependent personal work relations as 'the law of the contract of employment'. That is to say, by so doing we have immediately subscribed to an understanding of the employment relation, or more broadly the personal work relation, as an inherently individual and contractual one.

We probably thereby attract the concerns, traditionally felt very strongly by theorists of labour law, about accepting a dichotomy between the individual and the collective aspects of the subject of labour law. In its strongest form, that dichotomy appears as a distinction between individual employment law and collective labour law; but even in weaker forms, the drawing of that distinction is often viewed as involving a marginalizing or downgrading of collective interests and collective modes of action in our understanding of employment relations. From such a viewpoint, there is a slippery downward slope which descends from simply choosing to focus upon the individual and contractual aspect of personal work relations to regarding those relations as inherently individual and contractual ones.

We might succeed both in refining our legal analysis of personal work relations, and in meeting those concerns or criticisms, by recognizing that there may be different kinds and degrees of individuality and contractuality – or that particular notions of individuality and contractuality may stray nearer to or remain further from the prescriptive impulses of individualism and contractualism. The more strongly that a theorist or a law-maker asserts that personal work relations can best be described, in legal terms, as individual and contractual ones, the more likely it is that the assertion is driven by a prescriptive belief that the law of personal work relations should be shaped and guided by the values of individualism and contractualism.

We may identify those prescriptive beliefs as consisting of opinions that, in the legal regulation of personal work relations, the actors in those relations should be regarded as operating by themselves and for themselves as individuals; and that their relations should be primarily governed by the agreements which they make as individuals about the beginning and ending, and form and content of those relations. It may be observed that in the formation and articulation of such beliefs, the elements of individualism and of contractualism are powerfully mutually reinforcing.

However, although that dynamic of mutual reinforcement between individualism and contractualism may be a powerful one, it should not be viewed as one which inexorably comes into play as soon as personal work relations are legally analysed as individual contractual ones. That is because the individual contractual form of analysis has to be located within a spectrum, at one end of which it embodies a strongly prescriptive individualist and contractualist view of personal work relations, but at the other end of which it constitutes a formal façade for a view of personal work relations as strongly collectivized and status-based.

The existence of that spectrum, and therefore the understanding of individuality and contractuality as capable of being nuanced or graduated concepts, may be substantiated by comparative analysis as between different European legal systems. Those legal systems generally make some use of forms of analysis in which personal work relations are construed as individual and contractual ones, though we have argued that there is variation between national legal systems in the extent to which that construction is the predominant one. The French '*contrat de travail*', we are told, is, of course, a contract 'bestowing upon the work relationship it engenders a *contractual dimension*'. But the employment relationship: 'possesses . . . an extra-contractual dimension in which a number of rights are inscribed which are prerogatives attached to the character of the employee, rather than contractual rights flowing from the contract and its legal regime'.[13] Even to the extent that the individual and contractual form of analysis is used, there seems to be real variation in the extent to which it is on the one hand upheld *au pied de la lettre*, and viewed as

---

[13] J. Pélissier, A. Supiot, and A. Jeammaud (2008) *Droit du Travail*, 24th ed., Paris: Dalloz, p. 702. Our translation from the French original.

an ideology for the law of personal work relations, or on the other hand treated as a convenient formal cloak for or rationalization of a rather different reality.

We should, however, be careful of invoking the idea of a generalized discrepancy, differently perceived by different legal systems, between individual contractual forms and substantive 'realities' of a different kind. Perceptions of 'reality' often themselves have a normative colouring, and involve a purposive selection of that which the observer wants to regard as the important elements of 'reality'. We might do better to identify the key focal points at which this discrepancy is usually thought to occur. This means concentrating on those sources of norms for the formation, conduct, and termination of personal work relations which are wholly or largely external to the individual parties to those relations. Pre-eminent among those sources are collective bargaining and legislation, especially of the worker-protective kind. Another crucially important set of sources, though less clearly external to the parties, consists of judicial norm-making taking forms such as those of terms implied by law or 'general clauses'. Our question then becomes this – how and how far do different legal systems reconcile the individual contractual analysis of personal work relations with the regulation and the constraining of those relations by legislation, collective bargaining, and judicial norm-making?

This question, which is of course very hard to answer, is best addressed in two stages, at each of which we identify a different variable. The first variable concerns the extent to which, in the different legal systems, personal work relations are in fact regulated and constrained by legislation, collective bargaining, and judicial norm-making. We could say that each legal system has its own 'intervention formula' which expresses its particular location within that variable. For example, in a given system personal work relations might be highly regulated and constrained by collective bargaining, moderately by legislation, and minimally by judicial law-making. But another system may see the judiciary taking the lead in regulating personal work relations, with legislation aiming at a relaxing regulation for the sake of introducing more flexibility in the labour market, and collective bargaining only being marginally relevant.

The second variable, inevitably conditioned by the location of the particular system within the first variable, concerns the way in which each particular system manages to reconcile its own 'intervention formula' with a legal characterization, at least at a formal level, of personal work relations as individual contractual ones. Our point here is that there is not necessarily the direct correlation which one might imagine between the locations of a particular legal system within the two variables. For example, a system in which personal work relations were in fact quite highly regulated and constrained by collective bargaining, legislation, and judicial law-making, might nevertheless be unexpectedly prone to characterize personal work relations, formally at least, as individual contractual ones. This discrepancy between the two variables need not imply that the law-makers or theorists of the system in question are disingenuous in using the contractual characterization for personal work relations, but rather that they have their own particular understanding of what that characterization means and signifies.

In order to assess the behaviour of particular legal systems within the two variables which we have identified,[14] it may be helpful to make use of a notion of standardization which we could regard as one of the items in our comparative law toolkit. The questions then become, how far does a given legal system standardize, or allow the standardization of, the terms and conditions (in the widest sense) of personal work relations; and how far is that degree of standardization regarded as compatible with a view of personal work relations as essentially individual and contractual ones. We are using the notion of 'standardization' to refer to the making or imposing of standards or norms which apply uniformly or at least very similarly to many personal work relationships rather than specially to one particular personal work relationship.

There are, as we have indicated, various different kinds or sources of standardization, any of which could possibly be regarded as impinging upon the characterization of the personal work relation as an individual contractual one. As we have also indicated, it is useful to distinguish between external and internal standardization, though the two types do merge into one another at their margins. We shall consider in turn, as external sources, legislation and collective bargaining, and also the possible occurrence of external unilateral standardization by employers or by workers (consisting in the collective but unilateral imposition of terms and conditions of employment in the widest sense). Finally we shall refer to the phenomenon of internal unilateral standardization, which may in certain very limited situations be effected by workers, but is in practice largely confined to, and extensively effected by, employers.

Our inquiry, therefore, in relation to each of these kinds of standardization is as to how strongly and firmly the standards in question are imposed upon individual personal work relations. Where the standards are externally imposed or sourced, the question is how far and in what ways the arrangements between employer and worker may derogate from those standards. So far as those external standards can be regarded as legal norms, a way of asking that question is to consider whether they constitute *jus cogens* or *jus dispositivum*, that is to say mandatory law or optional law. We shall pursue that inquiry, in the first instance, with regard to employment legislation (in the widest sense), and to standards derived from collective agreements between employers and organizations representative of workers.

With regard to legislative standards, the answer to this set of questions might seem so obvious as to render the questions superfluous; it would seem self-evident that employment legislation has mandatory effect save in so far as it positively allows for derogation. However, such a stark view would considerably over-simplify the difference between *jus cogens* and *jus dispositivum*. The stark view would ignore the fact that legal standards may be formulated or interpreted in various ways as 'hard' or 'soft' ones. Variations in 'hardness' or 'softness' may consist in differences of substance as to the precision and directness of the norms in question, or in differences of procedure as to the manner in which the norms are construed

---

[14] A further variable is introduced in the course of this work; in Chapter 6 it is identified and elaborated as the 'integration variable'; see above p. 74 and below, pp. 226–27.

and applied. 'Legislation', moreover, is far from being a single homogeneous notion; different kinds or degrees of derogability may be associated with different sources or levels of legislation.

Significant examples of the variations which may occur in the derogability of employment legislation, and significant differences in this respect between European national legal systems, are to be found in the context of the formulation and implementation of EU law. A very clear instance is provided by the differences in national implementation of the Working Time Directive, and in particular its 48-hour standard for the maximum length of the working week. That standard was, at the insistence of the UK government, enacted as one which could be implemented by national legislation so as to leave it open to waiver by the individual worker, a process expressly contemplated by Article 22(1) of Directive 2003/88.[15] The British implementing legislation took the fullest advantage of this opportunity for allowing individual opting-out of the 48-hour standard, a practice that – until recently – was certainly unusual if not unique among European national legal systems, particularly since it effectively allows employers to insist upon waiver of the 48-hour standard by the worker as a precondition for appointment to the employment for which he or she applies. But as a testimony to the fact that the kaleidoscope sustaining the traditional regulatory paradigms of EU Member States in the social sphere has been dramatically shaken in recent years, the Commission noted in 2010 that, whereas: 'in 2000, the UK was the only Member State to make use of the opt-out [ . . . ] following recent enlargements, the use of the opt-out within the EU has expanded further, and *a total of sixteen Member States now explicitly provide for use of the opt-out*'.[16]

We should be cautious about drawing over-large conclusions from national policy decisions with regard to particular labour standards; but underlying such particular decisions, there do seem to be significant national variations in the approaches to derogability from labour standards in general. We may discern a broad contrast in this respect between the approaches of, on the one hand, the English common-law-based system, and, on the other hand, some continental European Civil-law-based systems. In English employment law, worker-protective legislation tends for the most part to be interpreted quite literally, without any special disposition on the part of the courts to construe it purposively in favour of the worker. Indeed, there was one episode in the history of the development of the legislation concerning unfair dismissal in which that legislation was characterized by the appellate courts as capable of operating as a 'rogue's charter' and was accordingly viewed as appropriate for construction in favour of the employer to avoid that perceived malfunctioning.[17] Even the express provisions in British employment

---

[15] Directive 2003/88/EC of the European Parliament and of the Council of 4 November 2003 concerning certain aspects of the organization of working time, [2003] OJ L 299/9.

[16] Commission Staff Working Paper, 'Detailed report on the implementation by Member States of Directive 2003/88/EC concerning certain aspects of the organization of working time ("The Working Time Directive")', SEC (2010) 1611/2, at 87–8.

[17] Cf. *Devis (W.) & Sons Ltd v. Atkins* [1977] AC 931, ICR 662 (HL) *per* Lord Diplock at 672 D–H.

legislation against contractual derogation from workers' statutory rights are themselves apt to be construed without any special protectiveness towards the worker.

In the employment law of various continental European legal systems, approaches are taken to the question of derogability from worker-protective legislation which are to a greater or lesser degree in contrast with that of English employment law. There generally seems to be a stronger sense of the inherent prevalence of legislation over contract. Indeed, as discussed in Chapter 2, the hierarchical superiority of legislation as a source of the norms of personal work relations is, in a number of those systems, perceived as a matter of fundamental and ultimately constitutional principle, especially though not solely at those levels of legislation which are themselves identified as supra-national, constitutional, or expressive of fundamental human rights. Perhaps the clearest though by no means the only expression of this approach is to be found in the French notion of *ordre public social* (social public policy), which has exactly those connotations, though admittedly that notion is less firmly entrenched in French employment law than it was 30 or 40 years ago. Similarly Treu (2007) in respect of Italian law, suggests that: 'Labour law is regarded as having in general an "imperative" nature (of public policy).... This nature implies that private agreements deviating from the law are in principle null and void.'[18]

Comparable contrast may be drawn with regard to norms derived from collective bargaining, especially collective bargaining involving a multiplicity of employing enterprises rather than a single one. In English employment law, these norms figure as very clearly optional, rather than mandatory ones. A number of legislative provisions which formerly accorded statutory force and effect to such norms in various prescribed conditions have been repealed in recent years,[19] so that this genre of legal enforcement of collectively bargained standards has largely disappeared. Moreover, as a matter of judge-made common law, workers asserting that collectively bargained norms form part of the terms and conditions of their personal work contracts have to show that those terms were originally and have remained validly incorporated into the individual contract in question. Judicial approaches to this question of incorporation are such as, in certain ways, to make that a more difficult burden for workers than employers to discharge.[20]

In many continental European employment law systems, we find that collective agreements are, by contrast, more deeply embedded in personal work contracts, so that the norms established by those agreements far more closely correspond to the notion of *jus cogens* than under English law. In many of those systems, the notion of *erga omnes* effect – that is to say the idea that the collective agreement automatically extends to all employers and all workers within the categories covered by the collective bargaining process in question – is either imposed by legislation or

---

[18] T. Treu (2007) *Labour Law and Industrial Relations in Italy*, Alphen aan den Rijn: Kluwer Law International, at 20.

[19] The Wages Councils were abolished by TURERA 1993, s. 35; at the time of writing the proposal to abolish the Agricultural Wages Boards has not been implemented though implementation is believed to be imminent.

[20] Cf. *Henry v. London General Transport Services Ltd* [2002] IRLR 472 (CA).

regarded as an inherent one. Moreover, in many such systems, there is a precept which is often regarded as having almost constitutional force that a hierarchically subordinate source of employment norms may deviate from a hierarchically superior set of such norms only if the overall result is not to the disadvantage of the worker – that is the principle against derogation *in pejus*. So, just as a collective agreement will not be allowed, in principle, to deviate from legislation *in pejus* so far as the worker is concerned, so an individual contract may not deviate *in pejus* from collectively bargained norms.

These principles are, as we have indicated, less sacrosanct than they once were in many European systems, but still retain real ideological and practical significance. Treu offers us a valuable standpoint from where to assess the persisting, albeit declining, relevance of these general rules in the context of Italian labour and industrial relations. We are told that while in principle imperative provisions of labour law cannot be modified *in pejus* by collective agreements: 'the rule on invalidity laid down by Article 2113 of the Civil Code does not apply to waivers or compromises reached between, or with the assistance of, the collective partners'.[21] And in recent years, we understand, Italian industrial relations have become no strangers to collective agreements that, at various levels, may appear to derogate *in pejus* from legislative – or even constitutional – provisions.[22]

Other forms of externally sourced standardization have much less importance, in relation to personal work contracts, than legislation or collective bargaining. Unilateral collective co-ordination of the terms and conditions of personal work relations or contracts, by employers or by workers, is probably of greater significance in some kinds of contracting for personal services, for example, in some areas of professional work, than it is in the case of dependent employment relationships. In some continental jurisdictions the unilateral co-ordinating functions of trade or professional associations may be important ones.[23] However, such activity quite quickly encounters objections and obstacles, both at EU and national levels, from competition law,[24] and probably should not be regarded as impinging very much upon the individual contractuality of the legal construction of personal work relations in the national legal systems which are under consideration in this work.

A different and potentially much more potent threat to the individual contractuality of the legal construction of personal work relations, is posed by the whole phenomenon of internal standardization of those relations by employers acting singly rather than in co-ordination with others. This is the issue of the personal

---

[21] T. Treu (2007) *Labour Law and Industrial Relations in Italy*, Alphen aan den Rijn: Kluwer Law International, at 20. Compare also above at pp. 73–74.

[22] Cf. F. Carinci (2009) 'Una dichiarazione d'intenti: l'Accordo quadro 22 gennaio 2009 sulla riforma degli assetti contrattuali', *Rivista Italiana di Diritto del Lavoro*, p. 177; F. Carinci (2010) 'Se quarant'anni vi sembran pochi: dallo Statuto dei lavoratori all'Accordo di Pomigliano', *WP C.S.D.L.E. 'Massimo D'Antona'*, IT – 108/2010. Compare also above at pp. 73–74.

[23] Cf. J. Pélissier, A. Supiot, and A. Jeammaud (2008) *Droit du Travail*, 24th ed., Paris: Dalloz, p. 1048.

[24] For a useful treatise cf. M. T. Carinci (2008) 'Attività professionali, rappresentanza collettiva, strumenti di autotutela', *WP C.S.D.L.E. 'Massimo D'Antona'.IT* – 69/2008. But see also Case C-94/04, *Cipolla v. Fazari* [2006] ECR I-11421.

work contract as a *contrat d'adhésion*, that is to say an arrangement made on standard or 'boilerplate' terms and conditions offered by an employer on a uniform or almost uniform basis to whole groups or types or sections of workers. It must be said that personal work contracts are, generically, as open as 'consumer contracts' to the charge of being standardized by organizational power vis-à-vis the individual human contracting party, albeit that in this case the latter figures as the provider of services rather than as the user of them.

We have therefore outlined the extent of the standardization of the terms and conditions of personal work relations, both from external and internal sources, and we have depicted some differences in this respect between national legal systems. This leads on, as we have indicated, to a further set of questions as to how far, in different European national legal systems, personal employment relations are legally constructed as individual contractual ones despite the different kinds and degrees of standardization to which they are subject in those different legal systems. Just as that set of questions is a highly complex one, so also is the set of answers which we have to offer.

At one level, there is a deceptively simple answer. In European national legal systems, there is a strong general disposition to construct personal work relations as individual contractual ones. This may be despite strongly held ideological objections to standardization. From the perspective of enterprise protection, the standardization brought about by worker-protective legislation and collective bargaining will be seen as imposing dangerous rigidities. From the different perspective of worker protection, the standardization effected by employers acting jointly or severally will often be seen as in its nature oppressive. But there is nevertheless a high degree of convergence upon the view that these policy objections to the various kinds of standardization, although they may generate demands for deregulation on the one hand or re-regulation on the other, are not fatally inimical to the legal construction of personal work relations as individual contractual ones. However, this convergence of English and European legal systems upon the construction of personal work relations as individual contractual ones is more apparent than real. In the following subsections, we shall expound a theory of layered regulation which will suggest a more diverse reality behind this façade of apparent uniformity.

## C. The Law of Personal Work Contracts as Layered Regulation

As we indicated in the previous chapter, our theory of layered regulation begins by asserting that we can refine and improve our understanding of the legal construction of personal work relations by considering the normative ordering of personal work relations as being composed of a number of layers of regulation. We will proceed to develop this notion of layers of regulation more fully, but we can give it some initial meaning by saying that it corresponds essentially to the notion of 'sources' of regulation, but envisages those sources as being superimposed or layered one upon the next, though not necessarily in a hierarchical sense in which norms in higher layers would take precedence over or have greater force than norms in lower layers.

We use this initial conception of the normative ordering of personal work relations as layered regulation to make two claims or suggestions about the legal construction of personal work relations as individual and contractual ones. The first claim or suggestion is that when personal work relations are legally constructed as personal work contracts, those 'contracts' represent a certain selection of layers of regulation, which between them form a stratum of normative layers, conceptualized and imagined by lawyers as personal work contracts. The second claim or suggestion is that we can use this notion of layered regulation in a comparative way, because in different legal systems or legal traditions, the stratum which is identified and conceptualized as that of the personal work contract may be differently imagined and composed. That is to say, each legal system or tradition seems to construct its own distinctive set of regulatory layers when formulating its idea of the personal work contract.

We revert to the task of providing a fuller explanation of our notion of 'layers of regulation'. Our idea is that it is useful to imagine the many different kinds of normative ordering that are brought to bear upon personal work relations as being piled upon each other in a set of layers. We may usefully conceive of those layers as being arranged not necessarily, as we have indicated, hierarchically according to their normative authority, but rather according to their immediacy to the personal work relations in question – though the precise ordering is not crucially important to the use to which we put this theory. Moreover there is scope for difference of opinion as to how finely the layers should be differentiated or sub-divided, and we shall find that some at least of the layers are porous ones.

In that way, we might arrive at the following archetypal set of layers of regulation of personal work relations:

1. the regulations or norms which are made and deemed to be agreed by and between the worker and the employer or employing organization. These regulations or norms will typically be put forward or imposed by the employer or employing organization. They could be regarded as constituting a kind of self-regulation by the parties to the personal work relations in question, or as a kind of internal regulation by the enterprise or work organization in question;

2. norms derived from collective bargaining, whether at enterprise level, or below or above that level. Each collective agreement at any such level might be regarded as a layer of regulation;

3. norms derived from national legal systems, whether constitutional, legislative or administrative, and whether national or subnational. Again, enacted norms or items of legislation could each be regarded as constituting a layer of regulation in and of itself;

4. norms derived from supra-national legal systems, such as those of the ILO or the European Union;

5. norms derived from common or judge-made law, or from jurisprudence in the continental European sense of authoritative judicial rulings; and

6. norms derived from legal treatises or doctrine in the continental European sense.

Thus far, this might seem to be nothing more nor less than a conventional account of the 'sources of employment law'. Less conventional and more controversial might be the suggestions or claims which we advance concerning the ways in which the legal construction of personal work relations, as individual and contractual ones, takes place in relation to these layers of regulation. In order to explain those suggestions or claims, we shift into another metaphor, derived from photography, and we represent each layer of regulation as a lens or filter through which the picture – that is to say the legal construction – of personal work relations is obtained. Just as a photographic image may be taken through several lenses or filters, so the legal construction of personal work relations may be regarded as a picture built up through one or several layers of regulation. In the way that each lens, or filter, frames and colours, and shapes the ultimate picture, so the legal construction of personal work relations is informed by each layer of regulation which is applied to the personal work relation in question.

Using these metaphors, we may be able to refine our understanding of the ways in which the legal vision of personal work relations is constructed by legal systems or traditions in general, and by different European legal systems or traditions in particular. As we have observed earlier, European legal systems and traditions seem to converge upon a view or construction of personal work relations as archetypally individual and usually contractual ones. When, in a particular legal system or tradition, personal work relations are thus construed as individual and contractual ones, this means that the system or tradition has arrived at its view or construction of personal work relations by concentrating upon a particular layer or stratum of regulation which is identified as the individual and contractual one. The personal work relation is viewed through a regulatory lens or set of lenses through which a contractual image is formed.

This elaborate metaphorical imagery might at this point in the argument seem quite superfluous. It might seem quite obvious that the legal vision of personal work relations as contractual ones is arrived at by viewing those relations through the first of the normative layers or filters which we specified, namely the regulations or norms made and deemed to be agreed by and between the worker, and the employer. This is, quintessentially, the contractual layer of regulation, and it might be thought entirely to define and express the legal construction of personal work relations as individual and contractual ones.

However, we suggest that the legal construction of personal work relations as individual and contractual ones is, normally if not universally, a more elaborate conception in which several layers of regulation are involved. For example, the construction of personal work relations as individual and contractual ones in English law is not arrived at solely by concentrating on that first layer of regulation. It also crucially invokes and depends upon the fifth layer of regulation which we specified, viewing personal work relations through the norms and doctrines of the common law as articulated by the judges of the courts of common law.[25]

If it is accepted that the legal construction of personal work relations as individual contractual ones may itself be a complex conception involving more than one layer of regulation, some immensely challenging arguments start to present themselves. It becomes apparent that when, in different legal systems or traditions, personal work relations are constructed as individual and contractual ones, the conception may differ in important ways as between systems and traditions. Those who use the legal language of individual contracts to characterize personal work relations may well be speaking within an idiom which is specific to their own legal system and tradition. They may be invoking a local and system-specific notion of the personal work contract which refers to a particular set of layers of regulation, differently selected as compared with other legal systems or traditions. The legal construction of personal work relations as individual and contractual ones may in that sense mean one thing in the English legal system and quite another in that of another European country.

Even thus far, the argument which is being put forward may appear to be uncontroversial and unsurprising. However, it starts to yield unexpectedly interesting results when it is applied methodically to the various layers of regulation which were identified earlier. In particular, we begin to discern that there may be a generic difference between systems and traditions in the way that they incorporate (or do not incorporate) two particulars layers of regulation within their conceptions of the personal work contract, namely those of collective bargaining and legislation. We shall amplify this observation in the course of this and later chapters, but it is worth elaborating upon it somewhat at this juncture.

In order to pursue our inquiry into the inclusion of particular layers of regulation in the contractual construction of personal work relations, we need to specify somewhat more precisely the exact nature of the issue about inclusion. There are two distinct questions involved. Firstly, does the legal system or tradition in question treat a particular layer of regulation as being applicable to and binding upon the personal work relation in question? Secondly, if and to the extent that a legal system or tradition does treat a particular layer of regulation as applicable to and binding upon the personal work relation, is that layer of regulation regarded as forming part of the construction of that relation as an individual contractual one? These two questions may as we shall see be interdependent, but they are distinct ones, each with their own importance.

Both the distinctness and the interdependence of those two questions will become clear if we ask them with regard to the inclusion of collective bargaining in the individual contractual construction of personal work relations. Here we find that quite a strong generic contrast emerges between the common law tradition as represented by English law and a continental European Civilian tradition as represented by a number of national legal systems. Each legal system has its own set of

---

[25] Including for this purpose the employment tribunals and the Employment Appeal Tribunal (EAT).

principles and rules to determine whether and how far collective agreements are applicable to and binding upon particular personal work relations, that is to say its rules about the applicability of and derogability from those agreements. However, we can venture the broad generalization that in many continental European legal systems, there is a strong tradition of regarding collective agreements as applicable to and binding upon personal work relations.

Indeed, as already discussed in Chapter 2, in that tradition collective agreements have very often been accorded concrete legal effect *erga omnes* (ie with respect to all workers within the labour market sector concerned), whether by legislation or as a matter of general constitutional or quasi-constitutional principle, in the sense that derogation from those agreements *in pejus* (ie to the disadvantage of the worker) is controlled or prohibited. In that tradition, these often inderogable norms derived from collective agreements would probably be regarded as forming part of the individual work contracts of the workers in question; but that characterization would not be regarded as especially significant or controversial, or as being crucial to the legal standing of those norms.

The approach of English law with regard to norms derived from collective agreements has been a very different one. Even if at times the practical outcomes have been comparable with those in other European systems with regard to the applicability of and derogability from norms derived from collective bargaining, the conceptual approach has been underlyingly divergent. In this respect much more strongly committed to a liberal notion of freedom of contract, English law has taken the default position (in the absence of specific legislative provision to the contrary) that norms derived from collective bargaining are applicable to particular work relations only if and to the extent that they form part of individual personal work contracts. At one time it might have been necessary to restrict this observation to private sector personal work relations, but the contractualization of public sector personal work relations has proceeded to the point where that caveat is unnecessary. In English law, norms derived from collective bargaining must pass reasonably exacting tests if they are to be regarded as being and remaining 'incorporated into' personal work contracts.[26]

As we have indicated, this approach does not necessarily operate as one which is more exclusive of norms derived from collective bargaining, as compared with the different continental European approach which we have depicted. The English approach is tempered by notions of implied incorporation, which bridge the gap between collective agreements and personal work contracts, even perhaps offering to do so in a systematic way. However, there may still be a real contrast in practical outcomes between the two approaches, and the conceptual or philosophical contrast between them is a very significant one. In this respect, the legal construction of personal work relations as individual and contractual ones is more of a fundamental and exigent reality in English law and in the English approach, and more of a conventionalized and convenient description in the continental European tradition.

---

[26] Compare above at p. 71 and M. Freedland (2003) *The Personal Employment Contract* Oxford: OUP at pp. 280–286.

A somewhat similar contrast can be drawn between the English legal system and tradition and the legal systems and traditions of many European countries with regard to the relationship which they make between personal work contracts and the third layer of regulation which we have identified, that is to say formally enacted norms derived from national legal systems (that is to say, essentially, national legislation). In the case of norms derived from collective bargaining, we observed how legal systems might differ from each other both in the extent to which they regarded those norms as applicable to and binding upon particular personal work relations, and in the ways in which those collectively bargained norms, which were applicable to and binding upon personal work relations, were related to the personal work contracts in question.

In the case of norms derived from national legislation, issues about applicability and bindingness do not arise in quite the same way as with collectively bargained norms, to the extent that national legislation will typically identify itself as binding – as *jus cogens* rather than *jus dispositivum* – and will prescribe its own sphere of application (although there may be major issues for adjudication in both those respects). So those engaged in the legal construction of personal work relations do not generally have fundamental choices as to whether to regard national legislation as constituting an applicable layer or applicable layers of legislation, for it clearly does in general terms count as such.

However, legal systems and traditions do have major choices to make as to the legal analyses by which they link up or apply national legislation to personal work relations, and it is in this respect that we find especially interesting divergences of approach. In English labour or employment law, there seems to be a marked tendency, driven by a strong liberal notion of freedom of contract, to maintain the theoretical integrity and autonomy of the personal work contract by regarding legislative norms as largely separate and distinct from the norms of the personal work contract itself.

In this way of envisaging the legal construction of personal work relations, the contractual layer of regulation and the legislative layer of regulation remain clearly separable from each other; the analysis is one of fission rather than fusion. Since, as we have previously observed, in the English legal tradition the 'contractual' layer of regulation seems to integrate within itself the judge-made 'law of contract', this could be regarded as an instance of the classic antithesis of common law and statute law which figures so largely in English jurisprudence. In our particular context, it is perhaps better understood as a distinction between the 'contract law' and the 'statute law' of personal work relations. It is in this way, for example, that English law has, ever since unfair dismissal legislation was first enacted in 1971, continued to maintain and develop as two separate bodies of law the common-law-based law of (contractually) wrongful dismissal, and the statute-law-based law of unfair dismissal.[27] Many similar illustrations of this kind of separation will present themselves in the course of the ensuing chapters.

---

[27] S. Anderman (2000) 'The Interpretation of Protective Employment Statutes and Contracts of Employment' 29 *ILJ*, 223.

In this respect the approach of English law appears to be a singular one. In continental European legal systems, the assumption seems to be that legislative norms both give shape to, and form an integral part of, the personal work contracts to which they apply. It is, for example, hard to find a counterpart in continental European jurisdictions of the dual system of regulation of termination of employment, contractual on the one hand and statutory on the other, which we have observed in the case of English law. In Italy, successive 'legislative interventions have overlapped with the rules [contained in the Civil Code] so that the general regime for dismissal in open-ended employment relationships (...) is today contained in a series of legislative sources that have succeeded each other over time'.[28] This special regime applies to the majority of personal work relations, while some groups of workers (such as domestic workers, professional athletes, managers) remain subject to the general rules on termination with notice derived from Articles 2118 and 2119 of the Italian Civil Code. Equally, the termination of the contract by the employee remains overwhelmingly subject to the general Civil law regime, contained in the Civil Code.

As for France, 'while the conclusion of a contract of employment remains largely subject to the principle of the freedom of the parties to choose each other, this no longer implies the freedom of contractual termination as a logical corollary. The act of hiring carries the necessary acceptance of a *statut professionnel* [regime of terms and conditions of employment] pre-established by statute and collective agreements, of which the mechanisms and conditions of termination form an integral part.'[29] The distinction between general contract law and special labour law rules is, if anything, even more marked in Germany, where unfair dismissal legislation is intrinsically linked to the procedural involvement of key labour institutions such as works and staff councils.[30] If in those jurisdictions common law and legislation in some instances provide distinct methods of termination of personal work contracts, or distinct remedies for or responses to wrongful termination, they nevertheless do so within integrated systems, rather than on a categorically distinct basis.

This contrast of approaches, though no doubt an imperfect one in the sense that counter-examples might be found, is nevertheless profound and far-reaching. To the extent that there is, in this respect, something amounting to a 'continental' approach, we find that, according to that approach, the stratum of regulation which would be regarded as the 'contractual' one, instead of being the thin common-law-based one which characterizes the English law approach, identifies itself as a thick stratum into which are aggregated the further layers of collective bargaining, national legislation, and, in effect, very often supranational norms too. If and to the extent that this contrast of approaches holds good, it has very significant consequences. When the 'thick stratum' approach is taken, the whole conception

---

[28]  E. Ghera (2007) *Diritto del Lavoro – il rapporto di lavoro*, Bari: Cacucci, 182.
[29]  J. Pélissier, A. Supiot, and A. Jeammaud (2008) *Droit du Travail*, 24th ed., Paris: Dalloz, at 526.
[30]  M. Weiss and M. Schmidt (2008) *Labour Law and Industrial Relations in Germany*, Alphen aan den Rijn: Kluwer Law International, 123.

of the personal work contract and of the way in which it is shaped and regulated may be different from, even antithetical to, the approach of English law.

Thus, according to this 'thick stratum' approach to the regulatory foundations of the personal work contract, it is quite natural and in no way counter-intuitive for a personal work contract to be accorded its basic shape and structure by legislative, and often codified norms. We often find, for example, that when, in various continental European legal systems, it is wished as a matter of public or governmental policy to alter the rules concerning the duration and termination of particular types of personal work relations, that aim is achieved by the legislative introduction of a new contractual model, or by the legislative re-modelling of an existing contract type. This would not be the naturally chosen mode of regulation under the English law approach.

We could take this argument one step further and suggest that, in the extreme case at least, we are confronting two different mindsets with regard to the legal construction of personal work relations. In both mindsets, the legal construct is nominally an individual and contractual one. But whereas in the English law approach that legal construct actually embodies only a thin stratum made up of layers of regulation regarded as genuinely 'contractual' in character, in the contrasting continental European approach the corresponding, ostensibly 'contractual' stratum of regulation is, as we have observed, actually a thick one which includes a wider range of regulatory types. In the former 'thin stratum' model, there is a lot of normative regulation of personal work relations which is perceived as external to the core contractual construction of those relations, whereas in the latter 'thick stratum' model, most of the normative regulation of personal work relations is internalized within the core contractual construct of them.

One very significant implication of that contrast is as follows. Under the 'thin contractual stratum' approach, a considerable difference or tension opens up between legal construction of personal work relations as, on the one hand, contractual ones, and, on the other hand, as simply being legally recognized and regulated relationships. The two conceptions refer to different strata of regulatory layers. Under the 'thick contractual stratum' approach, by contrast, the 'contractual' layers of regulation and the 'relational' layers of regulation are much more fully fused together into a single stratum. In that latter frame of mind, the difference or tension between the 'personal work contract' and the 'personal work relationship' is much less sharply felt, and may even dwindle into non-existence, other than – of course – when the law itself explicitly excludes particular personal work relations from this multilayered protective apparatus, as is often the case for managerial workers.[31]

If the foregoing argument appears to be a coherent one, we cannot however regard it as satisfactorily concluding our initial depiction of the legal contractual construction of personal work relations without entering one major caveat. Our analysis has extended itself freely across the sphere of 'personal work relations' and has invoked the correspondingly broad notion of 'personal work contracts'. We

---

[31] A more detailed comparative analysis of the status of managerial workers is developed in Chapter 5, pp. 190.

sought to explain and justify the use of those two broad notions in the initial chapters of this work. Nevertheless, it must be acknowledged that when, in this chapter, we have begun to sketch out in greater detail our notion of the legal construction of personal work relations as contractual ones, much of the argumentation has in fact been concentrated on the narrower sphere of 'employment relations'; and at many points where we have referred to 'personal work contracts', the terminology of 'the contract of employment' would have been equally applicable and might even at times have been more appropriate. If we are to avoid the charge of making too easy or glib an elision between 'contracts of employment' and 'personal employment contracts' and 'personal work contracts', we need to revert to the question of the position of the contract of employment, as such, in the larger sphere of personal work contracts which we are in the course of constructing.

## Section 2:  The Personal Work Contract as a Definitional Category and the Place of the Contract of Employment within that Category

In this section we seek to address a set of issues which has hitherto been left unresolved in our account of the legal construction of personal work contracts. We recognize some problems which have to be tackled if we are to regard the personal work contract as a viable definitional category. In a first and introductory subsection (A) we identify this set of issues as the problems of the questionable division of personal work contracts into two apparently irreconcilably distinct contract types, those of the contract of employment and the contract for services. In a second subsection (B) we use a comparative methodology to assess the status and validity of the binary divide between the two contract types. All this forms a preamble to the next section in which we suggest an approach which might resolve these difficulties by placing the binary divide within a multidimensional framework for the analysis of personal work contracts.

### A.  The Problems of the Binary Divide

In this subsection we therefore acknowledge a set of problems which, if not adequately addressed, might be thought seriously to vitiate our analysis of the legal construction of personal work relations as individual and contractual ones. Our heading cryptically identifies that set of issues as 'the problems of the binary divide'. This alludes to a set of difficulties stemming from the fact that the category of contracts which we have identified and focused upon as the subject of our analysis, that of the personal work contract, is by no means a well-established or well-accepted one. It could be said that by adopting and developing this category, our analysis, far from following the contours of orthodox contractual typology, cuts across those contours in a cavalier fashion by disregarding or overriding a well-understood and deeply entrenched distinction – the 'binary divide' – which is fundamental to the legal construction of personal work relations as contractual ones, between two very different contract types, those of the contract of employment and the contract for services.

Moreover, another associated criticism might be made of our analysis. As we shall hope to show in detail in the ensuing chapters, the legal construction of dependent personal work relations as contracts of employment is very much better developed and more fully analysed than the legal construction of other personal work relations as contracts for services. This is arguably true both in respect of English law, and in respect of other continental systems, in spite of the circumstance – which we will further explore in the next subsection – that in countries like France or Italy, the legal typologies sustaining some contracts for services are comparatively more developed and structured by their respective civil codes.

It might be thought that our analysis simply extrapolates or reads across from contracts of employment to all personal work contracts, and that we have assumed rather than proved that our larger analytical category, that of the personal work contract as a whole, can satisfactorily be treated in this way. In order to anticipate and meet those objections, we have to provide a carefully reasoned account both of the coherence of the 'personal work contract' category and of the role of the binary divide within that category. We consider those issues in relation to each other, looking first at the internal architecture and then at the external envelope of the personal work contract as a definitional category. We follow that sequence because we take the view that it is essential to get the binary divide into its proper perspective in order to obtain a clear view of the category as a whole.

We begin that discussion by pursuing one stage further our argument with an imaginary interlocutor who is sceptical about our adoption of the 'personal work contract' category, and who believes that we are understating the importance of the binary divide between contracts of employment and contracts for services. The imaginary interlocutor therefore asserts that the only satisfactory way for us to identify and analyse the category of personal work contracts is by recognizing that it is made up of two essentially separate sub-categories, those of the contract of employment on the one hand and the contract for services on the other. (We and the imaginary interlocutor are agreed that when we speak of the 'contract for services' in this context, we mean the *personal* contract for services, a point upon which we expand in the next section of this chapter.)

A very possible response to that argument would be for us to accept that we should indeed think of our definitional category of the personal work contract as an essentially dualistic typology, and that it should accordingly be presented and analysed in two separate parts or divisions, one consisting of the contract of employment and the other consisting of the (personal) contract for services. This might form a more readily recognizable portrayal of the existing positive law concerning the legal contractual construction of personal work relations. However – and this is a proposition which is crucially important to the whole argument of the present chapter – we take the view that this response would be an exaggerated one, which would ignore the difficulties which we believe to be associated with the binary divide. So our next steps are to explain and assess those difficulties, as a preliminary move to arriving at a balanced approach to the binary divide, that is to say one which neither overstates nor understates the viability of an analysis which is constructed around the binary divide.

By invoking the notion of a 'balanced view' of the binary divide as a categorical system for the legal contractual construction of personal work relations, we imply or claim that we can recognize and assess the virtues and vices of the binary divide as an analytical concept or tool. So we should compose a picture of the 'pros' and 'cons' of the binary divide. Its main claim to analytical virtue is that the existing law of personal work contracts does seem to be very strongly committed to it and dependent upon it. Accounts or renderings of the positive law of personal work contracts all seem to attest to the categorical contrast between the two contract types of the contract of employment and the contract for services. So much is this the case that it might on the face of it be thought to be perverse not to place the binary divide at the heart of an analytical account of the law of personal work contracts, and it might therefore appear that the whole enterprise of constructing a single overarching category of personal work contracts depends upon this central pillar. To do otherwise, it might be said, would be like trying to construct an analysis of the English law of homicide without recognizing the key distinction between murder and manslaughter.

This argument might be taken one stage further. It might be said that the binary divide is not primarily a legal typology, envisaged and imposed by the legal system, but rather a reflection of an institutional practice of personal work relations which is at least partly independent of the process of legal classification. This 'independent institutional' view of the binary divide might appear in either of two forms, one more extreme than the other. The less extreme form of this argument would content itself with the assertion that, although the binary divide might as a historical fact be a legally imposed phenomenon, or a product of legal ordering, it has nevertheless become so deeply embedded in the economic and social practice of personal work relations that it no longer owes its place to legal ordering.

The more extreme form of the argument would assert that the binary divide has never been a legally imposed phenomenon, but on the contrary has always consisted of a legal recognition of an essentially societal or pre-legal organization of personal work relations as either dependent or independent ones which is merely reflected in legal ordering. The argument in either form supports the observance of the binary divide as a central feature of the analysis of the legal construction of personal work relations as contractual ones, because it suggests that an analysis which was not cast in that mould would be or would rapidly become out of touch with the practicalities of personal work relations, shaped and influenced as those practicalities are by the forms and assumptions of the existing positive law.

However, although those arguments appear to be very strong ones, counter-arguments present themselves which concentrate on and bring out the problems which may nevertheless beset the binary divide as a categorical analysis of the contract law of personal work relations. The counter-arguments might start by admitting the foregoing 'independent institutional' arguments, even in their more extreme versions, and by accepting that the binary divide is quite deeply embedded in the practice of personal work relations. Nevertheless, even if it is thought that the binary divide was originally a pre-legal phenomenon rather than a legally imposed one, it might still be concluded that the binary divide had become ossified in and by the legal construction of personal work relations, so that it no longer had an institutional existence which was independent of legal construction and regulation of personal work relations. In other words, this argument would suggest that the binary divide might have lost its independent societal vigour or validity, and might be held in place only by the processes of legal regulation which support it and which create requirements or incentives for employers and workers to adapt the practice of personal work relations to the binary divide.

This brings us to the heart of the problem which we might have with the binary divide; it is that the distinction between the contract of employment and the (personal) contract for services may have become a largely or entirely self-referential one, an example of legal autopoiesis,[32] that is to say a distinction maintained within an enclosed sphere of legal argumentation having no firm connection with realities outside that sphere. We shall return shortly to the question of whether that is a justified assessment; if so, the binary divide could be regarded as a false dichotomy in the legal contractual construction of personal work relations. Suspending final judgment on that point for the time being, we proceed to indicate the grounds on which the binary divide might be regarded as, to say the least of it, a suspect dichotomy. We also identify some other problems which might be associated with that dichotomy; these are the difficulties of false unities, false symmetries, and false opposites. We proceed to elaborate upon all those possibly problematical features of the dual typology of personal work contracts.

There is no shortage of reasons for regarding the binary divide as being at least a suspect or dysfunctional dichotomy if not a completely false one. The main evidence of this dysfunctionality has been the endless controversy over very many years as to how to draw the distinction between the contract of employment and the contract for services, or between the employee and the independent contractor. Three basic approaches seem to compete or interact with each other: (1) the working person[33] is to be regarded as an employee employed under a contract of employment if but only if he or she works under the control of the employer (using the idea of control in a loose and extended sense); (2) the working person is to be regarded as an employee employed under a contract of employment if but only if he or she is integrated into the organization of the employer; and (3) the working person is to be regarded as an independent contractor employed under a contract or contracts for services if but only if he or she is in business on his or her own account.

There is a deep lack of resolution as between these three approaches, and moreover there are further disagreements about the way in which any of these approaches, or any combination of them, is to be operated. Further doctrines emerge which seem to modify or elaborate those three basic approaches to the

---

[32] G. Teubner (1986) *Autopoietic Law: A New Approach to Law and Society*, Berlin: DeGruyter.

[33] We introduce the terminology of the 'working person' as a categorically neutral one to identify the relational roles of the persons who, in the context of contracts of employment, figure as 'employees'.

test for the binary divide, but without making their application or their inter-relationship especially clearer. These modifications may be expansive or restrictive of the scope of employment under a contract or contracts of employment. The 'economic reality test' seems to be an inclusionary modification, to the effect that a personal work relationship is to be regarded as giving rise to a contract of employment if there is an 'economic reality' of dependence by the working person for security of employment and income upon the work-purchaser, even if there is an appearance of absence either of control over the working person on the part of the work-purchaser or of integration into the organization of the work-purchaser. On the other hand, the 'mutuality of obligation test' is an exclusionary modification, amounting to a rule that employment under a contract or contracts of employment exists only if the working person and the work-purchaser are in a state of continuing mutuality of contractual obligation.[34]

Over and above these emergent modifications to the basic test for the binary divide, we find a number of further, and equally contested, discussions about how the test or tests are to be applied. There is a discussion about how the basic tests, devised for and around bilateral personal work relations, are to be applied to multilateral personal work relations: do these represent a separate category? The answer seems to be that they do not, but the question keeps re-presenting itself. Then there is a discussion about whether or how far the application of the test or tests is a question of fact and thus to be determined entirely at first instance, or a question of law thus entirely open to reconsideration in the appellate courts. The solution to this conundrum is generally to sidestep it by identifying the issue as one of 'mixed fact and law', but that simply leaves it in place as a continuing controversy.

Yet a further and fairly perpetual debate about the binary divide concerns the question of whether it should be drawn in a uniform way regardless of the purpose for which or context in which it is being applied: should the classification be made uniformly in the context of employment law, tax law, the law of vicarious liability, social security law, and so on, or should it on the other hand be drawn in a way which is functional or instrumental to policy considerations in each different context? The general preference seems to be for a single universal standard across the different contexts, but that again is far from settled, and instrumental divergences do from time to time occur. These uncertainties all combine to produce a situation in which courts and tribunals have to adjudicate upon the application of the binary divide armed with no more than indications or pointers, rather than firm rules or clear doctrine, as to how to do so.

These various difficulties in defining and applying the binary divide certainly identify it as a dysfunctional distinction; but a more careful assessment is needed in order to decide whether it should be regarded as a false dichotomy. It would be a false dichotomy if it had never corresponded or had ceased to correspond to the

---

[34] For a comparative analysis of these tests, and of some of the effects, see A. Supiot (2001) *Beyond Employment*, Oxford: OUP, 10–17; N. Countouris (2007) *The Changing Law of the Employment Relationship: Comparative Analyses in the European Context*, Aldershot: Ashgate, Chapter 2; G. Casale (ed.) (2011), *The Employment Relationship – A Comparative Overview*, Oxford: Hart.

realities of personal work relations. That is a very difficult evaluation to make and indeed it is not easy to determine what might be the empirical basis for that judgement. A safe assertion, derived primarily from the evidence of case-law, would be that even if the dichotomy corresponded reasonably closely with social and economic realities fifty or sixty years ago, it has progressively been blurred by the growth of arrangements for personal work which are genuinely intermediate or ambivalent as between dependent employment and fully independent contracting for personal work. This ambivalence occurs with regard to any or all of the criteria of distinction, whether those are expressed in terms of control, integration, or economic dependence. Even if it is still possible to find many instances in practice of contracts of employment which embody unequivocally dependent personal work relations, and perhaps also many instances of personal contracts for services which embody unequivocally independent personal work relations, there can be little doubt that there is a clustering of personal work contracts into an enlarging grey area between those two supposed polar opposites.

Thus we come close to affirming that the binary divide has become a false dichotomy – a distinction which lawyers have to maintain and apply, and around which those engaged in personal work relations have to formulate their arrangements, because it is so deeply embedded in the legal ordering of personal work relations, but one which has become largely self-referential and no longer anchored in social and economic practice not itself dictated by legal ordering. However, before arriving at a firm conclusion to that effect, we propose to subject that hypothesis to a comparative scrutiny, since we would have to be more cautious about viewing the binary divide as a false dichotomy if it turned out to be uniformly maintained throughout European legal systems. But before carrying out that comparative scrutiny, we think it will be useful to identify some other false constructs which may be associated with the binary divide. We refer to the further possibilities of false unities, false symmetries, and false opposites; we shall suggest that each of these kinds of analytical error may occur as a corollary to the binary divide.

We begin with the possibility of false unities; this is the possibility that the two categories which are separated by the binary divide, that is to say the contract of employment and the personal contract for services, may each be falsely conceived of as unitary or homogenous ones. This could occur as a corollary to the existence of a sharp binary divide; the more that the world of personal work contracts is perceived as divided into two categories, the more compelling it seems to regard each of those two categories as unified or uniform ones. It can, we think, be safely asserted that this 'false unity' effect is quite strongly present in the legal contractual construction of personal work relations. To be more precise, we can say that there is one rather prominent 'false unity': the sharp binary divide which cuts through the sphere of personal work contracts does seem to be strongly associated with a view of 'the contract of employment' as a category which is in significant ways unified and homogeneous.

This kind of unification and attribution of homogeneity is to some extent inherent in the very notion of a category of contracts; by recognizing a category such as the 'the contract for the sale of goods', we attribute some degree of commonality to all the contracts within that category. But the evolution of the contract of employment in English law, especially in and from the second half of the twentieth century, does seem to have been driven by a specially powerful centripetal force which appears to compress all such contracts into a kind of analytical uniformity. There are, as we shall see shortly, some particular drivers in this direction, such as a policy thrust towards the reduction or elimination of distinctions between the contracts of 'blue collar' and 'white collar' workers.

Those forces have brought about a habit of analysis or perception which could be regarded as the false unity of the contract of employment. Moreover, this false unity of the contract of employment does seem to have a very real impact upon the way in which, in turn, personal contracts for services are understood and analysed, especially when this impact is combined with that of the binary divide itself. As we have previously indicated, one of the *leitmotifs* of our work is our perception that personal contracts for services are very under-researched and under-analysed both in absolute terms and by comparison with contracts of employment. If we imagine a map of the whole territory of personal work contracts, it would be a precisely detailed one on the side of contracts of employment, but a hazy and incomplete one on the side of personal contracts for services.

So we find that on to this sparsely detailed map of the territory of personal contracts for services, there are projected images which are in reality largely shadows of the more clearly drawn features of the contract of employment. This can and sometimes does produce, on the one hand, false symmetries with, and, on the other hand, false opposites to, the law of the contract of employment. There is one particular false symmetry: because of an assumed basic symmetry between the two bodies of law which are separated by the binary divide, the unity which is – in our suggestion falsely – attributed to the category of contracts of employment, is, with even less good reason, attributed also to the law of personal contracts for services. By a compounding of illusion, a false unity is replicated by reason of a false symmetry. As soon as one begins to chart and analyse personal contracts for services in any degree of detail, it becomes apparent how heterogeneous a category they in fact form. This, as we shall point out later, may be even more obvious in continental Civil law jurisdictions that expressly recognize different and varyingly diverse categories of contracts for services, while still viewing them as species of a less than coherent genus.[35] As we shall explain more fully in due course, the construction of them as a uniform contract type falls apart upon the slightest detailed scrutiny.

There is also a further conceptual error which seems prone to occur as a cumulative consequence of the false dichotomy (between contracts of employment and personal contracts for services), and the false unity of each of those two contract types, and the false symmetry between them, which we have identified in the

---

[35] Cf. the Italian Civil Code, where Article 2222 caters for the general category of *contratto d'opera*, whereas various special typologies are regulated by Articles 1655 c.c. (*appalto*), 1678 c.c. (*trasporto*), 1776 c.c. (*deposito*), and 1703 c.c. (*mandato*). See further Chapter 7 at pp. 269–70.

preceding paragraphs: we can think of this as the problem of false opposites. That is to say, there is a sequence of reasoning whereby, if personal work contracts are regarded as divided into two symmetrically homogeneous contract types, it is concluded that they must be fundamentally different to or opposite to each other in at least some significant respects (for otherwise there would be no basis for the binary divide). Here again, moreover, we find that the 'dark side of the moon' phenomenon comes into play: because the personal contract for services is relatively under-analysed by comparison with the contract of employment, some features of the personal contract for services seem to be ascertained by deducing that they must be different from or indeed opposite to the corresponding attributes of the contract of employment.

This would seem to be especially true with regard to certain structural features and implied terms which are deemed to be expressive of the fundamental nature of the contract of employment; it seems accordingly to be assumed that personal contracts for services must have different or opposite structural features, or implied terms in those particular respects. Three such key areas may be identified, two of them relatively recent and the third of much longer standing. Firstly, almost throughout its development during the last twenty years, the implied obligation of mutual trust and confidence seems to have been regarded as a special attribute of the contract of employment: it seems to have been assumed that no such implied obligation would attach to a contract for services, even if that were a personal contract for services. In the following Chapters 4 and 5 we will discuss how, and to what extent, these particular elements apply across legal systems, often by reference to functionally equivalent general clauses, such as that of good faith in contracts in general, and contracts of employment in particular.

Secondly, we may note the emergence during the last decade or so of a doctrine to the effect that the notion of mutuality of obligation applies either in a unique way or at least with special force to the contract of employment. Hence we encounter the view that the presence of mutuality of obligation has become not only a prerequisite for the existence of a contract of employment but also a basis for distinguishing between the contract of employment and the contract for services. In this way it has become an assumption that the contract for services, even when it is a personal contract, does not exhibit mutuality of obligation in the way that the contract of employment must necessarily do. In the following chapter we will further discuss how, in respect of this particular structural element, English law tends to stand out in comparison with other continental European systems.

By thus specifically invoking the idea that the contract for services may be a personal contract, we are, potentially at least, challenging the third, most deep-seated and longest-standing of the assumed contrasts between the contract of employment and the contract for services, namely the idea that, among all contracts for the performance of work, it is the contract of employment which is the personal one in a unique, or at least very special, sense. Various doctrines in the law of contracts of employment derive from this perception of the contract of employment as personal in a very special sense – our two earlier instances of doctrines perceived as special to the contract of employment, namely the ideas of the obligation of mutual trust and confidence and of continuing mutuality of obligation, can both be regarded as in some sense derived from the idea of the contract of employment as a specially personal one, and so also might we regard the special application of the doctrine of restraint of trade to contracts of employment, and also the special approach to remedies for wrongful termination which has developed with regard to contracts of employment.

In all these cases, the legal construction of the contract of employment depends in part at least upon a presumed contrast or opposition between that construction and the corresponding (though less fully articulated) construction of the personal contract for services: that is to say, at each of these points it seems to be presumed that, because these are identifying attributes of the contract of employment, the (personal) contract for services cannot and does not display those features. Our argument is that, although there may indeed be such a contrast or opposition in certain circumstances, it is quite unsafe to reason from the presumed existence of a generic or systemic contrast of any of the three kinds we have cited above. In other words, there is a real danger that this kind of reasoning may lead to the creation of false opposites.

In this subsection we have thus sought to show how the binary divide between contracts of employment and personal contracts, which seems intrinsic to the analysis of personal work contracts in English law, could be regarded as a false dichotomy. We have also suggested that several other false or unsafe conclusions might have followed from a dogmatic commitment to the idea of the binary divide; that is to say, we have also suggested that there may be false unities, false symmetries, and false opposites in the scheme of analysis which revolves around the binary divide. However, we have made these assertions in a tentative way. That is because we perceive that our arguments might be viewed as themselves being fallacious if the categorical errors or difficulties which we are alleging in the case of English law were found to exist in the same way and to the same extent in many other European legal systems. If so, it might be thought that it was misconceived to mount this analytical attack upon a multiplicity of employment law systems. So in the next section we subject our 'false dichotomy' argument to a comparative scrutiny vis-à-vis other European legal systems.

## B. A Comparative Assessment of the Binary Divide

In the foregoing subsection we advanced arguments for regarding the binary divide, which splits the analysis of personal work contracts into the two hemispheres of the contract of employment and the personal contract for services, as an inherently unsatisfactory one, with associated problems of false unities, false symmetries, and false opposites. But we advanced those arguments cautiously because of a consciousness that we were questioning an analysis which was not only deeply embedded in English employment law and contract law but was possibly also a universal one throughout European legal systems. Although it may on occasion be the right and the obligation of theorists of labour law to challenge existing analyses which are upheld even worldwide, the fact that an analysis is entertained on a universal or near-universal basis should at least engender some respectful caution towards it. So in this subsection we attempt to offer a comparative assessment of the standing of the binary divide within European legal systems, in order to test out the strength of our critique of it.

Let us state the universalist argument in its strongest form in order to evaluate it. In its strongest form, the argument would run that most employment law systems display a clear distinction between dependent employment and independent working, and that they regard employment law as being concerned with the former kind of work and not with the latter. Moreover, in its strong form the argument would go on to assert that in most European employment law systems this dichotomy permeates the analysis of personal work contracts, and that it is of such embeddedness and long standing that it can be directly compared with the distinction made in Roman law between *locatio conductio operarum* and *locatio conductio operis*, literally the hire of services and of service, but corresponding respectively to the contract of service and for services. This would seem to accord such an impeccable pedigree to the binary divide that it would be absurd to cast doubt on its intrinsic soundness.

A comparative scrutiny of that universalist argument turns out to reveal both its strengths and its weaknesses. On the positive side, it can be said that European employment law systems have possessed in common a strong disposition to distinguish between employment and self-employment, and to regard the former as the province of labour law and the latter as beyond the province of labour law. It can also be said that that European employment law systems have drawn this binary divide between the included relations of employment and the excluded relations of self-employment in broadly similar ways. Albeit with significant variants in detail between systems, the language of control, dependence, integration, and economic reality is spoken throughout these systems in order to make this distinction.[36]

However, that, we suggest, is more or less where the universality of the binary divide ends, so far as European legal systems are concerned; and our comparative assessment suggests that the perception of the binary divide as both universal and perpetual within European legal systems is an illusory one. The employment law systems of Europe did considerably converge upon a pattern of binary division of personal work relations in and during the second half of the twentieth century; but they did so from quite diverse starting points in quite diverse ways, and such temporary uniformity as came about during that period has since begun to dissolve under the pressure of fresh changes in the policy and practice of the regulation of the labour market as between national systems. Moreover, the picture of the binary divide is further fragmented by divergences between systems as to how far and in what sense the divide is a specifically contractual phenomenon. We shall expand upon and seek to justify these assertions in the ensuing paragraphs.

To consider the evolution of the binary divide in a number of European employment law systems is to be made aware of its historically contingent character

---

[36] A. Supiot (2001) *Beyond Employment*, Oxford: OUP, 10–17; N. Countouris (2007) *The Changing Law of the Employment Relationship: Comparative Analyses in the European Context*, Aldershot: Ashgate, Chapter 2.

in each system, not least in the English one. In the British context, Deakin (2001) memorably pointed up the way in which the drawing of the binary divide in employment law was largely the result of the re-mapping of the sphere of personal work relations for the purposes of state social security provision which was effected by the legislation introduced in 1946 to usher in the post-war welfare state, its architecture having been essentially designed by the Beveridge Report of 1943.[37] The hammering home of the wedge between employment and self-employment was achieved not least by means of a deliberate – and at the time far from intuitive, indeed rather artificial – unification of employment relations, hitherto themselves sharply stratified as between white-collar salaried employees and blue-collar wage-earning workers: those two groups were treated as one and as such collectively differentiated from the contrasting domain of self-employment.

It may well be true to say that a binary divide between employment and self-employment did become a fairly uniform common feature of post-war welfare state social security systems throughout Europe. But in the sphere of employment law and the regulation of personal work relations more generally, the geometry seems to have been much more variable. Considerable variation can be perceived in various respects; for example, in the extent to which employment law was, ideologically and as a matter of national policy, confined to the sphere of 'subordinate employment' and if so in the meaning which was attached to the idea of 'subordinate employment'. Another area of important variation consists in the question of how far and how fast the multifarious distinctions between white-collar salaried employees and blue-collar wage-earning workers were reduced or eliminated.[38] A further, very complex and elusive, set of variations, which we shall consider in detail later in this work, revolves around the issue of how 'professional' work is understood and regulated in different European legal systems.

Moreover, comparative assessment strongly suggests that a new set of variations between European employment law systems, across and around the binary divide, is starting to occur as those systems both develop new regulatory dimensions – most notably by extending the law of discrimination in employment – and adapt themselves to increasingly post-Fordist labour market patterns and structures. Thus, sometimes of their own accord, but in many cases under the pressure of requirements in EU Directives, most European employment law systems have framed their laws concerning discrimination in the employment field so as to include self-employment within the scope of 'employment' for that purpose. In fact it is quite striking how relatively quietly and uncontroversially the binary divide has been bridged in that context; but there is a wide variety in the ways and degrees in which and to which that transition has been made.

---

[37] S. Deakin (2001) 'The Contract of Employment: a Study in Legal Evolution', ESCR Working paper No. 203, 31.
[38] For a comparative discussion of these historical evolutions see N. Countouris (2007) *The Changing Law of the Employment Relationship: Comparative Analyses in the European Context*, Aldershot: Ashgate, 15–25.

Again, it is notable how many experiments have taken place within the last twenty years or so in the devising of legal formulae by which to accord selected employment rights to new intermediate categories of semi-dependent personal work relations, the best-known of these being the *parasubordinati* of Italian law, the *arbeitnehmerähnliche Personen* of German law, and the 'worker' category in English employment law. The Spanish notion of 'TRADEs', the acronym for '*trabajadores autónomos económicamente dependientes*', or 'economically dependent autonomous workers', introduced in 2007 by the Spanish *Ley 20/2007, de 11 de julio, del Estatuto del Trabajo Autónomo*, offers another example of this genre of experimentations.[39] Even legal systems such as the French one, that have hitherto sought to put this particular genie back in the bottle it came from by reverting to legal presumptions of employment status, are now flirting with the idea of regulating quasi-dependence. The 2008 'Antonmattei-Sciberras Report'[40] reopened the debate in France – a legal system where, until a few years ago, the notion of economic dependence was dismissed as 'too imprecise'[41] – by advocating 'the creation ... of a legal regime for the economically dependent worker'.[42]

Moreover, the binary divide is the subject of quite rapid and complex degradation from another direction; the exponential growth of temporary agency employment and various forms of labour subcontracting is provoking the evolution of legal forms of recognition of those multilateral personal work relations which often straddle or circumvent the binary divide. This growth is challenging the traditional binary divide, as well as the rules and institutional arrangements that had been set up to sustain it, across several European jurisdictions. As noted by Antonio Ojeda Avilés (2010): 'in quite a few cases the contracting-out is essentially reduced to the labour force alone, [thus raising] the old problem of pseudo-contracting and of labour-only contracting'. But, he asserts, the blurring of categories occurs at an even deeper level: 'The present reality has led to an expansion in services and from there to an expansion of contracts for services, where the dividing line between contracts and pseudo-contracts practically does not exist.'[43]

[39] J. R. Mercader Uguina and A. de la Puebla Pinilla (2007) 'Comentario a la Ley 20/2007, de 11 de julio, del Estatuto del Trabajo Autónomo', 20, *Relacione Laborales*, 99; F. Valdès Dal-Ré and O. Leclerc (2008) 'Les nouvelles frontières du travail indépendant. A propos du statut du travail autonome espagnol' *RDT*, 296; J. Cabeza Pereiro (2008) 'The Status of Self-employed Workers in Spain', *ILR*, 91; A. Ojeda Avilés (2010) *La Deconsrtucción del Derecho del Trabajo*, Madrid: La Ley, 394–424.

[40] P. H. Antonmattei and J. C. Sciberras (2008) *Le travailleur économiquement dépendant: quelle protection?*.

[41] J. Pélissier, A. Supiot, and A. Jeammaud (2000) *Droit du travail*, Paris: Dalloz, 151.

[42] '*La création, ... d'un statut du travailleur économiquement dépendant*', in P. H. Antonmattei and J. C. Sciberras (2008) *Le travailleur économiquement dépendant: quelle protection?*, 22. Cf. also P. H. Antonmattei and J. C. Sciberras (2009) 'Le travailleur économiquement dépendant, quelle protection?', *Droit Social*, 221. Our translation from the French original.

[43] A. Ojeda Avilés (2010) *La Deconsrtucción del Derecho del Trabajo*, Madrid: La Ley, 2010, 140. Our translation from the Spanish original: '*La realidad actual ha llevado a una expansion de los servicios y de ahí a la de las contratas de servicios, en donde la línea divisoria entre contrata y seudocontrata práticamente no existe.*'

However, if we stand back from these complex recent evolutions and take a long historical and comparative view, we can see that perhaps the most important and underrated variable of all in the evolution of the binary divide consists in the question of how far it constitutes a dichotomy specifically between contrasting *contractual* types. This is a question which we should understand and seek to answer by reference to the different evolution, as between European employment law systems, of the contract of employment as the central institutional category. Our answer to the question will consist of depicting two successive evolutions which took place in varying degrees and at varying times in European employment law systems, and which between them gave rise to the binary divide as a specifically contractual phenomenon.

These two evolutions are ones which are widespread among continental European Civil-law-based employment law systems, though they occur at different times and in rather different ways; the situation with regard to English common-law-based employment law is somewhat different, and we shall revert to that shortly. The first of these evolutions can be described as the liberal contractualization of personal work relations. It is archetypally represented by the articulation in the French Civil Code, and in various other national civil codes which were modelled upon or influenced by it, of propositions whereby latter-day counterparts of the *locatio conductio operarum* and *locatio conductio operis* of Roman law were identified as contract types falling within the domain of private law. These were developments which occurred during, and indeed themselves represented, the heyday of the 19th-century ideal of freedom of contract, and the movement 'from status to contract', never more so than in the securing of a contractual understanding of what were then regarded as 'master and servant' relations.

Those who wish to view as universal and perpetual the binary division of personal work relations and more particularly personal work contracts, into the two opposites of employment and self-employment, might well regard their position as vindicated by these evolutions. However, it should be stressed that there were many variations on the theme of the duality between *locatio conductio operarum* and *locatio conductio operis*. Simon Deakin has pointed out that in many respects the two versions of the *locatio conductio* contained in Article 1780 of the French Civil Code — that is to say the *louage d'ouvrage* and the *louage de services* — were only 'loosely' based on the Roman law notions of, respectively, *locatio conductio operarum* and *locatio conductio operis*. In each case, the link to Roman law concepts was more tenuous than it might seem at first sight. The concepts used in the Civil Code were adaptations – they were 'the same as the old *locatio conductio* in name only'.[44] He goes on to explain that: 'under the system of the *Code civil*, those falling under the concept of the *louage de services* were domestic servants (*domestiques*) and day labourers (*journaliers*), leaving the *louage d'ouvrage* to cover all others'.[45]

---

[44] S. Deakin (2005) 'The Comparative Evolution of the Employment Relationship', ESRC Working Paper No. 317, 9.
[45] Ibid.

By contrast, the Italian Civil Code of 1865 notion of *persone* (persons) contained in Article 1627, n.1 was considerably wider in scope than the French category of *gens de travail*, as the Italian *locator operarum* could also be the skilled manual or clerical worker even when a 'producer of works of the mind'.[46]

The essence of these exercises in the contractualization of personal work relations was to emphasize the proximity of *locatio conductio operarum* to *locatio conductio operis*, and not the distance between them. Such provisions demonstrated that what we would now regard as dependent employment relations could be codified as contractual ones just as much as independent personal work relations could be; the idea was to apply the notion of *locatio conductio*, as the contractual hiring of a person's work capacity, to general service (*operarum*) as much as to specific work assignments (*operis*).

So we would argue that the various occurrences of liberal contractualization of personal work relations in the 19th century, although on the whole following the contours of the ancient distinction between *locatio conductio operarum* and *locatio conductio operis*, did not especially reinforce or solidify the binary divide between employment and self-employment as a contractual classification; it was rather that they drew upon a received distinction between general services and specific task assignments. There was, however, in many European legal systems a second and consequential evolution which, in some ways ironically, did very much reinforce or solidify the binary divide between employment and self-employment as a contractual classification. This was a phenomenon which we have touched upon at various earlier points, but which we should now consider more specifically; we may refer to it as the social autonomization of the contract of employment.

When we speak of the social autonomization of the contract of employment, we refer to those foundational episodes in the making of labour law in Europe in which, from around the beginning of the twentieth century, various law-makers and theorists appreciated and sought to act upon their understanding of the fact that the liberal contractualization of personal work relations which had taken place during the 19th century had been, to say the least of it, rather a mixed blessing for much of the workforce. In exchange for varieties of status which might have servile incidents, they were exposed to the vicissitudes of an enhanced freedom of contract of which employers could easily be the real beneficiaries. Normative strategies were evolved which consisted essentially in seeking to reconcile the placing of personal work relations within the general domain of the private law of contract with the special needs of the workforce for a more socially protective regime.

The method of achieving that reconciliation was to insist that the contract for subordinate employment, although accommodated within the general private law of contracts, was nevertheless specially characterized by a generic inequality of bargaining power between employers and workers, which followed from the very character of the relationship as one of subordination. Hence the proper regulation

---

[46] '*produttor(e) di opere della «mente»*'; B. Veneziani (2003) 'Contratto di lavoro, potere di controllo e subordinazione nell'opera di Ludovico Barassi', in M. Napoli (ed.), *La Nascita del Diritto del Lavoro – Il 'contratto di Lavoro' di Lodovico Barassi cent'anni dopo*, Milano: Vita e Pensiero, 405.

of this particular type of contract demanded a distinctively socially protective approach which would compensate for that subordination and inequality of bargaining power. This was the *social autonomisation of the contract of employment*: the price that had to be paid for its realization was the driving of a deep wedge between the world of employment contracts and the contrasting world of private law commercial contracts.

Rather ironically, contracts for services were often placed on the wrong side of that divide so far as social protection was concerned, even if they were personal contracts for services representing personal work relations in which the workers concerned, although not qualifying as subordinated, were nevertheless considerably vulnerable to the insecurities of liberal freedom of contract. So far as concrete legislation is concerned, one could regard this particular form of institutionalization of the contract of employment – its social autonomization – as having been pioneered in the Netherlands with its Contracts of Employment statute of 1908. In a very important newly published study, Knegt (2008) and his colleagues have, while celebrating the ideals which motivated that legislation, nevertheless focused their work on the way in which the contract of employment has become 'an exclusionary device'.[47]

If our argument is accepted that it was these processes of social autonomization of the contract of employment which were crucial to the intensification of the binary divide between contracts of employment and other personal work contracts in most European legal systems, important conclusions can be drawn from that. Firstly, this serves to demonstrate that the intensification of the binary divide, which was thus an identifying characteristic of emergent European labour law systems from the beginning of the twentieth century onwards, was far from being the naturalistic and neutral acceptance of a category division which was already ineluctably enshrined in the law. It represented, on the contrary, a series of policy decisions taken at different times and in different ways which had the common feature that they were instrumental to the development of an autonomous corpus of socially oriented labour law within the national legal system in question.

Secondly, and by the same token, the fact that these intensifications of the binary divide typically represent instrumental policy decisions on the part of legislators means that, however laudable those decisions and the theoretical arguments behind them might have been from a social point of view, they were nevertheless somewhat contrived ones in terms of their legal logic. As such, they ran the risks of engendering those unities, symmetries, and oppositions which we have argued earlier may easily turn out to be false ones. Those who are pursuing the social autonomization of the contract of employment may readily be led by the force of their own policy objectives to envisage the domain of the contract of employment as a homogeneous one, and to regard the domain of the contract for services as a symmetrically homogeneous and contrasting one.

---

[47] R. Knegt (ed.) (2008) *The Employment Contract as an Exclusionary Device – An Analysis on the Basis of 25 Years of Developments in The Netherlands*, Antwerp: Intersentia.

The conclusion which is emerging from this comparative assessment is therefore that the making and intensification of the binary divide during the nineteenth and twentieth centuries was a set of contingent developments, which occurred asynchronously and in a diverse way in various continental European legal systems. This sense of the binary divide as a circumstantial and heterogeneous phenomenon rather than a uniform and inevitable one is reinforced when one reverts to considering how and when it occurred in the English common-law-based system. There, the picture was a very different one. The first evolution, that of the liberal contractualization of personal work relations, took place much more gradually and casuistically than in continental Europe; there was no moment of making of a Civil Code in which the two contract types were formally identified as incidents of a system of private law.

As to the second evolution, that is to say the social autonomization of the contract of employment, we would argue that in the English common-law-based system this development occurred much later and took a rather different form, as compared with the continental exemplars of this trend. In a way, we could see this as a natural consequence of the gradualism of the first evolution in English law; because no Civil Code had decisively contractualized personal work relations, there was less of a perceived need to establish the social autonomy of the contract of employment. In fact, although, as we have seen, this took place in the context of social security law in 1946, we would argue that it did not occur in the context of employment law until the enactment of the Contracts of Employment Act in 1963.

From that time on, however, during the remainder of the 1960s and the 1970s, there was a rapid and extensive legislative juridification[48] of the employment relationship in the UK, in the course of which the contract of employment, or more particularly being employed under a continuous contract of employment or series of such contracts, became the qualification or gateway to a raft of statutory employment rights and protections. So the process whereby the contract of employment is first the subject of social autonomization and then later comes to function as an exclusionary device occurred late in the day but very rapidly and completely in English employment law.

So our comparative assessment of the making and the working of the binary divide has certainly reinforced our doubts about its inevitability and universal uniformity in the legal contractual construction of personal work relations. In the next section of this chapter we move to suggesting a particular mode of analysis of personal work contracts which we hope will build in a useful way upon those conclusions.

---

[48] Cf. G. Teubner (ed.) (1987) *Juridification of Social Spheres – A Comparative Ananlysis in the Areas of Labor, Corporate, Antitrust and Social Welfare Law*, Berlin: De Gruyter, cf. especially G. Teubner, 'Juridification – Concepts, Aspects, Limits, Solutions', pp. 3–48, and S. Simitis, 'Juridification of Labour Relations', pp. 113–162.

## Section 3: The Contractual Construction of Personal Work Relations – Towards a Multidimensional Analysis

In the previous sections of this chapter, we have first provided a comparative account of the way in which, in English law and in the employment law systems of other European countries, personal work relations are constructed as contracts, and we have sought to develop a theory about layers of regulation in order to show how that contractual construction may differ in its nature as between those legal systems. This began to heighten the sense that there is a great diversity over time and as between legal systems in the legal construction of personal work relations as contractual ones. In the second section that awareness of diversity was heightened by an analysis which questioned the binary divide of personal work contracts as between contracts of employment and personal contracts for services; our conclusion was that the binary divide, far from being a universal constant, was a contingent and variable phenomenon in the ways in which it had come about and had operated in different legal systems. In this section we shall argue that those arguments and those conclusions serve to justify, indeed to necessitate, a method of analysis of the domain of personal work contracts which will recognize and do justice to these kinds of diversity.

We begin with a further point about diversity. In the extended realm of personal work contracts which we have envisaged by fundamentally breaking the bounds of the contract of employment, we find an enormous variety of factual patterns of work arrangements. Not only is this true, for example, for arrangements with sportspersons, it also applies to people working in entertainment and in the media, and also to a growing army of people providing consultancy services and stand-in services of every kind. As employment lawyers, we have seemed to approach this diverse world entirely from the contract of employment outwards. That is to say, we analyse such arrangements by considering whether they constitute contracts of employment. If they do not, we consider whether they can be analogized to contracts of employment. If they cannot, we tend to conclude that they are outside our province, some kind of business contract with which we are not really concerned. We are prepared to recognize diversity *within* the contract of employment, and we are becoming more accustomed than we were to recognizing diversity on the *margins* of the contract of employment; but we have still been allowing ourselves to be rather tightly constrained by the contract of employment paradigm.

The authors of this work are now tending away from that approach towards a rather different approach which involves being more willing to look at personal work contracts as a whole, and does not insist upon the contract of employment as a ubiquitous paradigm. According to this approach, personal work contracts are conceived of as a large group or family of contracts, some of which fall into the sub-category of contracts of employment while others do not; and we bear in mind in this connection that we have concluded that the drawing of that line between contracts of employment and other personal work contracts is a notoriously difficult, and ultimately unsatisfactory pursuit.

Within the overall category of personal work contracts, contracts of employment may well be heavily numerically preponderant, though that preponderance is tending to decline slightly, and is in any case hard to assess exactly.[49] Within the overall category, moreover, the law and practice of the contract of employment is more fully articulated than is the law and practice of other personal work contracts, which is, as we have said, often somewhat obscure. For these reasons there will be a natural tendency to regard the contract of employment as the dominant head of the family of personal work contracts. But it would be quite wrong to regard all the other members of the family simply as lesser siblings of the contract of employment. The approach which we are seeking to take regards the other members of the family as being interesting in their own right. Our approach moreover asserts that we can better understand the contract of employment itself by taking this holistic perspective upon the whole family of personal work contracts.

That then is our broad approach. The next step in our argument consists in explaining our way of constructing and analysing the family or group of personal work contracts. The aim is to understand what personal work contracts have in common and what differences there are between them; and, in particular, we have been seeking a better way of doing this than by simply working with the two categories of the contract of employment on the one hand and the independent personal contract for services on the other hand. Our way of doing this has been to seek to build upon analytical work which had previously been done on the margins of the contract of employment.[50] We will argue that this analytical work can be used to construct a multidimensional picture of the family or group of personal work contracts; and we will seek to introduce one new dimension into the analysis, or at least give it a more prominent place than it has previously had.

So let us identify this analytical work on the margins of the contract of employment, to which we have just referred, and explain how it starts to create several dimensions in the analysis of personal work contracts. A number of labour law scholars have engaged in this pursuit, such as, in particular, the first author of this work writing in conjunction with Paul Davies,[51] Hepple,[52] Collins,[53] Deakin,[54]

---

[49] Cf. B. Burchell, S. Deakin, and S. Honey (1999) *The Employment Status of Workers in Non-standard Employment*, London: Department of Trade and Industry.

[50] See M. Freedland, 'Re-thinking the Personal Work Contract' in (2005/6) *Current Legal Problems* Vol. 58, Oxford: OUP, 517, a part of which is recapitulated here.

[51] P.L. Davies and M. Freedland, 'Employers, Workers and the Autonomy of Labour Law' in H. Collins, P. L. Davies, and R. W. Rideout (eds) (2000), *Legal Regulation of the Employment Relation*, London: Kluwer; and 'Changing Perspectives on the Employment Relationship in British Labour Law' in C. Barnard, S.W. Deakin, and G. S. Morris (2004) *The Future of Labour Law : Liber Amicorum Sir Bob Hepple QC*, Oxford: Hart Publishing.

[52] 'Restructuring Employment Rights' (1986) 15, *ILJ*, 69.

[53] 'Independent Contractors and the Challenge of Vertical Disintegration to Employment Protection Laws' (1990) 10, *OJLS*, 353.

[54] 'The Many Futures of the Contract of Employment' in J. Conaghan, M. Fischl, and K. Klare (eds.) (2001) *Labour Law in an Era of Globalisation; Transformative Practices and Possibilities*, Oxford: OUP and cf. the further development of this work in S. Deakin and F. Wilkinson (2005) *The Law of the Labour Market*, Oxford: OUP.

and, in the younger generation of labour lawyers, Davidov,[55] Barmes,[56] and the second author of this work.[57] The main starting point for this analysis in recent labour law scholarship has been the debate about the enlargement of the personal scope of labour laws, which was initiated by the groundbreaking pieces of writing by Hepple in 1986[58] and by Collins in 1991.[59] That debate has gathered pace since then, stimulated by legislative initiatives in the UK and other European countries. Such initiatives include the recognition in German labour and social law of a category of *arbeitnehmerähnliche Personen*,[60] or employee-like workers, in Italian labour and social law of the *para-subordinati*,[61] or quasi-subordinated workers, and the use of the 'worker' category in some of the employment legislation introduced by New Labour governments in the UK since 1997.[62]

That has been a discussion which concentrates on one particular dimension of analysis of employment contracts, namely the dimension of the 'worker' in which we reconsider and re-analyse the concept and definition of the employee, worker, or employed person. That analysis focuses upon various types or descriptions of workers, on the margins of the 'employee' category, descriptions which to a greater or lesser extent become part of the legal parlance through which employment legislation is interpreted and applied. Examples of such types or descriptions are those of 'free-lancers',[63] 'consultants',[64] 'casuals' ('regular' or otherwise),[65] 'on-call workers',[66] 'outworkers' or 'homeworkers',[67] 'gang-workers',[68] 'contract-workers',[69] and 'agency-temps'.[70] The issue of the analysis has tended to be whether these

---

[55] 'Who is a Worker?' (2005) 34, *ILJ*, 57.
[56] 'The Continuing Conceptual Crisis in the Common Law of the Contract of Employment' (2004) 67, *MLR*, 435.
[57] *The Changing Law of the Employment Relationship: Comparative Analyses in the European Context* (2007) Aldershot: Ashgate.
[58] See above, n. 52.
[59] See above, n. 53.
[60] The *arbeitnehmerähnliche Personen* were first identified as a category by section 12a of the 1974 law on collective agreements (*Tarifsvertragsgesetz*) and defined as '*Personen, die wirtschafltlicht abhängig und vergleichbar einem Arbeitnehmer sozial schutzbedürftig sind*', that is to say: 'persons who [in spite of their formal independence] are economically dependent and, like an employee, in need of social protection'. See further M. Weiss and M. Schmidt (2008) *Labour Law and Industrial Relations in Germany*, Alphen aan den Rijn: Kluwer Law International, p. 47.
[61] The emergence of the notion of *parasubordinati* in the Italian legal domain is traditionally linked to Law 533/1973, modifying for this purpose Article 409(3) of the Italian Civil Procedure Code, which prescribed that the rules of procedure for labour litigation also apply to the 'relationship of agency, of commercial representation and other relations of collaboration materialising in a continuous and coordinated provision, predominantly personal, even if not of subordinate character'. *Parasubordinazione* has been absorbed in the concept of '*lavoro a progetto*' introduced by the so-called 'Biagi Law', Decreto Legislativo 276/2003, Articles 61 and following.
[62] Such as the National Minimum Wage Act 1998, s. 54.
[63] Cf. *Hall (Inspector of Taxes) v. Lorrimer* [1994] ICR 218 – a tax case, but much cited in the context of employment law.
[64] As in *MHC Consulting Services Ltd v. Tansell* [2000] ICR 789.
[65] As, most famously, in *O'Kelly v. Trusthouse Forte Plc* [1983] ICR 728.
[66] As in the leading case of *Carmichael v. National Power Plc* [1998] ICR 1167.
[67] As in *Nethermere (St Neots) Ltd. v. Gardner* [1984] ICR 612.
[68] Cf. *New Century Cleaning Co Ltd v. Church* [2000] IRLR 27.
[69] See *Harrods Ltd v. Remick* [1998] ICR 156, and also *Tansell*, see above n. 64.
[70] See, recently, *Bunce v. Postworth Ltd* [2005] IRLR 557.

descriptions of workers can be fitted into or approximated to the category of 'employee' in conditions, as Hugh Collins famously identified them,[71] of vertical dis-integration of production, in the era, therefore, of the so-called 'flexible firm'. There have also been such discussions about whether the 'employee' or 'worker' categories extend to people engaged in work or in occupations as volunteers, or as trainees, including particularly pupil barristers.

In recent writings,[72] the first author of this work and Paul Davies have sought to develop an argument that we should recognize a second distinct dimension to this analysis, which has to do with the way we identify or conceive of the employer or employing organization. That is to say, we have suggested that what starts out as a minor sub-theme in the analysis of the concept of the worker, a question of 'who is the employer of the worker?' deserves to end up as a whole separate theme or dimension of discussion, a question of 'within what kind of enterprise or organization is the worker employed?'. And in fact that turns out to be the real problem of classification with several of the types or descriptions of workers that we have identified, such as gang-workers, agency-temps, or contract workers. The issue would be better understood and analysed in terms of whether workers fit into or can be approximated to the category of 'employee' when they are employed in a particular kind of complex and multilateral employing organization, set-up, network, or arrangement. For example the discussion about the employment status of pupil barristers, as in *Edmonds v. Lawson*,[73] involves analysis of the very singular organization or set-up constituted by the barristers' set of chambers. So another distinct dimension has been added.

We now want to suggest that it is time to recognize and elaborate some more dimensions to the discussion. As well as analysing the 'worker' dimension and the dimension of the employer or employing organization, we need to consider various aspects of the nature or quality of the relationship as distinctive further elements in the analysis of the group or family of personal work contracts. As with the 'employer' dimension of the discussion, these further dimensions also grow out of the discussion of types or descriptions of 'worker'. Just as the idea of the agency worker signals a discussion about an intermediary employing enterprise, so the reference to the casual worker or the on-call worker invites discussion of the nature and quality of the employment relationship, in this case with particular reference to its continuity, mutuality, or bindingness. We think it is appropriate to couple those issues with concerns about the personality or substitutability of the worker in the work arrangement, and to elevate that whole set of issues to the status of a set of further dimensions of the analysis and understanding of personal work contracts. There is much scope for argument about how many such dimensions of differentiation to single out; a useful structure might be:

---

[71] H. Collins (1990) 'Independent Contractors and the Challenge of Vertical Disintegration to Employment Protection Laws', 10:3, *OJLS*, 353–80.
[72] See above, n. 51.
[73] [2003] ICR 567.

1. the worker;
2. the employing enterprise;
3. duration and continuity;
4. personality; and
5. purpose or motivation.

The succeeding paragraphs will elaborate upon those last three, less recognized, dimensions.

Firstly then we denote a dimension of duration and continuity. This would identify the common theme running through the discussions about the employment status of the 'regular casuals' in *O'Kelly v. Trusthouse Forte*,[74] the 'homeworkers' or 'outworkers' in *Nethermere v. Gardner*,[75] the trawlermen with gaps between voyages in *Hellyer Bros v. McLeod*,[76] the on-call tour guides in *Carmichael v. National Power plc*,[77] and the various workers the duration of whose contracts are specified by task or outcome rather than by calendar time.[78] The discussion of these practical examples should remind us, by the way, that in any particular factual personal work situation, the analysis of the legal contractual status of the work relationship or relationships in question may take place in more than one of the several dimensions, sometimes in all of them. In a given fact situation, there may well be issues about the personality of the worker, the structure of the employing organization or set-up, and about the duration and continuity of the arrangements between the worker and the employing set-up.

A further dimension of differentiation between personal work contracts which it is useful to single out is that of personality or 'personalness'. This is the dimension in which it is measured and considered how strictly the work contract insists, and in practice ensures, that performance of the work or provision of the services or securing of the outcome in question be carried out by the contracting person himself or herself. We have of course identified the requirement of performance in person as one of the key defining or limiting features of the whole category of contracts which we are seeking to establish and defend. However, we do not envisage this as a requirement which is formulated in absolute terms, so that the slightest allowance in the contract as formed or performed for deviation from performance in person identifies that contract as being outside the category.

Indeed, that is quite far from being the case, for the case-law interpreting the definitional requirement of personal performance for many statutory employment rights exacts only that personal performance must be the 'predominant purpose' of the contract, rather than an absolute attribute.[79] Moreover, further case-law seems to be identifying diminishing non-absolute degrees of personality as definitional

[74]  *O'Kelly v. Trusthouse Forte Plc* [1983] ICR 728 [1984] QB 90.
[75]  *Nethermere (St Neots) Ltd v. Gardner* [1984] ICR 612.
[76]  [1987] ICR 526.
[77]  *Carmichael v. National Power plc* [1999] ICR 1226.
[78]  Cf. *Wiltshire County Council v. NATFHE* [1980] ICR 455.
[79]  Cf. *Mirror Group Newspapers Ltd v. Gunning* [1986] ICR 145, *Sheehan v. Post Office Counters Ltd* [1999] ICR 73 (and, in the tax context, *IRC v. Post Office Ltd* [2003] IRLR 199).

requirements for, respectively, contracts of employment and 'workers' contracts' falling outside the contract of employment category.[80] In that case-law, this definitional requirement is being seen as one facet of the notion of 'mutuality of obligation'; we think that is something of a misconception, because the existence of a discretion on the part of the working person to provide work or service through a substitute does not necessarily reduce the bindingness of the work contract, and certainly does not eliminate its obligational core. However, even if we disagree with that way of analysing the issue of the personality of the work obligation, we should nevertheless regard it as representing a very important dimension of analysis of convergences and differences within the realm of personal work contracts.

The last of the dimensions which we wish to single out is that of the purpose or mode of the contractual relationship. We put this forward as a distinct dimension in order to confront the implicit and normally unquestioned reductive analysis of all personal work contracts which would envisage all of them as having the single purpose of providing for the exchange of work for remuneration, the work being provided either in the modality of subordination of the worker or in the modality of autonomy of the worker. Instead, we suggest that we can usefully identify a variety of purposes and/or modalities of personal work contracts, which between them constitute a very significant dimension of convergence and divergence between personal work contracts. Quite strongly differentiated varieties of modality and purpose are those, for example, of personal work contracts which are in the nature of training contracts or apprenticeships, or which are vehicles for volunteering, or for public service, or for authorship or innovation. If cautiously developed – for it could easily be overused – this will we think prove to be an informative analytical slice to cut across the domain of personal work contracts.

Having thus established a multiplicity of dimensions for the analysis of the types or descriptions of personal work contracts, there is one further major step in the analysis which we now need to take. This consists of using this multidimensional analysis to complete the journey away from analysis strictly centred upon the contract of employment, and towards the construction of our family of personal work contracts. We shall seek to develop that construction in a spatial form. At the moment it seems to us that the analytical map of personal work contracts is essentially a one-dimensional one, perhaps best portrayed as a series of concentric circles with the contract of employment at its centre, occupying most of the total space.[81] There are then some outer rings or penumbra constituted of personal work contracts (or relationships) in which the working persons concerned fall outside the definition of 'employee' but within the looser definitions of 'worker' or 'person employed'. Beyond them is an outer darkness in which any personal work contracts or relationships not so included would simply be outside the realm of, and unknown to, employment law.

[80] Cf. *Byrne Brothers (Formwork) Ltd v. Baird* [2002] ICR 667, *Express & Echo Publications Ltd v. Tanton* [1999] ICR 693.
[81] Cf. H. Collins, K. Ewing, and A. McColgan (2005) *Labour Law: Text and Materials*, 2nd ed., Oxford: Hart Publishing, 172.

So this is the world of employment law mapped around the contract of employment; the less a given personal work contract or relationship fits or approximates to the central modality of the contract of employment, the further it moves to the periphery until it falls away entirely. Moreover, in this conception, the single dimension of movement is that from the subordination of the contract of employment to the autonomy of the independent contract for services. This accurately portrays the analysis which legislators and courts have recently followed and currently seem to follow. Collins (1990) argued for a two-dimensional or bi-axial way of drawing the boundaries of employment relations, the two dimensions being those of risk and bureaucratic control.[82] This was a very powerful insight, but he acknowledged that it would be hard to translate into a workable legal test for the presence or absence of an employment contract or relation that would be suitable for application by the courts,[83] and so, inevitably, it has proved to be.

What we propose instead is a rather larger and looser analytical framework for personal work contracts which will be multidimensional, an openly constructed sphere. It will be openly constructed in two senses; firstly, in the sense that it will have a porous exterior, less firmly ring-fenced from other associated kinds of contracts than is our existing diagram centered upon the contract of employment. We revert to that point later. More important at this stage is the way that the space inside this sphere is envisaged. It is not that there is a central core of that space reserved for the contract of employment, forming a planet around which other personal work contracts rotate. It is not even that there is a clearly defined shape which envelops the contract of employment and separates it from other personal work contracts. It is rather that there is free movement or access throughout that space to locate particular kinds or variants of personal work contracts within the various dimensions.

It is that facility of movement within a loose multidimensional framework which really permits the construction of a family of personal work contracts on a more free-thinking basis than has been possible within the existing contract of employment-centred scheme. There is no bright-line binary divide or partly or wholly rejected out-group within this family of contracts. It becomes easier in this construct to recognize specific typologies *within* the contract of employment; but, even more important, also to accept typologies which *transcend the boundaries* of the contract of employment. One could cite many instances of these transcendent typologies; some of the most important ones, as we shall discuss further in Chapter 4, are to be found in the dimension of duration and continuity. For example, fixed-term contracting may as well occur in the form of the contract of employment as in the form of the independent personal services contract. More controversially perhaps, we would take the view that 'umbrella' or 'global' contracts are not necessarily always contracts of employment, and that, on the other hand, task-limited or outcome-limited personal work contracts may quite readily take the form of contracts of employment, contrary

---

[82] H. Collins (1990) 'Independent Contractors and the Challenge of Vertical Disintegration to Employment Protection Laws', 10:3, *OJLS*, at 378.
[83] Ibid.

to the perception that task limitation or outcome limitation is a strong or even decisive indicator against a contract of employment.[84]

The 'family of personal work contracts' analysis thus serves to identify convergences between contract types which are normally perceived to be very distinct, especially between the contract of employment and the personal contract for services. It may also illuminate divergences between contract types which are usually treated as homogeneous; for example, we think it can be used to disentangle short-term, medium-term and long-term personal work contracts, a set of differences which we think has been unduly suppressed by a rather monolithic analytical approach to the contract of employment.

Having, we hope, in the course of this chapter established the basis for regarding 'the personal work contract' as a satisfactory definitional category for the primarily contractual part of our analysis of the legal construction of personal work relations, and having also, we hope, shown cause for not regarding that category as irrevocably split by the binary divide between contracts of employment and personal contracts for services, we are now almost ready to proceed with our detailed analysis of the family of personal work contracts which we have envisaged. There is just one preliminary issue about the organization of our analysis remaining to be resolved. It is the question of what if any role to accord to that binary divide, given that on the one hand we have questioned its standing, utility, and viability, but that on the other hand we have to accept that it is, for all its difficulties, deeply embedded and institutionalized in the existing law of personal work contracts, and indeed in the employment law systems (and social security and fiscal systems) of European countries at large.

In *The Personal Employment Contract*, the first author of the present work, at that stage working with the composite category of 'the personal employment contract' and the two sub-categories of the contract of employment and the 'semi-dependent worker's contract', despite having expressed scepticism about the binary divide, nevertheless judged it necessary 'to conduct our analysis of the law of personal employment contracts in a way which recognizes and adverts to these two sub-categories'.[85] This was for two reasons: firstly, because it was felt that there was a great disparity between the highly developed state of the law concerning contracts of employment and the much less developed state of the law concerning semi-dependent workers' contracts, and that 'an analysis which ignored that disparity would be a misleading one';[86] and secondly because 'much of the statute law of personal employment contracts makes and enforces that distinction'.[87] In the present work, we take a similar view. Indeed, we recognize this is an even greater necessity in the present work, because our overall definitional category – the

---

[84] Compare below, pp. 290–308, where we consider further whether and how far the formulation of a personal work contract around a particular task or assignment should be regarded as marking out that contract as being a personal work contract *other than* a contract of employment.

[85] M. Freedland (2003) *The Personal Employment Contract*, Oxford: OUP, at 31.

[86] Ibid.

[87] *op cit* at 31–2.

personal work contract – is a somewhat wider one, as accordingly is our second sub-category, that of the personal contract for services.

Nevertheless, in *The Personal Employment Contract*, the first author of the present work was rather concerned about: 'in part...reintroduc[ing] the very distinction between the contract of employment and the contract for services which was argued...to be such an unsatisfactory one'.[88] However, in the present work, operating from a comparative perspective and using the notion of the 'family of personal work contracts', we feel more confident about such an approach. From those fresh starting points, we can feel more certain that a partial re-admission of the two sub-categories might be not merely necessary but also productive. It will enable us to show how the law of personal work contracts can be regarded as a composition in which the grand themes are developed and articulated in the sphere of 'the contract of employment', while significant variations upon those themes occur in the sphere of 'the personal contract for services'. Not only does the study of those variations serve to avoid what would otherwise be an analytical omission with regard to personal contracts for services; it also enables us better to understand the composition as a whole, and to appreciate its central themes more fully. We hope to succeed in substantiating this claim in the four succeeding chapters.

---

[88] *op cit* at 32.

# 4

# The Formation and Structure
# of Contracts of Employment

## Introduction

In the previous chapter, we considered the ways in which, in English law and in that of other European countries, personal work relations are, generally speaking, constructed as contractual ones. We discussed the different meanings which the idea of contractual construction of personal work relations seems to bear in different legal systems; we sought to establish and define our definitional category of personal work contracts; we considered the standing of the binary divide by which that category is divided into the two sub-categories of contracts of employment and personal contracts for services; and we proposed a multidimensional method of analysis of personal work contracts which might deal with some of the difficulties attaching to the binary divide. In the rest of this Part of our work we start to develop that multidimensional analysis further, applying it on a comparative basis in order to try to understand the conditions of formation, the personal and organizational structure, and the economic structure of personal work contracts. We therefore consider in more precise detail the conditions of recognition of personal work contracts and the ways in which personal work relations or arrangements are regulated both by the imposition of those conditions or requirements and by the assignment of consequences to failures to meet those conditions or requirements.

As we explained in the previous chapter, although we take the view that personal work contracts should as far as possible be regarded as a family or group of contracts not fundamentally divided into contracts of employment and personal contracts for services, we shall nevertheless differentiate between those two categories. Despite our misgivings about the viability and normative suitability of this binary divide, we nevertheless make use of it as a tool of descriptive analysis; in this and the next two chapters we concentrate upon those personal work contracts which are regarded as contracts of employment. In order to give both a composite picture and a breakdown of the ways in which the formation and structure of contracts of employment are approached and regulated, we begin by considering the purpose and effect of the conditions of formation which are exacted for those contracts by the English and other European legal systems (Section 1), and we continue by sketching out the personal structures or models and the economic structures or models which are imposed upon those contracts by those legal systems (Sections 2 and 3).

# Section 1:  The Conditions of Formation of Contracts of Employment

## A.  The Nature and Functions of Conditions of Formation

In this section, we consider in a comparative way the functions and effects of the ways in which conditions of formation of contracts of employment are formulated in different European systems. This functional approach to conditions of formation is taken in conscious contrast to a classical approach in which the conditions of formation tend to be isolated from their intended and actual consequences. The classical approach, and our contrasting approach, both apply to the questions both of whether there is a contract at all and what kind of contract it is. But we are interested not only in whether a contract of employment, seen here as a particular kind of personal work contract, has been formed, but also in the issue of why those questions are being asked. This functional context is an ephemeral or changing one, whereas the classical approach seeks a decontextualized and as far as possible perpetual account of the conditions of formation. For example, the case-law about the duration of employment contracts is highly contextual; the early law about 'hirings' evolved in the context of battles between parishes about whether individuals had become entitled to support in and by a particular parish by reason of settlement therein on the basis of a hiring for a year or more.[1]

Moreover, we shall concentrate especially upon the intended and actual effects of failure to meet the conditions of formation. This is an extremely important and somewhat neglected set of regulatory issues. Some significant comparative contrasts present themselves; in the English system, there seems to be a tendency simply to leave the worker to bear the consequences of the conclusion that he or she does not have any kind, or a particular kind, of personal work contract, whereas in continental European systems there seems to be more of a tendency to make worker-protective corrections, e.g. by processes of 're-qualification', or by anyway preserving some of the intended effects of the personal work relationship or arrangement.

The law which determines the basic conditions for the valid formation of contracts has a different role in the context of personal work contracts, and contracts in employment in particular, from that which it has in relation to contracts in general. In the law of contracts in general, our concern with the basic conditions for the making of valid contracts is normally in order to know whether an enforceable contractual right or obligation has arisen. That may be our concern in the context

---

[1] For a detailed account of this system and its implications for the development of the law of the contract of employment, see S. Deakin and F. Wilkinson (2005) *The Law of the Labour Market*, Oxford: OUP, pp. 112–24.

of personal work contracts; but more often the function of the basic conditions will be to determine whether a claimant has a gateway to statutory employment rights which depend upon the existence of a valid personal work contract between the worker and the employing entity, or, especially, upon the existence of one particular type of personal work contract, the contract of employment. So, in the cases which are discussed in expositions of the law of contract in general, the basic conditions for the making of valid contracts are usually applied to particular promises, undertakings, or courses of conduct, in order to determine whether they might support an action in contract to enforce them. In the employment context, the basic conditions are more often applied to know whether a personal work relationship or arrangement, which has a factual existence, has assumed the character of a legally valid personal work contract and if so of which type.[2]

We can go one stage further, and assert that what we are accustomed to think of as the conditions or requirements for the formation of valid contracts constitute, in the case of employment contracts, stages in a process of regulation of personal work relations. This is a process by which legal effects and consequences are assigned to personal work relations or arrangements; but the process is an interactive one in which the assignment of legal effects and consequences both influences and is influenced by the practice of employing institutions and workers in the personal work arrangements which they make. So we can envisage an extensive continuum of requirements for the recognition of personal work contracts and rules about the effects of failures to meet those requirements, by means of which legal systems both shape and determine the legal consequences which they assign to personal work arrangements and, in turn, shape and influence the actual practice of making personal work arrangements. We shall argue that this continuum extends not only to the classical 'conditions of formation' of personal work contracts, and of contracts of employment in particular, but also to the treatment of vitiating factors such as conflict with legislation and public policy, and also, even more broadly, to the personal and economic structures which legal systems impute to or impose upon personal work contracts. We reserve consideration of those personal and economic structurings to a later section of this chapter, concentrating in this section upon requirements and vitiating factors.

In respect of these requirements and vitiating factors, some initial comparative contrasts can be drawn; these generally follow from theoretical observations which we have developed in earlier chapters. The 'gateway' function which the conditions of formation have in the English common law system of personal work contracts applies somewhat differently in many continental European Civilian-based systems, for in many such systems there is not the same differentiation between the contractual and the statutory layers of regulation; as previously explained, there tends to be the one 'thick' layer of combined contractual and statutory regulation, as the Italian expression 'prevalent concurring of statutory sources in the shaping of

---

[2] M. Freedland (2003) *The Personal Employment Contract*, Oxford: OUP, p. 60.

the contractual regulation[3] paradigmatically suggests. The conditions of formation of personal work contracts, and especially of contracts of employment, tend to apply to determine whether the personal work relations in question accede to that layer of regulation, a layer that the parties can only modify consensually '*in melius*', since it has the character of '*ordre public relatif, dit "social"*' (relative public policy, known as 'social').[4]

This leads on to a more fundamental dichotomy between two types of approach to the conditions of formation of personal work contracts. We will depict those two contrasting approaches, and we will offer the hypothesis that the contrasting approaches are taken respectively by the English common-law-based system and by many continental European Civilian-law-based systems. This contrast in approaches harks back to our general discussion in Chapter 2 about contrasting legal methodologies. The first approach tends to develop the conditions of formation of personal work contracts, and contracts of employment in particular, in a lightly regulatory way which aspires to neutrality as between workers and employing organizations. The second approach by contrast tends to develop the conditions of formation of personal work contracts, and of contracts of employment in particular, in a strongly regulatory and worker-protective way.

The first approach is one in which courts or tribunals develop or interpret the conditions of formation of personal work contracts in a way which basically defers to the choices of employing organizations and workers as to the ways in which they arrange or contract for their personal work relations. The conditions or requirements of formation of personal work contracts are applied by courts or tribunals to determine, *ex post* – that is to say after and in light of the arrangements the parties have themselves made – in order to determine whether a valid personal work contract has been made and of what type. According to this approach, courts or tribunals are not *a priori* concerned to coerce those arrangements into any or any particular contractual type. A clear example of this approach can be found in the remark made by Ralph Gibson LJ, that: 'A man is without question free under the law to contract to carry out certain work for another without entering into a contract of service. Public policy has nothing to say either way',[5] and, we may add, standard contractual reasoning by and large applies – with little or no modification – to the formation of personal work contracts.

The second approach is one in which courts or tribunals work with a more specifically predetermined set of contractual models and interpretative '*doctrines*' dictated by public policy considerations and deviating from standard contract law, in order to decide, *ex ante*, whether a valid personal work contract has been made, and of what type. The issues surrounding the '*qualification de contrat de travail*' (characterization as contract of employment) is not only a matter of public policy, but is actually a matter of '*ordre public social*', 'the mere will of the parties being powerless in

---

[3] E. Ghera (2007) *Diritto del Lavoro*, 16th ed., Bari: Cacucci p. 63. Our translation from the original '*prevalente concorso della fonte legale nella determinazione del regolamento contrattuale*'.
[4] J. Pélissier, A. Supiot, A. Jeammaud (2000) *Droit du Travail*, 20th ed., Paris: Dalloz, p. 93.
[5] *Calder v. Kitson Vickers & Sons (Engineers) Ltd* [1988] ICR 232, 250.

subtracting [the claimant in the case] from the social regime that necessarily springs from the conditions of performance of his work'.[6] This approach might, as thus described, appear to be a more exclusionary approach than the first one, more apt to produce the outcome that no personal work contract in general or no contract of employment in particular has been formed. However, as discussed above, this approach is typically coupled with the assumption or even an enacted rule that a personal work arrangement should or must be identified as a personal work contract of some kind, and indeed as a contract of employment in particular if the arrangement is in substance one for dependent employment.

A strong example of this dynamic is visible in Article 8.1 of the Spanish Workers' Statute, providing for a (rebuttable) legal presumption that personal work relations be treated as contracts of employment. The use of this presumption by Spanish courts is also paradigmatic of the legal dynamic hitherto described. 'The legal presumption is used in jurisprudential practice both to clarify finally as a work relation any relationship where there is an exchange of work for salary, but also frequently to attribute this same nature to agreements where there may be doubts about whether they should be framed under other contractual arrangements close to the contract of employment.'[7]

Though Italian law does not provide for a similarly explicit legal presumption, it is clear that the interpretative canons applying to the construction of the contract of employment fail to relate neatly to the general principles of contract law. As Edoardo Ghera argues, 'in general private autonomy can determine the concrete qualification of the contract... Vice versa, in the contract of employment the parties' will is prevented from severing subordination from statutory protection. Precisely because it cannot be severed from the legal type of the contract of subordinate employment, that in contrast with the other legal types presents itself as a rigid model or type for the mandatory regulation of *interests*, one can talk about the "non-negotiability of the legal type".'[8] The 'type' is therefore a *legal* one, more than a contractual one. The parties' contractual arrangements are certainly relevant, but public policy severely constrains their range of movement. For German courts 'only in borderline cases can account be taken of how the parties have labelled a particular contract'.[9] '[I]t has to be stated that [German] courts tend to extend the scope of labour law as far as possible.'[10] This approach has

---

[6] Ass. plén., 4 mars 1983, Bull. civ., Ass. plén., n° 3. Our translation from the original *'la seule volonté des parties étant impuissante à soustraire M. (....) au statut social qui découlait nécessairement des conditions d'accomplissement de son travail'*.

[7] A. Martín Valverde, F. Rodríguez-Sañudo Gutiérrez, and J. García Murcia (1996) *Derecho del Trabajo*, 5th ed., Madrid: Technos, p. 462. Our translation from the original.

[8] E. Ghera (2007) *Diritto del Lavoro*, 16th ed., Bari: Cacucci p. 66. Our translation from the original and of *'indisponibilità del tipo legale'*. Emphasis original.

[9] BAG of 8.6.1967, BAGE 19, 324, 330, in S. Deakin, P. Lele, and M. Siems (2007) 'The Evolution of Labour Law: Calibrating and Comparing Regulatory Regimes', Centre for Business Research, University of Cambridge Working Paper No. 352, September 2007, 6.

[10] M. Weiss and M. Schmidt (2008) *Labour Law and Industrial Relations in Germany*, AH Alphen aan den Rijn: Kluwer, 47.

an underlyingly worker-protective purpose or tendency, and can be clearly contrasted with the one adopted in English law.

It will be apparent that in either of these approaches, and especially in the second one, the process of application of conditions of formation of personal work contracts is very closely linked up with processes of classification and subclassification of those contracts. In particular, the differentiation of conditions of formation as between contracts of employment and personal contracts for services figures as an important regulatory technique, which may be deployed in an instrumental way. For this reason, it is appropriate for us to develop our discussion of conditions of formation in a way which recognizes that there are these two distinct regulatory contexts.

However, in accordance with the arguments which were advanced in the final section of the previous chapter, we suggest that it would be inappropriate and retrogressive to present a view of the formation and structure of personal work contracts as corresponding to a simple dichotomy between the contract of employment and the personal contract for services. We therefore make the point that not every personal work contract which is not a contract of employment is necessarily a personal contract for services; and we organize our discussion so that it concentrates initially and mainly upon contracts of employment – because it is mainly on that terrain that the law of personal work contracts has been and is mapped out – and so that it then continues by looking at the (more limited) material relating to personal contracts for services and other personal work contracts.

The arguments so far set out in this chapter suggest that it is useful to try to create a single discourse about the conditions of formation for personal work contracts in general, and within that discourse to distinguish as necessary between contracts of employment on the one hand and other personal work contracts, especially personal contracts for services, on the other hand; that we should consider the conditions of formation as constituting regulatory requirements, the significance of which can only satisfactorily be understood by reference to the consequences of failure to fulfil them; and that the imposition of conditions of formation forms part of a larger process of structuration of personal work contracts. On those assumptions, we proceed to examine the following kinds of conditions of formation for contracts of employment: contractual intention, capacity, restraint of trade, legality, and formality.

## B. Employment-Specific Contractual Intention

Within the law of personal work contracts there is a particular body of law or doctrine which deploys ideas about contractual intention to distinguish between the personal work relationships which do and do not give rise to valid personal work contracts. This body of law or doctrine corresponds to or covers the same ground as the general contract principles concerning intention to create legal relations and, to some extent, consideration; but it has become so specialized and functionally adapted to the demands of employment law that this is not a direct correspondence.

We therefore consider it under the heading of employment-specific contractual intention.

One important respect in which this specialized body of law fails to relate neatly to the general principles of contract law, is that, within this specialized body of law, the doctrines concerning contractual intention, on this one hand, and consideration, on the other hand, are interconnected in a particular, and more than normally complex, sense. This is mainly because of problems about the extent to which and the sense in which personal work contracts consist of an exchange of work and remuneration. We address that set of problems later in this chapter, when we consider further the internal and economic structure of employment contracts. Most of the issues concerning the requirement of consideration will be discussed under that heading; the present discussion is about contractual intention.

It will help to explain the relationship between contractual intention in general contract law, on the one hand, and in the law of personal work contracts, on the other hand, if we identify it in the former context as intention to create legal relations and in the latter context as intention to make a personal work contract, and, more particularly, as an intention to make a contract of employment or intention to make some other kind of personal work contract. The former terminology, sanctioned by customary usage in the discourse of contract law, really refers to an intention that a given transaction or relationship shall give rise to a legally binding contract of whatever sort. The latter is put forward here as meaning an intention that a personal work relationship shall give rise to a legally binding personal work contract in general or contract of employment in particular.

The best way of understanding this body of law, and the sense in which it is about the intention of the parties to a transaction or relationship, is to realize that neither the general doctrine of intention to create legal relations nor the law concerning intention to make a contract of employment simply envisages the presence or absence of the requisite contractual intention. Instead, they envisage the parties as choosing between alternative modes of conducting their transaction or relationship, only one of which gives rise to a contract in general or to a personal work contract in particular, and possibly to a contract of employment. It is this idea of choice between alternative modes of relationship which makes intention to create legal relations or intention to make a personal work contract, or a contract of employment, a distinct requirement for the making of valid contracts in general or personal work contracts, and contracts of employment, in particular. The requirement is that the parties to the transaction or relationship shall have intended to choose the contractual mode for the conduct of it, and furthermore shall have intended to choose the particular mode of the contract of employment for doing so.

At this stage it should perhaps be noted that different legal systems provide different doctrinal and jurisprudential adjustments aimed at accommodating these peculiar characteristics of the intention to create contractual personal work relationships. Arguably one of the most extreme examples of these national adjustments can be found in the Italian regulation of the so-called 'obligatory hiring of disabled workers benefitting from a reserved quota of jobs available in the enterprise'.[11] In these extreme cases the employer's will is radically limited both in respect of the intention to create a relationship and in respect of the intention to create it with a particular worker. However, even in respect of these hard cases, it is argued that: 'although the conclusion of the contract and its content are imposed by the force of statute and are not freely determined by the will of the parties', the law 'does not give rise to the elimination of the contract, but rather the imposition upon the entrepreneur of an obligation to stipulate a contract with the worker placed into work by the competent [job placement] authorities'.[12]

In this sense, intention to make a personal work contract is something more complex than simply a specialized version of intention to create legal relations. That is to say, the law concerning intention to make a personal work contract envisages a decidedly more complex series of alternative intentions than does the general law of intention to create legal relations. In the general law of contracts, intention to create legal relations is one of two alternative modes of transaction or relationship, the other being the rather quaintly styled 'agreement binding in honour only'. This evokes the notion of an agreement which does give rise to moral obligations of a certain kind but not to legal or contractual obligations (legal and contractual obligations being effectively equated for this purpose).

In the specific context of personal work relationships, the intention to make a personal work contract – that is to say, the choice to conduct the personal work relationship in the mode of a personal work contract – amounts in fact to a series of choices between quite an extensive set of alternatives, both within and beyond the domain of personal work contracts. The most important choice of alternative modes or models within the domain of personal work contracts is, in terms of orthodox analysis, between the contract of employment and a personal work contract which is not a contract of employment and therefore must be some kind of personal contract for services. We have previously discussed the way in which law-makers and adjudicators both formulate and decide upon the way that this particular choice is deemed to have been made.

But, especially for the purposes of English law, there is a further set of alternatives to the personal work contract mode, that is to say a set of situations in which the parties are regarded as having chosen a non-contractual mode for their personal work relations. These alternatives do not really come within the category of 'agreements binding in honour only'. They are variants on a theme to the effect that personal work relationships may be conducted on the footing of a set of obligations which are essentially looser, more diffuse, and less reciprocally related to each other than is the case with personal work contracts. Such obligations may amount to legal obligations of some kind – and this will often be the case in continental European systems; they may even amount to contractual obligations of some kind; but they are seen as not being sufficiently concrete and reciprocally

---

[11]  E. Ghera (2007) *Diritto del Lavoro*, 16th ed., Bari: Cacucci, pp. 309–14 (our translation).
[12]  Ibid. 62–3.

related to ground an intention to enter into a personal work contract, still less a contract of employment.

There are a number of groups of personal work relationships which, especially in English law, have at times been regarded as falling wholly or partly within that set of alternatives, and so not giving rise to personal work contracts, or at least not contracts of employment. These groups include, in various different senses, the work relationships of apprentices and trainees, holders of certain public or private offices or appointments, and voluntary workers.

## I. Apprentices and Trainees

The analysis, in terms of intention to make a personal work contract, of arrangements for apprenticeship, and for other varieties or combinations of work, work experience, and training, is indeed an interesting one. Various alternative constructions of such arrangements present themselves. Historically speaking, the relationship of master and apprentice gradually assumed a contractual character, especially in the course of the nineteenth century. In fact we can probably regard this as having happened earlier, and more decisively, than was the case with the relationship of master and servant. That was because of the very long-standing practice of embodying apprenticeship arrangements in the form of deeds or indentures of apprenticeship, a degree of formality deemed necessary for the mutual protection of the interests of the master or the apprentice or his parents.

The emerging contractual nature of this relationship developed clearly outside the notion of contract of service, precisely because of the judicial focus on the legal intentions of the parties.[13] The words of Dunn LJ in *Wiltshire Police Authority v. Wynn* are emblematic in this respect: 'Where the primary object of the contract is teaching or learning, then there is no contract of service. . . . The fact that the conditions of engagement are consistent with a contract of service is not decisive if the principal object of the relationship is teaching and learning.'[14] It would thus be erroneous to place emphasis 'on the terms of engagement of the police cadet rather than on the principal object of the relationship'.[15] This represents a situation, fairly uncommon in the practice of English employment law, where a personal work arrangement is analysed according to quite a highly preconceived, prestructured, and formalized contractual pattern.

The distinction between contract of service and contract of apprenticeship was eventually reflected in the statutory definition of the contract of employment, defined as 'a contract of service or apprenticeship'.[16] Nevertheless, a significant controversy remains with regard to formal traditional apprenticeship contracts as to whether they are to be regarded, at least, as a specific subset of the contract of employment or as their own special kind of personal work contract. This remains

---

[13] Cf. *Horan v. Hayhoe* [1904] 1 KB 288; *Wiltshire Police Authority v. Wynn* [1980] ICR 649.
[14] *Wiltshire Police Authority v. Wynn* [1980] ICR 649, 661.
[15] Ibid.
[16] ERA 1996, s. 230(1).

unresolved both in UK legislation and case-law. While some decisions have effectively recognized the contract of apprenticeships as a subset of the contract of employment,[17] some others have clearly failed to do so, and some have even rejected the possibility that the trainee might fall under the statutory definition of 'worker'.

The issues concerning personal work relationships with a strong or predominant element of training all presented themselves in the leading case of *Edmonds v. Lawson*[18] in which the Court of Appeal decided that a pupil barrister was not a 'worker' within the meaning of the National Minimum Wage Act 1998. The arrangement for pupillage was regarded as contractual in character, but not as amounting either to a contract of employment or to that wider category of personal work contract embodied in the statutory definition of the 'worker'.

It is, we suggest, both satisfactory and useful to consider the issue in that case as being that of whether the parties to the pupillage arrangement had the requisite intention to enter into a contract of employment or at least some other form of 'worker's' contract. At the same time, it must be admitted that the question could at least as well be regarded as the instrumental one of whether this was an arrangement to which the minimum wage legislation should apply. On that view, the appearance of a search for the 'contractual intention of the parties' might be a deceptive one. In 2006 the Court of Appeal further complicated this already intricate area of personal work contracts regulation by stating that 'If... the appellant was receiving less than the national minimum wage, it points to the agreement being one of apprenticeship',[19] effectively suggesting that 'receipt of less than the minimum wage can be consistent with apprenticeship'.[20] That is a perception which might be heightened in the case of the very many combinations of work and training in which agencies of the state or other funding bodies are involved.[21] In such instances, the nature and structure of the arrangement will generally have been prescribed by the state or other funding body to an extent which would render an analysis in terms of 'contractual intention' frankly fictitious.

This point is of considerable practical relevance, given that, particularly since the New Deals launched by the Labour government in 1998,[22] the making of arrangements for apprenticeship and job training – often referred to as the 'modern apprenticeship agreements' or 'modern apprenticeship pacts' – only rarely takes that traditional form. Instead we find more complex and less clearly delineated

---

[17] *Dunk v. George Waller & Son Ltd* [1970] 2 QB 163; *Wallace v. CA Roofing Services Ltd* [1996] IRLR 435.

[18] [2000] ICR 567 (CA).

[19] *Flett v. Matheson* [2006] ICR 673, 684.

[20] *Her Majesty's Commissioners for Revenue & Customs v. Rinaldi-Tranter* [2007] WL 3389518, para. 38.

[21] This set of issues already emerged with the Youth Training Scheme in the 1980s. Cf. *Hawley v. Fieldcastle & Co. Ltd* [1982] IRLR 223; *Daley v. Allied Suppliers Ltd* [1983] IRLR 13.

[22] M. Freedland, P. Craig, C. Jacqueson, and N. Kountouris (2007) *Public Employment Service and European Law*, Oxford: OUP, at 323.

combinations of work, work experience, training, and education.[23] It becomes much more difficult to determine whether such arrangements, which often involve state agencies interested in the provision of job training, constitute personal work contracts of any kind and if so of what kind. As noted by the EAT in *Thorpe v. Dul*,[24] 'the modern apprenticeship agreement in this case is not a contract of apprenticeship ... the funds for paying [the trainee] came from the Learning and Skills Council through the college'.[25]

On the other hand, even in such instances there is no shortage of illustrations of a marked preference in recent times, on the part of those devising such complex and multilateral arrangements, for combining work and training, to cast those arrangements in contractual terms, and to ascribe contractual intention to those involved in them.[26] The results are sometimes rather tentative and inconclusive. The EAT has affirmed that 'despite use of the description "employer" it is clear that the true purpose of the agreement and the intention of all ... parties to it, was not that [the trainee] should be employed in her work placement'.[27] But it has also admitted that whilst it is 'hard to imagine a case in which a worker would be found to have no recognized status at all ..., trainees are difficult to classify, and we do not think it appropriate to come to a conclusion on this issue'.[28] This is arguably an area in which the benefits of the broader scope of application of anti-discrimination statutes, and of the Working Time Regulations 1998,[29] applying as they do to trainees who are employed neither under a contract of service nor a contract of apprenticeship, could progressively start to emerge. So even in such a context, the analysis in terms of intention to make a particular kind of personal work contract remains a useful one – though such discussions stray well beyond the confines of the contract of employment as such.

This analysis can be usefully contrasted with the rather more predictable and structured approach of some – but certainly not all – continental European jurisdictions, where the pre-characterization of these arrangements as particular types of contracts of employment is far more evident. French law – which until 1971 considered apprentices as parties to a *'contrat d'éducation'*[30] (contract for education) rather than one of employment – has since become clear about the fact that the 'contract of apprenticeship is a contract of employment of a particular type'.[31] The trainee is thus a 'salaried worker ... benefitting ... from the totality

[23] R. Walker and M. Wiseman (2003) 'Making Welfare Work: UK Activation Policies Under New Labour', 56 *Iss Rev* 3. For a 'quadripartite' agreement cf. *Her Majesty's Commissioners for Revenue & Customs v. Rinaldi-Tranter* [2007] WL 3389518.

[24] [2003] ICR 1556.

[25] [2003] ICR 1571.

[26] *Flett v. Matheson* [2006] EWCA Civ 53; *Wilson t/a Reds v. Lamb* [2007] WL 2817984.

[27] *Her Majesty's Commissioners for Revenue & Customs v. Rinaldi-Tranter* [2007] WL 3389518 para 33.

[28] *Her Majesty's Commissioners for Revenue & Customs v. Rinaldi-Tranter* [2007] WL 3389518 para 19.

[29] Working Time Regulations 1998, reg. 42, applying to 'non-employed trainees'.

[30] Loi du 16 julliet 1971.

[31] Article L 6221-1 Code du Travail. 'Le contrat d'apprentissage est un contrat de travail de type particulier.'

of labour legislation and collective agreements to the extent that they are not incompatible with his status'.[32] Nor do the more recent *'contrats aidés'* (subsidised contracts) modify this fundamental choice of French labour law. The *'contrat d'avenir'* (contract for one's future) for instance clearly provides that those working under it are covered by 'a private law fixed-term contract of employment concluded under Article L. 1242–3' of the Labour Code.[33]

The German situation is arguably more complex, but ultimately well illustrated by the few cases on the status of Turkish nationals undertaking training in Germany referred to the European Court of Justice (ECJ). As Weiss and Schmidt pointed out, 'technically speaking, the contract between an apprentice and an employer is not a labour contract. But according to [legislation] the rules and principles governing the labour contract are to be applied'.[34] Section 10(2) of the *Berufsbildungsgesetz* (Vocational Training Act) of 2005,[35] provides that: 'The legal provisions and principles governing contracts of employment shall apply to initial training contracts, insofar as this is not incompatible with the nature and purpose of the contract and the provisions of this Act.'

This ambivalence has been stigmatized by the ECJ on a number of occasions. The Court, in defining the concept of 'worker' for the purposes of EU free movement legislation, affirmed that a person engaged in 'activities which ... have been carried out in the course of vocational training [or] periods of apprenticeship in an occupation that may be regarded as practical preparation related to the actual pursuit of the occupation in question' must be considered to be a 'worker',[36] and that the fact that 'the remuneration of the person concerned is provided using public funds' cannot 'have any consequence in regard to whether or not the person is to be regarded as a worker'.[37] The tendency therefore seems to be towards regulating these 'training contracts' by analogy to ordinary contracts of employment, whilst being clear that they constitute a *sui generis* kind of personal work contract.

## II. Public Office-Holders and Appointees

The English common-law-based system is unusual, by contrast with continental European Civil-law based systems, in the extent to which it has tended to leave the legal status of public office-holders and appointees as an open issue dependent primarily on judicial analyses as to the presence or absence of personal-work-specific contractual intention. There seems to be a generally increasing readiness to find

---

[32] J. Pélissier, A. Supiot, A. Jeammaud (2000) *Droit du Travail*, 20th ed., Paris: Dalloz, at 227.

[33] Cf. Article L 5134-41 *Code du Travail*. Similarly, for the *'contrat de professionnalisation'* and the *'contrat initiative-emploi rénové'*, cf. respectively Articles L 6325-1 and L 5134-69.

[34] M. Weiss and M. Schmidt (2008) *Labour Law and Industrial Relations in Germany*, AH Alphen aan den Rijn: Kluwer, p. 70.

[35] Of 23 March 2005, *Federal Law Gazette* [BGBl.], Part I, 931 (our translation).

[36] Case C-188/00, *Bülent Kurz (né Yüce) v. Land Baden-Württemberg* [2002] ECR I-10691, para [33].

[37] Case C-1/97, *Birden v. Stadtgemeinde Bremen* [1998] ECR I-7747, para [28].

such personal-work-specific contractual intention in the personal work relations of public office-holders and appointees, but such a tendency has to be understood by reference to the regulatory contexts in which those analyses take place.

We should begin by observing that office-holding is not usually viewed as actually being incompatible with the existence of a personal employment contract, and indeed that such a notion of incompatibility as may have existed in the past seems to be fast diminishing. In *R v. Civil Service Appeal Board, ex p Bruce*,[38] a case in which – quite ironically – it was the Crown that was seeking to establish the existence of a contract of employment to defeat the judicial review claim of the civil servant, the abstract possibility of the creation of a contract of employment was firmly acknowledged. Nevertheless, office-holding still retains quite some importance as an alternative legal account of certain personal work relationships, and precisely as a consequence of the emphasis placed by courts on the intention of the parties. In *ex p Bruce* the Divisional Court concluded that while the 'contractual elements of offer and acceptance and consideration were all present...a fourth element must be present, namely, an intention to create legal relations on the part of the parties' – which did not appear to be present in the case before it.[39]

The idea of office-holding as a non-contractual, or even at times a counter-contractual, way of conceptualizing some personal work relationships involves a number of factors, some or all of which are encountered in each of the particular personal work relationships in question, and which interact with each other. The most important of these factors seem to be:

(1) that any payment which the office-holders receive is made by virtue of their holding the office in question rather than in respect of work done, so that there is not a contractual exchange of work and payment; (2) that office-holders are appointed to occupy positions within institutional structures rather than being employed by an employing entity in the contractual sense; and (3) that the office-holding is governed by a normative regime with some other basis or starting point than the contractual one.

With regard to civil servants, there was for a very long time a considerable degree of uncertainty as to whether and when the presence of such factors resulted in the absence of intention to embody the relationship between the civil servant and the Crown in a personal work contract of any kind or a contract of employment in particular; but the prevailing view seemed to be that there was no such intention, particularly because the civil servant, although enjoying considerable de facto security of tenure, was (and still is) technically speaking employed 'at pleasure', that is to say susceptible to dismissal at will. With the rapid growth in the 1960s and 1970s of statutory employment rights generally confined to employees working under contracts of employment, the contractual status of civil servants would have become a very contentious issue indeed, had not that question been largely side-

---

[38] [1988] ICR 649.
[39] Ibid 665.

stepped by legislative provisions extending the principal statutory employment rights to civil servants regardless of their contractual status.

If this meant that the contractual status of civil servants was not to be the determinant of their key statutory rights, it did not however mean that their contractual status ceased to be important. That issue of contractual status assumed a different, but still very significant, function in the 1980s; as the jurisdictional and conceptual separation between public law and private law became a more pronounced one, the contractual status of civil servants figured as a crucial element in decisions as to whether the common law rights and obligations of civil servants sounded in the public law of judicial review of administrative action or in the private law of the contract of employment. The outcome of that debate was an increasingly firm attribution of specific contractual intention to the personal work relations of civil servants.[40] There have certainly been many indications of a growing contractual mentality on the part of government departments with regard to the personal work relations of civil servants; it would seem fair to say that this has coincided with a judicial perception that the conceptual and practical apparatus of judicial review does not provide the appropriate regime for the resolution of employment disputes concerning civil servants.

A similar approach has manifested itself with regard to other public office-holders or appointees whose personal work relations can convincingly be approximated to an employment model; this seems to have progressed to the point where it is only the holding of judicial office or the office of constable (whether as a police officer or as a prison officer) which is generally regarded as being incompatible with a specific contractual intention. Other public office-holders or appointees seem very readily to be regarded as employees with contracts of employment, and that conclusion is not incompatible with the existence of statutory incidents to their personal work relations which confer some kind of special tenure. For example, the remnants of academic tenure which are still maintained by or under special statutory provision are certainly not viewed as inconsistent with a specifically contractual[41] view of academic employment.

There have been similar indications in the case-law in which, over the corresponding time period, the question of the contractual status of relations between independent professional office-holders or appointees and public authorities has been under consideration. In a pair of leading cases in which the primary alternatives in contention were that the independent professional either had a public service work relationship or a contract for services with the public authority, the courts certainly on both occasions decided that the relationship was one of private law rather than of public law, though in that case they preferred to regard it as a private law statutory relationship, rather than as a contract for

---

[40] M. Freedland, 'Contracting the Employment of Civil Servants – a Transparent Exercise?' (1995) 87 PL 224.

[41] The provisions in question are those of s. 202–208 of the Education Reform Act 1988, concerning academic tenure. The contractual view is visible for example in *University of Nottingham v. Eyett* [1999] IRLR 87.

services.[42] But once more this is an area in which no definitive and concluding answer can be expected from the existing case-law.[43]

The development of case-law concerning the employment status of ministers of religion probably provides the clearest illustration of the trends which we have discerned in the evolution of thinking about work-specific contractual intention. It used to be in this context that there was the strongest disposition to regard office-holding as fundamentally different from and even incompatible with contractual employment status and therefore to attribute an absence of intention to create legal contractual relations.[44] In recent years, and in a legislative context where most statutory employment rights depend upon this question, there has been a new willingness to accept the existence of the requisite intention for the formation of contracts of employment between ministers of religion and the religious institution for or within which they work.[45]

In these various situations of public or religious office-holding or appointment, we can thus see that English law makes some use of notions of work-specific contractual intention in order to decide how to construct and how to regulate these personal work relations where the bonds between the working person and the institution are at once too strong and too weak to fit easily into the stereotype of the personal work relation constructed as a contract of employment. That is to say, the bonds are too strong because the expectations of loyalty and commitment to public or religious service are so great as to confer upon the working person a status which is in some sense or other specially protected; but on the other hand the bonds are too weak in the sense that it is often regarded as inappropriate to regard them as sufficiently concrete or materialistic to amount to or be enforceable as contractual ones.

In most continental European legal systems, there is much less need to rely on subtle constructions of work-specific contractual intention in order to decide whether and how far such public office-holders and appointees enjoy employment rights, because in those systems special statuses or regimes have usually evolved for such offices or appointments, and those special statuses or regimes concretize the differences between those personal work relations and the ones which are embodied in contracts of employment. For instance in Italy laws such as the Law of 23 October 1992, n. 421, Law 15 March 1997, n. 59 and Legislative Decree 30 March 2001, n.165, produced what some authors have usefully defined as the 'contractualisation of work relationships with public administrations and their subjection to the norms of the Civil Code and special laws'.[46] The 2008 White Paper on the Future of the Public Service noted how France remains strongly anchored to a 'public law treatment' of the personal work relations of the 'agents

---

[42] *R v. Derbyshire County Council ex parte Noble* [1990] ICR 810 (CA), *Roy v. Kensington and Chelsea Family Practitioner Committee* [1992] 1 AC 624.

[43] Cf. *Lincolnshire County Council and Another v. Hopper* [2002] ICR 1301.

[44] *Diocese of Southwark v. Coker* [1998] ICR 140.

[45] *Percy v. Church of Scotland* [2005] UKHL 73, *New Testament Church of God v. Stewart* [2007] IRLR 178.

[46] E. Ghera (2007) *Diritto del Lavoro*, 16th ed., Bari: Cacucci, 22. Our translation.

employed by public operators for the purposes of executing a public service of administrative character.... Nothing similar [occurs] in Italy, the United Kingdom, and, to a lesser extent, in Germany, where the majority of such agents are regulated by common labour law and collective agreements.'[47]

For its part, the Spanish Law 7 of 2007 – the Basic Statute for Public Servants – introduced a very strongly articulated distinction between different classes of civil servants and public sector workers based on the type of personal work arrangement applying to their employment relationship. As such the Statute draws a main distinction, within the broad 'public servants' category, between '*functionarios de carrera*' (career civil servants) and other classes of '*personal laboral*' (working personnel).[48] The former remain 'linked to a Public Authority through a statutory relation regulated by Administrative Law',[49] and are the only ones that can exercise 'the functions that imply the direct or indirect participation in the public powers or the safeguard of the general interests of the State and of the Public Administration'.[50] Article 11 of the Law describes as '*personal laboral*' whoever 'by virtue of a contract of employment formalized in writing ... provides remunerated services for the public administrations'.[51]

## III. Volunteers

In recent years, arrangements for voluntary work by 'volunteers' have assumed an increasing importance in the labour market, which can be associated with a general growth of a mixed public and private and charitable services sector. This increasing importance is also linked to an increase in the labour supply for voluntary work from a growing number of retired workers wishing to remain economically or socially active, and furthermore attributable to an increased use of various combinations of voluntary work with work experience and training as methods of obtaining initial access to the labour market or of maintaining a preliminary footing in a particular occupation or sector. As a result, issues of whether and when volunteers are working under personal work contracts in general and contracts of employment in particular, so as to entitle them to statutory employment rights including employment equality rights, have assumed quite a crucial significance.

Although it is the absence of remuneration as such which identifies personal work arrangements of these kinds as volunteering in the first place, the line between volunteering and paid employment has been increasingly blurred by arrangements for payment of expenses, sometimes on a generous basis. In those circumstances,

---

[47] J.-L. Silcani (2008) *Livre Blanc sur l'Avenir de la Fonction Publique*, Paris: La documentation Francaise, 44. Our translation. For a comprehensive and updated analysis of some of these issues see A. De Becker (2011) 'The Legal Status of Public Employees or Public Servants: Comparing the Regulatory Frameworks in the United Kingdom, France, Belgium, and The Netherlands', 32 *CLLPJ*, 101.
[48] Art. 8.
[49] M. de Sande Pérez-Bedmar (2007) 'El Estatuto Básico del Empleado Público: Comentario al Contenido en Espera de su Desarollo' 18, *Relaciones Laborales*, 58. Our translation.
[50] Ibid.   [51] Ibid.

arguments against contractual status for such arrangements based upon the absence of consideration have tended to fall away; and the discussion of work-specific contractual intention in cases of volunteering is a rather indecisive and casuistic one. A new line of argument seems recently to have been introduced into this discussion, since it has been held that a voluntary worker did not have a personal work contract such as to qualify her for employment equality rights, in that the personal work relation in question, although perhaps giving rise to some kind of unilateral contracts for work actually performed, did not display sufficient continuing mutuality of obligation to constitute a contract of employment or other contract personally to execute any work or labour.[52] A similar conclusion was reached by the EAT and the Court of Appeal in *X v. Mid Sussex Citizens Advice Bureau*, where a volunteer offering legal advice under a voluntary agreement 'binding in honour only', was found 'not [to] owe sufficient or any obligations to the bureau in relation to the provision of her services to create any mutuality of obligation', and thus to fall outside the scope of disability discrimination legislation, both domestic and European.[53]

This steers the debate towards two different directions. The first one points at what we define as the economic structure of personal work contracts, and we return to it later under that heading. The second one revolves around the concepts of 'worker' and 'employment and occupation', as referred to in European anti-discrimination legislation, and whether these concepts ought to include personal work relations of a voluntary nature, an issue to which we return in Chapter 10. For the time being, and for the sake of completeness, we ought to point out that the Equality Act 2010 may provide some relief to volunteers under English law, in the different sense that, according to the Equality and Human Rights Commission (EHRC), the latter may be considered as 'service users'.[54]

We may conclude this discussion of work-specific contractual intention with the comparative observation that this whole approach to the contractual status of volunteering might seem unfamiliar and surprising to continental European legal sensibilities. In a number of such systems, a clearer line is drawn between remunerated contractual employment and voluntary work, which is regarded as simply in a different category of activity, as such subject to its own distinctive regime. This line tends to be policed quite actively by the judiciary. Since 'gratuitous performance can cast a strong suspicion of fraud',[55] 'the courts remain very cautious about assigning an altruistic character to such activity, and impose an

---

[52] *South East Sheffield Citizens Advice Bureau v. Grayson* [2004] ICR 1138 (EAT).

[53] *X v. Mid Sussex Citizens Advice Bureau* [2010] ICR 429, confirmed in *X v. Mid Sussex Citizens Advice Bureau* [2011] EWCA Civ 28.

[54] Section 29 of the Equality Act 2010, cf. EHRC: 'Your rights to equality from voluntary and community sector organizations (including charities and religion or belief organizations) – Vol 3' (July 2010).

[55] E. Ghera (2007) *Diritto del Lavoro*, 16th ed., Bari: Cacucci, 55. For a reconstruction of the Italian debate cf. C. Cester (ed.) (2007) *Il Rapporto di Lavoro Subordinato: Costituzione e Svolgimento – II*, Milano: Wolters Kluwer Italia Giuridica, pp. 150–69.

extensive conception of remunerated work'.[56] In more recent times some systems have actually stopped worrying about the possible misuses of voluntary work and have actually sought to address directly the regulation of what have effectively become highly regulated personal work contracts.

France is a paradigmatic example of this tendency. With the introduction of Law no. 2006-586 of 23 May 2006 on volunteering and engagements for education, the foundations were laid for the recognition of a 'a volunteering contract that does not carry a link of legal subordination'[57] and that is normally not expected to last more than two years.[58] The legislation provides for the payment of an 'indemnity' to the voluntary worker and caters for a large number of benefits and entitlements.[59] This law followed the introduction of another set of special provisions on other forms of voluntary work, such as those of Law no. 2005-159 of 23 February 2005 on the voluntary work contract for international solidarity, and *Ordonnance* no. 2005-883 of 2 August 2005 on voluntary work in the armed forces for young unemployed workers.

Comparative analysis would thus appear to suggest the emergence of a new category of personal work contracts applying to 'voluntary workers'. The latter category encompasses a vast range of personal work relationships in which the parties manifest a contractual intention to establish a relationship in which a quid pro quo is indeed understood to be in place, albeit perhaps in terms that differ from the canonical exchange of wage for labour, but by reference to training, benefits in kind, and sometimes monetary compensation. A 2007 consultation document produced by the UK Department of Trade and Industry (DTI) acknowledged the possibility of distinguishing between 'voluntary workers' and 'volunteers',[60] but it maintained that the current exclusions from minimum wage provided by s. 44 of the Minimum Wage Act 1998 should be kept in place and, if anything, extended to 'apply to people who participate in the national framework for youth volunteering'.[61]

In this section, we have examined the central conditions of formation of contracts of employment, that is to say the conditions which identify the basic model of what is required for the formation of a contract of employment. We have devised and presented a notion of employment-specific intention as a conceptual umbrella under which to group together the various ideas which are used for this identification. We have suggested that English law has a relatively fluid approach to the ascertainment of employment-specific intention, in some contrast to other European

---

[56] J. Pélissier, A. Supiot, A. Jeammaud (2000) *Droit du Travail*, 20th ed., Paris: Dalloz, 162. Cf. J. Savatier (2000) 'Entre bénévolat et salariat: le statut des volontaires pour le dévelopement', *Droit Social*, 146 (our translation).

[57] Article 1, *Loi n 2006-586 du 23 mai 2006 relative au volontariat associatif et à l'engagement éducatif.*

[58] Ibid., Article 7.

[59] Including a right to an '*indemnité*'. Cf. ibid., Article 9.

[60] DTI, 'National Minimum Wage and Voluntary Workers – Consultation Document (June 2007), 10.

[61] Ibid. 5, 18–21. Cf. G. Davidov (2009) 'A Purposive Interpretation of the National Minimum Wage Act' (2009) 72(4), *MLR*, 581, 596.

labour law systems which tend to take a rather more rigidly taxonomical approach. In the next section, we pursue this comparative inquiry by considering other factors in the legal regulation of the making of contracts of employment, factors which come into play once the basic identification of employment-specific intention has taken place.

## Section 2:  Other Factors in the Making of Contracts of Employment

Our focus in this Section is upon doctrines or provisions which, while not identifying the basic model for the formation of contracts of employment in the way that employment-specific intention does, nevertheless operate as factors in the legal regulation of the making of contracts of employment. Under that heading, we look firstly at vitiating factors consisting of illegality or conflict with public policy (subsection A) and secondly at the requirement of formality or for the provision of information in or associated with the making of such contracts (subsection B). Our main line of comparative argument will be that, whereas there is a fair degree of convergence between European labour law systems as to the requirements which are imposed by these doctrines or provisions, there is nevertheless quite significant divergence as to the effects which are accorded to failure to fulfil these requirements. We shall suggest that those divergences are indicators of differing degrees of worker-protectiveness in the application of those substantive requirements, and that this observation may represent a useful comparative finding.

## A.  Illegality and Other Vitiating Factors

### *I.  Illegality and Vitiating Factors in General*

We can identify a number of doctrines of contract law which create factors vitiating the validity or enforceability of personal work contracts. Most important among these are doctrines concerning illegality and compliance with public policy; in Western European legal systems, doctrines concerning capacity have largely lost their original importance. In the context of personal work contracts, the most significant aspects of illegality are those of working as an immigrant without entitlement to work and working under arrangements tending to evade taxation. The most significant aspect of compliance with public policy concerns the doctrine of restraint of trade.

These factors vary in the degree to which they are concerned with, on the one hand, the protection of the particular worker who is the subject of the personal work arrangement in question, or, on the other hand, the protection of societal interests more generally, including the integrity of the legal system as a forum, for the enforcement of obligations, which might be jeopardized by the entertaining of claims arising from relations tainted by illegality or conflict with public policy. For example, doctrines concerning capacity are primarily worker-protective; some areas of illegality such as that of illegal immigration are primarily concerned with the general protection of society; some doctrines of public policy such as that of restraint of trade are equivocal as between the particular interest of the worker and the general interest of society, or the smooth functioning of the market.

This variation in worker-protectiveness can be seen as having consequences for the effects which are accorded to the vitiating factors. The more that the vitiating factor has a worker-protective function, the more it becomes appropriate to regard the vitiating factor as not depriving the worker of the opportunity to rely on the contract as valid, and to enforce, in whole or in part, the rights or claims which it confers upon him or her. However, even at the worker-protective end of that spectrum, there may still be a perceived problem about the integrity of the legal system in enforcing or giving effect to legally tainted arrangements or contracts.

Even where the vitiating factor does not have a worker-protective function, the contrary problem is encountered, namely that a finding of contractual invalidity or unenforceability by reason of a vitiating factor is apt completely to undermine the whole structure of statutory protection of workers. That is especially true in a system, such as the English system of employment law, where statutory employment rights and equality rights in employment tend to be conditioned upon the existence of a valid personal work contract, often indeed a contract of employment as such. Courts and tribunals may hesitate, in the face even of an illegality or conflict with public policy which has no worker-protective function, to allow a worker to be comprehensively outlawed from employment rights and equality rights associated with employment.

It should already be evident that the regulatory demands and pressures, in this area of regulation of personal work contracts, are complex ones. So far as illegality is concerned, we can find or postulate a trend to treat lack of personal entitlement to work as fairly comprehensively negating personal work contractual rights and status, especially as working without personal entitlement to do so or employing a worker to do so is more and more intensely and comprehensively criminalized by immigration legislation. The case of tax fraud is a far more finely balanced one, in which the regulatory pressures interact with each other in a more complex way. The question of how far the worker is or should be treated as complicit in the tax evasive aspects of his or her personal work arrangements becomes an especially intractable one when the tax evasion consists of presenting a personal work relation as one of self-employment by the worker when it should properly have been presented as one of employment under a contract of employment. That is especially understandable in view of the inherent difficulty of drawing the distinction between employment and self-employment to which we have previously referred.

There are many adjudicatory techniques which courts and tribunals can and do draw upon in order to hold this balance; they can, for instance, consider whether the contract was illegal 'as formed' or 'as performed', the latter not vitiating the contract from the outset; or they can look at the extent of the worker's involvement in the mispresentation of the character of the arrangement or contract. The elaboration of such techniques of casuistry has progressed to the point where there is controversy as to whether this should be recognized as an overtly discretionary process of adjudication, despite dogmatic denials that this could be the case.[62]

In the discussion and development of the law of illegality as a factor vitiating personal work contracts, there does not seem to be any generic difference between its application to contracts of employment and, on the other hand, to other personal work contracts. But that perception may reflect nothing more substantial than the relative paucity of case-law concerning the effect of illegality upon personal work contracts other than contracts of employment. As this latter category is itself more of a residuary or exclusionary one than is the category of the contract of employment, and as presence in this category gives much inferior access to employment rights, there might turn out to be a greater judicial willingness to grant admission to the category by limiting the impact of this vitiating factor upon it.

In comparative terms, we can observe that continental European legal systems seem to have as their starting point a more firmly dogmatic doctrine of nullity by reason of illegality, so far as the general law of contract is concerned. However, this is significantly moderated by techniques for treating vitiating factors as resulting only in prospective unenforceability rather than retrospective invalidity. Moreover, there seems in some such systems to be a willingness to deploy such techniques in an overtly worker-protective way in the sphere of personal work contracts. In this respect, well-developed notions of 're-characterization' of contracts may improve the facility for worker-protective responses to the presence of vitiating factors, especially when those factors themselves consist of misrepresentation of personal work contracts as between the different contract types.

The rather dogmatic starting point of continental European systems is aptly represented by the stance of Italian contract law that considers illegality, often termed as *illceità* (wrongfulness),[63] as a vitiating factor affecting one or more elements of the contract often by reference to 'imperative norms', and triggering *nullità* (nullity) which itself is, along with '*annullabilità*' (annullability) (similar but broader than the English notion of 'voidability') and '*rescindibilità*' (rescindibility), one of the three main general types of contractual invalidity.[64] Similarly French contract law sees nullity, in its two forms of *nullité totale* (total nullity) and *nullité partielle* (partial nullity), as the general sanction for the 'inobservance of the rules of formation and validity of contracts',[65] with the notion of 'total nullity' being strongly linked to the concepts of '*ordre public*' and illicitness of cause and object.[66] According to Sabbath: 'in the civil law countries, rescission of a voidable contract has the effect of rendering the contract void *ab initio*, whereas in the English system

---

[62] M. Pilgerstorfer and S. Forshaw, 'A Dog's Dinner? Reconsidering Contractual Illegality in the Employment Sphere' (2008) 37 *ILJ*, 279.

[63] But on the possible distinction between the two see P. Cendon (ed.) (1997) *Commentario al Codice Civile, vol 4 artt. 1173–1645*, Torino: Utet, 1997, 729.

[64] Cf. Chapter 12 in M. Bianca, *Diritto Civile Vol 3, Il Contratto*, 2nd ed. Milano: Giuffré, 609. A slightly different taxonomy is provided by Chapter XXXVII in A. Torrente and P. Schlesinger (2007) *Manuale di Diritto Privato*, 18th ed., Milano: Giuffre, 587.

[65] B. Starck, H. Roland, and L. Boyer (1998) *Droit Civil – Les Obligations 2. Contrat*, 6th ed, Paris: Litec, 353.

[66] B. Nicholas (1992) *The French Law of Contract*, 2nd ed., Oxford: Clarendon Press, 128.

the repudiated agreement is treated by the law as having terminated from the date of such repudiation'.[67]

The divergence between English law and continental European systems in respect of illegality and invalidity becomes more marked when analysed in the more specific context provided by employment contracts. It has been noticed that in English law 'the general rules governing the application of the doctrine of illegality to claims based in contract apply equally when the contract concerned is one of employment'.[68] Indeed, in the employment sphere, general contract law principles apply not only to breach of contract claims 'but also to claims enforcing statutory employment rights where the existence of a legally valid and enforceable contract of employment is a statutory pre-condition to the right'.[69] Employment contracts are thus subject to the very same notion of illegality and invalidity as standard commercial contracts, anchored to the '*ex turpi*' maxim,[70] although in recent years English courts and tribunals have sought to liberate themselves from its stranglehold.[71]

By contrast most continental systems display a number of peculiarities when it comes to declaring contracts of employment null and void. These peculiarities, in their different forms, all pursue the rather specific policy aim of preserving those effects of the illegally formed contract that may benefit the worker. This public policy aim acts as a corollary to the general labour law principle of *favor* for the worker.[72] This outcome is often pursued by means of subtle distinctions between different grounds of illegality. A paradigmatic example is the French notion of '*ordre public*', 'confusing to the English lawyers... [as it brings together] ideas between which he does not normally see a connection'.[73] French lawyers further 'distinguish between a traditional *ordre public*... and... *ordre public économique et social*... [which] is more likely to be relevant to the question of excluding an objectionable term from a contract or including one which is required by, for example, the policy of protecting the weaker party to a bargain',[74] and typically a contract of employment. Nicholas lucidly attributed the inability of English law to achieve a similar distinction to the fact that 'we still see statutes as isolated

---

[67] E. Sabbath (1964) 'Effects of Mistake in Contracts: A Study in Comparative Law', 13, *The International and Comparative Law Quarterly*, 803.

[68] M. Pilgerstorfer and S. Forshaw (2008) 'A Dog's Dinner? Reconsidering Contractual Illegality in the Employment Sphere', 37 *ILJ*, 279.

[69] Ibid.

[70] *Hall v. Woolston Hall Leisure* [2000] IRLR 578; S. Forshaw and M. Pilgerstorfer (2005) 'Illegally Formed Contracts of Employment and Equal Treatment at Work', *ILJ*, 158.

[71] *Enfield Technical Services Limited v. Payne*; *BF Components Limited v. Grace* [2008] IRLR 500. But see the general acceptance of the status quo as expressed in The Law Commission, 'The Illegality Defence' (March 2010).

[72] E. Ghera (2007) *Diritto del Lavoro*, Bari: Cacucci, 66.

[73] B. Nicholas (1992) *The French Law of Contract*, 2nd ed., Oxford: Clarendon Press, 129.

[74] Ibid., 130.

irruptions into the ordered framework of the Common law, each perhaps giving effect to a policy, but embodying as a whole no general ideas'.[75]

Lord Wedderburn caustically noted that the Italian concept of 'inderogability *in pejus*' 'is (unhappily) deeply offensive to classical common law "freedom of contract"'.[76] It is interesting to explore how inderogability, and the corollary doctrine of '*sostituzione automatica delle clausole difformi*' (automatic substitution for non-compliant clauses) interact with the doctrine of illegality to create a framework effectively aimed at rescuing the validity of essential aspects of contracts of employment in the presence of invalidating elements. Admittedly, if the object of the contract itself is illicit – as it would be if for 'activities prohibited by criminal law or for immoral performances'[77] – then 'common contract law principles, and article 2126(1) of the Civil Code exclude the conservation of the effects of the invalid contract'.[78] However if a contract is set up as a sham arrangement aimed at evading tax and social security obligations, the application of Article 2126 will effectively invalidate both the simulated and the dissimulated contracts, but, 'where possible [there will be] an automatic substitution with the imperative regulation of the relationship'.[79] In all the other, less radical and structural, cases of illicitness, 'the invalidity will be temporarily ineffective and valid obligations will derive from the relationship'.[80] In any case, even in the presence of the most radical cases of illegality deriving from the breach of worker-protective statutes and norms, the doctrine of the 'inefficacy of invalidity' in the context of contracts of employment – introduced on the back of Article 2126(2) of the Italian Civil Code – will guarantee a 'right to remuneration'.[81]

The notion of '*favor*' [construction or interpretation in their favour] that public policy doctrines in some of the continental, Civil law, systems afford to workers has the ability to pierce through legal formalism in an undeniably worker-protective way. While French law, for instance, would typically see the illegality of a contract concluded with an illegal immigrant as a 'breach of a rule of *ordre public général*',[82] it would nevertheless hold that the resulting nullity 'is . . . original and operates without retroactivity', so that most of the rights arising from the work relationship are maintained.[83] Similarly Italian case law is predominantly in favour of the 'conservation of the contract of employment if [the residence permit] is irregular . . . and of the de facto performance rule if the residence permit is missing

---

[75] Ibid.
[76] Lord Wedderburn (1992) 'Inderogability, Collective Agreements, and Community Law', 21, *ILJ*, 245, 249.
[77] E. Ghera (2007) *Diritto del Lavoro*, Bari: Cacucci, 68 (our translation).
[78] Ibid.
[79] Ibid. 82.
[80] Ibid. 69.
[81] Ibid.
[82] A. Supiot (2007) 'Le Statut des Travailleurs Migrants Extracommunautaires en Droit Français', in Various Authors, *Lavoratore Extracomunitario ed Integrazione Europea – Profili Giuridici*, Bari: Cacucci, 66. Our translation.
[83] Ibid.

or, upon its expiry work has continued'.[84] Spanish law has addressed the problems deriving from contractual illegality by means of statutory intervention, once more in an attempt to preserve the rights of the worker deriving from the employment relationship.[85] As for English law, and in spite of the timid departure made by the Court of Appeal in *Protectacoat Firthglow Ltd v. Szilagyi*[86] – with regard to sham contracts of employment – decisions such as *Vakante* remain broadly effective for the purpose of denying even basic anti-discrimination rights to asylum seekers falsely claiming that they had a right to work in the UK.[87]

## II. Restraint of Trade

The common law doctrine of restraint of trade plays a pivotal role in the formation of personal work contracts. At a basic level, this doctrine may well serve to invalidate contracts where the weak bargaining position of a worker has led to an unfair agreement under which the employing entity undertakes minimal obligations in return for total commitment by the worker. Cases such as *Instone v. Schroeder Music Publishing Co Ltd*[88] strongly suggest that the doctrine applies well beyond unfair agreements emerging in the context of contracts of employment, and has a more general scope of application.[89]

It is also well accepted that the doctrine applies whenever specific clauses improperly restrict access to employment under a personal employment contract.[90] This application of the doctrine of restraint of trade should be read in parallel with the perhaps more pervasive effects of some 'doctrines' inspired by or deriving from EU law and prohibiting even non-discriminatory national rules which effectively impede or hinder access to employment.[91]

A further question arising in the context of the formation of personal work contracts is whether the effects of the doctrine necessarily affect the validity of the contract as a whole, effectively preventing it from carrying on, or can instead be used to strike down some particular terms and clauses even during the currency of the contract. This is a vital question in the context of personal work relations as the worker may well have an interest in carrying on the terms of the contract, bar the ones that effectively amount to an unlawful restraint of trade. This question

---

[84] B. Veneziani (2007) 'Il Popolo degli Immigrati e il Diritto al Lavoro: una Partita Incompiuta', Various Authors, *Lavoratore Extracomunitario ed Integrazione Europea – Profili Giuridici*, Bari: Cacucci, 430.

[85] See F. G. Abelleira (2004) 'Valides y Efectos del Contrato de Trabajo del trabajador Extranjer sin Autorización para Trabajar', *Relaciones Laborales*, 523.

[86] [2009] IRLR 365. Cf. A. C. L. Davies (2009) 'Sensible Thinking About Sham Transactions', 38(3), *ILJ*, 318. Compare also now *Autoclenz Ltd v Belcher* [2011] UKSC 41.

[87] *Vakante v. Addey and Stanhope School* [2005] ICR 231. But cf. the distinctions introduced in *Blue Chip Trading Ltd v. Helbawi* [2009] IRLR 128 and in *Allen v Hounga* [2011] UKEAT 0326/10/LA.

[88] [1974] 1 WLR 1308 (HL).

[89] Cf. M. Freedland (2003) *The Personal Employment Contract*, Oxford: OUP, 79–82.

[90] *Nagle v. Feilden* [1966] 2 QB 633 (CA).

[91] Cf. Case C-415/93, *ASBL Union Belge des Sociétés de Football Association v. Bosman* [1996] 1 CMLR 645.

effectively spans across formation and performance.[92] While the common law accepts the possibility that a clause may be struck out during the currency of a contract,[93] the answer to this question will effectively depend on the nature of the clause or term actually invalidated on the ground of the restraint of trade. If the invalidated term is a negative one, and its supervening invalidity does not frustrate the contract in a substantial and fundamental way,[94] the contract is more likely to be maintained, as courts are relatively well accustomed to inhibiting such clauses. However if the term is a positive one, common law courts may be more reluctant to substitute their judgment for the one of the parties and grant specific performance of a positive obligation.

Continental systems are arguably less accustomed to the balancing of economic freedom considerations in the context of the formation of personal work contracts. In fact, restraint of trade is less prominent as a distinct doctrine or principle. But perhaps a similar effect comes about from more rigid legislative control of contract types. Some facets of the continental notions of '*ordre public*' and 'inderogability', as discussed in the previous subsection, arguably provide a function equivalent to the doctrine of restraint of trade, at least to the extent that they can be used to limit the '*autonomia negoziale*' of the parties to the contract. The Italian doctrines of '*indisponibilità del tipo contrattuale*' (non-availability of the contractual type) and '*inderogabilità in pejus della disciplina legale*', (*in pejus* inderogability of the legal regime)[95] coupled with the corollary doctrines of automatic substitution of pejorative clauses ('*sostituzione legale delle clausole difformi*'), and of the, ever present,[96] '*forma vincolata*' (mandatory form), provide indeed a very rigid legislative control of contract types. Ghera emphasizes that all these devices confer upon the 'legal type of the contract of subordinate employment' the characteristics of a 'rigid model of imperative regulation of *interests*', and aptly speaks of a 'restriction of contractual autonomy within the limits of the inherent or genetic function of the relationship and the reduction of its regulatory function within the limits designated by statute and collective agreements'.[97]

## B. Formality and Information

The lack of any significant requirement of formality for the formation of standard contracts of employment is a feature that is shared by personal work contracts at large. At common law, contracts of employment can also be formed orally and impliedly and statute has so far merely restated this general position. This is in stark contrast with most continental European, Civil law-based, systems where, as we are

---

[92] Cf. M. Freedland (2003) *The Personal Employment Contract*, Oxford: OUP, 79–82 and 178–186; also S. Deakin and G. Morris (2009) *Labour Law*, 5th ed., Oxford: Hart, 316–22.

[93] *John Michael Lapthorne v. Eurofi Ltd* [2001] EWCA Civ 993.

[94] On frustration in personal work contracts, cf. S. Deakin and G. Morris (2009) *Labour Law*, Oxford: Hart, 418–20.

[95] For a vivid comparative analysis of these contexts see Lord Wedderburn (1992) 'Inderogability, Collective Agreements, and Community Law', 21, *ILJ*, 245, 250.

[96] M. D'Onghia (2005) *La Forma Vincolata nel Diritto del Lavoro*, Milano: Giuffrè, 78.

[97] E. Ghera (2007) *Diritto del Lavoro*, Bari: Cacucci, 66. Our translation.

going to see, the general – but qualified – rule of informality in the formation of contracts of employment is usually accompanied by a pervasive formalism in the formation of non-standard contracts of employment and a significant number of other personal work contracts.

English law does of course display an increasingly elaborate set of statutory information requirements for contracts of employment which, while not imposing *stricto iure* restrictions of form on the formation of contracts of employment, are nevertheless centrally significant in the legal regulation of the formation of those contracts. But crucially, none of these worker-protective and dispute-resolutory particulars are required as a matter of substance nor are they sanctioned by invalidity. On the other hand some of them explicitly attribute to the judicial interpreter the power to 'draw any inference which it considers it just and equitable' when the substance[98] is not observed by the employing entity, a formula which may include an inference of invalidity on the part of the tribunal.

These legislative requirements of information in the making of contracts of employment are primarily those which were originally imposed by the Contracts of Employment Act 1963, and are now contained in Part I of the Employment Rights Act 1996, which confers upon the employees employed under contracts of employment the right to a written statement or specific particulars of employment. This layer of regulation has been shaped further by the requirements of the EC Directive of 1991 concerning 'an employer's obligation to inform employees of the conditions applicable to the contract or employment relationship'.[99] However, the notoriously narrow British implementation of this Directive so far as personal or relational scope is concerned,[100] and of other EU instruments dealing, directly or indirectly, with the formation of various personal work contracts,[101] has effectively led to a strengthening of the binary divide, and towards the further marginalization of casual work relations from the sphere of contracts of employment.

This regulatory framework can be usefully contrasted with the different attitude of a number of continental European systems towards contractual formalism in the formation of personal work contracts. For instance, while it is clear that 'the French State has not regarded it as necessary to impose the requirement of a written contract'[102] for the formation of a standard contract of employment, such a requirement is explicitly included in the French *Code du Travail* with regard to the formation of a number of atypical contracts of employment and other personal work contracts. Thus Article 1242-12 of the French labour code provides that 'the fixed-term contract of employment is established in writing and requires

---

[98] Cf. Regulation 9(4) of The Fixed-term Employees (Prevention of Less Favourable Treatment) Regulations 2002, SI. 2034/2002.

[99] Council Directive 91/533/EEC of 14 October 1991, OJ L288, 18.10.1991, 32–5.

[100] C. Barnard (2003) *EC Employment Law*, 3rd ed., Oxford: OUP, 605; M. Freedland (2003) *The Personal Employment Contract*, Oxford: OUP, 83.

[101] N. Countouris (2007) *The Changing Law of the Employment Relationship – Comparative Analyses in the European Context*, Aldershot: Ashgate, 189.

[102] J. Pélissier, A. Supiot, A. Jeammaud (2000) *Droit du Travail*, 20th ed., Paris: Dalloz, 299–300. Article L 1211-1 of the Labour Code provides that: '*Le contrat de travail est soumis aux règles du droit commun. Il peut être établi selon les formes que les parties contractantes décident d'adopter.*'

the exact definition of its purpose'. This feature is hardly unique to French law. Section 14 paragraph 4 of the German *Teilzeit und Befristungsgesetz* (Law on Part-Time Work and Temporary Employment Contracts) of 2000 similarly indicates that 'in order to be effective, a fixed term to an employment agreement must be in written form'.[103] It is worth emphasizing the structural function of form in the context of some atypical contracts of employment, such as fixed-term and temporary work. Under Article 1242-12 of the *Code du Travail*, in the absence of written form, a fixed-term contract 'is presumed to be an open-ended contract'.[104]

A similar principle applies in the context of the Italian regulation of agency work where the written form is required as a condition of validity, and the consequences of its breach have been elaborated by the legislation and its interpretation in an evidently worker-protective way. If the agency fails to enter into a formal written contract with the worker, the formal defect is dealt with, under Article 21(4) of legislative decree n. 276/2003, by means of 'the absolute nullity of the contract that nevertheless does not have any negative repercussion on the juridical position of the workers'. Thus, the worker-protective rationale of the formal requisite is not conducive to the survival of the flawed contract, but to the subjective transformation of the employment relationship, in the sense that the workers concerned . . . are considered for all purposes as *dependents of the user company* (principle of effectiveness).'[105] As explained by the *Corte Costituzionale*: 'the lack of the written form as a condition of validity cannot as a general rule lead to the complete dissolution of the employment relationship without irremediably contradicting its protective purposes'.[106]

The progressive social acceptance of part-time work as a legitimate form of flexible work contract by most continental European legal systems has been reflected in the slow but steady relaxation of the formal requirements surrounding its formation. Italian scholars are clearly of the view that, since the reform of 2000, the requirement of concluding a part-time contract in writing is now only imposed as a matter of evidence.[107] (Workers may nevertheless require a conversion of the flawed contract into a full-time one, if the employer fails to discharge the burden of proof imposed on him by statute.[108]) Similarly in the French regulation of part-time work, 'the written form is not a condition of validity for the part-time contract'.[109]

---

[103] S. Lingemann, R. von Steinau-Steinrück, and A. Mengel (2008) *Employment & Labor Law in Germany*, München: Verlag C. H. Beck, 15.

[104] In the original: '*est réputé conclu pour une durée indéterminée*'.

[105] M. D'Onghia (2005) *La Forma Vincolata nel Diritto del Lavoro*, Milano: Giuffrè, 184. (Our translation: emphasis added.)

[106] *Corte Costitituzionale* 15 Luglio 2005, n. 283. Our translation.

[107] Article 2(1)(8) of Decreto Legislativo n. 61 of 2000. Cf. E. Ghera (2007) *Diritto del Lavoro*, Bari: Cacucci, 349; M. D'Onghia (2005) *La Forma Vincolata nel Diritto del Lavoro*, Milano: Giuffrè, pp. 212–13.

[108] Article 8 of Decreto Legislativo n. 61 of 2000; M. D'Onghia (2005) *La Forma Vincolata nel Diritto del Lavoro*, Milano: Giuffrè, 213.

[109] J. Pélissier, A. Supiot, A. Jeammaud (2000) *Droit du Travail*, 20th ed., Paris: Dalloz, 333. Our translation of the original: '*l'écrit n'est pas une condition de validité du contrat à temps partiel*'.

There is hardly any doubt about the existence of a negative correlation between the presence of strict and structural formal requirements for the formation of personal work contracts and the general social acceptance of specific types of atypical contracts departing from the standard contract of employment. However, this element alone cannot fully explain the policy choices made by various legal systems in respect of formal requirements in the formation of personal work contracts. For instance quasi-subordinate work relations are probably seen with much suspicion in most Civil law systems, and often perceived as a Trojan horse in the citadel of the standard contract of employment.

Nevertheless, the formal requirements that accompany their formation in countries such as Italy or Spain are arguably less stringent than those involved in the formation, for instance, of fixed-term or part-time contracts of employment. Thus, the comprehensive regulation of the Spanish contract for 'economically dependent autonomous work' provides that this type of contract 'must be formalized in writing'.[110] This requirement, strong as it may be, effectively amounts to a rebuttable legal presumption: 'When a particular duration or task is not fixed in the contract, it shall be presumed, unless the opposite is proven, that the contract was agreed for an undetermined time.'[111] Similarly, a less than satisfactory drafting of the Italian 'Biagi Law' of 2003 appears to have hitherto prevented Italian interpreters from reaching a unanimous position on whether the requirement of written form for '*contratti di lavoro a progetto*' (project work contracts) is to be considered as a substantive formal requirement or an evidentiary one.[112] A '*circolare*' issued by the Italian Ministry of Welfare in 2004[113] expressed the view that the requirement was an evidentiary one, although formalism remains a characteristic of these personal work contracts to the extent that 'if they are set up without the identification of a specific project, work programme or part of it . . . they are then considered open-ended relationships of subordinate employment from the date of the establishment of the relationship'.[114]

This tendency, visible in a number of continental European systems, to provide stricter formal requirements for the formation of atypical contracts of employment, and looser ones for other personal work contracts that are traditionally perceived as being closer to self-employment, may be explained by the dominance of 'freedom of contract' in an area of law that has been traditionally perceived as falling outside the territory of labour law. Even the Spanish *Ley 20/2007*, for all its worker-protective preoccupations, provides that autonomous workers' contracts 'can be

---

[110] Article 12 of *Ley 20/2007, de 11 de julio, del Estatuto del Trabajo Autónomo.*

[111] J. R. Mercader Uguina and A. de la Puebla Pinilla (2007) 'Comentario a la Ley 20/2007, de 11 de julio, del Estatuto del Trabajo Autónomo, 20, *Relacione Laborales*, 99. Our translation.

[112] Cf. D. Garofalo (2004) 'Statuto Protettivo del Lavoro Parasubordinato e Tutela della Concorrenza', in M. Rusciano and L. Zoppoli (eds.), *Mercato del Lavoro. Riforma e Vincoli di Sistema della Legge 14 Febbraio 2003 n. 30 al Decreto Legislativo 10 2003 n. 276*, Napoli: Editoriale Scientifica, 231. *Contra* E. Ghera (2005) 'Sul Lavoro a Progetto', *Rivista Italiana di Diritto del Lavoro*, 208.

[113] *Circolare* 1 of 8 January 2004.

[114] Article 69(1) of D. Lgs 276/2003. Cf. E. Ghera (2007) *Diritto del Lavoro*, Bari: Cacucci, 360–1. Our translation.

concluded both in writing and orally',[115] (although the same provision adds that 'each of the parties can demand from the other, at any given moment, the formalization of the contract in writing').

A type of personal work contract in which the tension between the two regulatory territories is particularly visible is the personal work contract of self-employed commercial agents, as regulated by Council Directive 86/653/EEC.[116] Article 13(2) of the Directive explicitly states that implementing Member States 'may provide that an agency contract shall not be valid unless evidenced in writing' but few of them have actually chosen to take up this opportunity. Article 85 of the German *Handelsgesetzbuch* (Commercial Code) simply provides that any party may request from the other written evidence of the terms of the contract. Similarly Article 1742(2) of the Italian Civil Code reads: 'Each party has the right to obtain from the other a copy of the contract signed by that other.'

Even the French Commercial Code, which until recently required a written agreement for the conclusion of a commercial agent's contract, now merely provides, in Article L. 134-2, that 'each party has the right, on demand, to obtain from the other party a signed writing specifying the content of the agency contract'. However national rules usually provide that some particular terms of these contracts must be concluded in writing in order to be valid. For instance, partly under the auspices of Directive 86/653/EEC,[117] regulation 20(1) of The Commercial Agents (Council Directive) Regulations 1993, a 'restraint of trade clause shall be valid only if and to the extent that – (a) it is concluded in writing'. This intricate regulatory panorama is further complicated by the fact that some systems accept the possibility that similar services of commercial intermediation and agency may be provided under contracts that, for all purposes, are approximated to the regulation of contracts of subordinate employment, as in the case of the French contract of *voyageur, représentant ou placier*.[118]

## Section 3: The Personal and Organizational Structure of Contracts of Employment

In the course of this chapter, we are seeking to develop the perception that the legal construction of employment relations as contractual ones imposes – to a greater or lesser extent as between labour law systems – a certain particular legal vision of the nature and structure of those relations. Such a vision may be imposed in a positive sense: when a labour law system encounters a certain employment relation, it may ascribe a certain contractual nature and structure to it. Alternatively, such a view may be imposed negatively: when a labour law system encounters a certain

---

[115] Article 7 of *Ley 20/2007, de 11 de julio, del Estatuto del Trabajo Autónomo*. Our translation.
[116] Council Directive 86/653/EEC of 18 December 1986 on the coordination of the laws of the Member States relating to self-employed commercial agents, [1986] OJ L 382/17.
[117] Article 20(2)(a).
[118] Cf. Article L 7313-1 *Code du Travail*.

employment relation, it may refuse to admit that relation to the category of employment contracts because it is judged to lack a certain contractual nature and structure. In this section, we shall consider the way in which particular contractual visions are imposed upon employment relations, in one or other of those senses, with respect firstly to the individuality of those relations (subsection A), and secondly with respect to their bilaterality and personality, features which we consider with regard to the structure of relations within the employing organization and then with regard to the structure of relations between employing organizations where more than one such organization is involved in the employment relation (subsection B).

## A. The Bilaterality, Individuality, and Personality of Contracts of Employment

It is a common feature of European national labour law systems that the core typology which they developed in the course of the twentieth century – that of the contract of employment – evolved from earlier models of the kind known to English law as the relation of 'master and servant'.[119] While other models and regulatory pressures eventually contributed to its shaping and construction,[120] to this day the contract of employment continues to display the characteristics of bilaterality, individuality, and personality typical of master and servant relations.[121] These characteristics are not just of a descriptive nature. On the contrary, they have progressively become deeply embedded structural features of the contract of employment, which is perceived as being bilateral, individual, and personal – that is to say as a contractual relation between two individual persons, the employer and the employee.

We may elaborate those features in the following way:

1. bilaterality – contractual employment relations are conceived of as being essentially between two parties, an employer and an employee, each regarded as unitary entities;

2. individuality – each party is seen as contracting as a sole entity; and

3. personality – each party is seen as a human being or, if a legal person, then in a very anthropomorphic way.

Stated as such, these features may seem axiomatically obvious as necessary structural components of contractual employment relations. We wish to argue that they should be regarded as being rather historically contingent, and open to scrutiny as normative assumptions with profound effects of their own. A good way to develop

---

[119] B. Veneziani (1986) 'The Evolution of the Contract of Employment' in B Hepple (ed.), *The Making of Labour Law in Europe: A Comparative Study of Nine Countries up to 1945*, London: Mansell, 45–50; cf. also, for English law in particular, S. Deakin and F. Wilkinson (2005) *The Law of the Labour Market*, Oxford: OUP, pp. 61–74.

[120] S. Deakin and F. Wilkinson (2005) *The Law of the Labour Market*, Oxford: OUP, Chapter 2.

[121] M. Freedland (2003) *The Personal Contract of Employment*, Oxford: OUP, at 36–9.

that argument is by means of comparative inquiry. We proceed to suggest that each of these three features is very strongly manifested in the approach of English law to the construction of contractual employment relations, but that the latter two at least may be less deeply embedded in the approach of other European national legal systems.

In developing this argument, it will be important to distinguish between the different ways in which these features of bilaterality, individuality, and personality operate at one and the same time to define not only the way in which we understand contractual employment relations but also the way in which we construct our notions of the participants in or parties to those relations, that is to say 'the employer' and 'the employee'. It is worth reminding ourselves that, although difficult issues of taxonomy of work relations or work contracts have often been perceived as rasing a free-standing question of 'who is an employee?', that is a question which cannot be considered in isolation from the questions of how we construct our understanding of 'the employer' and of the relations between employer and employee. In this subsection, we suggest how the three features of bilaterality, individuality, and personality have informed the answers to all these questions; in the next two subsections, we consider how the resulting constructs of contractual employment relations create certain ways of understanding employment relations both within and between the work organizations in which those relations are arranged and conducted.

It is rather difficult to decide how bold to be in venturing generalizations across European legal systems about the exact nature and significance of the transitions which those systems made in the course of the later part of the nineteenth century and the earlier part of the twentieth century from a primarily servile-relational view to a primarily contractual view of arrangements for personal work or service in conditions of subordination or dependency. Cautiously confining ourselves in the first instance to the case of English law, we can observe that an early nineteenth-century framework of 'master and servant relations', which itself strongly displayed the features of bilaterality, individuality, and personality, was gradually subsumed into a pattern of contractual employment relations. This superimposition of a contractual pattern took place in such a way as to leave the personal character of the relation intact, while greatly reinforcing its bilateral and individual character.

At a high level of generality, we can assert that other European legal systems rather similarly subsumed their analogous conceptions of 'master and servant relations' into contractual conceptions of those relations. For many of those systems, this transition was represented by the abandonment of notions in the nature of servile status, and the embodiment of the essentially contractual notion of the '*locatio conductio operarum*' in national Civil codes of private law.[122] However, we have to be very cautious about regarding this as remotely resembling a uniform pattern of development; and even to the extent that it was a uniform pattern of

---

[122] Cf. N. Countouris (2007) *The Changing Law of the Employment Relationship – Comparative Analyses in the European Context*, Aldershot: Ashgate, pp. 16–25.

development, it would be succeeded by very diverse evolutions of national labour law systems from any such common starting point.

We can begin to consider that diversity by concentrating in the first instance upon the individuality of contractual employment relations, a feature which is, as we have said, implicit in the original vision of 'master and servant relations' and is apt to be reinforced by the construction of those relations as contractual ones. We suggest that this reinforcement effect has been especially strong in English law, so that in this system, the vision of the contractual employment relation as an individual one rather than a collective one has remained an especially sharp and clear one.

This intensely individual vision of contractual employment relations which English law maintains manifests itself at two levels, at one of which it is relatively uncontroversial but at the other of which it is quite egregious by comparison with other European legal systems. At the uncontroversial level, the individual vision of contractual employment relations requires that employees cannot, save in exceptional circumstances, contract jointly with each other as partners, either in a formal or an informal sense. Other European legal systems would tend to say the same – such joint contracting would generally be regarded as identifying the workers as having formed a business organization, as such contracting neither individually nor 'personally' in the sense of each individual worker's arranging to carry out the work in question himself or herself. If English law seems to make only minor exceptions – for example by apparently allowing contracts of employment to be formed around a 'job-share' arrangement whereby two workers divide a single job between them – it would seem unlikely that other European legal systems, which incidentally also recognize arrangements such as the Italian *lavoro ripartito*[123] (shared work) and the German *Arbeitsplatzteilung* (work sharing),[124] would be much readier to regard such arrangements as constituting contracts of employment.

Much more singular to English law is its insistence on conceptualizing contractual employment relations as strictly individual ones even where they fall within the ambit of arrangements for collective bargaining or collective representation which apply to the employees in question. This is a stance or position which manifests itself in the notion that the impact of collective agreements upon contractual employment relations is not a direct one – so that the collective agreement itself determines the terms and conditions of employment of those workers who are within its ambit – but an indirect one so that the collective agreement, so far as it does determine the terms and conditions of employment of the workers within its ambit, does so by incorporation of its terms into individual contracts of employment.

By contrast, many other European labour law systems seem much readier to regard collective agreements as a primary source of contractual terms and conditions of employment for workers within their ambit. The French case is possibly the most paradigmatic example of this approach, by accepting the so called '*effet impératif*' of collective agreements, whereby 'a collective agreement imposes itself

---

[123] Article 41 of Decreto Legislativo n. 276 of 2003.

[124] S. 13(1) *Tedzeit- und Befristungsgesetz* (Act on Part-time work and fixed-term employment contracts) of 2001.

in its contents . . . [i]t regulates contracts of employment as a statute would do'.[125] By the same token 'collective agreements underpin contracts of employment as legislation would do; . . . [the] solution of the incorporation of terms of a collective agreement into a contract of employment is rejected by [French] jurisprudential' analysis[126]. This is, we suggest, a difference which is more than merely technical or conceptual. It would exaggerate this contrast to suggest that collective agreements have a mandatory or automatic impact on contractual employment relations in other European labour law systems, but no such impact under English labour law. Nevertheless, a European-wide diminution in the impact of collective bargaining in the last twenty or more years does seem to be especially marked in the United Kingdom; and we might regard the particularly easy technical dispensability of collectively bargained terms from individual contracts of employment, which English law ensures, as making some contribution to that tendency.

We have established in initial outline the ways in which, somewhat differentially as between European national labour law systems, the contractual analysis of employment relations tends to assign to those relations the features of bilaterality, individuality, and personality. In the next subsection, we pursue this discussion further so as to identify the implications of this analysis for the understanding of the organizational structure of contractual employment relations.

## B. Organizational Structure

In the previous subsection, we identified the propensity of contractual construction of employment relations to characterize those relations as bilateral, individual, and personal ones; and we opened an inquiry as to whether that potential has been generally uniformly realized in European national labour law systems at large. We noted that English law strongly displays this propensity in imposing an individual-istic vision of contractual employment relations upon its treatment of collective bargaining, while other legal systems seem more willing to build a collective dimension into their core conception of contractual employment relations.

In this subsection we seek to identify the assumptions about organizational structure which may be implicit in or may be imposed by contractual constructions of employment relations. Making the assumption – admittedly questionable as anything more than a method of organizing our discussion – that we can satisfac-torily distinguish the boundaries of the 'employing enterprise' or the 'employing organization', we concentrate initially upon intra-organizational structural issues, and then upon inter-organizational ones. Both those discussions specially focus, in different ways, upon the bilateral and personal features of contractual constructions of employment relations.

---

[125] J. Pélissier, A. Supiot, A. Jeammaud (2008) *Droit du Travail*, 24th ed., Paris: Dalloz, 1335. Our translation.
[126] Ibid., 1337. Our translation.

Before entering into those discussions, it will be useful to say something about their normative implications. We have identified the propensity or potential of contractual analyses of employment relations to characterize those relations as bilateral rather than more widely multilateral, as individual rather than collective and the parties to them as personal rather than organizational. Underlying that set of assertions is a set of concerns which is both descriptive and normative. We could summarize those concerns in the following way: it might be regarded as both descriptively inaccurate and normatively inappropriate for employment relations to be understood and regulated as bilateral and individual ones between parties regarded as personal ones.

It is of course the normative concerns which are the more important ones; the functions of legal construction of employment relations are regulatory ones, and the provision of an accurate and convincing narrative analysis of those relations, although very significant, is a task which is secondary and instrumental to that primary function. The real question is whether and how far misleading narratives give rise to regulatory shortcomings. The answers to that question will of course depend on the precise normative perspective from which we are making our assessment. From the broadly worker-protective perspective which is taken in this work, the principal normative concerns would be of two kinds, one larger but less immediate than the other. The larger but less immediate concern is with the potential of contractual constructions of employment relations to generate regulation which is not holistic or coherent because it is founded on inaccurate description of employment relations. The more localized and more immediate concern is with instances where contractual constructions of employment relations give rise to specific failures of regulation which result from inaccurate description of employment relations.

We might feel both those concerns at both those levels with the way in which, in English law, the contractual construction of employment relations imposes a characterization upon the employing party to such contractual relations as a personal one, that is to say as a single person, which even if consisting of a legal corporate entity rather than a human being, is still conceived of in a decidedly anthropomorphic way as if it were a single human being, corresponding to the 'master' in earlier constructs of employment relations as being between 'master and servant'. It should be said at the outset that there is no such objection to conceiving of the employee as personal in that sense, once a servile description of that person has been avoided. Indeed, one of the key assertions of this book is that there is a positive importance to thinking about workers in general as human beings for whom there is a positive value of 'personality in work', and there is much modern legal thought, some of it embodied in current contractual constructions of employment relations, which is virtuous in that respect.

However, if it is broadly speaking descriptively and prescriptively appropriate to think about the employee as participating in employment relations as a single human being (while recognizing that those relations have a significant collective dimension), it is quite otherwise so far as the 'employer' is concerned. It is only in a small minority of contractual employment relations that the 'employer' consists of a single human being not operating through the medium of a corporate legal vehicle; and even if that corporate legal vehicle is no more than a nominal institutionalization of a single human entrepreneur, the very fact of incorporation and the resulting requirements of institutional practice tend to transform the character of the 'employer' into that of a very small business organization.

Yet, in a curious paradox, the persistence in English law of a strongly personalized and individualized contractual construction of the 'employer' has a surprising potency to hide the internal dimensions and complexities of the employing enterprise behind a façade upon which we might paint, in caricature, the image of a human (and still archetypally male) 'boss' wearing a single top hat and smoking a single cigar. And this façade may sometimes seem just as impervious as the 'black box' into which some economic theories place the internal structures of the corporate business enterprise, or the 'corporate veil' behind which they are concealed by some of the doctrines of company law.[127]

We can point to instances in which this mode of construction of 'the employer' and its occlusion of the realities of the internal organization of the employing enterprise, gives rise to particular regulatory failures. For example, it has reinforced a falsely symmetrical doctrine that specific enforcement of the contract of employment in the form of requiring reinstatement of a wrongfully dismissed employee would be as oppressive of 'the employer' as specific enforcement of the contract in the form of an order to resume work would be for the employee. By comparison, continental European systems display a far more 'intrusive' attitude, ranging from the strongly 'coercive' approach adopted by Italian courts on the basis of Article 18 of the *Statuto dei Lavoratori*, to the more malleable protection offered by German jurisprudence where, in spite of the pro-employer 'escape clause' contained in section 9 *Kündigungsschutzgesetz* (Law on Collective Bargaining), 'once there is a strong indication of the illegality of the dismissal, the employee's interest in continuing working prevails over the employer's interest'.[128]

We can also discern, in a larger sense, a more general lack of doctrinal coherence which results from the personalized and individualized conceptualization of 'the employer' in the English law of contractual employment relations. For example, the expounding and application of the 'implied obligation of mutual trust and confidence' quite often requires a delineation of the elements of organizational or personal behaviour which are regarded as representing the conduct of 'the employer'. This particular exercise of ascription of organic or vicarious liability to the employing enterprise is apt to prove rather unsatisfactory when it has to be carried out according

---

[127] It should be noted that the economic theories in question and the company law doctrines in question are very distinct from each other; the point made here is that they, albeit in different ways, denote the exclusion from visibility of the internal dimensions of the firm or corporate enterprise. The economic theories are especially associated with the ideas of R. H. Coase, cf. for a recent overview S. Medima (ed.) (2008) *Coasean Economics: Law and Economics and the New Institutional Economics*, The Hague: Kluwer, and for an overview of doctrines representing the 'corporate veil' cf. Gower and Davies (2008) *Principles of Modern Company Law*, 8th ed., London: Sweet & Maxwell, Chapter 8 'Limited Liability and Lifting the Veil at Common Law'.

[128] M. Weiss and M. Schmidt (2008) *Labour Law and Industrial Relations in Germany*, AH Alphen aan den Rijn: Kluwer, 132.

to a doctrinal viewpoint which tends to deny the existence of internal hierarchies, something which makes it difficult to dissect the working of such structures when the need presents itself.

There are some indications that this strongly personal characterization of 'the employer' in the contractual construction of employment relations might be particular to English law. It is risky to generalize about other European labour law systems, but – as noted in the previous paragraph – the doctrinal objection to reinstatement of dismissed employees based upon the individual and personal characterization of the 'employer' does not seem to be encountered in those systems, at least not in such a pronounced form.

Moreover, we do encounter in some of those systems a greater readiness to integrate into their contractual constructions of employment relations a more complex narrative of hierarchy and cross-connections within the employing enterprise. Thus, some labour law systems such as the German one seem to embody in their notion of the corporate contractual employer an idea of the employing enterprise as having its own internal constitution. This core idea is embodied in the *Betriebsverfassungsgesetz* (Works Constitution Law) itself as the notion of a 'works constitution'.[129] Moreover, a number of systems regard those employees who are also managers as having a more distinctive place within their constructions of the employing enterprise than is conceded by the corresponding constructions of English law.

If we turn our attention from the intra-organizational aspects of this analysis to its inter-organizational aspects, we find that the effects of these characterizations are even more significant. Especially important is the way in which contractual constructions of employment relations largely insist upon an analysis of those relations as bilateral ones between an individual employee and an individual 'employer'. In a practical environment in which employment relations are often multilateral ones in which employing functions are shared or distributed between a multiplicity of persons or enterprises, we shall argue that these bilateral contractual constructions become especially controversial. We shall suggest that this may be especially the case in English law because of its reluctance to take a worker-protective functional approach to the contractual construction of employment relations in this inter-organizational dimension.

In order to develop that argument, it will be useful to distinguish between certain different ways in which these contractual constructions of employment relations may operate and take effect. If we say that a particular legal system or labour law system insists upon constructing contractual employment relations as bilateral ones, we may mean this in one or other or both of two different senses. We may on the one hand mean that a particular labour law system recognizes contracts of employment only or exclusively as bilateral ones – in other words that the system requires bilaterality as a condition for the recognition of contracts of employment. We might on the other hand mean that the system in question positively imposes

---

[129] Cf. M. Weiss and M. Schmidt (2008) *Labour Law and Industrial Relations in Germany*, AH Alphen aan den Rijn: Kluwer, 222 onwards.

the conclusion that this condition is satisfied wherever an employment relation factually exists – in other words that the legal system operates in an inclusive way to ensure that its own 'entry conditions' are fulfilled.

These are very real regulatory alternatives, and the choice between them becomes urgent in practical environments where there are all kinds of incentives towards the arranging of employment relations in multilateral configurations, either by the interposition of intermediary persons or organizations such as labour subcontractors or employment agencies, or by the creation of groups or networks of enterprises linked together by relations of supply or co-ordination or investment, between which functions of management of employment relations are distributed. There are yet further regulatory choices in the face of such incentives. At one extreme, the legal system could set about creating truly multilateral constructions of contractual employment relations to adjust to those realities. At the other extreme, the legal system could seek to limit or prescribe the making of arrangements for employment on a multilateral basis – such prohibitions upon the intermediation of private employment agencies used to be widespread. But the two regulatory alternatives which we have singled out are those which are most significantly in play in European labour law systems at the present day.

It should be noted that these are regulatory choices only in the sense of representing extreme ends of a theoretical spectrum, and that in reality legal systems will often rely on a mixture of modes of regulation. Continental labour law systems often present themselves as regulatory regimes composed of mixtures of legal prohibitions and legal presumptions effectively ensuring that 'the provision of labour for a profit is in principle prohibited; it is even criminally sanctioned',[130] and that the main exception to this rule, temporary agency work, is constructed around a contract between the worker and the agency the '[temporary agency contract], which is, necessarily, a fixed-term contract'.[131] But this paradigm, which is reflected in the approach adopted by the Temporary Agency Work Directive,[132] does not exclude the fact that some of these systems are capable, indeed much more than the British one, of recognizing joint or multiple employers in situations of contracting out or employment through an intermediate agency.[133]

In English law, our observation is that the first of the two regulatory alternatives which we have singled out is preferred, while the second one is generally eschewed.

---

[130] J. Pélissier, A. Supiot, A. Jeammaud (2008), *Droit du Travail*, 24th ed., Paris: Dalloz, 459. Cf. Article L. 8231-1 *Code du Travail*. Our translation.

[131] Ibid., 470. Our translation of the original: 'contrat de mission [qui] est, obligatoirement, un contrat à durée déterminée'. Cf. N. Countouris (2007) *The Changing Law of the Employment Relationship – Comparative Analyses in the European Context*, Aldershot: Ashgate, Chapter 3; though on Italy, doctrinal analysis is increasingly inclined to accept that the original prohibitions on labour subcontracting may have been removed by the 'Biagi Law', cf. L. Corazza, 'La nuova nozione di appalto nel sistema delle tecniche di tutela del lavoratore' (2009), *WP C.S.D.L.E. 'Massimo D'Antona'.IT* - 93/2009.

[132] Directive 2008/104/EC of the European Parliament and of the Council of 19 November 2008 on temporary agency work [2008] OJ L 327/9, Article 3(1)(c).

[133] Cf. L. Ratti (2009) 'Agency Work and the Idea of Dual Employership: A Comparative Perspective' 30, *CLLPJ*, 835; L. Corazza, *'Contractual integration' e rapporti di Lavoro – Uno studio sulle tecniche di tutela del lavoratore*, Padova: Cedam.

That is to say, the system tends to require bilaterality as a condition for the recognition of contracts of employment, but does not seem committed to imposing the conclusion that this condition is satisfied wherever an employment relation factually exists. So the triangulation, or the more elaborate multilateralization, of an employment relation may easily have the result that there is held to be no contract of employment between the worker and the enterprise which is factually the main employer, and may even have the result that there is held to be no contract of employment between the worker and any of the persons or enterprises involved.

The taking of this particular regulatory approach manifests itself especially clearly in the way that the English courts have in recent years handled cases where claimants engaged in temporary agency work relationships have sought to establish that they have a continuing contract of employment either with the employment agency or with the enterprise which is the end-user of their services. Their fortunes in making such claims have varied; but there have been two recurring themes in the numerous decisions at first instance or on appeal. The first is that the tribunals and courts seem not to hesitate to hold that there is no contract of employment with one of the possible employers even where that may produce the outcome that the worker has no contractual employment status with any employer, and indeed no contractual status at all.[134]

The second, and perhaps even more telling, manifestation of this approach consists in the way that a doctrine of 'necessity' is applied to determine whether, in a situation of temporary agency work, there is a contract of employment in force between the worker and the end-user of his or her services.[135] This doctrine is applicable in those instances in which there is no express contract between the worker and the end-user; it is a doctrine which creates a strong presumption against the finding or implying of a contract of employment between the worker and the end-user, the yard-stick of 'necessity' being that no other legal construction of the facts is felt to be convincing. There seems to be little or no perception in such cases that the implication of a contract of employment might be judged to be 'necessary' in the very different sense that any other legal construction would deprive the worker of a legally protected status vis-à-vis the end-user, and might deprive the worker of a legally protected status vis-à-vis any of the persons or enterprises involved in the set of arrangements under which he or she works.

It is instructive to consider whether different approaches are taken in other European labour law systems. Generally speaking, the idea of the contract of employment as an essentially bilateral rather than a more broadly multilateral one does seem to be fairly universal. However, other systems seem on occasion to take a rather more elastic view of what might be regarded as constituting the contractual 'employer'; such views feed into the notion of the continuity of the 'employing enterprise' which provided national exemplars for the EU Acquired Rights Directive.[136]

---

[134] Cf. *Muschett v. HM Prison Service* [2010] IRLR 451.
[135] See *James v. London Borough of Greenwich* [2007] IRLR 168; [2008] ICR 545.
[136] The challenges arising for English law are further discussed at pp. 256–7.

Moreover, many other European labour law systems seem committed to a view that a contract of employment and a contractual employer must be discoverable somewhere within a triangular or multilateral employment arrangement. So, in the situations of temporary agency employment which are increasingly tolerated and prevalent, the underlying question seems to be whether to regard the agency or the end-user as the contractual employer, rather than the very different question of whether there is any contractual employer and contract of employment at all.[137] The generally preferred choice is to presume that the agency is the contractual employer, but that in a sense is a secondary though still very important point, and – as stressed above – the ability of some continental European systems to deal with the legal complexities arising from work relations with multiple parties is, to say the least, noteworthy, with statutes such as the German *Arbeitnehmerüberlassungsgesetz* (Law on Hiring-out of Workers) of 1972 regulating 'the specific peculiarities result-ing from the splitting of the employer's functions between hirer-out and hirer'.[138]

It is useful at this point to revert to our earlier discussion, which we conducted in the context of considering the intra-organizational construction of contractual employment relations, and which identified the two kinds or levels of normative concern which we might wish to express with regard to such analyses. That is to say, we distinguished between a more general concern with descriptive accuracy and normative coherence, and a more specific concern with particular regulatory failures or shortcomings to which such analyses might give rise. Our discussion of the inter-organizational construction of contractual employment relations has given rise to concerns at both those levels. In the next and concluding section of this chapter, we turn to consider whether and if so how far similar concerns might arise with regard to a large aspect of the contractual construction of employment relations which we may designate as their economic structuring.

## Section 4: The Economic Structure of Contracts of Employment

In this section, we conclude our discussion of the formation and structure of employment contracts by posing a fundamental but unfamiliar question; that is to say, to what extent do contractual constructions of employment relations in European legal systems impose certain particular economic structures upon em-ployment relations? We use the terminology of 'economic structures' to identify those elements in employment arrangements which create and specify, at a basic level, exchanges or processes of exchange of work and reward and define the duration and continuity of those exchanges. Drawing on a notion of 'imposition' which was developed in the previous section, we consider firstly whether and how far a two-level economic structure is imposed upon employment relations by the

---

[137] Cf. N. Countouris (2007) *The Changing Law of the Employment Relationship – Comparative Analyses in the European Context*, Aldershot: Ashgate, Chapter 3.

[138] M. Weiss and M. Schmidt (2008) *Labour Law and Industrial Relations in Germany*, AH Alphen aan den Rijn: Kluwer, 64.

construction of them as contracts of employment (subsection A), and secondly what patterns of duration and continuity are imposed, and thirdly and finally, what kind of interrelations between working time and remuneration or reward are so imposed (subsection B).

## A.  A Two-Level Economic Structure?

At this stage in our analysis of the construction of employment relations as contractual ones, we consider one of the most fundamental and difficult aspects of that construction. The issue is whether and how far a two-level economic structure is imposed upon employment relations by the construction of them as contracts of employment. Two alternative possibilities present themselves for consideration. On the one hand, the view could be taken that all contracts of employment by their nature have a two-level economic structure consisting of, at one level, one or a series of short-term or unitized 'spot' exchanges of work or services for remuneration, or reward, and, at another level, of obligations which bind the employee and the employing enterprise into a continuing contractual relation. On the other hand, the different view could be taken that some contracts of employment may exist solely on the first of those two levels. This is a question of very great theoretical and practical importance; it is very determinative of the way in which the regulation of casual employment is handled by the labour law system in question.

Our own views have evolved over time in relation to that issue. The first author of this work, when first writing about the English law of contracts of employment, took the former view and went so far as to identify 'the mutual undertakings to maintain the employment relationship in being which are inherent in any contract of employment properly so called'.[139] Moreover, this was regarded as a feature of contracts of employment which might generically distinguish them from other personal work contracts. Writing much more recently about the English law of personal work or employment contracts more generally, the first author moved towards a more open and inclusive formulation of the obligations which may identify a continuing contractual relation between employer and employee, and suggested that this modified formulation might be applicable to personal work or employment contracts in general, simply as an identifier of their relational quality, even if the contractual relation were of very short duration.[140]

We now seek to place that view of the position or stance of English law within a wider comparative context. From the wider European comparative perspective which is taken in the present work, we argue that the modified formulation of the two-level economic structure of employment contracts should be regarded as a description of the position of English law, rather than as a necessary or universal position for the contractual construction of employment relations in any European

---

[139] M. Freedland (1976) *The Contract of Employment*, Oxford: Clarendon, at 20.
[140] M. Freedland (2003) *The Personal Employment Contract*, Oxford: OUP, at 86–92, especially at 91–2.

labour law system. From that comparative perspective, it becomes clear that the idea of the two-level structure, and in particular the idea of continuing mutuality of obligation as a necessary or inherent feature of employment contracts, seems to be more prominent, and to play a more significant normative or regulatory role, in English law than in many other European labour law systems, where in spite of the existence of analogous concepts, it would be hard to identify 'functionally equivalent' notions, with comparable exclusionary effects.[141]

So our argument is that the two-level analysis of the economic structure of employment contracts, and the notion of continuing mutual obligation, may be applicable in various stronger and weaker versions as between different European labour law systems. In order to make out this argument, it will be useful to return to the suggestion, which we advanced when considering the organizational structure of contractual employment relations, that, if contractual constructions of employment relations may be said to 'impose' particular visions or structures of those relations, that 'imposition' may take a variety of forms, each with normative or regulatory effects which are different from those of other forms of 'imposition'. Hence we will suggest that different versions of the idea of continuing mutuality of obligation, even if they seem similar at an abstract and conceptual level, may play out very differently as between different labour law systems. This argument opens the way to a normative critique of the role which is accorded to the idea of continuing mutuality of obligation in any particular labour law system.

This argument can be developed in much the same way that we earlier developed our argument about the 'imposition' of a bilateral structure upon contractual employment relations. If we say that a particular legal system or labour law system insists upon constructing contractual employment relations as ones of continuing mutual obligation, we may mean this in one or other of two different senses. We may on the one hand mean that a particular labour law system recognizes as contracts of employment only those employment relations exhibiting continuing mutuality of obligation – so that the system requires mutuality of obligation as a condition for the recognition of contracts of employment. We might on the other hand mean that the system in question positively imposes the conclusion that this condition is satisfied wherever an employment relation factually exists, or at least in the great majority of such cases – in other words that the labour law system operates in an inclusive way to ensure that its own contractual 'entry conditions' are normally fulfilled so far as continuing mutuality of obligation is concerned.

We have thus established a simple contrasting typology of exclusive and inclusive approaches to the 'imposition' of a two-level economic structure, and of the idea of continuing mutuality of obligation, upon contractual employment relations. However, applying that typology to particular legal systems may be a complex matter. Particular systems may present relatively weak or relatively strong versions of each approach, and may indeed combine the two approaches in various mixtures. Moreover, exclusive requirements of continuing mutuality of obligation, or on

---

[141] On this point see N. Countouris (2007) *The Changing Law of the Employment Relationship – Comparative Analyses in the European Context*, Aldershot: Ashgate, pp. 69–70.

the other hand inclusive positive attributions of continuing mutuality of obligation, may be indirectly imposed or effected under different conceptual headings. Different labour law systems may formulate their foundational or epistemological constructions of employment contracts in very different ways where these questions of economic structure are concerned, and may themselves change very much over time in these respects.

Despite those very real complexities and subtleties, some tentative comparative observations can nevertheless be made. In English labour law, the two-level construction of contractual employment relations seems to have assumed the character of a powerfully exclusive requirement of continuing mutuality of obligation, which is not matched by a corresponding willingness to attribute or to presume in favour of the presence of that continuing mutuality of obligation in the face of arrangements for employment which are casual or intermittent ones. The overall effect is that the contractual construction of employment relations in English labour law has tended to become markedly exclusive with regard to precarious personal work arrangements, increasingly permitting such arrangements to be constituted so as to fall outside the scope of protective legislation predicated upon the presence of a continuing contract of employment.

We have not been able to identify a correspondingly exclusive approach in other European national labour law systems. It is possible that a similar exclusiveness might be manifested in other systems through a narrow approach to the notion of 'subordination' and a correspondingly broad approach to the notion of 'independence' in the context of precarious employment arrangements, but we believe that this is a diminishing tendency in European national labour law systems. Admittedly, these systems in general require that contracts or employment relationships be premised on an exchange of remuneration for work as part of their *synallagma*, *causa*, or – as common lawyers might say – their consideration. And surely enough, as we will point out in the following subsection, they will all require that these reciprocal obligations be maintained over a period of time, so as to have a 'duration in time of the obligation of functional availability of the worker vis-à-vis the enterprise'.[142] However, we believe that none of these elements affects or even influences continental European jurisprudential or doctrinal construction of contracts or relationships in a manner that is functionally equivalent – that is to say equivalent both in structure and effect – to our domestic concept of 'mutuality of obligations' as construed by English judicial reasoning. Nevertheless, before we can be fully of confident of such a conclusion, it will be necessary to develop this discussion somewhat more fully with regard firstly to contractual constructions of the duration and continuity of employment relations, and secondly with regard to the ways in which working time is constructed and is linked to remuneration or reward within such relations. Those will be the tasks of the next subsection.

---

[142] E. Ghera (2007) *Diritto del Lavoro*, 16th ed., Bari: Cacucci, at 46 (our translation).

## B.  Duration, Continuity, and the Provision of Remunerated Work

In the previous subsection, we opened an inquiry as to whether and how far the contractual construction of employment relations by different European labour law systems brings about or imposes a conception of those relations as having a two-level economic structure and as therefore including some degree of mutual obligation with regard to the continuity of the exchange of work and reward. We argued that European labour law systems can in general be said to have such a perception of contractual employment relations: however, we went on to suggest that they differ in the extent to which they on the one hand require such mutual obligation as a condition for the recognition of a contract of employment, but also on the other hand in the extent to which they assign such mutual obligation to arrangements which they recognize as those of contractual employment. We concentrated primarily on the requirement of mutual obligation as a condition of recognition, and concluded that English law imposed such a requirement in a particularly strong and distinct way by comparison with other legal systems.

We now concentrate primarily on the contrasting possibility that labour law systems may positively assign various kinds and degrees of continuing mutual obligation to employment relations as an inherent consequence of their recognition as contracts of employment. In other words, we now consider the capacity of contractual construction of employment relations to operate in an inclusionary and constructive sense in imparting continuing mutual obligation to those relations. In this respect, there are two key issues. The first concerns job security; it is the question of whether the construction of employment relations as contractual ones involves some degree of imposition of job security in the form of an imputation of some minimum duration and continuity to those relations. The second concerns income security; it is the associated but distinct question of whether the construction of employment relations as contractual ones involves some minimum degree of income security in the form of an imputation of some minimum guarantee of remunerated work or at least of remuneration during a given period of employment. We consider those two questions in turn.

It should be noted that these questions are directed particularly at the effects of the construction of employment relations as contractual ones. Thus with regard to job security, our question is not the general one of what degree of job security is imposed upon employment relations by each national labour law system taken as a whole, but the more specific one of what degree of job security is, for each labour law system, inherent in its particular vision of the employment contract. It is admittedly difficult to separate the specific question from the general one, if only because, as we have previously argued, labour law systems differ in the extent to which they regard regulation derived from legislation or from collective bargaining as integrated into their essential vision of employment contracts. Such differences are apt to mean that when we attempt to compare the vision of the employment contract which each labour law system has with regard to job security, we are not comparing like with like in any true sense.

Nevertheless, there is still some validity and utility in developing a comparative understanding of the contractual vision of job security which particular labour law systems have evolved and currently maintain. Assessed in that way, the contractual vision of job security in English labour law is an essentially blurred one. That is largely because there has never been a prescriptive approach to the duration of employment contracts. There is an underlying freedom to make contracts of employment either for a fixed term of more or less any chosen length or on the basis of termination by notice, or indeed for a fixed term but terminable by notice. Moreover, an employment relation may consist of a succession of such contracts.

This is not to say that this freedom is in no way constrained or controlled. Quite important limits have been placed upon it by legislation which, where a contract of employment is terminable by notice, stipulates the minimum length of such notice – in the case of notice by the employer to the employee, an increasing minimum according to the employee's period of contractual employment,[143] and by other legislation which in certain circumstances converts a fixed-term contract of employment into a 'permanent' one.[144] Moreover, the legislation which confers rights against unfair dismissal quite crucially controls the relationship between contracts of employment terminable by notice and fixed-term contracts of employment by providing that the expiry of a fixed term is to be regarded as a dismissal for the purposes of that legislation.[145]

However, although there are those significant constraints upon the freedom to choose the duration of the contract of employment, it is still a freedom which is present in the background of English labour law, and which imparts an essential lack of clarity to any supposed distinction between fixed-term and open-ended contracts of employment. We could say, at a deeper level, that the English law's conception of the contract of employment has never systematically differentiated between permanent or secure employment and casual or precarious employment. This conception, while not as overtly libertarian or anti-regulatory as the idea of the 'at-will contract of employment' in the laws of the USA, is nevertheless rather at variance with any claim on the part of English labour law to maintain a doctrine of mutual obligation as a sustaining or defining feature of employment contracts in any positive sense.

Many continental European national labour law systems have, historically at least, taken a very different approach. Many such systems have distinguished much more sharply and directly than English law does between the open-ended and the fixed-term contract of employment. They have tended somewhat more strongly to characterize the open-ended contract of employment as a 'permanent' one in that robust controls upon termination have tended to be viewed as integral to the very nature of the contract itself – whereas in English law controls exerted, for example and

---

[143] Currently imposed by Employment Rights Act 1996, s. 86.
[144] Regulation 8 of The Fixed-term Employees (Prevention of Less Favourable Treatment) Regulations 2002, SI. 2002/2034.
[145] Employment Rights Act 1996, s. 95(1)(b).

especially, by the law of unfair dismissal have, even if equally robust, nevertheless not been regarded as integral to the conception of the contract of employment itself.

Moreover, continental European national labour law systems also tended historically to place controls upon the use of fixed-term contracts of employment in ways that English law did not,[146] so much so that those controls could be regarded as part of the very conception of the contract of employment which the systems in question had evolved. If those controls have been weakened in recent years, they have nevertheless left behind the sense that this relaxation involves a modification of that core conception of the contract of employment itself. This approach to the contractual construction of employment relations is evidenced in the fact that propositions for the greater use of more 'flexible' models for those relations have, in many continental labour law systems, to take the form of proposals to introduce new types of employment contract, such as the 'single contract of employment'[147] – whereas in English law the contractual construction of employment relations has such 'flexibility' built into it that no such radical transformations of contract types are necessary.

A rather similar set of observations can be made and a somewhat similar set of comparative contrasts can be tentatively proposed, with regard to the associated set of issues concerning the continuity of employment. The question here is whether and how far the contractual construction of employment relations by different European national labour law systems tends towards treating those relations as amounting to contracts of employment which continuously span both periods when the employee is 'working' or 'at work' and periods when he or she is not 'working' or 'at work'. That is a very complex question which we encounter in various conceptual and practical forms – for example, as a question about when the contract of employment may be 'suspended'. It is a question which brings into issue the very meaning of 'working' or 'being at work', itself a deeply intricate debate in which many factual and contextual variants have to be considered.

We can make a beginning on the analysis of these deeply complex questions, about the ways in which different labour law systems construct employment relations as contractual ones, by recognizing that these questions arise in different contexts where different time horizons may apply. Thus we might be considering this set of questions as a relatively long-term one or as a relatively short-term one. As a relatively long-term question, let us say for period of a week or more, it will contractually arise as an issue of job security; as a short-term question, let us therefore say for periods of up to a week, it will contractually arise as an issue of income security. We proceed to consider those two sets of issues, beginning with that of employment continuity.

---

[146] N. Countouris (2007) *The Changing Law of the Employment Relationship – Comparative Analyses in the European Context*, Aldershot: Ashgate, Chapter 3.

[147] P. Cahuc and F. Kramarz (2004) *De la précarité à la mobilité: vers une sécurité sociale profession-nelle*. Paris: La Documentation française; Disegno di Legge n.1481/2009, 'Disposizioni per il super-amento del dualismo del mercato del lavoro, la promozione del lavoro stabile in strutture produttive flessibili e la garanzia di pari opportunità nel lavoro per le nuove generazioni'.

Assessed comparatively, the set of issues about employment continuity and job security therefore becomes the question of how far and when European national labour law systems will envisage as continuous contracts of employment those employment relations where weeks or longer periods in which the worker is 'at work' or 'working' are intermitted with weeks or longer periods in which the worker is not 'at work' or 'working'. However, we can specify the set of issues more precisely, since if there is complete clarity of understanding or obligation concerning the resumption of work, it will normally be regarded as uncontroversial in all such labour law systems to envisage the contract of employment as continuous throughout the intermitting periods – for example during weeks of absence on paid holiday. So our set of issues becomes, more precisely, the question of envisaging contracts of employment as continuing through intermitting periods when there is less than complete clarity of understanding or obligation concerning the resumption of work after each intermitting period.

The tendency of English labour law in this respect is a fairly strong and clear one. The case-law of the modern era of worker-protective employment legislation displays an increasing reluctance on the part of courts and tribunals to regard periods of intermittent employment as constituting continuous contracts of employment.[148] This tendency is very undermining of the protection of job security because of the way that legislative measures to protect job security are largely dependent upon the existence of continuous contracts of employment. The tendency has nevertheless manifested itself increasingly powerfully in a reluctance or refusal to construct 'global' or 'umbrella' contracts of employment where periods of working are intermittent and where the resumption of work at a predetermined date is not fully guaranteed.[149] Moreover, that tendency has been visible even where the time horizons are very close ones, so that there have been various instances where contractual continuity has been denied even where the periods of work and of intermission are very short ones. The result of such approaches to the construction of employment relations is to deny continuing contractual status to an increasingly extensive range of arrangements for casual or occasional employment even where the worker is in practice economically dependent upon a single employing enterprise and frequently engaged for short periods of work by and with that enterprise.

If the tendency of English law is a clear and strong one in this respect, the task of comparative evaluation is nevertheless a very difficult one. It is made the more difficult by the fact that the requirement of continuing mutuality of obligation as a precondition to the existence of a continuous contractual employment relation has not, generally speaking, been allowed by other European labour law systems to assume the effect of a distinctive exclusionary device which English labour law has

[148] See M. Freedland (2003) *The Personal Employment Contract*, Oxford: OUP, at 102–3.
[149] Ibid. However, a powerful argument has been constructed by A. Davies (2007) 'The Contract for Intermittent Employment', 36, *ILJ*, 102 to the effect that there is the basis for a more positive recognition of such contracts in cases such as that of *Cornwall CC v. Prater* [2006] IRLR 362.

accorded to it.[150] This makes it very hard to assess how far and when the other labour law systems would treat the issue of contractual continuity if it did have the same high degree of prominence in those systems. In a sense the very absence from those systems of an equally prominent exclusionary requirement of contractual continuity seems to imply a greater readiness to assume that contractual continuity exists so far as it is necessary in a wide range of employment relations. However, we should acknowledge the possibility that a comparable exclusionary effect might be exerted in other doctrinal guises.

Another similar set of observations can be made and another similar set of comparative contrasts can be drawn with regard to the continuity of employment at the micro-level of the arrangements which are made for the exchange of work and remuneration within each working week. There is a large and complex set of questions about the many different ways in which 'week' may be defined and in which remuneration may be related to 'work', and in which the legal construction of employment relations may regulate all those factors, but rather than attempting a full-scale analysis of that whole set of questions, we shall at this stage focus upon one particular aspect of it, which is a key issue of income security. This is the question of how far the contractual construction of employment relations by different national systems of labour law secures to the worker any guaranteed minimum of opportunity for remunerated work or at least for remuneration within any given week during some or all of which an employment relation subsists.

In English law, the contractual construction of employment relations has not generally speaking been seen to require the imposing of any such minimum guarantees. We shall see in a later chapter that the courts at one stage seemed inclined to impose constraints upon the assertion of unlimited managerial powers to lay workers off in the sense of having them standing idle and in consequence earning no wages for periods of hours or days (or even longer periods). However, that tendency was not strongly or consistently maintained, and in recent years courts and tribunals have been more inclined to pursue the reverse logic, in which the absence of express guarantees against unlimited lay-off has been seen to point to the absence of a continuing contract of employment. Hence it would seem that English law accepts the validity of so-called 'zero-hours' contracts under which the worker has no fixed hours of remunerated work.[151] It is, however, still to be hoped that if courts or tribunals were pressed with the difficulty of reconciling such contracts with their own insistence upon an irreducible minimum of continuing mutual obligation, they might impose some appropriate guarantees as a matter of necessary construction of any contract of employment, rather than simply accepting the absence of a continuing contract.

---

[150] N. Countouris (2007) *The Changing Law of the Employment Relationship – Comparative Analyses in the European Context*, Aldershot: Ashgate, pp. 68–71.

[151] *Manpower UK Ltd v. Vjestica* [2005] All ER (D) 259 (Dec). It should be noted however that the person working under such an arrangement may be denied employee status on the ground of lack of mutuality of obligation, as in *Stevedoring and Haulage Services Ltd v. Fuller* [2001] IRLR 267 (CA), cf. P. Leighton, 'Problems Continue for Zero-hours Workers' (2002) 31 *ILJ*, 71.

This set of questions about the minimum guarantee of income security is one which is so essential to the core conception of the contract of employment that it is, paradoxically, difficult to ascend to a vantage point from which a common vision between different labour law systems can be obtained. Nevertheless, there is some reason to think that English law is towards the permissive extreme of what we might conceive of as a spectrum of positions as between different European national labour law systems. Other such systems operate less permissive approaches to the contractual construction of employment relations in various senses. Thus they may maintain regimes of guaranteed minimum weekly hours of work and/or remuneration, whether realized by collective bargaining or by legislative intervention, which form elements in the core and non-derogable conception of the contract of employment, as exemplified for instance by the *'indennità di disponibilità'* (retainer for availability) imposed for inactive periods of 'on-call' work in Italy. Moreover, they may be more inclined than the courts and tribunals of English labour law to characterize or 'qualify' actual employment arrangements in such a way as to impose such a conception of the contract of employment as generic to the contract type in itself.[152]

It will be apparent that these reflections upon the economic structures which are recognized or imposed in and by the contractual construction of employment relations reach a point where the conditions of formation of contracts of employment become inseparable from the approaches to the content, performance, and termination of those contracts. That continuity of issues and concerns is pursued into the next two chapters of this work.

---

[152] By Article 36 of D. Lgs. 276/2003.

# 5

# The Content and Performance of Contracts of Employment

## Introduction

In the previous two chapters, we have considered the ways in which, in English law and in that of other European countries, personal work relations are, generally speaking, constructed as contractual ones; we have proposed a multidimensional method of analysis of personal work contracts which might deal with some of the difficulties attaching to the binary divide; and we have started to develop that multidimensional analysis further, applying it on a comparative basis in order to try to understand the conditions of formation, the personal and organizational structure, and the economic structure of contracts of employment. In the present chapter we seek to take that analysis on to its next stage by examining the doctrines and regulatory techniques which have evolved to ascertain the content of contracts of employment in relation to their performance, that is to say, their content analysed not so much as at the outset of the personal work relation in question but rather as a function of the actual evolution of the personal work relation, and as a working out of the contractual rights and obligations originally established when the contractual relation was formed. We could think of these doctrines and regulatory techniques as representing the ways in which contractual content is related to or matched with the factual conduct or outcomes of personal work relations.

In English law, there has been a strong tendency to effect this content/conduct matching by means of terms which are implied into or deemed to be incorporated in contracts of employment. We begin by identifying the way in which a whole body of doctrine has evolved with regard to the 'implied terms' of contracts of employment, and especially the major subset conceived of as 'terms implied in law', and we consider the ways in which an elaborate arsenal of regulatory techniques has been developed in the form both of principles prescribing how and when terms are implied into contracts of employment in general, and of articulations of certain overarching or specific terms to be implied into particular contracts of employment (Section 1). We continue by discussing some specific areas in which the law of contracts of employment interprets, and assigns effects or outcomes to, the eventualities which present themselves or the steps which the parties take in the course or conduct of personal work relations; the areas or locations in question are those of performance of contracts and the regulation of the wage-work bargain (Section 2), variation of contracts or of their terms (Section 3), and suspension of contracts (Section 4). Our principal concern in these analyses will be to display both the continuities between these bodies of doctrine and their connections back to our previous discussion of the formation and structure of contracts of employment, and forward to our subsequent discussion of their termination and transformation.

This chapter will form a further stage in our investigation of the legal construction, in the English legal system and other European legal systems, of personal work relations in general and, in these chapters, those personal work relations in particular which are regarded as taking the legal form of contracts of employment. Our concern is with the way in which each legal system fashions its own distinctive legal construction of the contract of employment – its own law of the contract of employment; and our further concern is with the way in which the distinctiveness of each of those constructions shapes and differentiates the regulation of the personal work relations in question. The area or topic of the content and performance of contracts of employment is a fruitful one in which to pursue those concerns, and in which to test and further develop certain of the comparative hypotheses which we have begun to advance in earlier chapters.

There are, as we have previously suggested, many kinds of variation or variable in the ways that contracts of employment are constructed, and indeed conceived of, by different European legal systems. There is one such variable upon which we suggest that it will be especially useful to focus in this chapter. This is a variable which concerns the manner in which and the extent to which the various sources of regulation of employment relations are viewed as being integrated into the contract of employment. Another way in which we might identify this variable is to see it as a question whether, if each source of regulation is viewed as constituting a layer of regulation, that layer forms part of the composite layer of regulation which is envisaged as forming 'the contract of employment' by and in each legal system – that being one respect in which we have suggested that European national legal systems differ considerably one from the next.

However, perhaps the most useful way to think about this variable is to regard it as giving rise to a spectrum or continuum of modes of legal construction of the employment contract, at one extreme of which all the sources of regulation of contractual employment relations would be regarded as integrated into the 'contract of employment'. At the other extreme, all the sources of regulation which could be viewed as external to the agreement made between the parties themselves would be excluded from the contract of employment. These extremes might be styled as, respectively, the fully integrated contract of employment and the fully dis-integrated contract of employment. The actual patterns of legal construction of contracts of employment in European legal systems seem to fall between these extremes; but they vary considerably as to how far they tend to one extreme or the other, thus enabling us to distinguish between relatively integrated and relatively dis-integrated visions of the contract of employment as between the various legal systems.

In this chapter, we shall explore the significance of this variability in the integration of sources of regulation. Two preliminary general points may be made; they concern the extent to which this variable can be regarded as a useful tool for comparison between European employment law systems. The first of those points is a caveat about regarding this variable as giving rise to a simple contrast between an English common law approach and a continental European Civil law approach. It will emerge that English law provides an example of a very disintegrated approach, and it will also emerge that examples of more highly integrated approaches are to be found in other European employment law systems. Nevertheless, we should beware of concluding that this represents a generic contrast between an English law approach and an approach taken by all other European legal systems; and we should be still more wary of concluding that any such episodic contrasts are straightforwardly attributable to a general antithesis between common law and Civil law.

Our second preliminary point, about the utility of the high-integration/low-integration contrast as a tool of comparative law, concerns the degree of protection of workers which is associated with this contrast. We can venture a very tentative hypothesis that high-integration approaches are associated with high levels of protection of workers, and low-integration approaches with low levels of protection of workers. We can offer that hypothesis in the following sense, that the sources of regulation which are external to the arrangements made by employees and employers – the most important of which are employment legislation and collective bargaining – have generally speaking tended to be protective of workers in their impact upon terms and conditions of employment. The more highly such sources of regulation are integrated into contracts of employment, the more the resulting conception of the contract of employment will therefore tend to be protective of workers.

In the course of this and the ensuing chapter, this hypothesis will be extensively elaborated and explored. It will be suggested that, in situations of low integration of external sources, contracts of employment are more apt to be constructed according to default models which are more protective of the interests of employers or employing enterprises than of the interests of their employees. It will also be suggested that in situations of low integration of external sources, the regulation of terms and conditions is accordingly apt to be less cogent and more easily displaced by contractual provisions.

However, it is important to be clear from the outset that we do not envisage, and will not arrive at, anything amounting to a rigid equation of high integration of external sources into contracts of employment with a high level of protectiveness towards workers, or of low integration of sources with low levels of protectiveness towards employees. And it is still more important to be clear that we will not compound any such rigid equation with a generic contrast between the approaches of English common law on the one hand and the approaches of civilian legal systems in other European countries. We proceed, as previously indicated, to begin to explore these essentially cautious hypotheses in the context of the implied terms or guiding principles as to the conduct of employment relations, which might be regarded as embodied in contracts of employment, and then we carry the discussion through to the treatment of performance, variation, and suspension of contracts of employment.

## Section 1:  Implied Terms and Guiding Principles

### A.  Implied Terms and the Regulation of Content and Performance

In this section, we seek to lay the foundations of our analysis of the ways in which the law of personal work contracts both constructs and regulates the content and performance of contracts of employment. We shall argue that the principal regulatory technique which is used for this purpose in the English law consists of the implying of terms into contracts of employment. We shall go further and suggest that the law governing the implying of terms into contracts of employment amounts to a body of guiding principles for the interpretation of the content and regulation of the performance of contracts of employment.

By identifying the legal doctrines concerning implied terms in contracts of employment as representing both a set of regulatory techniques and a body of guiding principles, we seek to open up a comparison with the bodies of law in certain continental European legal systems which to our minds are the corresponding ones, but which are formulated differently and do not use the language of implied terms, instead being couched in conceptions of 'general principles' or 'general clauses'. Some of these general principles or 'clauses' owe their genesis to doctrines that effectively predate the establishment of employment and labour law as autonomous legal disciplines. This may be said, for instance, for the principles of '*bonne foi*', or '*buona fede*' or '*Treu und Glauben*', deriving as they do from the general law of contract and applying, not without some important adaptations, to contractual employment relationships. Other such principles may be more recent and their development can be seen as being endogenous or internal to labour law, and indeed often deriving from the judicial interpretation of principles and institutions first enshrined in labour statutes or collective agreements. A good example of this latter dynamic is the English concept of 'mutual trust and confidence', produced by the highly complex interaction between the common law of the contract of employment and the law of unfair dismissal.[1]

Even where such implied terms or general principles were originally external to labour law, the labour law context has inevitably had a transformative effect on the contents and functions of these implied terms and general principles. For instance, the traditional general contract law concept of '*buona fede*' in Italian labour law bears little resemblance to the notion of 'good faith' as applied to labour relations. Furthermore, according to some distinguished scholars, '*buona fede*' has been used as the means either to establish or influence and reinterpret other general obligations

---

[1]  M. Freedland (2003) *The Personal Employment Contract*, Oxford: OUP, at 155; see further below at 224–31 and 241–50.

and principles imposed on the parties of the employment relationship, such as the obligation to protect the liberty and dignity of the worker,[2] the principle of 'proportionality', and that of 'justification'.[3] These principles and objectives have moreover often been enshrined in labour codes and labour legislation,[4] and their judicial and doctrinal elaboration has therefore developed even more distinctively as a consequence of the implying of these terms from such legislation.

Having in that way opened up a certain particular line of comparative inquiry, we shall seek to develop it by posing a set of comparative questions, designed to focus attention upon the key variables between European legal systems as to the ways in which they have each developed their own set of regulatory techniques and guiding principles with regard to the content and performance of contracts of employment. There are three such key questions.

Firstly, how far does each set of regulatory techniques and guiding principles give rise to norms for the content and performance of contracts of employment which are on the one hand mandatory or inderogable, or on the other hand displaceable by express contractual provision?

Secondly, how far is each set of regulatory techniques and guiding principles one which is specific to contracts of employment (or contracts of employment in particular) or on the other hand simply a local application of the general regulatory techniques and guiding principles of contract law at large?

Thirdly, what if any policy orientation does each set of regulatory techniques and guiding principles have, and in particular does it have a worker-protective, or on the other hand an employer-protective orientation?

The framing of those three key questions might suggest the possibility of making quite a direct or like-for-like comparison between legal systems with regard to the regulation of the content and performance of contracts of employment. However, arguments developed in earlier chapters begin to suggest that we have to be rather sceptical about the extent to which our comparisons really will be direct or like-for-like ones. In particular, our argument initially put forward in Chapter 2 and developed in Chapter 3 about the different nature and thickness of the layer of regulation regarded as 'contractual', as between employment law systems, indicates that the body of law which is perceived as the 'law of contract' governing the content and performance of personal work contracts may be quite differently constructed and understood as between the various European employment law systems.

We can in fact now go one stage further down that path of argument; we suggest that a dominant theme, perhaps the dominant theme, in understanding the

---

[2] D. Garofalo (2004) 'Mobbing e Tutela del Lavoratore tra Fondamento Normativo e Tecnica Risarcitoria' in Various Authors, *Scritti in Memoria di Massimo D'Antona*, Milano: Giuffrè, 821. The main direct influence on this principle in Italian law derives however from Article 2087 of the Italian Civil Code and Article 41 of the Italian Constitution. Cf. R. Casillo (2008) 'La Dignità nel Rapporto di Lavoro', 71, *Working Paper 'Massimo D'Antona'*, 6.

[3] A. Perulli (2002) 'La Buona Fede nel Diritto del Lavoro' 53, *Rivista Giuridica del Lavoro*, 3.

[4] The entire Titolo I of the Statuto dei Lavoratori deals with 'liberty and dignity of the worker'. The *loi de modernisation sociale du 17 janvier 2002*, introduced 'good faith' in Article L 1222-1 of the French Labour Code.

different ways in which the 'law of contract' governing the content and performance of contracts of employment is constructed as between the various European
employment law systems, has to be the differences in the ways of dividing that
territory between common or judge-made law on the one hand and statutory or
codified law on the other. As a broad generalization, we can venture the proposition
that the English law of contracts of employment is unusual, among European legal
systems, in the extent to which it maintains a strong separation between common
or judge-made law on the one hand and statutory or codified law on the other, and
also in the extent to which it still accords the primary role to common or judge-
made law in the regulation of the content and performance of contracts of
employment, at least in a conceptual sense but to a considerable extent in a practical
sense too.

Pursuing that theme, we can begin to sketch out some tentative answers to our
three questions, which we can then treat as hypotheses which we will test in the
course of the more detailed discussion which will ensue. The first of these tentative
answers or hypotheses is that English common-law-based regulation of the content
and performance of contracts of employment, essentially focused as it is upon the
implying of terms into contracts of employment, presents itself as basically *jus
dispositivum* in character, tending to operate by providing default terms which can,
in broad theoretical terms at least, be displaced by express contractual provision,
although in some respects it does consist of mandatory norms, especially where
national or EU legislation can be regarded as directly affecting the terms and
functioning of contracts of employment. Somewhat in contrast, the regulation of
the content and performance of contracts of employment in other European systems,
frequently code-based or primarily legislative, and sometimes also of a constitutional
nature, in character, more readily presents itself as *jus cogens* in character, its norms
typically appearing to be inderogable, or derogable only in very limited conditions.

That broad generic contrast would, if sustained by detailed evidence, be a
significant one, and we hope indeed to be able to sustain that thesis in general
terms. It is however important to realise that this is not a simple like-for-like
comparison between legal systems. The regulation of the content and performance
of contracts of employment is not, generally speaking, effected by means of simple
norms which can be directly compared as between legal systems. Comparative law
rarely consists of such simple analogies, but hardly ever less so than in this instance,
because in this area regulation is usually based upon broad evaluative behavioural
notions such as those of 'good faith' or 'contractual co-operation'. As we shall see at
various points in the course of this chapter, the deployment of these broad
evaluative behavioural notions is in its nature such a discretionary operation that
theoretical distinctions between mandatory and displaceable norms may melt away
in the practice of case-law development.

This sense of the malleability of legal doctrines in this particular area is reinforced
when we attempt to provide tentative working answers to our second and third
questions. These two questions are best answered in conjunction with each other;
the question of whether and how far each legal system has a body of regulation of
contractual content and performance which is distinctive to contracts of employ-

ment is inextricably bound up with the question of whether and how far each legal system has taken a predominantly employer-protective or worker-protective approach to this area of regulation. Furthermore, the two questions are best answered by envisaging the present body of regulation as having been constituted by a series of historical evolutions which are very broadly comparable as between European legal systems, but which have taken place at differing speeds, to differing extents, and with significant differences in legal methodology.

If we take a long historical perspective across European legal systems, we can in fact usefully discern three reasonably distinctive phases into which these evolutions can be grouped; there is a nineteenth-century phase in which general contractual liberalism is combined with personal-work-specific notions of obligations of loyalty and discipline owed by workers to employers. There is a twentieth-century phase, occupying the first three-quarters of that century, during which, in the specific area of contracts of employment, an overlay of worker protection is developed and in varying degrees infuses the regulation of contractual content and performance. That is succeeded by the current phase, in which the regulation of the content and performance of contracts of employment seems to be characterized by a complex interplay between on the one hand liberal deregulation and on the other hand the general protection of individuals envisaged at once as right-bearing citizens and contractual consumers – a protectiveness of which workers are beneficiaries only to a rather uncertain extent.

It is, we suggest, in the second of these phases that quite a significant divergence seems to occur between the English common-law-based system on the one hand and many continental European Civilian and code-based systems on the other, so far as the regulation of the content and performance of contracts of employment is concerned. Although the third and current phase has been a more convergent one, the divergent positions which evolved during the second phase have nevertheless led to still rather divergent outcomes during this third phase; in other words, the recent evolutions have been dependent upon path divergences which identified themselves and opened up in the second phase.

Expanding somewhat upon this suggestion that a significant divergence opened up between the English common-law-based system and other European systems in the second of these three phases, we would say as follows. In many continental European legal systems there occurred in the course of the first three-quarters of the twentieth century, and particularly in the aftermath of the Second World War, an autonomization of the regulation of the content and performance of contracts of employment, whereby the domain of subordinated work relations was identified as distinctively requiring a redressing of an inequality of bargaining power between employer and worker which was perceived as a generic or systemic one. That redress was normally effected by legislative measures and sometimes by a distinct codification of labour law.

English law was, on the other hand, throughout most of this period characterized by a voluntarist approach according to which the amelioration of the situation of the worker was seen as the function of collective bargaining rather than of legislation, with the result that the older common-law-based regulation of the content and performance of contracts of employment remained largely intact and unchanged. The regulation of the content and performance of contracts of employment was not strongly autonomized, and to the extent that it did become autonomous, that was more on the basis of the older 'law of master and servant' than on that of the redressing of inequality of bargaining power. There was indeed a swing towards worker-protective legislation towards the end of this phase, in fact from the 1960s onwards; but that never succeeded in displacing the common-law-based substratum, which therefore remained in place as the basic layer of regulation of the content and performance of contracts of employment, largely preserving its underlying employer-protective orientation.

The effect of this appears to be that, in the third and current phase, direct comparison of the ways of regulating the content and performance of contracts of employment, as between the English law of contracts of employment and that of other European systems, is difficult because, as the result especially of divergences in the previous phase, English law is distinctive in its methodology – operating primarily through implied terms rather than through mandatory principles, and in according a lower degree of autonomy to the law of contracts of employment, and seemingly in its orientation too – being underlyingly employer-protective rather than worker-protective. But it is important for us not to overstate the value of our preliminary views; they do no more than provide working hypotheses with which to examine in greater detail the actual state of the law with regard to the implied terms of contracts of employment, and the associated doctrines which are applied to the regulation of the content and performance of contracts of employment.

Before doing so, we might elaborate our working hypotheses one stage further by relating them somewhat more fully to the development of general contract law in the English common-law-based system and in continental European Civil-law-based systems. We could consider that development of general contract law in two phases; we can identify a first phase lasting from the nineteenth to the mid-twentieth centuries during which the market-liberal doctrinal foundations of modern contract law were established and consolidated. We can also identify a second phase from the mid-twentieth century onwards which is especially characterized firstly by the growth of an overlay of consumer protection upon those earlier market-liberal doctrinal foundations, and secondly by the development of a greater role for legally-recognized fundamental rights in the evolution of contract law.

We might imagine that there would be a general tendency for the autonomy of the law of contracts of employment to be eroded during that second phase. That is to say, we might suppose that the growth of the consumer protection and the increasingly strong articulation of fundamental rights in general contract law would bring general contract law and the law of contracts of employment back into parallel with each other. On the whole, however, there has been less re-integration of the law of contracts of employment into the general contract law than one might have expected. The reasons for this are very complicated, but we can elaborate our working hypotheses by giving a tentative account of them. It is again useful to differentiate in broad terms between the English common-law-based system and continental European Civil-law based systems.

In many continental European Civil-law based systems, by the time that the growth of an overlay of consumer protection and the development of a greater role for legally-recognized fundamental rights occurred in general contract law, the law of contracts of employment had already taken on a quite distinctively worker-protective character. This, as we have suggested, was the main basis for the autonomy of labour law in general and the law of contracts of employment in particular. That autonomy was sufficiently strong and well-established as to be resistant to the re-integration of the law of contracts of employment into the general contract law, even when general contract law itself began to take a more welfarist and rights-based path, especially in favour of consumers.

The story has been a rather different one in the English common-law-based system. As we have previously suggested, the development of a distinctive genre of worker protection in the law of contracts of employment occurred more slowly and less systematically in the case of English law. However, this has not meant that the English law of contracts of employment has been ripe for re-absorbtion into the general law of contract as the latter has itself become more welfarist and rights-based in character. Almost on the contrary, the English law of contracts of employment has tended to be perceived as more specialized and distinctive as time has gone on. The development of individual worker protection in English labour law has been regarded as a primarily legislative or statutory phenomenon; and when this growth of worker-protective legislation began, rather belatedly and in a rather limited way, to infuse the law of contracts of employment, that served to confer a new kind of partial autonomy upon the law of personal work contracts – in particular, upon the law of the contract of employment.

So in that rather complex way, the law of contracts of employment has either, in the case of many continental Civil-law-based systems, remained rather distinctive from general contract law, or, in the case of the English Common-law-based system, has latterly seemed to draw away from general contract law by developing its own special kind of worker protection upon an underlying foundation of employer protection. In order to sketch in the details of this picture, we proceed to consider the special role which implied terms now play in the English law of contracts of employment, and to compare and contrast the conception and working of implied terms with the conceptions and working of doctrines such as that of 'good faith' in the law of contracts of employment in many continental European systems. Our argument develops in three further stages; it looks first at implied terms or doctrines concerned with fidelity and the protection of the interests of the employing enterprise, secondly at implied terms or doctrines which identify the obligations of the employing enterprise to take care of the health, safety, and wellbeing of the employee, and thirdly and finally at implied terms or doctrines which, in an overarching way, interrelate and build upon the first two sets of obligations, deploying broader notions of mutuality, good faith, and fair dealing.

However, we feel the need to conclude this introductory section with a short word of warning as to some of the possible methodological pitfalls of the comparative analysis we are about to undertake. We seek to draw attention to the fact that while different systems have all developed functionally equivalent devices for the regulation of the aforementioned aspects of the employment relationship, they have done so by reference to nominally and conceptually different terms and principles. These terms and principles can in some cases bear a misleadingly similar *nomen juris* while often performing considerably different functions, as is the case for the French concept of '*bonne foi*' and the English notion of 'good faith'. To quote the French Cour de Cassation, 'Good faith broadly understood (loyalty, solidarity, proportionality and care for the contractual balance) imposes itself in all the phases of the life of the contract: negotiation, information, conclusion, execution, interpretation, modification, renegotiation, inexecution, breach and its consequences.'[5] Moreover, as noted by Pélissier, Supiot, and Jeammaud: 'the actioning of a contractual term is subject to some very general rules of our law. First and foremost, that of article 1134, alinéa 3 of the Civil Code prescribing the performance in good faith of any contract'.[6] As we will further discuss in the present and in the following chapter, neither the 'gap-filling' nor the 'interpretative' functions that English lawyers tend to accord to the principles of 'good faith' and 'mutual trust and confidence'[7] can be easily equated, or even associated, with the structural, general, and non-derogable effects that French law accords to the '*bonne foi*' principle.

Nevertheless, some terms and principles that have a very distinct conceptual and terminological heritage can often develop as legal devices performing broadly comparable functions in the regulation of the performance of the employment relationship. This is, we suggest, the case for the implied term of 'mutual trust and confidence' – with the caveat discussed in the previous paragraph – and the continental notions of '*buona fede*', '*bonne foi*', or '*Treu und Glauben*'.[8] There are, moreover, important principles and implied terms, such as the one requiring the parties to the contract to perform their obligations while taking due care of the other's welfare (to use a neutral formula), that have been established in ways that are intimately intertwined with structurally different legal doctrines and cultures, and that are therefore only comparable by reference to the functions performed and objectives pursued, rather than to significantly similar concepts or sources of regulation. This is arguably the case for the English notion of 'care' when compared to continental codified and

---

[5] Cour de Cassation, *Rapport du groupe de travail de la Cour de cassation Sur l'avant-projet de réforme du droit des obligations et de la prescription* (15 juin 2007). Our translation from the original French.

[6] J. Pélissier, A. Supiot, A. Jeammaud (2008) *Droit du Travail*, 24th ed., Paris: Dalloz, 711. Our translation.

[7] M. Freedland (2003) *The Personal Employment Contract*, Oxford: OUP, 122–7; Cf. H. Collins (2007) 'Legal Responses to the Standard Form Contract of Employment' (2007), 36(1), *ILJ*, 2, 9; *contra* Lindsay J. (2001), 'The Implied Term of Trust and Confidence', 30(1), *ILJ*, 1.

[8] On similar methodological lines cf. N. Nogler (2008) 'Why do Labour Lawyers Ignore the Question of Social Justice in European Contract Law?', 14, *ELJ*, 483; C. Vigneau (2004) 'L'Impératif de Bonne Foi dans l'Exécution du Contrat de Travail', *Droit Social*, 706. Cf. also, in a different comparative context, D. Cabrelli (2005) 'Comparing the Implied Covenant of Good Faith and Fair Dealing with the Implied Term of Mutual Trust and Confidence in the US and UK Employment Contexts' 21, *IJCLLIR*, 445.

statutory obligations to 'preserve the physical integrity',[9] or to 'ensure the safety and preserve the physical and mental health'[10] of the worker.

It will soon become apparent how central and crucial to this chapter, and indeed to this work as a whole, is the question of how to approach comparatively and systematically terminological and linguistic differences without doing violence to the often nuanced but always important conceptual differences embodied in the terms used. Indeed the mere inclusion of a section referring to 'implied terms' may cause surprise and even concern among continental Civilian jurists for whom the English common law notion of 'implying' a term into the contract of employment is, as indicated above, typically resolved by reference to the hierarchy of normative sources, and the associated principles of inderogability and *favor* [construction in favour of the worker]. In France, for example, 'the regime of normative sources orders employment relations in a way that obviously restrains contractual freedom: any clause of the contract that may deprive the worker of a guarantee or an advantage introduced by the law of the state is null', this being, moreover, 'by virtue of the "fundamental principle in labour law according to which, in a case of conflict between rules, it is the one that is more favourable to the worker that must be applied"'.[11] In this sense the continental 'general principles' or 'general clauses' tend to be found in specific statutory sources, either in the form of codified provisions or in special legislative enactments, rather than exclusively or predominantly in jurisprudential reasoning 'implying' them in work relationships, so that they become applicable on the basis of their relative position in the hierarchy of normative sources.

However, we still suggest that, in spite of these fundamental differences, it should still be possible to examine these various normative propositions as rules or principles prescribing how the parties are to act or stating what rights and duties they have in relation to each other. Furthermore, and in spite of the different roles of the judiciary in the English common-law-based and continental European Civilian systems, it should still be possible to advance the idea that the body of law governing the content and performance of personal work and employment contracts can be seen as underpinned by a set of guiding principles of interpretation emerging from judicial/jurisprudential analysis. It is on the basis of these considerations that we proceed to a more detailed enquiry into the functions and contents of these terms and principles and their effects on the regulation of content and performance of personal work and employment contracts.

---

[9] '*Di tutelare l'integrità fisica*'. Article 2087 of the Italian Civil Code. A similar obligation of constitutional character is derived from Articles 32 and 41(2) of the Italian Constitution.

[10] '*Assurer la sécurité et protéger la santé physique et mentale*'. Article L-4121-1 *Code du Travail*.

[11] J. Pélissier, A. Supiot, A. Jeammaud (2008) *Droit du Travail*, 24th ed., Paris: Dalloz, 708, referring to *Soc. 27 mars 2001, Bull. Civ. V, n 106; 4 févr. 2003, Dr. Soc. 2003.352, obs C. Radé*. Our translation.

## B. Fidelity, Obedience, and the Protection of the Interests of the Employer or Employing Enterprise

It can be regarded as axiomatic to the employment law systems of European countries that contracts of employment have it as a core characteristic that the employee owes a duty to protect, and serve the interests of, the employer or employing enterprise. This duty can be typically broken down into a number of implied obligations, which are the legal manifestation of the subordination of the worker to the authority of management in the employing enterprise. It is commonly accepted that this situation of legal and sociological subordination implies the acceptance of the authority of the employer or employing enterprise to direct and control the work of the employee, something that many labour law systems refer to as a 'duty of obedience'. At the same time, this duty demands some degree of obligation not to prejudice the interests of the employer or employing enterprise, and in that sense imposes an obligation of loyalty and fidelity.

As a preliminary observation it needs to be pointed out that while it is arguable that these two duties reinforce each other, and support a strong view of the protection of the interests of the employing entity, their genesis is – both conceptually and historically – fairly autonomous and distinct. Obedience, as the other side of the managerial prerogative, is almost inseparably linked to the emergence of the modern and pre-modern notions of the subordinate contract of employment. Gaeta (2001) provided a fascinating reconstruction of the early twentieth-century debate between Philipp Lotmar and Lodovico Barassi on this very point. Lotmar, according to this reconstruction, was inclined to consider the 'power to direct' as a legal effect of the contract, whereas Barassi took his argument to the point of seeing obedience and subordination as a constitutive element of the contract of employment.[12] Similarly, the English notion of obedience can trace its origins back to the master and servant model,[13] and there is no question that the duty it embodies is an essential characteristic of the employment relationship. Thus it could still quite recently be said that: 'There is certainly nothing more essential to the contractual relation between master and servant than the duty of obedience.'[14]

The implied duty of fidelity has a rather different historical development, which, while inevitably connected to the emergence of the contractual relations in the employment context, owes a great part of its conceptual apparatus to contract law *tout court*. This, as we shall soon see, is particularly evident in continental European Civilian systems, where a duty of fidelity was first imposed by courts through the interpretation of the duty of 'good faith', expected in all contractual relations, and varyingly prescribed in the various nineteenth-century civil codes. But the same is also true of the English notion of fidelity, implied in spite of the absence of a general obligation of good faith in contractual relations. While we are inclined to view the

---

[12] L. Gaeta (2001) 'Lodovico Barassi, Philipp Lotmar e la Cultura Giuridica Tedesca', *GDLRI*, 179.

[13] 'The general rule is obedience': *Turner v. Mason* (1845) 14 *Meeson and Welsby* 112, 118.

[14] *Wilson v. Racher* [1974] ICR 428, 434.

duty of fidelity and confidentiality as fairly distinctive to contracts of employment,[15] their genesis owes much to the notions of 'trust and confidence' and even to ideas of 'good faith' implied in a wider range of contractual relationships. As it was put by Lord Esher MR in *Robb v. Green*: 'The question arises whether . . . in a contract of service the Court can imply a stipulation that the servant will act with good faith towards his master. [ . . . ] I think that in a contract of service the Court must imply such a stipulation as I have mentioned, because it [ . . . .] is impossible to suppose that a master would have put a servant into a confidential position of this kind, unless he thought that the servant would be bound to use good faith towards him.'[16]

These obligations are so deeply embedded in most conceptions of the contract of employment that it is often hard to assign a particular legal source to them. In English law they seem to consist of terms 'implied in law', which can be derived from the very nature of the contract as one which embodies a dependent employment relation. Even in the comparatively more intensely regulated French system, 'no legal disposition explicitly bestows upon the employer a "prerogative" or a "power of direction"' and there is a clear understanding that there are 'rules which . . . can be implicit'.[17] Having said that, continental European Civilian systems go a long way towards providing an explicit statutory or codified basis for these implicit obligations. A duty of obedience is effectively contained, for instance, in Article 2104 of the Italian Civil Code, while Article 2105 explicitly refers to an '*obbligo di fedeltà*'. French jurisprudence and case-law had traditionally derived a fairly similar '*obligation de loyauté*' from the duty of 'good faith' contained in Article 1134, al.3 of the *Code Civil*,[18] but eventually the Law of 1 August 2003 explicitly introduced such an obligation in Article L. 1222-5 al. 3, providing that: 'The employee remains subject to the obligation of loyalty vis-à-vis his employer.'

Although at a basic level it would seem to constitute a universal proposition, European legal systems differ as to the rigorousness of these duties, and as to the extent to which they can be shaped and manipulated by express contractual terms. The following sections endeavour to investigate the detail of this proposition, but at this stage we suggest that one useful way to think about these variations, both within and between national systems, is to examine the extent to which they involve the recognition of different subcategories of contracts of employment, to which these obligations apply in a differential way.

As a duty of acceptance of the authority of 'the employer' to conduct the employing enterprise, the obligation of fidelity seems to extend to all kinds of contract of employment. In English law, a duty of obedience originally formulated in the context of domestic and industrial employment seems to have extended, in theory at least, to all kinds of employment. This is also true of the analogous

---

[15] See the landmark decision in *Faccenda Chicken Ltd v. Fowler* [1986] ICR 297 (CA).
[16] [1895] 2 Q.B. 315, 317.
[17] J. Pélissier, A. Supiot, A. Jeammaud (2008) *Droit du Travail*, 24th ed., Paris: Dalloz, 721. Our translation.
[18] Ibid., 716.

continental European Civilian concepts. Veneziani reminds us of the perceptive analysis of Barassi in respect of the Italian concept of subordination. While acknowledging that the intensity and level of subordination is inversely correlated to the degree of independence and autonomy enjoyed by each individual worker, he confirmed that 'The hard core of the subordination remains unaltered in the physionomical traits so effectively described by Barassi: "This applies both to the factory worker and to the bank director".'[19]

However, as a duty to display more discretionary kinds of loyalty, or to serve the interests of the employer in more far-reaching ways, the obligation of fidelity seems to attach more strongly to employees in the managerial or professional grades of the employing enterprise. In English law, there is a particular heightening of the duties of employees who can be regarded as 'senior' or 'senior managers' with regard to disclosure of their own conduct or that of others which could be injurious to the interests of the employing enterprise.[20] A similar situation applies to the French '*dirigeants*', whose employment status is often shaped by both a contract of employment and by a set of contractual arrangements governed by corporate and commercial law known as '*mandat social*'. For them, the traditional duties of loyalty and fidelity deriving from their employment relationship only operate as a first layer of obligations, to which the duties owed to the company[21] and the shareholders[22] need to be added. These are strong obligations, and the Italian Court of Cassation has found them to apply, on the basis of Articles 2104 and 2105 of the Civil Code, to senior '*dirigenti*' (managers), even during periods of inactivity or during the temporary suspension of the employment relationship for health reasons.[23]

This may represent a partial re-stratification of contracts of employment, following the general homogenization, from the 1960s onwards, of the contracts of employment of 'staff' employees and other workers, that is to say of 'white-collar' and 'blue-collar' workers. The new point of division seems more likely to be between managers and associated professional employees on the one hand, and other employees on the other. In English law this seems unlikely to evolve as a sharp technical categorization, but it does seem likely to influence the way in which the duty of fidelity is interpreted and applied in particular cases. On the other hand, it has been pointed out that in French law, for example, a progressive rehomogenization – with heightened notions of fidelity spreading towards the lower echelons of the enterprise's workforce – can be said to have occurred.[24] But the fact remains, as the following sections of this chapter will endeavour to highlight, that the protection of the interests of the employing entity is served by a mixture

---

[19] B. Veneziani (2002) 'Contratto di Lavoro, Potere di Controllo e Subordinazione nell'Opera di Lodovico Barassi', *GDLRI*, 43.

[20] Cf. *Sybron Corprn* v *Rochem Ltd* [1983] ICR 801, and M. Freedland, 'High Trusts, Pensions and the Contract of Employment' (1984) 13 *ILJ*, 25.

[21] Cass. com., 27 février 1996.

[22] Cass. com., 24 janvier 1995.

[23] Cass. Sez. Lav. n. 24591 del 20 novembre 2006.

[24] J.-E. Ray (1991) 'Fidélité et Exécution du Contrat de Travail', *Droit Social*, 376.

between different levels of intensity of the duty of obedience and the duty of loyalty expected of the workforce.

## C. Care and the Protection of the Welfare of the Worker

Having considered the principal kinds of implied terms or implied obligations which are protective of employers or employing enterprises, we turn our attention to those which are protective of the interests of the worker. Over a long historical period – let us say from the beginning of the twentieth century – it can be observed that the initial focus of the law of contracts of employment consisted in imposing the prescriptions, identified in the previous subsection, for fidelity or loyalty on the part of the worker. Of secondary significance for law-makers, at least until the middle of the twentieth century, was the formulation of obligations of the employer for the care and the protection of the welfare of the worker.

Indeed, until the mid-twentieth century, the law of contracts of employment might even take a negative position so far as the care and protection of the welfare of the worker was concerned, regarding the workplace as a location in which the general development of delictual liability, for injury caused by fault, should be restricted so far as injuries to workers were concerned. This was the position taken in English law under the doctrine of 'common employment' whereby the employee was deemed, by entering into the contract of employment, to accept the risk of and waive the employer's liability for injury caused by fellow workers in 'common employment' with him or her.

This stance can be contrasted with the incremental approach adopted, for instance, by Italian labour legislation and health and safety legislation. As briefly discussed in the introductory section of this chapter, Article 2087 of the Italian Civil Code expressly imposes upon the employer a duty 'to adopt . . . the measures that . . . are necessary to protect the physical integrity and the moral personality of the providers of work'. This norm is built on a series of strong juridical foundations, partly contained in statute, partly in general contract law. Ghera (2007) referring to the Royal Decree n. 230 of 18 June 1899 – possibly the first statute on this subject-matter – suggests that 'the objective of the protection of . . . the physical integrity of the worker has been present right from the origins of [the modern Italian] legal order'.[25] But it is also important to emphasize that this sort of statutory intervention developed and evolved in parallel to the progressive extension of the contractual duty of good faith so as to impose upon each party to the contract an obligation to protect the other party.[26]

Moreover, Barassi reminds us that it was through the general contractual duty of good faith that Italian law derived the more specific 'obligation to treat the employee humanely and to create for him a healthy working environment'.[27]

---

[25] E. Ghera (2007) *Diritto del Lavoro*, Bari: Cacucci, 111.
[26] Ibid, 113.
[27] L. Barassi (1901) *Il Contratto di Lavoro nel Diritto Positivo Italiano*, Milano: Società Editrice Libraria, 556.

Thus, from its introduction in 1942, Article 2087 of the Civil Code could count on the conceptual apparatus already developed in general contract law to impose a duty to protect the parties to a contract of employment. It is in this trajectory that one can see the further development of the Italian 'duty to protect' by means of its inclusion in Articles 32 and 41(2) of the 1948 Constitution. Subsequent statutory prescriptions, such as those contained in the *Statuto dei Lavoratori* (Workers Statute) or in Legislative Decree 626/1994 'identified some [further] specifications of the duty to protect',[28] and further intertwined the statutory, contractual, and collective threads of the Italian version of the 'duty of care'.

Eventually, English law abandoned the negative positions previously described; and in European legal systems there was a general development of legislation concerning health and safety at work, from modest beginnings in the mid-nineteenth century, which gathered pace and momentum in the second half of the twentieth century. To the question, how far has that development of health and safety legislation permeated the law of contracts of employment, giving rise to a general prescription for the care and the protection of the welfare of the worker, there seem to be two contrasting paradigms for European legal systems. Particular legal systems can be seen as in varying degrees aligned to one or other of these paradigms.

On the one hand, there is a paradigm of high protection of the health, safety, and welfare of workers. In this paradigm, the law of contracts of employment incorporates and builds upon the foundations of worker-protective health and safety legislation which may itself derive from the elaboration and application of general contractual duties to the context of the employment relationship. The legislation establishes not only a set of particular rules about health and safety in the work place, but also a set of principles which form part of the norms of the contract of employment and which the courts further elaborate upon. France is arguably a good example of this regulatory paradigm. Successive statutes, amendments of the *Code du Travail*, and court decisions, have produced a very dense and integrated regulatory network in the area of health and safety. As Pélissier, Supiot, and Jeammaud (2008) argue,[29] this network is of course composed of substantive provisions specifying exacting duties, and also contains an articulated regime of both Civil and criminal liabilities, provisions for the establishment of several bodies in charge of health and safety, and a series of individual and collective rights. But it is also, and crucially, composed of a general *'obligation de sécurité'*.[30] As pointed out by those authors, 'the norm creating a duty of safety does not prescribe a precise obligation, but charges the debtor with doing "everything that is useful and possible in order to obtain a result". . . . Imposing a duty of safety represents an economy of regulation, of multiplication or reiteration of particular provisions.'[31]

---

[28] Ibid, 115.
[29] J. Pélissier, A. Supiot, A. Jeammaud (2008) *Droit du Travail*, 24th ed., Paris: Dalloz, 834–7.
[30] Ibid, 837.
[31] Ibid. Our translation.

There is a contrasting paradigm in which, even if there is strongly worker-protective health and safety legislation, that remains separate from the law of contracts of employment, so that contracts of employment do not themselves contain or generate strong principles in favour of protection of the health, safety, or welfare of workers. The English law of contracts of employment seems to correspond to this paradigm. There has been a strong legislative development of norms of health and safety, in and from the Health and Safety at Work Act 1974 (HSWA 1974). But this does not seem to have to have permeated the law of contracts of employment. While the 'duty of care' principle is of course mentioned by HSWA 1974, the statutory and the common law regimes do not produce a normative network as integrated as the one present in some continental European Civilian countries.

This less than perfect integration became apparent in recent years before the ECJ, when the UK government, in order to escape liability for the – according to the Commission – unsatisfactory implementation of Article 5 of Directive 89/391, argued that its health and safety regime was not contained solely in the 1973 Act but 'that the employer is also liable for damage resulting from a failure on his part to discharge the duty of care in relation to workers provided for under the common law'.[32] The Court eventually found for the UK after accepting that the contested provision did not actually require the imposition of a no-fault type of liability upon the employer. But it is interesting to note how even the Commission had failed to recognize this evident, and peculiarly British, disjunction between statute and the common law.[33] This fact, however, had not escaped the attention of AG Mengozzi who noted that, under the system in force in the UK, 'employers are subject to civil liability only in relation to breaches of the specific obligations placed on them by particular provisions of law but not in relation to the failure to discharge the general duty to ensure safety set out in HSWA 1974, s.2(1). However, it appears from the case-file that, in common law, the employer will be subject to a form of civil liability if he is in breach of his duty of care to his workers.'[34]

We may add to this set of considerations that in the English law of contracts of employment, the legislature has been, at least until the last couple of decades and in some ways even until today, content for the courts to construe contracts of employment as doing little if anything more than replicating the general law of delict so far as the health and safety of the worker is concerned. So, far from being integrated as in some continental European Civilian systems, the employer's contractual liability for the health and safety of the worker has tended to be generally co-extensive with, even interchangeable with, its liability for the tort of negligence.

This has resulted in a relatively cautious approach, so far as the English law of contracts of employment is concerned, to the emergent liability of employers to

---

[32] C-127/05, *Commission v. UK* [2007] ECR I-4619, [34].

[33] AG Opinon [128]: 'This form of liability was not considered in the application, in keeping with the assumption on which the Commission based its view concerning the strict nature of the employer liability required by the framework directive.'

[34] AG Opinion [127].

workers in respect of mental injury caused by stress suffered in the workplace or in the work situation. The largely interchangeable contractual or delictual liability has emerged more as a response to episodic post-traumatic stress disorder (PTSD) to which the worker has been exposed by the negligence of the employer than as the construction of a positive continuing managerial responsibility for the protection of the mental health and well-being of the employee.[35] There has been a comparable tendency to stick to a rather narrowly tort-based approach to the employer's liability under the English law of contracts of employment with regard to the provision of references for the employee. The courts seemed to be moving in the direction of the recognition of a general duty to protect the economic well-being of the employee as well as his or her physical well-being; but a more restrictive approach subsequently set in.[36]

Thus far, having considered the employee's implied duties of fidelity, obedience, and loyalty to the employer, and the employer's implied duties of care and protection towards the employee, we have noted a general historical tendency for English law, while not necessarily being less protective than continental Civilian systems towards the worker, nevertheless to be relatively reluctant to integrate its protection of workers into the construction of the contract of employment itself. In the next subsection we turn to consider whether and if so how far English law has in recent years transformed its approach by harnessing a worker-protective notion of an obligation of mutual trust and confidence to that contractual construction.

## D.  Towards a Principle of Mutual Trust, Good Faith, and Fair Dealing?

In the previous two subsections it was established that there are two main sets of duties for the regulation, by the law of the contract of employment, of the content and performance of those contracts. These consist of a set of prescriptions for fidelity and obedience on the part of the worker towards the employer, and another set of prescriptions for care of the health and safety of the worker. As between European legal systems, these are common themes, though there is considerable variation in the ways in which and the rigour with which these prescriptions are imposed.

In this subsection we go on to consider to what extent those two sets of prescriptions have merged or expanded into or are in the course of merging or expanding into an overarching prescription for good faith and fair dealing in the content and performance of employment contracts, applying – albeit in different ways – to both workers and employers. This is a promising hypothesis since, as we briefly discussed above, some of these duties actually originally derive from a re-elaboration of the general notion of good faith and fair dealing in contractual relations. Our argument will be that many European legal systems do

[35] See M. Freedland (2003) *The Personal Employment Contract*, Oxford: OUP, p. 145.
[36] See M. Freedland (2003) *The Personal Employment Contract*, Oxford: OUP, p. 146, and cf. S, Middlemiss (2004) 'The Truth and Nothing but the Truth: the Legal Liability of Employers for Employees' References', 33 *ILJ*, 59.

display such tendencies. The English law of contracts of employment can be included in this conclusion. However, English law displays this tendency in its own rather special way, preferring an employment-specific conception of 'mutual trust and confidence' to the more general formulae of good faith and fair dealing. That differentiation has important causes and consequences which will be examined.

In some European legal systems, the law of employment contracts has over long periods of time contained prescriptions which are in the nature of requirements of good faith and fair dealing between the parties. These could usually be regarded as applications or developments, in the specific context of employment contracts, of general notions of good faith in the performance of contracts which permeated or were nascent in the general law of contract in the legal systems concerned. The *Code Napoléon* first codified 'good faith' in its Articles 1134 and 1135. 'In Germany, *bona fides* could conveniently be blended with the indigenous notion of *Treu und Glauben* (literally: fidelity and faith) [which] was ultimately destined to find its way into the famous § 242 of the German Civil Code of 1900.'[37] The Italian Civil Code of 1865, under the influence of the French Civil Code, similarly provided for the introduction of 'good faith' and 'equity' in Article 1124. By the early twentieth century Barassi could convincingly argue that the parties to a contract of employment were surely bound by the contractually agreed terms, but also by those moral duties that 'common conscience considers obligatory'.[38] The judicial praxis of the Italian *probiviri* (equivalent to modern-day arbitrators) further consolidated the relevance of *buona fede* both 'in the individual employment relationship, and [in] the good practices of industrial relations'.[39]

These prescriptions of good faith would not necessarily or typically have been developed in a very concrete way at the level of judicial doctrine, and might not, at that level, have amounted to very much in the way of the protection of the interests or well-being of workers. However, 'from what came to be considered as good faith behaviour [ . . . :], rules derived that were eventually transformed by the legislator into positive [statutory] duties, since back then the contract [of employment] still did not have a fully articulated regime'.[40] The norms derived from worker-protective legislation might have been regarded as a sufficient concretization of the general idea of good faith in the employment context, not requiring further supplementation by judicial doctrine.

Moreover, the principle of good faith had its periods of popularity as well as its periods of demise. The central decades of the twentieth century coincided with a

---

[37] S. Whittaker and R. Zimmermann (2000) 'Good Faith in European Contract Law: Surveying the Legal Landscape', in R. Zimmermann and S. Whittaker (eds.), *Good Faith in European Contract Law*, Cambridge, CUP, at 18.

[38] L. Barassi (1901) *Il Contratto di Lavoro nel Diritto Positivo Italiano*, Milano: Società Editrice Libraria, 561.

[39] A. Perulli (2002) 'La Buona Fede nel Diritto del Lavoro' 53, *Rivista Giuridica del Lavoro*, 5. Our translation from the original Italian.

[40] L. Castelvetri (2001) 'Correttezza e Buona Fede nella Giurisprudenza del Lavoro. Diffidenza e Proposte Dottrinali', *Diritto delle Relazioni Industriali*, 238. Our translation.

period in which the principle of good faith in general, and in particular in the context of work relations, was increasingly approached with some degree of suspicion by the continental European legal scholarship. Even before 1933, 'there were, and still are, German lawyers who [looked] askance at a principle which a judge can invoke whenever he wants to do justice and cannot find any other authority'.[41] This suspicion was only reinforced by the advent of the Third Reich, when 'the courts applied the principle to discriminate against the Jews'.[42] Unsurprisingly German courts and authors generally agree that *Treu und Glauben* cannot be invoked 'to replace the effects imposed by law and contract by what they in their taste consider to be reasonable and equitable in concrete cases'.[43]

During Italy's fascist period, the principle of good faith was similarly manipulated to serve some of the regime's legal and political *teloi*. The '*dovere di buona fede*' (duty of good faith) was flanked by the '*dovere di correttezza*' (duty of correctness) imposed by Article 1175 of the 1942 Civil Code. In its original formulation – eventually abrogated in 1944 after the regime's fall – the norm required the 'creditor' and the 'debtor' to adhere to this principle 'by reference to the principles of the corporatist legal order'. 'Evoking these general clauses, in the political strategy of the fascist regime, had the declared aim of shaping positive contract law around a notion of good faith enlightened by the principles of corporatist solidarity'.[44]

It is perhaps unsurprising therefore that the relevance and influence of good faith as a general clause in employment contracts declined in the aftermath of the Second World War. The principle was either perceived as irrelevant, since most good faith constructs had been or were being incorporated in labour law statutes, or as socially regressive, in that it had largely been used in the past 'with the aim of expanding the sphere of responsibilities of the worker'.[45] In some systems it was even perceived as ideologically suspect, in that it suggested an equality and bilaterality in the contractual duties of the worker and the corporate structure of the enterprise that was tainted by a paternalistic, and ultimately flawed, vision of industrial relations. As Camerlynck put it in respect of the suggestion that '*bonne foi*' and '*devoir de fidélité*' might apply to employment relations, 'this formulation reproduces a certain paternalism and [...] evokes the Germanic notion of allegiance [...]. It does not appear to correspond to the spirit which prevails in employment

---

[41] O. Lando (2007) 'Is Good Faith an Over-arching General Clause in the Principles of European Contract Law', in M. Andenas *et al.* (eds.), *Liber Amicorum Guido Alpa – Private Law Beyond National Systems* London: British Institute of International and Comparative Law 604.

[42] Ibid.

[43] Ibid., 604–5.

[44] L. Castelvetri (2001) 'Correttezza e Buona Fede nella Giurisprudenza del Lavoro. Diffidenza e Proposte Dottrinali', *Diritto delle Relazioni Industriali*, 239 (our translation).

[45] A. Perulli (2002) 'La Buona Fede nel Diritto del Lavoro', 53, *Rivista Giuridica del Lavoro*, 7.

relations within an enterprise of which the worker does not form a part, merely being in its service and from which he could be rejected at any time.'[46]

The evolution in the English law of contracts of employment has been in some respects a parallel one, but in certain ways very eclectic. The English law of contracts has traditionally and down to the present day refrained from adopting generalized prescriptions of good faith and fair dealing. The traditional scepticism towards the role of 'good faith' during contractual negotiations and during contractual performance is well documented and researched in both jurisprudential and scholarly analyses, in spite of some recent tendencies towards a more open engagement with the concept.[47] This is not saying that English contract law is not influenced by notions of good faith, but arguably 'it does not, as yet, recognize the existence of a doctrine of good faith. In this respect English law stands out from many other legal systems in the world.'[48] Undeniably, since the 1970s onwards, there has been extensive development, partly under the influence of EU law, of regulation of contract terms by reference to notions of 'fairness', especially in the context of 'consumer contracts', culminating with the adoption of the Unfair Terms in Consumer Contracts Regulations 1999. But contracts of employment have on the whole been excluded from that kind of regulation, either by express legislative provision or by judicial interpretation, especially consisting in a judicial reluctance to regard contracts of employment as falling within the conception of 'standard form contracts'. So in the English law of contracts of employment, there has been nothing directly corresponding to continental European examples of the elaboration of general private law notions of good faith and fair dealing.

However, in the last couple of decades there have been significant changes in the attitude of both continental European systems and the English system towards the role of good faith in contracts of employment and other personal work contracts. In some European systems there has been a reinforcement of prescriptions of good faith and fair dealing in the law of contracts of employment, generally speaking in a worker-protective sense. As Vigneau argues, 'for some years now the [French] judiciary has not hesitated to evoke contractual good faith to impose on the employer some requirements of good behaviour, thus increasing his share of obligations emerging from the contract of employment'.[49] This has tended to take place in parallel with quite a vigorous development of notions of good faith and fair dealing in European systems of private law, especially in the context of the protection of consumers as against the suppliers of goods and, increasingly, services. Sometimes this enhancement of requirements of good faith and fair dealing in the content and performance of contracts of employment has taken place by way of

---

[46] G. H. Camerlynck (1982) *Droit du Travail – Le Contrat de Travail – Tome I*, 2nd ed., Paris: Dalloz, 1982, 244. Our translation.

[47] Cf. E. McKendrick, 'The Meaning of 'Good Faith'', in M. Andenas *et al.* (eds.) (2007), *Liber Amicorum Guido Alpa – Private Law Beyond National Systems*, London: British Institute of International and Comparative Law, 687.

[48] E. McKendrick: 2005 *Contract Law*, 2nd ed., Oxford: OUP, 542.

[49] C. Vigneau, (2004) 'L'Impératif de Bonne Foi dans l'Exécution du Contrat de Travail', *Droit Social*, 711.

direct extension of such requirements from their primary context of consumer protection, as in the case of the reform of the German *Bürgerliches Gesetzbuch* (Civil Code) in 2002.[50] Sometimes the influence from the domain of consumer protection has been a more indirect one, as with the strengthening of the idea of '*bonne foi*' in the French *Code du Travail* and in its recent applications to contracts of employment by the French courts.

In the English law of contracts of employment, a very significant equivalent development did occur from the 1980s onwards. This consisted in the articulation and development of a powerfully prescribed obligation of 'mutual trust and confidence'. This was by definition and in its very conception reciprocal as between employers and employees. But it had the particular function of reinforcing the protection of employees, and of counter-balancing the very general requirements of fidelity or loyalty to which they had traditionally been subjected. This development was the unexpected and indeed ironical outcome of a very particular interaction between the common law of contracts of employment and the statute-based law of unfair dismissal. We shall show in the next chapter how those two systems developed as distinct (though interactive) ones.[50a] The statutory law of unfair dismissal had its own conception of dismissal. That included a notion of 'constructive dismissal' consisting of conduct on the part of the employer which was such as to entitle the employee to leave his employment but to claim that he or she had in effect been dismissed by the employer.[51] The legislation failed to make it clear whether the criterion for its notion of constructive dismissal was that of serious breach of contract, or, on the other hand, simply of generally unreasonable conduct on the part of the employer. In a conscious effort to secure a cautious and restrained approach to the idea of constructive dismissal, the Court of Appeal decided that the criterion should be the contractual one.[52] The ironical outcome was that this provoked the articulation of a vigorous implied contractual obligation of 'mutual trust and confidence' in order to support a strong conception of constructive unfair dismissal.[53]

In the remainder of this chapter, we shall consider the ways in which, and the extent to which, this rather esoteric development in the English law of contracts of employment resulted in a functional parallel with the treatment, in many European legal systems, of issues concerning the content and performance of contracts of employment according to broadly based notions of good faith and fair dealing. As pointed out in the previous sections and paragraphs, we will be comparing systems that considerably differ in the ways in which they approach the general and specific concepts of good faith and fair dealing in personal work relations. Perhaps more importantly, these systems also differ in the extent to which they incorporate these

---

[50] R. Zimmermann (2005), *The New German Law of Obligations – Historical and Comparative Perspectives*, Oxford: OUP, Chapter 5 'Consumer Contract Law and General Contract Law – the German Experience'.

[50a] Cf. In particular pp. 224–31 and 241–50.

[51] Cf. M. Freedland (2003), *The Personal Employment Contract*, Oxford: OUP, 385–387 and 422–425.

[52] *Western Excavating (ECC Ltd) v. Sharp* [1978] ICR 221.

[53] Cf. M. Freedland (2003), *The Personal Employment Contract*, Oxford: OUP, 155–162.

concepts into statutory provisions for the regulation of the performance, the variation, and the suspension of contracts of employment, provisions which themselves sometimes feed into the legal construction of contracts of employment.

Thus, systems like the British one provide only a marginal incorporation of these duties into statutes, and only a marginal incorporation of those statutory provisions into the core conception of the contract of employment itself. By contrast, countries like France or Italy have long incorporated the general and specific duties of fair dealing and good faith into some rather precise and prescriptive statutory norms, often inspired by their respective constitutional principles, which in turn are at least partly integrated into the regulation of contracts of employment as such. As a result, our analysis of contractual performance may appear to be rather asymmetric at times, with the focus variably shifting from statutory norms to implied contractual regulatory principles, in an effort to encompass the structural regulatory differences of the various legal systems.

However, in the next chapter, which is concerned with the termination and transformation of the contract of employment, we shall see that this alignment of the English law of contracts of employment with broadly based notions of good faith and fair dealing was rather a contingent and fragile one. At a crucial point in the development of the implied obligation of mutual trust and confidence, the courts would, partially at least, sever this new link between the law of contracts of employment and the law of unfair dismissal.[54] It remains to be seen whether and if so how far the implied obligation of mutual trust and confidence has retained, in the context of the regulation of the content and performance of contracts of employment, the capacity to operate as a general constraint upon the abuse of law, of rights, and of power on the part of employing enterprises. It may be that its exclusion from the regulation of dismissal has crucially undermined its ability to operate in that way even beyond the sphere of dismissal. Another possibility is that the mutual obligation of trust and confidence will enjoy a vigorous half-life in the limited sphere to which it has been consigned. That will become clearer in the subsequent sections of the present chapter.

## Section 2: Performance

### A. Integrated and Dis-Integrated Approaches to the Performance of Contracts of Employment

As we have indicated in the Introduction to this chapter, the present discussion forms a further stage in our examination of how European legal systems construct contracts of employment and each create their own distinctive body of 'law of the contract of employment' – our interest being in the ways that these constructions shape and affect the regulation of those personal work relations which are regarded as taking the legal form of contracts of employment. To recapitulate for a moment,

---

[54] Cf. *Johnson v. Unisys Ltd* [2001] ICR 480. See below at pp. 248–50.

we contend that a key variable as between these different national constructions of 'the contract of employment' and 'the law of the contract of employment' consists in the different treatment by each of those systems of the relations between the sources of regulation of the personal work relations in question, in particular as to the extent to which and the manner in which inputs from the various sources of regulation are regarded as falling within 'the contract of employment' or within the 'the law of the contract of employment'. The fact that there is wide diversity between national legal systems around this key variable means that the ideas of 'the contract of employment' and of 'the law of the contract of employment' differ considerably as between national legal systems – so much so that the appearance of a commonality of meaning between national terminologies may be an illusory one.

In this subsection, we seek to identify some contrasts between integrated and dis-integrated approaches to sources of regulations in the construction of contracts of employment with regard to the performance of those contracts or of the obligations which they are deemed to create or embody. As a preliminary step in the development of those contrasts, it will be useful to articulate, slightly more fully than we have previously done, the regulatory tendencies or regulatory implications which we ascribe to the two contrasting approaches, that is to say the integrative and dis-integrative approaches to the external sources of regulation of contractual employment relations. We are now, moreover, in a position to incorporate into that articulation some lessons from the preceding discussion in the preceding section of general principles, general clauses, and generically implied terms as elements or factors prescribing the content of contracts of employment.

Being careful to stress that we are at this stage seeking to identify general theoretical tendencies, or 'ideal-types', we can with that caveat identify the following contrasting implications of, on the one hand, integrative, and, on the other hand, dis-integrative approaches to the external sources of regulation of contractual employment relations. We suggest that dis-integrative approaches, which *ex hypothesi* maintain the separateness of external sources of regulation, thereby ensure the dominance of some underlying features of what we might regard as a kind of historical common law of contracts of employment which can be discerned in largely similar manifestations in European national legal systems quite generally. This historical common thread is woven of two strands, which reinforce each other. One is the individualistic liberalism of the law of contracts in general, and the other is the more specific notion of the prerogative of the employer to 'be master in his own house', largely translated into a modern vision of the managerial prerogative of the employing enterprise.

We suggest that those two historical strands are often found, in the long development of labour law in European national legal systems, to have interwoven with each other and to have created what we might regard as underlying default positions for the construction and regulation of contractual employment relations. In all European legal systems, those underlying default positions have to some degree, often to a very great degree, been modified or displaced by combinations of worker-protective legislation and collective bargaining. However, if that has been an evolution which

European legal systems have had in common, those systems have nevertheless varied considerably as to the speed and timing of that displacement – and in particular as to the extent to which the overlay of worker-protective regulation has been integrated into the conception which each system has of 'the contract of employment' and of 'the law of the contract of employment'. In other words, there is a contestation between integrative and dis-integrative approaches in the way that each European national legal system constructs its vision of the contract of employment, and a considerable variation between those systems in this very important respect.

We can now in light of the discussion in the previous section of this chapter, add the further reflection that this contestation between integrative and dis-integrative approaches may be played out by and through the general principles of the law of employment contracts or the general clauses or the generically implied terms which each legal system brings to bear upon or imports into the construction of contractual employment relations. Such general principles, general clauses, or generically implied terms might evolve in a given system so as to reinforce either tendency – the integrative or the dis-integrative one. In the remainder of this section of this chapter, quite a lot of our concern will be focused on the question of which of those two opposite effects has been more prone to occur in particular European legal systems. Before embarking on the further stages of that discussion, we explain why we are concentrating especially strongly upon English law as the principal location for our arguments.

The focus on English law, as the primary case with which comparisons are made, is one which is maintained throughout this work, and one which was explained from the outset. The argument for that methodology is especially strong with regard to the discussion of integrated and dis-integrated approaches to the regulation of the performance of employment contracts. That is because, in ways which we have begun to indicate, no aspect of the legal construction of personal work relations is more deeply embedded in the fabric of each national employment law system, or more intimately path-dependent upon the vagaries of each system, than this aspect is. It seems to us necessary to focus upon one particular legal system in order to make this particular discussion a meaningful one in any sense. We hope that it will emerge that, while English law provides the most prominent example of a dis-integrative approach among European legal systems, it nevertheless does not conform to any simple paradigm of that approach. We proceed in the following subsection to seek to demonstrate this with regard to its treatment of the relation between performance and remuneration, firstly with regard to the regulation of the wage–work bargain in general, and secondly at a more specific level on which the continuity of remuneration is related to differing conceptions of contractual performance, in some of which performance is conceived of as 'work' while in others it is conceived of more broadly as 'service' or 'willingness to work'.

## B. Performance and the Wage–Work Bargain

In this subsection and the next we take a broad sweep across the many ways in which employment law regulates the performance of contracts of employment in the sense of supervising the functioning of the wage–work bargain, that is to say the arrangements which determine the relation between work and remuneration. This involves the consideration of many different kinds of regulation, differentiated not only by their sources but also by their objectives; and each national employment law system has its own complex assemblage of layers of regulation in this area. That makes it quite difficult, and ultimately not very meaningful, to place particular elements from the different national assemblages of regulation alongside each other. Nevertheless, it is an area which is a fruitful one for the pursuit of our discussion of contrasts between integrated and dis-integrated approaches to the regulation of contractual employment relations. So we seek to develop that discussion by concentrating primarily on English law but offering some incidental comparative reflections.

On the whole, in this area as in several others, English law presents a case study, and the clearest instance among European legal systems so far as we are aware, of a dis-integrated approach in the sense that a strong separation is made between 'the contract of employment' and sources of regulation which are viewed as external to it, especially that of statute law. This certainly represents a strong historical trend, and one which was the dominant one until recent times, though it has been somewhat moderated in the last twenty or so years. As an historical trend, it has had the effect that the regulatory discourse in this area has been one which has accorded a low level of protection to employees' interests in the functioning of the wage–work bargain, both because of the default models which have been applied and because of the degree of deference to the parties' own contractual arrangements – therefore in practice those of the employing enterprise – which it has implied.

A telling illustration is to be found in the regulation of deductions from remuneration in respect of incomplete or defective performance of work. Under the common law, the 'doctrine of entire contracts' gave rise to a presumption or default model according to which remuneration for the whole of what we would now refer to as a payment reference period could be withheld for incompleteness of performance of work throughout that reference period even if it was a very long one.[55] A general principle of the law of equity which authorizes judicial intervention against 'fines or penalties' has provided little or no protection against fines or punitive deductions in the field of contractual employment relations.[56]

That common law substratum, affording a low level of protection to employees, has been overlaid but not displaced by a long history of legislative regulation, originating in the Truck Acts from the 1830s onwards, which has signally failed to remould the matrix for contractual employment relations. The legislative regime for the control of fines and deductions which has been in place since the enactment of the Wages Act 1986 is more deferential than ever to the contractual arrangements which employing enterprises choose to make in this regard, and moreover the claim against unauthorized or inappropriate deductions from wages which is supported by that legislation is viewed as not being in its nature a directly contractual claim.

[55] See M. Freedland (2003) *The Personal Employment Contract*, Oxford: OUP, at 201–4.
[56] Ibid. 208–9.

This approach can be usefully contrasted with the one adopted by some continental European systems, where statutory, and often codified, interventions have placed clear constraints on the common/contract law principles. Article L. 1331-2 of the French *Code du Travail* provides that 'fines or other pecuniary sanctions are prohibited', and although this provision does not operate as to exclude the '*exceptio non adimplenti contractus*',[57] French courts have interpreted this provision in such a way as to narrow down the influence of contract law, for instance by prohibiting 'any deduction from the salary applied by reason of bad performance of the work'.[58] Similarly Article 7 of the Italian *Statuto dei Lavoratori* has severely constrained the disciplinary powers of employers, and their abilities to impose fines on their workers. The French Court of Cassation has further interpreted the provisions of Article L. 1331-2 as applying to a 'travelling salesperson engaged on an exclusive basis'[59] for any 'deduction applied by the employer from [his] minimum remuneration'[60] for failing to reach his weekly quotas.[61] Article L. 1331-2 of the *Code du Travail* further provides in our translation that 'any provision or agreement to the contrary is considered as null and void'.

## C. Performance and the Continuity of Remuneration

A somewhat similar picture of the dis-integrated approach of English law presents itself in the rather more specific location of the treatment of interruptions to work and their effect upon the continuity of remuneration. We shall in a later section of this chapter revert to that discussion under the heading of suspension of the contract of employment or of obligations under that contract; but it is useful to reflect upon the way in which English law displays a dis-integrated approach even at the logically prior stage at which it regulates the basic relationship between the obligations of the employee under the contract of employment and the employee's entitlement to remuneration under that contract.

As in our earlier discussion of performance and the wage–work bargain, we find that English law brings to bear, upon this aspect of the relationship between the employee's obligations and his or her entitlement to remuneration, a body of common law doctrine which has scarcely been touched by other regulatory inputs. In this context, that body of common law doctrine has two relevant elements. One is the doctrine of 'entire contracts' or of 'entire contractual obligations', which as we have seen generally militates against the employee by making his or her entitlement to remuneration conditional upon complete performance of the corresponding duties or obligations. The other element is a doctrine which renders the entitlement to remuneration as sometimes conditional upon 'readiness and willingness to work' rather than upon the performance of work. It is a doctrine which, as we shall see, is

---

[57] J. Pélissier, A. Supiot, A. Jeammaud (2008) *Droit du Travail* (24th ed., Paris: Dalloz, 808. Our translation.

[58] Cass. soc., 2 décembre 1992, n 89–43162. Our translation.

[59] Our translation of '*VRP, engagé à titre exclusif*'.

[60] Our translation of '*ressource minimale forfaitaire*'.

[61] Cass. soc. 13 décembre 2006, n 05–40969.

at best only weakly protective of the interests of the employee and may even on occasion operate against those interests. We shall proceed to argue in a few specific contexts that these doctrines have appeared to represent 'the law of the contract of employment', somewhat to the exclusion of other sources of regulation which might be more protective of those interests.

The first such context is that of interruption to work brought about by interruption to demand for the services of the employee. In this context, the notion that the employee's entitlement to remuneration may be conditional upon his or her willingness to work rather than upon the actual performance of work will indeed tend to be protective of the employee. But the doctrine has historically amounted to no more than a weak presumption or default model, which could easily be displaced by contrary indications;[62] and it was moreover one which served to differentiate the socially and economically more favoured 'salaried employee' from the less favoured 'wage-earner'. That is a kind of differentiation which was reduced in later decades of the twentieth century (although it was in a sense succeeded by shifts in the labour market towards atypical forms of employment); but it was in a certain sense unduly perpetuated in the English law of the contract of employment, while the admittedly rather modest statutory provisions for guaranteed minimum remuneration during such interruptions, like the guarantee arrangements under collective agreements upon which the statutory provisions were modelled, failed to secure a substantial foothold in that body of law still underlyingly dominated by common law doctrine.[63]

The second such context in which the dis-integrated approach to continuity of remuneration can be discerned is that of sick pay. As a matter of common law doctrine a kind of presumption in favour of the continuation of remuneration during sickness was fashioned out of the idea that the condition of 'readiness and willingness to work' was satisfied where the employee could be said to be ready and willing to work 'if of ability to do so' – a qualification which included absence by reason of incapacitating sickness. However, that presumption was of little cogency and was limited in its social and economic field of application in rather the same way as the weak presumption in favour of continuity of remuneration during economic lay-off.[64] On the other hand, the legislative provisions requiring employers to provide payment for short-term sickness absence (with recoupment from the National Insurance system) have seemed to be viewed as creating 'statutory sick pay' which has no real place in the firmament of the common law of the contract of employment.

A rather more subtle form of this dis-integrated approach is to be found in the third such context to which we shall refer, namely that of interruption of performance by reason of industrial action in which the employee takes part. In the case of outright strike action, the cessation of remuneration is for the most part an

---

[62] See M. Freedland (2003) *The Personal Employment Contract*, Oxford: OUP, at 214–18.

[63] Ibid. 474–9 and compare R. McCallum (1989) 'Exploring the Common Law: Lay-off, Suspension and the Contract of Employment', 2 *Australian Journal of Labour Law*, 211.

[64] See M. Freedland (2003) *The Personal Employment Contract*, Oxford: OUP, at 214–18.

obvious consequence; but the position with regard to industrial action falling short of a strike is more controversial both at the doctrinal and practical levels. In this context the common law doctrine of 'entire contracts' may militate against the interests of the employee; and even the normally employee-protective notion of readiness and willingness to work as amounting to constructive performance of the conditions for continuation of remuneration may turn into one which is hostile to the employee's interests, as where, in *British Telecom plc v. Ticehurst*[65] it was invoked to require the employee to disclaim any intention of taking part in threatened future industrial action short of a strike as a precondition for continuation of remuneration. The application of such doctrines manifests a dis-integrated approach to external sources of regulation in the sense that the doctrine is developed and applied entirely without any reference to legislation conferring immunity from tort liability for industrial action, and equally without any reference to any legislation concerning freedom of association; such measures seem to be regarded as existing in a separate juridical realm from that of the law of the contract of employment.

Turning our attention to some of the continental European Civil-law based systems, we can usefully contrast the aforementioned approach of English law by reference to two fundamental, albeit inevitably general, sets of considerations. Firstly, and perhaps inevitably, continental notions of contract of employment are not completely shielded from the effects that general doctrines of contract law exert upon the contractual employment relationship. As such, the modern equivalent of the Roman law '*exceptio non adimplenti contractus*' inevitably still plays a role in Italian labour law, in the form of the 'exception of non-performance'[66] contained in Article 1460 of the Civil Code. Secondly, however, and this is an important qualification for the purposes of the argument developed in these subsections, statutory intervention and in specific doctrinal developments judge-made labour law, have substantially limited the scope of these contract law principles in the context of work relations, for instance by limiting the applicability of the common principles of restitution,[67] or by subjecting some typologies of partial and temporary non-performance to other special regulatory regimes, most commonly the one applying to suspension of employment relations, or – as in the case of German law at least since the Weimar period[68] – by placing squarely upon the employer the risk of the impossibility of accepting the provision of work: 'the employer, who usually makes the profit, was also supposed to bear the risk (*Betriebsrisikolehre*)'.[69] More generally, Weiss and Schmidt (2008) stress that German labour law makes an explicit exception to the common/contract law principle of 'no work, no pay', which can be found in the Civil Code, s. 615. 'Accordingly the employer is obliged to pay

---

[65] [1992] ICR 383.

[66] For a description of its effects, cf. E. Ghera (2007) *Diritto del Lavoro*, Bari: Cacucci, 147–8.

[67] With Article 1373(2) of the Italian Civil Code introducing an exception to the general principle of restitution contained in Article 2033.

[68] M. Weiss and M. Schmidt (2008) *Labour Law and Industrial Relations in Germany* (AH Alphen aan den Rijn: Kluwer, 112.

[69] Ibid.

remuneration if the employee offers to work, but the employer does not accept this offer.'[70]

Similarly, Ghera suggests that Italian labour law has 'progressively established the principle or general rule – albeit a non-absolute one, and thus subject to exceptions – of the so-called transfer to the employer of the risks arising from the inactivity of the worker (so-called lack of work) in case of the *supervening impossibility of the performance [of work] due to fortuitous causes or to* force majeure *pertaining to the worker*'.[71] Articles 2110–2111 of the Italian Civil Code thus expressly provide for the suspension of the employment relationship in cases of accidents at work, illness, pregnancy and maternity, and military service. This effectively introduces, as well as a right not to be dismissed, a right to the 'conservation of remuneration, or in its stead, to the attribution of an indemnity in the measure and for the time established by law, collective agreements, custom or equity'.[72] What we can infer from these considerations is not just the extent to which the substantive protection afforded by other legal systems differs from the ones enshrined in English law, but also – and in particular – the extent to which these specific labour law provisions and jurisprudential norms displace and marginalize the general common law principles that the contractual nature of the employment relationship, perhaps inevitably, cannot altogether exclude.

We revert to some of these issues in a later section under the heading of 'suspension' of contracts of employment or of obligations under those contracts; but before doing so we turn to pursue our discussion of contrasts between integrated and dis-integrated approaches in the associated context of variation of contracts of employment or of obligations arising under those contracts.

## Section 3: Variation

In this section, our exploration of contrasts between integrated and dis-integrated approaches to the legal construction of contractual employment relations moves into the area of regulation of the flexibility of those relations, and in particular the regulation of the latitude accorded to the employing enterprise to alter the employee's job specification or the location in or within which the employee is required to work. In this regard, English law presents a specially interesting case-study of a dis-integrated approach to the conceptualization and construction of the contract of employment. We firstly conduct that case-study in some detail (subsection A) and then engage in some comparative reflection around it (sub-section B).

---

[70] Ibid.

[71] E. Ghera (2007) *Diritto del Lavoro*, Bari: Cacucci, 148–9. Our translation. Emphasis original.

[72] Ibid., 149.

## A. The Contested Approach to Variation in English Employment Law

In this subsection, we will seek to show how the strongly dis-integrated approach of English law to the variation of contracts of employment or of their terms and conditions has had controversial regulatory implications, so that the approach itself should be regarded as a contested one. That situation may be better understood if we enumerate the principal ways in which variation may be regulated; there are three main points at which this kind of regulation of the flexibility of terms and conditions of employment might take place. Firstly, there might be regulation of the freedom of the employing enterprise to confer upon itself, from the outset of the contractual relation, the power to vary the terms and conditions of employment. Secondly, there may be controls upon subsequent bilateral variation of terms and conditions of employment; and finally there may be controls, which one might expect to be the strictest of the three types of regulation, upon the power of the employing enterprise unilaterally to impose subsequent variation of terms and conditions of employment. We could think of any of these types of control as the regulation of variation either for flexibility if it is permissive in character or for stability if it imposes strict controls.

In English law, we find that the common law of the contract of employment tends towards a permissive regime in all these three respects, and that this regime is the subject of a dis-integrated approach, so that it is rather strongly distinguished and separated from other kinds or sources of control of variation. This permissiveness is, in large measure, an expression of that historical combination of liberal contractualism and deference to managerial prerogative which we have remarked upon in an earlier section. It is reinforced by another important element in the common law of the contract of employment which is explained at length in the next chapter, namely the attribution to the employing enterprise of extensive implied powers of termination of the contract. Those extensive implied powers of termination give rise to almost equally extensive implied powers of unilateral variation, according to an implicit logic whereby, if the employing enterprise has a certain power to terminate the contract of employment, that power may be used to bring the old package of terms and conditions to an end and to offer a new one in its place.

As with various other aspects of the legal construction of contractual employment relations which have been discussed in this chapter, that permissive common law regime for variation has been maintained in isolation from any controls upon variation which might be derived from external sources of regulation. In the case of one particular kind of statutory regulation, this separation became problematic and gave rise to contention as to which regime should be regarded as the prevalent one. The statutory regulation in question was that of the redundancy payments legislation, which was originally introduced in 1965.[73] This provided a kind of control on

---

[73] By the Redundancy Payments Act 1965. Cf. S. Deakin and G. Morris (2009), *Labour Law*, 5th edn, Oxford: Hart, paras 5.166 to 5. 170, 'Diminished requirements for "work of a particular kind"'.

variation of terms and conditions of employment, in the sense that an employee, who contends that a variation of job specification or job location imposed by the employing enterprise is so significant as to amount to the withdrawal of the existing job, may claim a statutory payment on the footing that he or she has in effect been made redundant.

In order to apply that set of legislative provisions, it was necessary for tribunals and appellate courts to decide upon the degree of flexibility which was to be attributed to the specification of the employee's job definition, terms and conditions of employment, and place of work, when they were deciding whether the employee had been made redundant within the meaning of the legislation. The problem arose of whether those courts and tribunals were bound to accept the approach of the common law of the contract of employment, which would permit the employing enterprise to maintain a constantly flexible specification, or whether on the other hand they were free to impose a mode of specification which was more protective of the employee's acquired expectations of a narrower and more stable specification of the job and of the place of work. This became known as the choice between 'contractual' and 'factual' modes of specification.[74]

The appellate courts eventually inclined slightly towards the latter, more employee-protective, view. In a very influential article,[75] Anderman (2000) convincingly argued that it was appropriate, indeed essential, for the statutory regime to be developed as an autonomous layer of regulation in that way, and that the deference to contractual flexibility which was so characteristic of the common law regime should not be allowed to permeate the statutory one. Our argument seeks to go one stage further, and to draw attention to the way in which, in English employment law, the 'law of the contract of employment' has been allowed to insulate itself from integration with external sources of regulation such as that of worker-protective legislation. Our discussion proceeds by seeking to place that analysis in a European comparative perspective; by doing so, we hope to enlarge our understanding of the approach of English law itself.

## B. Variation From a Comparative Perspective

The variation of contractual terms in contracts of employment presents itself right from the outset as one of those areas marred with comparative difficulties. These difficulties derive from several distinct sources. Firstly, the topic poses, in and of itself, a series of conceptual complexities that are challenging enough when analysed within a single jurisdiction, let alone when assessed comparatively. By the term 'contractual variation' in the context of personal work contracts in general, and contracts of employment in particular, one can refer to a series of conceptually

---

[74] Ibid., para 5.169.

[75] Cf. S. Anderman (2000) 'The Interpretation of Protective Employment Statutes and Contracts of Employment', 29 *ILJ*, 223. The interpretative question to which this paragraph refers has recently been addressed by the UK Supreme Court in *Gysda Cyf v. Barratt* [2010] UKSC 41, see J. Prassl (2011) 'Interpreting Employment Protective Legislation: *Gisda Cyf v. Barratt*', 40 *ILJ*, 103.

distinct legal and relational dynamics.[76] One may refer to a variation of one or more contractual terms, or to a more radical contractual variation affecting the contract as a whole. Technical as this distinction may seem in some jurisdictions, it maintains a fundamental importance in others. In France, for instance, the Court of Cassation decided in the mid-1990s to introduce 'a new distinction; it was no longer necessary to distinguish between substantial and non-substantial modifications; it was necessary instead to distinguish between modifications of the contract and changes to working conditions'.[77]

Of course, variation in the context of any relational contract implying the performance of reciprocal and mutual obligations over an indefinite or long period of time, can also refer to the – perhaps inevitable – changes or developments in the dispositions of the relationship. The way these changes, which may not necessarily involve variations of terms or of the contract itself, are perceived by labour law systems tends to vary from country to country. It has already been noted that English employment law, when confronted with the need to define the terms and conditions of a personal work relationship, 'normally deals with the problem by constructing, by means of backward projection, an original personal work or employment contract, and by then considering how subsequent developments... come within the scope of the original contract or have resulted in a variation of the... contract or its terms'.[78] In other systems this type of variation is strictly controlled by statutory provisions. Italian labour law, for instance, accepts the natural evolution of the relationship and even, as we shall soon see, unilateral changes on the part of the employer, but confines them within a strict framework, provided by the combined application of Article 2103 of the Civil Code as amended by Article 13 of the *Statuto dei Lavoratori*, prescribing that these changes must not alter substantially, and certainly not *in pejus*, the worker's position in terms of job specification and pay.

Not only do we find ourselves comparing systems in which the influence of statute law on the changes affecting specific contractual clauses varies considerably, but we encounter different streams of legal thinking and jurisprudential reasoning over which kinds of changes and variations are deemed to be compatible with the original contractually agreed relationship, and which instead are to be seen as essentially incompatible, and effectively amounting to a unilateral breach and termination of the contract. This is an area in which simple distinctions between English common-law-based and continental European Civilian systems can hardly illustrate the diversity of approaches, and where there are significant divergences between continental systems such as, for instance, the French and the Italian one. We can, however, tentatively suggest that all these different approaches can be analysed by reference to a series of goals that all legal systems, albeit in different ways and with different nuances, seek to pursue, namely the protection of the

---

[76] Cf. M. Freedland (2003) *The Personal Employment Contract*, Oxford: OUP, 235–40.

[77] J, Pélissier, A. Supiot, A. Jeammaud (2006) *Droit du Travail* (23rd ed., Paris: Dalloz, at 463.

[78] Cf. M. Freedland (2003) *The Personal Employment Contract*, Oxford: OUP, 236.

interests of the employing entity, the protection of the worker's interests and the, arguably increasing, relevance of the concepts of good faith and fair dealing.

The present section explores the suggestion that both in England and in other European systems, the body of law regulating the variation of contracts of employment is actively preoccupied with protecting the interests of the employing entity. We do not advance the proposition that this is the sole or indeed the main preoccupation of this area of labour contracts regulation. Nor do we suggest that labour law systems allow a complete departure from the traditional '*pacta sunt servanda*' approach of general contract law. However there is an obvious readiness to accept a certain degree of unilateral '*jus variandi*' in the setting and modification of the working conditions contractually agreed, which betrays an implicit acceptance of the fact that 'ever since the notion of contract of employment was first elaborated, the performance of work has always been presented as a performance that can be subject to unilateral modifications at the employer's will, since he organizes the production and is therefore endowed with a power of initiative and direction of the workers' performance'.[79]

In some jurisdictions this power relationship is conceptualized in ways that suggest a dichotomy between the contractual framework sustaining the work relationship, and the relationship itself. In France, for instance, it is accepted that 'the performance of the contract of employment is placed under the sign of the subordination of the salaried worker in relation to the employer; he can modify the conditions of work performance. The changes of the conditions of work do not concern the contractual sphere; they are the expression of the power of direction of the head of the enterprise.'[80] Whilst we are warned by the *doctrine* that this is a 'contestable distinction',[81] these subtleties do not affect the fact that most legal systems regard, and indeed facilitate, the variation of general and specific working conditions as a reflection of managerial prerogative.

In fact, this specific manifestation of the power of direction engenders a corresponding obligation on the worker's part to obey and accept reasonable variations imposed by the employer. Article 2103 of the Italian Civil Code, as modified by Article 13 of the *Statuto dei Lavoratori*, provides for a very ample discretion in that sense, allowing the employer unilaterally to modify the working conditions of the employee 'horizontally', that is to say by reassigning her to tasks that, while factually different, are substantially equivalent to those contractually agreed, or 'vertically', that is to say by appointing him or her to a hierarchically and functionally superior job, with a correspondingly accrued remuneration. The concept of 'substantial equivalence' is often hard to define, but Italian courts have been known to accept, for instance, the role of mail delivery staff as equivalent to the one of counter staff in the Italian post office,[82] and there is an obvious willingness to do that when such equivalence is dictated by arrangements specified

---

[79] E. Ghera (2007) *Diritto del Lavoro*, 16th ed., Bari: Cacucci, at 105 (our translation).
[80] J. Pélissier, A. Supiot, A. Jeammaud (2006) *Droit du Travail*, 23rd ed, Paris: Dalloz, at 463.
[81] Ibid., 467 (our translations).
[82] Cassazione Sezioni Unite Civili, Sentenza 24 novembre 2006, n. 25033.

by relevant collective agreements.[83] But outright variations to the detriment of worker are also possible when this is seen as an '*extrema ratio*' (last resort) and when the only alternative is the dismissal of the employee, for instance by reason of bankruptcy or foreclosure of the employing entity.[84] But it should be noted that in this case the employer's exercise of the *jus variandi* is subject to a good faith requirement.[85] Conversely a refusal of the worker to comply with the demoting ordered by the employer will be a just cause for dismissal.[86]

If we now attempt a general assessment in which English law is considered in comparative relation to these continental European models, that assessment would be that, although quite significant similarities seem to have presented themselves, appearing to suggest a considerable degree of convergence between the common-law-based approach of English law and the Civilian approach of many continental labour law systems, English law nevertheless has a distinctive logic which accords to the employing enterprise an ultimately more deep-seated and extensive power of variation of terms and conditions and employment. We begin this summative assessment by referring to some apparent similarities and continue it by referring to the more fundamental differences.

The apparent similarities consist in occasional indications that English law regards the employer's power to vary the contract of employment as being derived from an essentially limited and specific right, corresponding to the *ius variandi* which is found in some continental labour law systems. Such an apparently limited and specific right might, for example, be conferred by the incorporation in individual contracts of employment of collective agreements containing generously formulated grading systems.[87] Moreover, cases such as *Catamaran Cruisers Ltd v. Williams* support the view that an employer can, without incurring liability for unfair dimissal, unilaterally impose variations to the contract of employment for 'business reasons so pressing that it was absolutely vital for the employer's business that the terms be accepted',[88] something that is strikingly similar to the Italian notion of *extrema ratio*.

On the other hand, English law often accepts that the contract of employment has specified the tasks which the employee may be required to perform, in a way which places the job specification beyond the reach of instant modification by the employer. Thus decisions such as *Bull v. Nottinghamshire and City of Nottingham Fire and Rescue Authority* clearly suggest that, while it is 'uncontroversial' that 'generally there [is] an obligation on an employee to obey his employer's instructions and to co-operate in the work that the employer wishe[s] him to do [ . . . ] the

---

[83]  Ibid (our translation).

[84]  Cass. 22 agosto 2006, n. 18269. See also Article 4(11), Legge 23 luglio 1991, n. 223, which however required an agreement between the parties, a requirement eventually abandoned in Sezioni Unite 7 agosto 1998 n. 7755, Cass. 9 marzo 2004 n. 4790.

[85]  Cf. E. Ghera (2007) *Diritto del Lavoro*, 16th ed., Bari: Cacucci, at 106–7.

[86]  Cass. 9 maggio 2007 n. 10547. Commented by E. Raimondi (2008) 'Rifiuto di Svolgere Mansioni Inferiori e Licenziamento per Giusta Causa: un Revirement nella Giurisprudenza della Cassazione?', *Rivista Italiana di Diritto del Lavoro*, 597.

[87]  Cf. for instance *Callison v Ford Motor Co Ltd* (1969) 4 ITR 74 (IT).

[88]  [1994] IRLR 386.

employer can only give instructions to his employee to do that which the contract requires the employee to do. Otherwise, it is not a question of the instruction being lawful or unlawful, but rather that the tasks are not open to the employer to require of his employee.'[89] This can be effectively contrasted with the leeway granted to employers in reformulating the means and processes under which their employers are to pursue the contractually agreed tasks.[90] This distinction between a power to modify unilaterally the *working conditions* under which the workforce is to perform the contractually agreed tasks, and the reluctance to accept – other than in exceptional circumstances – unilateral variations of substantial elements of the contractual arrangement, is present in a number of European labour law systems. As Dockès (2004) has put it: 'the legal source of the power of the employer, the contract of employment is thus also one of its principal limits'.[91]

All that said, we suggest, however, that English is ultimately distinctive and in contrast to many European Civilian systems in its underlyingly libertarian approach to variation of the terms and conditions of the contract of employment. Whereas many of those other systems historically viewed the employing enterprise as having a limited *jus variandi* within a framework of control in which the stability of the contract was quite robustly maintained, English law has historically regarded the employing enterprise as being free to stipulate for an almost infinitely variable job specification, both as to the location at which the employee may be required to work and as to the tasks which the employee may be called upon to perform. Moreover, English law has also been willing to accord to the employing enterprise a power of variation which is derived from the power to terminate the contract of employment, so that if the contract of employment is terminable upon short notice without the need for cause to be shown, then it is seen to follow that it is variable upon equally short notice and without the need for justification.[92]

It is of course quite true English law places significant controls upon such powers of variation through the law of unfair dismissal, in principle and often in practice enabling the employee to claim that an imposed variation of the terms and conditions of employment amounts to an unfair dismissal. However, that is an indirect control upon powers of variation which, according to the dis-integrated approach so deeply embedded in the thinking of English law about contractual employment relations, does not actually reach down to the foundational level at which the contractual powers of variation are understood and legally constructed. Even in this context, we can usefully contrast the English approach with the one adopted, for instance, in German labour law. Even leaving aside the robust role that work councils maintain in the context of changes of terms and conditions of employment, under section 2 of the *Kündigungsschutzgesetz* (Protection Against

---

[89]  *Bull v. Nottinghamshire and City of Nottingham Fire and Rescue Authority* [2007] ICR 1631 (CA).

[90]  *Cresswell v. Board of Inland Revenue* [1984] ICR 508 (QBD).

[91]  Our translation of the original: '*Source juridique du pouvoir de l'employeur, le contrat est donc aussi l'une de ses principales limites*'. E. Dockès (2004) 'De la supériorité du contrat de travail sur le pouvoir de l'employer', in A. Arsequel, *et al.* (eds.) (2004) *Analyse juridique et valeurs en droit social: Mélanges en l'honneur de Jean Pélissier*, Paris: Dalloz, at 9.

[92]  M. Freedland (2003) *The Personal Employment Contract*, Oxford: OUP, at 250–252.

Dismissal Act) a worker refusing to accept a contractual variation can, in order to avoid a dismissal, agree to work under protest, or to use Weiss and Schmidt's expression, 'accept the offer and at the same time declare a reservation. The implication of the reservation is that the justification for the dismissal can still be contested in court. If the dismissal is unjustified, the former working conditions apply; if it is justified, the new working conditions apply. But the employment relationship continues in any case.'[93] Moreover, the employer will also have to establish 'whether or not the change of working conditions is socially justified, whether it is for reasons concerning the employee's personality, for reasons concerning the employee's behaviour, or for economic reasons'.[94]

The mechanism which, in English law, seemed to present some possibility of burrowing down to those conceptual foundations – that of the implied obligation of mutual trust and confidence – has not hitherto been allowed to realize its full potential. In the next and final section of this chapter, we pursue that theme into the topic of suspension of the contract of employment.

## Section 4: Suspension

In this section, we bring to a conclusion a chapter which has developed largely as a case-study, with some comparative reflections, of the way in which 'the English common law of the contract of employment' became and has largely remained dis-integrated from the main sources of regulation of contractual employment relations which were external to the common law itself, and especially from worker-protective legislation. That case-study becomes especially interesting as the regulation of the content and performance of contracts of employment intersects more closely with the regulation of the termination of employment. We begin by identifying the topic of suspension as the one in which that intersection is at its most important, and in which the dis-integrated approach is most obviously conditioned by that intersection (subsection A). That discussion is then pursued more specifically in relation to the principal kinds or grounds of suspension, that is to say, economic lay-off, parenthood leave, suspension by reason of sickness or incapacity, suspension by way of industrial action, and finally disciplinary, investigatory, and precautionary suspension (subsection B).

### A. Approaches to the Regulation of Suspension, and the Intersection with Termination

Our analysis of the law of the contract of employment in this and the preceding chapter has reached a point where we can begin to address directly a question which has been hovering over the whole discussion. This question is whether the legal

---

[93] M. Weiss and M. Schmidt (2008) *Labour Law and Industrial Relations in Germany*, AH Alphen aan den Rijn: Kluwer, 144.
[94] Ibid., 145.

construction of employment relations (leaving aside for the moment the issues concerning other personal work relations) as contractual ones provides a framework for the regulation of those relations which is doctrinally coherent and adequate to the normative functions which it is called upon to serve. The topic of suspension provides a suitable focal point at which to advance a tentative answer which has gradually been emerging in the course of this and the previous chapter, and which will be further tested, and we think substantiated, in the course of the next chapter. We suggest that the topic of suspension in fact demonstrates particularly well the shortcomings of the construction of employment relations as contractual ones. We argue that this is especially true where, as in the case of English law, there is a dis-integrated approach to the law of the contract of employment almost amounting to a systemic disjunction between 'the contract of employment' as legally constructed and the main sources of worker-protective regulation, that is to say legislation and collective bargaining. We shall consider firstly the lack of doctrinal coherence and secondly the normative inadequacies which may be involved.

The lack of doctrinal coherence seems to manifest itself quite widely in European legal systems when it is perceived as necessary or appropriate to expound in contractual terms the phenomenon which can be recognized in factual terms as 'the suspension of employment'. There are a number of situations which occur in the course of the conduct of employment relations which can be so described; we might wish to say that there had been a 'suspension of employment' in situations where the employee is laid off temporarily because of a fluctuation in demand for the product of the employing enterprise, or a temporary interruption in produc-tion; or where the employee is in a state of sickness or incapacity not regarded as permanent; or where she is on maternity leave; or where he or she is on strike; or performing military service obligations; or where he or she has been placed on suspension by the employing enterprise for disciplinary or investigatory purposes, or placed on 'garden leave' on a precautionary basis pending the termination of employment. Such situations fall to be regulated by or under employment law, if only in the sense that employment law needs to specify the rights and obligations of employees in respect of such situations.

That specification of the rights and obligations of employees in respect of situations of 'suspension of employment' is quite often confused and confounded, and becomes more difficult rather than easier when such situations have to be explicated in contractual terms, that is to say under 'the law of the contract of employment' which obtains in the legal system in question. For at that point, it becomes necessary to say whether there has been suspension of the contract of employment itself, or only of the obligations which arise under the contract, and also to answer incidental questions such as whether there can be said to be suspension of the contract itself when only some and not all of its primary obligations are suspended. These are questions to which the doctrinal systems of employment law or indeed of general contract law do not normally provide coherent answers, so that the transposing of regulatory issues about the 'suspension of employment' into contractual terms tends to generate more heat than light.

A pertinent example is the debate surrounding what French labour lawyers define as '*concours de suspensions*' (conflict between suspension types), and pertaining to the way the juridical system approaches those situations where a worker's employment is initially suspended for a particular reason but at some point during the period of suspension another reason intervenes so as to affect and inhibit the worker's ability to return to work, for instance the classic case of a worker falling ill during a pre-arranged period of annual leave. The traditional approach of the French Court de Cassation has been that of relying on a 'chronological criterion ... it is the cause of suspension that first manifested itself chronologically that is considered as the reason for the lack of performance of the employment relationship'.[95] This approach has been forcefully criticized by the French *doctrine*, and – to us at least – would seem to suggest a residual influence of a narrowly contractual reasoning on the suspension of work relations, at least to the extent that French courts have been reluctant to accept that the legitimate grounds for suspending a work *relationship* can vary well beyond the ground for the original suspension of the contract itself.

In fact, Pélissier, Supiot, and Jeammaud (2008) – who vehemently criticize this approach – note that 'in the absence of a contrary contractual provision', a worker falling ill during a period of leave will not even be able to claim unpaid compensatory leave.[96] This is of course a jurisprudential approach that will now be subject to the groundbreaking interpretation of the ECJ in case C-277/08, *Francisco Vicente Pereda v. Madrid Movilidad SA*, suggesting that Article 7(1) of Directive 2003/88/EC must be interpreted as precluding national provisions or collective agreements from providing that a worker who is on sick leave during a period of annual leave 'does not have the right, after his recovery, to take his annual leave at a time other than that originally scheduled, if necessary outside the corresponding reference period'.[97]

Of greater concern, however, and perhaps more germane to the comparative purpose of this work, is our argument with respect to the normative inadequacies which we believe present themselves when the regulation of 'suspension of employment' is mediated through the contractual construction of employment relations, and when the legal system in question takes a dis-integrated approach to sources of regulation which are viewed as external to the contract itself – especially those of collective bargaining and worker-protective employment legislation. In this regard, as we have previously indicated, we believe that English law provides a particularly interesting case-study of a system which takes a dis-integrated approach, and presents some significant contrasts with some other European legal systems where more integrated approaches seem to be taken.

Accordingly, pursuing our suggestion that English law provides a case-study of a dis-integrated approach to the law of the contract of employment, we suggest that this approach to the treatment of suspension of employment gives rise to normative concerns for the following set of reasons. The dis-integrated approach, as we have

---

[95] J. Pélissier, A. Supiot, A. Jeammaud (2008) *Droit du Travail*, 24th ed., Paris: Dalloz, 503.
[96] Ibid., 504, fn. 4. Emphasis added.
[97] [2009] OJ C 267/21; [2009] ECR I-8405.

previously indicated, consists of, or at least tends towards, treating the main sources of worker-protective labour standards, that is to say collective bargaining and employment protection legislation, as essentially external to the legal construct of the contract of employment. Terms and conditions derived from collective bargaining may be incorporated into the contract of employment, and employment protection legislation may override or coercively transform the contract of employment, but, in the case of English law, these are imports or impositions *ab extra* into or upon a largely intact conception of the contract of employment as a creature of the common law.

Our normative concerns arise with regard to the character and effects of that common law conception. Our argument in this regard is that the common law conception of the contract of employment is not one which is basically protective of employees, nor even, it must be said, normatively neutral as between the employing enterprise and its employees. Rather to the contrary, it provides a starting position or default model for the legal construction of employment relations as contractual ones which in several respects maintain some values and assumptions pre-dating much of the worker-protective regulation which was put in place in the course of the twentieth century. This it does in three particular respects.

Firstly, this starting position or default model defers strongly to freedom of contract in the sense that, as we observed in the previous chapter, it creates a very wide latitude within which the parties are free to design the contract of employment as they see fit – this being, in practice, a freedom enjoyed by the employer or employing enterprise. That might seem to be no more than an expression, in this particular context, of an idea or ideal of freedom of contract which underlies the law of contracts in general. However, this starting position or default model goes further than that towards the orientation of the contract of employment in a particular direction in that, secondly, and as we have seen in the course of this chapter, it gives effect to a broad notion of managerial prerogative or managerial control with regard to the conduct of employment relations.

Thirdly and in a similar vein, the starting position or default model of the common law of the contract of employment also accords a high degree of power to the employer or employing enterprise with regard to the termination of employment. This aspect of the starting position or default model will be examined in full in the next chapter; but it is important to begin to take account of it in the argument of this section, since the treatment of suspension is to quite some extent shaped by it. It is indeed in that particular sense that the topic of suspension forms a bridge between the subject-matter of this chapter and that of the next one.

We therefore pursue this case-study, of the functioning of a dis-integrated contractual approach to the regulation of suspension of employment, into the main specific areas or circumstances where suspension of employment may occur, viewing that topic as being poised between the content and performance of the contract of employment and its termination. It might be thought that our argument portrays the approach of English common law to this topic as being irredeemably stuck in a pre-twentieth century past, and isolated from the advances in the protection of workers which occurred during that century. That is far from being the case; we shall show that there are various instances in which the common law judges have engaged with and even at times taken part in those advances. Nevertheless, we shall suggest that those episodes of protectiveness towards employees, in the legal construction of suspension of employment as a contractual phenomenon, have tended to be somewhat isolated and ephemeral by reason of the underlyingly dis-integrated approach which prevailed, and the consequential failure to achieve a lasting fusion between the doctrines of the common law of the contract of employment and the advances in regulation brought about by collective bargaining and worker-protective legislation.

## B. The Regulation of Suspension in Specific Circumstances

In this subsection, we therefore consider the nature and effects of the dis-integrated approach to the regulation of suspension more specifically in relation to the principal kinds or grounds of suspension, that is to say, economic lay-off, pregnancy, maternity or parenthood leave, suspension by reason of sickness or incapacity, suspension by way of industrial action, and finally disciplinary, investigatory, and precautionary suspension. It will be useful first to consider what might be the goals or outcomes of the regulation of suspension, and then to consider, in those specific contexts, how far the pursuit of those goals or outcomes is supported or impeded by the dis-integrated approach to regulation. We can identify those goals or outcomes firstly by reference to the claims which might fall to be protected by such regulation, and secondly by reference to the kinds of control or sanction which might be deployed to vindicate those claims.

The claims which might fall to be protected by such regulation are of quite diverse kinds, so much so that we might think of them as sometimes consisting of claims which employees might have for suspension of employment, and as sometimes consisting of claims against suspension of employment. Employees might have claims against economic suspension or temporary lay-off due to lack of demand for their services, or claims against disciplinary suspension or investigative or precautionary suspension. Those claims would tend to apply especially strongly to suspension without pay as opposed to suspension with pay, but might extend even to suspension with pay in the form of asserting an interest in working in order to maintain the employee's skills and professional reputation. Employees' claims in respect of suspension might on the other hand be claims in favour of suspension, in the sense that the employee might assert an interest in the continuation of employment during temporary absence. Thus the employee might make such a claim in favour of suspension – with or without pay – while absent by reason of sickness or incapacity, or during maternity or paternity leave, or – without pay – while taking industrial action.

The kinds of control or sanction which might be deployed to vindicate those claims are also diverse. They might consist of upholding employees' pecuniary claims to continuation of remuneration throughout the periods in question, or, less probably, to compensation for denial of the opportunity to work – as, for example, where the employee claims against suspension by way of economic lay-off. They might on the other hand consist of controls or sanctions relating to the termination of employment, that is to say either entitling the employee to treat the imposition of suspension as tantamount to a wrongful termination of employment by the employer – as for example, where the employee claims against an imposition of disciplinary suspension – or alternatively as entitling the employee to treat a dismissal by the employer as a violation of the employee's claim in favour of suspension – as for example where an employee is dismissed for taking strike action, or is refused the opportunity to resume her employment after maternity absence.

The body of English law which we may identify as the common law of the contract of employment varies considerably in its responsiveness to these different claims, and in its readiness to deploy these different controls or sanctions. Thus, it has been relatively responsive to the employee's claims against employers' assertions of wide or unlimited powers of economic or disciplinary suspension without pay,[98] and relatively willing to enforce those claims by awarding continued remuneration during such periods of purported suspension.[99] It has, on the other hand, been rather unresponsive to claims in favour of suspension during long-term sickness absence,[100] and positively averse to any claim of a right on the part of employees to suspension of the contract of employment during strike action.[101]

Common to all these variations, however, is the fact that where there have been legislative or governmental regulatory interventions to modify the common law position, such interventions have generally failed to alter or even join up with the core of doctrinal thinking which shapes the common law vision of the contract of employment. Thus, for example, there is a virtually complete disconnection between the common law body of doctrine concerning economic suspension of the contract of employment and the legislation which provides a modest level of guaranteed pay during periods of lay-off.[102] There is a similar disconnection between the common law concerning suspension of the contract of employment during sickness absence and the legislative provisions concerning statutory sick pay.[103]

---

[98] This argument refers to the body of case-law which developed from *Devonald v. Rosser & Sons Ltd* [1906] 2 KB 728 (CA) and *Hanley v. Pease & Partners* [1915] 1 KB 698 which Deakin and Morris have described as 'two landmark cases in the development of modern employment law' – S. Deakin and G. Morris (2009) *Labour Law*, 5th ed., Oxford: Hart, at p 333. See M. Freedland (2003) *The Personal Employment Contract*, Oxford: OUP, at pp 469–71 and 474–7.

[99] In *Hanley v. Pease & Partners*, Lush J awarded a sum equal to the wages for the day of wrongful suspension, holding that it was unnecessary to determine whether that represented a sum due or damages [1915] 1 KB 698. For a fuller discussion, see M. Freedland (2003) *The Personal Employment Contract*: Oxford: OUP, at pp. 470–1.

[100] In the sense that at least that there has been a growing reluctance to presume in favour of suspension with continuation of pay during long-term sickness – see M. Freedland (2003) *The Personal Employment Contract*, Oxford: OUP, at pp. 482–4.

[101] *Simmons v Hoover Ltd* [1977] ICR 61 (EAT). See M. Freedland (2003) *The Personal Employment Contract*, Oxford: OUP, at pp. 480–2.

[102] The statutory provisions are those of ERA 1996, ss. 28–35. See Deakin and Morris n. 98 above, p. 336.

[103] The statutory provisions are those of the Social Security Contributions and Benefits Act 1992 as subsequently amended – See Deakin and Morris n. 98 above, pp. 331–3.

But perhaps the most conspicuous disconnection is that which exists between the common law of the contract of employment with regard to industrial action and the whole elaborate statutory apparatus for the regulation of industrial action. It could of course be said at a certain level of analysis that the statutory apparatus is concerned with the law of tort and with the law of unfair dismissal rather than with the contract of employment, so that the disconnection is to that extent not surprising; but at a deeper level that way of thinking demonstrates the very point we are making. There could hardly be a stronger contrast with the way that French law is constructed in this respect: here, the notion of a right to strike which underpins the whole elaborate body of legal regulation of industrial action, devolving from the Constitution itself, is articulated by and through the contractual doctrine that 'The exercise of the right to strike cannot justify the breach of the contract of employment, other than in the presence of *faute lourde* [serious fault] attributed to the worker', which is contained in Article L. 2511-1 of the *Code du Travail*. Similarly, in Germany, 'during strikes and lock-outs the employment contract continues. A legal strike and a lawful lockout only suspend the employment contract.'[104]

We may identify from these observations of English law some effects which are characteristic of the dis-integrated approach. Two such characteristic effects may be discerned, one of which refers back to themes developed earlier in this chapter, and the other of which looks forward to a discussion which will be developed in the next chapter. The first characteristic effect of the dis-integrated approach is that, despite some worker-protective constructions of contracts of employment early in the twentieth century, and despite the early promise of the implied obligation of mutual trust and confidence, it has nevertheless proved counter-intuitive for the common law judges to develop generally worker-protective principles in relation to contracts of employment, or to act upon employees' claims with regard to suspension, especially where that would involve the articulation of positive rights for employees. In the latter respect, there is a decided reluctance to build such positive rights from sources of regulation which are still viewed as essentially external to contracts of employment, and hence to embed such rights into the core legal conception of those contracts.

By contrast, as indicated in the previous section, most continental systems have developed statutory rights and jurisprudential principles that have by and large been integrated into contractual reasoning to a considerable degree, as well as being sustained by their respective bodies of legislation on unfair dismissal. A pertinent example would be the treatment under French law of suspension due to long-term illness. Until the late 1970s, French courts effectively accepted the idea that the termination of a contract of employment due to the long-term illness of an employee did not amount to dismissal, a conclusion resulting from the traditional

---

[104] M. Weiss and M. Schmidt (2008) *Labour Law and Industrial Relations in Germany*, AH Alphen aan den Rijn: Kluwer, 214.

rationales of contract law.[105] Suspension could only last a certain period of time before the contract would be seen as discharged by the employee's non-performance took centre stage. This, however, changed in the 1980s, with French unfair dismissal legislation being systematically applied to these particular situations of contractual termination and to the enquiry as to whether the protracted period of absence due to ill-health could be seen as being a *'cause réelle et sérieuse de licenciement'* (real and serious cause for dismissal), something that would not be the case in and of itself. Instead, courts would have to ascertain whether 'this absence severely disrupts the functioning of the enterprise' and whether it was necessary permanently to replace the sick worker.[106]

Collective agreements will often play an important role here, for instance by setting a minimum period of time for workers to be absent before an employer can be allowed lawfully to terminate a contract of employment. But perhaps more importantly, in recent years French courts have started focusing on the actual *lawfulness* of the decision of the employer rather than on whether the actual circumstances constitute a sufficiently serious reason for dismissing the worker, by relying on Article L. 1132-1 of the *Code du Travail* which states that 'no worker can be sanctioned [or] dismissed ... by reason of his state of health'. Pélissier, Supiot, and Jeammaud note that this has effectively meant that 'all dismissals pronounced by reason of the absences resulting from the state of health of the worker ought to be annulled unless a *médecin du travail* (works doctor) has not verified the inability of the worker to maintain his employment'.[107]

The second characteristic effect of the dis-integrated approach is that the recognition of employees' claims with regard to suspension of employment, whether they are claims against suspension or in favour of suspension, and the deployment of controls or sanctions in support of those claims, tend to be undermined by reference to the very wide powers of termination of employment which are conceded to the employer or employing enterprise by the dis-integrated approach to the contractual construction of the employment relation. If the employer claims very wide powers to impose suspension of employment, it is easy, under the dis-integrated approach, to regard those claims as underpinned by the employer's wide powers of termination, so suspension is regarded as a 'merciful substitute' for a termination which could have been imposed. If the employer refuses to concede rights of suspension to the employee, it is equally easy, under the dis-integrated approach, to justify such a refusal on the basis that the employer could in any event have terminated the contract of employment in question.[108]

---

[105] Cf. S. Blanc-Jouvan, 'Initiative et imputabilité: un eclatement de la notion de licenciement' (1981) *Droit Social*, 207.
[106] J. Pélissier, A. Supiot, A. Jeammaud (2008) *Droit du Travail*, 24th ed., Paris: Dalloz, 515. Our translation.
[107] Ibid.
[108] Such thinking has been prominent in the older case-law concerning disciplinary suspension; see M. Freedland (2003) *The Personal Employment Contract*, Oxford: OUP, at p. 470.

So the wide powers of termination of employment which the English common law of the contract of employment confers upon the employer, powers which are preserved and nurtured by the dis-integrated approach, emerge as crucial conditioning features for the regulation of suspension, and as a juridical element which significantly inhibits the development of the positive rights of employees either in favour of or against suspension in various different kinds of circumstances. This is a theme which will be more fully developed in the next chapter in the context of the termination or transformation of the contract of employment.

# 6

# The Termination and Transformation
# of Employment Contracts

## Introduction

In this chapter, we complete our analysis of the legal construction of employment relations as contracts by concentrating on the termination of employment contracts and on the principal transformations which they may undergo. We begin by showing how, in this context, the layering of legal regulation of employment relations takes an unusual form in English law, such that there are two distinct systems of legal regulation of the termination of employment, one contractual and the other extra-contractual, which co-exist in a state of separation but interdependency (Section 1). Then, evoking and developing the continuity between the successive parts of our analysis of the law of employment contracts, we suggest particular senses in which the duration and the termination of employment contracts can each best be understood in relation to each other, and we advance a scheme of analysis of the duration and terminability of those contracts (Section 2).

In the following section we pursue further the idea of dual or dis-integrated regulation of the termination of employment, taking English law as the extreme case of such duality (Section 3). That section provides an analytical interlude exploring the ways in which European legal systems shape the duration and termination of employment contracts, particularly by reference to the conceptual and regulatory distinctions between 'fixed-term' and 'open-ended' contractual arrangements. Finally, in the concluding section we articulate a composite notion of the transformations which may take place in employment contracts (Section 4). Firstly we show how employment contracts may be transferred between employing entities; secondly we consider the various other transformations which may occur in the course of the life of those contracts.

## Section 1: The Role of Contract Law in the Regulation
## of Termination of Employment

In this section we argue that inter-European comparisons suggest that contract law, and the conceptions of employment contracts to which it gives rise, may play significantly different roles, as between legal systems, in the regulation of the termination of employment. Each European state may be envisaged as having its own system for the legal regulation of termination of employment. We initially show how such systems may be single integrated ones or may on the other hand consist of more than one distinct subsystem (subsection A); and we then develop further, in this context, our theory as to the contrast between integrated and dis-integrated approaches to the contractual regulation of the termination of employment (subsection B).

## A. Integrated and Dis-integrated Systems of Legal Regulation of Termination of Employment

One of the central functions of labour or employment law consists in the regulation of the termination of employment relations. By that we refer to the prescribing of the circumstances in which, and the terms on which, employment relations may lawfully be terminated, and the ascribing of consequences to and remedies for unlawful termination. We can think of the apparatus of rules, principles, and doctrines, which each European state has evolved to carry out that function, as constituting its own system of regulation of the termination of employment relations.

At this stage in our book, our aim is to isolate and analyse comparatively that part of the various national systems for the legal regulation of the termination of employment relations which can be regarded as contractual regulation or regulation by contract law. As we have argued earlier in this work, it is for various reasons important to single out in this way the specifically contractual aspect of the legal regulation of employment relations. Chief among those reasons is the fact that this specifically contractual part or aspect of the legal regulation of employment relations seems to have its own special standing or legitimacy as compared with the other parts or aspects of that body of regulation. That is to say, the contractual type of legal regulation commands the high ground which liberal systems of private law accord to normative structures which can be viewed as contractual ones. They are viewed, rightly or wrongly in particular cases, as the product of the exercise of individual choice and freedom of contract.

It seems to be especially true of the legal regulation of the termination of employment relations that importance is attached to the establishing and main-taining of a specifically contractual set of foundations. In different ways, both law-makers and those involved in the advancing, defending, and deciding of claims concerned with the termination of employment relations wish to feel that they are reflecting or implementing the contracts in which those relations are legally embodied. Accordingly, the decisions which law-makers or adjudicators make, about the kind and degree of job security that should attach to particular employment relations or categories of employment relations, tend to be expressed as statements about the contractual norms applying to the employment relations in question.

So we find that in most European legal systems, there is a system of regulation of termination of employment which, whilst of statutory or collective origin, is essentially constructed around and on the basis of contracts of employment. In these systems, the termination of employment relations may be heavily regulated; but this regulation typically takes the form of mandatory construction or explicit legislative modification of employment contracts. Thus, the outcomes of such regulation present themselves as contractual ones, albeit in an extended sense rather than in a narrow sense. In that way, such systems maintain a kind of doctrinal unity as part of a basically contractual order. These therefore form unified or integrated contract-based systems for the regulation of termination of employment relations.

Even in the case of such unified or integrated contract-based systems, there may be elements or aspects of the regulation of termination of employment relations which would normally be regarded as separate ones, falling outside the contract-based system of regulation. For example, legislative provisions requiring consultation with workers' collective representatives about proposed redundancies might be regarded as quite distinct from the contract-based system of regulation of termination of employment. Indeed, in many European states, the whole notion of retirement at pensionable age and consequential entitlement to a pension seems to fall within the domain of social security law rather than forming part of the contract-based system of regulation of termination of employment. There may therefore be significant inroads into the notion of a unified or integrated contract-based system of regulation of termination of employment.

However, in most European legal systems it would seem that these inroads do not encroach upon the essential integrity or unity of the contract-based system of regulation of termination of employment. In this respect, English law seems to be unusual. It has evolved so as to produce two distinct systems of regulation of termination of employment, the one superimposed upon the other but remaining essentially separate from it. This is an evolution of profound doctrinal and practical significance which we proceed to detail in the later sections of this chapter. Before doing so, we proceed firstly to develop further our analysis of the differences between integrated and dis-integrated approaches to the termination of employment relations (subsection A), and then secondly in subsection B to offer an overall conspectus of the application of those approaches in European labour law systems generally.

## B. Regulation and Integration in the Contractual Construction of the Termination of Employment

In this subsection, we put forward a general argument or theory about the relation between regulation and integration in the contractual construction of the termination of employment. It is an argument or theory to which we have been building up in earlier chapters, and which applies in some measure to all aspects of the legal construction of employment relations as contractual ones, but which can be made out especially clearly in the context of the termination of employment.

The argument or theory which we put forward is one which seeks to advance our analysis of the way in which the termination of contracts of employment is constructed and regulated in and by different European labour or employment law systems. Our suggestion, reformulating and building upon ideas put forward earlier in this work, is that, as between those systems, there are two key variables in the way that the termination of contracts of employment is constructed and regulated; one has to do with the level or intensity of regulation, while the other has to do with the degree to which that regulation is integrated into the legal construction of the contract of employment itself. We shall expand upon each of those two key variables in turn, and then consider how they relate to each other or interact with each other.

The first of our two key variables is relatively well recognized; it can be thought of as the 'regulation variable'; this identifies the fact that national labour or employment law systems vary considerably in the extent to which the termination of the contract of employment is subject to mandatory legal regulation, either by direct legislative standard-setting, or by legal enforcement of standards derived from collective bargaining. This is a relatively familiar variable; it is often discussed as the distinction between *ius cogens* and *ius dispositivum*,[1] or between 'status and contract'[2] in the law of the contract of employment. If the termination of the contract of employment is intensely regulated, then the contract itself is perceived, in the extreme case, as more in the nature of *ius cogens* than *ius dispositivum*, and even as a status which is contractual in name only.

However, before we conclude our discussion of this relatively familiar variable and turn our attention to the second and less familiar one, we should note that this first variable does not take the form of a simple contrast between *ius cogens* and *ius dispositivum*, or between 'genuine contract' and 'status pretending to be contract'. Those represent the opposite positions on a theoretical spectrum which is not in practice populated at its extreme ends but at various points on a continuum between those extremes. There are many legal rules and doctrines which operate to create not only extreme positions but also intermediate positions on that spectrum – we can think of these as 'cogency rules'. Thus if we take the example of a control upon collective dismissals or redundancies, that might be imposed in one legal system as an absolutely mandatory rule, but might be the subject of tightly limited derogation in another system, and of much less tightly limited derogation in a third system – these would represent different cogency rules locating the control upon collective dismissals or redundancies at different points on the mandatory regulation spectrum. So our 'regulation variable' also has a 'cogency variable' built into it.

That much is reasonably straightforward, but we now have to consider the second variable which we initially identified in Chapters 2 and 3 and developed

---

[1] See M. R. Freedland (2002) 'Jus Cogens, Jus Dispositivum, and the Law of Personal Work Contracts', Chapter 12 of P. Birks and A. Pretto (eds.), *Themes in Comparative Law in Honour of Bernard Rudden*, Oxford: OUP. Cf. in particular pp. 58–62.

[2] See, for instance, O. Kahn-Freund (1967) 'A Note on Status and Contract in Modern Labour Law' 30, *MLR*, 635.

in Chapter 5 but which we now apply in the context of the regulation of the termination of employment. We can think of this as the 'integration variable'; as in those earlier chapters it will require careful explanation to clarify what it is and how it interacts with the 'regulation variable' which we have previously identified. That explanation, illustrated with comparative examples, gives rise to the central argument of this subsection.

Our argument with regard to the 'integration variable' is the following one. We have observed that labour law systems may vary as to the extent to which they impose mandatory regulation upon their contractual employment relation, and as to the degrees of cogency or rigour with which that regulation is imposed. We also suggest that they may also vary as to the extent to which such regulation, although it bears upon and affects the contractual employment relation, actually forms part of, that is to say is integrated into, the legal construction of the contract of employment itself. We suggest that, in some labour law systems, mandatory regulation affecting the termination of the contract of employment has tended to be viewed as actually being embedded in the legal vision or conception of the employment contract itself, so that the mandatory regulation comes to define the contract and to be inseparable from it. That might be regarded as the 'integrated paradigm' of the termination of the employment contract. In other labour law systems, the same kind and degree of mandatory regulation affecting the employment contract might nevertheless be regarded as separate from the employment contract itself. That, for its part, might be regarded as the 'dis-integrated paradigm' of the termination of the employment contract.

Having identified our two key variables, we now seek to show how these variables, interacting with each other, may determine the very meaning and understanding of the termination of the contract of employment in different employment law systems. We suggest that we can draw some significant comparative contrasts between some particular labour law systems by deploying our two notions of a 'regulation variable' and an 'integration variable'; and we suggest that contrasts in respect of the integration variable are especially important in determining what the termination of the contract of employment means in each such system.

As an aid to comparison between systems, it will be useful to regard our two variables, the regulation variable and the integration variable, as forming two axes from which a quadrant may be constructed, and four zones can be identified, within which particular labour law systems can be located: see Fig. 6. 1.

We will suggest that, so far as the termination of employment contracts is concerned, we can locate many continental European labour law systems within zone 1 as being of the high regulation/high integration type (HR/HI), and that English labour law provides an especially interesting intermediate case in zone 2, being quite high on the regulation axis but low on the integration axis. However, before proceeding to develop those comparisons, we need to take our general argument or theory one stage further. In order to understand both how particular labour law systems became located in their respective zones and how that determined the meaning which each system attached to the termination of the contract of employment, it will be helpful (at the usual risk of over-generalization

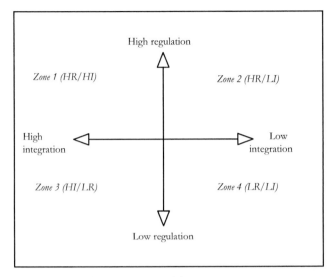

**Fig. 6.1.** The regulation and integration variables

and over-simplification) to identify some common historical starting points and some divergent patterns of evolution away from those starting points.

If we take as our historical starting point the state of affairs at the very beginning of the twentieth century, we can fairly safely generalize to the effect that the legal systems we are talking about were all in zone 4 with regard to the termination of the employment relation; there was low regulation, at least in the sense of regulation for the protection of workers, and such regulation as did exist could not be said to be integrated into anything which recognizably amounted to a general regime for the termination of contracts of employment in any modern sense of that notion.

This does not mean, however, that the conceptual space, which was in the course of the twentieth century gradually occupied by the idea of the contract of employment in general[3] and the termination of the contract of employment in particular, was at the outset an empty one, a kind of legal *carte blanche* upon which a new contract of employment, and a new regime for its termination, was notionally written every time a worker was engaged for employment. Far from it, for each legal system had its own default models for contractual employment relations and their termination, in which the exercise of the notional freedom of contract of employers and employees was quite firmly channelled into conventionally established and

---

[3] And, as the first author of this work has argued elsewhere, the idea of a 'standard' contract of employment – see his chapter in H. Arthurs and K. Stone (eds.), *Employment Regulation after the Demise of the Standard Employment Contract*, Russell Sage, forthcoming.

legally supported patterns of 'master and servant' relations. Those default models were largely characterized by the large or maximal disciplinary power and managerial prerogative accorded to the employer, and the small or minimal job security accorded to the employee.[4]

In France the *'principe du droit de résiliation unilatérale'* (the right of unilateral termination) was seen, effectively until the early 1970s, as 'inherent to the indeterminacy of the duration of the contract', although the *loi du 19 julliet 1928* had subjected 'abusive terminations' of open-ended contracts of employment to the special remedy of damages.[5] It was, in many ways, a step forward in terms of the emancipation of the contract of employment from the more coercive and premodern 'master and servant' models of regulating work relations, at least to the extent that it implied that workers could unilaterally terminate open-ended contracts of employment without seeking the mutual consent of their masters. An analogous principle, known as *'recesso ad nutum'* (rescission) subject to a notice requirement, was introduced in Italy by Article 9 of the Royal Decree n. 1825 of 1924, as an exception to the general rule contained in Article 1123 of the Civil Code of 1865. The principle would eventually be enshrined in Article 2118 of the Civil Code approved in 1942, which in its second paragraph explicitly introduced the principle of 'indemnity in lieu of notice'. This rule was subject to the exception contained in the following Article 2119, allowing for a termination without notice, by either party, in the presence of a 'just cause'. Similar rules were present in Germany where, however, 'originally the length of the notice period was up to the individual parties' often leading to 'very short periods of notice'.[6]

If this represented a common starting point at the beginning of the twentieth century for the legal systems with which we are concerned, it was overlaid in the course of the century, to a greater or lesser extent as between different legal systems, by worker-protective legal regulation consisting either of directly enacted labour standards or of legal support for collectively bargained labour standards. In this respect German labour law had undoubtedly a head start over other European systems. As early as 1920, at the height of the Weimar social ambitions, section 84 of the *Betriebsrätegesetz* (Works Councils Law) limited the grounds of justified dismissal and increased the involvement of works councils in individual dismissal procedures. This collectivism was in accordance with the general theory underlying German labor law during

---

[4] Cf. B. Veneziani, who argues that by the end of the nineteenth century there were two conceptions of 'subordination' – an English one centred on the employer's power of control, and a continental one centred upon the continuous availability of the worker over a period of time – but that: 'In practice these two conceptions of subordination ... were simply two sides of the same coin, namely the acceptance of the power exercised by the employer' – in B. Hepple (ed.) (1986) *The Making of Labour Law in Europe*, London: Mansell, at 65.

[5] J. Pélissier, A. Supiot, A. Jeammaud (2008) *Droit du Travail*, 24th ed., Paris: Dalloz, 567, 581. Our translation. The authors point out that in practice courts were extremely deferential to the reasons alleged by employers for terminating contracts.

[6] M. Weiss and M. Schmidt (2008) *Labour Law and Industrial Relations in Germany*, AH Alphen aan den Rijn: Kluwer, 122.

the Weimar Republic',[7] and had few if any counterparts in other European systems until after the Second World War.

It was not until 1947 that Italian industrial workers saw the powers of their employers to unilaterally terminate their contracts of employment under the Civil Code provision restrained by inter-sectoral collective agreements.[8] These provisions, which were consolidated in subsequent years by other collective agreements,[9] are widely credited with subjecting the powers of employers to the concept of '*giustificato motivo*' ('justified reason') for terminating contracts of employment. This latter concept was eventually incorporated, clarified, and expanded in statute with the adoption of Law 604 of 1966, effectively establishing the first systematic departure of Italian unfair dismissal legislation from its codified contractual base, which became residual and supplementary in character. The worker-protective apparatus introduced by Law 604/1966 – partly revised by Law 108/1990 – was further reinforced by Law 300/1970, better known as the '*Statuto dei Lavoratori*', particularly by strengthening the remedies available to workers in case of unfair, *rectius* unjustified, dismissal.

By comparison with Germany and Italy, France was slow to move beyond the minimalist position which in Fig. 6.1 above appears as 'zone 4', but this departure from a narrower contractual framework occurred with the adoption of Law of 13 July 1973. 'Only the employers' obstructionist stance explains a prolonged legislative inertia and the absence of collectively agreed rules.'[10] This reform, as well as catering for a number of procedural guarantees in case of dismissal, introduced the key principle that contracts of employment could only be terminated '*pour une cause réelle et sérieuse*' (a real and serious reason). It was from and by this kind of worker-protective overlay upon an earlier employer-protective foundation that the legal conception and practice of the contract of employment in general and its termination in particular was essentially formed.

That analysis in itself supplies some explanation for divergences between legal systems as to the meaning and content which they accorded to the termination of the contract of employment – both the starting position and the subsequent regulatory overlay varies from one legal system to another within those general parameters. These represent the different positions which we would assign to different national conceptions of the termination of the contract of employment on the vertical 'regulation' axis of our diagram. That, however, is where our second variable comes into play, creating different positions on the horizontal 'integration' axis of our diagram. To recapitulate for a moment, the point here is that, as different legal systems built up the worker-protective overlay to greater or lesser

---

[7] A. Seifert and E. Funken-Hötzel (2004) 'Wrongful Dismissal in the Federal Republic of Germany' 25, *CLLPJ*, 489.

[8] Cf. G. Giugni (1953) 'Verso il tramonto del recesso ad nutum dell'imprenditore. La disciplina interconfederale dei licenziamenti nell'industria', *RDL*, 201.

[9] Most notably with the inter-confederal agreement of 18 October 1950.

[10] J. Pélissier, A. Supiot, A. Jeammaud (2008) *Droit du Travail*, 24th ed., Paris: Dalloz, 567. Our translation.

degrees, they also varied in the degree to which those regulatory superstructures were integrated into the previously existing infrastructure.

If we take some actual current examples, we find that there is some correlation between the two variables, so that most legal systems fall into zones 1 or 4 where a system is either high (zone 1) or low (zone 4) on both axes. Many continental legal systems fall into zone 1, in the sense that their worker-protective regulation seems to be deeply integrated into their conceptions of the contract of employment in general and its termination in particular. The provisions of the French *Code du Travail*, of the German *Betriebsverfassungsgesetz*, and of the Italian statutes on termination, including the relevant parts of the *Statuto dei Lavoratori*, all seem to have formed an integral part of those respective national conceptions. The residual exceptions to this particular model of high integration and regulation usually concern work relations that individual national systems view as peripheral to the traditional scope of labour law, those of professional athletes, managers, domestic workers, or which, while included within its scope are explicitly subject to relatively less intense levels of integration.

A typical exception of this kind of dis-integration can be found in the way Italian law excludes '*lavoratori domestici*' (domestic workers) from the statutory protections offered by unfair dismissal legislation.[11] These workers remain covered by Articles 2118–2119 of the Civil Code, by a number of provisions contained in collective agreements, and by the provisions contained in Law n. 339 of 2 April 1958. What is interesting, for the purposes of the argument built in the present section and chapter, is the extent to which Italian scholars contrast the relationship between the Civil Code and statutory provisions in the case of domestic workers with the more integrated relationship between unfair dismissal law as it applies to workers in general and Articles 2118–2119 of the Civil Code. While the former is described as being 'complementary', with both regimes 'having to be considered as applicable',[12] the latter is best described as one where statute has rendered Article 2118 'merely residual',[13] with statutory norms contained in Laws such as 604 of 1966 having substantially modified the very concept of 'just cause' contained in the original wording of the Civil Code articles.[14]

A somewhat similar example of exclusion can be found in the various national systems exempting from unfair dismissal legislation small enterprises employing a reduced number of workers. So, for instance, German labour law explicitly excludes from the scope of application of the 1951 *Kündigungsschutzgesetz* businesses employing fewer than ten employees, and Italian labour law similarly excludes from the scope of Article 18 of the *Statuto dei Lavoratori* employers with fewer than fifteen dependent workers. The result is that these workers are protected by the default mechanisms provided by standard 'wrongful' dismissal and by those statutory provisions that are not subject to any particular qualifying requirement or

---

[11] Cf. Article 4(1) of Law 108/1990.
[12] E. Ghera (2007) *Diritto del Lavoro*, Bari: Cacucci, 276. Our translation.
[13] Ibid., 183.     [14] Ibid., 191.

threshold, a particular configuration of low/mid-level regulation, but accompanied by a high level of integration, which Italian labour lawyers describe as *parallelismo delle tutele* (the parallelism of protections).

We shall go on to argue that the case of English labour law is an especially interesting one in which the two variables of regulation and integration do not co-relate closely; it provides an instance of quite high worker-protective regulation, but which has not been integrated into the core conception of the termination of the contract of employment. We shall seek to show, in particular, that there is a real disjunction between the common law of contractually wrongful dismissal, and the legislative regulation of unfair dismissal. However, before pursuing that especially interesting case-study, we should offer a more general overview of ways in which the duration and the termination of contracts of employment are related to each other in different European national employment law systems.

## Section 2: The Duration and Termination of Employment Contracts – a European Regulatory Spectrum

In this section we advance an argument, which largely follows from the discussion in the previous section, that there is a wide variety of different ways in which the law of contracts of employment may contribute to the regulation of the termination of those contracts; and we suggest, moreover, that these different ways of contributing to the regulation of the termination of those contracts also serve in turn to define the duration of those contracts. This variety of patterns of regulation can best be understood by separating out two different aspects of those patterns, that is to say, firstly, the regulation of the time of contractual termination, which we consider in subsection A, and, secondly, the grounds and procedures for termination which we consider in subsection B.

### A. Regulating the Time of Contractual Termination

Our earlier discussions have established that European legal systems vary considerably in the strictness with which they regulate the terms and structures of employment contracts. All these systems have their own rules and principles and doctrines which to some extent shape and control the terms and structures of employment contracts; but these rules and principles and doctrines vary considerably in the degree to which they constrain freedom of contract. At one extreme, there are examples of strong regulation whereby terms and structures are imposed on a mandatory basis. At the other extreme, there are examples of weak regulation giving rise to terms and structures of employment contracts having no more than a default status whereby they are presumed to apply in the absence of indications that the parties have discarded them and have made some other form of agreement. It can be said that the terms and structures of contracts of employment may be strongly prescribed or weakly prescribed.

That, however, is by no means the only kind of variation between European legal systems in the ways that they regulate the termination of contracts of employment. For there is also significant variation in the extent to which the terms and structures which are prescribed (whether strongly or weakly) are protective of job security. Analysing the manner in which, and the degree to which, prescribed terms and structures protect job security is a complex matter. We shall argue that this analysis involves some terms and structures and legal doctrines or rules which actually between them *define* the duration of contracts of employment, and other terms, structures, and legal doctrines or rules which *may affect* the duration of those contracts.

The terms and structures and legal doctrines or rules which between them define the duration of contracts of employment are of two types. Firstly, and most obviously, there are prescribed terms and structures, and legal doctrines or rules, which in one way or another specify the time at which a contract of employment shall terminate or may be terminated. Secondly, there are prescribed terms and structures and legal doctrines or rules which define the duration of contracts of employment in less obvious and more indirect ways. This they do by specifying the grounds upon which a contract of employment may be terminated or the procedures by which a contract of employment may be terminated. We shall consider in turn these different ways of defining the duration of contracts of employment, and the ways in which those different modes of definition interact with each other.

This two-part typology, of the terms and structures and legal doctrines or rules which between them define the duration of contracts of employment, therefore begins with prescribed terms and structures and legal doctrines or rules which in one way or another specify the time at which a contract of employment shall terminate or may be terminated. However, although those prescribed terms and structures, and legal doctrines or rules figure in the typology as the ones which define the duration of contracts of employment in relatively direct and obvious ways, even they do not lay down the duration of contracts of employment in any simple sense.

In fact, the rules, doctrines, or prescribed terms, which relatively directly define the duration of contracts of employment, generally make a basic distinction between two contrasting modes or approaches to the specifying of duration. That distinction is between contracts said to be 'fixed-term' ones and contracts said to be 'open-ended' or 'of indeterminate duration'. The notion of the fixed-term contract of employment is a reasonably though not entirely clear one; there are some marginal issues, such as whether we can regard the contract for the duration of a particular task or project as a kind of fixed-term one, that undoubtedly deserve further attention.

There are various different ways in which European legal systems regulate the use of fixed-term contracts of employment. There may be a prescribing of the minimum, or indeed the maximum, duration of such contracts; and there may also be controls on the use of successive fixed-term contracts, or upon what can be regarded as the abusive use by employers of the fixed-term contracting mechanism. The Fixed Term Work Directive 1999 required EU Member States to maintain controls of this kind upon the use by employers of fixed-term employment contracting;[15] that Directive has been implemented in a variety of different ways, and more or less rigorously according to the degree to which the legislators and courts in each Member State are sympathetic or hostile to fixed-term contracting.[16]

The contrasting notion, that of the 'open-ended' contract of employment, is a surprisingly complex and elusive one, all the more so when considered on a comparative basis as between different European employment law systems. In understanding the ways in which the laws of employment contracts define the duration of this central contract-type, we confront an initial paradox. The duration of this contract seems to be defined by non-definition; it is specified as unspecified; it is determined as indeterminate. This position appears to be a common one across many European employment law systems. But behind this paradoxically and deceptively common façade lies a set of deep-seated real differences in approach as between European employment law systems.

The reality is that the notion of the 'open-ended contract of employment' has perhaps always been, and has certainly become, rather a fictitious one. The employment relations which are identified as being legally embodied in the 'open-ended contract of employment' are actually, in normal practice, the subject of rather elaborate normative arrangements for their duration and termination which vary very much as between national employment law systems, and as between employing enterprises so far as national employment law systems allow scope for such variation. So the 'open-ended contract of employment' is in truth a contract of employment intended as a long-term one but with complex closure arrangements.

Understanding those complex closure arrangements in a comparative way as between European employment law systems requires very careful analysis. Each national employment law system evolves its own more or less tightly prescribed set of closure arrangements for the 'open-ended contract of employment'. National systems differ widely in the set of closure arrangements which they prescribe, and in how tightly the prescription is imposed. For example, one system may require a formal dismissal procedure to be followed while another may not. One system might exempt small- or medium-sized enterprises from such procedural requirements while another may not.

However, there is a further and more subtle kind of variation between national systems. Even to the extent that different national systems share the same or very similar sets of closure arrangements, they may nevertheless differ very much in the

---

[15] Council Directive 1999/70 concerning the framework agreement on fixed-term work concluded by ETUC, UNICE and CEEP [1999] OJ L 175/43.
[16] The European Commission (Employment, Social Affairs & Inclusion) has provided the following Reports on the state of implementation of the Directive in EU Member States: Commission Staff Working Document – National implementation measures of Directive 1999/70/EC (EU-15) SEC (2006) 1074; Commission Staff Working Document – National implementation measures of Directive 1999/70/EC (EU-10) SEC (2008) 2485; Implementation Report on Directive 1999/70/EC concerning the Framework Agreement on fixed-term work concluded by UNICE, CEEP and ETUC (Czech Republic, Estonia, Cyprus, Latvia, Lithuania, Hungary, Malta, Poland, Slovenia and Slovakia) (March 2007). For a comparative discussion of recent development in the UK, see A. Koukiadaki (2009) 'Case-law Developments in the Area of Fixed-term Work', 38, *ILJ*, 89.

degree to which the set of closure arrangements is embodied in the contract of employment itself, so as to define the duration of the contract. That is to say two things: firstly, a particular kind of closure arrangement may or may not be embodied in the contract of employment. Secondly, even if a particular kind of closure arrangement is embodied in the contract of employment, it still may or may not be regarded as actually forming part of the definition or model of the duration of the contract of employment. To pursue the previous example, legislatively prescribed dismissal procedures might or might not form part of the contract of employment. Even if forming part of the contract of employment, they might well not be regarded as forming part of the definition or model of the duration of the contract.

Against that background, it is useful to identify the range of closure arrangements which comparative analysis shows to be embodied in contracts of employment in some national employment law systems but not in others. It is also important to analyse the ways in which the different types of closure arrangement may combine and interlock with each other. Closure arrangements for so-called 'open-ended' contracts of employment seem to fall into the following categories:

1. arrangements or norms concerning notice;
2. arrangements or norms concerning grounds for termination;
3. arrangements or norms concerning procedure for termination;
4. arrangements or norms concerning probation; and
5. arrangements or norms concerning retirement.

We proceed to enlarge upon each of these and then to consider how they may be interrelated, and how far they are embodied firstly in contracts of employment and secondly in contractual duration models.

Arrangements or norms concerning notice are an almost universal feature of contracts of employment in European legal systems, and they are usually embodied in contractual duration models. It could almost be said that the so-called 'open-ended contract of employment' is in its nature a contract of employment terminable by notice. However, there is wide variation between European legal systems as to the length of notice which is prescribed, and as to whether or how far payment of remuneration during notice, or payment in lieu of notice, is prescribed. So for instance the statutory minimum notice periods range from the seven months prescribed in paragraph 622(7) of the German *BGB* (Civil Code) for workers with at least twenty years' continuous service, to the twelve-weeks limit imposed by ERA 1996, s. 86(1)(c) for those with more than twelve years of continuous employment.

Moreover, and unlike the position taken up in *Delaney v. Staples*,[17] Italian jurisprudential analysis expresses a fundamental,[18] but not unanimous,[19] preference for the

---

[17] [1992] 1 AC 687, 692.
[18] Cass. 21 novembre 2001 n. 14646, and Cass. 15 maggio 2007 n. 11094.
[19] Cf. Cass. 21 maggio 2007 n. 11740.

idea that the duty to give '*preavviso*' is primarily discharged by means of remuneration during notice rather than, as French labour lawyers would say, as a '*préavis non travaillé*' – literally 'unworked notice'. While French labour law seems more willing to accept payment in lieu of notice, Article L. 1234-5 of the *Code du Travail* clarifies that 'The failure to give notice, notably in case of dispensation by the employer, does not produce any diminution of the remuneration and other benefits that the worker would have received had he continued at work till the expiry date of the notice'. This implicitly points to the fact that there is some further variation as to the extent to which those prescribed arrangements for payment during notice or in lieu of notice are built into contractual duration models. Norms concerning payment during notice will tend to be built into contractual duration models, but those concerning payment in lieu of notice will tend to be more distanced.

As we will further discuss in the following section, in relation to arrangements or norms concerning grounds for termination we find a wide set of variations between European legal systems. Those systems converge upon a generally accepted notion of what those grounds consist of; the list normally comprises misconduct, incapacity, and redundancy, though of course these grounds will be construed in different ways across the various systems. But there is wide variation as to whether and if so how tightly such a set of grounds for termination is prescribed; there is further variation as to whether, if so, those prescriptions are embodied in contracts of employment, and still further variation as to whether, if so, those prescriptions form part of contractual duration models. In so far as there is a typical position as between European legal systems, it is probably one in which the grounds of termination are fairly tightly prescribed, are embodied in the contract of employment, and do form part of the contractual duration model; but we should be very cautious about regarding this as representing a general norm. This is an 'ideal-type' or model that may well fit the French approach to termination, which neatly prescribes, in Articles L-1232 and L-1233 the substantive details underpinning '*licenciement pour motif personnel*' or '*économique*' – dismissal for personal or economic reasons – but is arguably less suited to describing the slightly more scattered approach adopted, incrementally, by Italian unfair dismissal legislation.

The situation is somewhat similar with regard to arrangements or norms concerning procedures for termination. Again, we find a wide set of variations between European legal systems. Those systems converge upon a generally accepted notion of what those procedures consist of. In the case of misconduct, or incapacity, the core procedural requirements are the giving of reasons to the worker concerned,[20] the holding of a hearing to decide,[21] and the allowing of an appeal against a decision to dismiss. In the case of dismissal for redundancy, there is a similar convergence upon more collectivized procedures, often with the involvement of administrative bodies and labour inspectorates,[22] and there are requirements of EU

---

[20] Cf. for instance Article L1232-6 *Code du Travail*, or Article 2(2) of *Legge 604/66*.
[21] Article L1232-2 *Code du Travail*.
[22] Cf. Articles L1233-19 to L1233-20 *Code du Travail*.

law which determine this convergence.[23] But, that said, there is, here again, wide variation as to whether and if so how tightly such a set of procedures for termination is prescribed;[24] there is further variation as to whether, if so, those prescriptions are embodied in contracts of employment and or collective agreements.[25] It is hard to say whether, if so, those prescriptions form part of contractual duration models; probably on the whole they do not.

We conclude this analysis by referring to the two remaining kinds of closure arrangements which we have identified, namely those relating to probation and to retirement. The paradoxical character of the 'open-ended contract of employment' is manifested most clearly by reference to these two kinds of closure arrangement. European legal systems frequently allow or even provide for 'open-ended contracts of employment' to begin with periods of probation; these constitute closure arrangements in the sense that they are mechanisms for the termination of contracts of employment on the basis of the employee's failure to satisfy the conditions for confirmation of the contract beyond its initial probationary phase, and typically without unfair dismissal legislation playing any significant role in controlling the employer's discretion. French and Italian law, for instance, both allow the parties to a contract of employment to lay down a specific '*période d'essai*'[26] or '*patto di prova*'.[27] During the '*période d'essai*',[28] as confirmed by the French Court of Cassation, the employer's discretion in terminating the contract on the basis of the worker's failure to satisfy the conditions for confirmation[29] is effectively only constrained by anti-discrimination legislation.[30] More generally, the non-confirmation of probation is a right, limited by the abuse of rights doctrine,[31] which is predominantly governed by common/contract law reasoning and applies from the day the contract is concluded.

European legal systems frequently allow or even provide for 'open-ended contracts of employment' to end with or to be ended by the retirement of the employee – by which we normally mean the withdrawal of the employee from full-time or career employment by reason of reaching an age, such as the age of 60 or of 65, which has

---

[23] Cf. Council Directive 98/59/EC of 20 July 1998 on the approximation of the laws of the Member States relating to collective redundancies [1998] OJ L 225/16.

[24] Article L. 1235-2 of the French *Code du Travail* reinforces the procedural requirements introduced by *loi 30 décembre 1986* and *2 août 1989*, by means of specific pecuniary sanctions.

[25] Many continental systems do of course encompass '*procédure conventionelles*', but they are typically seen as being a '*garantie de fond*', with statute providing an inderogable floor of rights. Cf. J. Pélissier, A. Supiot, A. Jeammaud (2008) *Droit du Travail*, 24th ed., Paris: Dalloz, p. 579.

[26] Article L 1221-19 of the *Code du Travail*.

[27] Article 2096 of the Italian Civil Code.

[28] Which is limited to two months, though – under Article L. 1221-21 – it can be further extended by another two months, in the presence of a collective agreement. In fixed-term contracts it cannot extend beyond thirty days, Article L. 1242-10.

[29] Though taking into account other conditions or factors unconnected to the worker's performance would be seen as an '*abus de droit*' – Cass Soc. 20 novembre 2007, n. 06-41.212.

[30] Cour de Cassation, 16 février 2005, no. 02-43.402.

[31] '*La rupture de l'essai est un droit, limité par l'abus de droit*'. P. Lokiec et S. Robin-Olivier (2008) 'La période d'essai', *RDT*, 258.

been identified either at national level or at enterprise level as the 'default retiring age' for workers in the category concerned.

A comparative overview of how the concept of 'default retirement age' is approached in the UK and in France is enlightening in this respect. France did not have a 'default retirement age' as such until the Law of 30 July 1987. Prior to that, the French Court of Cassation jurisprudence affirmed that 'no legal or regulatory provision fixes an age at which a worker must obligatorily leave his work and take up his retirement',[32] and by and large the retirement of a worker was conceptualized as a peculiar form of dismissal or resignation – peculiar in that it would not attract any kind of severance pay – depending on the party instigating it. A contrasting evolution has occurred in the UK, where the imposition of a 'default retirement age' has been largely forbidden with effect from October 2011.[32a] What is interesting for the purposes of our argument, is that neither lawfulness nor the illegality of the 'default retirement age' contradicts our hypothesis that the 'open-ended' contract of employment is really far less open-ended than its name suggests. French labour law had successfully devised a number of ways for a default termination of contracts in the absence of a 'default retirement age' and no doubt so will English labour law, possibly taking the lead from the apparent benevolence of EUCJ jurisprudence towards such arrangements.[33]

So these various types of closure arrangement crucially affect the duration of 'open-ended' contracts of employment. Where those types of closure arrangement are present, the contract of employment is in fact constituted as a contract for an initial probationary period and then, if confirmed, until retirement (subject to earlier termination on certain conditions, for example by reason of misconduct or redundancy). This is the real or factual duration model of the typical career appointment or 'standard' contract of employment. The paradox is that in the laws of the contract of employment of most European countries, the more that these kinds of closure arrangement become regulated and contested, the more that they seem to be kept separate from the theoretical duration model of the 'open-ended contract of employment' – which remains in being as a symbol or icon increasingly isolated from the surrounding factual and legal realities.

However, behind that simple paradox lies a complex set of variations between European national systems as to the way that these types of closure arrangement figure in the law of contracts of employment. Although in most systems the symbolical notion of the 'open-ended contract of employment' is still encountered, it is understood more literally in some systems and less literally in others. There are many systems in which the legal construction and regulation of retirement, although not seen as negating the notion of the 'open-ended contract of employment', would nevertheless be seen as integrated into the law of contracts of

---

[32] Cass. Soc. 1er mars 1972, D. 1972.540. Our translation.

[32a] See the Employment Equality (Repeal of Retirement Age Provisions) Regulations 2011 (SI 2011/1069).

[33] Cf. Joined Cases C-250/09 and C-268/09, *Georgiev v. Tehnicheski universitet – Sofia*; Case C-159/10, *Fuchs v Land Hessen* (Case C-159/10) (not yet reported at the time of writing).

employment. In those systems, it is as if the notion of the 'open-ended contract of employment' has become a conventional (if rather misleading) description for contracts which are recognized by the law of contracts of employment as being subject to termination by retirement, as well as in other ways.

There is an at least equally extensive set of variations between European employment law systems in their handling of probation arrangements. Most such systems accept that probation arrangements are to some degree compatible with the notion of the 'open-ended contract of employment', or with the notion of the fixed-term contract of employment,[34] and that such arrangements can therefore be regarded as part of such contracts. However, in some systems though not in others,[35] it is recognized (whether in legislation or in judicial doctrine or in both) that if the probationary period is of long duration, it may be incompatible with the notion of either the 'open-ended' or the 'fixed term' contract of employment so that if such an arrangement is permissible at all, it has to be made by means of some special category of personal work contract.[36]

So from all these different kinds of closure arrangement, there can be composed for each national system a picture of the duration model or series of duration models which are prescribed for the so-called 'open-ended contract of employment'. But that is no simple task, because of the many different ways in which these closure arrangements may be combined with each other to produce radically divergent outcomes. A very important example of such divergences consists of the different ways in which arrangements for termination by notice interlock with arrangements for termination on specified grounds, and with procedural conditions for termination.

At one extreme, these arrangements might be fully cumulative, so that the employee could be dismissed only with notice, on specified grounds, and conditionally upon compliance with procedural safeguards. At the opposite extreme, dismissals might be permitted without any of those requirements. In between lies a whole mass of possible combinations of one, two, or all three of those kinds of requirement. Moreover, each of those requirements might be pitched at a highly worker-protective level, or at a lower level at which it is less worker protective. Finally, as we have seen, even where some or all of those requirements are present, systems may differ in the extent to which they identify those requirements as integrated into contracts of employment or prescribed by the law of contracts of employment.

---

[34] Although in this case the use of probationary clauses is narrowly supervised by the courts, that will on balance require them to be introduced in writing upon the conclusion of the contract. For Italy cf. *Cassazione 14 ottobre 1999, n. 11597.*

[35] English law does not prevent the inclusion of long-term probationary arrangements in contracts of employment, even beyond the qualifying period for protection against unfair dismissal, though the non-confirmation of probation may constitute an unfair dismissal.

[36] We venture to suggest that the '*periode de consolidation*' contained in the '*contrat nouvelle embauche*' (which was abolished by Law 596 of 25 June 2008), did serve the purpose of extending probation beyond the normal limits for the standard CDI, thus circumventing French unfair dismissal legislation. But similar effects can often be obtained by a misuse of 'training contracts' and '*stages*'. Cf. J. Pélissier, A. Supiot, A. Jeammaud (2008) *Droit du Travail,* 24th ed., Paris: Dalloz, p. 300–4.

## B. Specifying the Grounds and Procedures for Contractual Termination

Thus far, we have been considering the range of closure arrangements which may, in national legal systems, be prescribed by the law of employment contracts, and which may, in those national legal systems, form part of the duration model of so-called 'open-ended contracts of employment'. In order to complete our understanding of the nature of the European regulatory spectrum which exists with regard to the duration and termination of employment contracts, we need also to refer to certain aspects of the laws of contracts of employment which, although not conventionally regarded as forming part of the closure arrangements or duration models for those contracts, nevertheless do have a significant bearing upon those arrangements for duration and closure. There are in particular two aspects which require attention: firstly, the regulation of termination of contracts of employment other than by the employer unilaterally, and secondly, the provision of remedies for the contractually wrongful termination of the contract of employment.

Firstly, then, we should explain the significance of the regulation of termination of contracts of employment other than by the employer unilaterally. We mean by this the ways in which the law of employment contracts prescribes or controls the termination of contracts of employment other than by the employer unilaterally; and it is useful to specify that termination other than by the employer unilaterally might consist of termination by the employee, or bilateral termination by both parties (that is to say termination by agreement), or termination independently of the parties by judicial ruling or by operation of law.

In each national system, the law of employment contracts in some sense prescribes or controls the conditions for the termination of contracts of employment other than by the employer unilaterally, just as it prescribes the conditions for the termination of contracts of employment by the employer unilaterally. The two sets of prescriptions or controls are complementary to each other. In many situations, termination of the contract of employment other than by the employer unilaterally may provide a way of side-stepping the prescriptions or controls which are placed upon unilateral termination by the employer. So the prescriptions or controls which are placed upon termination other than by the employer unilaterally have the function of supplementing and indirectly sustaining the prescriptions or controls which are placed upon unilateral termination by the employer – or they may fail to do so, and thus may undermine that latter set of prescriptions or controls.

For example, the law of contracts of employment of a particular national system might rigorously control the employer's power to terminate the contract of employment by way of mandatory retirement; but that same law of contracts of employment might allow great latitude for the termination of contracts of employment by bilateral agreement between employer and employee, including bilateral agreement for the retirement of the employee. Historically, this has been an approach followed by French labour law, especially before the adoption of the aforementioned Law of 30 July 1987. A principled stance against mandatory retirement by reference to a default age was accompanied by a more relaxed approach of the Cour de Cassation in accepting the lawfulness of termination clauses varyingly known as *'clauses guillotine'* or *'couperet'*, holding that 'no legal provision prevents the social partners... from providing that the open-ended contract of employment will come to an end *de plein droit* [by operation of law] when the worker attains the age agreed for his retirement'.[37]

Even more fundamentally, the strong prescription against unilateral termination by the employer may well be undermined by a loose regulation of termination by mutual consent. This has been a problematic aspect of English labour law,[38] and is increasingly becoming a vexed question in continental European systems. In Germany, for instance, 'expectations that the courts would establish conditions limiting the freedom to conclude a contract terminating an employment contract have turned out to be futile',[39] and the practice of signing an *Aufhebungsvertrag* (termination agreement) remains practically unchallenged. In France, since the Law of 25 June 2008 granted an explicit codified legal basis for such agreements,[40] this area of employment protection legislation has been substantially weakened, though the provisions of L. 1231-4 of the *Code du Travail* limit the use of automatic termination clauses agreed in the contract, including clauses of the kind in issue in *Brown v. Knowsley BC.*[41] Obviously the weak prescription or the absence of prescription in respect of mutual termination arrangements will often undermine the strong prescription otherwise imposed by unfair dismissal legislation. We would be unlikely to regard this as actually forming part of the duration models of contracts of employment; but in a sense we should do so, because it does indirectly affect the ways and circumstances in which contracts of employment may be terminated and hence, somewhat more indirectly, the duration which those contracts may have or be projected to have.

In this aspect of the law concerning the termination of employment contracts – as in various others – we can envisage a regulatory spectrum. At one extreme would be systems in which the prescriptions for or controls over termination of the contract of employment other than by the employer unilaterally were strong ones designed to buttress or underpin a strong set of prescriptions for or controls over unilateral termination by the employer. At the opposite extreme would be weak prescriptions or controls, reflecting either a generalized preference for freedom of contract with respect to these arrangements, or even a view that it was specifically important to the efficient functioning of the labour market for employers to have a high degree of flexibility with regard to such arrangements. Our investigation

---

[37] Soc. 24 avr. 1986 *Droit Social* (1986) 460. Cf. Cour de Cassation, *Bulletin d'information no. 485 du 15/01/1999*. Our translation.

[38] Cf. *Sheffield v. Oxford Controls Co Ltd* [1979] IRLR 133 and *Sandhu v. Jan de Rijk Transport Ltd* [2007] IRLR 519.

[39] M. Weiss and M. Schmidt (2008) *Labour Law and Industrial Relations in Germany*, AH Alphen aan den Rijn: Kluwer, 119.

[40] Articles L 1237-11 to 1237-16 of the *Code du Travail*.

[41] *Brown v. Knowsley Borough Council* [1986] IRLR 102.

would appear to suggest a slow but visible shift of a number of European labour law systems towards this latter end of the spectrum.

If we turn our attention, secondly, to the provision of remedies for the contractually wrongful termination of the contract of employment, it will be even more clear that this is an aspect of the laws of employment contracts which has a significant bearing upon the arrangements for their duration and closure, although not conventionally regarded as directly forming part of the closure arrangements or duration models for those contracts. Generally speaking, national systems of employment contract law prescribe quite specifically or control quite rigorously the remedies for contractually wrongful termination of the contract of employment. That is to say, those systems lay down the conditions in which the contractually wrongful termination of the contract of employment may be nullified or reversed, and also the conditions in which compensation may be payable by the employer to the employee in respect of the contractually wrongful termination of the contract of employment. We propose further to investigate this particular assertion in the following section.

We have thus established the existence of a wide range of possibilities for diversity in the manner of regulation of the termination of contracts of employment, and we have indicated how that diversity may occur in the several dimensions of the time of termination, of the grounds and procedures for termination, and of the controls or remedies placed upon contractually wrongful termination. In the next section, we seek to build upon those notions of diversity by taking English law as a case-study of a rather eclectic set of regulatory choices within that range of possibilities, that is to say a set of choices which between them amount to the creation of a dual system of legal regulation of the termination of employment. Some of our analyses and findings in respect of English law will be contrasted with the approach adopted in some continental legal systems.

## Section 3: English Law as a Case-Study in the Dual Regulation of Termination of Employment

Our argument now focuses upon one of the points at which English law is at its most singular in its contractual construction of employment relations. This singularity consists in the way that the general controls upon the fairness of dismissal, put in place by legislation from 1971 onwards, were superimposed upon the law of the contract of employment without, however, fundamentally modifying the legal vision of the contract of employment itself. This appears to be in significant contrast to continental European legal systems, in which the corresponding controls have seemed to be regarded as affecting the legal construction of the contract itself. In this section, we firstly consider how and why this essentially dis-integrated approach was taken (subsection A), and we secondly argue that this approach has been conducive to the maintenance of a conspicuously low level of protection of job security within the framework of the construction of employment relations as contractual ones (subsection B).

## A. The Separation Between Contractually Wrongful Dismissal and Unfair Dismissal in English Law

In the English legal system, the legislature and the courts have created and maintained two systems for the regulation of termination of employment, the 'wrongful dismissal system' and the 'unfair dismissal system'; their separate but symbiotic existence has been a matter of profound consequence which differentiates English law from that of many other European legal systems. In this subsection we describe firstly how that separation came about and secondly the effects which can be ascribed to it.

By comparison with many other European states, the UK was relatively late in the twentieth century in undertaking anything which amounted to a systematic regulation of the duration and termination of employment relations. By the time that, in the later 1960s, the need to do so became a matter of urgent policy debate in the UK, many other European states, as noted in the previous section, had engaged in legislative or codificatory activity in this area which amounted to the systemic regulation of the duration and termination of employment relations. Moreover, in many such systems, it appeared quite normal and natural for this regulation to consist of or at least to imply the systematic shaping of employment contracts.

When, in the early 1960s, British governments embarked upon what was to become an extensive series of proposals or programmes for legislation to enhance or protect the employment rights of workers, the initial inclination seems to have been to proceed in a manner familiar to many continental European states, namely by legislative subjection of contracts of employment to minimum labour standards which would serve to underpin, and ultimately to define, the 'standard' contract of employment. This seems to have been the intention embodied in the Contracts of Employment Act 1963, which provided for certain minimum periods of notice to terminate contracts of employment, for certain rights to payment of remuneration during such minimum periods of notice, and for the giving of written particulars to employees of certain of the terms and conditions of their employment.[42]

It was most probably the assumption of the drafters of this legislation that all those three measures would be regarded as directly affecting the content or at least the minimum content of contracts of employment so as to enhance job security.[43] That indeed seems to have been the actual effect of the provisions prescribing the

---

[42] Cf. M. Freedland (1976) *The Contract of Employment*, Oxford: Clarendon Press at 306.

[43] Cf. Hansard, HC Deb 14 February 1963 vol. 671 cc1503–618, esp. John Hare's introduction to the Bill: 'The objects of the Bill are, first, to lay down minimum periods of notice to terminate employment, and, secondly, to require employers to give their employees written statements about the main terms of their contracts of employment. The Bill is a part of the Government's plans to provide greater security for workers.'

minimum period of notice. However, something different has, over a period of time, occurred with regard to the other two measures, for they have come to be regarded as having created legislative or 'statutory' rights which are in their nature distinct from the contracts of employment upon which they come to bear.

Thus, firstly, there is said to be a 'statutory' right to payment during the minimum period of notice, which is conceived of as essentially independent of the contract of employment itself. And, secondly, the required written particulars are known as the 'statutory particulars', and are clearly identified as not constituting the contract of employment itself, in the absence of clear indications that the parties have specially identified them as such. Instead, 'It is, of course, quite clear that the statement made pursuant to section 4 of the Act of 1963' – that is, the Contracts of Employment Act – 'is not the contract; it is not even conclusive evidence of the terms of a contract.'[44] Other employment law systems make a somewhat similar differentiation between the terms of the contract and information about those terms,[45] a distinction that may be implicitly accepted by Directive 91/533 itself.[46] But the identification of that difference as being between the 'contractual' and the 'statutory' seems to be singular to British employment law.

Thus even at the very moment at which the British legislature started to shape a 'standard' contract of employment, its efforts were understood and construed as the addition of legislative superstructures which did not actually alter the common-law-based infrastructure of the contract of employment as a contract type. This separation of common-law-based infrastructure and legislative superstructure was maintained as further legislative rights for employees were created. This was especially true in relation to the legislative scheme for minimum redundancy payments which was introduced by the Redundancy Payments Act 1965. This placed a legislative floor of standardization beneath the redundancy payments schemes which were at that period created and put into effect by many public and private employing enterprises, often brought about by collective bargaining, and which were incorporated into the contracts of employment of many workers. A perfectly clear distinction emerged and was continually thereafter maintained between 'contractual' and 'statutory' entitlements to redundancy payments.

In 1971, with the introduction of unfair dismissal legislation as part of the Industrial Relations Act 1971, that fissure between 'contractual' and 'statutory' rights with regard to the termination of employment was enormously widened. In

---

[44] Ackner LJ citing with approval Lord Parker in *Robertson v. British Gas Corporation* [1983] ICR, 351, 354.

[45] Cf. M. D'Onghia (2005) *La Forma Vincolata nel Diritto del Lavoro*, (Milano: Giuffrè, 144–5). And some of the MPs debating the Bill thought that this could have been the case in respect of the Contracts of Employment Act 1963: 'It is oddly titled, a "Contracts of Employment Bill". That has a legalistic sound, but my legal advisers say that the phrase should be "Terms of Employment" and that it is wrong to talk of contracts of employment since the Bill deals with terms of employment' (Mr. Arthur Holt MP), Hansard HC Deb, 14 February 1963, vol. 671 cc1555.

[46] Article 2(1) requiring that the employer notifies the essential aspects of the contract or employment relationship, rather than the contract itself. Council Directive 91/533/EEC of 14 October 1991 on an employer's obligation to inform employees of the conditions applicable to the contract or employment relationship, [1991] OJ L 288/32.

this legislation, the right not to be unfairly dismissed was constructed in a way which made it almost entirely independent of the existing body of law concerning contractually wrongful dismissal. The notion of 'unfairness' was defined quite differently from that of contractual wrongfulness; the concept of 'dismissal' was assigned a wider meaning than in the context of contractually wrongful dismissal; the remedies for unfair dismissal were significantly different from those for contractually wrongful dismissal; and the law of unfair dismissal was to be administered, both at first instance and at the first appellate stage, by a specialized hierarchy of tribunals and courts quite distinct from the courts of common law in which cases of contractually wrongful dismissal were adjudicated.

On this occasion, the impulse to differentiate between the previously existing body of regulation and the new one was especially strong. There was a perception that the law relating to dismissal from employment was in need of radical reform, whereby the new law of unfair dismissal would provide a kind and degree of job security that the contract law of wrongful dismissal had signally failed to create. Moreover, the new law of unfair dismissal was enacted as part of a larger programme, the authors of which had the aim of juridifying employment relations, both collective and individual, in a consciously different mode from that of the existing common law of contract and tort. These were the main ingredients in a recipe which produced a new and separate second system for the legal regulation of the termination of employment.

This separation of the legal regulation of the termination of employment relations into two distinct systems has been a phenomenon of very great significance. It has a special importance which has been rather under-recognized and is best revealed by European comparative analysis. It is very well known that the principal regulatory system for the termination of employment relations has become that of the law of unfair dismissal. It is also well understood that there have been very significant interactions between the two systems, in the sense that both the legislators and the courts have drawn upon contractual concepts as the starting points for many of the novel conceptions embodied in the unfair dismissal system. Attention has been extensively focused too upon the ways in which that has fed back into the development of the contractual concepts themselves, nowhere more conspicuously than in relation to the notion of constructive dismissal and to the evolution of the implied obligation of mutual trust and confidence.

These interactions between the two systems of legal regulation of the termination of employment relations, and this evidence of a kind of symbiosis between them, has given rise to a certain perception of the division of this area of legal regulation into two systems, as a healthy and dynamic one. It does, however, have at least one consequence of a negative kind so far as the protection of the job security of workers is concerned. For it means that the older paradigm for the legal regulation of the termination of employment, which was produced by the law of contractually wrongful dismissal, was never actually replaced by the new paradigm, which was produced by the law of unfair dismissal. The earlier contractual paradigm, essentially a creature of the common law, co-exists with the statutory paradigm which has been created and superimposed by the law of unfair dismissal.

There are even distinct hints that the courts regard the contractual paradigm for the legal regulation of the termination of employment as representing the real or true law which underlies what they perceive as a more ephemeral and politically instrumental body of law laid upon the top of it.[47] By contrast, in many continental European legal systems, the legal regulation of the termination of employment relations has evolved by way of a far more deep-seated reformulation of underlying paradigms. In such systems there is no essential separation between two paradigms. Notions of job security often very similar to those which inform British unfair dismissal legislation have been integrated into core notions of standard contractual employment relationships. This was in many ways something to expect as a natural consequence of the more structured and integrated relationship between the various sources of regulation of the employment relationship, a point that we have developed in Chapters 2 and 3 of the present work. But it was arguably also the consequence of a precise policy choice, explicitly or implicitly embodied in the various statutes and regulatory instruments controlling unfair dismissal, aimed at rendering the contractual and common law norms underpinning what English lawyers would call wrongful dismissal, residual in character. In the following subsection, we enlarge upon the consequences of this very important comparative phenomenon.

## B. The Low Protection of Job Security in the English Law of Employment Contracts

In the previous subsection we have explained how, in English labour or employment law, the regulation of the termination of contractual employment relations has become fragmented into two quite distinct subsystems, that is to say on the one hand the law of wrongful dismissal which forms part of the common-law-based law of the contract of employment, and on the other hand the law of unfair dismissal which is, by contrast, entirely of statutory origin, deriving in the first place from the Industrial Relations Act 1971. In this subsection, we consider the significance and consequences of that dis-integrated approach to the regulation of the termination of employment relations. Our argument is that, by comparison with other European labour or employment law systems, that of English law is subjected to a discernible pressure against the development of legal protection of job security by reason of that dis-integrated approach. It is of course impossible to be sure how much of an effect that dis-integrated approach has upon the overall level of legal protection of job security, especially during a period when there is no shortage of other deregulatory pressures. Nevertheless, we can point to some concrete effects of that approach, even if it is hard to assess their impact in the larger scheme of legal regulation of contractual employment relations. In other words, we suggest that the

---

[47] Cf. M. Freedland (2003) *The Personal Employment Contract*, Oxford: OUP, at pp. 292–305, esp. pp. 298–305, 'Lawfulness in Termination – A Theory of Adjudication'.

dis-integrated character of the body of English law concerning the termination of contractual employment relations tends in some degree to restrain or reduce the level of protection of job security which that body of law provides, and we seek to advance some detailed explanation for that.

As we have previously begun to indicate, the key to the understanding of this phenomenon – this negative impact on the protection of job security – consists in recognizing that the dis-integrated approach has the result that these two sub-systems of legal regulation function in partial (though by no means complete) independence from each other, so that each sub-system has its own regulatory orientation; and that, in this fragmented situation, the common law of the contract of employment seems to embody and express some negative attitudes towards the protection of job security which have been more deeply displaced in legal systems where a more integrated approach prevails. The common law of wrongful dismissal, invigorated by its relative autonomy from the statute law of unfair dismissal, has marched on through an era of growth in legislative protection of job security, still displaying occasional capacities for rearguard actions and doctrinal ambushes. We proceed to examine the positions from which those capacities are derived.

The first and most crucial of these doctrinal positions concerns the largely unrestricted freedom to contract for termination of employment by notice or by expiry of a fixed term or by a combination of the two. That freedom is strongly asserted and maintained by the common law of the contract of employment, almost as an unquestioned axiom. It has been marginally constrained, but by no means abolished, by legislation conferring rights to statutory minimum periods of notice, and by legislation converting fixed-term contracts into 'permanent' ones in certain specified circumstances. It is of great comparative significance to note that many other European labour law systems considerably constrained that freedom for much of the twentieth century, even if in more recent years some of those restrictions have been somewhat relaxed.[48] It almost amounts to a philosophically distinctive feature of the English common law of wrongful dismissal that it confers an unrestricted power of termination by notice or by the expiry of a fixed term. We could refer to it as the unrestricted power of termination by notice or expiry.

The second such doctrinal position consists of the conferring upon employers, by presumed implication into contracts of employment, of wide powers of summary (that is to say immediate) dismissal by reason of misconduct or want of capability on the part of the employee. These quite sweeping managerial disciplinary powers were moreover untrammelled by any procedural requirements. This is an area in which English law can be contrasted with the way in which some continental European labour law systems regulate those power. As discussed above, the Italian Civil Code of 1942 introduced in Article 2119 a concept of dismissal for '*giusta causa*' (just cause) without notice which, we believe, could be seen as functionally equivalent to the English common law concept of 'summary dismissal' due to a repudiatory breach of contract. Both these concepts did of course evolve over the

---

[48]  Cf. N. Countouris (2007) *The Changing Law of the Employment Relationship*, Aldershot: Ashgate, Chapter 3.

years under the auspices of common law reasoning, partly as a reflection of changing 'current social conditions'.[49]

However, and this is an important point, we would argue that the development of unfair dismissal legislation in the two countries has produced far deeper inroads into the Italian notion of '*giusta causa*' than into the English law concept of 'summary dismissal' for repudiatory breach of contract. In fact cases such as *Delco Ltd v. Joinson*,[50] suggest that even in claims of unfair dismissal, common and contract law concepts of gross misconduct will infiltrate and ultimately dominate judicial reasoning. By contrast, Italian scholars would suggest that the opposite trend has affected the relationship between Article 2119 and successive statutory interventions in the area of unfair dismissal. While this notion pre-dates the one of 'justifiable reason' introduced by Law 604/1966, 'on a systematic level [just cause] configures itself as a species of the wider genus of the notion of justifiability of dismissal established by Article 1, para. 1, L. n. 604, according to which "in an open-ended employment relationship... the dismissal by the employee can only occur for a just cause according to Article 2119 of the civil code or for a justifiable reason"'.[51] The introduction of the notion of justifiable reason beside that of just cause has 'therefore pushed legal scholarship and jurisprudence to a reconsideration of the latter notion, evidently, by reference to the former'.[52] The result has been a progressive convergence between the codified notion of 'just cause' and the – much narrower – statutory concept of 'justifiable subjective reason'.[53] By comparison English law has maintained very broad underlying powers of summary dismissal, in spite of the overlay of unfair dismissal legislation.

Nevertheless, although those wide powers of summary dismissal have tended to be regarded as emblematic of the low protection of job security in the common law of wrongful dismissal, we are of the view that it is actually the unrestricted power of termination by notice or expiry which is ultimately more expressive of the whole stance of the common law towards the termination of contractual employment. The fact that wide implied powers of summary dismissal are conferred on grounds related to the conduct or capability of the employee pales into insignificance by comparison with the largely unrestricted power to contract for termination by notice or expiry, especially as those kinds of termination are not required to be for good cause shown, either in a substantive or a procedural sense.[54] These are two aspects of the termination of work relations that continental European systems generally address much more effectively, partly due to the fact that their statutory provisions

---

[49] *Wilson v. Racher* [1974] ICR 428, (Edmund Lawson LJ). Cf. M. Freedland (2003) *The Personal Employment Contract*, Oxford: OUP, 324–5.

[50] [1991] ICR 172 (EAT). Cf. M. Freedland (2003) *The Personal Employment Contract*, Oxford: OUP, 327.

[51] E. Ghera (2007) *Diritto del Lavoro*, (Bari: Cacucci, pp. 187–8), see further pp. 191–3.

[52] Ibid (our translation).

[53] T. Treu (2007) *Labour Law and Industrial Relations in Italy*, AH Alphen aan den Rijn: Kluwer, 108.

[54] Cf. M. Freedland (2003) *The Personal Employment Contract*, Oxford: OUP, 305.

are not subject to the qualifying periods attached to English unfair dismissal legislation and, subject to the presence of probation clauses, apply from the outset. That, we suggest, is the largest elephant in the room of the common law of wrongful dismissal, though there are others to which we now turn our attention.

The other principal doctrinal positions of the common law of wrongful dismissal, which complement those which we have so far described, are concerned with the remedies which are available to enforce claims of contractually wrongful dismissal; and, as is often the case with doctrinal positions concerning remedies, they have an enormous impact upon the substantive law of the termination of the contract of employment. There are two key doctrinal positions of this kind; one concerns the unavailability of specific enforcement of contracts of employment, while the other relates to the damages which may be awarded for contractually wrongful dismissal.

The doctrine of the common law (including the law of equitable remedies) which proscribes the specific enforcement of contracts of employment is a long-established and deeply entrenched one which has admitted of only minor exceptions.[55] Although it has a worker-protective function as a form of protection against enforced labour, it is clear that some at least of the judges who developed and applied this doctrine were at least as much concerned with ensuring that employers could not be compelled unwillingly to employ particular servants. As a rule which therefore ensured that the remedies for wrongful dismissal would be limited to pecuniary ones, this doctrine contributes to a notion that dismissal in breach of the contract of employment is itself a pecuniary wrong rather than a wrong in any more extensive sense.

That notion of dismissal in breach of the contract of employment as a purely pecuniary wrong is itself complemented by a further doctrinal position of the law of the contract of employment, which consists of a rule that damages for wrongful dismissal are normally to be based upon and limited to compensation for loss of remuneration and other pecuniary benefits in respect of the period of contractually promised employment of which the employee was deprived by the wrongful dismissal. This stance was taken up, decisively, by the judges of the House of Lords, in the leading case of *Addis v. Gramophone Company* in 1908,[56] and has been more or less consistently maintained since then. It is of the very highest significance, because this remedial doctrine works in tandem with the unrestricted power of termination by notice or expiry which we identified earlier. It is those doctrinal positions which between them effectively define the wrongfulness of wrongful dismissal as consisting of no more than the failure to pay remuneration and any other pecuniary benefits for the contractually stipulated period of notice, or the statutory minimum period of notice, or the unexpired fixed term of the contract.

---

[55] Ibid. at 368–376, 'The Specific Remedies/Termination Complex Presented'.
[56] *Addis v. Gramophone Co Ltd* [1909] AC 488 (HL). Cf. M. Freedland (2003) *The Personal Employment Contract*, Oxford: OUP, pp. 355–368, 'The Sources and Scope of the Limited Damages Rule'.

The series of interlocking doctrinal positions that we have thus described forms and constitutes the core of a body of English law about the termination of the contract of employment which is firmly oriented towards a low level of protection of job security. In circumstances which we considered in the previous subsection, a body of legislation concerning unfair dismissal was introduced for the very purpose of providing a higher level of legal protection of job security, taking different or contrary doctrinal positions at all those key points; but, in a classic manifestation of a dis-integrated approach, the unfair dismissal legislation created a layer of regulation which was distinct from the law of wrongful dismissal. The two systems were required to co-exist in what almost amounted to an enforced symbiosis of legal opponents. We proceed to consider the outcomes of that difficult interaction.

The interaction between those two dis-integrated layers of regulation, the law of wrongful dismissal and the law of unfair dismissal, has in fact been an enormously complex and interesting one, because the legislators who designed the unfair dismissal legislation, although distancing themselves from or reversing many of the doctrinal positions of the law of wrongful dismissal, nevertheless relied heavily upon that body of law to provide some of the key technical concepts for their new body of law. In particular, the statutory notion of 'dismissal' was itself defined by reference to the termination of the contract of employment, thus invoking the common law of wrongful dismissal in order to explicate the statute law of unfair dismissal. This created a link between these two regulatory domains, across which there was a tension and the possibility of a pull in either direction; the common law of wrongful dismissal might pull the statute law of unfair dismissal towards a low job-security and less worker-protective approach, or the statute law of unfair dismissal might pull the common law of wrongful dismissal towards a high job-security and more worker-protective approach.

There was a period – essentially during the 1990s – when this tug of war seemed to be going in favour of the law of unfair dismissal. That is to say, the functional requirements of the law of unfair dismissal seemed to be demanding and producing some worker-protective evolutions in the common law of the contract of employment, particularly though not solely in the shape of the creative evolution of the contractual notion of 'constructive dismissal'.[57] This took the doctrinal form of the rapid and radical expansion of an obligation of mutual trust and confidence, which, as we saw in the previous chapter, was articulated in the context of the law of unfair dismissal as a generically implied term in contracts of employment.

However, there was to be an unexpected turn in the contrary direction early in the following decade, consisting of the decision of the House of Lords in the case of *Johnson v. Unisys Ltd*[58] in which it was held, most curiously, that the legislators who had enacted the unfair dismissal legislation in 1971 must have intended that the implied obligation of mutual trust and confidence, although unrecognized at that time, was to be inapplicable to common law contractual claims for wrongful dismissal. In effect, the older doctrinal positions of the common law of wrongful

---

[57] Cf. M. Freedland (2003) *The Personal Employment Contract*, Oxford: OUP, pp. 338–41.
[58] *Johnson v. Unisys* [2001] ICR 480 (HL).

dismissal were reasserting themselves, especially the restrictive approach to damages for wrongful dismissal associated with the decision in *Addis v. Gramophone Company*.[59] This decision seemed to administer a lasting counter-check to the development of the implied obligation of mutual trust and confidence, and in particular to inhibit its capacity to contribute to the development of substantive and procedural safeguards for employees facing dismissal, not only in the common law of wrongful dismissal but even in a sense in the law of unfair dismissal too.

It is always risky to attempt to draw bold comparative conclusions from such contingent and path-dependent evolutions. However, it is quite convincing – and arguments in the previous chapter pointed somewhat in the same direction – to regard the implied obligation of mutual trust and confidence as an integrative principle capable of bringing about a fusion of different strands or layers of worker-protective regulation in much the same way as doctrines of good faith or *ordre public social* might do in other European legal systems. If so, it is especially significant to observe how the dis-integrated approach of English law to the regulation of the termination of contractual employment relations has seemed in the end to militate against such developments. The particular view expressed in *Johnsons v. Unisys* that for the judiciary to construct a general common law remedy for unfair circumstances attending dismissal would be to go contrary to the intention of Parliament, would amount – in comparative terms – to saying that the equivalent continental European notions of unfair dismissal should be immune from any reasoning based on the breach of common law notion of good faith in contractual relations.

Continental European systems appear to have moved beyond these rather contrived arguments. Italian courts, for instance, have accepted that the manner of dismissal can cause injury to a person's feelings, dignity, and honour, capable of attracting damages at least since the 1980s.[60] The French Court of Cassation has been undisturbed by the possibility that the termination of a contract of employment could both be fair, in the sense of complying with the just cause requirements of French labour law, and attract contractual damages under Article 1382 *Code Civil* for the *conditions vexatoires* (vexatious manner) in which the dismissal occurred.[61] In the next and final section of this chapter, we pursue this line of thought from the topic of termination of contracts of employment into the topic of transformation of those contracts from one state or condition to another.

---

[59] *Addis v. Gramophone Co Ltd* [1909] AC 488 (HL); the relationship between the two cases is considered in M. Freedland (2003) *The Personal Employment Contract* Oxford: OUP, at pp. 359–365.

[60] Cassazione 22 Luglio 1987 n. 6375. Cf. M. L. Vallauri (2010) 'L'argomentazione della "Dignità Umana" nella Giurisprudenza in Materia di Danno alla Persona del Lavoratore' 128(4), *GDLRI*, 659, 679–80.

[61] Cf. Cass. Soc. N. 05–42143 du 8 novembre 2006. Or indeed that it might attract both labour law and contract law remedies; cf. Cass. Soc. 08-44094 du 16 mars 2010.

## Section 4: The Construction of Transformations in Contractual Employment Relations

In this section we complete our comparative inquiry into the working of the contractual construction of employment relations by considering the various senses in which the relation may be transformed from one state or mode of existence into another. We shall continue, as in the previous section, to be especially interested in comparisons and contrast between integrated and dis-integrated approaches to contractual construction. We shall therefore continue to focus quite strongly on English law as a case-study of a relatively highly regulated system but one where a highly dis-integrated approach is maintained to that regulation. However, that will not be the sole point of our inquiry; we shall also be interested in some difficulties in the contractual construction of the transformation of employment relations which are experienced more or less equally as between systems where integrated or dis-integrated approaches to contractual construction are taken. We shall first consider transformations in the identity of the employer or in the ownership, or control of the employing enterprise (subsection A), and we shall then consider other kinds of transformation in the nature or character of the employment relation, concentrating especially on what we have previously identified as changes in the mode of existence of the employment relation (subsection B).

## A. Transformations in the Identity of the Employer or in the Ownership or Control of the Employing Enterprise

In this subsection we begin our comparative inquiry into the contractual construction of transformations in the employment relation by looking at the way in which the law of the contract of employment treats transformations in the identity of the employer or in the ownership or control of the employing enterprise – and for reasons which will become evident, we shall focus particularly upon the notion of the 'transfer of an undertaking' and shall consider the part which that plays in the contractual construction and treatment of such transformations. As in the immediately preceding sections of this chapter, our principal comparative argument will be that there are significant differences in the contractual construction and treatment of such transformations according to whether an integrated or a dis-integrated approach is taken to the contractual construction of such transformations, that is to say according to whether the prevailing vision of the contract of employment is one which integrates or fails to integrate external sources of regulation, especially worker-protective employment legislation and collective agreements; and we shall continue to treat English law as providing a case-study in a system which, unusually among European labour law systems, combines a relatively high overall level of regulation with a very low level of integration of regulation viewed as external into the contract of employment as legally constructed.

The heading which we have given to this subsection itself feeds into our argument about the significance of the differences between integrated and dis-integrated approaches. By referring to transformations in, on the one hand, 'the identity of the employer' and, on the other hand 'the ownership or control of the employing enterprise', our heading identifies two different ways of conceptualizing changes in the character or nature, or constitution of the employer or employing enterprise. The idea of transformation in the 'identity of the employer' looks at such changes from the narrow perspective of the contract of employment itself; from that narrow perspective, the employing organization is conceived of as the contractual opposite or counterpart of the employee, the other party to an essentially bilateral contract of employment. To look upon such changes from that perspective is more consistent with dis-integrated approaches to contractual construction than with integrated ones.

By contrast, the idea of transformations in the 'ownership or control of the employing enterprise' looks at such changes from a broader perspective in which labour law itself connects up with those aspects of commercial and corporate law which determine the legal organizational patterns in which economic activity and employment take place, and which regulate the exercise of ownership or control of the organizations in question. To look upon such changes from that perspective is, we suggest, more consistent with integrated approaches to contractual construction than with dis-integrated ones.

This is a contrast which, we suggest, reaches right into the history of labour law and of the evolution of the legal construction of employment relations as contractual ones. If, pursuing the argument which we presented earlier in this chapter, we identify the foundational doctrinal positions for the law of the contract of employment just before the birth of labour law in its modern sense, therefore at the end of the nineteenth century, we find that those foundational doctrinal positions at that juncture are ones which firmly identify the contractual employer as a single independent human or corporate person – the 'master' of the law of master and servant becoming reconceptualized as the employing party to the contract of employment.

During the twentieth century, more and more complex organizational patterns would be recognized for the conduct of economic activity and of employment in that activity, and for the ownership and control of the organizations in question – and there was great variation in the ways in which and extents to which the labour law systems of the different European countries accorded rights and statuses to workers in the structures or constitutions of those organizations. As those evolutions occurred, the visions or conceptualizations of the employing enterprise and its relation to its employees would tend to diverge as between different national labour law systems, and so in particular would visions and conceptualizations of the nature of the employing party to the contract of employment, and of the effect on those conceptualizations of changes in ownership or control of the employing organization.

Those conceptualizations would diverge in particular (though not solely) as between systems where integrated and dis-integrated approaches were taken to the contractual construction of employment relations. Where integrated approaches were taken, evolutions in the regulation of organizational structures and of the role of workers in those organizational structures would tend to be reflected in the contractual construction of employment relations; where dis-integrated approaches were taken, contractual construction would tend to persist in a nominally contractualized version of master and servant relations.

If we pursue that observation into specific European legal systems, with English law figuring, as before, as the archetypal instance of a system which takes a dis-integrated approach, we do so at some risk, as ever, of over-generalizing the apparently generic contrasts between what are in truth highly contingent and path-dependent national evolutions; but the results of this analysis seem sufficiently interesting to justify the taking of that risk. The generalization which we advance is that in labour law systems where a highly integrated approach is taken to the contractual construction of the employment relation, there seems to be a greater readiness or capacity to regard the contract of employment as attaching to an organization, or even to an activity, which has a continuity capable of surviving changes in its institutional form or in its ownership or control. Where that capacity is shown, it generally represents an integration into the conceptualization of the contract of employment, of legislative or doctrinal positions which accord the worker various kinds of rights as a stakeholder or constitutional status vis-à-vis the employing enterprise.

If, however, we take English law as the illustrative case of a less integrated approach, we find that there has been much less of a disposition to conceptualize the contract of employment as attaching to an organization or activity in which the worker has stakeholder rights or a constitutional status capable of surviving changes in institutional forms or in ownership. Instead, the English common law of the contract of employment has shown rather a contrary disposition, perpetuating its origins as a nominally or lightly contractualized version of the law of master and servant. From that perspective, the contract of employment is viewed as being highly personal as between the employee and a specific employer, whether that employer is a human being or a legal corporate entity – the latter type of corporate employer being treated very much as an anthropomorphized equivalent of the former human archetype.

That generally persistent tendency on the part of the English judges who developed and expounded the common law of the contract of employment reached its zenith in the decision of the House of Lords in *Nokes v. Doncaster Amalgamated Collieries Ltd*,[62] in which it was held that the contract of employment of a coalminer could not be regarded as having been validly transferred from the mining company which had originally employed him to the company which had been formed by an amalgamation, taking place under a statutory procedure, between the original employing company and various other mining companies. Lord Atkin's judgment in particular famously vindicated the employee's 'right to choose for

[62] [1940] AC 1014.

himself whom he would serve' and therefore to resist his transfer 'without his knowledge and possibly against his will from the service of one person to the service of another'.[63]

It is important to be cautious against over-generalizing the significance of a decision taken in very specific and contingent circumstances; the amalgamated company was following a practice by then rather singular to mining companies of taking contractual proceedings against workers as a disciplinary sanction (often used to control collective industrial action), so that it was natural for the court to be specially concerned with the protection of the employee's claim against automatic transfer of the contract of employment from one employer to another, whereas the concern is more usually, as we shall see, with the protection of the employee's rights and expectations in the event of changes in the legal identity of the employer. Moreover, the decision was taken at a period – in 1940 during the Second World War – when it was especially compelling to envisage the role of the court as that of preserving individual (contractual) freedom against oppression by corporate or corporatist institutions.

The decision in that case can also be seen as an egregious one in other ways; it was somewhat artificial to pronounce a *de facto* transfer of employment from one corporate employer to another as invalid in contractual terms, when equally fundamental changes in the ownership and control of the employing organization could be accomplished, and have since that time on countless occasions been accomplished, behind the veil of a single unchanged corporate identity by means of acquisition of equity in the company concerned. Nevertheless, for all its singularity, the decision is expressive of a pronounced trend in English law towards a highly individualized and individualistic construction of the contract of employment, and manifests an intuitive resistance to the historical replacement of the human employer by the corporate conglomerate which can be and was in this instance regarded as an alien creature of statute law.

Albeit in a less declamatory way, this remained as the basic stance of the English common law of the contract of employment towards changes in the nature or ownership or control of the employing organization. If those transformations did not amount to a formal change in the identity of the corporate employer, they generally speaking left the contract of employment intact – although even if that was the case, the contract of employment would, as we have seen in the previous sections of this chapter, be legally constructed so as to confer very little security upon the employee, either for the employment itself or, *a fortiori* for the particular set of terms and conditions and for any seniority rights in the enterprise which the employee enjoyed. If on the other hand those transformations did amount to a formal change in the identity of the employer, they generally speaking seemed to bring the contract of employment to an end without ensuring that there was any transfer of even such limited contractual rights to a new *de facto* employer.[64]

---

[63] [1940] AC 1026.
[64] Cf. generally M. Freedland (2003) *The Personal Employment Contract* Oxford: OUP, pp. 491–505 'Transformation of Parties (I) – Partial Transformation'.

When, from the mid-1960s onwards, the English law of the contract of employment was supplemented by an expanding set of statutory employment rights, it became the standard practice for the legislator, where those rights depended upon or varied according to the employee's seniority in employment, to provide that statutory continuity of employment would be deemed to exist and to be preserved as between successive periods of employment with 'associated' companies or upon the sale or other transfer of the business or part thereof in which the employee in question was employed. In other words, there was in those situations a transfer of statutory continuity of employment which survived a change in the corporate identity of the employer. However, in a way which we have previously identified as typical of the dis-integrated approach of English law to the contractual construction of employment relations, these notions of continuity do not seem to have extended to the underlying contract of employment itself.

In a number of continental European labour law systems, there were evolutions towards more extensive transfers of employment rights upon the transfer of an undertaking from one human or corporate owner to another. Such initiatives were viewed, much more readily than in the English case, as implying the transfer of the contract of employment itself; and when those initiatives involved legislation, there seems to have been little of the resistance, which we have noted as typical of the dis-integrated approach of English law, to regarding such legislation as impacting upon the legal construction of the contract of employment itself. This was famously true of the relevant article in the French *Code du Travail* first introduced with the Law of 19 July 1928, and much the same reversal of the traditional contractual stance seems to have occurred in Germany with its amendment to the *BGB* in 1972.[65] French authors use revealing expressions such as '*transmission automatique*' (automatic transfer), noting that 'the transfer of the contracts to the new user is mandated by the law and is a matter of *ordre public*'.[66]

The dis-integrated approach and traditional contractual stance of English labour law does seem to have placed it in a rather singular position, by comparison with many other European jurisdictions, with regard to the effects of transfers of undertakings upon contracts of employment, so that when the Acquired Rights Directive[67] of 1977 was enacted, to apply throughout the EC what was in essence the French doctrine of transfer of employment rights and indeed the contract of employment itself upon the transfer of the undertaking in which the employee is employed, it had an especially radical and indeed disruptive effect upon English law. We consider extensively in the final chapter of this work the differential bearing of EU law measures upon different national legal constructions of employment relations, but it will be useful at this point to consider for a

---

[65] Section 613a *BGB*.

[66] Our translation of: '*la transmission des contrats au nouvel exploitant s'opère de plein droit [et] est d'ordre public*'; J. Mouly (2008) *Droit du Travail*, Paris: Bréal, 145.

[67] Directive 77/187 EEC on the approximation of the laws of the Member States relating to the safeguard of employees' rights in the event of transfer of undertakings, businesses or parts of businesses, [1977] OJ L 61/26; amended by Council Directive 98/50 of 29 June 1998, [1998] OJ L 201/98, the two now consolidated into Council Directive 2001/23/EC of 12 March 2001, [2001] OJ L 82/16.

moment the particular problems of implementation of the Directive which were presented to English law largely by reason of the dis-integrated approach of the latter to the contractual construction of the kind of transfers of employment with which the Directive was concerned.

Thus it is well known to those familiar with the TUPE Regulations[68] by which the Directive was implemented in English law, that this implementation involved three quite distinct sets of new provisions for English law; there was firstly a set of provisions for the transfer of relevant contracts of employment upon an event qualifying as a 'transfer of an undertaking or a part thereof', secondly a set of provisions providing for the treatment of such transfers under the law of unfair dismissal, and thirdly a set of provisions providing for consultation with the representatives of employees about a proposed transfer of undertaking. It is perhaps less generally understood that this represents a degree of separateness of the law of the contract of employment from the other aspects of the transfer regime which is hardly encountered in other European labour law systems.

Here it is important to emphasize that, while the introduction in 1977 of the Acquired Rights Directive[69] has undoubtedly contributed to the convergence and harmonization of the various national rules on transfer of undertakings, the relative degree of integration between contract and statute have displayed a number of relevant national distinctions. In light of the European Court's jurisprudence, it is no doubt accurate to state that the Directive's provisions have displayed the 'principle of the automatic transfer to the transferee of . . . the contracts of employment' and that such transfer, other than being automatic, is indeed also 'mandatory'.[70] But it is probably important to note that the Court has accepted that employees maintain 'the option of refusing' to have their contracts of employment transferred to the transferee, and that 'in such a case, the position of the employee depends on the legislation of the individual Member State: the contract binding the employee to the transferring undertaking may be terminated either by the employee or by the employer or the contract may be maintained with that undertaking'.[71]

Here we can see a number of national variations. English law accepts that an employee has the right to object to the automatic transfer of his contract of employment if he or she so wishes, if he or she informs either the transferor or the transferee. However, 'In that case the objection terminates the contract of employment and the employee is not treated for any purpose as having been dismissed by either the transferor or the new employer. Moreover the employee is considered to have resigned and . . . [t]he transferor may re-engage the transferee on whatever terms they agree, though the continuity of employment will be broken.'[72] Italian labour law and Article 2112 of the Italian Civil Code, by contrast, appears to be more reluctant to take the view that the workers' objection to a transfer of undertakings can effectively

---

[68] The Transfer of Undertakings (Protection of Employment) Regulations 2006 (TUPE), SI 2006/246.
[69] See above n. 67.
[70] Case C- 51/00, *Temco Service Industries v. Samir Imzilyen and Others* [2002] ECR I-00969, [35].
[71] Ibid., [36].
[72] BIS (2009) *Employment Rights on the Transfer of an Undertaking*, 11–12.

be of any relevance in halting the transfer of the contracts of employment from the transferor to the transferee, possibly failing to respect the EUCJ's jurisprudence.[73]

French labour law, while opposing the idea that a worker may object to a transfer of his contract,[74] will more readily accept that, in spite of the '*ordre public*' nature of the transfer, the three parties involved can agree for the workers, or for some of them, to continue working for the transferring undertaking, and even contemplates the possibility that such continuation in the relationship be exclusively agreed between the employee and the transferor.[75] However, undoubtedly the most worker-protective approach is adopted by the mainstream German jurisprudence on transfers, partly reflecting a historical sensitivity to any forms of coercion vis-à-vis 'human resources'.[76] 'According to the Federal Labour Court's established case law the employee whose employment relationship is supposed to be transferred automatically to the new owner or leaseholder had the right to contradict the transfer and opt *to remain employed by the old employer.*'[77] Obviously, under German law, strong fundamental norms contained in the *Grundgesetz* (Federal Constitution) and guaranteeing that 'All Germans shall have the right freely to choose their occupation or profession, their place of work and their place of training',[78] are structurally integrated by courts in both statutes and contracts.

This argument about the dis-integrated approach of English law to the contractual construction of employment relations also serves to illuminate some of the particular conceptual and practical difficulties which have been encountered in giving effect to the Directive so far as its impact on contracts of employment is concerned. For example, when in the leading case of *Litster v. Forth Dry Dock Ltd*[79] the House of Lords sought to control dismissals effected by the transferring employer shortly before the transfer of the undertaking in question with a view to pre-empting the occurrence of a TUPE transfer of contractual and statutory liabilities to the transferee of the undertaking, it was hard to construct those controls in contractual terms, and it is open to question whether a satisfactory conceptual basis existed or was found for doing so.

Indeed, the dis-integrated approach of English law can be seen as exerting its effects on the employees subject to a transfer in a number of different ways. Firstly, and by contrast to a number of other European systems, English law will accept that a pre-emptive dismissal is only 'prohibited' and 'ineffective', as opined by Lord

---

[73] V. Speziale (2006) 'Il trasferimento d'azienda tra disciplina nazionale ed interpretazioni "vincolanti" della Corte di Giustizia Europea' *WP C.S.D.L.E. 'Massimo D'Antona' IT - 46/2006.*

[74] A. Supiot (2006) 'Les salariés ne sont pas à vendre. En finir avec l'envers de l'article L.122-12, alinéa 2', *Droit Social*, 264.

[75] Soc. 9 janvier 1985. Cf. J. Pélissier, A. Supiot, A. Jeammaud (2008) *Droit du Travail*, 24th ed., Paris: Dalloz, p. 495.

[76] A. Supiot (2006) 'Les salariés ne sont pas à vendre. En finir avec l'envers de l'article L.122-12, alinéa 2', *Droit Social*, 267.

[77] M. Weiss and M. Schmidt (2008) *Labour Law and Industrial Relations in Germany*, AH Alphen aan den Rijn: Kluwer, 143. Emphasis added. Cf. also Y. Viala (2005) 'Le maintien des contrats de travail en cas de transfert d'entreprise en droit allemand', *Droit Social*, 200.

[78] Artikel 12(1) reading: '*Alle Deutschen haben das Recht, Beruf, Arbeitsplatz und Ausbildungsstätte frei zu wählen*'.

[79] *Litster v. Forth Dry Dock and Engineering Co* [1989] IRLR 161.

Oliver in *Litster*,[80] in the comparatively narrow sense of being wrongful[81] and, now under TUPE 2006, reg. 7(1),[82] providing employees affected by the termination with the protections derived from unfair dismissal legislation. This is in stark contrast with other continental systems that have implemented – in our view correctly – the Acquired Rights Directive, and the Court of Justice's jurisprudence that 'the employees . . . whose contract of employment or employment relationship was terminated with effect from a date prior to that of the transfer . . . must be regarded as *still in the employ of the undertaking* on the date of the transfer, with the result, in particular, that the employer's obligations towards them are *automatically transferred from the transferor to the transferee*',[83] by subjecting such unlawful pre-transfer dismissals to the doctrine of nullity, in its 'relative' sense.[84]

A second visible manifestation of the dis-integrated approach is to be found in TUPE 2006, reg. 4(4), which renders 'void' any contractual variation by reason of the transfer which is not an 'economic, technical, or organizational reason'. This new provision, allegedly introduced to 'reflect the Government's view of the correct interpretation of the [Acquired Rights] Directive in this regard',[85] was in all likelihood required to comply with the Court's interpretation that 'the transfer of the undertaking itself may never constitute the reason for [an] amendment'.[86] What is interesting, for the purposes of our argument in this section, is that the limited introduction of a 'nullity' doctrine in this area of English law has had no systematic bearing on its overall architecture of employees' rights in the case of a transfer of undertaking. Moreover, by virtue of decisions such as *Berriman v. Delabole Slate Ltd*,[87] it appears that when a transfer of contracts of employment does take place, the existing terms and conditions of such contracts are for a period of time more strongly protected against variation by the transferee employer than they were in the hands of the transferor employer, or indeed than they ever are under the English law of employment contracts as it normally functions.

However, it is important not to commit the grave comparative error of exaggerating or over-systematizing contrasts between different legal systems. Many European labour law systems have struggled at length with difficulties in implementing the Acquired Rights Directive as originally enacted and as subsequently amended

---

[80]    Ibid., 172.

[81]    Cf. M. Freedland (2003) *The Personal Employment Contract*, Oxford: OUP, 510–11.

[82]    TUPE 2006, SI 2006/246.

[83]    Case 101/87, *P. Bork International A/S, in liquidation v. Foreningen af Arbejdsledere I Danmark*, [1988] ECR 03057, para. [18].

[84]    For this notion of 'relative' nullity cf. Soc. 20 mars 2002, arrêt Maldonado, and J. Mouly (2008) *Droit du Travail*, Paris: Bréal, 147, noting that: '*La jurisprudence la plus récente a donc ouvert un choix au salarié entre la poursuite du contrat et l'octroi de dommages-intérêts par le cédent*'. (The most recent case law has thus given the employee a choice between maintaining the contract and seeking damages from the transferor'.)

[85]    DTI, TUPE Draft Revised Regulations Public Consultation Document, (March 2005), para. 45.

[86]    Case 324/86, *Foreningen af Arbejdsledere i Danmark v. Daddy's Dance Hall A/S* [1988] ECR 00739, [17].

[87]    [1985] ICR 546.

over time;[88] difficulties in doing so have been by no means confined to English law, and have indeed extended to the French labour law system despite the fact that it was that system which provided the model for the Directive itself. That reminds us that there are difficulties and complexities in the handling of transformations of employment relations which are to a greater or lesser extent common to European labour law systems generally, regardless of whether the system in question takes an integrated or a dis-integrated approach to the contractual construction of employment relations. Now we turn our attention to some transformations presenting issues which are in that sense general ones across European labour law systems at large.

## B.  Other Transformations

We have now, in the course of this chapter and the previous one, touched upon, in varying degrees of detail, what would normally be regarded as a complete catalogue of the principal evolutions which the employment relation, constructed as a contract of employment, may undergo – we have considered its variation, its suspension, its termination, and the transformations which may occur in the identity of the employer or in the ownership or control of the employing enterprise or organization. Our principal concern has been to consider the differences in the contractual construction of those evolutions, as between different European national labour law systems, which can be ascribed to the combination of different levels of worker-protective regulation of those evolutions with different approaches to the integration of such regulation into the construction of the contract of employment itself.

In this subsection we briefly conclude this section and this chapter and our sequence of chapters on the contract of employment by considering a further set of evolutions in the employment relation constructed as a contract of employment, which would not normally be recognized as such, but which we think deserve to be regarded as a significant genre of other transformations in their own right. Our principal concern in so doing will be, on this occasion, not so much with the contrasts between different European national labour law systems by reason of different levels of regulation and integration of that regulation into the contract of employment, but rather with the difficulties which are faced by those systems, more or less in common with each other, in building this particular genre of transformations into their constructions of the employment relation as contractual ones – and ultimately into their definition and construction of the employment relation itself.

We proceed to identify the 'significant genre of other transformations' which we have in mind. In the course of our discussion of those transformations in the employment relation as contractually constructed which can be classified as

---

[88]  Cf. A. Supiot (2006) 'Les salariés ne sont pas à vendre. En finir avec l'envers de l'article L.122-12, alinéa 2', *Droit Social*, 264; also C. Marzo and F. Lecomte (2010) 'Le Refus d'être Transféré: Droit Comparé', *Droit Social*, 698.

'suspension', we evoked the idea that it was useful to think of the employment relation, as contractually constructed, as evolving between different modes or states of existence. We depicted the idea of suspension as representing an evolution from the full employment mode into what may be designated as a sub-employment mode – though we made the point that it was rather difficult to be clear as to how that sub-employment mode of existence of the employment relation fitted into the contractual conceptualizations of the employment relation which different national labour law systems have created for themselves. We now suggest that, somewhat similarly, there are a number of other evolutions which the employment relation may undergo which it would be useful to think of as transformations into a 'post-employment' mode of existence of the employment relation – but we take the view that it is even more difficult to be sure how that post-employment mode of existence of the employment relation fits into the various different national contractual conceptualizations of the employment relation, and indeed that these evolutions eventually present difficulties for the definition of the employment relation itself.

It will be evident that the notion which we are invoking, of transformations of the employment relation into post-employment modes of existence, is a difficult and slippery one, and that this difficulty and slipperiness is redoubled when it is a question of how they fit into legal constructions of the contract of employment. Indeed, it might be thought that this notion is not merely difficult and slippery but actually counter-intuitive or self-contradictory, since it appears to suggest that the employment relation and perhaps also the contract of employment may be deemed to be in existence although the 'employment' in question has ended.

However, we take the view that our notion of transformation of the employment relation into post-employment modes of existence, however elusive it may become under close scrutiny, may nevertheless represent at least the beginning of a solution to a real analytical problem. This problem consists in the fact that the employment relation may evolve into or give rise to situations in which, although it would normally be said that the contract of employment had come to an end and although it might be said that the employment relation, whether constructed as a contract of employment or in any other way, had come to an end, we would still recognize that there are work-related legal relations between the former employee and the former employer.[89] That is a problem which is apt to be ignored or evaded in conventional contractual constructions of the employment relation.

It will be helpful to provide some illustrations of these situations where there may be said to be work-related legal relations between the former employee and the former employer. It should be noted that the list is not intended to be exhaustive, and that these work-related legal relations may exist in various combinations with each other in the overall situation of a given former employee. Examples of such situations are as follows:

---

[89] Cf. M. Freedland (2003) *The Personal Employment Contract*, Oxford: OUP, at pp. 106–108, and 405–407 where the idea of the post-employment phase of the contract of employment is set forth and explained.

1. after the ending of employment in the ordinary sense, the ex-employee is under obligations not to compete, or to respect the confidentiality of information or know-how;
2. after the ending of employment in the ordinary sense, the former employee and formal employer remain in legal relations with reference to the occupational pension arrangements which applied to the employment in question;
3. after the ending of employment in the ordinary sense, the former employee and formal employer remain in legal relations because there is some understanding about future resumption of employment; or
4. after the ending of employment in the ordinary sense, the former employee and former employer remain in legal relations because they have entered into some different kind of personal work relation such as that of 'self-employment'.

It is then useful to consider how each of those situations on the one hand represents a transformation of the employment relation into post-employment mode but is on the other hand difficult to fit into the conventional contractual construction of the employment relation.

The first situation, that where the ex-employee is under obligations not to compete with the former employer and/or obligations of confidence or confidentiality, is the one which it is easiest to recognize as representing a kind of after-life of the contractual employment relation. There are nevertheless aspects of these post-employment legal relations which it is difficult to fit into the contractual construction of the employment relation. Firstly, there are various conceptual and practical difficulties with the analysis and treatment of obligations which arise under the contract of employment but which arise or apply after the employment in question has ended and therefore after the contract of employment itself is regarded as having been terminated. Secondly, the legal relations in question may, to varying degrees in different legal systems, be regarded as only partly contractual in character; for example, English law regards post-employment obligations of confidence and confidentiality as being partly of restitutionary rather than contractual character. Thirdly, the legal relations in question are essentially multilateral rather than bilateral in character – in so far as subsequent employers of the ex-employee come into the picture – and as such the more difficult to treat simply or primarily as contractual ones. French law seems to be more willing to conceptualize these legal relations as, at least partly, contractual in character to the extent that the mandatory '*contrepartie pécuniaire*', the pecuniary compensation, imposed on employers is perceived as deferred salary.[90] But it is revealing that, while undoubtedly linked to some aspects of the performance of obligations arising from contracts of employment, the mutual obligations arising from French restrictive covenants have been essentially shaped and heavily 'integrated' by the jurisprudential intervention of the

---

[90] Soc. 7 févr. 2006. Cf. J. Pélissier, A. Supiot, A. Jeammaud (2008) *Droit du Travail*, 24th ed., Paris: Dalloz, p. 371.

Court de Cassation that leaves very little leeway to the parties affected and is non-derogable in character and is much inspired by public policy considerations.[91]

The second situation, where the former employee and former employer remain in legal relations with reference to occupational pension arrangements, presents similar difficulties, and may also present its own complications, with regard to its construction as a transformation of the contract of employment into post-employment mode. Like all four of our illustrative situations, it arises after the contract of employment has been in a conventional sense terminated. As in the first situation, the legal relations which it involves may be only partly contractual in character – or indeed may not be contractual in character at all – and may be multi-lateral ones involving a pension provider other than the former employer. More-over, there is a tendency to regard 'pensioners' as being retired from the labour market and so in a situation which has nothing to do with their former contractual employment relation. Yet in truth their situation does amount to a transformation of their contractual employment relation into post-employment mode in various senses: firstly in the general sense that the pension can be seen as representing deferred remuneration from employment or a protection of income security which is derived from employment, and secondly in the particular sense that the pension arrangements are likely to involve continuing obligations which can be regarded as work-related as between the former employee and former employer.

The third situation, where employment has ended in the ordinary sense but there is some understanding between former employer and former employee about future resumption of employment, seems much easier than the previous two to regard as a transformation of the employment relation into post-employment mode rather than a simple termination of it. Indeed, it can be difficult, both analytically and in a practical sense, to distinguish between this situation and the situation where employment is merely suspended – which we have previously identified as a transformed continuation of the employment relation in sub-employment mode. However, it is conspicuously difficult to fit this situation into the contractual construction of the employment relation especially in labour law systems, such as that of English law, where the continuing existence of a contract of employment is uncompromisingly premised upon there being some degree of specifically contractual obligation of resumption of work both on employer and employee. But it is doubtful whether continental European systems would in analogous cases be able to see the contractual employment relationship extending beyond the duration of the actual work or employment. Therefore it is far more likely that any promise about future employment or re-employment will be treated as a prima facie self-standing 'preliminary contract'.[92]

The fourth situation, where after the ending of employment in the ordinary sense, the former employee and former employer have entered into some different

---

[91] Cf. L. Dardalhon (2005) 'La liberté du travail devant le Conseil constitutionnel et la Cour de Cassation' 64, *Revue française de droit constitutionnel* (Paris), 755–80; also, R. Vatinet (2002) 'Les conditions de validité des clauses de non-concurrence: l'imbroglio', *Droit Social*, 949.

[92] Cf. Cass. 4 giugno 2003 n. 8889.

kind of personal work relation such as that of 'self-employment', is in some senses easier, but in one other sense more difficult, than the other three situations to regard as a kind of continuation of the employment relation or the contract of employment in post-employment mode. It is easier in the sense that the former employer and former employee have continued to be in a bilateral contractual personal work relation; but it is more difficult in that this relation is not one of employment as such. Yet such a relation might genuinely deserve recognition as a transformation of the pre-existing contractual employment relation; the relation of an ex-employee now in a position of self-employed consultancy to the former employer may refer back to and be in some sense continuous with the former contractual employment relation in a way which distinguishes it sharply from a relation of self-employment which is formed entirely *de novo*.

By considering these situations which in our submission demonstrate, on the one hand, the functional need for a capacity to recognize transformations of the employment relation into post-employment mode, but on the other hand the difficulties of achieving that recognition within the compass of the contractual conceptualization of the employment relation, we have indeed arrived at our conclusion to this set of chapters about the contract of employment. The chapter, and the sequence of chapters as a whole, have amounted to an exploration of the problems and limits of the legal construction of personal work relations through lenses which are almost exclusively focused upon the contract of employment as the central organizing and definitional category for labour law.

That exploration has indicated how variations between national labour law systems, both as to how highly contractual employment are regulated by worker-protective labour standards and as to the degree of integration of that regulation into the legal conceptualization of the contract of employment itself, may create inherent difficulty in arriving at a common understanding as between legal systems of what we mean by 'the contract of employment'. In systems where a highly dis-integrated approach is taken, the contractual construct of the employment relation may give an incomplete and false picture of the totality of the ways in which the contractual employment relation is regulated. On the other hand, in systems where a highly integrated approach is taken, a truer picture may be obtained, from the contractual construct of the employment relation, of the totality of the regulation of that relation. This may, however, be at the price of making its characterization as a contract appear at best misleading and at worst deceptive in presenting what is in truth a status imposed by *ius cogens* as a contract offered up as *ius dispositivum*.

The final chapters of this work are devoted to considering the possibilities for breaking out of this contractual frame. However, there is one more crucial step to be taken while still within the contractual frame of analysis. While contesting the feasibility of a satisfactory binary division of the domain of personal work contracts into contracts of employment on the one hand and other personal work contracts on the other hand, and while also contesting the suitability of a nearly exclusive concentration of the analysis of labour law on the contract of employment rather than upon other personal work contracts, we have nevertheless felt it to be justified to subscribe to both of those positions for working purposes in order to understand in its own terms the conventional analysis of the legal construction of personal work relations. A necessary next step towards our ultimate analytical goal therefore consists in considering the part of the domain of personal work contracts which we have hitherto neglected, that of personal work contracts other than the contract of employment. That is the task of the next chapter.

# PART III

# THE PERSONAL WORK RELATION AS A LEGAL NEXUS

# 7

# Personal Work Contracts Other Than the Contract of Employment

## Introduction

This chapter explores the category of personal work contracts which lie beyond the contract of employment – or, to be more precise, which lie at the margins of and beyond the contract of employment. We begin by arguing that this category is, to a singular extent which is revealed by European comparative analysis, an evolving and mutating one (Section 1). Having identified the category as an essentially elusive one, we proceed to consider in the three succeeding sections whether the contracts which fall within it can be regarded as being regulated in ways which are analogous to the modes of regulation of contracts of employment which were considered in the preceding chapters. So we successively consider the regulation of the formation and structure of these contracts (Section 2), their content and performance (Section 3), and their termination and transformation (Section 4).

## Section 1: The Legal Categorization of Personal Work Contracts Other Than the Contract of Employment

In this section, we make a series of assertions or claims which are crucial steps in the development of our analysis of the legal construction of personal work relations. Firstly, we suggest that the logic of our own analysis leads to the recognition of a category of contracts consisting of personal work contracts other than the contract of employment (subsection A). Secondly, we consider three possible approaches to the analysis of that category, moving from an implicit traditional approach to our own preferred approach (subsections B to D).

### A. The Category Identified

In the first Part of this work, we delineated the category of 'personal work relations' as the relational domain of labour law; in this second Part we are engaged in the analysis of the legal construction of the great majority of personal work relations as contractual ones. So this Part of the work seeks to provide a general analysis of the category of 'personal work contracts'. In the preceding three chapters we have been concerned with the predominant subset of personal work contracts, namely the contract of employment. Since our concept of the 'personal work contract' is a wider one than that of the 'contract of employment', it follows that we also recognize another subset of the personal work contract consisting of personal work contracts which are not contracts of employment. Hence we can speak of 'personal work contracts other than the contract of employment', or, more succinctly, of 'other personal work contracts'.

Thus far, the category of other personal work contracts is simply one which we have chosen to invent as a logical element in our own overall analysis of personal work relations and personal work contracts. So we need to substantiate that element of our analysis more fully, filling in what is at the moment no more than an empty space in our notional diagram of the legal construction of personal work relations. Several possible approaches present themselves. The legal analysis of the conceptual space which we have delineated as the 'other personal work contract' category is not at all well developed – obviously this category is not analysed under that name or heading, because that is a name or heading invented by us, but nor is there a well-developed analysis of it under any other name or heading. However, we can discern an existing, though largely implicit, analysis whereby all other personal work contracts are regarded as contracts for services.

So that constitutes the first possible approach to the analysis of the 'other personal work contract' category. We regard that as the traditional (if largely implicit) approach; but we doubt very much whether that provides an adequate or robust analysis in the context of contemporary labour legislation and contemporary labour market practice – that critique is presented in the next subsection, B. We then go on to consider a different possible approach to the analysis of the 'other personal work contract' category which consists of breaking it down into two sub-divisions, one representing contracts for semi-dependent personal work relations and the other representing contracts for fully independent personal work relations. This is to some extent supported by contemporary labour legislation but seems to us to present its own set of difficulties. That approach and its difficulties are considered in the following subsection, C.

Finally, in subsection D, we put forward a third possible approach which is our own preferred one. Having considered and been sceptical about an essentially unitary analysis of the other personal work contract category (in subsection B), and an essentially binary analysis in subsection C, we go on to argue for an analysis in which the other personal work contract category is seen as consisting in a mutating and evolving grouping or family of contracts. That category, viewed in that way, is also represented by us as being in a loose and evolving relationship with the contract of employment category itself.

## B. The Traditional View of Other Personal Work Contracts as Contracts for Services

In this subsection we seek first to articulate and then to challenge a certain implicit analysis of the category of personal work contracts other than the contract of employment or, as stated above, of 'other personal work contracts'. This implicit analysis is the product of the binary view of personal work contracts which, we have suggested, is in some shape and form common to European employment law systems and indeed to European legal systems more generally. European legal systems, so far as they engage in systematic or comprehensive analysis of the legal construction of personal work relations, generally seem to envisage those relations, so far as they are contractual ones, as falling into two legal categories, namely the contract of employment on the one hand and the contract for services on the other. This is the binary divide to which we have referred; it seems to exist as a bright line in the legal systems of European countries, although we might question whether and how far an apparent set of linguistic equivalents between legal systems is in fact reliable.

That binary view of the domain of personal work contracts gives rise to an analysis of other personal work contracts which is an implicit one, or at least is largely implicit rather than explicit, in the following sense. As we have remarked or argued in earlier chapters, European legal systems have generally speaking each evolved a strongly articulated conception of the contract of employment as a core institution of labour or employment law. National conceptions of the contract of employment, although quite diverse in some respects, seem to have it in common that they are to some degree unified. In particular, they tend to be unified by or around a generic contrast with a different type of personal work contract, which is thought to be essentially characterized by the independence of the working person from the work recipient or work purchaser whereas the contract of employment is essentially characterized by the subordination of the worker to the employer.

The most vivid example appears to be provided by the '*Libro V*' (Book 5) of the Italian Civil Code, dealing with matters '*Del Lavoro*' in general, and providing the paradigmatic contrast between '*lavoro subordinate*' (subordinate work) in Article 2094) and '*lavoro autonomo*' (autonomous work) exemplified by the '*contratto d'opera*' (contract for services) referred to in Article 2222).[1] As noted by Supiot, the decision made by the drafters of the Italian Civil Code to establish a separation, a divide, between 'subordinate employment' and 'contracts for services' was rendered all the more tangible 'detaching the employment relationship from

---

[1] In the Italian Civil Code one finds a relatively articulated subdivision of various species of the '*contratto d'opera*' genus, in particular in Article 1655 ('*appalto*'), Article 1678 ('*trasporto*'), Article 1776 ('*deposito generico*'), and Article 1703 ('*mandato*') with the latter being further articulated into three subspecies, that is to say '*commissione*' (Article 1731 of the Code), '*spedizione*' (Article 1737), and '*agenzia*' (Article 1742).

the law of obligations (treated in the book 'Of Obligations'), by dedicating to it a distinct book (entitled 'On Employment').[2] This particular divide was rendered even more palpable in French law where it was actually decided to create an altogether separate locus for the regulation of contracts of employment, as opposed to contracts for services, in the form of a *Code du Travail*. Thus in France we find that the binary divide is expressed in a formal as well as conceptual and regulatory, distinction between the *'contrat de travail'* which, while not being explicitly defined in the *Code du Travail* is thoroughly regulated in its scope, formation, performance, and termination in the *Livre II* of the First Part of that Code, and 'certain *contrats de louage*, more particularly with the *contrat de louage d'ouvrage*'[3] which have traditionally been regarded as falling unde Article 1787 of the *Code Civil*.

In Germany, the binary divide, while present, is scattered across a variety of sources. The *BGB* appears to display some of the features of the binary divide, by reason of the contrast between the concept of *'Dienstvertrag'* (service contract), contained in s. 61 and that of *'Werkvertrag'* (work contract), contained in s. 631. But the *BGB* provides, at best, only a partial textual source for the emergence of the binary divide. Indeed as noted by Deakin (2005)[4] originally '...there [was] no clear reference in the *BGB* to the binary divide between employees and the self-employed: "at the time the *BGB* was drafted...the distinction between employment and services had not been established, so the term *Dienstvertrag*...covered both types of agreement. This means that in the context of Art. 611 [*BGB*], *Dienstvertrag* refers both to the contract for service...and the contract of employment." The modern notion of the employment relationship or *Arbeitsverhältnis* came later, as in France, with the adoption of protective legislation and the legal accommodation of collective bargaining'.

However, the notion of *Diensvertrag* has been used to implement the Acquired Rights Directive in German law,[5] and although German case law and commentaries will typically recur to the 'self-employed' definition contained in s. 84 (1) of the *Handelsgesetzbuch*,[6] the concept of 'contract to produce a work' contained in s. 631 *BGB* will include contracts concluded between businesses and 'independent contractors', very much like the French concept of *'contrat de louage d'ouvrage'* often also referred to as *'contrat d'entreprise'*, which Camerlynck noted 'constitutes, with the contract of employment, one of the two fundamental and contrasted juridical

---

[2] A. Supiot (1994) *Critique du Droit du Travail*, Paris: PUF, 19.
[3] A. Brun and H. Galland (1958) *Droit du Travail*, Pairs: Sirey, 244. Our translation.
[4] S. Deakin (2005) *The Comparative Evolution of the Employment Relationship*, Working Paper No. 317, ESRC Centre for Business Research, University of Cambridge, p. 10 (quoting V. Sims).
[5] See BGB Title 8, Heading and Official Note.
[6] Cf. M. Weiss and M. Schmidt (2008) *Labour Law and Industrial Relations in Germany*, AH Alphen aan den Rijn: Kluwer, 45; W. Däubler (1999) 'Working People in Germany' 21 *CLLPJ*, 80; R. Wank (1999) 'Workers Protection – National Study for Germany for the ILO', ILO, 2.

mechanisms in the capitalist economy'.[7] Interestingly, and revealingly, the ECJ referred, rather crudely, but not wholly inappropriately, to 'paragraph 611 et seq. and paragraph 631 et seq. of the BGB relating to contracts of employment and contracts for services',[8] undoubtedly taking the point that a number of 'contracts to produce a work' will be performed by self-employed independent contractors.

That is in essence the idea or nature of the binary divide which runs through the foundational analysis of personal work contracts in European legal systems. In previous chapters we have argued that this binary divide analysis tends to impute a false duality to the domain of personal work contracts as a whole, and a false unity to each of the two contract types which is identified by its separation from the other. And in the chapters which precede this one, we have considered in detail how far and in what sense it is useful to deconstruct the unitary category of the contract of employment. It was possible and meaningful to engage in that kind of analysis because in most if not all European legal systems the contract of employment is a highly regulated legal category. Indeed, the regulation of that category of contracts has tended to be envisaged as one of the core functions, perhaps even in a sense the core function, of labour or employment law. There is an abundant body of explicit analysis of the contract of employment in European employment law which can be scrutinized to see how far and in what sense it is right to regard it as a unitary category. Supiot acutely observes that European systems have proceeded on these 'unifying' trajectories in more than one way.[9] He notes that in those legal systems where the tendency to the unification of the contract of employment is stronger, such as for instance in France, Portugal, in Spain or in Germany, 'we can see some varieties of employees to whom one tries to apply the common labour law in a measure compatible with the specificity of their tasks'.[10] Elsewhere, in countries dominated by a more casuistic type of approach, such as Denmark or the UK, 'the tendency is rather to subject them to special regimes'.[11]

The situation is very different when we turn to the analysis of other personal work contracts. As we have indicated, the legal construction and regulation of the contract of employment in European legal systems has to an important extent taken place by way of asserted contrast with a supposedly different or even opposite category of contracts, the contract for services. Although it has to some extent dissolved in recent times, there was for much of the twentieth century a kind of orthodoxy of labour or employment law which identified the contract of employment as the appropriate definitional concept with which to designate the proper sphere of labour or employment law. Part of that orthodoxy consisted in the corresponding belief that contracts for services were outside the proper sphere of

---

[7] G. H. Camerlynck (1968) *Traité de Droit du Travail – Contrat de Travail*, Paris: Dalloz, at 73. Our translation from the original French.

[8] Case C-209/90, *Commission v. Walter Feilhauer* [1992] ECR I-02613, para. 36.

[9] A. Supiot (1994) *Critique du Droit du Travail*, Paris: PUF, 35.

[10] Ibid. Our translation of the original: '*on y voit des variétés de salariés auxquelles on s'efforce d'appliquer le droit commun du travail dans la mesure compatible avec la spécificité de leur tâche*'.

[11] Ibid. Our translation of the original: '*la tendence est plutôt de les soummetre à des statuts spèciaux*'.

labour law, even if they were personal work contracts for performance by the worker in person. From this perspective the personal contract for services was a category conceptualized in a negative or exclusionary way; it was in its very conception the contract type for personal work contracts beyond the sphere of regulation of labour or employment law.

From that exclusionary perspective of labour law, it seems to have been assumed that, by a kind of symmetry of opposites, the personal contract for services constituted a single contract type for all other personal work contracts, which in its own way has the same unitary character as the contract of employment. *Ex hypothesi* this contract type was not constructed or regulated within the sphere of labour or employment law; it was tacitly assumed that this contract type was constructed and regulated within the different sphere of general private contract law. When personal work contracts are classified or treated as not being contracts of employment, it has apparently been thought to follow that this locates them within a more or less unitary private law regime which applies to contracts for services in general, and to personal contracts for services in particular. While nobody seems to have stated this explicitly, everybody seems to have assumed it implicitly.

Comparative analysis suggests that this assumption, that there is a unitary category of personal contract for services matching the unitary category of contracts of employment, is especially strong in English law, though it can also be discerned in other European legal systems. In English law, the assumption is confirmed by occasional discussions as to whether triangular personal work relationships might give rise to a 'tertium quid' or third type of contract; the suggestion of a third type affirms the view of the contract of employment and the personal contracts for services as the two established types. In other European legal systems, the assumption is visible in typologies which replicate or descend from the classical duo of the *locatio conductio operarurm* and the *locatio conductio operis*. We noted above how the various articulated typologies and subtypologies of personal contracts for services contained in the Italian Civil Code are still conceptualized as ultimately being part of the '*contratto d'opera*' genus.[12] In France the separation between those contracts regulated by the *Code Civil* and *Code du Travail* brought about a conceptualization of the two 'false unities' even more strongly than elsewhere. In many ways, whatever was going on in the *Code Civil* was beyond the ambit of interest of labour lawyers and labour law, who could focus their attention exclusively on the *Code du Travail*. We suggest, however, that this assumption was never a fully warranted or robust one, and moreover that even to the extent that it was ever sustainable, it has ceased to be so. We will argue for those two claims successively.

The assumption that there is a unitary category of personal contracts for services matching the unitary category of contracts of employment has, we suggest, been an unwarranted one in the following sense. The assertion of the existence of a unitary category of personal contracts for services would be meaningful only if we could identify a body of regulation or exegesis, or legal or labour market practice, which

---

[12] Cf. also E. Ghera (2007) *Diritto del Lavoro*, Bari: Cacucci, 43–4.

gave substance to the category. That is to say, we could regard the personal contract for services as a substantial and meaningful category of contract if there were a legal discourse which in a recognizable and distinctive way prescribed the conditions of validity and the functioning and interpretation of contracts of this type. We put this forward as a general test for the recognition of a contract type. We acknowledge that its application will be difficult and debateable in any given case; the taxonomy of species of contracts could be regarded as being just as subtle and shifting as the taxonomy of plants and animals. Moreover its application will have different outcomes in different legal systems, varying both with the nature of economic activity and with the manner, and density of legal regulation of contracts in and by each legal system. Nevertheless we think it is sustainable and workable as a principle of recognition of distinctive and meaningful contract types.

Applying this test, we find that none of these existential conditions for the unitary category of personal contract for services seems to be satisfied. There seems to be no textbook or treatise or practitioners' handbook for this category. At a more profound level, neither does there seem to be any real notion of distinctive regulation or even distinctive interpretation of such a category of contracts. The contracts which might between them compose this category in fact seem to exist in a kind of uncertain no-man's land between the domains of labour contracts on the one hand and commercial contracts for services on the other. Camerlynk's juxtaposition of the *contrat de travail* to other '*conventions voisines*' – (similar agreements) – 'also having as their object the accomplishment of a remunerated performance'[13] is paradigmatic in that sense. As described by Brun and Galland in 1958, these '*coventions voisines*' were actually neither very similar to the contract of employment, nor particularly convergent upon a single regulatory framework. They comprised at least sixteen different typologies of personal work relations, ranging from those applicable to professional sportspersons to the regulation of commercial agents and '*dirigeants de sociétés anonymes*' (corporate executives), to professionals such as doctors and pharmacists.[14] And neither did it escape the attention of the two authors that the application, to some of these personal contracts for services, of some of the protections typically bestowed upon employees – for instance in the case of some '*mandataires*' (company directors) – was 'highlighting on the one hand the *particularisme* of Labour Law, and on the other its fragmentation',[15] thus demonstrating – we would say – both the false unity of the contract of employment and the false unity of the 'personal contract for services' category, and ultimately questioning the binary divide itself.

This is true in different senses as between different European legal systems. To identify those different senses, we can usefully invoke the notion of a broad contrast of ideal-types as between the English common-law-based and European civilian legal systems. As we have seen in earlier chapters, that contrast of ideal-types can be

---

[13] G. H. Camerlynck (1968) *Traité de Droit du Travail — Contrat de Travail*, Paris: Dalloz, at 71. Our translation.
[14] A. Brun and H. Galland (1958) *Droit du Travail*, Paris: Sirey, pp. 243–304.
[15] Ibid. 291. Our translation.

understood as giving rise to a spectrum of approaches ranging from, at one extreme, an English common-law-based approach which minimizes the prescription of contract types and leaves wide scope for innovation of contract forms by private and individual actors, to, at the other extreme, an approach in which contract types tend to be taxonomized *a priori* by the legal system in question. In English law itself, at the non-prescriptive end of the spectrum, we find, as we might *ex hypothesi* expect, a singularly low degree of regulation or concertation of the personal contract for services in any shape, manner, or form, but in particular as a composite category. We could go so far as to assert that in English law the personal contract for services does not seem to exist as a composite category. The idea that there must be such a category by reason of a necessary symmetry with the contract of employment turns out to be an illusion.

In English law, moreover, an adjacent and relevant category has for a long time been recognized; it is that of the law of agency, which clearly constitutes a 'specific contract' or identified subset of the law of contracts, distinguished by its essential notion of the contract for the representation of another, of the principal by the agent.[16] This helps to prove by contrast the point about the non-existence of the personal contract for service as a category. If, as logic might be thought to demand, the personal contract for service were articulated as a category in the way that the contract of agency has been, it would have been necessary to spell out the relationship between these two contract types, that is to say to identify the degree of overlap between the two contract types, in a way perhaps similar to that of some continental European systems. As it is we can say confidently that this would be a mutually incomplete overlap, but we would be very hard pressed to define its extent at all fully. In the previous paragraphs we already highlighted the extent to which some continental European legal systems equally struggle to maintain a level of internal coherence and conceptual consistency in respect of their own notions of agency contracts, and the relationship of the various kinds of contractual arrangements that derive from the broad category of agency contracts, either to the contract of employment or to the contract for services.

This overlap between agency contracts and the supposed category of personal contracts for services is rendered even more complex and problematical by the articulation in English law of a novel category of 'commercial agents', something made necessary by the requirements of EU law.[17] Where commercial agents are personal ones, in the sense of being human persons operating as individuals, the contracts under which they work would seem to form a particular subset of agency contracts in general; but if we are thinking of the personal contract for services as a single composite category, personal commercial agency contracts would also be strong candidates for membership of that category. So if we identify a special

---

[16] *Chitty on Contracts* (2008) 30th ed., Chapter 31, para. 31-001.
[17] Council Directive 86/653/EEC of 18 December 1986 on the coordination of the laws of the Member States relating to self-employed commercial agents [1986] OJ L 382/17. Cf. the Commercial Agents (Council Directive) Regulations 1993, SI 1993/3053. Cf. also European Commission, 'Report on the application of Article 17 of Directive 86/653/EEC on the co-ordination of the laws of the Member States relating to self-employed commercial agents', COM (1996) 364.

category of 'personal commercial agency contracts' that category has to be located at a very complex interface between the quite well-established category of agency contracts and the apparent but actually very inchoate one of the personal contract for services. This is a complex set of issues that the Directive itself implicitly recognizes by creating a number of exclusions and exceptions, in Articles 1(2) and 2, to its personal scope of application. In spite of these exclusions, or possibly because of them, litigation – both before the ECJ and domestically – has arisen precisely to clarify the scope of the notion of 'commercial agent', as distinguished from that of an agent 'contracting on behalf of the principal but in its own name'.[18]

We can extend this set of observations to other, though less well-defined, categories which overlap with the apparent category of personal contracts for services. Key examples would be contracts for professional services, sports contracts, and entertainment contracts. Each of these represents, in English law, an inchoate contract type which, so far as its outlines can be discerned, would necessarily intersect with but not coincide with the also inchoate category of personal contracts for services. They would intersect, in the sense that some of these contracts would take the form of personal contracts for services.[19] But they would not coincide, because, on the one hand, such contracts might take the form of contracts of employment. On the other hand, they might not constitute personal work contracts in any sense, but rather contracts made by professional practitioners, or sportspersons, or entertainers operating with others – partners or assistants, or employees – as professional practices or business organizations therefore making business-to-business or business-to-consumer contracts. Moreover, we can of course envisage personal contracts for services which would not be contracts for professional services, sports contracts, or entertainment contracts.

Comparative inquiry yields similar conclusions for other European legal systems. A very valuable set of sources in this respect consists of the preparatory scholarly work for the articulation of the Draft Common Frame of Reference for European Private Law, in particular the efforts which have been made to establish the basis for a Common Frame of Reference for the category of 'Service Contracts'.[20] The studies of national systems which were undertaken for this purpose generally confirm the idea that, within Civilian systems, it is reasonably satisfactory to designate a category of 'service contracts' which is generically associated with the historical category of

---

[18] Case C-85/03, *Mavrona & Sia OE v. Delta Etairia Symmetochon AE* [2004] OJ C 94/17. Domestically cf. *Sagal (Trading as Bunz UK) v. Atelier Bunz GmbH* [2009] EWCA Civ 700.

[19] An interesting example is provided by the contractual arrangement for the supply of 'personal services' by a rugby coach in *Lambden v. Henley Rugby Football Club, Henley Rugby Football Club Ltd*, Appeal No. UKEAT/0505/08/DA.

[20] There are two principal sources of this kind. The first one is the volume prepared by M. Barendrecht *et al.* (2007) *Principles of European Law – Service Contracts (PEL SC)* (Sellier and OUP) under the aegis of the Study Group on a European Civil Code. The second one, derived from and building upon the first one, is Volume II, Book IV, Part C, 'Services' of C. von Bar and E. Clive (eds.) (2009) *Principles, Definitions and Model Rules of European Private Law – Draft Common Frame of Reference (DCFR)* Sellier, prepared by the Study Group on a European Civil Code and the Research Group on EC Private Law (Acquis Group).

*locatio conductio operis.*[21] However, an analysis in any detail reveals a rather kaleido-scopic picture, in which those categories fragment into complex relations with other categories.[22] Moreover – and this is the crucial point – neither any of these national categories nor the proposed supranational category of 'service contracts' confines itself to, or singles out within itself a sub-category of, contracts for personal performance by a human service provider[23] – a delineation which in our argument is centrally necessary to the construction of an intellectually coherent and functionally adequate body of law in the field of service provision.

So the law of 'other personal work contracts' seems to be in the course of an evolution whereby very loosely defined new typologies emerge and intersect with pre-existing – and also quite loose or inchoate – typologies, which moreover often fail to make the distinction between personal work contracts and other work contracts which we regard as being of quintessential importance. This strongly suggests that, if there ever was the possibility of regarding the personal contract for service as a unitary category comprehending all other personal work contracts, that possibility is fast receding into nothingness. If that view is accepted, two main alternative possibilities present themselves as offering the best analysis of the 'other personal work contract' category. We consider the first of those in the next subsection.

## C. Other Personal Work Contracts as a Dual Category

We have argued in the previous subsection that the analysis of other personal work contracts as constituting a unitary category of personal contracts for services cannot satisfactorily be sustained. An alternative approach appears to emerge from the recent evolution of English labour law and the labour law of other European systems. Although the notion of other personal work contracts is not explicitly

---

[21] See PEL SC pp. 148–53, from which it appears that in many European jurisdictions there is a legal category corresponding to the idea of the 'service contract' or 'services contract', for example, the *Werkvertrag* in Germany and Austria, and the *opdracht* in the Netherlands, and that some of those legal categories are obviously derived from or related to the *locatio conductio operis*, such as the *louage d'ouvrage* in France and Belgium, the *contratto d'opera* in Italy, and the *contrato de obra* in Spain. It is worth pointing out that the decision on the part of the authors of PEL SC and DCFR to unify these national conceptions under the head of 'service contracts' rather than of 'services contracts' risks an underlying confusion by reason of the fact that the terminology of 'service contracts' was historically largely synonymous with that of 'employment contracts', at least to the extent that it was *opposed to* that of 'contracts for services' in contractual formulations of the employment/self-employment dichotomy.

[22] Ibid. Thus, as also noted above, in Germany and Austria there is an overlap between the *Werkvertrag* and the *Dienstvertrag*, in France and Belgium the *louage d'ouvrage*, itself a terminology now generally superseded by that of the *contrat d'entreprise*, stands in a complex relation with the idea of *mandat* which is equivalent to agency, in Italy the *contratto d'opera* is a subset of the category of *lavoro autonomo*, in Spain there is a duality between the *contrato de obra* and the *contrato de servicio* which does not correspond neatly to the dichotomy between employment and self-employment, and so on.

[23] Ibid. It seems fully clear that the notion of 'service contracts' as deployed in PEL SC and DCFR is not so confined, nor is that of the *Werkvertrag* or the *contrat d'entreprise*. It may be arguable that the *contratto d'opera* in Italy, and the *contrato de obra* in Spain were historically regarded as personal work contracts, but if so that is now much less clear than it formerly was.

recognized, many European labour law systems can be regarded as identifying it as a dual category consisting of two sub-types, one of which is at least partly within the domain of labour law, while the other is largely entirely outside the domain of labour law. In this subsection, we shall suggest that, although this analysis appears on the face of it to be an attractive one, it is ultimately no more satisfactory than the unitary approach which was considered in the previous subsection and is in certain respects even more problematical than the unitary approach.

This dual category approach to other personal work contracts has been quite strongly favoured by the English legislator in recent years. This has taken the form of using the category of 'worker' as the defining concept for the personal scope of certain significant items of worker-protective labour legislation. In such legislation, the concept of the 'worker' is normally defined as follows:-

'worker' [ ... ] means an individual who has entered into or works under (or, where the employment has ceased, worked under)–
   (a) a contract of employment, or
   (b) any other contract, whether express or implied and (if it is express) whether oral or in writing, whereby the individual undertakes to do or perform personally any work or services for another party to the contract whose status is not by virtue of the contract that of a client or customer of any profession or business undertaking carried on by the individual; and any reference to a worker's contract shall be construed accordingly.[24]

In that formulation, limb (b) precisely evokes our 'other personal work contracts' category; but it will be apparent that limb (b) divides that category of contracts into two subcategories, namely: (1) 'other personal work contracts' which are between client or customer and profession or business; and (2) all other 'other personal work contracts', that is to say those which are not between client or customer and profession or business. So there we have the dual subcategory approach to 'other personal work contracts'; some of them, the ones between client or customer and profession or business undertaking, are treated as outside the scope of the labour legislation in question, but the rest of them, the ones that are not concluded between client or customer and profession or business undertaking, are bracketed with contracts of service or apprenticeship and are treated as within the labour legislation in question. So the crucial break, between those personal work contractual relations which fall within the personal scope of labour legislation and those which do not, is placed not, as in the traditional way, between contracts of service (and apprenticeship) and 'other personal work contracts', but rather between the two different kinds of 'other personal work contracts'.

This may seem to represent a surprisingly methodical approach on the part of the English legislator. Quite untypically, it places English law in the vanguard of a new taxonomical approach to the personal scope of labour legislation by comparison with other European labour law systems, while English law more usually lingers in the reluctant rearguard of such categorical developments. However, it is quite likely

---

[24] ERA 1996, s. 230(3).

that the drafters of this legislation were following their usual pragmatic and non-categorical approach; they probably regarded themselves more as redefining the 'employee' concept in a modern and inclusive way than as splitting the other personal work contracts category into two parts.[25] That is to say, this formula may have been intended to represent a flexible and inclusive approach to the existing 'employee under a contract of employment' concept. But even if so, it in fact logically creates a precise division between two new sub-categories of other personal work contracts.

Comparable evolutions have occurred – though, as we have indicated, in an apparently less systematic way – in other European labour law systems. Two similar kinds of evolution may be identified, though each is subtly different from the other and from the evolution of the 'worker' concept in English law. The 'worker' concept in English law, as we have seen, embraces two categories of personal work contract, namely (1) the contract of service or employment (including the contract of apprenticeship), and (2) all other 'other personal work contracts', that is to say those which are not between client or customer and profession or business undertaking. The latter category is identified in a partly negative way; it is identified as a personal work contract which is neither on the one hand a contract of employment nor on the other hand an 'other personal work contract' which is between client or customer and profession or business undertaking. It is an intermediate category identified by exclusion of the two categories regarded as being on either side of it.

In some continental legal systems, we find that analogous notions have developed but have been defined positively rather than negatively. We can single out two such patterns of development; firstly, the notion of the 'employee-like person', and, secondly, the notion of the 'economically dependent worker'. We proceed to examine those two notions in turn, and to consider how far any or all of the three notions – that is to say, the 'worker', the 'employee-like person' and the 'economically dependent worker' – succeeds or succeed in effecting a satisfactory sub-division of our category of 'other personal work contracts'.

The articulation of a positive notion of 'employee-like persons' famously occurs in the German and the Italian legal systems, in the forms respectively of the *'arbeitnehmerähnliche Person'*[26] and the *'parasubordinati'*.[27] These are instru-

---

[25] A strong indication of this consists in the fact that the governmental drafters of the policy document *Fairness at Work* regarded the category of 'worker' as including all working persons other than the 'genuinely self-employed' – that being evidently intended as a narrower more stringently tested category than 'the self-employed' *tout court*. The logic of that would seem to be that the binary division between 'employees' and 'the self-employed' was simply being resituated, the two categories being respectively identified as 'workers' and those working under client or customer, and profession or business undertaking contracts. Cf. *Fairness at Work* (May 1998), para. 3.18.

[26] See s. 12a of the *Tarifvertragsgesetz* of 1974; M. Weiss and M. Schmidt (2008) *Labour Law and Industrial Relations in Germany*, AH Alphen aan den Rijn: Kluwer, 47–8; W. Däubler (1999) 'Working People in Germany' (1999) 21 *CLLPJ*, 88–9. Cf. in general N. Countouris (2007) *The Changing Law of the Employment Relationship*, Aldershot: Ashgate, 71–81.

[27] Traditionally derived from Article 409(3) of the Civil Procedure Code, the main contractual type under which it is currently articulated is the *'lavoro a progetto'* regulated under Article 61 of Legislative Decree 276/2003. See further A. Perulli (2011) 'Subordinate, Autonomous and Economically Depen-

mental categories, in the sense that they are articulated with the purpose of identifying a set of workers who it is thought should be treated similarly to, though not in identically the same way as, employees. It should be said that the articulation of these notions of employee-like persons has not hitherto put down deep roots in those labour law systems; in so far as that has occurred, it has been more in the context of social security legislation than in the context of labour legislation.

Equally widespread in continental legal systems, and more particularly occurring in the context of labour legislation, is the articulation of the notion of the 'economically dependent worker'.[28] This is a phenomenon which is quite similar to, but subtly different from, the articulation of the idea of the employee-like person. The articulation of notions amounting to that of the 'economically dependent worker' does occur to a significant extent in the context of labour law, as a purposive conception of a set of workers to whom worker-protective legislation should be in whole or in part extended. These notions are apt to be put forward as much by judges as a matter of interpretation of legislation as by legislators themselves engaged in the primary formation of legislation.

Thus far, notions of the 'economically dependent worker' very closely resemble notions of the 'employee-like person', but there is a significant difference. Whereas notions of the 'employee-like person' seem to differentiate unequivocally between the employee and the employee-like person, designating the latter as similar to but at the same time different from the former, notions of the economically dependent worker are much more equivocal as to whether they represent a distinct category from that of the employee, or on the other hand, no more than a new and somewhat more inclusive way of identifying the 'employee' category itself. That is a highly subtle ambiguity, but one which is of great functional significance. For, if the former view is taken, it follows that these workers, although they should as such be treated similarly to employees, need not be treated identically to them. Whereas if the latter view is taken, then economically dependent workers must as such be treated identically with employees, because they belong to the same single category.

We could exemplify these two distinct conceptual positions by reference to the approach taken, respectively, by Spanish and French law in respect of some personal work relationships characterized by high levels of economic dependence. In particular the treatment in Spanish law of the contractual category of 'economically dependant autonomous workers',[29] is indicative of a tendency to conceptualize such personal work contracts as a distinct category – or possibly a subcategory – of the 'autonomous work' category characterized by a high degree of economic

---

dent Work: A Comparative Analysis of Selected European Countries', in G. Casale (ed.), *The Employment Relationship – A Comparative Overview*, Oxford: Hart, 165–8; also the critical analysis by V. Pinto (2006) 'La Categoria Giuridica delle Collaborazioni Coordinate e Continuative e il Lavoro a Progetto', in P. Curzio (ed.), *Lavoro e Diritti a Tre Anni dalla Legge 30/2003*, Bari: Cacucci, 431.

[28] On the notion of economic dependence and its historical evolution cf. O. Razzolini (2010) 'The Need to Go Beyond the Contract: "Economic" and "Bureaucratic" Dependence in Personal Work Relations', 31 *CLLPJ*, 267.

[29] '*Trabajadores autónomos económicamente dependientes*' introduced in *Ley 20/2007, de 11 de julio, del Estatuto del Trabajo Autónomo*.

dependence upon a single 'client'.[30] These workers are covered by a fairly comprehensive worker-protective regulatory framework,[31] far more comprehensive than the one accorded to their functionally equivalent German counterparts,[32] which, however, does not seek to bring them within the realm of labour law. By contrast, the Seventh Part of the French *Code du Travail* (*Dispositions Particulières à Certaines Professions et Activités*) (Provisions Specific to Certain Professions and Activities) introduces a number of '*présomptions de salariat*' – legal presumptions of employment – in respect of a range of other personal work relations which, while not strictly speaking ones of employment, are characterized by a high degree of economic dependence.[33] As we indicated earlier, there seems to have been some ambiguity in the intentions of the UK legislators who articulated the notion of 'worker'. However, in the event they committed themselves to a formulation which does add a clearly distinct new category to that of the employee under a contract of employment, namely the person working under a personal work contract which stands outside and beyond the contract of employment though not being, on the other hand a business-to-customer or profession-to-client contract.

We may question whether these various evolutions are giving rise to a satisfactorily recognizable dual categorization of 'other personal work contracts'. A satisfactorily recognizable dual categorization would establish two distinct types of 'other personal work contracts', one of which was similar to the contract of employment while the other was not, and one of which should be integrated into the regulatory regime of labour law in a way which was similar to that of employment contracts while the other should not. This cannot really be said to have been achieved to date. The evolutions which we have cited in continental jurisdictions have not created a fully developed notion of the employee-like person within the sphere of labour law as such. The notion of the economically dependent worker has, as we have shown, remained rather ambiguous as to whether it is distinct from that of the employee. Moreover, neither of those two notions are specifically contractual ones; in so far as they establish new categories, those are not necessarily contractual categories. This is an important point to which we revert in the next chapter.

By contrast, British labour legislation does on the face of it appear to have established a clear distinction between two types of personal work contract beyond the contract of employment, namely, on the one hand, the 'worker's' contract (not being a contract of employment) and, on the other hand, the profession-to-client or business-to-customer personal work contract. However, a detailed examination of the case-law creates doubt about whether such an evolution is really taking place; we suggest that this case-law, properly understood, points more towards the

[30] A. Ojeda Avilés (2010) *La Deconsrtucción del Derecho del Trabajo*, Madrid: La Ley, 394–424.

[31] E. Sánchez Torres (2010) 'The Spanish Law on Dependent Self-employed Workers: A New Evolution in Labour Law', 31 *CLLPJ*, 231.

[32] S. Sorge (2010) 'German Law on Dependant Self-employed: A Comparison to the Current Situation under Spanish Law', 31 *CLLPJ*, 249.

[33] Cf. O. Razzolini (2010) 'The Need to Go Beyond the Contract: "Economic" and "Bureaucratic" Dependence in Personal Work Relations', 31 *CLLPJ*, 289.

evolution of *various* types of personal work *relation* beyond the contract of employment than to the evolution of *two* types of personal work *contract* beyond the contract of employment.

The British case-law on the definition of the 'worker' suggests that there are two respects in which a person in a work relation may be identified as a 'worker' although he or she does not work under a contract of employment. Firstly, he or she may be identified as a 'worker', though not one working under a contract of employment, in that the work relation, although not displaying sufficient *mutuality of obligation* to give rise to a contract of employment – because of a wide discretion on the part of both parties about whether and when the individual is actually engaged to work – nevertheless displays a sufficient degree of mutuality of obligation to qualify the individual as a 'worker'. Secondly and rather similarly, he or she may be identified as a 'worker', though not one working under a contract of employment, in that the work relation, although not sufficiently *personal* to the individual in question to give rise to a contract of employment – because of a wide provision for substitutability of the individual by other individuals – nevertheless displays a sufficient degree of 'personal-ness' or personality to qualify the individual as a 'worker'.[34]

This appears on the face of it to create a nicely articulated category of personal work contract which is intermediate between the contract of employment on the one hand and the genuinely independent personal contract for services on the other – with degrees of personality and mutuality of obligation as the variables which locate this category between the other two. However, there are serious difficulties with such a scheme, which it is useful to identify first in relation to the requirement of personality and then in relation to the requirement of mutuality of obligation. With regard to the requirement of personality, we firstly encounter the difficulty that this scheme is a very elaborate one, for it postulates no less than four distinctive degrees of personality. That is to say, the scheme seems logically to recognize: (1) the highest degree of personality, sufficient to sustain a contract of employment; (2) a lower degree of personality, but sufficient to sustain a 'worker's' contract which is not a contract of employment; (3) a still lower degree of personality, but sufficient to sustain a personal work contract which is not a 'worker's' contract; and (4) an absence of personality such as to identify a work contract, or contract for services, which is not a personal work contract at all. We may think that this is too elaborate a scheme to be practically viable.

---

[34] A very helpful judicial analysis is provided by Elias J as the President of the Employment Appeal Tribunal in *James v. Redcats (Brands) Ltd* [2007] IRLR 296. Rather confusingly, it has become customary for both of the dimensions of analysis identified in this paragraph to be regarded as questions of 'mutuality of obligation'; we suggest that it is nevertheless important to maintain an analytical distinction between the two questions of: (1) the presence and firmness of the obligations to provide and to perform work; and (2) the extent to which such work has to be performed by the worker in person. Both questions were at issue in this case; both were resolved in favour of the worker; the reasoning of Elias J regards the second issue as one of personal-ness or personality rather than of mutuality of obligation in the way which we have argued is appropriate.

Moreover, and no less significantly, there is a logical objection to such a scheme in so far as it implies that there is a linear spectrum of personality or personal-ness from the contract of employment at one extreme to the non-personal contract for services at the other extreme. The fallacy is that the two intermediate categories do not fit neatly along such a spectrum. We might find a personal work contract which was neither a contract of employment nor a 'worker's' contract – therefore a profession-to-client or business-to-customer contract – but which still had a high requirement of personality. An example might be the briefing of a particular well-known barrister to work on a particular case. So it does not follow that as the personality of a work relation decreases or increases, it necessarily becomes more or less like a contract for services. In other words, personality does not work as a simple linear indicator of a notional transition from the contract of employment to the contract for services, and still less is there a series of clear benchmarks along any such line.

We can observe the same set of difficulties with the idea that there are, correspondingly, descending degrees of mutuality of obligation from the contract of employment to the worker's contract and from the worker's contract to the profession-to-client or business-to-customer contract for services; and with this argument we also encounter a further and very significant difficulty. As with the degrees of personality, it is firstly to be observed that there is no simple linear spectrum of mutuality of obligation from the contract of employment to the contract for services with two clearly discernible divisions along the way (that is to say, firstly between the contract of employment and the other workers' contract, and secondly between the other workers' contract and the profession-to-client or business-to-customer contract for services). Thus, we might find a profession-to-client or business-to-customer contract for services which displayed a high level of mutuality of obligation – again, the briefing of a barrister to work on a particular case might provide a good example.

Moreover, there is a further and quite fundamental difficulty with the notion of stepped degrees of reduction in the rigorousness of the requirement of mutuality of obligation as a way of distinguishing between contracts of employment, other workers' contracts, and profession-to-client or business-to-customer contracts for services. It might make sense to think of degrees of reduction of personality as a way of distinguishing between different types of work contracts – though even there we have argued that there is no neatly stepped linear series. But we have to remember that the requirement of mutuality of obligation is, at bottom, not a way of distinguishing between contract types but rather a way of deciding whether a given personal work arrangement gives rise to any kind of contract at all.[35] And we also have to remember that the requirement of mutuality of obligation for contracts of employment has itself been envisaged as an 'irreducible minimum'[36] – which implies that this is itself a very low threshold.

---

[35] Cf. Elias J in *James v. Redcats (Brands) Ltd* [2007] IRLR 296, 297.
[36] *Nethermere (St. Neots) Ltd v. Gardiner* [1984] ICR 612, 623 C–G *per* Stephenson L.J.; *Carmichael and another v. National Power plc* [2000] IRLR 43, *per* Lord Irvine.

So it would follow that, if there are to be stepped degrees of reduction in the rigorousness of the requirement of mutuality of obligation as a way of distinguishing between different types of personal work contract, we have to look for two further 'irreducible minimum' levels of mutuality of obligation below that which is required for the contract of employment, firstly for other workers' contracts, and secondly for profession-to-client or business-to-customer contracts for services. And each of these miniscule levels of mutuality of obligation has to be compatible with the existence of a contract of any kind, when the very purpose of the doctrine of mutuality of obligation is to draw a clear bright line between those personal work arrangements which do amount to contracts and those which are insufficiently concrete or firmly obligational to qualify as such.

So we arrive at the conclusion that the idea of splitting up the category of 'other personal work contracts' into two clearly separated subcategories cannot be regarded as one which is well established on a satisfactory basis. We would argue that even in continental European labour law systems, the idea has not really taken root, despite the presence of some apparent tendencies in that direction. The Spanish case of 'economically dependent autonomous workers', often cited as the epitome of this tendency, is in our view better understood as an attempt to bestow a higher level of protection to some workers falling in what Supiot[37] and Perulli[38] have described as the 'grey area' between subordination and autonomy, rather than a radical reconceptualization, or even a clarification,[39] of that 'grey area' itself. Comparative analyses also illustrate that some European countries,[40] as well as part of the doctrinal debate,[41] are resisting the idea of an intermediate category of other personal work relations, and are relying on a number of legal devices, ranging from presumptions to an outright rejection of the notion of quasi-dependency, to

---

[37] A. Supiot (2001) *Beyond Employment: Changes in Work and the Future of Labour Law in Europe*, Oxford: OUP, 219.

[38] A. Perulli (2011) 'Subordinate, Autonomous and Economically Dependent Work: A Comparative Analysis of Selected European Countries', in G. Casale (ed.), *The Employment Relationship – A Comparative Overview*, Oxford: Hart, 140.

[39] It is conceptually artificial and normatively unsatisfactory to bestow a more protective regime, as the Spanish legislation does, upon workers deriving 75 per cent of their income, and to exclude those who receive any lesser proportion of their income.

[40] When the Luxembourg Government was prompted by the 2006 Commission Green Paper to take a stance in respect of 'the concept of *"economically dependent work"*', it forcefully argued that it found: '*très artificielle l'introduction de la notion de travail économiquement dépendant qui ne serait ni du travail salarié ni du travail indépendant*'. This was seen as a mere means to '*réduire la protection liée au statut de salarié*', the problem being, in their view, the existence of 'sham self-employed to be requalified *ex officio* as salaried workers'; Contribution du Gouvernement du Grand-Duché de Luxembourg au LIVRE VERT 'Moderniser le droit du travail pour relever les défis du XXIe siècle' (30 March 2007), 10. Available at: http://ec.europa.eu/employment_social/labour_law/answers/documents/1_2_fr.pdf.

[41] M.G. Garofalo (2003) 'La legge delega sul mercato del lavoro: prime osservazioni', *RGL*, 362; M. Hascöet (2007) 'Le contrat de projet: le nouveau visage de la parasubordination en Italie', *Droit Social*, 879; M. Pedrazzoli (2006) 'Le complicazioni dell'inutilità: note critiche sul lavoro a progetto', in L. Mariucci (ed.) (2006), *Dopo la flessibilità, cosa? Le nuove politiche del lavoro*, Bologna: Il Mulino, 119; R. Dalmasso (2009) 'Salariés, travailleurs indépendants et travailleurs économiquement dépendants: vers une troisième catégorie juridique régissant la relation de travail ?' available at http://gree.univ-nancy2.fr/digitalAssets/51826_DALMASSO.pdf.

re-label the varieties of other personal work relationship as essentially autonomous or subordinated ones. In English labour law, the idea of such a distinction has been firmly embodied in legislation, but presents real difficulties when the attempt is made to develop it in case-law. In particular, the idea that there are two satisfactorily separable *contractual* sub-categories turns out to be rather hard to maintain, even if two such groups of personal work *relations* can be distinguished from each other. We return to that point in the next chapter; at this point, we turn to consider how the category of other personal work contracts might best be analysed if, as we have argued, it cannot satisfactorily be regarded either as a single homogeneous category of personal contracts for services or as a dual category.

## D. Other Personal Work Contracts as a Family of Contracts

In the previous two subsections, we have successively argued that there are significant difficulties about constructing the category of other personal work contracts either as a single essentially homogeneous category of personal contracts for services or as a dual category of, on the one hand, employment-like contracts and, on the other hand, fully independent contracts for personal services. In this subsection, we argue for our own preferred analysis of the category as a loose and heterogeneous grouping or family of other personal work contracts; and we suggest how that analysis provides the conceptual link between the previous and subsequent chapters of this work.

So our argument is that the category of 'other personal work contracts', that is to say personal work contracts other than the contract of employment, should be conceived of and analysed as a loose grouping or diverse family of contracts, not especially unified or necessarily having a very great deal in common with each other, and not representing a homogeneous contract type or even two internally homogeneous subcategories. We suggest that this argument holds good at more than one level and in more than one sense. In the two previous subsections we have sought to show that alternative possible views of this category either as a single homogeneous one or as two internal homogeneous subcategories are not very sustainable, either because legislation and case-law in European labour law systems has not generally proceeded on such a view, or because, in the few instances where the attempt has been made to develop such an approach with any degree of theoretical rigour, it has proved difficult to achieve that objective.

When, as we are doing, we argue against those approaches and in favour of a looser and more diversified conception of this category, it might appear that we are simply content to settle for a view of it as no more than a rag-bag of contractual oddments having only this in common, that they are personal work contracts which have failed to qualify as contracts of employment (or which have been successfully framed by employing enterprises as not being contracts of employment). However, we suggest, to the contrary, that our 'loose grouping' view of this category can be more positively maintained, both at a technically analytical level and as a tool or instrument for the policy development of labour legislation. We have been accustomed to view 'other personal work contracts' through an optic of exclusion, seeing them as a single contract type united by their externality to labour law, or at least as a double contract type, one part of which is united by its partial externality and the other part by its total externality. This amounts to a kind of negative homogenization of the category of 'other personal work contracts'.

Once we cease to view other personal work contracts through that particular optic, we can, as labour lawyers, become much more interested in what personal work contracts are rather than in what they are not – and in why they might fall within the domain of labour law rather than in why they do not. We begin to see that other personal work contracts represent the legal constructions of a wide range of personal work relations which exist within a richly interesting variety of normative and institutional frameworks which intersect with those of labour law itself. As we pursue this line of thought, there come to mind a number of very interesting and important (though very loosely defined) categories of personal work relations which are regarded as primarily (though not entirely) located beyond the sphere of the contract of employment.

These categories are of two broadly distinct, though somewhat overlapping, types. On the one hand, there are categories which refer to occupations or occupational sectors – so, occupational categories – for example (to speak of the British labour market): (1) the professions or liberal professions; (2) commercial travellers and agents; (3) sportspersons and those working in entertainment and the media. On the other hand, there are categories which refer to work arrangements or work patterns – so, work arrangement categories – for example (again to speak of the British labour market): (1) freelancers; (2) consultants; and (3) homeworkers. This begins to sketch out a picture which becomes even more complex and interesting when we bring into consideration the corresponding or similar categories which are encountered in other European labour markets, for example in France the *artisan* and the *voyageur représentant placier* (traveling salesperson), or the Italian complex categories of *lavoratori a domicilio* (home-workers), who may offer their services either through a contract of employment or a contract for services.[42]

By drawing on these primarily empirical rather than primarily legal categories, we can begin to construct a vision of the domain of other personal work contracts which is informative in several respects. Firstly, we can arrive at a more contextual understanding than would otherwise be possible of the interface between the domain of contracts of employment and the domain of other personal work contracts – and we can better understand why it is so profoundly difficult and unsatisfactory to draw a clear boundary between those two domains. As long as we are envisaging the 'other personal work contract' as a single homogeneous type (or even as two sub-types), we cherish the illusion that it must be possible systematically to distinguish it from the contract of employment. Once we accept that the domain of 'other personal work contracts' is an essentially polycentric or amoebic one, it becomes clear why law-makers and adjudicators are endlessly driven to adduce and manipulate more and more '*indicia*' in a vain attempt to isolate the

---

[42] Cf. L. 13 marzo 1958 n. 264 and L. 18 dicembre 1973 n. 877 Article 1.

contract of employment from it. Thus, to identify one key instance of this polycentricity, we can observe that the isolation of the contract of employment from other personal work contracts is a very different kind of exercise when attempted on the one hand in the context of highly specialized professional work and on the other hand in the context of casual manual work.

Thus the understanding of the domain of other personal work contracts as a polycentric one serves to show why its interface with the domain of contracts of employment is such a complex and ultimately indeterminate one. The understanding of the domain of personal work contracts as a polycentric one secondly makes us realize that, as such, this domain also has a very complex rather than a simple interface with other contract types. This challenges any simple perception that, if the interface between the contract of employment and other personal work contracts forms the inner boundary of the domain of other personal work contracts, the outer boundary consists of a single interface with non-personal or commercial contracts for services. Instead, we begin to perceive a complex outer boundary, reflecting the polycentricity of the domain itself. Particular kinds of other personal work contracts interface with various other contract types according to their particular nature. Personal franchise contracts will verge upon non-personal franchise contracts, personal agency contracts will verge upon (non-personal) commercial agency contracts, personal work-training contracts will verge upon education contracts – and so on.

There is, however, a third and even more important insight which can be obtained from regarding the domain of other personal work contracts as an essentially polycentric one. It becomes apparent that this domain is one in which there are many different kinds of contractual practice, shaped or affected by many different kinds of occupational regime. Thus we might find widely divergent contractual practices and occupational regimes as between, for example, a 'liberal' but highly regulated profession such as that of general medical practice, and, on the other hand, a more loosely defined and less regulated occupation such as that of management consultancy. We can include in this diversity a wide variety of mechanisms of normative co-ordination which lie wholly or partly beyond the scope of legal regulation, such as collective bargaining or the formulation of standard terms or standard contracts by trade or professional associations. Those divergences become very greatly elaborated when we compare contractual practices, normative co-ordination mechanisms, and occupational regimes as between European countries.

Moreover, and this is a very important point, those divergences may and often do represent deeper variations in the basic orientations of the normative co-ordination mechanisms and occupational regimes which apply in different parts of the domain of other personal work contracts. This brings us to a point at which there appears to be a contrast between the domain of the contract of employment and the domain of other personal work contracts, at least in the tone of the regulatory discourses which take place within each of those two domains. Let us for the sake of argument, albeit at some risk of over-simplification, accept that the regulatory discourse which takes place in the domain of the contract of employment is oriented towards the reconciliation of managerial power with the protection of workers, this generally being regarded as a matter of the correction or adjustment of a paradigmatic inequality of bargaining power between management and workers, at least when workers are operating as individual rather than collective actors.

If that view of the orientation of the regulatory discourse in the domain of the contract of employment is at risk of being over-simplified, there is a largely unquestioned contrasting assumption about the orientation of the regulatory discourse in the domain of other personal work contracts which is, in our view, quite undoubtedly over-simplified. The largely unquestioned contrasting assumption is that in the domain of other personal work contracts – misleadingly, as we have argued, lumped together as contracts for services – the regulatory discourse is quite uniformly that of private and indeed basically commercial contract law. In fact the regulatory orientations within this domain are much more diverse and complex, especially when considered comparatively between European legal systems. In various different locations within the domain of other personal work contracts, we find that the avowed neutrality between contracting parties which is the supposed hallmark of private and commercial contract law is heavily overlaid or even displaced by concerns with: (1) the protection of the employing party, or purchaser of services, who may be regarded as a 'consumer' of a service provision; or (2) the regulation of competition between service providers; or (3) the protection of the factually weaker party without a paradigmatic assumption as to which party that is; or (4) wider public interests such as the welfare of those affected by the service provision in question. We could regard the concerns which EU law has of each of these four kinds as in some sense representing the corresponding concerns within national systems.[43]

That observation can be used to build upon the idea of polycentricity in the domain of other personal work contracts in the following way. For it confirms that the domain of other personal work contracts is a polycentric one not only in the sense that it comprises a wide variety of different kinds of personal work relations, but also in the sense that there is a correspondingly wide variety of regulatory approaches. So the domain of other personal work contracts can be regarded as one comprised of various localities within each of which a singular regulatory approach might be taken. Moreover, we can further observe, especially from a European comparative perspective, that some of these localities may be more subject to the regulation of labour law than others – as for example is the case in English law for

---

[43] Cf. M. Freedland (2008) 'Private Law, Regulation and Governance Design and the Personal Work Contract', in F. Cafaggi and H. Muir-Watt (eds), *Making European Private Law – Governance Design*, Cheltenham: Edward Elgar, 227. Some of these preoccupation seem to underlie the work carried out by the 'Study Group on Social Justice in European Private Law' and by the 'European Social Contracts Code Group', cf. 'Social Justice in European Contract Law: a Manifesto' (2004) 10:6, *ELJ*, 653; and EuSoCo Group, 'Public Consultation on the Green Paper from the Commission on policy options for progress towards a European Contract Law for consumers and businesses' (January 2011); L. Nogler and U. Reifner (2010) 'Social Contracts in the Light of the Draft Common Frame of Reference for a future EU Contract Code', in L. Antoniolli, F. Fiorentini (eds.), *A Factual Assessment of the Draft Common Frame of reference*, Sellier, pp. 365–407. A further discussion of these points is conducted in Chapter 10 of the present work.

that part of the domain in which the personal service providers in question fall within the statutory definition of 'workers'.

Those observations together lead on to a further and perhaps yet more important insight into the polycentric nature of the domain of other personal work contracts. This insight is that there is a close, indeed integral, connection between the different kinds of contract which are found within this domain and the different regulatory approaches. Although there is nothing like a precise one-to-one fit between contract types and regulatory approaches, nevertheless we can find close associations between contract types and regulatory approaches. For example, European legal systems share a certain regulatory approach to the contracts of commercial agents,[44] which is distinctively protective of those agents vis-à-vis their principals: an EU Directive effected a co-ordination of national regimes to this effect.[45]

Moreover, as we have argued earlier in this work, these associations between regulatory approaches and contract types are sometimes so close that it is appropriate to understand the contract type as having evolved, or even as having been devised, precisely as the vehicle and embodiment of a particular regulatory approach. Again as we have suggested earlier,[46] the contract of employment could itself be regarded as the supreme example of such an evolution, or rather as a set of examples since distinctive evolutions of this kind occur as between different historical periods and different legal systems. That is by now quite well understood as a matter of the theory of labour law.[47] However, our suggestion is that, especially when viewed from a comparative perspective, the domain of other personal work contracts has become an even more fertile ground for evolutions of this kind.

By that we mean as follows. For much of the twentieth-century period of development of labour law in European legal systems, the domain of other personal work contracts existed as the largely unregulated epiphenomenon of the domain of the contract of employment: the domain of the contract of employment was by definition or conception the sphere within which the regulation of labour law developed and applied, while the domain of other personal work contracts represented a more shadowy conception of an outer world of personal work relations charcterized and described largely in terms of the absence of labour law regulation, rather than by the presence of any different system of regulation. Indeed, so much is this the case that our claim that we can designate a domain of other personal work contracts is in a sense an act of retrospective and creative reconstruction, a carving-out of a set of 'personal work contracts' from a sphere of contracts for works or services which might or might not be stipulated for provision by the service-providing contractor personally – that sphere being loosely governed, almost by

---

[44] Cf. S. Mégnin (2003) *Le Contrat d'Agence Commerciale en Droit Français et Allemand*, Paris: Litec; I. Billotte, P. Kenel, T. Steinmann (2005) *Le Contrat d'Agence Commerciale en Europe* (Paris: Bruylant/LGDJ/Schulthess, 2005).

[45] Council Directive 86/653/EEC of 18 December 1986 on the co-ordination of the laws of the Member States relating to self-employed commercial agents [1986] OJ L 382/17.

[46] Cf. Chapter 3, Sections 1 and 2 in particular.

[47] Cf. A. Supiot (1994) *Critique du Droit du Travail*, Paris: PUF, esp. Introduction and Chapter 1.

default, by the general private law of contracts in a way which did not differentiate between personal and non-personal work contracts.

However – and this is the crucial point – we can observe, especially from a European comparative perspective, developments which indicate that this domain is starting to emerge from the shadows. On the one hand, new contractual conceptions are emerging which begin to mark out large parts of this domain, or even the whole of it, as being subject to some aspects of labour law or of the law of discrimination in employment. As we shall see shortly, the conceptions in English law of the 'worker', and of 'employment' in the context of discrimination law, provide important, though rather obscure and concealed, examples of this phenomenon. Not without some delay, some continental systems appear to have followed a similar path in according some level of protection against discrimination to some categories of people engaged under other personal work services.[48] On the other hand, certain more specific contract types are identified within this domain which are the subject of or the vehicles for particular regulatory interventions, approaches, or packages. As already indicated above, various continental designations of commercial agents or commercial travellers provide especially good examples, but there are many others.

We have thus, we hope, established a basis for thinking about the domain of 'other personal work contracts' as being populated by a family or loose grouping of contract types, with definitions and intersections which are evolving or mutating in complex ways. We have argued that this is a better way to understand and analyse this contractual domain than by thinking of it as a single contract type – the personal contract for services – or as consisting of two contract types – the quasi-dependent worker's contract and the fully independent personal work contract. Our argument has emphasized the importance of taking account of the diversity of regulatory contexts in which these contract types are articulated and developed. In the succeeding sections of this chapter, we seek to flesh out and expand upon those arguments by considering how they play out with regard to, firstly, the formation and structure, secondly the content and performance, and, thirdly, the termination and transformation of this family of 'personal work contracts other than the contract of employment'.

---

[48] Arguably the most visible example to date is provided by Articles 4 and 6 of *Ley 20/2007, de 11 de julio, del Estatuto del trabajo autónomo*; limited protection against harassment is offered to some German quasi-dependent workers by §7 *Sozialgesetzbuch-SGB*, s IV, Book IV. By contrast Italian '*lavoratori a progetto*' have not been afforded any such protection by the Biagi Law, though it is arguable that Article 3(1)(a) of *Decreto Legislativo 9 luglio 2003, n. 216, 'Attuazione della direttiva 2000/78/CE per la parità di trattamento in materia di occupazione e di condizioni di lavoro*', ought to provide at least some protection to autonomous workers, albeit limited to conditions for *access* to self-employment or occupation.

## Section 2:  Formation and Structure

In this section we start to develop in detail the notion of 'other personal work contracts' as a family or loose grouping of contracts which can be regarded as being partially or potentially within the purview of labour law. We argue that this is a domain within which personal work contracts are lightly and patchily regulated, certainly in English law but also in many other European legal systems. So we are trying to arrive at a legal analysis of the structure and formation of other personal work contracts by looking at a fragmentary and rather incomplete map of these contracts, a map drawn in diverse regulatory contexts which has a number of gaps and sometimes expresses surmises rather than clearly established outlines. Our analysis is developed in parallel with the analysis of the law of contracts of employment which was conducted in the preceding chapters, but it is much briefer because on this occasion we have much less straw from which to fashion our building bricks. In subsection A we consider what structures are attributed to other personal work contracts, and in subsection B we turn to the question of what rules or doctrines govern the formation of those contracts, with regard to the aspects of intention, formality, and legality.

### A.  Paradigm and Variety in Structure – the Personal Task Contract as a Paradigm for Other Personal Work Contracts?

In order to give as much shape and clarity as possible to our discussion of the structure of other personal work contracts, it is useful for us to consider whether and how far we can identify a general or typical structure, or paradigmatic structure, for other personal work contracts in the way that we sought to do for contracts of employment in earlier chapters. We very cautiously advance the suggestion that there is such a paradigm, consisting of the 'personal task contract'. Having said that, we need strongly to qualify that suggestion with a caveat: the paradigm is a very weak one, and the diversity between other personal work contracts is very considerable, so much so that the exceptions, far from proving the rule, almost overwhelm the rule. We seek to demonstrate this by considering the various regulatory contexts in which the paradigm and the exceptions seem to arise.

The paradigm for 'other personal work contracts' – so far as it can be satisfactorily identified at any level – can be located at that decidedly acontextual level at which legal systems establish and express their typologies for contracts in general. That articulation of general contract typologies takes place, in English law, in treatises on the law of contract or contracts which summarize and analyse the common law as modified by particular statutory interventions; in continental legal systems, as already indicated above in subsection 1B, the corresponding articulation generally speaking takes place in the form of Civil Codes and the bodies of judicial doctrine which interpret them.

Even at that very general level, it must be admitted that English law offers very little by way of a paradigm for 'other personal work contracts'; the category of 'other personal work contracts' is not recognized as such; that category would be regarded as a subset of the larger category of 'contracts for services' – which might or might not be for personal performance; and even that larger category has not really acquired a clear typical identity, as it has tended to be recognized in negative contradistinction to the contract of employment rather than in its own right. In those other European legal systems which formulated a Civil Code, and in doing so drew upon the Roman law distinction between the *locatio conductio operarum* and the *locatio conductio operis*, a somewhat stronger identification emerges; as mentioned earlier in this chapter, the modern equivalents of the *locatio conductio operis* are more clearly identified in their own right, and more directly focused upon the contract for services for personal performance.

Building on these admittedly rather shallow foundations, we can nevertheless, if only by means of inference, discern how English law gives rise to a paradigm for 'other personal work contracts', as do many continental European Civilian legal systems. This paradigm is that of the personal contract for services, namely a contract personally to carry out a particular task, by means of work or service provision, without entering into the general service of the purchaser of that work or service provision. We could refer to this paradigm as that of the 'personal task contract for services' or, less cumbersomely, simply as the 'personal task contract'. In English law the basic paradigm of the task contract for services has not generally differentiated between contracts which promise performance by the services provider in person and those which leave it to the services provider whether or not to provide the services in person. That differentiation between contracts for services in person and not in person has come into play only in the particular regulatory contexts of labour law and of the law of employment discrimination where the statutory formula has been used of 'any other contract [ie other than a contract of employment] for the personal execution of any work or labour'.

In its basic and classical form, the task contract for services is quite strongly differentiated from the contract of employment in its basic and classical form. The task contract for services, in its paradigmatic form, is a contract to produce a stated outcome by the input of work or services; as such its duration is defined by the outcome rather than by time, as is its relation between work or services and remuneration. Moreover, its manner of performance is a matter for the services provider, and, as we have indicated, that includes a freedom on the part of the services provider to decide whether to achieve the contractually stipulated outcome by personal performance or via the work of others.

However, the idea that 'other personal work contracts' have a single paradigmatic form and structure, consisting of the task contract for services, which is strongly and clearly differentiated from the contract of employment, is in truth no more than a notional one, at best a valid historical starting point rather than the characterization of a current reality. As soon as we focus in upon the *personal* task contract, and consider the way in which it is understood and constructed in specific modern regulatory contexts, we become aware of such a diversity of patterns and possibilities as to undermine the simple paradigm. This occurs in two particular ways or senses. Firstly, the apparent clear separation between the contract of employment and the personal task contract disappears; and, secondly, it becomes clear that there is a diversity of contracting patterns within the domain of 'other personal work contracts' which extends way beyond the direct interface between the contract of employment and the personal task contract. We shall enlarge upon those two phenomena in turn.

If we consider first the erosion of the separation between the contract of employment and the personal task contract, the point here is that, until the modern period of development of labour law from the early 1960s onwards, English law conferred almost unlimited freedom upon employers or purchasers of services – and, though often only nominally, upon workers or providers of services – to shape the structure of personal work contracts, both contracts of employment and other personal work contracts, as they saw fit. (This was a more extensive freedom than was conferred by many continental European legal systems, which were, very generally speaking, more prescriptive as to the forms and structures of personal work contracts.)[49]

The exercise of that freedom, as it were on both sides of the binary divide between contracts of employment and contracts for services, made it more and more difficult to maintain the distinction between the two contract types, as elements of outcome-based remuneration entered into the structure of contracts of employment, especially in industrial contexts but also in the emerging service sector,[50] while time-based contracting was always permissible for other personal work contracts. We could say that 'payment by results' gradually became almost as much of a feature of contracts of employment as of other personal work contracts.[51] On the other hand, the personal contract for services could be structured partly or even wholly on the basis of timed work remunerated as such, as may be the case with the contract of 'retainer' between solicitor and client.[52]

If we turn to consider the diversity of contracting patterns within the domain of 'other personal work contracts', a diversity extending beyond the direct interface between the contract of employment and the personal task contract, we find that the following very interesting evolutions seem to have occurred and to be occurring. Various kinds of new contract-types, with their associated contractual structures, seem to be identifying themselves within the domain of 'other personal work contracts'. We can usefully distinguish between, on the one hand, new contract-types and structures which are on a spectrum between the contract of employment and the non-personal contract for services and, on the other hand, other new

---

[49] On this point see the reconstruction and analysis carried out in the previous chapters, especially Chapters 1, 2, and 3. See in particular pp. 66–8 and 151–4. On the state of English law, cf. M. Freedland (2003) *The Personal Employment Contract*, Oxford: OUP, 306.

[50] *Pauley v. Kenaldo, Ltd* [1953] 1 All ER, 226.

[51] Cf. W. Brown (ed.) (1981) *The Changing Countours of British Industrial Relations*, Oxford: Blackwell, 115.

[52] *Halsbury's Laws of England* (2008) 5th ed. reissue, London: Lexis Nexis, Vol. 65(3) 'Solicitors', para. 763, 'meaning of "retainer"'.

contract-types and structures which are aside from that spectrum. It should, however, be observed that on the whole these evolutions seem to be more pronounced in some continental European legal systems than they are in English law. We proceed to enlarge upon these arguments.

If we consider firstly the evolution of new contract-types and structures which are on a spectrum between the contract of employment and the contract for services, we find that matters are in an interesting phase of development, the outcomes of which are rather uncertain. In English law, the legislator has since 1997, as we have previously seen, evoked the category of worker's contracts other than the contract of employment, this being the category of personal work contracts located by exclusion between, on the one hand, contracts of employment and, on the other hand, business-to-customer and professional-to-client personal work contracts. It is at the moment hard to say whether judicial and academic analysis will endow this negatively identified contract type with its own positive identity and structure. As we have previously indicated, there have been some tentative signs of the formulation of a contractual structure for this 'non-employee worker's contract' which is typified by reduced requirements of mutuality of obligation as compared with the rather tight requirements for contracts of employment; but it would be an exaggeration to say that a clear shape has emerged for this contract-type.

Some continental European legal systems seem to have gone somewhat further in articulating specific contract-types, with their associated structures, on the contract of employment/contract for services spectrum. In particular, there have been some experiments with the identification of a personal task contract for services as a conceptual vehicle for the conferring of some labour rights upon those working under such contracts. Perhaps the clearest example is the Italian *contratto a progetto*;[53] a rather more esoteric example is provided by the Portuguese *contrato de trabalho come regime especial*, a personal work contract identified by its association with a special social security regime for self-employed workers.[54] However, even for more taxonomically inclined continental European legal systems, it has not on the whole seemed very compelling to identify economically dependent personal work relations as novel contract-types as such; as we shall see in the next chapter, it has generally seemed more convincing to identify new types of personal work *status* in this area.

However, if the development of a diversity of specific types of 'other personal work contract' has been rather limited on the contract of employment/contract for services spectrum, it has been somewhat more extensive in other parts of the domain of other personal work contracts. As we have indicated earlier, it is of the greatest importance to realize that the evolutionary capacities of the domain of other personal work contracts are not confined to the carving of new notches on

---

[53] Cf. N. Countouris (2007) *The Changing Law of the Employment Relationship*, Aldershot: Ashgate, 71–81; cf. above Section 1.C.
[54] See European Foundation for the Improvement of Living and Working Conditions (2009) *Report on Self-employed workers: industrial relations and working conditions*, Dublin, at p. 34.

that linear spectrum. Those evolutionary capacities are being demonstrated, and are especially visible from a European comparative perspective, in the context particularly of multilateral personal work relations, both where: (1) there is a private sector intermediary between the worker or personal services provider and the end-user of his or her services; and also where (2) a public body or emanation of the state is involved in the personal work relation as the provider of employment services – in the sense of activity designed to place people in work – and/or as the provider or facilitator of training for work. We proceed to consider in more detail what has occurred and is occurring in those two (not mutually exclusive) contexts.

Let us begin then with the case where there is a private sector intermediary between the worker or personal services provider and the end-user of his or her services. Both as a matter of abstract theory and as a matter of comparative observation, it can be seen that there is a clear potential for the recognition of novel contract types in these multilateral personal work relations, contract types which, if they were deemed not to be contracts of employment, would logically fall within the category of 'other personal work contracts'. Indeed, it might be thought that in situations where there were multilateral personal work relations which did not fall within the bilateral contract types which are recognized as lying within the contract of employment/contract for services spectrum, there was a logic which would dictate that a novel contract type falling within the category of 'other personal work contracts' must be recognized, in order to avoid the conclusion that the worker has no personal work contract of any kind, and therefore falls outside all the statutory protections which are confined to those who have such contracts. That logic would permit a contracting out from labour law protections by the multilateralizing of the personal work relation.

In English law, there has been some disposition to accept that logic, but it must be said that the courts seem in recent years to have found it less than fully compelling. Thus, there was a stage at which the Employment Appeal Tribunal seemed disposed to treat the relations between a worker, the end-user of his services, and the labour-only subcontractor intermediary as amounting to an '*eiusdem generis*' contract,[55] though that was mainly to rationalize their view that there was no contract of employment as such. Latterly, there has been a tendency, in the context of temporary agency work relations, to deny the existence of a contract of employment between the worker and the end-user of his or her services, and on other occasions to deny the existence of a contract of employment between the worker and the intermediary employment agency, without regarding it as necessary for the court or tribunal to that the worker necessarily has a personal work contract of any kind with either the end-user or the agency.[56]

---

[55] *Construction Industry Training Board v. Labour Force Ltd* (1970) 3 All ER 220, 225. Cf. M. Freedland (2003) *The Personal Employment Contract*, Oxford: OUP, p. 44.

[56] Cf. *James v. London Borough of Greenwich* [2008] EWCA Civ 35; *Muschett v. HM Prison Service* [2010] EWCA Civ 25; Cf. P. Leighton and M. Wynn (2011) 'Classifying Employment Relationships – More Sliding Doors or a Better Regulatory Framework?' 40 *ILJ*, 5.

Many continental European legal systems, on the other hand, seem more accepting of the logic that a personal work contract must be devised to accord a legal construction to a multilateral personal work relation where the failure to do so would leave the worker without statutory protection. This may, of course, compel the finding of a contract of employment as such; but there are also indications that it will at least result in the formulation of some other kind of personal work contract. In some European legal systems, temporary agency workers have been regarded as having personal work contracts which, although close in nature to contracts of employment, have been distinctively different from 'standard' contracts of employment, sometimes so much so as to identify them as 'other personal work contracts'. This could probably have been said, for example, of the French *contrat de travail interimaire* (temporary agency work contract), though latterly the *'contrat de mission'* – the contract between the agency and the worker – has been more and more formally identified as a kind of *'contrat de travail á durée determinée'*, a fixed-term contract.[57]

This phenomenon of diversity of types of 'other personal work contracts', especially in the context of multilateral personal work relations, becomes more strongly evident where public employment services are involved, and where the personal work relations in question involve combinations of work with training for work. In English law, there seems to be some reluctance to formulate new contract types. In the leading case of *Edmonds v Lawson* (2000)[58], the Court of Appeal, in holding that a pupil barrister was not a 'worker' within the meaning of the National Minimum Wage legislation, decided that there must be deemed to have been some kind of contractual relationship between pupil and pupil-master, but declined to identify any specific contract-type. In the more recent case of *Flett v Matheson* (2006),[59] the Court of Appeal had to characterise the contractual relationship which arose in a 'Modern Apprenticeship' arising under a government scheme which created a tripartite arrangement between the apprentice, the employer, and a government-sponsored external training provider: declining to recognize this as a novel contract-type, the court simply decided that the involvement of the external training provider did not prevent the arrangement from being treated as a traditional contract of apprenticeship. Even as such, however, this provides an example of a personal work contract which is neither a contract of employment nor a contract for services but an 'other personal work contract' which is off the linear spectrum between employment and self-employment.

In many continental European legal systems, there seems to be a stronger disposition to characterise such personal work relationships (including here arrangements for combined work and training) as novel kinds of 'other personal work contracts', at least in the sense of employment contracts which are so distinct from 'standard' ones as to fall effectively within the domain of 'other personal work

---

[57] J. Pélissier, A. Supiot, A. Jeammaud (2008) *Droit du Travail*, 24th ed., Paris: Dalloz, at 470. See above p. 165.

[58] [2000] ICR 567.

[59] [2006] EWCA Civ 53; [2006] IRLR 277.

contracts'. There is for example a real proliferation of such contracts in French law and governmental practice; in addition to the fairly traditional *contrat d'apprentissage*, there have also been a *contrat de professionnalisation*,[60] a *contrat d'insertion Revenue Minimum d'Activité*,[61] and a *contrat jeune en entreprise*.[62] The articulation of these contract types – which represent the legal constructs accorded to a set of arrangements for work and training involving employing enterprises and public employment services – demonstrates a methodology of regulation by designing personal work contracts which is scarcely practiced by British governments and might indeed be regarded as so prescriptive as to be antithetical to the approach and spirit of English contract law. That observation leads on to some reflections about the role of requirements of intention, formality, and legality in the formation of 'other personal work contracts' which will be developed in the next subsection.

## B. Intention, Formality, and Legality in Formation

In the previous subsection we argued that a satisfactory account of the way in which 'other personal work contracts' are structured and characterized, whether in English law or in other European legal systems, has to be very attentive to the particular and diverse regulatory contexts in which that structuration and characterization takes place. We saw how the impression that there might be a general paradigm for other personal work contracts – consisting of a personal task contract for services – was largely, though not entirely, dispelled by analysis in specific regulatory contexts, so that it emerged as a paradigm which existed only at the rather abstract and a-contextual level of 'general contract law'. In this subsection, we will argue for an account of the treatment of intention, formality, and legality in the formation of 'other personal work contracts' which is even more strongly dependent upon the different regulatory contexts in which those concepts are deployed.

The notion of 'regulatory contexts' which we are invoking is such that the legal construction of personal work relations and personal work contracts may and often does take place in an enormous number and variety of specific regulatory contexts. Thus, in the present instance, we could say that there are many dozens of statutory contexts in which questions arise as to the contractual intentions of those entering into personal work relations which do not qualify as contracts of employment, as to the role of formality in the making of such arrangements, and as to the contractual legality of the arrangements which are so made. It seems useful and appropriate to group the specific regulatory contexts of both statute law and judge-made common law into three broad regulatory contexts, and to suggest that we can identify a distinctive regulatory approach in each of these contexts. The three broad regulatory contexts are those of: (1) general private contract law; (2) social security law and

---

[60] *Ordonnance no. 2006–433 du 13 avril 2006 relative à l'expérimentation du contrat de transition professionnelle,* as modified by *loi no. 2009–1437 du 24 novembre 2009.*
[61] Articles L 5134–74 à L 5134–99 *Code du Travail.*
[62] Details are to be found on the French public website *Avis Droit Social,* available online at http://www.avis-droit-social.net/insertion_professionnelle.php#cie. See also above p. 139.

the law of personal taxation; and (3) labour law including the law of employment discrimination and the law concerning health and safety at work. We proceed to develop the idea of different approaches to intention, formality, and legality in each of those regulatory contexts.

The first broad regulatory context to which we should make reference is that of general private contract law. We could think of this as the default context, that is to say the general underlying regulatory context in which requirements of intention, formality, and legality are articulated and applied if and to the extent that there is no specific regulatory context which imports its own distinctive considerations and dynamics. So in this default context, it follows that a certain kind of default position is taken up, which can be identified as the position of or under general private contract law. In English law certainly, and the same can be generally asserted for other European legal systems, that default position seems to be quite simply that, since 'other personal work contracts' do not in and of themselves constitute a distinctive genre of contracts, it is the general law of contracts at large, or at least the law applicable to services contracts in general, which determines what requirements of intention, formality, and legality apply to these contracts.

We might expect, and we do in reality find, that there are distinctive considerations and dynamics which bear upon the role of requirements of intention, formality, and legality in the other two broad regulatory contexts which we have identified, namely those of, on the one hand, social security law and the law of personal taxation, and, on the other hand, labour law including the law of employment discrimination and the law concerning health and safety at work. In both those two contexts, issues arise about avoidance or evasion of legal or other regulatory standards, which inform approaches to requirements of intention, formality, and legality with regard to other personal work contracts. Those issues about avoidance or evasion are distinct ones as between the two broad regulatory contexts, but, as we shall proceed to show, they intersect with each other.

In the context of social security law and the law of personal taxation, these issues arise from the fact that, in English law certainly and to a greater or lesser extent in other European legal systems, the social security and personal taxation regime is ordered in such a way as to create incentives both for employing enterprises and for working persons to construct their contractual relations as other personal work contracts rather than as contracts of employment.[63] Those incentives may be short-term ones, and it may be short-sighted on the part of working persons to respond to them – for example because they thereby receive inferior social security protection against longer-term risks and detriments – but those incentives are nevertheless quite strong ones. When employers and/or working persons do act upon those incentives, issues may arise as to whether there has been inappropriate avoidance, or evasion, of the social security and tax regime which applies to those working under

---

[63] For an English tax law perspective on the matter of employment status, cf. J. Freedman (2001) *Employed or Self-Employed? Tax Classification and the Changing Labour Market*, London: Institute of Fiscal Studies. For an Italian perspective cf. A. Uricchio (2006) *I Redditi dei Lavori tra Autonomia e Dipendenza*, Bari: Cacucci.

contracts of employment, and those issues may be addressed by and through the imposing of requirements of intention, formality and legality in the making of other personal work contracts.[64]

Similar but distinct issues about avoidance or evasion of regulatory standards arise in the context of labour law. The same set of incentives, coupled with some possibilities for trading labour law protections against short-term enhancements of the terms and conditions of work, operate to intensify the dynamic towards constructing personal work relations as other personal work contracts rather than as contracts of employment. The legislature or the courts could seek to control that dynamic of avoidance or evasion of regulatory standards in the ways that they fashion the requirements of intention, formality, and legality with regard to other personal work contracts. We proceed to consider how far and in what ways they have actually done so.

In more than one sense, in English law there has been a hesitancy or even a reluctance to pursue an anti-avoidance or anti-evasion approach to the analysis of intention in the formation of other personal work contracts, whether in the regulatory context of tax and social security law or in that of labour law. Almost to the contrary, there seems to be some disposition to take at face value choices apparently made by working persons to regard their work relations as those of self-employment, and so to cast their contracts in the mould of other personal work contracts rather than contracts of employment. One particular sense in which the courts express that disposition consists in sometimes taking the view that where working persons have intended their personal work contracts to be constructed so that they will be regarded as self-employed persons for tax and social security purposes, they cannot be allowed to 'approbate and reprobate' by then claiming employment rights on the footing that their contracts should be regarded as contracts of employment.[65]

Another sense in which the courts have expressed that disposition consists in the way that they have brought to bear the notion of the 'sham contract' upon their analysis of the intentions of working persons and their employers in the making of their contractual arrangements. The notion of the 'sham contract' can be used, in the regulatory contexts with which we are concerned, to express and act upon the conclusion that the parties have presented their contractual arrangements as being some form of personal work contract or set of work contracts which is not a contract of employment, when their intentions were to make arrangements which correctly understood amount to a contract of employment. So the notion of the 'sham contract' provides a particular kind of control upon avoidance or evasion of regulation attaching to contracts of employment; it provides something which is between an intention control and a legality control upon the making of other personal work contracts. However, it is a rather limited control, and the

---

[64] Cf. *Usetech Ltd v. Young (Inspector of Taxes)* [2004] All ER; Cf. also L. Oats and P. Sadler (2008) 'Tax and the Labour Market: Taxing Personal Services Income in the UK', *Journal of Applied Law and Policy*, 59.
[65] Cf. *Young & Woods Ltd v. West* [1980] IRLR 201.

courts have not hitherto seemed ready to use it in a purposive way to deal with situations where the apparent intentions of working persons, to construct their work relations as personal work contracts other than employment contracts, have been formed under pressure from their contractual counterparts.[66]

Finally on this theme, we may discern yet another instance of the same judicial disposition in the approach to requirements of formality. In Chapter 4, reference was made to the significance of the statutory requirements for employers to provide workers with written particulars of certain terms of employment – a set of requirements which applies to employees under contracts of employment. One could imagine the possibility of an instrumentally inclusive approach to the interpretation of the reach of those requirements into the penumbral region of personal work contracts which are on the borderline between contracts of employment and other personal work contracts. The actual dynamic of judicial interpretation of these statutory requirements is to the contrary effect – the restriction of the requirements to employees under contracts of employment has been taken very literally and has been very strictly applied, for example in the pre-eminently significant case of *Carmichael v National Power plc.*[67]

Examples of different approaches are to be found in other European jurisdictions. Sometimes, as discussed in Chapters 2 and 4 of the present work, legislation specifically controls the avoidance or evasion of the regulation of labour law by the casting of personal work arrangements in the form of personal work contracts other than contracts of employment. In many systems, there is a robust approach to 're-qualification' of other personal work contracts as contracts of employment by reference to what is presumed to be the true intention of the contracting parties, even if that involves some conflict with the indications from contractual forms which the parties have adopted. Such controls often go further than that which has hitherto been exerted in English law in the name of 'sham contracts'.[68]

The foregoing discussion hinges in part upon those differences in approach, as between European labour law systems, to which we have adverted in earlier chapters, with regard to the relationship between the doctrinal and statutory foundations of labour law on the one hand and general private contract law on

---

[66] Cf. M. Pilgerstorfer and S. Forshaw (2008) 'A Dog's Dinner? Reconsidering Contractual Illegality in the Employment Sphere', 37, *ILJ*, 279. See also above Chapter 4, III and cf. *Autoclenz Ltd v Belcher* [2011] UKSC 40.

[67] [1999] ICR 1226 (HL) – the worker's claim was to statutory particulars of her terms and conditions of employment under ERA 1996, s.1; because of the way in which that entitlement was confined to continuous contractual employment relations, this claim could be used to test the worker's entitlement to a wider range of statutory employment rights which were subject to the same restrictions. The House of Lords was conspicuously unwilling to give an expansive interpretation to these requirements even when those substantive employment rights were not directly at issue. Cf. H. Collins (2000) 'The Employment Rights of Casual Workers', 29, *ILJ*, 73.

[68] We regard legislation such as Italian Law N. 1369/1960, prohibiting various forms of labour only subcontracting and job intermediation, as the high watermark of this genre of continental approach to controlling some of the attempts to depart, consensually or not, from the standard format of the contract of employment. See further, N. Countouris (2007) *The Changing Law of the Employment Relationship*, Aldershot: Ashgate, 5–7; and see also above, n. 66.

the other. We continue by pursuing the discussion of those differences into the treatment of the performance and termination of other personal work contracts.

## Section 3: Performance and Termination

We have indicated in earlier chapters, and particularly in Chapters 5 and 6, that we regard as somewhat arbitrary the division of the regulation of personal work contracts into the three areas or phases of formation and structure, content and performance, and termination and transformation; and we have made the point that it is a division which is made rather differently as between various European legal systems. This observation is as true for other personal work contracts as for contracts of employment; but in a rather different sense, because in this instance, instead of being a way of organizing a great mass of regulatory and doctrinal material, this division represents an attempt to impart shape and form to a rather thin body of material. But that paucity of material only increases the need for a plan of conceptual organization, so we make use of that method of division in order to complete our account or overview of the law of other personal work contracts.

### A.  Performance and Content

When we turn, with the above-mentioned caveat, from consideration of the formation and structure of other personal work contracts to consideration of their performance and content, we have an even more heightened sense of the fragmentary character of their regulation as contracts, and of the rather speculative nature of our analysis of that regulation. Indeed, we could say that this is especially the case in English law by comparison with other European legal systems. We can make that assertion on the basis of several different, though interlocking, propositions.

Firstly, so far as the performance and content of other personal work contracts is concerned, the legal apparatus of interpretation or construction of these contracts is not, under English law, pervaded by a notion of 'good faith'. This is a real contrast with many other European legal systems where, in however loose a sense, underlying notions of performance in good faith are applicable. The general or default position of English contract law applies to such contracts in such a way as to negate the existence of a general doctrine of 'good faith' with regard to their content or performance. There follows from this a further divergence between the approach of English law and that of many other European legal systems which is quite striking in doctrinal or theoretical terms even if it is not very obvious or prominent in its practical consequences. This divergence concerns the continuity of construction and interpretation as between contracts of employment and other personal work contracts.

So far as contracts of employment are concerned, as we have seen in Chapter 5 of the present work, both in English contract law and in the contract law of many other European systems quite strong notions of obligation to loyalty and contractual co-operation apply to the employee, and in fairly recent years English contract law has evolved a notion of mutual obligation to trust and confidence which probably corresponds quite closely to an underlying notion of good faith in the content and performance of contracts of employment which is to be found in many other European jurisdictions. However, it follows from our foregoing arguments that in English law, this relatively intense form of good faith obligation in the context of contracts of employment is in quite sharp theoretical contrast with the asserted absence of a general notion of good faith in performance beyond that contractual sphere; whereas it equally follows from our foregoing arguments that in many other European systems, there may be a smoother incline from stronger forms of good faith obligation in the employment context to weaker forms of that obligation in the context of other personal work contracts. It is arguable that the obligation of mutual trust and confidence which English law recognizes as attaching to the performance of employment contracts should not be regarded as tightly confined to those contracts; but such an argument has to be made out against quite a steep gradient of doctrinal resistance, and is unlikely to yield more than an occasional and marginal spill-over of this obligation into the sphere of other personal work contracts.

A second aspect or manifestation of the fragmentary and inchoate character of regulation of the content and performance of contracts in this sphere consists in the limited role which is accorded to statutory norms in English law, again in some contrast with many other European systems.[69] In English law, statutory regulation has actually been extended rather significantly from the sphere of contracts of employment into the sphere of other personal work contracts in the last thirty years – to all such contracts with regard to the control of equal pay and employment discrimination, and to the subset of 'workers' contracts' with regard to protection of wages, working time regulation, minimum wage, and parity of treatment of part-time workers with full-time workers. However, we have previously remarked upon the way in which these have remained as layers of regulation which are quite separate from the layer of regulation which is regarded as contractual even so far as the contract of employment is concerned. Still less have these statutory norms managed to permeate the bedrock of contractual regulation so far as other personal work contracts are concerned. That is to say, those norms do not seem to have shaped the basic understanding of the content of those contracts and of the nature of the obligations of their performance.

Another and very different manifestation of the limited role accorded to statutory norms, and their failure to influence the core conceptualization of the content of other personal work contracts, consists in the fact that it has remained very unclear how far the whole statutory apparatus of control of unfair contract terms is applicable to other personal work contracts – and indeed, to the extent that it is applicable, whether and when it is the working person or the counter-party to the contract who enjoys the protection of that legislation.

---

[69] A noteworthy example of the higher level of taxonomical coherence of some continental systems can be found in the lucid monograph of A. Ojeda Avilés (2010) *La Deconsrtucción del Derecho del Trabajo*, Madrid: La Ley.

The third aspect which we wish to single out, of the fragmentary and inchoate character of regulation of the content and performance of contracts in this sphere, consists in the fact that, in English law, there is very little by way of topical regulation of the content or performance of specific kinds of other personal work contracts, and certainly not enough to begin to assemble a series even of fragments of topical regulation from which a composite body of regulation could be deduced. In this respect a contrast can be drawn with some other European systems in which, as noted in the earlier sections of the present chapter, such patches of topical or contract-specific bodies of regulation of content and performance do seem to exist. So far as English law is concerned, there is one exception which can be pointed out, namely that there is a body of regulation of the content and performance of contract between commercial agent and principal; but it is an exception which proves the rule in the sense that, as noted above in section 1B of this chapter, it has been created only by way of compliance with an EU Directive rather than as the result of domestic evolution within English law itself.

We proceed to consider the corresponding, and even more obscure, situation with regard to the termination and transformation of other personal work contracts.

## B. Termination and Transformation

With regard to the termination and transformation of other personal work contracts, it must be said that it is even more difficult than it was with regard to their content and performance to identify anything remotely approaching an established body of regulation by or under contract law – such regulation is very fragmentary and its conceptual shape remains largely unresolved. Again, as with performance and content, we make that assertion on several different though intersecting grounds. It is an assertion which can be confidently made for English law, but probably to a great extent for other European legal systems too.

In English law, it is very much easier to say what the regulation of contract law excludes than to identify what it includes with regard to the termination and transformation of other personal work contracts. The statute law of unfair dismissal – which in any event we have described in an earlier chapter as being separate and distinct from contract law – applies only to employees working under contracts of employment. The crucial legislation so far as transformation of contracts is concerned – the TUPE Regulations – is limited in the same way.[70] The legislation controlling discrimination in employment does cover the termination of

---

[70] In the current version, namely the Transfer of Undertakings (Protection of Employment) Regulations 2006, the employment transfer effect of the Regulations is provided by regulation 4 which applies to 'contracts of employment' defined by regulation 2(1) to mean 'any agreement between an employee and his employer determining the terms and conditions of his employment'. This, in our view, imposes a restriction of the transfer effect to contracts of employment as such, even though the definition of 'employee' in regulation 2(1) as meaning 'any individual who works for another person whether under a contract of service or apprenticeship or otherwise but does not include anyone who provides services under a contract for services' may be a somewhat wider one.

other personal work contracts as well as of contracts of employment; but the controls which it imposes, highly significant though they are, do not seem to have been recognized as part of the contract law of other personal work contracts, just as they have not, as we have seen, become part of the contract law applying to contracts of employment.

Moreover, if the statute law relating to the termination and transformation of contracts of employment is excluded from other personal work contracts, and if the employment discrimination legislation, although applicable to other personal work contracts, seems to have failed to establish itself as part of their contractual makeup, there is equally an exclusion, or marginalization, of much of the common law regulation which applies to the termination or transformation of contracts of employment, so far as other personal work contracts are concerned. Neither the common law of summary dismissal – that is to say the default terms giving the employer extensive contractual rights of summary dismissal in response to the employee's misconduct or want of capability – nor the common law of wrongful dismissal – that is to say the doctrines of contract law which define and limit both wrongful dismissal and the remedies for it – would seem at all likely to extend beyond the contract of employment (although they are not as firmly confined to the contract of employment as the statute law of unfair dismissal is).

In English law, that seems to leave something of a vacuum as to what are the applicable rules and principles regarding the termination and transformation of other personal work contracts, with nothing much more to fill it than some specific regulation of termination of the contracts of commercial agents, which, as we have said, exists only by reason of the need to comply with an EU Directive. Beyond that, the analysis is an almost entirely speculative one. How far is there an adapted form of the obligation of mutual trust and confidence which might apply to the termination of other personal work contracts, given that the exclusion of that doctrine from the law of wrongful dismissal seems to apply only to contracts of employment? How far is there an adapted form of the doctrine of non-transferability of contracts of employment which was overtaken by the TUPE Regulations for contracts of employment as such but might survive and apply to some other personal work contracts? How far if at all are other personal work contracts presumed to be terminable by reasonable notice in the way that contracts of employment are underlyingly so presumed to be? There is no conclusive answer to any of those questions. The foregoing observation, that there is in effect an almost empty space at the heart of our analysis of the contract law of other personal work contracts, leads on to the conclusion of this chapter as a whole.

## Section 4: The Narrowness of the Contractual Perspective

The arguments and analyses which we have put forward in the course of the foregoing sections have increasingly and cumulatively pointed up the essential paucity or thinness of the material upon the basis of which we have been seeking to put together an account of the contract law of other personal work contracts, especially so far as English law is concerned. For some who read these arguments and analyses, that might seem to indicate the futility, and even the inappropriateness, of our endeavour to create an account of the contract law of other personal work contracts in the first place. Such critics might regard this as the predictable outcome of trying to construct a particular legal narrative which has no authentic place in the doctrinal discourse of labour law.

We draw a different conclusion. We believe that the discovery of this particular legal vacuum demonstrates the narrowness of the contractual perspective, and the inadequacy of the contractual frame of reference as one from which or within which to survey and understand the legal construction, and therefore the legal regulation, of personal work relations. It is this which is vividly displayed by the rather unconvincing outcome of our effort to analyse the legal construction of a certain large set of personal work relations – those falling beyond the sphere of employment contracts – through the medium of contract law. Our view is not that there is no legal construction and almost no meaningful legal regulation of that large set of personal work relations, but rather that the legal construction and legal regulation which does exist is obscured or even concealed when one looks at it from a purely contractual perspective. It is that narrowness, and even distortion, of vision which we seek to address or correct in the remaining chapters of this work.

As a first step in that direction, and as a way of enlarging our understanding of the conceptual and practical vacuum which has been encountered in the earlier sections of this chapter, we suggest that it will be useful to bring to bear upon our analysis some crucial insights which were provided by Gerard Lyon-Caen (1990) in his pioneering monograph *Le droit du travail non salarié*.[71] His purpose in that work, as is part of ours in this work, was to provide an account of the law of personal work relations other than those of employment which would be complementary to the account of the law of employment relations which forms the subject matter of labour law itself.[72] He pursues the hypotheses that it may in this way be possible to construct '*un droit du travail non salarié sur le modèle du droit du travail (salarié)*' – labour law for workers other than employees on the model of labour law (for employees) – and also to some extent to discover 'legal principles which are common to employment and work other than employment'.[73]

His methodology, like ours in this chapter, was to take as his starting point the contractual basis for *le droit du travail non salarié*. He therefore initially considers as we have done the boundary between contracts of employment, that is to say

---

[71] G. Lyon-Caen (1990) *Le droit du travail non salarié*, edns. Paris: Sirey – (*DTNS*). Since that pioneering work, other authors have no doubt contributed to this particular aspect of the labour law debate, both domestically, and from comparative and European perspective. We refer the readers to the works by A. Couret *et al.* (1996), *Les Frontières du salariat – actes du colloque org. les 26 et 27 oct. 1996 à l'Université de Cergy-Pontoise*, Paris: Dalloz; P. Morgado Panadero (ed.) (2010), *Empleo, trabajo autonomo y economia social*, Madrid: Comares; also A. Ojeda Avilés (2010) *La Deconsrtucción del Derecho del Trabajo*, Madrid: La Ley.

[72] His account was confined to French law and EU law, rather in the way that ours is based primarily on English law but extends to EU law and makes some comparisons with other European national legal systems.

[73] Lyon-Caen, n. 71 above, pp. 7–9. Our translation of the original French.

contracts for *travail salarié* and contracts for personal work in other forms, that is to say contracts for *travail non salarié*,[74] and his construction of the '*régime du travail non salarié*' which forms the second part of his work is a primarily contractual one. He found the elaboration of this construction as difficult as we have done, remarking upon the extreme lack of coherence of the fragments of legal regulation which he was trying to assemble together,[75] and, at another point in the work, upon the sheer multiplicity of the forms which contracts for *travail non salarié* may take.[76]

However, Lyon-Caen was by no means defeated in his undertaking by the shortcomings of a purely contractual analysis of *le droit du travail non salarié* – as we too hope not to be. On the contrary, he had a number of profound insights into the various ways in which it was on the one hand necessary but also on the other hand possible to transcend the restrictions of contractual analysis in order to arrive at a deeper understanding of the basis or bases of *le droit du travail non salarié*. To this end, he drew a distinction between '*le travailleur independent individuel*' and '*le travail non salarié exercé en société*', which we may respectively translate as 'the individual independent worker' and 'personal work in a joint enterprise'.[77] In successive subsections we briefly consider the insights which are afforded by Lyon-Caen's analyses under those two headings.

## A.  The Individual Independent Worker

In Lyon-Caen's dual conception of the regime for personal work other than as an employee, this first division – that of *le travail independent individual*,[78] individual independent work – is easier to understand for English lawyers and to assimilate to the thought patterns of English law, if only because it is built on contractual foundations.[79] But for Lyon-Caen this infrastructure of bilateral contracts between the individual independent worker and his or her clients – in his view consisting of a multiplicity of contract types according to the professional activity in question[80] – is itself overlaid by other legal structures. Those other legal structures include the *rapports collectifs de travail*, the collective relations of work which consist of the apparatuses of regulation or collective self-regulation which are maintained through or by professional bodies or trade associations.[81] They also include the important

[74]  See *DTNS* pp. 1–4 in which the author reflects upon: '*l'opposition: travail salarié, travail non salarié*', and the first title of the work on '*Les incertitudes de la distinction en droit Français*'.

[75]  He speaks at one point of '*une poussière de réglementations*', p. 7.

[76]  Ibid., at p. 115.

[77]  Ibid., p. 104: '*Il est tentant de presenter la théorie juridique du travail non salarié en ramenant celui-ci à l'entrepreneur individual. Mais chacun sait qu'un nombre croissant d'activités sont exercées en société*'.

[78]  This is a notion which for Lyon-Caen is effectively synonymous with that of *L'activité professionnel*, cf. pp. 105, 107.

[79]  Ibid. p. 107 where he refers to it as having the legal construct of '*une prestation exécuté dnas le cadre d'un contrat*', and cf. p. 115 – '*L'activité professionnel s'exerce à travers des contrats, comme le salariat s'exerce à travers le contrat de travail.*'

[80]  He proposes a system of classification of these contract types at pp. 117–21, whereby they are divided into '*contrats de services*', '*contrats portant sur les biens*', and '*sous-traitance*'.

[81]  Ibid., pp. 133–6: '*L'organisation corporative*'.

structuration which is provided by the social security system as it applies to individual independent workers – that is to say, loosely speaking, to the self-employed.[82]

This is relatively familiar territory for labour lawyers generally, and for those operating within the mind-set of English labour law. Lyon-Caen also introduces a further dimension of the regime for individual independent work which is harder to grasp from an English law perspective – it is that of *patrimoine et revenu profession-nels*.[83] The latter term translates well enough as 'income from professional activity', but the former is much more difficult; perhaps the best equivalent is 'professional capital' – it conveys the notion that the worker's occupation has a proprietary aspect or dimension.[84] It is an idea combining notions such as those of *la clientèle* – the goodwill of a business – *le fonds de commerce* – roughly speaking the assets of a business – and that of *offices ministériels* – office-holding as a quasi-proprietary or fully proprietary concept.

Lyon-Caen regarded these as notions which were coming together or should be brought together in the formation of a full and rounded understanding of the juridical regime for individual independent work. It is especially interesting that he regarded as significant, in this melting pot of legal concepts, the then recent legislative introduction to French law of the *société unipersonelle*[85] – the one-person company – as an expression of a trend towards the recognition of individual independent work as a form of business organization with assets distinguishable from the purely personal ones of the worker in question, rather than simply as a congeries of personal work contracts. This very innovative perception leads on in turn to his second set of novel insights into the evolving nature of *le droit du travail non salarié*, which is considered in the next subsection.

## B. Personal Work in a Joint Enterprise

If, in those reflections on the dimensions of individual independent work relations which were beyond contract Lyon-Caen was treading an unfamiliar path and breaking new ground, this was doubly the case with his further perception that there was a whole emergent domain of *le travail non salarié exercé en société*, which we translate as 'personal work in a joint enterprise'.[86] A fully exact translation is difficult, because the idea of work *exercé en société* has strong connotations of work carried out in the framework of a corporate organization, but our perception is that it has to be viewed as a somewhat broader notion of work carried out in some form

---

[82]    Ibid., pp. 140–9: '*Protection Sociale*'.

[83]    Ibid., pp. 124–32. The author asserts that this topic is under-recognized and under-theorized even in French law which is his source: '*Une theorie du patrimoine et du revenu professionnels reste a faire. Elle fait cruellement defaut*' (p. 124).

[84]    Labour lawyers should not be deterred by this; it is an idea vigorously pursued into the domain of employment itself by Wanjiru Njoya in her monograph (2007) *Property in Work – The Employment Relationship in the Anglo-American Firm*, Aldershot: Ashgate.

[85]    As constituted in French law in the form of the '*Entreprise unipersonnelle à responsabilité limitée (EURL)*' by the *loi du 11 juillet 1985* – see *DTNS* at p. 125.

[86]    Delineated and analysed in *DTNS* at pp. 153–93.

of equal or joint association with others, at least in a comparative context in which such forms of association may be less tightly tied to the idea of incorporated legal personality, and more able to reside in constructs of unincorporated association or partnership. Lyon-Caen is well aware of this difficulty or ambiguity in his construct; he says very elegantly that: 'The massive importance of legal personality [*personnalité morale*] causes some disturbance in the legal regime for work other than employment', and he develops his idea of '*le travail non salarié exercé en société*' as an intimate combination of the two notions of '*le travail associé*' (which we may translate as 'work in association or partnership with others') and '*la role de la personnalité morale*'.[87]

Within the particular conceptual space which he has thus created, Lyon-Caen explores, in the compass of French law, two emerging species or locations of '*le travail non salarié exercé en société*' – personal work in a joint enterprise. On the one hand, he identifies the impressive number of types of corporate vehicle which had been created for the for the conduct of '*le travail associé*', such as the older '*sociétés civiles professionnels*'[88] and the multiplicity of newer types confirmed or created by the Law of 29 November 1966.[89] On the other hand – and this is an even more provocative suggestion – he discerns the emergence of a distinctive body of law describing a genre of personal work relations which he designates as '*le travail de gestion*'.[90] Again this defies exact translation in a comparative legal context, but it amounts to the notion of work as a manager of and organic office-holder in, but not as an employee of, a business organization – therefore, in terms of English law, most obviously as a non-executive company director, but the equivalence may not be complete.[91]

This elaborate and highly innovative construct which Lyon-Caen devised has much to offer to our present work. It heightens the sense of the contestability of the project upon which he was engaged in that monograph, and of our rather similar project in this work, because it demonstrates the way in which these projects bring into, or at least onto the edges of, the sphere of labour law a set of personal work relations traditionally regarded as beyond that sphere both in a descriptive and in a normative sense – starting to introduce new clients into the protectorate of labour law whose admissibility would be denied from a traditional standpoint. This was a danger of which Lyon-Caen was very conscious; he alludes to it at the end of his monograph, as we will do in the Conclusion to ours.[92]

Of more immediate significance, however, to our concerns in this chapter has been the way in which Lyon-Caen's innovative constructs have substantiated our

---

[87] Ibid., at p. 153.
[88] Ibid., at pp. 158–60.
[89] Ibid., at pp. 160–8. A somewhat similar, though perhaps more specific, constitutive role was played in English law by the Limited Liability Partnerships Act 2000.
[90] Ibid., at pp. 170–93.
[91] The role is that of '*dirigeant mandataire*' – see ibid. at p. 170 – which is contrasted with that of '*directeur salarié*', the latter probably having its equivalent in English law in the executive or senior manager who is not a director of the company.
[92] Ibid., Conclusion, p. 195; and below, Conclusion, pp. 433–46.

hypothesis that an adequate account of the legal construction of personal work relations beyond the scope of the contract of employment cannot be provided on a purely contractual basis – a further and more richly resourced set of analyses turns out to be required, of the kind that he provided in the context of French law. Moreover, his analysis had, as he clearly perceived, significant implications not just in its immediate location of *le droit du travail non salarié* but also for its counterpart domain of *le droit du travail salarié* itself – for example, he was concerned to point out how far *le travail de gestion* could, exceptionally in the eyes of French law, be combined with the holding of a contract of employment.[93] In this way, Lyon-Caen's monograph anticipates and encourages the scepticism about the sufficiency of a contractual analysis of personal work relations which we have developed and expressed, not only in this chapter in the context of personal work contracts other than the contract of employment but also in earlier chapters with regard to the contract of employment itself.[94] That scepticism, and the resulting identification of the need to provide a more overarching legal construction of personal work relations, form the starting points for the remaining parts of our present work.

---

[93] Ibid., pp. 186–93 '*Cumul d'un mandat social et d'un contrat de travail*'.

[94] Comparative work along analytical trajectories that share some of Lyon-Caen's concerns has more recently emerged in other jurisdictions. Cf. A. Ojeda Avilés (2010) *La Deconsrtucción del Derecho del Trabajo*, Madrid: La Ley.

# 8

# Contract, Relation, and Nexus in the Legal Construction of Personal Work Relations

## Introduction

This chapter has a key function in this work. Its point of departure is found in the preceding chapters, which increasingly pointed up the difficulties and shortcomings of the legal construction of personal work relations in purely contractual terms – that was specially evident in the immediately preceding chapter on other personal work contracts. So in this chapter the attempt is made to propose an approach to the legal constructions of personal work relations which would address those difficulties and shortcomings.

That approach is set forth and explained in two stages. At the first stage (in Section 1), the ideas of 'the personal work relation' and 'the personal work nexus' are developed as generic concepts, and it is suggested that these concepts provide the foundational elements for an analysis of the legal construction of personal work relations which transcends the restrictions of the existing contractual construction of most such relations. At the second stage (in Section 2), it is shown how those concepts can be applied in specific personal work situations; for this purpose, the theory of layered regulation which was introduced earlier in Chapter 3 of the present work is further developed.

The development of this approach in the present chapter will, we hope, be regarded as making possible and leading on to proposals in subsequent chapters for, firstly, a particular way of reconsidering the binary divide between the two main types of personal work contract (Chapter 9) and finally for reconsidering the role of EU law and European comparative law in the legal construction of personal work relations (Chapter 10). So a great deal turns on the arguments of the present chapter.

## Section 1:  The Personal Work Relation and the Personal Work Nexus as Generic Concepts

### A.  The Shortcomings of the Contractual Analysis of Personal Work Relations

As we indicated in the short Introduction to this chapter, the preceding set of chapters increasingly pointed up some significant shortcomings of the contractual analysis of personal work relations. When we speak of shortcomings, we refer to obstacles to the obtaining of a full understanding of the ways in which personal work relations are legally constructed and legally regulated, those two being inseparably connected. It is our view that when the legal construction of personal work relations is analysed from a solely contractual perspective, the vision which is obtained is apt to be an incomplete or distorted one. This we suggest is true both with regard to the understanding of the legal construction of personal work relations in any one legal system and with regard to the conducting of meaningful comparisons between legal constructions of personal work relations in different European legal systems. It will be the task of this chapter to propose an alternative mode of analysis which seeks to avoid those shortcomings; a first step is to identify those shortcomings more fully.

In identifying the shortcomings of contractual analysis which we encountered in the preceding chapters, it is useful to distinguish between shortcomings in the analysis of the legal construction of personal work relations within a single legal system and those which present themselves when we attempt to make a comparative analysis as between European national legal systems. So we begin with the shortcomings of analysis which were encountered in relation to a single legal system, that of English law. In relation to English law, our findings have been that the contractual analysis of personal work relations creates or encourages an understanding of the legal construction of those relations which is unduly narrow and overly dichotomized in several crucial respects.

Firstly, in English law the contractual analysis of personal work relations has developed as a very dominant one. This has encouraged an approach to the legal construction of personal work relations according to which those relations are viewed as normally, and indeed almost exclusively, having the legal character of individual contracts rather than being in the nature of individual or collective relationships. So this approach is one which insists upon a dichotomy between the contractual and the relational, and another dichotomy between the collective and the individual, and which places personal work relations firmly on the contractual and individual sides of those dichotomies.

Secondly – and this is a finding very closely associated with the first one – in English law the dominance of the contractual analysis of personal work relations has taken the form of an imposed view of personal work relations as falling within one of two rather monolithic contract types – the contract of employment and the personal contract for services. This in our suggestion is another overly dichotomized approach to the understanding of the legal construction of personal work relations which gives rise to an unduly narrow view of the process and dynamics of that legal construction.

Thirdly, English law in its analysis of personal work relations makes a further deep dichotomy as to the sources of regulation; this is the deep dichotomy between common law and statute law, that is to say between judicial casuistic regulation and legislative regulation. Our finding, as emerging from the analysis carried out in earlier chapters, has been that this dichotomy is deeply built into the construction of personal work relations as contracts. That contractual analysis brings about a view of personal work relations as being legally constructed by and around the common law of contracts in general and of the contract of employment in particular. In another words, there is a marked dichotomy between the common-law-based doctrines of contract law and the regulations which are superimposed upon that by statute law. Some legislative interventions are seen as being directly modificatory of the common law of contracts in general or the common law of the contract of employment in particular; but very often legislative interventions are seen as being quite dissociated from the contractual analysis, existing on the far side of the dichotomy between contract law and statute law. The most vivid examples of such dissociation have emerged in Chapter 6, in respect of the analysis of the regulatory framework sustaining the substantive and procedural rules for the termination of contracts of employment.

Finally, there is another dichotomy which is built into the contractual analysis of personal work relations; it is the dichotomy between the relations of public law and those of private law. Although English law generally avoids a very sharp distinction between public law and private law,[1] there is a real sense in which the contractual analysis of personal work relations does feed into a real public law/private law dichotomy. That is to say, the overwhelmingly prevailing construction of personal work relations as contractual ones, coupled with the location of contract law in the domain of private law, marks out almost all those relations as ones of private law – and effectively excludes from view the remaining ones which survive as relations of public law because and so far as they cannot be fitted into the contractual analysis.

Moreover, these dichotomies and restrictions upon vision, which are such strong features of English law's contractual analysis of personal work relations, quite often operate in mutually intensifying and self-reinforcing ways. Thus, the dichotomy between contract and relationship combines with the binary divide between employment and self-employment to produce a particularly strong separation between the contract of employment and all personal work relations which do not fall into the category of the contract of employment. The dichotomy between common law regulation and statutory regulation tends to become aligned with that set of distinctions and to reinforce it; in English law the legal constructs which are generated by statutory regulation, in the sphere of personal work, more often take

---

[1] Cf. M. R. Freedland (2006) 'The Evolving Approach to the Public/Private Distinction in English Law', in M.R. Freedland and J.B. Auby (eds.), *The Public-Private Divide – Une Entente Assez Cordiale?*, Oxford: Hart Publishing, 93.

the form of novel relational forms than of novel contractual forms, though the latter are by no means unknown. Yet a further effect of mutual reinforcement as between these various tendencies used to occur (though less commonly does today) when the fact that employment took place under a statutory scheme of regulation was seen as identifying a relationship of public law rather than a private law contract of employment.

From this rather restricted viewpoint, our survey of the contractual construction of personal work relations did indeed seem to produce a somewhat incomplete and fragmented vision so far as English law was concerned. With regard to those personal work relations which are constructed as contracts of employment, it proved difficult, from within the framework of the contractual analysis, to comprehend or do analytical justice to a great body of statutory regulation. With regard to those personal work relations which are not constructed as contracts of employment, it was rather difficult, from within that framework of analysis, to identify anything amounting to a body of regulation at all – we found ourselves caught in something of a regulatory vacuum.

This sense, that there were serious shortcomings in the analysis of the legal construction of personal work relations from a contractual perspective, was only intensified when we tried to extend that analysis in a European comparative dimension. In this larger arena, there was a further set of problems; it consisted of the possibility that, from the restricted perspective of contractual analysis, apparently equivalent legal constructions of personal work relations might present themselves, which would, on a more holistic view, be revealed as 'false friends', that is to say not equivalent to each other at all. Thus, while it is a well-known problem that the boundary between contracts of employment and personal contracts for services may be differently drawn as between European legal systems, there turned out to be more insidious dangers that the dichotomy between 'contract' and 'relationship' may be differently conceived,[2] or that there may be nothing truly corresponding to the dichotomy which English law draws between the regulation and construction effected by 'common law' on the one hand and 'statute law' on the other.[3]

Our effort was to address these shortcomings as far as possible within the compass of contractual analysis. Thus we sought to create a scheme of contractual analysis of personal work relations which would be as open-minded as possible to the inherent 'unsatisfactoriness' of the binary divide between contracts of employment and personal contracts for services, and which would recognize that it was preferable to conceive of a family or loose grouping of personal work contracts composed of many rather than just two varieties of personal work contract. However, some of the analytical deficiencies, which we have identified above, remained impervious to remedy from within a solely contractual frame of reference.

---

[2] Cf. Section 1.A of Chapter 3, and more generally Chapters 1 and 2.
[3] An analysis of the concepts of 'false unities', 'false symmetries', and 'false opposites' was first developed in Section 2.A of Chapter 3.

In the next subsection, we begin to present suggestions for a scheme of analysis which might more fully address those remaining shortcomings.

## B. Concepts for a Different Method of Analysis

In this subsection, we seek to introduce and begin to put forward a scheme of analysis of the legal construction of personal work relations which will represent our attempt to transcend the restrictions and deal with the shortcomings of the primarily contractual analysis which has been developed earlier in this work. This alternative scheme of analysis has been in various ways foreshadowed in earlier chapters but can now be articulated in a more concrete form. Our suggested scheme of analysis asserts the need for a particular set of new conceptual organizing notions. As has been indicated in earlier chapters, we propose to use the ideas of 'personal work relation' and the 'personal work nexus'. We now seek to explain how those concepts function within our suggested scheme of analysis, and in particular how they can be deployed either as generic or as specific ones.

In order to explain further these two concepts, and the functions which our scheme of analysis assigns to them, we invoke the idea that an adequate scheme of analysis of the legal construction of personal work relations has to be envisaged as one which has to be conducted at two different levels. At each of these two levels, a particular kind of conceptualization of personal work relations take place. One of those two levels – let it be regarded as the macroscopic or 'macro' one – is a taxonomical level in which all personal work relations are mapped out and classified into categories. The other of those two levels – let it therefore be regarded as the microscopic or 'micro' one – is a structural level in which the structural features of particular personal work relations are identified or assigned.

The distinction which we are making between these two levels of analysis can usefully be imagined by thinking of these levels as degrees of focus or magnification of a map or design-diagram of the legal construction of personal work relations – choosing the degree of focus or magnification can be compared with zooming in on or zooming out from a design-diagram of personal work relations. If we zoom right out so that we are looking at the whole diagram of all personal work relations, we see it as a classificatory map which locates particular personal work relations as dots on the map – of each one of which we are taking an external view. If we zoom right in, we are looking – as it were internally – at particular personal work relations. So we have two focus-levels – a broad and distant focus-level on the macro-map of personal work relations in general and a narrow and close-up focus-level on the micro-map of particular personal work relations.

We suggest that such a scheme of analysis, taking place at these two focus-levels, corresponds to the processes of normative characterization of personal work relations which take place in actual legal systems and in the development of legal doctrine within and around those systems. We return in the next section of this chapter to the amplification of the idea of normative characterization. Suffice it to say at this stage that the developments of the legal construction of personal work relations which take place at these two focus-levels are of course integrally linked –

in other words, normative characterizations of personal work relations consist of the product of the formulations which take place on each of these two levels. Our scheme of analysis involves the separating of the two focus-levels in order to understand the composite construction better. It is in order to develop this scheme of analysis, at its two distinct levels, that we propose to deploy the notions of the 'personal work relation' and the 'personal work nexus'. As a preliminary to doing that, we need to explain slightly more fully the ways in which the legal construction of personal work relations takes place at each of those two levels.

In order further to explain this idea of the legal construction of personal work relations as taking place on two distinct levels, let us take the example – in fact the most obvious and paradigmatic example – of the legal construction of a certain large set of personal work relations as contracts of employment. Our dual-focus scheme of analysis sees this as involving, on the taxonomical (macro) level, the classification or characterization of that large set of personal work relations as contracts of employment – so that a certain area on a notional map of all personal work relations is designated as the area of contracts of employment. Our dual-focus scheme of analysis sees something different as occurring on the other, structural (micro), level. On that level, each personal work relation within that large set is assigned, or is identified as having, a certain normative shape or structure – for example, within a particular legal system, it might be assigned or identified as having the structure of being made between an individual employee and an individual employer or employing enterprise either for a fixed duration or for termination by reasonable notice, and as according the employer a certain degree of control over the way in which the employee works.

The giving of this example may serve to make our dual-focus scheme of analysis more comprehensible, but perhaps only at the cost of casting doubt on its utility. It will be obvious from this example that the aspects or parts of the process of legal construction which we have allocated to the two respective levels are fully interdependent, so that it cannot be said that the one is logically distinct from and prior to the other. In other words, we cannot say on which level we find the chicken and on which the egg in this process of the legal construction of a set of personal work relations as contracts of employment. So it may accordingly be wondered whether this separation of the process into two levels of focus is meaningful or helpful.

That doubt might well be warranted if the example which we have given were a complete and fully representative one – that is to say, if it depicted fully and accurately what is involved in the process of legal construction of a set of personal work relations. In fact, we envisage that process as being a far more complex one than is suggested by the example we have given – an example, therefore, which is an essentially over-simplified one. Those complexities will be explained in the next section of this chapter, when we return to the idea of normative characterization, and we hope that by so doing we will be able in turn to demonstrate the utility of our dual-focus scheme of analysis. However, even in advance of that explanation and justification, we hope to have developed our scheme of analysis far enough to enable us to demonstrate the need for and the role of the concepts of the 'personal work relation' and 'the personal work nexus' in that scheme. So we now proceed to attempt that demonstration.

Our argument is that, in order satisfactorily to carry out the dual-level scheme of analysis which we have outlined, and in order fully to understand the dual-level processes of prescriptive legal construction of personal work relations which are the subject of that analysis, we crucially need to be able to deploy two neutral or baggage-free analytical concepts or terminologies – and our suggestion is that the 'personal work relation' and the 'personal work nexus' are ones which fit that purpose well. When we refer to 'neutral or baggage-free' analytical concepts or terminologies, we have in mind the aspiration of avoiding terms which are invested with particular significance in the context of existing legal constructions – in other words, terms which 'take sides' in existing debates or dichotomies.

We have previously – much earlier in this work – committed ourselves to using the concept and terminology of 'the personal work relation' in just that way. We have deployed that terminology to identify a generic conception of all personal work arrangements in their legally constructed forms. It has appeared to work reasonably well in carrying the meaning we have sought to impose on it. However, now that we have made the distinction between the two focus-levels of our analysis, we find that a still more neutral or baggage-free conception and terminology is needed in order to frame and develop the analysis at the close-up focus-level at which we seek to understand the internal structure of particular personal work relations. It is the notion of the 'personal work nexus' which we have chosen to bear that quite heavy analytical burden. Our reasons for doing so, and the micro-level analysis itself, are developed more fully in the next section of this chapter.

## Section 2: The Personal Work Relation as a Complex Network or Nexus

In the previous section of this chapter, we reintroduced the idea of the personal work nexus into our scheme of analysis of the legal construction of personal work relations, and explained its role in that scheme of analysis. The personal work nexus was presented as a 'generic concept', representing the internal structure of the personal work relation in a way which was as neutral as possible, that is to say as free as possible of the baggage of existing classificatory concepts or terminologies. In this section, the conception of the personal work nexus is fleshed out: it is explained how it offers a way of thinking of the personal work relation as a complex network constructed around the worker (subsection A); and how it represents a particular way of combining the ideas of contract and relationship (subsection B).

## A. The Personal Work Nexus as the Internal Structure of the Personal Work Relation

In the previous section in which the idea of the personal work nexus was introduced as a key element in our scheme of analysis of the legal construction of personal work relations, it was explained that its role in the analysis was to serve as a generic and neutral concept representing the internal structure of the personal work relation. This neutrality or freedom from baggage was depicted as consisting, above all, of freedom from conceptual constraints of certain distinctions or dichotomies which had come to dominate the existing analysis. We return in the next subsection to the matter of escaping from existing dichotomies; it will suffice at this point to remind ourselves that our scheme has the purpose of doing that.

One major consequence of that particular objective is that our organizing concepts may be negatively or evasively defined and therefore amorphous – more concerned with avoiding the pitfalls of existing analyses than with building structures which are robust in themselves. Our response to that problem is to refer to the real and genuine complexity of personal work relations both in a practical and in a legal sense, and to recognize that complexity by envisaging personal work relations as having a relatively simple legal base but one which is overlaid, almost of necessity and certainly in most instances, with a series of complex extensions. It is that combination of simple bases within complex superstructures which leads us to suggest a way of thinking about the personal work relation as a complex network – an idea which we attempt to encapsulate in our conception of the personal work nexus.

Our notion of the personal work nexus is that of a network which is the legal embodiment of an arrangement or relation into which the worker enters in order to work for another or others normally for remuneration or reward. It is the personal work relation opened out and made transparent so that its internal structure is visible. That concept is in essence a simple one, sometimes as we shall see deceptively simple, but an elaborate network of legal connections may assemble itself within and around that basic notion. Our suggestion is that the idea of the personal work nexus, as the fully expanded and opened-out vision of the internalities of the personal work relation, operates to demonstrate both the need for such an analysis, and, at the same time, of the possibility of accomplishing it.

We suggest, therefore, that the analysis of the structure of the personal work relation as a personal work nexus is an essentially liberating one, which frees the analysis in certain critical respects from existing strongly felt but intellectually cramping constraints. The most significant of those constraints is that of the dominant paradigm of the contract of employment – that is to say, the domination of the model of the personal work relation as a bilateral contract between a worker and an employer which is essentially characterized by subordination of the worker to the employer or dependence of the worker or the employer. The personal work nexus analysis, by centring itself upon the *worker*, allows us to understand the relation in a way which is not cast within that theoretical mould from the outset – it provides a larger, looser matrix for understanding the structure of the personal work relation.

In order to develop this idea of the personal work nexus as offering a liberating analysis of the internal structure of the personal work relation, it will be helpful to return to and reflect further upon our notion of the normative characterization of personal work relations. It will be recalled from earlier pages of this work that we regard it as useful to think of acts of legal regulation of personal work relations as involving the assignment of both category and consequence to those relations, as where we say, for example, that a given worker has a contract of employment with a given employer and is therefore entitled not to be unfairly dismissed by that employer; it is that integrally connected operation of assigning category and consequences which we have identified as normative characterization.

We might usefully deconstruct our own notion of normative characterization somewhat further. The normative element consists of assigning a certain set of legal consequences in a certain stated set of conditions. The characterization element consists of using a relational category definition as a way of bracketing together and identifying the set of conditions in question. Thus, in the example we are using, the idea of 'the contract of employment' functions as a way of bundling together the main conditions in which a worker has the right against an employer not to be unfairly dismissed.

However, it is to be noted that when a relational category definition is used in that way as a shorthand term for the bundle of conditions in which a certain norm or set of norms applies, it is very likely to represent a simplified or elliptical summary of an elaborate set of conditions. Thus, to pursue our example, treating 'the contract of employment' as the qualifying category for unfair dismissal rights really involves using that category as a label or heading for an elaborate set of conditions which normally includes the requirement that the worker in question must have been 'continuously employed under' a contract of employment for a qualifying period of one year. Moreover, the relational category concept which is used in this way may be specifically defined for the purpose of a particular legal norm or set of norms: and even if it is not specifically defined for that particular purpose, it will still have a meaning which is specific to the legal system in which it is used, as that legal system stands at the time in question. For example, the 'contract of employment' as a relational category might be specifically defined in a particular legislative context as including or excluding a contract of apprenticeship: and, if it were being used as a relational category under English law at the present day, it would take its shape from current English law, which might be a very different shape from that of English law fifty years ago or French law today.

In that connection, it is also to be noted that an act of normative characterization, by carrying out that linking together of category with consequences, itself has a transformative effect upon the category in question. To pursue our example yet further, where a personal work relation is identified as a contract of employment so as to trigger the attachment of a right on the part of the worker not to be unfairly dismissed by the employer, the character of the contract of employment in question is itself thereby transformed. The contract of employment has become a contract of employment with unfair dismissal rights attached to it. We may debate whether that alters the fundamental nature of that contract of employment, but we would agree that at least its attributes have been altered in a very important way.

There is a further and final point to be made by way of deconstruction of our notion of normative characterization. If – as we intend – the arguments advanced in the immediately preceding paragraphs have served to identify the outcomes of normative characterization as very varied, complex, and specific each to its own particular regulatory context, there is one more very important reason for regarding them in that light. We have sought to show how processes of normative characterization are interactive and reiterative, so that the outcomes bounce off each other and build upon each other. But those outcomes interact not only with each other as normative legal constructs, but also with the patterns and constructions which those involved in the making and conduct of personal work relations place or seek to place on their own dealings or arrangements.

In other words, even as legal actors engage in normative characterizations of personal work relations, and by doing so create an enlarging multiplicity of relational categories which interact with each other, so also do those legal actors interact with the practice and practicalities of making and conducting personal work relations. The practical actors in those interactions, especially employing entities, are, often very inventively, testing out the limits of the scope for manoeuvre which the normative systems in question allow to them. These experiments in the exercise of whatever 'freedom of contract' happens to be afforded to them by the legal system in question in their turn play a crucial role in shaping the relational categories which are the outcomes of normative characterization.

A good illustration of this interplay, between legal processes of normative characterization and practical processes of work contracting, is to be found in the developing practice of work arrangements in which the worker is in a personal work relation with an employing entity or network but in which there are no fixed or guaranteed hours of remunerated work. These arrangements are variously described as 'on-call', 'intermittent',[4] or 'on-demand'[5] work, or sometimes referred to as 'zero-hours contracts'.[6] There are major and continuing controversies in many European legal systems as to how these arrangements fit into existing legal relational categories which are the outcomes of processes of legal normative characterization

---

[4] Controversially introduced in Italy by the so called 'Biagi Law', D. Lgs, 276/2003. Cf. the critical analysis of D. Gottardi, 'Lavoro intermittente. Commento agli artt. 33–40', in E. Gragnoli and A. Perulli (eds.) (2004), *La Riforma del Mercato del Lavoro e i Nuovi Modelli Contrattuali* (Padova: Cedam), 496. For the French '*contrat de travail intermittent*' see Articles L. 3123-31 to 37 of the *Code du Travail*. Cf. also, in respect of Spain, J. Gorelli Hernández, 'El contrato de trabajo fijo discontinuo', in Ojeda Avilés (ed.) (2003), *Modalidades de Contrato de Trabajo*, Madrid: Tecnos Editorial, 281.

[5] For example in Case C-313/02, *Wippel v. Peek & Cloppenburg GmbH & Co. KG* [2004] ECR I-9483.

[6] *Fasuyi v. Compass Contract Services (UK) LTD*, Appeal No. UKEAT/0194/10/MW; *Mr K Kennaugh v. Mr D Lloyd Jones*, Appeal No. UKEAT/0236/09/RN; *Manpower UK Ltd v. Mr V Vjestica*, Appeal No. UKEAT/0397/05/DM.

of personal work relations.[7] There are some instances where new or adapted legal normative characterizations start to form themselves around those practical developments at a European level.[8]

By deconstructing our notion of the normative characterization of personal work relations in those ways, we hope to have carried out some groundwork for our analysis of the personal work nexus as the internal structure of the personal work relation. Our deconstruction of the notion of normative characterization indicates that great numbers of processes of normative characterization of personal work relations take place as part of the continuing development of labour law systems, in a continuing and interactive way. The deconstruction also shows how each of those processes or acts of normative characterization produces its own set of category definitions of personal work relations; and moreover that these sets of category definitions represent complex analyses of personal work relations which may be very diverse both as between national labour law systems, within each national labour law system, and over time as those systems are in states of continuing evolution.

Our argument is, therefore, that these diversities represent potentially huge numbers of differently framed conceptions or characterizations of personal work relations. We think that this multiplicity of conceptions or characterizations can best be understood and analysed, not only by reference to the enveloping notion of the personal work relation which we constructed earlier in this work, but also by an equally comprehensive framework for thinking about the actual and possible varieties of internal structure of personal work relations which exist within that envelope. It is that comprehensive structure of analysis of the internal structure of personal work relations which we embody and seek to actualize in the notion of the personal work nexus.

Our notion of the personal work nexus as the internal structure of the personal work relation is the following one. To say that the personal work nexus consists of the internal structure of each personal work relation signifies that it describes how that relation is made up – what are its internal mechanisms or working parts – whereas its external face or characterization consists of its place on the map of all personal work relations or of legal relations at large. So in that sense, if we conceive of each personal work relation, with its own legal construction, as an entity or molecule, the personal work nexus consists of the internal structure of that molecule. Somewhat in the way that scientists conceive of molecules as having an internal structure consisting of atoms linked up in particular configurations by chemical bonds, we conceive of the internal legal construction of each personal work relation as consisting of a set of participants linked up by a particular set of

---

[7] In Italy, for example, the distinct treatment of intermittent work was abolished in 2007 with *Legge 24 dicembre 2007, n. 247*, only to be reintroduced in 2008, upon the return of a new centre-right government, with Article 39(11) of the *decreto legge 25 giugno 2008 n. 112*.

[8] For example with regard to arrangements and regulations which distinguish between 'active' and 'inactive' on-call time, as reflected in the abortive proposals for a new Working Time Directive COM (2004) 607 final, Article 1.

legal connections, each of which has its own nature or character and its own duration. The personal work nexus, and indeed the personal work relation itself, is made up of the totality, or bundle, of those legal connections. This conception obviously requires explanation and elaboration, which we now seek to provide.

Perhaps the best way of explaining this conception of the personal work nexus is by contrasting it with the model which is normally used to understand the internal structure of personal work relations – and which we have ourselves regarded as sufficient in the past. We do not contrast the personal work nexus with the normally used model in the sense of arguing that the normal model is incompatible with the personal work nexus analysis. We do contrast the normal model with the personal work nexus in the sense of arguing that the normal model is incomplete and to that extent analytically deficient as compared with the personal work nexus model. We proceed to develop our notion of the personal work nexus around that contrast.

The contrast between the normal model of personal work relations and the personal work nexus analysis may be developed as follows: essentially it consists in the fact that the normal model is that of a single bilateral legal connection between a worker and an employer – a legal connection which has a single clearly identified nature or character, such as that of being a contract of employment. The personal work analysis, by contrast, asserts that the internal structure of the personal work relation is typically a far more complex one, which may have more than two participants and which may involve several legal connections each with its own nature and duration rather than just one such connection, the nature and duration of which identifies and defines the personal work relation as a whole.

In order to clarify this contrast between the normal model of personal work relations and the personal work nexus analysis, it may be helpful to put forward a distinction between primary and secondary legal connections in the legal construction of personal work relations. As we have previously indicated, when personal work relations are legally constructed or normatively characterized, that is normally done by seeking out a bilateral legal connection, usually a contractual one, between a worker and an employer and treating that as identifying, and exhaustively embodying, the legal relation as a whole. We suggest, however, that such a legal connection should be viewed only as the primary legal connection, in a way which recognizes that there may also be secondary legal connections which form part of the personal work nexus. Moreover, we suggest that even the primary legal connection itself should be regarded as often being complex and multi-faceted, its nature or identity varying according to the particular regulatory context in which it is being analysed.

Obviously this notion of primary and secondary legal connections requires further elaboration. Before proceeding to that, it will be helpful firstly to give an illustration of how this notion might work, and then to proceed to reflect on some larger consequences or implications of the discussion as it has developed thus far. We take as our illustration the statutory concept of 'contract workers' which figures in the legislation concerning the various kinds of discrimination in employment, and the application of that concept to a franchise situation in the leading case of

*Harrods Ltd v Remick.*[9] Section 7 of The Race Relations Act 1976, in common with the other types of such legislation, made special provision for the situation where any work for a person ('the principal') is available for doing by individuals ('contract workers') who are employed not by the principal himself but by another person who supplies them under a contract made with the principal. The special provision consists in effect of applying the obligations of the law concerning employment discrimination to the principal with regard to the contract worker. The issue in that case was whether that special provision applied to the Harrods department store in favour of workers employed by or seeking employment with an enterprise (Shaeffer Pens (UK) Ltd) retailing its goods within the store under a franchise or concession. The Court of Appeal upheld a tribunal finding that on the facts the workers were or would be 'working for' Harrods so as to bring the special provision into play.

This decision, and indeed the legislative provision which was under consideration in it, provide a remarkably telling illustration of the significance of our theories of 'normative characterization' and 'primary and secondary legal connections'. Both the special provision itself and its application in the *Harrods* case constitute instances of normative characterization. The special provision identifies or characterizes a certain defined set of work relations – where a 'contract worker' is 'working for' a 'principal' – as attracting the norms of employment equality which prohibit or control discrimination in employment. The decision of the Court of Appeal identified or characterized in that same way the work relations which were under scrutiny in the particular case. Moreover, the legislative provision and the judicial decision served between them to establish and identify a certain kind of legal connection between a 'principal' and a 'contract worker' both at a general and a particular level – a legal connection consisting of the obligation of the 'principal' to observe the requirements of employment equality law with regard to the 'contract worker' (or somebody seeking to become a 'contract worker').

The question then arises whether that legal connection should be regarded as a 'primary' or a 'secondary' one. If, according to the traditional view which seems to prevail in English law, the primary legal connection for each and every personal work relation has to consist of a single bilateral link between a worker and an employer, then the legal connection between the principal and the contract worker could not be the primary one for that worker's personal work relation, because the principal is defined by the legislation in question as being a person other than the employer. But according to the different mode of analysis embodied in the notion of the personal work nexus, there may be more than one, there may even possibly be several, legal connections between the worker and users of his or her work, or controllers in some sense of his or her work relations: and the overall identifier of a personal work relation may consist of a complex set of those legal connections, so that each of those legal connections can be regarded as a primary one (in the sense of being part of the primary set).

---

[9] *Harrods Ltd v. Remick* [1998] 1 All E R 52.

So it was, we suggest, in the *Harrods* case. A traditional analysis would envisage the personal work relation of the claimant workers as consisting of and character-ized by their contracts of employment with their employer, Shaeffer Pens (UK) Ltd. Expressed in the terminology of primary and secondary legal connections, that would mean that there was a simple bilateral primary legal connection between Mrs Remick and Shaeffer Pens. That analysis would not be affected by the special provision of employment equality law which was under consideration in the case in question. The legal connection between the 'principal' and the 'contract worker' which was recognized and imposed by that special provision could only amount to a secondary connection which did not have any bearing upon the primary identity of the personal work relation in question as a bilateral contract of employment; for it would constitute only a secondary statutory extension of that relation. Our analysis, by contrast, regards the decision of the Court of Appeal as identifying a legal connection between Harrods and Mrs Remick which formed one of the primary components of the personal work nexus within which Mrs Remick was employed as a 'contract worker'.

This could appear to be a rather abstruse argument; but it has the most profound implications for labour law. It will be useful to take stock of where we have got to, and to consider where we go to from here. Essentially, by combining together the notions of normative characterization, of the personal work nexus, and of primary and secondary legal connections, we hope to have completed a preliminary mapping of the internal structure of personal work relations in a way which challenges traditional or received analyses. In the succeeding sections, we shall consider in greater depth the nature and variety of the legal connections which make up the personal work nexus, and also the significance of this analytical approach for the understanding of the comparative evolution of the legal construc-tion of personal work relations in different European legal systems. There is, however, one particular implication of our argument as so far developed which it is worth singling out at this juncture; this concerns the effect of our argument upon the perceived dichotomy between 'contract' and 'relationship' in the analysis of the legal construction of personal work relations.

## B. Contract and Relationship Within the Personal Work Nexus

Our point concerning the effect of our argument upon the perceived dichotomy between 'contract' and 'relationship' in the analysis of the legal construction of personal work relations is the following one. We regard the personal work nexus analysis as casting fundamental doubt upon the idea that, in the legal construction or normative characterization of personal work relations, there is a simple or complete dichotomy or antithesis between 'contract' and 'relationship'. Our argu-ment challenges an assumption which seems to underlie the received wisdom concerning the legal construction of personal work relations. That assumption, expressed in the terminology which we have been using, is to the effect that each personal work relation has its particular normative character, normally constructed around a bilateral legal connection between a worker and an employer, and that this single normative character consists either of some kind of contract or otherwise of some kind of relationship which is not contractual in its nature.

We hope to have pursued the personal work nexus analysis sufficiently far as to demonstrate that this assumption would be an unwarranted one, and that the characterizations of 'contract' and 'relationship' may be overlapping ones in at least two respects. Firstly, we argue that a personal work nexus may be made up of a number of legal connections, and that even the primary legal connection or connections may not be uniquely 'contractual' or 'relational' in a mutually exclusive sense. Secondly, we argue that a personal work nexus may be the result of a number of different normative characterizations, occurring in a number of different regulatory contexts even within the ambit of labour law, so that a personal work relation may be regarded as a 'contract' in one regulatory context but as a 'relationship' in another. The overall effect of those arguments is that a personal work nexus – and in consequence a personal work relation – may consist neither solely of a 'contract' nor solely of a 'relationship', but may instead sometimes consist of a contract within a relationship, or sometimes of a contract alongside a relationship, or sometimes even a relationship within a contract.

As we have said, these alternatives will be identified more fully and clearly in the succeeding sections of this chapter. At this juncture, it will suffice to make the point that this fluidity between 'contract' and 'relationship', which it has proved difficult to recognize or accommodate within a traditional analysis of the legal construction of personal work relations, becomes much easier to understand in the framework of the personal work nexus. Within that framework, the tension between 'contract' and 'relationship', and the sense that these are mutually exclusive analyses, largely disappears. In particular, it becomes straightforward to think about a contract within a relationship, rather than contemplating a stark choice between contractual and relational analyses. It is that core idea which we seek to express in the notion of 'contract and relationship within the personal work nexus'. Invoking that core idea, we can when necessary refer to 'the personal contract within the personal work nexus', or even to 'the personal work contract within the personal work relation' itself. Armed with those notions, in the next section we consider more fully the variety of legal connections which may compose or play a part in the legal construction of personal work relations.

## Section 3: The Legal Connections of Which the Personal Work Nexus is Composed

In this section we conduct a discussion which represents another crucial stage in the development of our view of the legal construction of personal work relations – indeed an existential stage, because upon it depends the establishment of a meaningful notion of the personal work nexus which will impart shape and definition to our idea of the personal work relation itself. We seek to achieve that by defining and describing the set of legal connections of or from which the personal work nexus is made up, and by locating within that set of legal connections the primary ones which act as the identifiers of personal work relations. We consider in turn – as distinct but interlinked aspects of that discussion – firstly the nature of these legal connections (subsection A) and secondly the suggested difference between primary and secondary legal connections (subsection B).

## A. The Nature of These Legal Connections

Our first task then is to provide our outline definition of the nature of the legal connections of or from which the personal work nexus is composed. We do this by taking the worker as the starting point, identifying him or her as the focal point or hub of the legal connections of or from which the personal work nexus is composed. We take that starting point because we conceive of the personal work relation as the relation in which the worker works for another or others (normally for remuneration or reward). From that starting point, we identify the legal connections of or from which the personal work nexus is composed; we think of those legal connections as the factors which determine the legal construction and effect of personal work arrangements by assigning legal significance to factual or narrative links between persons (human or legal) who can be regarded as involved in those arrangements as actors in the making or functioning of those arrangements. Various aspects of this conception require elaboration.

If this conception of legal connections is to be a convincing one, it will be necessary both to elaborate it, and at the same time to acknowledge and to justify some normative assumptions which are built into it. In this regard, we proceed to consider more fully, firstly, the worker-centric nature of our conception of the personal work nexus, and secondly its basis in the factual narrative of personal work arrangements. Our conception of the personal work nexus as being centred on the worker, although in one sense obvious, nevertheless in another sense represents a significant choice among possible alternatives. In particular, we could have envisaged the personal work nexus as being equally centred upon the worker and the 'employer'. Our preference for the worker-centric conception presents us with issues both analytical and normative.

We revert in the next chapter to the normative issues concerning the worker-centric conception of the personal work nexus. They consist of the possibility that a worker-centric conception of the personal work nexus, although on the face of it not in any way tendentious, underlyingly implies that labour law is 'all about' workers, perhaps even 'all about' the protection of workers – that is to say, normatively focused upon and systemically disposed towards workers and their protection. We think that such an extreme implication would be unwarranted, but that there is a charge of this kind to be answered; we shall in due course attempt to do so by advancing a particular normative notion of 'personality in work'.

That brings us back to the analytical concerns which we might have about the worker-centric nature of our conception of the personal work nexus, and about its basis in the factual narrative of personal work arrangements. Those are concerns about the amorphousness or lack of definition of the personal work nexus which might be thought to result from those two aspects of our conception of it. That is to say, as to its worker-centric nature, that if the personal work nexus is constructed from the worker outwards, rather than as a simply bilateral relation, we might worry about its lack of any definite relational shape. Equally, if it is based upon a broad or open-ended notion of the legally significant elements in the factual narrative of personal work arrangements, we might be concerned about its lack of any definite legal shape.

Our response to those concerns is, in the last resort, a positivist one: we believe that labour law systems do in fact construct personal work relations around the worker, and do in fact construct those relations as the legally significant elements in the factual narrative of personal work arrangements, and do in fact thereby construct those relations in highly complex ways so that they can easily appear to be amorphous and to lack clear legal definition. In other words, we believe that the apparently much clearer accepted vision of personal work relations as consisting of bilateral dealings between a worker and an 'employer' achieves its apparent clarity only by over-simplification and at the cost of obscuring a more complex reality to which it is quite hard to assign a single legal shape. We shall develop that positivist argument and attempt to tease out its significant implications in the next section of this chapter. However, before reaching that point, there are some important steps which we can take by way of analytical refinement of our conception of the personal work nexus. One of these concerns the difference between factual significance and legal significance in the identifying of legal connections; another concerns the distinction which we draw between primary and secondary legal connections.

Firstly, then, we consider how we might clarify our understanding of the nature of the legal connections which make up the personal work nexus by refining our analysis at the point where it differentiates between factual and legal significance. To recapitulate for a moment, we have so far identified our conception of the legal connections which make up the personal work nexus as having their starting point in the factual narrative of the making and functioning of personal work arrangements; we now seek to specify more precisely those factual starting points, and then to specify the circumstances in which some of those factual connections become legal connections. We initially delineated the factual connections as factual or narrative links between persons (human or legal) who can be regarded as involved in personal work arrangements as actors in the making or operating of those arrangements. We could develop that idea by thinking about work-related roles or functions. Thus we could say that a factual or narrative link consists of the having or exercising of a work-related role or function in the making or operation of a personal work arrangement or set of arrangements.

We could go on from there to delineate two main distinct though intersecting types of work-related roles or functions, namely those of 'determinative' roles or functions, and 'co-working' roles or functions. The former of those typologies transcends the traditional notion of the 'employer', while the latter introduces into the analysis of personal work relations an element which is unrecognized or in our view under-recognized in traditional analysis of those relations. We proceed to develop each notion in turn.

We think of 'determinative' roles or functions as those which involve taking or directly influencing decisions about the making or operation of a personal work arrangement or set of arrangements. Such determinative roles or functions may be played or carried out by individuals or organizations, for example as intermediaries between workers and end-users of their work, or as representatives of workers or employing enterprises, for instance in collective bargaining, or as in various senses insurers, guarantors, sponsors, or providers of some aspects of the personal work arrangements who have a significant degree of voice in the making or operation of those arrangements. An illustration of the latter type would be the role of a pension fund in giving or withholding agreement to the early retirement of an employee, and taking or participating in the decision as to what pension benefits the employee would receive upon early retirement.

We think of 'co-working' roles or functions as those which involve persons working in some kind of factual association with the worker who is the subject of a personal work arrangement or set of arrangements, in circumstances such that their doing so has some bearing upon that arrangement or set of arrangements. The factual association might consist of one worker working in the same organization as another, or in working for the same organization as another, or might arise in other ways. If one worker is in an organizational hierarchy of some kind with another, that may be as the hierarchical inferior, equal, or superior of that other. That factual association between the two workers might have some bearing upon the personal work arrangement or set of arrangements of each worker in all kinds of ways, for example because they are engaged in a 'job-share' as equals, or because one is the line-manger of the other. (It follows from these propositions, incidentally, that 'determinative' and 'co-working' roles may intersect or combine with each other; for example, if one worker is a hierarchical superior of another in an employing enterprise, then he or she may have a role which is both co-working and determinative vis-à-vis that other.)

The preceding paragraphs have been concerned with the connections which derive from the factual narrative of personal work arrangements. We now turn to specifying the ways in which those connections may assume or be assigned legal significance. There are many ways in which this may occur, but they can be reduced to two principal types, or modes; one of these can be conceived of as the 'liability mode', and the other as the 'conditionality mode'. A factual connection may be said to assume legal significance in a direct and obvious way in liability mode when legal rights and obligations are associated with it, as in the most obvious case where contractual rights and obligations are associated with the personal work arrangement between the worker and the employing enterprise.

On the other hand, a factual connection may be said to assume legal significance in a less obvious and direct way in conditionality mode, when a factual connection does not have legal rights or obligations running across it between the parties to it, but when it provides the conditions for legal rights and obligations across other connections. Two illustrations may be given. The first is the case where two workers are hierarchically equal workers employed by the same employing organization, and one worker bullies and harasses the other not so gravely as to be liable in tort to that other but so that the employing enterprise is held liable to the harassed worker for constructive unfair dismissal in respect of its failure to control the harassing worker's behaviour: that would amount to a legal connection between the two workers because of the way that the one worker's actions conditioned the obligations of the employing enterprise to the other worker. The second illustration is the case where a female worker and a male worker are hierarchically equal workers employed by an employing enterprise, and where the male worker is a comparator by reference to whose situation the female worker has an equal pay claim against the employing enterprise. Here again there is a legal connection between the two workers not in liability mode but in conditionality mode.

By this path of argument and definition, we have identified in outline at least the nature of the legal connections which make up the personal work nexus. It will have become apparent that the personal work nexus may be composed of a potentially bewildering number and variety of legal connections between all kinds of actors having roles or functions in the making or operation of the personal work relation in which a worker is engaged. In order somewhat better to organize our understanding of this highly complex and multifarious personal work nexus, it will be useful to revert to the earlier-mentioned distinction between primary and secondary legal connections and to develop that distinction: that will be undertaken in the next subsection.

## B.  Primary and Secondary Legal Connections

At this point it is useful to remind ourselves of our objective in putting forward and developing our conception of the personal work nexus. That objective is to create a conceptual framework which will be helpful in the understanding and analysis of the legal construction of personal work relations. So our central concern is with the ways in which the makers of labour law – whether as legislators, adjudicators, or theorists – think and reason and act when engaging in processes of legal construction of personal work relations, those being processes of continuing interaction with the primary participants in the making and operation of personal work arrangements. So far in this chapter, we hope to have demonstrated how these processes can usefully be understood as consisting or resulting in the creation of an often very elaborate nexus of legal connections centred upon the worker and linking him or her with a wide range and variety of actors or participants in his or her personal work arrangement. We have argued that this personal work nexus constitutes the internal structure of the personal work relation, so that the personal work relation can be regarded as consisting of the personal work nexus, which in turn consists of the set of legal connections with and around the worker in question.

However, although we hope thereby somewhat to have advanced our understanding of the processes of legal construction of personal work relations, there are some important further steps which can usefully be taken, one of which consists of differentiating between primary and secondary legal connections. The legal construction of personal work relations, as we envisage it, does not consist simply of establishing and giving effect to a multiplicity of legal connections in their raw and unorganized state. We suggest that the legal construction of personal work relations also involves, and indeed turns upon, intermediate processes of legal ordering – these are at the heart of the activity which we have designated as the normative characterization of personal work relations. They are processes whereby the various legal connections which can constitute or form part of the personal work nexus are organized into recognized groups or sets which are identified or classified as particular types of personal work relation, such as, for example, 'employment under a contract of employment'. In this subsection it is argued that we can better understand these processes of legal ordering by invoking a distinction between primary and secondary legal connections.

We have previously argued that processes of legal construction of personal work relations make use of a conceptual mechanism which we have identified as that of normative characterization, whereby personal work relations are identified or characterized in particular ways for particular normative purposes. We now advance the argument that this mechanism operates by singling out a particular legal connection or set of legal connections, which is regarded as identifying or characterizing the personal work relation in question. That particular legal connection or set of legal connections becomes as it were the vehicle for the legal construction of the personal work relation in question. It is this legal connection or set of legal connections, operating as an identifier of the personal work relation and as a vehicle for the normative operation in question, which we are designating as the primary legal connection or set of connections in the personal work nexus. In this scheme of analysis, all other legal connections forming part of the personal work nexus are defined as secondary legal connections.

Before we go on to develop more fully this notion of the primary legal connection or set of legal connections which acts as the identifier of a personal work relation, and of the secondary legal connections which exist but do not act in that way, we pause to reflect for a moment on why and in what sense this notion might contribute to a better understanding of the legal construction of personal work relations. Our answer to that question is that we believe that this notion provides one of the keys to a 'best-fit' analysis, in the Dworkinian sense,[10] of what the makers and adjudicators of labour law do when they engage in the legal construction of personal work relations. That analysis is primarily descriptive and explanatory, hoping to provide the clearest possible explanation of what they in fact do; but it has a certain prescriptive element in that it suggests how they might best do it. As we have said, we revert in due course to identifying the normative stance from which we maintain that prescriptive element.

So we suggest that we can best understand what the makers and adjudicators of labour law do, when they engage in the legal construction of personal work relations, if we view them as choosing or defining a primary legal connection or set of legal connections, which they use as the identifier of the personal work relation in question, and as the vehicle for the process of legal regulation in which

---

[10] See R. Dworkin (1986) *Law's Empire*, Cambridge, MA: Harvard University Press, esp. Chapter 2 'Interpretative Concepts'.

they are engaged. As we have previously argued, this choosing or defining of a primary identifier of the personal work relation is often represented as a very simple operation of fastening upon a single bilateral link between the worker and a counter-party who or which is therefore by definition 'the employer'. We take the view that a 'best-fit' analysis would represent this as a more complex and sophisticated operation.

We argue that this more complex and sophisticated operation should be envisaged as the choosing or specifying, from among all those persons, human or legal, who have legal connections with the worker and are thus in some sense participants in the personal work nexus and relation, the person(s) for whom the worker is regarded as working and their relevant legal connection(s) with the worker for the purpose of the legal regulation which is in question. That choice or specification identifies, in a particular regulatory context, the primary legal connection(s) between the worker and a person or set of persons who can be considered as the primary participants in the personal work nexus – in a broad sense the user or users of the worker's work. For any given personal work relation, the choice or specification of the primary legal connections and primary participants may vary as between different regulatory contexts, so that a particular legal connection may be a primary one in one regulatory context, but a secondary one in another regulatory context.

It will be useful at this point to illustrate the working of this theory by applying it to the case of *Harrods Ltd v. Remick*[11] which we analysed earlier. It will be recalled that the decision was that, for the purposes of the legislation concerning employment discrimination, the employees of the holder of a franchise or concession located within the Harrods department store could be regarded as 'working for' Harrods Ltd within the meaning of a provision concerning 'contract workers', so as to render Harrods Ltd liable to give effect to the legislation vis-à-vis those 'contract workers', of whom the claimant Mrs Remick was one. In the terms of our analysis, this amounts to saying not only that, in the particular regulatory context of employment discrimination legislation, there was a legal connection between Harrods Ltd and Mrs Remick, forming part of her personal work nexus (consisting of the rights and obligations under that legislation), but also that the provisions concerning 'contract workers' had identified that legal connection as a primary one, identifying a relation between the worker and a company for whom she could be regarded as working although that company was not her 'employer' in the ordinary sense.

We can also use this example to demonstrate our contention that the primary legal connections may be differently specified in different regulatory contexts. Let us suppose that, in the same fact situation, Mrs Remick had complained that the actions of Harrods Ltd (in enforcing a discriminatory dress code throughout their store) had amounted to or brought about a constructive unfair dismissal on the part of her immediate employer, Shaeffer Pens UK Ltd, the holders of the franchise or

---

[11] [1998] ICR 156. See above pp. 321–2.

concession from Harrods. The unfair dismissal legislation makes no analogous provision extending liability in respect of 'contract workers'. So whereas in the regulatory context of employment discrimination law there was a primary legal connection in liability mode between Mrs Remick and Harrods Ltd, in the different regulatory context of unfair dismissal legislation there would have been a secondary legal connection between them, in conditionality mode, in the sense that the conduct of Harrods Ltd would have conditioned the operation of the primary legal connection between Mrs Remick and her employer, Shaeffer Pens (UK) Ltd.

Thus far, we hope to have shown that personal work nexus analysis, and the differentiation between primary and secondary legal connections within the personal work nexus, yield the following benefits or refinements by comparison with more traditional analyses of the legal construction of personal work relations. Firstly, they provide a more sophisticated and inclusive account of the links to which legal significance may be accorded between workers and work-users – in the terminology of our argument, the primary legal connections within the personal work nexus. Secondly, they also produce a clearer and fuller recognition of the legal significance of a further set of links between the worker and others who are actors in the factual narrative of his or her personal work arrangements – in the terminology of our argument, the secondary legal connections within the personal work nexus. In the next and concluding section of this chapter we shall suggest that these illuminations might cast considerable light upon our more general understanding of the legal construction of personal work relations.

## Section 4: The Personal Work Nexus and the Personal Work Relation

Our discussion of the personal work nexus and of the analytical benefits which we can derive from using this conception has reached the point at which it will be useful to consider the significance of that discussion for our understanding of the legal construction of the personal work relation itself. In this section we will seek to conduct that further discussion, drawing firstly upon a theoretical perspective (subsection A) and then upon a comparative perspective (subsection B).

### A. A Theoretical Perspective

In the previous sections of this chapter we set out our conception of the personal work nexus, and we have sought to show how that conception might provide us with a better understanding of the internal structure of the personal work relation than is afforded by traditional analyses. In this subsection we now seek to develop a theoretical notion of how this internal structure of the personal work relation influences the legal construction of each personal work relation, and enables it to be externally positioned on an analytical map of the whole category of personal work relations.

We suggest that the key to understanding the way in which the personal work nexus shapes and defines the personal work relation is to be found by further considering the process of normative characterization which we evoked earlier in this chapter. It will be recalled that we designated as normative characterization the processes whereby legislators, adjudicators, and in a different way theorists, assign character or identity to particular personal work relations in particular regulatory or normative contexts. We can now expand upon that idea, using the notion of the personal work nexus which we have now established. We now suggest that processes of normative characterization make a complex and interactive link between the personal work nexus and the personal work relation; they use the personal work nexus both to identify or characterize a personal work relation, and to attribute certain normative consequences to that relation. Moreover, in a further twist of the taxonomical screw, that often has the effect of recharacterizing the personal work relation itself – or even, in some cases, of recognizing a wholly new type of the personal work relation itself.

A couple of illustrations will be helpful. Let us start by drawing yet again upon the example of *Harrods Ltd v. Remick*. We have seen earlier how the legislation concerning the application of employment race discrimination law, as construed in that decision, affirmed the existence of a primary legal connection not only between Mrs. Remick and her immediate employer, but also between her and Harrods Ltd, which was regarded as the 'principal for whom' she was working. So that served to extend the personal work nexus to include another primary participant, and it had the normative consequence that Harrods Ltd, as that additional participant, was subjected to the obligations of employment race discrimination law. Moreover – and this is the crucial further step in our argument – this also operated to recharacterize the personal work relation itself, as Mrs Remick was now identified not just as an employee but also as a 'contract worker'.

This kind of transformation of the personal work nexus, and with it the personal work relation itself, is by no means confined to situations where the nexus and the relation are extended to include additional participants – such transformations may equally well occur where there is a single primary legal connection between two primary participants. To illustrate that possibility, we take the example of the provision of the Fixed-term Employee Regulations which, in the case where a worker has been employed under a succession of fixed-term contracts of employment for four years or more, and where the use of fixed-term contracting is not justified on objective grounds, nullifies the restriction on the duration of the ultimate contract of employment, so that the worker ceases to be a fixed-term employee.[12] So, in the terms of our argument, where that effect occurs, the nature of the primary legal connection and therefore of the personal work nexus in question has been transformed from that of a fixed-term contract to an open-

[12] The Fixed-term Employees (Prevention of Less Favourable Treatment) Regulations 2002, SI 2002/2034, s. 8.

ended one. Moreover, this amounts to an out-and-out normative recharacterization of the personal work relation itself, something marked by the legislation itself when it identifies the worker in question as having become a 'permanent employee' – a concept which, it must be said, the legislation signally fails to define.

We can take this argument to a further stage; both of our two examples illustrate the possibility, to which we alluded above, that operations of normative characterization may so fully reconstitute the personal work nexus in question that they amount to a complete recharacterization of the personal work relation and to the recognition of a wholly new type of personal work relation. Thus the legislation which was applied in *Harrods Ltd v. Remick* served not only to establish a new primary legal connection between the 'principal' and the 'contract worker' but also thereby established what we think deserves to be regarded as a new kind of multilateral personal work relation between the principal, the worker, and the contractual employer. Thus again, the legislation concerning Fixed-term Employees, which formed our second illustrative case, serves not only in certain circumstances to alter the duration of the primary legal connection between the employee and the employer – by removing its restriction to a fixed term – but also thereby fundamentally recharacterizes the personal work nexus in question and – crucially for the purpose of our argument – establishes what we think deserves to be regarded as a new kind of personal work relation, namely that of the 'permanent employee'.

This way of understanding the capacity of normative recharacterizations of the personal work nexus to bring about the evolution of new kinds of personal work relation has very significant implications for the whole of our theory about the legal construction of personal work relations. Those implications will be most effectively teased out by pursuing this argument from a European comparative perspective, which we attempt to do in the next subsection.

## B. A Comparative Perspective

The theoretical analysis which we conducted in the previous subsection has sought to demonstrate how adaptations to or changed constructions of the personal work nexus, effected by combinations of legislation and judicial interpretation, may result in the evolution of new forms or patterns of personal work relations. In this subsection we shall consider those processes of evolution from a European comparative perspective. We shall argue, firstly, that this analysis from a European comparative perspective demonstrates the sheer variety of these new patterns and the way in which they exist both in nominate and innominate forms. We shall secondly argue that this variety is heightened and complicated by the fact that it is embedded in rules about or approaches to legal construction or characterization of personal work relations which themselves vary between legal systems and within legal systems. We shall thirdly and finally argue that this analysis throws up enormous challenges to any system of taxonomy of personal work relations, such that, although our personal work nexus analysis may be helpful in meeting those challenges, further techniques of analysis are nevertheless required.

So we consider firstly the argument concerning the sheer variety of new forms or patterns of personal work relations which are revealed by our personal work nexus analysis. The logic of that analysis is that new forms or patterns may be created or recognized by many kinds of regulatory measures or adjudications in a great variety of specific regulatory contexts within the field of labour law alone. It follows that this potential for variety is vastly magnified when we move to considering it on a European comparative basis, if only because the range of regulatory contexts is thereby so very greatly extended. So much is this the case that examples are necessarily quite random ones. National legislation concerning the protection of wages, or the regulation of health and safety at work, is a very fruitful source of context-specific patterns of personal work relations. A good example, we believe, is provided by the constantly developing body of Italian (labour) law seeking to regulate (labour, or 'labour-intensive') subcontracting. As noted by Corazza (2009) this body of law, in one of its most recent developments, has introduced a 'variegated system of remedies, where both the contractor and the principal assist each other to guarantee the worker against those risks of under-protection represented by the fragmentation of the entrepreneurial activities'.[13] A further area where context-specific personal work relations are fast developing is that of national legislation concerning the various kinds of employment equality claims. As Speziale (2010) acutely observes, the relevant EU anti-discrimination Directives – coupled to the national implementing regulations – are applicable in the case of complex personal work relations which depart from the classical bilateral 'employer–employee' scheme and are applicable in the case of subcontracting practices 'extending the protection against discrimination beyond subordinate employment, albeit without the principal also becoming an employer'.[14]

In the previous subsection it began to become apparent, even when we were drawing our illustrations from only one national system, that this great and evolving variety of context-specific patterns of personal work relation is often shrouded in a terminological or taxonomical fog. Again, this effect is greatly magnified when these evolutions are considered from a European comparative perspective. We can see from that perspective that one national legal system may endow a certain regulatory-context-specific personal work relation with a particular terminology, which appears deceptively and falsely to have an exact equivalent in the language and terminology of another legal system. Moreover, an analogous personal work relation, evolving in a different regulatory context in another national legal system, may be identified by a different terminology, or may be wholly or partly innominate in the sense that a distinctive terminology is not accorded to it.

It will be useful to elaborate and illustrate this particular notion of the comparative taxonomical fog. The first manifestation of it which we alluded to in the

---

[13] L. Corazza (2009) 'La nuova nozione di appalto nel sistema delle tecniche di tutela del lavoratore', *WP C.S.D.L.E. 'Massimo D'Antona', IT 93/2009*, at 17. Our translation from the original Italian.
[14] V. Speziale (2010) 'Il datore di lavoro nell'impresa integrata', *WP C.S.D.L.E. 'Massimo D'Antona', IT – 94/2010*, 17. Our translation.

previous paragraph represents the familiar idea of the 'false friend'; but its decep-
tiveness may be seated at quite a deep conceptual level. For example, we have noted
in earlier chapters the way in which the linguistic equivalents of the 'contract of
employment' in other legal systems may represent significantly different juridical
conceptions from that of the contract of employment in English law. The terminology of 'contract workers' is fraught with even greater dangers of this kind, so
much so as to have become one of the key reasons for the collapse of the ILO
negotiations on the 'Contract Labour' Draft Convention in 1998.[15] But a no less
dense taxonomical and terminological fog arises from the different regulation that
applies, across but also within, different legal systems, to 'home-workers',[16] 'domestic workers',[17] 'professional sportspersons',[18] 'travelling salespersons', or journalists,[19] just to name a few. The second and opposite manifestation of the
comparative taxonomical fog which we identified consisted of cases where an
analogous personal work relation is differently labelled as between legal systems.

  Examples of this differential labelling effect may for instance result from divergent or inconsistent, national or supranational, definitions of what constitutes work
provided through an 'employment agency' and work provided through an 'employment business', partly because of the persisting terminological confusion over
the notions of 'agency' and 'business'.[20] No less confusingly, some legal systems
such as the British one will refer to 'on-call work contracts' as a quasi-synonymous
term for 'zero-hours' work[21] often, but not necessarily, provided through an
employment agency, whereas in other continental jurisdictions such as Italy, 'on-
call work' will attract a specific regulatory regime, which is quite distinct from the
one applicable to temporary agency work.[22]

---

[15]  International Labour Conference (ILO), *Contract labour – Fifth item on the agenda Report V (1) to
the International Labour Conference 86th Session 1998* (Geneva, 1997); ILO, *International Labour
Conference Report V – The Scope of the Employment Relationship – Fifth Item on the Agenda* (Geneva,
2003), p. 6.

[16]  In Italy, for instance, the presence of a substitution clause in a home-worker contract constitutes
the dividing line between dependent and independent home worker; cf. L. 13 marzo 1958, n. 264 and
L. 18 dicembre 1973, n. 877, Article 1. In some UK legislation the protections afforded to employees
or workers is explicitly extended to home workers on the basis that they may not have to perform the
required service in person, as recognized by Elias, J in *James v Redcats (Brands) Ltd* [2007] IRLR 296.

[17]  The vast range of national approaches in respect of this particular form of personal work can be
observed in ILO, *Decent Work for Domestic Workers – Report IV(1)* (International Labour Conference,
99th Session, 2010).

[18]  Cf. the special regime applying in Italy under *L. 23 marzo 1981, n. 91*. Cf. Spadafora (2004)
*Diritto del Lavoro Sportivo*, Torino: Giappichelli.

[19]  See the *Septième Partie* of the French *Code du Travail* (*Dispositions Particulières à Certaines Professions et
Activités*; and G. Lyon-Caen (1990) *Le droit du travail non salarié*, Paris: Sirey.

[20]  A marked contrast persists in the meaning of the two terms, which becomes apparent when
comparing the use made of them in the Employment Agencies Act 1973, s. 13(2)–(3) with other UK
and supranational provisions such as Regulation 4 of the Agency Workers Regulations 2010, SI 2010/
93 and Article 1 of ILO Convention C181, Private Employment Agencies Convention, Geneva, 1997.

[21]  *Manpower UK Ltd v Vjestica*, Appeal No. UKEAT/0397/05/DM of 2005.

[22]  Cf. for example the position in Italy where the contract for *'lavoro intermittente'* attracts a specific
regulatory regime (Article 33 of the D. Lgs 276/2003), which is distinct from the one applicable to a
*'contratto di somministrazione a tempo indeterminato'* (open-ended agency work contract, cf. Articles
20–8 of the D. Lgs 276/2003).

However, we suggest that the comparative taxonomical fog becomes most impenetrable in the third and most subtle of the manifestations which we have discerned, namely that a type of personal work relation which is recognized and labelled in a certain way in one legal system may have a close analogy in another legal system, but one which is wholly or partly innominate in that other system. Let us at this point elaborate the idea of wholly or partly innominate types of personal work relation. We suggest that wholly or partly innominate types of personal work relation arise where processes of legal regulation cast personal work relations in genuinely distinctive moulds or forms, but do so without according labels or complete labels to those distinctive forms. This is, we suggest, an under-recognized phenomenon of very frequent occurrence. New kinds of personal work contract or personal work relation are created, but without being endowed or fully endowed with a name which will secure conceptual recognition for them.

A typical form of partial but incomplete nomination occurs, especially with regard to multilateral personal work relations, where one of the participants is labelled but not all the participants are labelled and the relation itself is not labelled. In English law an illustration is to be found in the legislation concerning the licensing of 'gangmasters'.[23] That legislation recognized and regulated, for a certain rather narrow sector of the labour market, a particular kind of personal work relation with what we would argue was a complex personal work nexus involving the customers of or contractors with the 'gangmaster' as primary participants. But only one of the participants is nominated, namely the immediate employer; neither the worker nor the relation as a whole is labelled.

Once one has accepted the possibility of this phenomenon, examples of it are to be found all about us. In English law, many such examples result from the implementation of EU Directives, themselves often modelled upon legal character-izations which it is difficult to reproduce directly within the particular conceptual framework of existing national employment law. In a sense, the largest and most striking example is the particular kind of transferable employment contract or relationship which is created by the TUPE Regulations in implementation of the Acquired Rights Directive.[24] Another good example consists of the contract or relationship into which the fixed-term contract of employment is transformed in certain conditions by the Fixed-term Work Regulations which implemented the Fixed-term Work Directive.[25]

It will in our view turn out to be the case that another new personal work relationship has been ushered into existence by the Agency Work Regulations which implement the Temporary Agency Work Directive.[26] In an even more

---

[23] We are referring in particular to The Gangmasters (Licensing) Act 2004, s. 4.

[24] Transfer of Undertakings (Protection of Employment) Regulations 2006, SI 2006/246; Council Directive 2001/23/EC of 12 March 2001, [2001] OJ L 82/16.

[25] Regulation 8(2)–(3) of The Fixed-term Employees (Prevention of Less Favourable Treatment) Regulations 2002.

[26] The Agency Workers Regulations 2010, SI 2010/93, implementing Directive 2008/104/EC of the European Parliament and of the Council of 19 November 2008 on Temporary Agency Work [2008] OJ L 327/9.

extended sense, we can observe the emergence of new and as yet innominate personal work relations from the legislation about 'flexible working', in the sense that the employment contract or relationship to which the provisions about 'flexible working' applies is distinctive in character from the employment contract or relationship to which those provisions do not apply. Conversely, the far more taxonomically disposed continental European legal systems are increasingly experimenting with creating legal types out of complex work relations emerging in the context of 'groups of enterprises' or 'enterprise networks',[27] in a way that remains beyond the level of inventiveness of the English common law tradition.

It is hardly necessary to point out how obviously this phenomenon, of innominate or partly innominate emergent personal work relations, will be the subject of enormous, almost infinite, diversity as between different national legal systems. One legal system may label an emergent personal work relation in a way that evokes no obvious analogy in another legal system; this may be because the closest analogy which could be found in the other system exists in a wholly or partly innominate state. An example starts to present itself in the shape of a notion found in several continental European systems, the terminology for which translates into English as the idea of the 'single employment contract' – the *contract unique* in France, *contratto unico* in Italy, and so on.[28] The idea seems to be that of a single or universal model of the contract of employment with inbuilt notions of differential application according to the seniority of the worker in the job in question – initially probationary, with a progressive subsequent accretion of rights to job security. It is debatable how far an analogous notion can be identified in English labour law or in the practice of personal work arrangements in the jurisdiction of English law; but it is pretty clear that in so far as there is an identifiable analogy, it exists in a largely or entirely innominate form.

Even that depiction arguably understates the complexity of our inquiry into the sources of comparative diversity between different patterns of legal construction of the personal work nexus and the personal work relation. In an early chapter of this work, we identified the possibility that apparently similar characterizations of a

---

[27] Cf. A. Ojeda Avilés (2010) *La Deconsrtucción del Derecho del Trabajo*; Madrid: La Ley, Chapters 5 and 8.

[28] P. Cahuc and F. Kramarz (2004) *De la précarité à la mobilité: vers une Sécurité sociale profession-nelle*, Paris: La Documentation française. On the basis of these proposals the UMP produced the report *Repenser le contrat de travail en instaurant un contrat de travail unique* available online at www.u-m-p. org/site/index.php/ump/debattre/dossiers/economie_emploi/repenser_le_contrat_de_travail_en_ instaurant_un_contrat_de_travail_unique; Disegno di Legge n. 1481/2009, 'Disposizioni per il super-amento del dualismo del mercato del lavoro, la promozione del lavoro stabile in strutture produttive flessibili e la garanzia di pari opportunità nel lavoro per le nuove generazioni'. See also, T. Boeri and P. Garibaldi (2008) *Un Nuovo Contratto per Tutti*, (Milano: Chiarelettere); *Propuesta para la reactivación laboral en España*, available online at www.crisis09.es/propuesta/. Also available in English online at www.crisis09.es/PDF/restart-the-labor-market.pdf. Cf. also J. Kenner (2009) 'New Frontiers in EU Labour Law: From Flexicurity to Flex-Security', in M. Dougan and S. Currie, *50 Years of the European Treaties: Looking Back and Thinking Forward*, Oxford: Hart, 305. The OECD has advocated the adoption of this contractual model as a measure to foster a 'sustainable recovery' in Greece, after the country's 2010 'bail-out', cf. OECD (2010) *Greece at a Glance: Policies for a Sustainable Recovery*, Paris: OECD, 12.

personal work relation as between legal systems – such as are involved in the use of terminologies corresponding to the 'contract of employment' – may well represent very different ways of combining layers of regulation.[29] Thus, English law seems much more reluctant than some other European legal systems to integrate layers of statutory regulation into its notion of the contract of employment.

Moreover – and this is a very elusive but important point – comparison between the ways in which typologies of personal work nexus and personal work relation are articulated in different legal systems has to consider the complicating factor which is introduced by differences, as between legal systems, in their methodologies of legal characterization or legal construction of personal work relations. So for instance where one system may, in the absence of a particularly delineated and pre-defined type of 'contract', refrain from acknowledging any personal work relationship whatsoever, other systems may more readily accept that, even in the absence of a 'contract' type, the presence of one or more particular personal work nexuses may imply the existence of a personal work relation. Thus, for instance, whereas English labour law – as already noted in Chapter 7 – will refuse to imply a contractual relationship between a user company and a worker supplied through an intermediary agency, in France it is accepted that 'it is not accurate to say that, since there is no contract linking the temporary worker to the user company, there is no legal nexus between the two. An aggregation of rights and obligations ties the one to the other.'[30] These are variants which exist in a complicated spectrum from *jus cogens* to *jus dispositivum*, and our understanding of the processes of normative characterization has to be attuned to that kind of diversity. It is a point to which we return in the next chapter.

This latest step in our discussion, with its observation of a terminological fog around the personal work nexus, seems to take us further away from, rather than closer to, the possibility of using personal work nexus analysis to arrive at a new taxonomy of the personal work relation. Nevertheless, we hope to be able to show that this step was more in the nature of a clearing of the ground than of an admission of defeat, so that advance towards some new taxonomy may yet be attainable. However, that depends on some yet further analytical steps which we hope and intend to take in the next chapter.

---

[29] Cf. Chapter 3, in particular see Section 1.C.

[30] Our translation of '*ce n'est pas parce qu'il n'y a pas de contrat liant le travailleur temporaire à l'entreprise utilisatrice qu'il n'existe pas de lien juridique entre eux. Un ensemble de droits et d'obbligations les unit l'un à l'autre.*' J. Pélissier, A. Supiot, A. Jeammaud (2008) *Droit du Travail*, 24th ed., Dalloz: Paris, p. 473.

# 9

# The Personal Work Profile and the Idea of Personality in Work

## Introduction

In the previous chapter, we presented and developed the idea of the personal work nexus as representing the internal structure of the personal work relation. We deferred until this chapter the consideration of how that analysis might contribute to the making of a taxonomy of personal work relations. We reach the point of proposing a taxonomy in this chapter; but in order to do so, we regard it as necessary to take yet more analytical steps, and to introduce some further concepts which encapsulate those steps. We bring these steps and concepts together under the headings of the personal work profile and the idea of personality in work.

The purpose and desired effect of articulating these two notions is to provide as strong a framework as possible, both at the descriptive and the normative level, for viewing the legal construction of personal work relations from the perspective of the worker herself or himself. We believe that it is a tacit assumption of modern labour law[1] that this is the most appropriate perspective from which to analyse personal work relations, and that it is useful to make that assumption an overt and declared one.[2] If the open assertion of this often tacit assumption is important for labour law in general, it is doubly so for the legal construction of personal work relations in particular, because that is an aspect of labour law in which this tacit assumption comes under strain and comes into question. This is especially true, as we have sought to show in earlier chapters, when the exclusive model of the personal work relation is taken to be that of the individual contract of employment, a model which in its nature imagines that relation as being founded in agreement between an employee and 'an employer' whose claims and interests are often regarded as equally 'personal' ones.

---

[1] The point about 'modernity' is of course a complex one. We may wish to see this concentration upon the worker as an assumption inherent in the very notion of 'labour law' itself, and in its emergence as a branch of law distinct from general private law but different in its orientation from earlier notions of 'the law of master and servant' – a view which underpinned the comparative study of Bob Hepple and his colleagues, B. Hepple (ed.) 1986 *The Making of Labour Law in Europe*, London: Mansell.

[2] As famously accomplished by Lord Wedderburn (1966) by the titling and in the writing of his treatise on labour law *The Worker and the Law* (originally Harmondsworth: Penguin).

In earlier chapters, we have explored extensively the workings of the contract of employment paradigm for the legal construction of employment relations, and we have considered its extensibility or the viability of other contractual models for the legal construction of personal work relations other than those of employment. In the preceding chapter, we began to develop a frame of reference for the legal construction of personal work relations, that of the personal work nexus, which would be systemically more inclusive than the contractual construction as to the legal links which it recognizes between the worker and other actors in an enlarged set of personal work relations. In this chapter, we introduce the notion of the 'personal work profile' as the basis for a yet more comprehensive or holistic way of understanding the legal construction of personal work relations, and moreover as a way of locating that understanding around the situation of the worker herself or himself. We then seek to use that analysis as the basis for an identification of the normative claims which workers may be regarded as having vis-à-vis other actors in the personal work relations in which they are engaged – an identification which we conduct under the heading of the idea of 'personality in work'. This will involve a sequence of analytical steps.

In the first section, we take the first of those analytical steps. This consists of identifying a further analytical element in the legal construction of personal work relations which we identify by the terminology of the 'personal work profile' of each worker. We advance and seek to deploy the idea of the personal work profile not as a status or relationship in and of itself, but as a technique of analysis for understanding in what sense and to what extent particular personal work relations should be regarded as secure, autonomous or freestanding, or precarious – and for better understanding the ways in which the existing legal categories of personal work relations are articulated and applied. We argue that, seen through the lens of the personal work profile, personal work relations, and working lives at large, appear as far more multi-faceted and multidimensional than the traditional binary divide suggests. From the personal work profile perspective, elements that are traditionally concealed behind the normative implications and underpinnings of the employee/self-employed distinction, acquire a clearly visible dimension that casts a new light on the concepts of security, precariousness, and autonomy in employment or work. For instance the vexed question of work or employment under multiple contracts, or the issue of work or employment by a primary carer for a disabled dependent, acquire a distinct normative dimension typically obscured by the binary divide and the regulatory rationales – or ideas of labour law – normally attached to it.

In the second section, preparing the way for our deployment of the notion of the personal work profile, we first suggest an analytical method of classification of personal work relations or profiles into three loose groupings, those of secure, autonomous, and precarious work. We then suggest that, using a comparative method of analysis, each of these groups can be further divided up. Then we consider the ways in which the evolutions of the labour market produce certain dynamics of movement between and around these different groupings. We suggest that an analysis of these dynamics can give us a further set of elements for identifying ways and directions in which the idea of labour law may have to evolve in order to realize a set of prescriptive regulatory objectives, a point to which we return in the third section of this chapter.

In the third section, we suggest ways in which, embellished with the notion of the personal work profile, our method of descriptive classification of personal work relations might contribute to the prescriptive regulation of those relations. We pursue further the idea that there are emergent new forms of personal work relation or profile, often fully or partly innominate; and we suggest that this might represent a particular way of thinking about the roles of *jus cogens* and *jus dispositivum* in the legal construction of personal work relations.

In the fourth and final section we give a preliminary indication of the ways in which this scheme of analysis might play a part in the future normative development of labour law. For this purpose we introduce the idea of 'personality in work', as a combination of the values of dignity, capability, and stability in personal work relations.

## Section 1:  The Idea of the Personal Work Profile

### A.  The Personal Work Profile and the Personal Work Situation

In the previous chapter, we have advanced and developed a technique of analysis of personal work relations, which, by using the idea of the personal work nexus, starts to get behind or underneath existing legal constructions of personal work relations and therefore to identify ways in which existing legal constructions sometimes fail to respond to the realities of personal work arrangements. We now introduce another such technique of analysis, which seeks to advance further down that path by invoking and using the idea of the 'personal work profile'. This serves to place the personal work nexus analysis in the larger context of the whole work and work-related situation within which each personal work relation operates.

Our starting point for the idea of the personal work profile is our perception that personal work relations cannot satisfactorily be understood, classified, or, ultimately, regulated in isolation from the overall 'personal work situation' of the worker in question. That personal work situation may be that the worker simply has one personal work relation through his working life. But that is a rarity; much more common is the personal work situation in which the worker has more than one personal work relation occurring concurrently or sequentially, and where the one or more personal work relations are combined or interspersed with states which can be thought of as work-related, such as those of being in unpaid work – for instance as a carer for a dependent, or being an unemployed jobseeker, or being on long-term sickness absence, or even being retired from work. We suggest that it is useful to conceive of such personal work situations as constituting the personal work profile of each working person, made up primarily of one or more personal work relation and secondarily of one or more work-related state.

We suggest that the idea of the personal work profile, as thus located in the personal work situation of each working person, can be used as an analytical technique in various ways. We can use the idea of the personal work profile to illuminate the ways in which a particular working person may be engaged or involved in a multiplicity of personal work relations or work-related states at any given moment, and to show how those personal work relations and work-related states may have implications for each other. Thus, within a personal work profile there might be two or more personal work relations which, while remaining sufficiently separate as not to fuse together into a single complex personal work relation, might nevertheless have normative implications for each other – as for instance in the debate about whether the employer in a personal work relation has to take account, for the purposes of working time regulation, of the hours which the worker works for another employer in a separate personal work relation.[3]

Thus again, within a personal work profile there might be a work-related state which has normative implications for the primary personal work relation in which the worker is engaged – as for instance where being in the work-related state of carer for a disabled relative transforms the primary personal work relation into one where there is a right to 'flexible working'. That is, therefore, a legal classification or adjudication which is carried out by reference to the personal work profile of the worker in question – where the personal work profile of the worker in question includes a qualifying work-related state as a carer, the primary employment contract or relationship is thereby transformed into this special kind of flexible work contract or relationship.[4] Such developments instantiate our conception of the analysis of personal work relations by reference to the larger personal work situation or personal work profile of each working person.

It is important for us to be clear about how this conception of the personal work profile relates to that of *statut professionnel* – best translated as 'labour force membership' – which has been identified as an analytical concept in existing labour law scholarship, as we discussed in an earlier chapter of this work, by Supiot and his colleagues in the 'Beyond Employment' project.[5] Our conceptions of the personal work situation and the personal work profile are, in descriptive terms, quite similar to those of the *statut professionnel* or labour force membership. However, the way in which we seek to develop and deploy the idea of the personal work profile is different from the way in which the idea of the *statut professionnel*/labour force

[3] This is a debate with very real consequences; the inability of some EU national legal systems to encompass the idea that discrete but simultaneous personal work relations ought to be approached and regulated by reference to the overall personal work situation of the worker in question was one of the causes of the collapse of the new Working Time Directive negotiations in 2009: 'Finally, no substantive agreement could be reached on the issue of multiple contracts. For workers covered by more than one employment contract, Parliament considered that working time should be calculated per worker and not per contract', COD/2004/0209: 29/04/2009 – EP/Council: Conciliation Committee, results.

[4] European Union law is an increasingly fertile territory for the development and recognition of such complex work situations. In Case C-303/06, *Coleman v. Attridge Law* [2008] ECR I-5603, for example, the ECJ effectively recognized that domestic work performed as the primary carer of a disabled dependant may well have important normative effects upon the personal work relationship of the carer, by virtue of the linking concept known as discrimination by association. See generally below Chapter 10, Section 3.A, pp. 44–16.

[5] A. Supiot (2001) *Beyond Employment*, Oxford: OUP, 24. See above, pp. 24–6.

membership is developed and deployed by Supiot and his colleagues. As we have earlier observed, they advance the idea of the *statut professionnel*/labour force membership as an element in an over-arching personal status for the working person involving responsibilities both for employers and for the state as guarantor of social security and regulator of the labour market, and, by the same token, correlative rights for the working person – identified as 'social drawing rights'. We regard that as a very important basis for the design, on a strategic level, of labour law, social security law, and employment policy. However, we envisage the personal work profile as an analytical concept with a more specific function. We advance and seek to deploy the idea of the personal work profile not as a status or relationship in and of itself, but as a technique of analysis for better understanding the ways in which the existing legal categories of personal work relations are articulated and applied. This will we hope become clearer in the next subsection, in which we further elaborate our notion of the personal work profile as a concept which frames particular work relations within the working life or career of each working person who is the subject of the work relation or relations in question.

## B. The Personal Work Profile and the Working Life or Career

In the previous subsection we put forward the notion of the personal work profile as a way of placing personal work relations within a larger framework which is located upon each working person as the subject of those personal work relations. The first step towards the setting up of that larger framework consisted in invoking the idea of the personal work situation or profile of each working person, and identifying that personal work situation or profile as the complex or congeries of the work relations and work-related states in which the working person is involved. As thus expressed, the notion of the personal work profile might appear to lack a time-dimension; it might present itself as a snapshot of the working person's personal work relation(s) and work-related states at a given moment at which the personal work profile is described and analysed.

The purpose of this subsection is to assert that the personal work profile does in our conception have such a time-dimension, and to elaborate that time dimension as one which extends over the working-life or career of the working person in question. We mean to say that, if the personal work profile is located in the present reality of the working person's personal work situation at the moment of its description, integral to that present reality is a past constituted by the earlier working life or career of that working person, and a future consisting in the projected subsequent development of that working life or career. This may appear to be a rather abstract or ethereal assertion; but it can we think be shown to have very concrete consequences.

For instance – and it is a very major instance – it is very noticeable that in many European legal systems, the taxonomy system for personal work relations – whether it is a binary or a tri-partite one – is very often, one might say typically, applied with reference to a single personal work relation or single personal work contract at a given moment in time. The working person is classified as an 'employee' or a 'worker' or an 'independent contractor' by reference to one particular personal work relation or personal work contract which is in issue at a particular juncture. This kind of classification of working persons themselves, *ratione personae*, rather than of their personal work relations, may itself be problematical in some important general ways – historically at least, it could amount to very questionable assignments of lowly status as 'servants' or 'workmen'. However, this way of taxonomizing (and thereby regulating) personal work relations gives rise to a more specific analytical problem; it fosters the illusion that this taxonomy can satisfactorily be effected, indeed can satisfactorily exist, at the level of each particular personal work relation or personal work contract assessed at a given moment in time, when in fact such taxonomies, in so far as they are sustainable at all, can only satisfactorily be operated on the basis of the personal work profile as a whole and considered as existing and evolving over a period of time.

Thus we suggest that the binary divide between 'employment' and 'self-employment', or between 'dependent employment' and 'independent contracting' has increasingly been identified as the distinction between two contract types – the contract of employment and the personal contract for services – a distinction regarded as one capable of being applied to a particular contract at a given moment in time. Yet we think that the binary divide evolved historically as, and can still best be understood as, a contrast between those personal work *profiles* which involve one personal work contract or relation with one employer over a significant time period and, on the other hand, those personal work profiles which involve multiple short-term personal work contracts or relations with many different employers or work-users over a comparable time period.[6] Indeed, this is in a way implicit in the very terminology which is used to identify personal work profiles which do not have the character of dependent employment. The terminologies of 'independent contractor' or 'self-employed worker' invoke the historical fact that the people in those personal work situations were viewed as working for many persons over a significant period of time and therefore dependent on no one person during that time. Only thus can we explain the otherwise very curious notion of 'self-employment' itself – it draws on the idea that persons employed by no others are therefore employed by themselves.

From that particular discussion, we might draw the conclusion that the legal notion of 'self-employment' works better and makes more sense as a taxonomy for the personal work profile as a whole than as a taxonomy of any one contract or relation within that profile. If so, we might begin to realize that the legal notion of 'employment' as a directly contrasting taxonomy also and by the same token works better and makes more sense as a taxonomy for the personal work profile as a whole

---

[6] On time as a determinant characteristic for different work relations cf. the very perceptive V. Bavaro, 'Tesi sullo Statuto Giuridico del Tempo nel Rapporto di Lavoro Subrdinato', in V. Bavaro and B. Veneziani (eds.) (2009) *Le Dimensioni Giuridiche dei tempi del Lavoro*, Bari: Cacucci, p. 11. In *Wage Labour and Capital* Marx provides a vivid description of the importance of the temporal element in the provision of labour at the outset of the industrial revolution: 'The capitalist, it seems, therefore, *buys* their labour with money. They *sell* him their labour for money. But this is merely the appearance. In reality what they sell to the capitalist for money is their labour *power*. The capitalist buys this labour power for a day, a week, a month, etc. [ . . . ]. Labour power, therefore, is a commodity, neither more nor less than sugar. The former is measured by the clock, the latter by the scales.' K. Marx (1978) *Wage Labour and Capital*, Peking: Foreign Languages Press, pp. 18–19.

than as a taxonomy of any one contract or relation within that profile. As will be very clear from arguments advanced in earlier chapters, we are sceptical about the feasibility and appropriateness of maintaining a binary divide between 'employment' and 'self-employment' as the general categorical system for personal work contracts or personal work relations. However, we strongly suggest that, so far as this is a feasible and appropriate categorical system for those contracts or those relations, it is much more sustainable if it is constructed and applied within the macroscopic framework of the personal work profile of each working person to whom the category system is being applied than if it is constructed and applied at the more microscopic level of particular personal work contracts or particular personal work relations or nexuses.

We shall argue in the last two sections of this chapter that these conclusions about the analytical importance of the personal work profile have profound regulatory consequences and normative implications. However, at least one preparatory step is still necessary before articulating those arguments; in the next section, we set out our proposed taxonomy of personal work relations with which we suggest that the idea of the personal work profile can usefully be combined.

## Section 2: A Critical Taxonomy of Personal Work Relations

A constantly recurring theme of the present work has been the unsatisfactoriness, in various analytical and normative senses, of the taxonomies of personal work relations or profiles which are explicit or implicit in European national labour law systems. In this section, we come to the point of proposing a taxonomy of personal work relations which is critical of and challenging to existing taxonomies both in its methodology and in its substance. We articulate that taxonomy, and advance our claims for it as one which is in some senses alternative to existing taxonomies, in two stages. At the first stage, we seek to establish a starting point consisting of a broad tri-polar classification or grouping of personal work relations or profiles (subsection A). At the second stage, we amplify and elaborate our taxonomy, from that tri-polar starting point, into a scheme of seven empirical categories (subsection B).

### A. A Tri-Polar Starting Point

In this subsection we take the first step in presenting a taxonomy of personal work relations or profiles which consciously differentiates itself from those which currently exist in European national labour law systems. This analysis is not a static one; it depicts the taxonomies of personal work relations in European national legal systems as being in various states of flux. These states of flux are between binary and tri-partite taxonomies of personal work relations. Binary taxonomies are those which distinguish simply between employment and self-employment, or between dependent and independent work. Such taxonomies persist, albeit not without some struggle, in legal systems such as the French one. Tri-partite taxonomies are those which distinguish between employment, employment-like work, and self-employment, or between dependent, semi-dependent, and independent work. European national labour law systems generally started with a binary taxonomy, and some have remained in that state (though having tended to enlarge the employment category).

Meanwhile, some other national labour law systems – such as that of the UK – are moving towards using mixtures of binary and tri-partite taxonomies, binary for some purposes and tri-partite for others. There is a noticeable centrifugal drive away from the pure binary divide and towards more complex and fragmented taxonomies. Even in France – a legal system where, until a few years ago, the notion of economic dependence was dismissed as 'too imprecise'[7] – the 2008 *Antonmattei-Sciberras Report* reopened the academic and policy debate by advocating 'the creation... of a legal regime for the economically dependent worker'.[8] There is no doubt, however, that the most significant advance in that sense has been produced by the widely commented upon[9] 2007 Spanish Law 20/2007, of 11 July, the Statute on Autonomous Work, introducing and regulating the contractual category of 'economically dependent autonomous workers'.[10]

Reformist arguments in these states of flux generally concentrate on modifying these taxonomies by pressing either for enlargement of the employment category within a binary taxonomy, or for greater use of tri-partite taxonomy, or both. Rather than taking up a particular position within that debate, we prefer to advance a separate critical taxonomy which transcends existing descriptive taxonomies and aims to provide a basis for the critical evaluations of the working of the descriptive taxonomies, and for regulation on the basis of those evaluations. Our critical taxonomy is not intended to be used directly to provide a new set of legal categories. That might be terminally disruptive of an already very complex and fragile set of existing legal taxonomies. Instead, our critical taxonomy is advanced as possibly providing ways of adapting and adjusting the formulation and application of existing categories. We have, as it were, temporarily freed ourselves of the responsibility for creating a legal taxonomy in order to obtain a critical perspective upon existing legal taxonomies.

---

[7] J. Pélissier, A. Supiot, and A. Jeammaud (2000) *Droit du travail*, Paris: Dalloz, 151.

[8] P.H. Antonmattei and J. C. Sciberras (2009) *Le travailleur économiquement dépendant: quelle protection?* (Novembre 2008), 22. Cf. also P.H. Antonmattei and J. C. Sciberras, 'Le travailleur économiquement dépendant, quelle protection ?', *Droit Social*, 221.

[9] J. R. Mercader Uguina and A. de la Puebla Pinilla (2007) 'Comentario a la Ley 20/2007, de 11 de julio, del Estatuto del Trabajo Autónomo', 20, *Relacione Laborales*, 99; F. Valdès Dal-Ré and O. Leclerc (2008) 'Les nouvelles frontières du travail indépendant. A propos du statut du travail autonome espagnol' *RDT*, 296; J. Cabeza Pereiro (2008) 'The Status of Self-employed Workers in Spain', *ILR*, 91.

[10] Article 12 of *Ley 20/2007, de 11 de julio, del Estatuto del Trabajo Autónomo*. Available online at www.boe.es/boe/dias/2007/07/12/pdfs/A29964-29978.pdf. This has been recently supplemented by *Real Decreto 197/2009, de 29 de febrero*. Cf. J. R. Mercader Uguina and A. de la Puebla Pinilla, (2007) 'Comentario a la Ley 20/2007, de 11 de julio, del Estatuto del Trabajo Autónomo', 20, *Relacione Laborales*, 99; F. Valdès Dal-Ré and O. Leclerc (2008) 'Les nouvelles frontières du travail indépendant. A propos du statut del travail autonome espagnol' *RDT*, 296; J. Cabeza Pereiro (2008) 'The Status of Self-employed Workers in Spain' *ILR*, 91; cf. J. Fudge (2010) 'A Canadian Perspective on the Scope of Employment Standards, Labor Rights, and Social Protection: The Good, the Bad, and the Ugly', 31, *CLLPJ*, 253.

From that critical perspective, we advance a different taxonomy which consists not of hard legal categories, but rather of typologies which we regard as 'soft' ones in two senses. They are soft in the sense that they are loose descriptors rather than legal terms of art, and also in the further sense that they describe transient locations in a rapidly changing or fluctuating world of personal work arrangements or relations. With those explanations or caveats, we advance a set of three typologies for personal work relations or profiles; we suggest that it is useful to make a critical analysis of personal work relations or profiles which distinguishes between them according to whether they are:

1. relations or profiles of 'secure work'; or
2. relations or profiles of 'autonomous or freestanding work'; or
3. relations or profiles of 'precarious work'.

We advance this taxonomy as one which is quite different in nature from existing bi-partite or tri-partite legal taxonomies in that, whereas existing taxonomies, whether bi-partite or tri-partite, assume or assert that there is a spectrum or axis from 'dependence' to 'independence', this taxonomy denies the existence of a single spectrum or axis, or for that matter a single set of concentric circles. Our analysis prefers to envisage a set of more elaborately differentiated kinds of personal work relation, and to group those relations into three loosely defined locations. Those three locations are each envisaged as coalescing around the three respective core ideas or 'poles' of security, autonomy, and precarity; it is in that sense that this analysis is put forward as a tri-polar one. The particular suggestion of this tri-polar scheme is, therefore, that there is no straight line which can be drawn between 'secure', 'autonomous', and 'precarious' work, such as would for example locate 'precarious work' as a half-way house between 'secure' and 'autonomous' work in a way that is often implicitly assumed in the formation and application of legal categories. Crucially, we think that the suggestion that precarious work is a such a half-way house, on a spectrum between security and autonomy, tends to exaggerate its virtues and understate its problems in normative terms.

We furthermore suggest that this analysis, although it gives rise only to 'soft' typologies, nevertheless allows us to identify certain dynamics of development in the practice of personal work relations or profiles, which tend to be obscured by existing legal taxonomies. The general perception seems to be, from within existing legal taxonomies, that there is a dynamic from dependent towards independent personal work relations, and that conceptions of dependent or semi-dependent employment should be advanced to keep pace with that dynamic. We suggest that there is a rather more complex set of dynamics which can better be understood by using our set of three soft typologies. The most significant of these dynamics are those whereby both secure personal work relations or profiles and autonomous or free-standing personal work relations or profiles are tending to metamorphose into precarious work relations or profiles (probably reversing a much earlier set of dynamics whereby both autonomous or free-standing and precarious personal work relations or profiles tended to metamorphose into secure ones).

There are also some further dynamics whereby some personal work relations may metamorphose into other kinds of relation or state, which are not personal work relations at all. Some personal work relations, especially autonomous or freestanding ones, may metamorphose into non-personal work arrangements whereby the working person operates within a corporate commercial framework rather than within a personal work relation at all. Some personal work relations, especially precarious ones, may metamorphose into work arrangements which are so informal or non-obligational that they fail to come within the framework of legally recognized personal work relations. The British labour market provides us with a newly emerging example of these particular trends; the  current Government's 'Big Society' policy, seeking *inter alia* to 'give communities the right to bid to take over local state-run services'[11] as well as to 'give public sector workers a new right to form employee-owned co-operatives and bid to take over the services they deliver [and] become their own boss',[12] is likely to accelerate the transformation of secure forms of employment into precarious work relations, and give centre stage to voluntary or community work relations of an explicitly non-obligational character. We argue that it is the complexity of these dynamics, and the difficulty of reconciling them with essentially single-spectrum legal taxonomies, that has created great difficulties for the analysis and policy-making of labour law. In the next subsection we seek to develop this line of thought, and our critical taxonomy itself, by exploring some further categories into which we think that our tri-polar structure can be loosely divided.

## B. A Scheme of Empirical Categories

The next step in presenting our argument consists in establishing a practical or empirical typology of personal work relations or profiles which will supplement and expand upon the tri-polar analysis which was advanced in the previous subsection. The notion of a practical or empirical typology – as opposed to a legal taxonomy – of personal work relations is essentially a socio-economic one; so labour lawyers proposing such a typology are operating outside their own immediate expertise, and are encroaching upon that of labour economists or sociologists. This would not be too grave a matter in itself, for these areas of expertise overlap with that of the labour lawyer, and legal ordering is important among the factors which inform and shape the practical or empirical typology of personal work relations. A greater problem is that a labour lawyer when suggesting such a typology, rather than straying *too far* from his or her own legal discipline, will not stray *far enough* – that is to say, will remain entrapped within the legal frame of reference, and will propose a typology which simply reflects the legal categories from which the very aim of the exercise is to break free.

---

[11] Cabinet Office, *Building the Big Society* (May 2010) 1.
[12] Ibid., 2.

To propose a typology which had that character, and to purport to use it as a basis of evaluation and criticism of the corresponding legal categories would of course be to engage in autopoiesis or self-referential argument. That, we dare to suggest, is what employment lawyers very often do when seeking to sustain and to apply the binary division of personal work relations and of personal work contracts into those of 'employment' on the one hand and 'self-employment' on the other hand, since that binary division is one very largely invented and imposed by legal systems of labour market administration. But we are very aware of the risk of falling into more complex and apparently sophisticated forms of the very same analytical error. Very conscious, therefore, of these hazards, we nevertheless suggest that it may be useful to identify the following seven leading types of personal work relations:

1. 'standard employment' work relations or profiles;
2. the personal work relations or profiles of 'public service' or of 'public office';
3. the personal work relations or profiles of those engaged in 'liberal professions';
4. the personal work relations or profiles of individual entrepreneurial workers, such as 'freelance workers' and 'consultants';
5. the personal work relations or profiles of 'atypical' workers such as 'casual', 'temporary', and 'part-time' workers;
6. the personal work relations or profiles of those engaged in preparatory work, such as 'trainees', 'apprentices' or 'interns', and
7. the personal work relations or profiles of volunteers.

We also suggest that these seven types can usefully be related back, in a reasonably precise way, to the tri-polar critical typology which we put forward in the previous subsection. That is to say, we suggest that these seven types can be roughly aligned with the tri-polar typology as follows: type (1) standard employment and type (2) public service work relations or profiles roughly correspond to or instantiate the notion of 'secure work'; type (3) liberal professional and type (4) public service work relations or profiles roughly correspond to or instantiate the notion of 'autonomous work'; type (5) atypical work relations or profiles; type (6) preparatory work relations, and type (7) personal work relations or profiles of volunteers, roughly correspond to or instantiate the notion of 'precarious work'.

One or two points of detail may usefully be made about this scheme. It is not intended to be a comprehensive typology covering all possible personal work relations. The categories are not only therefore incomplete but also not mutually exclusive, so that they are overlapping and intersecting ones; this is a point to which we revert later. We have enclosed terminologies in quotation marks where we believe that they emerge from, or at least are identifiable within, a reasonably pan-European discourse of practical or empirical personal work relations which is authentically distinguishable from the legal analysis of those personal work relations, though necessarily interconnected with that legal analysis for the reasons which we have previously given. We think this is true even of the 'standard employment' type, though we acknowledge that this category is the one which is most open to the suspicion of being simply a back-formation or reflection of a legal typology.

Rather differently, the notion of 'individual entrepreneurial workers' which we have invoked as category (4) is one which we have invented in order to group together a number of existing practical or empirical types such as 'freelancers' and 'consultants'. This represents a deliberate resisting of the temptation to use the terminology of 'the self-employed' or 'independent contractors' to identify this category, because they are so obviously reflections of *legal* categories; but we are conscious that our argument becomes difficult here. Equally open to debate is its invoking of the notion of 'atypical personal work relations or profiles' in order to assemble, in category (5), a number of practical typologies; here the difficulty is not so much that it steers either towards or away from a legal category, as that it alludes to a very imprecise socio-economic characterization.

There are on the other hand other genuinely *practical or empirical* typologies which could be invoked, but which we believe to be cross-cutting ones rather than additional ones; the most important of those are 'agency workers' (meaning workers employed through employment agencies) and 'contract workers'(meaning workers employed on a 'contracted-out' basis through subcontractors); personal work relations of these kinds are to be found to a greater or lesser extent within categories (3) to (6) of the system outlined above. It is hoped by means of these various caveats and explanations to have established a sufficiently robust typology of personal work relations or profiles to act as the foundation of the legal superstructure which the next subsection of this chapter seeks to build up.

## C. The Legal Construction of the Empirical Categories

In this next stage of our argument, we consider the legal nature of personal work relations or profiles in each of the practical or empirical categories which were identified in the previous section. Since one of the starting points for the whole of our argument in this part of our work is that the legal construction of personal work relations can usefully be envisaged as a set or a variety of different kinds of personal work nexus, this stage of the argument therefore involves considering what kinds of personal work nexus are associated with each of our practical or empirical categories when those categories are passed through the filter of legal construction. By way of reminder, we point out that this analysis is posed against a generally accepted legal construction of the world of personal work relations which imposes on it a binary division into the two contrasting types of 'employees' and 'independent contractors', or, more specifically, into the two contractual categories of 'contracts of employment (or of service)' and 'contracts for services'.

In order to apply our personal work nexus analysis to our seven practical or empirical types of personal work relations, one or two further definitions or refinements are needed. Firstly, we should, as we argued in the last chapter, draw certain distinctions between different types of personal work nexus. Personal work nexuses may differ from each other in more than one dimension. They may differ in the extent to which they are contractual in character; they may be wholly contractual, wholly non-contractual, or partly contractual and partly non-contractual. They may also differ as to how many sides or links they have; they may be bilateral or multilateral. Again, this analysis is posed as a challenge to a generally accepted much simpler paradigm for the legal construction of personal work relations in which those relations are viewed as universally or nearly universally having the legal character of bilateral contracts.

One further element of definition is then needed in order to explain the relationship between that simpler accepted paradigm (in which personal work relations are almost systemically reduced to bilateral contracts) and the more complex or multifarious analysis which we are proposing. As we have indicated, in the simpler more generally accepted analysis, the bilateral contracts in terms of which personal work relations are legally construed are subjected to a binary division into contracts of employment with employees and contracts for services with independent contractors. In that system of construction, enormous analytical effort is concentrated on drawing a bright line between those two types (an illusory quest in our view); but the outer perimeters of the whole double category of contracts are left relatively undefined. In particular, little care or energy is devoted to distinguishing between those contracts for services which fall within the domain of personal work relations, and those which are outside that domain but are within the whole large domain of services contracts in general.

That turns out to be a serious issue when, as happens more and more frequently in current European practice, the scope of employment legislation is extended beyond that of employees with contracts of employment to include other workers who therefore, according to this binary system, are normally regarded as working under contracts for services; criteria are needed to delineate this expanded sphere of employment law from that of commercial contract law in general, but those criteria tend to be lacking. In the system of analysis which we are trying to construct, much importance is attached to the articulation of those criteria; they are crucially needed to define the *personal* character of the personal work contract and indeed the personal work relation or profile, the latter being more expansive concepts, but ones which are nevertheless limited to work relations which are focused upon the doing of work or provision of services *primarily by an individual operating as such* rather than by a multi-personal organization. In short, the system of analysis based on the concepts of the personal work contract and relation or profile and the personal work contract requires a distinction between the *personal* contract for services (in the above sense) and the contrasting *non-personal* contract for services.

Armed with these distinctions, we can usefully analyse the legal construction of personal work relations or profiles within the practical or empirical categories which we have identified. We will attempt to do this both statically and dynamically; that is to say, we will consider both the predominant current analysis of personal work relations or profiles within each of our seven categories, and also the dynamics whereby personal work relations or profiles tend to transmute within and between our seven categories. At this point, however, we need to remind ourselves that the practical or empirical categories and the legal categories do not evolve totally independently of each other – changes in the legal character or construction of personal work relations or profiles are generally linked to changes in the character and functioning of the practical or empirical categories of those relations or profiles, though there are significant phenomena of mismatching between practical work relations or profiles and the legal construction of them. So the dynamics which we shall seek to identify, although primarily describing legal evolutions, are also secondarily empirical ones. In the following analysis we shall refer to personal work relations, reverting later to the extension of the analysis to personal work profiles.

Thus we begin with (1) 'standard employment' personal work relations. The legal construction of those work relations is, as noted in the chapters forming Part 2 of the present work, overwhelmingly strongly oriented towards the contract of employment – though we have argued in the previous chapter that this bilateral contractual construction of 'standard employee' relations often belies a more complex reality which ought to be reflected in the recognition of an only partly contractual personal work nexus in which the worker is accepted as having legally significant though non-contractual vertical, horizontal, or diagonal links with other workers and managers within, or connected to, the employing enterprise, for example because the employing enterprise and other workers or managers might be delictually liable for harassment of the worker in question, or of a prohibited form of discrimination against that worker.

There is at the same time a practical dynamic according to which some 'standard employee' personal work relations evolve either towards individual entrepreneurial work relations, or towards casual temporary and part-time work relations, for example where the remuneration of the worker is more strongly related to performance or output than it previously was, or in that the employment security of the worker is reduced, thus transferring more risk of downturn in demand to the worker than was previously placed upon him or her. However, it should be noted that such changes, fundamental though they may be from a socio-economic perspective, often do not displace or even disturb the legal construction of the personal work relations in question; much of that dynamic of entrepreneurialization or precarization of 'standard employee' personal work relations can be absorbed within the 'soft texture' of the contract of employment. On the other hand, the parties to standard employee personal work relations may be under strong incentives created by fiscal and regulatory regimes to reconstitute them in the practical form of individual entrepreneurial work relations or casual work relations, and more particularly in the legal form of the personal contract for services.

(2) The personal work relations of public service or public office. The inclusion of this type of personal work relations in our system of categories dramatically illustrates the diversity of legal constructions of personal work relations in general, and the unsatisfactoriness of envisaging those relations as falling into a simple binary division between contracts of employment and personal contracts for services. Although the particular personal work relations of public officials or functionaries in substance usually resemble versions of 'standard employee' work relations in which the worker benefits from strong protection of security of employment and income, the legal construction of those relations is usually radically different from that of standard employee relations, being in terms of a public law status which would in many systems not be regarded as a contractual

one, because the view is taken that the public official should be 'above the fray' of contractual work relations.

European legal and administrative systems diverge considerably as to how widely they accord the status of public official or public functionary. There is quite a widespread practical dynamic towards the approximation of these work relations to those of standard employee relations, indeed towards versions of standard employee relations which transfer some degree of economic risks to the worker; but European state legal systems diverge considerably in the extent to which they have inbuilt resistances to those changes. The UK employment law system has been very open to this kind of adaptation, while many other European systems erect much higher barriers around the separate public law status of public officials.

(3) Personal work relations in liberal professions. The logic of the binary legal conception of personal work relations would suggest that these particular work relations would fall squarely within the category of personal contracts for services – indeed, that they would represent the very archetype of this legal category, since professions have historically been described as 'liberal' precisely because those engaged in them are seen as operating on an autonomous basis rather than as subordinate 'servants'. However, the legal construction of these personal work relations is in reality much less straightforward. There is considerable divergence between European systems as to the regulatory regimes which have been devised for the practice of various different liberal professions – law, medicine, architecture, and accountancy for example – but one can generalize by saying that those practising these professions often do so within highly complex personal work nexuses involving, as legal actors in various ways, public authorities, or publicly accountable professional bodies, and, in another sense, professional colleagues who work together in various forms of partnership or collegiality.

The dynamics of movement from those kinds of personal work nexuses are also very complex and interesting. Historically, those dynamics have often tended to be towards a greater involvement of the public state – especially in the work of lawyers and doctors – so that those engaged in these professions came more to resemble public officials or functionaries. However, a more recent and quite pervasive dynamic has seemed to be towards a further 'liberalization' or even 'privatization' of these professional roles, identifying these work relations more squarely within the domain of private law. One might expect that this would involve a clearer characterization of these work relations as those of personal contracts for services. The reality is a more complex one, in which the relations of professional partnership or collegiality of individual practitioners tend to be transformed into professional enterprises often resembling commercial enterprises. This is comparable with a dynamic situation which exists within the sphere of individual entrepreneurial work relations, to which we now turn our attention.

(4) Individual entrepreneurial work relations. A picture is emerging in which none of the types of personal work relations which we have identified is as simple or

as stable, either in its practical existence or in its legal construction, as one might have imagined. This fourth typology, that of individual entrepreneurial work relations, is a no less deceptive one in that sense. Although the terminology is admittedly one which we have coined, it seems to identify a well-established form of personal work relations – those of the autonomous individual or personal provider of services – with a clearly corresponding legal construction – that of the personal contract for services. As noted in Chapters 7 and 8, these personal work relations, those of the self-employed or independent contractor, seem to occupy a well-defined space in the labour market historically reserved for the commercial and artisanal counterparts of the liberal professional.

That is a deceptive simplicity, because contemporary European labour markets and the regulatory regimes in which they operate, although they seem on the face of it to encourage and favour this type of personal work relations, also impose powerful dynamics of movement away from these relations and transform their practical mechanics and legal construction. There are in a sense pressures in several directions away from this type of personal work relations and away from their stereotypical legal form of the personal contract for services. In labour markets and regulatory regimes which exact organizational competence and competitiveness, it is hard for an individual to sustain an entrepreneurial role as a sole operator. He or she may be impelled by those forces towards the greater security of 'standard employee' work relations, or forced to settle for casual or temporary work relations. At the level of legal construction, the worker may be under pressure to move from work relations characterized by personal contracts for services to those represented by the contract of employment.

There is also another dynamic in a very different direction, indeed an almost diametrically opposed one. If the less successful individual entrepreneurial worker is driven by the adversities of sole operation towards fully dependent or semi-dependent employment relations, the more successful one seems to come under an equally strong set of pressures to extend and elaborate the organizational structure of his or her personal work relations. A number of observers have usefully identified this phenomenon in terms of the evolution of 'networked' employment arrangements involving 'networks' or teams of workers, and we have earlier remarked upon this as providing a good example of the evolution of complex personal work nexuses.[13] However, we are of the view that very often, the evolution of individual entrepreneurial work relations is not so much towards the elaboration of networks of workers but rather towards the transformation of the sole operator into a multipersonal small employing enterprise.

This might occur, for example, where an individual entrepreneurial worker in, let us say, the plumbing trade takes on assistants and begins to function as a very small-scale employer. The institutional forms for this kind of functioning as a very

---

[13] A very useful set of papers on this topic is to be found in a special issue of the *BJIR* – Vol. 42, issue 4 of December 2004 – on the topic of 'Changing Contours of Employment and New Modes of Labour Regulation', cf. in particular D. Marsden, 'The "Network Economy" and Models of Employment Contract', pp. 659–684. See also above at pp. 329–36.

small enterprise vary considerably between European countries; but we think they would have this in common, that the work relations of the individual entrepreneur with the purchasers or users of his or her services cease to be *personal* work relations; in legal terms, such relations move from the primary form of personal contracts for services to the primary form of non-personal contracts for services, that is to say in other words ordinary commercial or business contracts; and the work relations therefore fall outside even the enlarged domain of employment law which we have identified for the purposes of our general arguments in this work.

(5) The personal work relations of atypical workers. This discussion has to begin with a reiteration of the rather impressionistic character of this typology, and in particular of its overlap with, and indeed its lack of precision in relation to, the categories of 'standard employment' work relations and individual entrepreneurial work relations. This category, already depicted in its outline in Chapter 4 of the present work, consists in the effect of personal work relations which are marginal to 'standard employee' work relations not so much because of any preference on the part of the workers in question for autonomous and entrepreneurial forms of working, but rather because those workers do not have favourable access to the 'standard employee' sector of the labour market. The dynamics of the evolution of these work relations and of their legal forms is therefore and in fact rather different from those which were identified for 'standard employee' work relations or for individual entrepreneurial work relations; but, as in the latter case, we can observe that these dynamics tend in two very different or opposing directions.

One such dynamic is towards the classification and treatment of marginal work relations more and more in the manner of or like 'standard employee' work relations. The legal systems of different European countries vary as to their adaptability in this respect; some are more disposed than others either to treat marginal work relations as falling within the legal category which they apply to 'standard employee' work relations – typically that of the contract of employment; but there seems to be a common trend among those systems either to construct marginal work relations in that way or to devise legal conceptions of *similarity* with 'standard employee' work relations, which can be deployed in order to impose regimes similar to those applicable to 'standard employee' work relations, whether in terms of employment law or in terms of taxation and social security provision.

There is, however, a contrary dynamic, which we think perhaps has not been identified as clearly as it deserves to be in view of its very real practical and legal significance. This is a dynamic whereby the various practical and legal actors involved in the conduct or regulation of marginal personal work relations contrive to deepen the separation between marginal work relations and 'standard employee' work relations, in other words increasing the social, economic, and/or legal marginalization of those in this sector of the labour market. One significant manifestation of this marginalization may consist of increasingly structuring such work relations in the form of temporary agency employment or labour subcontracting, especially if the protective apparatus of employment law and social security is weakened by the interposition of employment agencies or labour subcontractors.

There is a further very important point about the way in which this dynamic away from 'standard employee' work relations may operate; it is one which has major implications for the legal construction of the personal work nexus in marginal work relations. As we have previously implied, the further marginalization of already marginal work relations away from 'standard employee' work relations does not typically project them towards individual entrepreneurial work relations. Instead, it projects them towards the 'informal' or 'grey' sectors of the labour economy in which work relations are characterized not by the positive autonomy of the workers but rather by the absence of legal regulation and protection. As a matter of the legal construction of those work relations, this may amount to a tendency *away* from contracts of employment, but not *towards* personal contracts for services in the way that the binary legal conception of personal work relations might suggest, but rather towards legally indeterminate or legally defective kinds of personal work nexus which fall below the horizons of contractually based employment law systems.

(6) The personal work relations of trainees or apprentices or interns. As already noted in Chapter 4, these personal work relations are especially interesting for the purpose of this analysis because of the intervention into them of the active labour market policies and public employment services of various European states. In practical terms they display some of the characteristics of 'standard employee' work relations – often in especially strongly integrated but subordinated forms – but also some of the aspects of marginal work relations, especially as expectations of subsequent employment security following successful completion of training or apprenticeship are reduced by post-Fordist patterns of work organization. State intervention tends to take the form of supporting and facilitating the creation and maintenance of these types of work relations as a way of combating unemployment, especially among young entrants to the labour market. In practice those interventions often result in the formation of multilateral personal work relations in which the state is an active participant via its public employment services.

The legal construction of these personal work relations has generally taken the form of special variants upon the contract of employment; in some employment law systems, for example the French one, there is a tendency to identify these as new contractual forms such as the '*contrat unique d'insertion*'.[14] These represent complex forms of personal work nexus in which public authorities may be formally recognized as legal actors. The dynamics of these personal work relations are also especially interesting; there is a tendency for them to undergo a degradation from educational variants upon 'standard employee' work relations to marginal or casual work relations. Such transitions are sometimes acutely controversial, because of suspicions that governments may be introducing them in order to effect a more generalized downgrading of 'standard employee' work relations to marginal or casual work relations. That was the essential explanation for the controversy in

---

[14] Article L. 5134-19 of the French *Code du Travail*.

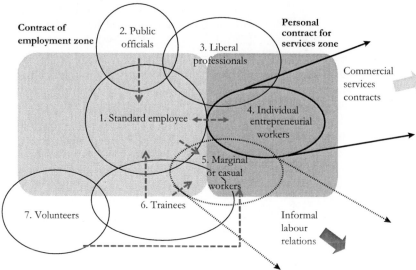

**Fig. 9.1.** The domain of personal work relations.

France about the proposed introduction of the '*contrat première embauche*' – here, the debate about a particular species of personal work contract or nexus reached the level of a national political crisis.

(7) The personal work relations of volunteers. As we noted in Chapter 4, it is a complex question whether and when arrangements for personal voluntary work may be constituted as contracts of employment, and we might also regard it as an equally complex question, the answer to which will vary as between national legal systems, whether and when such arrangements might be regarded as constituting other forms of personal work contract. In earlier formulations of our typology of practical or empirical categories of personal work relations, we had taken the view that arrangements for work by volunteers should only very exceptionally be regarded as coming within the domain of personal work relations, and even then not as a separate category.[15] We are now of the different view that such arrangements have grown in their incidence, and in their significance to the functioning of labour markets, to the point where they should be regarded as coming within the domain of personal work relations and as a distinct category thereof – though still in complex and debatable conjunctions with other categories, especially those of trainees and marginal workers.

The foregoing analysis is perhaps best understood as a map of the domain of personal work relations and of the different kinds of personal work nexus which may exist within that domain. We now present our attempt at drawing that map (see Fig. 9.1.). It depicts the different types of personal work relations which have

---

[15] As for example in M.R. Freedland (2007) 'Application of Labour and Employment Law Beyond the Contract of Employment' 146, *International Labour Review*, 3 at pp. 7–15.

been identified and discussed earlier in this section. It also seeks to show the dynamics of movement between and from those different types of work relations as we have described them in the course of this section. Finally, it illustrates the zones of application of the classical types of personal work contract which are constructed by employment law systems as the legal expression of those relations, namely those of the contract of employment and the (personal) contract for services.

We hope that this diagram may help to give a graphic reality to the domain of personal work relations which we have sought to identify, and also to convey the sense of the variety of types of personal work nexus which may arise within that domain. The map seeks to show how the different types of personal work relations overlap and connect with each other. Although the map shows how all the other types of personal work relation and of personal work nexus interconnect with 'standard employee' work relations and with the contract of employment, it also seeks to demonstrate that the other types should not be regarded as a mere periphery to that particular work relation and work nexus, still less a *uniform* periphery entirely occupied by individual entrepreneurial work relations and the personal contract for services. In order to heighten the emphasis upon that crucial point, the diagram depicts the respective spheres of the contract of employment and of the personal contract for services, showing that they do not between them occupy the whole domain of personal work relations, and that the interface between them is a complex but limited one.

The diagram also, we hope, gives further illustration and support to the arguments which we have presented by showing the dynamics of movement between the different types of work relation and work nexus. This depiction challenges an accepted or traditional conception by showing how the dynamics of movement do not consist simply of centrifugal movements away from or centri-petal movements towards 'standard employee' work relations, nor for that matter simply of two movements, between the legal forms of the contract of employment and the personal contract for services. The movements are shown instead to be complex intersectoral ones, sometimes indeed extending beyond the domain of personal work relations into the sphere of commercial or non-personal business relations in which the prevalent legal form is the non-personal services contract, or moving out to the zone where marginal work relations shade off into the relations of the informal economy.

The setting out and explanation of this diagram has completed this part of our discussion of the taxonomy of personal work relations. However, this diagram and explanation, by focusing particular attention on the dynamic elements in our taxonomy of personal work relations, has paved the way for the next part of our discussion of the taxonomy and regulation of personal work relations. That will be the part of the discussion in which we return to the argument presented in the first section of this chapter to the effect that the notion of the personal work profile would serve as a useful conceptual tool both in the taxonomy and in the regulation of personal work relations. To develop and complete the argument will be the task of the next section of this chapter.

## Section 3: The Personal Work Profile in the Taxonomy and Regulation of Personal Work Relations

In this section we draw together several strands of the arguments which have been developed in the preceding sections, and thereby hope to make good our contention for the idea of the 'personal work profile' as having a major positive part to play in the legal construction and, more especially, in the regulation of personal work relations. We seek to make out this argument in two steps; firstly, by elaborating the idea of 'normative characterization' of personal work relations as a primarily regulatory process (subsection A), and secondly by showing how the concept of the personal work profile might be regarded as having an especially important role in processes of normative characterization of personal work relations, and, by extension, in the legal regulation of those relations in a more general sense (subsection B).

### A. The Personal Work Profile and the Idea of Normative Characterization

The argument of this section will be that the taxonomy of personal work relations which we sought to establish in the previous section can itself be better understood and used as the basis for the legal construction and regulation of personal work relations if it is deployed in conjunction with the idea of the personal work profile which was articulated in the first section of this chapter. At this point in the argument, we return to and further elaborate upon the notion of 'normative characterization of personal work relations' put forward in the previous chapter; we use it to identify a process or activity which seems to us to be at the core of the legal construction and regulation of personal work relations, and which forms the point of entry for the idea of the personal work profile into that body of legal construction and regulation.

We begin by elaborating afresh upon what we mean by 'normative characterization' of personal work relations, a term that we see as an aspect or dimension of the 'legal construction' of personal work relations. By 'legal construction' of personal work relations we mean the whole process of ascribing legal form and structure to personal work relations, and of determining what legal norms or legally recognized norms (for example, valid contractual terms) apply to those personal work relations. There is a major aspect of that whole process which is normally thought of as the taxonomy or classification of personal work relations, carried out for the purpose of determining whether a particular norm or set of norms applies to a particular personal work relation. (For example, under English law we classify a personal work relation as being or not being a contract of employment in order to know whether the law of unfair dismissal applies to it or not.) This aspect is also thought of as being the determining of the 'personal scope' of labour law or of any particular law or set of laws which might be applicable to personal work relations.

However, we believe that the taxonomy or classification of personal work relations cannot satisfactorily be separated out from the rest of the process of legal construction of personal work relations as a distinctive or self-contained element in the process. And in fact we believe that much trouble and confusion comes about from trying to regard 'taxonomy' or the determination of 'personal scope' as a self-contained activity. We think it is preferable to think about 'taxonomy' or the determination of 'personal scope' as itself being part of a very complex activity which we have identified as the 'normative characterization' of personal work relations. That is to say, we identify as the 'normative characterization' of personal work relations a complex activity which is a combination of taxonomy with regulation. The element of regulation consists of ordaining that a certain norm or set of norms applies to a particular personal work relation or set of personal work relations. The element of taxonomy consists of providing and applying the category which identifies that personal work relation or set of personal work relations. These two activities are integrally linked to each other; they combine into a complex activity which applies a certain legal normative framework to any particular personal work relation within any particular legal system. This combined activity thereby assigns a certain normative *character* to any particular personal work relation; hence our choice of the terminology of 'normative characterization' to designate this complex activity.

The very idea of 'normative characterization', as we have previously and now articulated it, serves to demonstrate how intimately the legal categories of personal work relations are bound up with particular sets of norms in particular legal systems at particular moments in time. The idea of 'normative characterization' reminds us that when we invoke and deploy a notion such as 'the contract of employment', we are identifying a certain set of personal work relations which are subject to a certain normative regime and which derive a certain legal character from that regime. So it will be apparent that our idea of 'normative characterization' depicts an activity which is very contingent upon the particular legal and practical context in which it takes place, and very dependent on the path by which that context was created. In the remainder of this chapter, we further develop the idea of 'normative characterization' and think about ways of illuminating the activity which it depicts. We begin by distinguishing between two different modes in which 'normative characterization' may take place.

Normative characterization may take place in a purely descriptive mode; or it may take place in a purely prescriptive one. It is in a purely descriptive mode where it classifies personal work relations with regard to an existing set of norms simply as a matter of applying existing legal systems, and with no aim of altering the ways in which personal work relations are regulated. It is in a purely prescriptive mode where it proposes a classification for personal work relations with regard to a set of norms in a way that consciously overrides existing legal systems and does imply fundamental alteration to the ways in which those systems are regulated. In this purely prescriptive mode, normative characterization involves both reclassification and re-regulation of personal work relations. We can envisage a spectrum between these modes of normative characterization, so that the modes of description and prescription are combined in varying degrees.

This is true of the normative characterization which is carried out in various senses by the various actors in the legal construction of personal work relations – legislators, judges, legal policy makers, and theorists. Generally speaking, each of these legal actors seeks to find a single mode of normative characterization in which to operate. Judges will tend to operate in a largely or entirely descriptive mode, legal policy makers and theorists will tend to choose a more prescriptive mode. Legislators may at times follow the contours of existing legal constructions of personal work relations, and may at times fundamentally modify those constructions. But of late, the participants in the discussion about the role of taxonomy in labour law have been beset with uncertainty about what is the right mode of normative characterization in which to operate – in particular, as to whether to operate entirely in descriptive mode, or in gently prescriptive mode, or in strongly prescriptive mode. The discourses both of policymakers and theorists display great ambiguity in this respect.

It may be helpful at this point to emphasize the width of variety of the techniques of normative characterization which have a genuinely regulatory aspect or effect. We believe that the whole discussion, of the activity which we are identifying as the normative characterization of personal work relations has been impoverished by a tendency to assume that the arsenal of regulatory weapons is a very limited one. That is to say, the available techniques often seem to be envisaged as being limited to either: (1) adjustment of the place at which to make the binary divide between contracts of employment and personal contracts for services; or (2) the introduction of a third intermediate contract type; or (3) the treatment of personal work relations as relationships rather than contracts as a way of opening out the contractual categories. These are very important techniques, but there are various other ones which should command our attention.

Among such further techniques we should count rules or doctrines of law which create presumptions in favour of one particular contractual or relationship analysis of any given personal work relation – for example a rule or doctrine that a specified set of personal work relations shall be presumed to take the legal form of contracts of employment.[16] Equally, we should also count as such techniques rules or doctrines of law which authorize or require characterization of personal work relations in ways which override the stated intentions of the participants in those relations that they should fit into one category or avoid another category – for example rules or doctrines which tackle 'disguised employment' or 'sham contracts'.[17] Such rules or doctrines may combine to create general notions of controlling the abusive adoption of legal forms with the purpose or effect of defeating the application of labour laws – that is to say that such notions may amount to anti-dodging measures to protect the integrity of labour laws.

We suggest that one important further step can be taken in evolving the idea of 'normative characterization of personal work relations' as a larger, more dynamic

---

[16] The paradigm in this sense remains the *présomption de salariat* contained in the recently renumbered Article L7313-1 of the French Labour Code, in spite of its important qualification by Article L7313-1 bis. See also above p. 54.
[17] A. C. L. Davies (2009) 'Sensible Thinking About Sham Transactions: *Protectacoat Firthglow v Szilagyi*', 38, *ILJ*, 318.

way of thinking about the role of classification or taxonomy in the development of labour law. That further step consists of recognizing and being alert to the ways in which the law-makers and doctrinalists of labour or employment law are in fact constantly inventing or discovering novel forms not just of personal work contract or personal work relationship as we recognized in the previous chapter but also new patterns of personal work profile in the sense in which we have identified that latter notion in this chapter. This continual process of invention or discovery takes place around or within the existing grand categories of employment or self-employment, but eventually disrupts or transforms those grand categories themselves.

Hence we can use the notion of the personal work profile to re-visit in a new way the phenomenon of constant reinvention of novel forms of contract of employment or other personal work contract or relation, upon which we remarked in the previous chapter. This is an idea which Deakin (2004) encapsulated in the notion of the 'many futures of the contract of employment',[18] and which is instantiated by Anne Davies' articulation of the idea of the 'intermittent employment contract'.[19] We have previously observed that this may create new kinds of personal work contract or relation which have not been endowed with a name which will secure conceptual recognition for them. We have argued that these may amount to fully or partly innominate personal work contracts or relations; we now suggest that they can also often be regarded as the evolution of new kinds of personal work profile.

A rich source of these new kinds of personal work profile or new elements in personal work profiles is to be found in those national implementations of EU Directives which in the previous chapter we identified as constituting new and sometimes innominate forms of personal work contract or relation. So, for English law, we could think of the TUPE Regulations, in their implementation of the Acquired Rights Directive,[20] as instituting new kinds of personal work profile containing 'elements of transferred employment'. Similarly, we could think of the Fixed-term Work Regulations which implemented the Fixed-term Work Directive[21] as creating new kinds of personal work profile embodying 'transitions from fixed-term to permanent employment'. Then again, we could regard the Temporary Agency Work Regulations which implement the Temporary Agency Work Directive[22] as instituting and regulating 'temporary agency personal work profiles' of a novel kind.

---

[18] S. Deakin (2004) 'The many futures of the contract of employment', in J. Conaghan, R. M. Fischl, K. Clare (eds.), *Labour Law in an Era of Globalization*, Oxford: OUP, pp. 177–96.

[19] A. C. L. Davies (2007) 'The Contract of Intermittent Employment', 36, *ILJ*, 102–18.

[20] The Transfer of Undertakings (Protection of Employment) Regulations 2006, SI 2006/246; Council Directive 2001/23/EC on the approximation of the laws of the Member States relating to the safeguarding of employees' rights in the event of transfers of undertakings, businesses or parts of undertakings or businesses, [2001] OJ L 82/16.

[21] The Fixed-term Employees (Prevention of Less Favourable Treatment) Regulations 2002, SI 2002/2034; Council Directive 1999/70/EC of 28 June 1999 concerning the framework agreement on fixed-term work concluded by ETUC, UNICE and CEEP, [1999] OJ L 43.

[22] The Agency Workers Regulations 2010, SI 2010/93; Directive 2008/104/EC of the European Parliament and of the Council of 19 November 2008 on temporary agency work [2008] OJ L 9.

Moreover, just as we have earlier observed the emergence of new and as yet innominate personal work relations from the legislation about 'flexible working', so we could begin to identify such relations as combining sequentially to form something amounting to 'flexible working profiles'. Rather similarly, we believe that the implementation of the Employment Discrimination Framework Directive 2000/78 will not only turn out to have generated new kinds of employment contract in which arrangements for retirement are newly and differently articulated, but will also give rise to differently envisaged personal work profiles or career progressions taken as a whole. This kind of evolution is already perceptible in the UK in the transition from the approach taken in the Employment Equality (Age) Regulations 2006[23] to the different regulatory approach which has most recently been instituted.[24] We suggest and argue that these emergent new forms of personal work profile instantiate the idea of 'normative characterization' in its full and complex sense; that is to say, they are much more than simply emerging new taxonomies; they are also in and of themselves instruments of regulation. They are, indeed, very subtle instruments of regulation, capable of being highly tuned, in at least two dimensions. We proceed to display those two dimensions in the succeeding paragraphs.

Firstly, these newly emerging types of personal work relation or profile constitute complex regulatory instruments in that they represent new forms of regulation which, in various ways, fall between *jus cogens* and *jus dispositivum*. That is to say, they do not, on the one hand represent mandatorily imposed terms and conditions for the making or conduct, or termination of personal work relations; nor, on the other hand, do they represent mere default or optional terms and conditions for the making, or conduct or termination of personal work relations. (In that sense, the 'default retirement age' is a misnomer.) Instead they represent complex instruments of control over the making, conduct, or termination of personal work relations, imposing elaborate constraints often of a procedural kind (such as that a particular normative arrangement is allowable only if agreed according to certain individual or collective procedures).

Secondly, these newly emerging types of personal work relation or profile constitute complex regulatory instruments in that they represent, in and of themselves, carefully nuanced positions on a 'flexicurity' spectrum. In this respect, they are rather unlike the traditional forms of labour law regulation, which consisted in a much more direct way of protective interventions in favour of defined sections of the workforce. The new generation of regulatory instruments, taking this form of

---

[23] Council Directive 2000/78/EC establishing a general framework for equal treatment in employment and occupation, [2000] OJ L 303/16; Employment Equality (Age) Regulations 2006, SI 2006/1031, now embodied in Equality Act 2010.

[24] UK Department for Business, Innovation and Skills, 'Phasing Out the Default Retirement Age: Government Response to Consultation' (January 2011). Cf. the Employment Equality (Repeal of Retirement Age Provisions) Regulations 2011, SI 2011/1069.

novel legal characterizations, may as easily create models for the conduct of personal work relations which are retrogressive rather than progressive when measured against older patterns of legal intervention, and which would accelerate the processes of precarization of personal work relations.

One such example of retrogressive legal intervention may be provided by some reform proposals aimed, ostensibly, at reunifying various forms of atypical work contracts through the introduction of a new, unifying, 'normative characterization', variably referred to as '*contrat unique*',[25] '*contratto unico*',[26] or '*contrato único*'.[27] These suggested reforms have the objective of replacing both 'atypical' and 'standard' contracts, and their distinctive regulations, with a new and unifying contractual structure which, while in principle of an indefinite duration, would derogate from standard employment protection legislation and provide for a progressive accrual of rights according to seniority and continuity in employment. There is substantial support from some European quarters for this third type of deregulatory approach, with the 2007 *Flexicurity Pathways Report* overtly suggesting that '[t]he flexibility of standard contracts and the security of non-standard contracts could be enhanced by having a system where certain entitlements (on top of the basics) and elements of protection are being built up gradually'.[28]

A no less pertinent example of retrogressive legislation is offered to us by a *decreto delega legislativa*, adopted by the Italian Parliament in early 2010.[29] Among other things, this statute seeks to allow the parties to a contract for the provision of personal work to include terms specifying that, in case of grievances, they may bring the matter before ad hoc arbitration committees, whose decisions – unless the mandate given to an arbitrator, or an applicable collective agreement, explicitly provides otherwise – may not be appealed before the ordinary jurisdiction of the *pretore del lavoro*.[30] This reform is supposed to encourage alternative dispute resolution (ADR) mechanisms and reduce the backlog of cases pending before the notoriously log-jammed Italian courts; however, in fact, its effects are to strengthen the '*certificazione*' procedures set up by Law 276/03,[31] by allowing the

---

[25] P. Cahuc et F. Kramarz (2004) *De la précarité à la mobilité: vers une Sécurité sociale professionnelle*, Paris: La Documentation française. On the basis of these proposals the UMP produced the report *Repenser le contrat de travail en instaurant un contrat de travail unique* available online at www.u-m-p. org/site/index.php/ump/debattre/dossiers/economie_emploi/repenser_le_contrat_de_travail_en_ instaurant_un_contrat_de_travail_unique.

[26] Disegno di Legge n.1481/2009, 'Disposizioni per il superamento del dualismo del mercato del lavoro, la promozione del lavoro stabile in strutture produttive flessibili e la garanzia di pari opportunità nel lavoro per le nuove generazioni'. See also, T. Boeri and P. Garibaldi (2008) *Un Nuovo Contratto per Tutti*, Milano: Chiarelettere.

[27] *Propuesta para la reactivación laboral en España*, available online at www.crisis09.es/propuesta/. Also available in English at www.crisis09.es/PDF/restart-the-labor-market.pdf.

[28] European Expert Group on Flexicurity, *Flexicurity Pathways – Turning Hurdles into Stepping Stones* (June 2007), 12. See also explicit references at pp. 32, 35.

[29] DDL 116–B available online at www.lavoro.gov.it/NR/rdonlyres/E4890E6F-EB00-4C3C-89C3-AAAD34DBD0DC/0/collegatolavoro.pdf.

[30] Article 31(5). A provision that may well not withstand the scrutiny of the Italian Constitutional Court.

[31] Cf. N. Countouris (2007) *The Changing Law of the Employment Relationship*, Aldershot: Ashgate, p. 68.

parties to *ex ante* 'certified' self-employment contracts to protect their choice of the nature and regulatory regime applying to their personal work relation – dare we say their very personal 'normative characterization' – from any unwelcome *ex post* judicial interference.

In this subsection we have sought to demonstrate that there is a process or genre of legal taxonomy and legal regulation of personal work relations which it is useful to think about as the 'normative characterization' of those relations. We have also tried to develop a critical analysis of that process or genre, and to show that this process or genre plays a significant role in the development of labour or employment law. In the next subsection we proceed to sketch out more fully a special role for the idea of the 'personal work profile' in the normative charcterization of personal work relations, and in their regulation in an even more general sense.

## B. The Personal Work Profile as a Regulatory Framework

In the previous section of this chapter we concentrated on the taxonomical and descriptive aspect of the normative characterization of personal work relations. In this section, our attention has turned towards its regulatory and prescriptive aspect; we have made the point that there are a number of different techniques for regulating personal work relations by means of normative characterization. These techniques of regulation by normative characterization can be used to respond to concerns which were identified by the critical analysis which we advanced in the previous section. In the preceding subsection we have sought to identify the variety of those techniques; in this subsection we develop the idea of the personal work profile as providing an important additional technique for that purpose. We make that claim in the form of suggesting that the idea of the personal work profile provides a framework for understanding and developing, or modifying various existing normative formulations for the legal construction and regulation of personal work relations; formulations which we might think of as the 'regulatory narratives' of personal work relations.

In order to make out that claim, we begin by briefly recapitulating the arguments so far advanced in this chapter, indicating how we see those arguments as paving the way towards our present proposition. Our initial contention in the first section was that it was useful and important for our analysis of the legal construction of personal work relations to be able to look at those relations from a macroscopic perspective across the career or working life of the working persons involved in those relations. We then in the second section suggested an approach to categorizing those relations at a more microscopic level, which took a tri-polar starting point from which a set of seven loosely-defined groups of relations were put forward; it was an approach which emphasized the fluidity and mutability of the categories which could be discerned at that level. Earlier in this section, we depicted the processes of legal construction of personal work relations which take place in this context of fluid and mutable categories as being regulatory ones as well as analytical ones, a duality which we embodied in the idea of normative characterization. Those arguments culminate in the proposal which we now put forward for the idea of the personal work profile as a framework for consciously engaging with and engaging in the legal regulation of personal work relations from the macroscopic perspective of the working life or career.

In that proposal which we thus put forward, the element of 'consciousness' is crucially important. Our point here is that the idea of the personal work profile as a framework for the legal regulation of personal work relations represents not so much a new way of carrying out that legal regulation as a conscious recognition of how that legal regulation is currently, has for a long time, and perhaps always has been and will be carried out. For we suggest that those engaged in the theory and the practice of legal regulation of personal work relations do in fact generally think of and represent that regulation as being projected across the working lives or careers of the working persons who are the subjects of that regulation. They (in which we include ourselves) construct and seek to implement normative formulations for those working lives or careers, which we may designate as 'regulatory narratives'. The design and manipulation of those regulatory narratives is at the very core of much of what labour law does; we suggest that the idea of regulating by reference to the personal work profile provides a usefully self-conscious way of understanding this, and the basis of a valid critical stance from which to evaluate what is so done.

This point about self-consciousness is therefore at the heart of our proposition about the utility of the idea of the personal work profile as a regulatory framework. Analysis by reference to the idea of the personal work profile may illuminate the fact that legal constructions of personal work relations, which appear to be purely descriptive categorizations of the state of those relations at a given moment, may in a larger sense be highly normative recipes for those relations which are projected in time through the careers or working lives of the working persons in question – hence constituting regulatory narratives in the sense in which we are using that terminology. This proposition or thesis requires illustration, and we shall now proceed to argue that, once the idea of the personal work profile is understood as a way of being self-conscious about currently existing analyses, such powerful examples present themselves as to suggest that the idea of the personal work profile can be applied quite ubiquitously to much of the discourse of legal regulation of personal work relations.

So if we think of personal work profiles as consisting of normative characterizations of personal work relations, which extend themselves over the whole of or an extensive span of the working life or career of the working person in question, it follows that very obvious examples are to be found in those terminologies which assign an enduring role or personal character to the working person in question – such as that of 'servant' in 'master and servant' relations or 'workman' in 'employer and workman' relations. In such examples, those legal formulations speak from eras when those work-related ascriptions did indeed assign a working person to a certain role which endured through his or her working life – they represented a person's 'station in life'. But even in what is hopefully a less socially and economically static condition of society and of labour markets, legal descriptions of personal work relations which assign a role to the working person – such as that of 'employee' or 'apprentice' – still convey a sense both of projection of that role across the whole or a part of the career of the working person in question, and of placing that person within a certain normative ordering of working lives.

However, our use of those illustrations should not be taken to suggest that these assignments of personal roles to working people constitute the sole or even the leading examples of personal work profiles as regulatory frameworks. Nor should these examples point us towards thinking of personal work profiles as located in notions of 'status' rather than of 'contract'. On the contrary, we can regard the idea of 'the contract of employment' itself as being, in some of its manifestations or presentations, a formulation for the regulation or ordering of employment relations over the whole or long spans of the working lives or careers of employees engaged in those relations. This quality of normative projection over the working life or career of the working person is very evident in some particular conceptual variants upon the idea of 'the contract of employment' such as the 'standard' or the 'implicit' or even the 'psychological' contract of employment.

We can pursue that kind of argument still further: there is even a certain sense in which the idea of the 'at-will' contract of employment represents not so much the single instantly terminable engagement for employment as instead the notion of a continuing regime for working life in which the working person is continually at risk of immediate termination of his or her employment (though he or she enjoys a notionally symmetrical freedom immediately to withdraw from that employment). And this is indeed a particular kind of personal work profile in the further sense that its proponents argue for it as a normatively appropriate, indeed optimal, regulatory framework for employment relations extending if necessary across whole working lives.

The claims which we have just made for regarding notions such as that of 'the standard contract of employment' or 'the at-will employment contract' as examples of personal work profiles may seem to be surprising ones. Indeed, in the case of the at-will employment contract, the claim may even appear as a paradoxical one in its attempt to represent the freedom to make the most non-committal of arrangements for employment as a kind of regulatory framework projected across the working lives or careers of workers engaged in those arrangements. However, even in this paradoxically extreme form, these examples make the important point that contractual constructions of personal work relations do constitute normative frameworks for the long-term conduct of those relations, albeit that such frameworks may sometimes be of a deliberately deregulatory character.

If, as we hope, that insight is a valid one, it gives rise to some further reflections about the utility of the idea of the personal work profile. For it suggests that evolutions in the typologies and formulations of personal work relations in general and personal work contracts in particular may, at a deeper level, represent changes to the personal work profiles of the workers affected by those evolutions – that is to say, changes to the regulatory frameworks which govern not just their personal work arrangements at any given moment but also the continuities and changes in those arrangements over the span of their careers or working lives. One very telling example of this is to be found in proposals for 'single' contracts of employment; this is an emergent new typology of personal work contracts which is precisely aimed at creating an evolution of the worker's entitlements over a long or even full-career time span, and as unifying many hitherto diverse contractual employment arrangements into that common form. This is therefore at one level a new contract type but one which can also at another level be considered as extending across the entirety of a personal work profile.

There is also another sense in which the dynamic and evolutionary character of personal work contracts and personal work relations can best be understood from the perspective of the personal work profile – that is to say within a regulatory narrative or regulatory framework extending across the working lives or careers of those working under those contracts and in those relations. In the previous section of this chapter, we set out our suggested taxonomy of personal work relations in a way which emphasized the fluidity of the categories which we were proposing, and the powerful dynamics of movement between those categories – especially the dynamics of movement from secure work relations, and even to some extent from autonomous work relations, towards precarious work relations. We depicted those movements as being evolutions in the way that the labour economy or the labour market functions, and suggested ways in which evolutions in the legal construction of personal work relations form part of that functioning.

However, this fluidity of categories, and these movements between categories, are phenomena whose significance is not confined to the rather general and abstract level upon which we consider the functioning of the labour market and the part that the legal construction of personal work relations plays in that functioning. The movements between categories, such as the displacements from secure work relations towards precarious work relations, are ones which occur within the working lives or careers of particular workers, and which shape or reshape their personal work profiles. This is relatively obvious when those movements happen in the course of the career of particular workers, so that they personally experience a change, for example from secure full-time permanent employment to precarious part-time temporary agency employment, during their working life. It is in a less obvious sense equally true when they have an experience of working life and a career path which is, perhaps from its outset, a very different one from that of a comparable person entering upon working life at an even quite shortly previous time by reason of changes in the functioning of the labour market and/or its legal regulatory environment.

This is the key point in our proposition about the importance of regulating personal work relation from the perspective of the personal work profile. It is not simply an assertion of the sentimental proposition that workers should be viewed as human beings rather than units in the statistics of the labour market and of its legal classifications. It is an assertion of the far more immediately practical point that many of the claims or needs which labour law recognizes, and therefore many of the entitlements or protections which it provides, are and have to be conditioned upon the legal construction and regulation not just of a particular personal work relation in which he or she is engaged at a particular moment but upon his or her personal work profile in a larger and more time-extended sense. Thus, many of labour law's protections are dependent upon the working person's accumulation of entitlements from engagement in one or more personal work contracts or relations over defined periods of time, or upon the coming and going of work-related states such as sickness absence for periods of time and over periods of time – or of course upon episodes and situations in working lives such as pregnancy and the incurring of caring responsibilities for dependents.

Much of what we have to say about the significance of the personal work profile follows from that central point. It follows that much of labour law's construction and regulation of personal work relations does, and rightly should, consist of the recognition and shaping of the regulatory narratives of working lives or careers. These are the formulations which we suggest should be articulated within the framework of the personal work profile. It further follows that labour law's classifications of personal work contracts or relations are better understood, and likely to be more satisfactorily deployed, if they are themselves regarded as being at a deeper level the taxonomies of personal work profiles. Our own suggested classifications, in particular our tri-polar division of personal work relations into 'secure', 'autonomous' and 'precarious' types, probably work best in this sense, as the depiction of different kinds of personal work profile.

There is also another kind of conclusion which we can draw from this argument about the significance of the personal work profile as a regulatory framework within which to understand and shape the legal construction of personal work relations. It means that we should approach the normative characterization of personal work relations – in the sense in which we have articulated that notion in the previous subsection – from the regulatory perspective of the personal work profile. But the same argument also serves to point to a functional continuity between the normative characterization of personal work relations and a wider range of legal instruments by which personal work relations can be shaped and adjusted: it is appropriate and useful to understand and deploy that whole range of legal instruments from the regulatory perspective of the personal work profile.

From that sequence of reasoning, we can identify an extensive array of techniques or interventions of labour law, which can be functionally linked together by the notion of regulation from the perspective of the personal work profile. This array includes not only:

1. characterizations of personal work contracts and relations and adjustments to the personal scope of employment legislation, but also:
2. other controls on 'atypical' forms of work such as the creation of claims to parity of treatment with 'standard' forms of work;
3. alterations to the regulation of the duration and termination of different forms of personal work contract and relation;
4. regulation of the patterns and forms of personal work contracts and relations on the basis of gender equality or age equality; and
5. development and implementation of notions of 'flexible' and/or 'family-friendly' work arrangements.

This brings our argument about the utility of the personal work profile, as a regulatory framework for the legal construction of personal work relations, to a concluding point, by which it will be linked to the next and final section of this chapter. The depiction of the normative characterization of personal work contracts and relations as part of an array of labour law techniques or interventions, all of which should in our suggestion be deployed within the regulatory framework of the personal work profile, should serve to highlight the enormous normative implications of adopting the personal work profile as a regulatory framework for the legal construction of personal work relations. There is a very real need for the making of clear and conscious normative choices and for articulating a well-thought-out normative approach for the handling of such an array of labour law techniques or interventions, or for the development of any one legal instrument within that array.

In that regard, it is crucial to remind ourselves that normative approaches to conducting labour law's regulation of personal work contracts and relations from the perspective of the personal work profile may as easily be deregulatory and reductive of protections for workers as they may be re-regulatory and enhancing of those protections. As we have indicated, proposals for a 'single employment contract' – which as we have said provide an example of regulation from that career-length perspective – are at best equivocal in this respect, and could at worst be thought to exert a potentially deregulatory thrust, by requiring the worker to build up gradually to entitlements to protections, for example against unfair dismissal, which would have been immediately or much more quickly conferred under earlier models of secure employment. Much the same thing could be said of many of the variants on the theme of 'flexicurity' – that being the supreme example of a policy approach which is precisely framed within and projected across working lives or careers and professes to achieve a reconciliation of the goals of 'flexibility' and 'security' over such extended timespans. This identifies to us very sharply indeed the necessity to articulate our own suggested policy goals for this kind of legal construction of personal work relations; that is the task to which we next turn our attention, seeking to carry it out under the heading of a notion of 'personality in work'.

## Section 4: The Idea of Personality in Work

Our discussion of the legal construction of personal work relations has reached a point at which it has evidently presented some novel suggestions about the ways in which personal work relations should be analysed and indeed about the ways in which they should accordingly be regulated. That discussion has also, in the course of, and by so doing, created its own need for a reconsideration of the normative basis of that regulation. In this section, we engage in that reconsideration, and put forward an idea of 'personality in work' as the outcome of that reconsideration. We begin by indicating why and in what respects our analysis of the legal construction of personal work relations has required this reconsideration of its normative basis and by presenting the idea of personality in work as a trio of values (subsection A).

We continue by analysing in greater detail this trio of values, composed by the concepts of *dignity*, *capability*, and *stability* in work relations (subsection B).

## A. Personality in Work as a Set of Values

We begin this subsection by presenting the argument that our analysis in the preceding chapters of the legal construction of personal work relations has served to throw into question the adequacy of the traditionally accepted normative basis per the regulation of those relations by labour law. We can identify the traditionally accepted normative basis as consisting of the idea of the redressing of the inequality of bargaining power as between the employer and the employee under the contract for subordinate employment.

Our analysis of the legal construction of personal work relations has by no means discredited that basic normative idea, which deserves its continuing status as the central ideological driver of labour law. Nevertheless, we suggest that our analysis has indicated the insufficiency in certain aspects of that central normative idea to the regulatory task which we believe confronts labour law in the domain of personal work relations which we have sketched out. This insufficiency, we suggest, presents itself in the following aspects. Firstly, the idea of inequality of bargaining power which constitutes the traditional normative basis of labour law is so much bound up with and bounded by the idea of subordination in personal work relations that is does not easily operate as a rationale for the regulation of those relations which lie beyond the scope of the contract for subordinate employment but within the larger scope of the personal work relations as we have defined and depicted it.

Secondly, we suggest that the idea of inequality of bargaining power as the traditional normative basis of labour law, just as it is intimately connected with the idea of subordination, is also infused with and bounded by the idea of a bilateral and typically also contractual relation between the employee and a single (contractual) counter-party to that relation, conceived of as 'the employer'. Our analysis of the legal construction of the personal work relation also casts doubt in that regard upon the sufficiency of the traditional idea of inequality of bargaining power between employer and employee as the normative basis of the legal construction of personal work relations. That is because our analysis has strongly suggested that the personal work nexus cannot satisfactorily, as a general or systemic proposition, be simplified down into a single bilateral connection across which alone all rights and responsibilities are held to flow.

Thirdly, we suggest that the idea of the inequality of bargaining power as the normative basis of the legal construction of personal work relations, in the form in which it is traditionally conceived and presented, suffers from a further kind of insufficiency as the normative basis for the legal construction of personal work relations. That insufficiency consists in the way that it tends to encourage dogmatic and sometimes false assumptions about the location or incidence of disadvantage and vulnerability within the sphere of personal work relations. That is to say, the notion of inequality of bargaining power as the animating normative idea of labour law is often interpreted as meaning that all employees in subordinate or dependent personal work relations are, automatically by virtue of that situation, to be regarded as disadvantaged and vulnerable – whereas, by implicit contrast, all other workers in non-subordinate or non-dependent personal work relations are to be regarded as not disadvantaged or vulnerable.

If either of those assumptions about inequality of bargaining power is seriously tested as a general or universal proposition as to the location of vulnerability or disadvantage in the sphere of personal work relations, it is revealed as an unreliable over-simplification. Inequality of bargaining power as the source or expression of vulnerability or disadvantage is not confined to subordinate or dependent personal work relations; it may well extend to non-subordinate or non-dependent personal work relations. It must also be said, more controversially for many labour lawyers, that inequality of bargaining power as the source or expression of vulnerability or disadvantage is not necessarily present in all subordinate or dependent personal work relations. It might be regarded as an immanent potential presence in all subordinate or dependent personal work relations; but it should not, we think, be viewed as a necessary actuality. And as an immanent potential source or expression of vulnerability or disadvantage, inequality of bargaining power straddles any perceived frontier between the subordinate and the non-subordinate so as to be present throughout the sphere of personal work relations.

We believe that it is possible to tackle these problems concerning the normative idea of inequality of bargaining power in the legal construction and regulation of personal work relations by re-conceiving that idea rather than by discarding it: we think it is important to try to get rid of the bathwater without throwing out this particular baby. Instead of focusing upon 'subordination' as an axiomatic source of grievance, a generic locator of inequality of bargaining power, we suggest that it makes better sense to focus upon a set of positive claims which workers have to certain kinds or qualities of treatment – claims which in our suggestion underlie the notion of inequality of bargaining power in subordinate work relations, and which extend in some measure to all personal work relations or profiles. We suggest that this set of claims can be encapsulated in the idea of 'personality in work', and that the notion of 'personality in work' can in its turn be broken down into the more particular ideas of respect for dignity, capability, and stability.

## B. The Component Values of Personality in Work: Dignity, Capability, and Stability in Work

In this section we proceed to elaborating on a set of ideas that are of pivotal importance for the present work, as they effectively constitute the normative basis sustaining the centrality of a number of the key concepts developed in the previous chapters, first and foremost the notion of 'personal work relation'. The three key concepts that we seek to develop in the next few paragraphs are the concepts of 'dignity', of 'capability', and of 'stability'. We discuss these key ideas under the umbrella notion of 'personality at work', and consider them as mutually reinforcing and essential elements of this composite notion.

As it will be recalled from our Introduction and from Chapter 1 of the present work, our present normative elaboration is essentially developed for two main reasons. Firstly, our argument goes, the failure to assign a carefully and suitably designed legal format to a work relation or arrangement falling within the broad category of 'personal work relations' would, we suggest, amount to a failure to respect the values of dignity, capability, and stability. Secondly, we suggest that these three concepts could be used as a basis to reshape and inform the regulation which labour law deploys within its domain. We advocate the importance of refocusing the normative rationale for labour regulation upon a set of positive claims which workers have to certain kinds or qualities of treatment – claims which in our suggestion underlie the notion of inequality of bargaining power in subordinate work relations, and which extend in some measure to all personal work relations. With this in mind we think that regulation should aspire to establishing strong protections in terms of: (1) *dignity* and decent conditions for workers; (2) maximising workers' access to the labour market and opportunities for skills development and *capability* building; and (3) controlling the costs and risks for employing entities and workers alike of entering into such arrangements by introducing and promoting elements of *stability*. Borrowing and paraphrasing Alleva's words, we seek to depart from the typological separation between dependence and autonomy and to recognize a more homogeneous regime for the regulation of 'personal work relationships', 'albeit with a possible internal diversification of the modalities of performance',[32] based on these three normative claims. There is, we believe, sufficient support for adopting a normative notion for personal work while allocating some elements of the protection afforded to particular workers on the basis of the specific modalities of performance of their work relation. As noted by the late Mario Giovanni Garofalo, a broad concept of 'work' (such as the one contained in Article 35 of the Italian Constitution), 'challenges the belief that the forms of protection that Parliament must guarantee must be identical for all forms of work; the protections accorded may well be different, not so much from a quantitative point of view, as from a qualitative one'.[33]

## I. Dignity

Dignity is a concept that does not need much introduction to social scientists in general and lawyers and labour lawyers in particular, as it has long been used, if

---

[32]  P. Alleva (2006) 'Nuove Norme per il Superamento del Precariato e per la Dignità del Lavoro', *Quale Stato*, 219.

[33]  Cf. M. G. Garofalo, '*Unità e pluralità del lavoro nel sistema costituzionale*' (2008) 30 *Giornale di Diritto del Lavoro e di Relazioni Industriali*, 30. Our translation from the original '*impedisce di ritenere che le forme di tutela che il legislatore ordinario deve garantire debbano essere identiche per i diversi tipi di lavoro; le tutele apprestate ben potranno essere tra loro diverse – non tanto dal punto di vista quantitativo, quanto da quello qualitativo*'.

often by reference to slightly different meanings,[34] to justify particular normative discourses. It appears in several international Covenants such as the Universal Declaration of Human Rights,[35] the Charter of Fundamental Rights and Freedoms of the European Union,[36] and is an important element of the ILO Declaration of Philadelphia[37] and of the ILO 'Decent Work' Agenda.[38] A number of national constitutions refer to notions of human or personal dignity in general, and often to more specific notions of dignity at work, as the normative basis for statutory norms seeking to protect labour rights as fundamental as the right not to be discriminated against and the right to health and safety.[39]

But for the purposes of our work, we take a particular view of the notion of dignity as ultimately amounting to a conceptual amalgam of the concepts of personal autonomy and equality. We are conscious of the fact that these three concepts – dignity, autonomy, and equality – are typically seen as being notionally distinct and, in some particular discourses, as being far from reconcilable and actually often in tension with each other. However we are comforted by the fact that we are not the only ones to see dignity as something of a composite concept. An important line of scholarship has convincingly argued that autonomy's 'value . . . is related to its being a constituent of the dignity of the human person',[40] a point we gladly espouse. As for the possible objection that freedom and equality are inevitably in tension with each other, we think that this very much depends on the respective notions of freedom and equality that one chooses to embrace. John Rawls' *Theory of Justice* provided, in many ways, a bold and original attempt to reconcile notions of liberty and equality in modern societies. In this sense we can also refer to the seminal work by the late Gerry Cohen, perceptively pointing out that freedom understood as 'self-ownership' is indeed reconcilable with equality of condition,[41] while also suggesting that other notions of freedom could and should be construed in the same way.[42]

---

[34] Cf. B. Hepple (2009) 'The Aims of Equality Law', in C. O'Cinneide and J. Holder (eds.), *Current Legal Problems 2008*, Oxford: OUP, 1; D. Roman (2005) 'Le Principe de Dignité dans la Doctrine de Droit Social', in S. Hennette-Vauchez et Ch. Girard (dir.), *La Dignité de la Personne Humaine, Recherche sur un Processus de Juridicisation*, Paris: PUF, 70; B. Veneziani (2010) 'Il Lavoro tra l'ethos del Diritto ed il Pathos della Dignità', 126(2), *Giornale di Diritto del Lavoro e di Relazioni Industriali*, 257.

[35] See in particular Articles 22 and 23.

[36] In particular Article 31.

[37] Declaration Concerning the Aims and Purposes of the International Labour Organization (Declaration of Philadelphia), II(a).

[38] Cf. A. Sen, 'Address by Mr. Amartya Sen, Nobel Laureate in Economics' (87th International Labour Conference, Geneva, 15 June 1999); D. Ghai (ed.) (2006) *Decent Work: Objectives and Strategies*, Geneva: ILO.

[39] Cf. for instance Article 1 of the German Constitution; Articles 3, 36, and 41 of the Italian Constitution; Articles 7, 10, and 35 of the South African Constitution.

[40] J. Griffin (2008) *On Human Rights*, Oxford: OUP, 151.

[41] G. A. Cohen (2005) 'Are Freedom and Equality Compatible?', in E. Goodin and P. Pettit (eds.), *Contemporary Political Philosophy – An Anthology*, Oxford: Blackwell, 416.

[42] Cf. the excellent analysis of Cohen's work in N. Vroussalis (2010) 'G. A. Cohen on Socialism' available online at www.theorein.org/vrousalis-cohen.pdf.

Of course neither the idea of freedom as self-ownership, nor the vision of equality as equality of condition, exhaust the possible conceptualizations of these two value-laden terms. And clearly the abstract possibility of reconciling autonomy and equality does not of course automatically imply that personal dignity could be seen as the synthesis of these two concepts. But we think that by elaborating a bit more on our visions of autonomy and equality, we may be able to suggest how to square this particular circle. Our vision of autonomy is one that predominantly focuses on the worker, and encompasses both the ability to take decisions about the life to pursue (including of course, one's working life), and the possibility of doing so in the absence of any undue constraints. We explored some of its characteristics in earlier published work focusing on the 'right to work', as a right to free, decent, suitable, and rewarding work.[43] Our vision has a number of essential components that readily translate into legal rights and entitlements. Such are, primarily, the classical negative freedom to work,[44] followed by a set of rights to engage into work relations that protect one's health and safety, fundamental human rights, and freedom of conscience.[45] It includes a set of entitlements to an income that is sufficient to the satisfaction of that person's fundamental rights and freedoms, and personal and family needs,[46] and finally a general entitlement to work that can help a person in her personal and professional progression.[47] Given the specific focus of our work, we are less concerned with issues of possible trade-offs between (the employer's) freedom and social and economic gains (for workers), a question that has preoccupied a number of political philosophers in the past.[48]

Equality, perhaps even more than dignity and autonomy, is a term that lends itself to multiple definitions.[49] This term appears to have lost much of its appeal in current policy discourses, in favour of other concepts such as 'fairness', or 'solidarity', which arguably convey different normative implications. We think that it still ought to play an important role in policy and normative discourses, and indeed there is no doubt that equality in the sense of non-discrimination would already feature in the concept of autonomy we have discussed in the previous paragraph. For reasons that will become apparent shortly, we do not feel overly prescriptive in respect of a particular equality model, though inevitably we do have our own preferences. In line with recent labour law scholarship, we find Sen's idea

[43] Cf. M. Freedland, P. Craig, C. Jacqueson, and N. Kountouris (2007) *Public Employment Services and European Law*, Oxford: OUP, Chapter 6.

[44] Ibid., at 226–7.

[45] Ibid. at 227–8.

[46] As noted by Cohen, personal freedoms are all too often 'compromised by lack of means', cf. G. A. Cohen (1998) 'Freedom and Money – In Grateful Memory of Isaiah Berlin', 7, available online at www.howardism.org/appendix/Cohen.pdf.

[47] Ibid., 228–30.

[48] H. L. A. Hart (1973) 'Rawls on Liberty and Its Priority', *University of Chicago Law Review*, 40 and his critique of J. Rawls (1971) *A Theory of Justice*, Cambridge: Harvard University Press; cf., A. K. Sen (2000) 'Social Justice and Distribution of Income', in A. B. Atkinson and F. Bourguignon (eds.) (2000) *Handbook on Income Distribution*, vol. 1, Amsterdam: North Holland, at 70.

[49] Cf. Part VI in E. Goodin and P. Pettit (eds.) (2005) *Contemporary Political Philosophy – An Anthology*, Oxford: Blackwell; B. Hepple (2009) 'The Aims of Equality Law', in C. O'Cinneide and J. Holder (eds.), *Current Legal Problems 2008*, Oxford: OUP, 1.

of 'basic capability equality' as particularly appealing and suitable for the purposes of labour law and social rights in general. We will return to this notion in the following subsection. But the reformed Rawlsian account of the 'difference principle', purged of some of the more extreme consequences of his 'priority of liberty principle',[50] may also be suitable to a reorganization of societal institutions (including the regulation of personal work relations), along more 'dignitarian' lines. In recent years Cohen's simple and disarmingly convincing idea of equality of opportunity as a 'correct[ion] for all unchosen disadvantages'[51] and seeking to ensure that 'differences of outcome reflect nothing but differences of taste and choice, not differences in natural and social capacities and powers',[52] has also contributed in a significant way to the debate. Equality, we believe, is a concept that ought to occupy a much more central role in labour law reform discourse.

But the reason why we feel we need not overly focus on a particular notion of equality, and indeed need not provide an exhaustive analysis of the concept of autonomy, or of the potential trade-offs between the two, is that our work is concerned with the justification, or rather the lack of it, for disparate regulatory protection for different typologies of providers of personal work services. Paraphrasing Sen's original question *Equality of What?*[53] we could say that our enquiry pertains to the similarly fundamental question of 'equality for whom?', or rather *Dignity for Whom?* a question which – in its immediacy – prompts us to explore the reasons why some typologies of providers of personal work are left outside employment protection legislation. As we now turn to explain, a focus on the concept of 'dignity' provides a powerful antidote to the main justifications as to why some workers should not be endowed with the protection of employment or labour law.

The concept of dignity, we believe, goes hand-in-hand with the idea of personality in work. Dignity is personal. It demands the protection of the person regardless of the specific arrangements for the performance of his or her personal work. In recent years, Griffin (2008) has offered a powerful account of 'personhood' as the generating concept for most of the conventional list of human rights, stressing precisely the importance of the concept of 'person' as the incipit to generate rights preserving human dignity.[54] Similar accounts can be found in Christian moral philosophy, with a recent encyclical stressing that 'activity has a human significance, prior to its professional one. It is present in all work, understood as a personal action, an *"actus personae"*',[55] though perhaps this is too broad a concept for the purposes of our normative analysis, and one we feel we need to qualify by reference to another facet of our concept of personal dignity. Personality, in our view, warrants dignity only to the extent that the services provided are truly

---

[50] A. K. Sen (2000) 'Social Justice and Distribution of Income', in A. B. Atkinson and F. Bourguignon (eds.), *Handbook on Income Distribution*, vol. 1, Amsterdam: North Holland, at 70.

[51] G. A. Cohen (2009) *Why not Socialism?*, Princeton: Princeton University Press, 18.

[52] Ibid.

[53] A. Sen (1979) 'Equality of What?', The Tanner Lecture on Human Values, Stanford.

[54] J. Griffin (2008) *On Human Rights*, Oxford: OUP, 2008.

[55] Benedict XVI, *Encyclical Letter 'Caritas in Veritate'*, Rome, 29 June 2009, para. 41.

and *predominantly* (though crucially not necessarily 'exclusively') a manifestation of one's *personal work*.

This has, in our view, a series of important consequences. It goes to the exclusion of those service providers who are not operating mainly and *predominantly* on the basis of their personal work, but rather *primarily* through their ability to organize other factors of production (and often the factors of production of others), labour and capital in particular. The ability to do so, we believe, makes the person akin to an employer or a commercial entrepreneur, or both, even where some degree of personal work may be present in the actual activity performed. In other words, to attract the protection granted by our notion of personality in work, the work needs to be *personal* in a complex or double sense: firstly, in the sense that the worker himself or herself provides it (rather than by arranging for some other person in his or her control to do it in his or her stead); and, secondly, in the sense that his or her personal work overwhelmingly shapes the service provided, over and above the amount of capital that he or she may be availing herself of to assist him or her, which ought to be marginal and ancillary.

The traditional justification for leaving outside the protective scope of labour law those workers who were not providing their services in a bilateral relationship with the employer-entrepreneur has been inextricably linked, we believe, to a particularly narrow view of the Marxist understanding of work relations in capitalist societies. These Marxist accounts 'try to condemn capitalism on the ground that it violates… bourgeois liberty: the labour contract, they say, is *fictio juris*, for it conceals a relationship substantially similar to the one between lord and serf',[56] effectively permitting and legitimizing the extraction of surplus-value from the worker. This analysis, correct or incorrect as it might have been, provided a relatively solid underpinning for employment protection legislation for much of the twentieth century. But by focusing exclusively on a particular manifestation and paradigm of work, perhaps still a dominant one, it also engenders a crucial theoretical weakness, which we seek to redress.

Exploitative or unfair work relationships regularly emerge outside the traditional paradigm described above, a fact that Marxists, we believe, would readily accept. These other personal work relations may of course not be exploitative or unfair, at least not in the traditional (and we would argue narrow) Marxist sense, but in terms of our normative critique and our normative propositions this makes little difference. Regulation will still have to make sure that work relations do not arise or develop in ways that harm the personal dignity of the worker (and this regardless of the ways in which they may, or may not, guarantee a certain protection and enhancement of the workers' capabilities, and regardless of their inherent stability). We believe that the dignity concept, and the next two we are about to discuss, may well serve as a normative and moral *raison d'être* for labour law in the twenty-first century.

---

[56] G. A. Cohen (1995) *Self-ownership, Freedom, and Equality*, Cambridge: CUP, pp. 162–3.

## II. *Capability*

The capability discourse[57] has long attracted the attention of labour and social law experts.[58] And unsurprisingly so, given its inherently progressive regulatory agenda, and its explicit interest for 'labour – whether it is rewarding or grindingly monotonous, whether the workers enjoy any measure of dignity and control, whether relations between employers and "hands" are human or debased'.[59] Undoubtedly, another factor determining its success and interest on the part of scholars in general, and labour lawyers in particular, has been its conceptual malleability, rendering capabilities just as relevant in the context of gender analysis,[60] and in the study of the market-structuring function of social standards,[61] in assessing and reconceptualizing the goals of international labour law,[62] and in the operation and development of European social policy,[63] from a domestic or a comparative perspective.[64] It has also rightly been noted that, at a certain level of abstraction, 'the capabilities approach is as equally consistent with Marxist political economy as it is with pluralism',[65] though some of the analytical constructs it has spawned have been criticized both from the left and from the more liberal end of the political spectrum.[66] The capability discourse is, as Supiot contends in respect of the notion of '*capacité*', '*une notion à haut potentiel*'[67] – a notion with great potential – but

---

[57] Cf. in particular A. Sen (1985) *Commodities and Capabilities*, (Deventer: North Holland), and A. Sen (1999) *Development as Freedom*, Oxford: OUP.

[58] Cf. A. Supiot (ed.) (1999) *Au delà de l'emploi: transformations du travail et l'avenir du droit du travail en Europe*, Paris: Flammarion, Chapter 7; C. Barnard, S. Deakin, and R. Hobbs (2001) 'Capabilities and Rights: An Emerging Agenda for Social Policy?', *IRJ*, 464; J. Browne, S. Deakin, F. Wilkinson (2002) 'Capabilities, Social Rights and European Market Integration, ESRC Centre for Business Research Working Paper No. 253.

[59] M. C. Nussbaum and A. K. Sen (1993) *The Quality of Life*, Oxford: Clarendon, 1.

[60] Cf. for instance M. Nussbaum (2000) 'Women and Equality: the Capabilities Approach', *ILR*, 227.

[61] S. Deakin and F. Wilkinson (2005) *The Law of the Labour Market*, Oxford: OUP.

[62] B. Langille (2009) 'What is International Labor Law for?', *Law & Ethics of Human Rights*, 47; R.C. Drouin (2009) 'Capacitas and Capabilities in International Labour Law', in S. Deakin and A. Supiot (eds.), *Capacitas – Contract Law and the Institutional Preconditions of a Market Economy*, Oxford: Hart, 97.

[63] S. Deakin (2005) 'The Capability Concept and the Evolution of European Social Policy', ESRC Centre for Business Research Working Paper, No. 303.

[64] S. Deakin and A. Supiot (eds.) (2009) *Capacitas – Contract Law and the Institutional Preconditions of a Market Economy*, Oxford: Hart. The editors make a point about distinguishing the notions of 'capacitas' from the original notion of 'capability'.

[65] E. Tucker (2010) 'Renorming Labour Law: Can We Escape Labour Law's Recurring Regulatory Dilemmas?', *ILJ*, 119.

[66] S. Fredman (2004) 'The Ideology of New Labour Law' in C. Barnard, S. Deakin, and G. Morris (eds.), *The Future of Labour Law – Liber Amicorum Sir Bob Hepple*, Oxford: Hart, 9, 14–16. For a review cf. E. Tucker (2010) 'Renorming Labour Law: Can We Escape Labour Law's Recurring Regulatory Dilemmas?', *ILJ*, 99, in particular sections 3 and 4.

[67] A. Supiot (2009) 'En Guise de Conclusion: La Capacité, Une Notion à Haut Potentiel', in S. Deakin and A. Supiot (eds.), *Capacitas – Contract Law and the Institutional Preconditions of a Market Economy*, Oxford: Hart, 161.

also a 'contested terrain, in which many different conceptions of the market order struggle for acceptance'.[68]

Given the wealth of elaborations on the capability approach to social rights and labour market regulation, we feel the need to spell out at least the basic framework of our own understanding of the capability discourse, and its overall purpose and function in the architecture of the 'personality in work' notion. Firstly, we approach the concept of capabilities from a predominantly *normative* perspective. We think that, at a prescriptive level, one of the objectives of labour law should be that of enhancing human capabilities for the purposes of fostering human autonomy and equality at work, and a rewarding existence.

From this perspective the capability approach can have the potential to unlock a number of regulatory discourses in both individual and collective labour law. It clearly points at 'employability' measures, but also, as noted by Deakin, at laws that offer 'protection against the risks of interruption to earnings through illness, unemployment and old age (social insurance law), guarantee freedom of association for the purposes of collective action (collective labour law), stabilize the employment relationship against the consequences of economic uncertainty and the arbitrary exercise of employer power (unfair dismissal law), and insert basic labour standards with respect to the wage-work bargain and maximum hours of work, can all be understood as underpinning the contractual capacity of the worker'[69] and, we would add, his or her ability to pursue a rewarding and dignified working life. From this viewpoint, the capability discourse transcends the strict boundaries of the contract of employment. It applies equally to any contractual relationship, and to any personal work relationship, by introducing a number of positive rights and duties aimed at enhancing the human and social capital of workers, regardless of a bilateral contractual relationship, and indeed as a prerequisite for any such work relationship being established in ways that are respectful of the workers' dignity, and in this sense we see it as reinforcing the dignity discourse developed in the previous subsection.

Our eclectic notion of capability also calls for social rights being 'inderogable' and imbued of elements of cogency 'as a limit to private powers'.[70] In this respect, capabilities and inderogability also emerge as mutually reinforcing concepts, and an antidote to socially regressive policy agendas. It is 'thanks to the capacity approach that it can be possible to avoid that this combination (between protection and flexibility) transforms itself, simply, into an obligation of adaptability of the individual to the transformations of the enterprise and of the labour market'.[71]

---

[68] S. Deakin (2005) 'The Capability Concept and the Evolution of European Social Policy', ESRC Centre for Business Research Working Paper, No. 303, 18–19.

[69] S. Deakin (2009) 'Capacitas: Contract Law, Capabilities and the Legal Foundation of the Market', in S. Deakin and A. Supiot (eds.), *Capacitas – Contract Law and the Institutional Preconditions of a Market Economy*, Oxford: Hart, 13.

[70] A. Vimercati (2009) 'Capacité et l'evolution du Droit du Travail Italien', in S. Deakin and A. Supiot (eds.), *Capacitas – Contract Law and the Institutional Preconditions of a Market Economy*, Oxford: Hart, 102. Our translation from the original French.

[71] Ibid., 102–3.

So rather than thinking of capability as a 'floor of rights', which would be *per se* an interesting proposition, we view it as a 'springboard' for social rights. Employment and activation policies in the UK and the EU provide abundant evidence of the existence of measures nominally aimed at enhancing workers' capabilities, but that are effectively subservient to short-term labour market demands.[72]

Last but not least, we see the capability notion as a springboard for a progressive regulation of collective labour law: 'Although Sen, in his writings, often gives a purely individualistic account of the development of capabilities, we can say that effective freedom of choice of salaried workers and, therefore, his power to act, are declined collectively.'[73] This is an important point, and calls for both a respect of the fundamental rights of freedom of association, collective bargaining, and strike action, as well for the societal support for forms of collective organization across the various layers of the increasingly segmented modern workforce. It should be clear, at this point, that our vision of capability is not completely disconnected from what could be termed as considerations of class interests and exercise of class power and dynamics. These are of paramount importance for both our notion of personality in work, and our concepts of layered regulation and inderogability.

## III. Stability

The final component of our notion of personality in work is stability. At a normative level we expect regulation to foster the stability of work relations. Stability is of course an important component of the capability discourse, and an essential element of our dignitarian analysis, but we still feel it needs to be discussed as a separate element, and for a number of reasons. Firstly, stability in employment has been the main victim of the overall liberalizing and deregulatory reforms adopted in recent decades. In fact, labour market deregulation, and the 'flexibiliza-tion' of work relationships, became increasingly perceived as some of the main ingredients for economic reform and sustained economic growth, which in turn promised to deliver more and better jobs in what appeared to be a virtuous neo-liberal macroeconomic spiral. As Karl Aiginger critically observed: '[w]hen analys-ing the reasons for slow growth in Europe during the nineties, many researchers (including those from the OECD, EU, and IMF) single out Europe's inflexible labour markets as the primary suspect'.[74] Much of the policy response focused, unsurprisingly, on the liberalization of some forms of atypical work contracts which, by their very nature, were temporary, under-remunerated, and particularly precarious. We say 'unsurprisingly' since already in the early 1990s the OECD was affirming that the 'development of various types of temporary contracts may

---

[72] Cf. M. Freedland *et al.*, n. 43 above.

[73] A. Vimercati (2009) 'Capacité et l'evolution du Droit du Travail Italien', in S. Deakin and A. Supiot (eds.), *Capacitas – Contract Law and the Institutional Preconditions of a Market Economy*, Oxford: Hart, 101. Our translation.

[74] K. Aiginger, 'Labour Market Reforms and Economic Growth – The European Experience in the Nineties' (WIFO Working Paper 232/2004), 3. Available online at: www.oecd.org/dataoecd/41/58/34943545.pdf.

present several advantages',[75] and that 'there is some evidence that the nature of technological change calls for more flexible forms of employment contract – such as fixed-term contracts – that fall outside the province of traditional employment protection legislation'.[76]

Consequently, by the late 1990s it was possible to observe that 'a number of countries have liberalised significantly the regulation of temporary employment in the past ten years, while a smaller number have liberalised EPL for regular employment or tightened specific components of EPL'.[77] Paradoxically, the proliferation of these precarious and temporary work relationships soon became the pretext for seeking more deregulation in the area of employment legislation. As candidly noted by the OECD in 2004, 'stricter rules applicable to regular contracts may tend to increase the incidence of temporary work and to limit the extent to which temporary contracts will be converted into permanent ones'.[78] Once more, according to the OECD, the way forward was more deregulation. As advocated as recently as 2004 by the then Chief Economist of the Organization: 'It is now time to move from second bests and palliatives to first best options. We need to give more balance to the currently polarized arrangements. It could mean reforming head-on permanent contracts with a view to minimizing separation costs.'[79]

It is no exaggeration to say that, over the past few decades, deregulation has applied a stranglehold to labour law reforms. In what appears to be a case of spill-over effect, deregulation of some areas of labour law triggered the demand for further flexibilization and deregulation of employment protection legislation. Some leeway was granted to policymakers in terms of channelling resources into labour market and activation policies, but that often meant a reduction of unemployment benefits and a tightening of eligibility requirements.[80]

But some economists are now questioning the overall value of these past reforms. As the Nobel laureate Joseph Stiglitz (2009) has put it:

we realize that many of our policy frameworks in recent decades have been making things worse [ . . . ] we have weakened our automatic stabilizers by weakening social protection, and we have destabilized the economy by making wages more flexible rather than providing job security. We have created greater anxiety, which, in times like this, increases savings rates and weakens consumption. All of these so-called reforms have made our economic system less stable and less able to weather a storm.[81]

[75] OECD (1993) *Employment Outlook 1993*, Paris: OECD, 111.
[76] OECD (1994) *Employment Outlook 1994*, Paris: OECD, 145.
[77] OECD (1995) *Employment Outlook 1999*, Paris: OECD, 48.
[78] OECD (2004) *Employment Outlook 2004*, Paris: OECD, 87.
[79] J.P. Cotis (2003) 'Reforming European Labour Markets: the Unfinished Agenda', address made to the Vienna Economics Conference 'Fostering Economic Growth in Europe', 12–13 June 2003, *The crisis, the 'cost' of job security, and a new role for public policy*, p. 6.
[80] Cf. M. Freedland, P. Craig, C. Jacqueson, N. Kountouris (2007) *Public Employment Services and European Law*, Oxford: OUP.
[81] J. Stiglitz (2009) 'The Global Crisis, Social Protection and Jobs', *International Labour Review*, 11.

The economic benefits of 'stability in work relations' are becoming increasingly evident, particularly in the aftermath of the recent economic downturn. 'What explains the resilience of continental Europe? Some of it was already built-in. Job-protection laws make it costly for firms to lay-off workers, and where posts are sacrificed, the newly unemployed are preserved from penury.'[82] There is indeed a growing sense that the often scorned continental European model of relatively high levels of employment protection, public subsidies, and incentives for employers to retain workers in employment, and public income support schemes for unemployed workers and those whose working hours are cut during recession, may contain most of the ingredients for an anti-recession recipe. 'Numerical flexibility' is no longer portrayed as a panacea for all labour market evils, on the contrary. The 2009 *OECD Employment Outlook* notes that employment protection legislation (EPL) provides a particularly useful stabilizer especially in respect of that section of the workforce, temporary and casual workers, that many labour market regimes have grown to see as the epitome of 'numerical flexibility'. 'EPL for temporary workers', the report reads, 'has a stronger negative impact on unemployment inflows than on outflows, suggesting that this type of regulation may reduce structural unemployment.'[83]

It should be clear, however, that we are not advocating stability in work relations as a market-building factor. Just as it was erroneous to assume that labour law deregulation would have structured macroeconomic performance, it would be illusory to claim that stability could become the new philosopher's stone to re-emerge from cyclical or structural economic downturns. Stability is part of our normative critique, and we intuitively feel the time has come to refrain from using labour law as a macroeconomic tool, and to promote stability in work relations for the sake of the protection and enhancement of 'personality in work'. In this respect we advance the claim that stability should be promoted across the board of 'personal work relations', although here we do accept that this may require a certain degree of internal diversification of the modalities by which stability is given to different typologies of work. Stability emerges therefore as a policy compass for labour law reform, rather than a one-size-fits-all rule embracing all personal work relations. To put it simply, stability will both have to shape the regulation of contractual termination rules in a way that promotes job security for workers and allows them to enjoy dignity and capability entitlement to the full, to control the ability of employers to employ workers on a succession of fixed-term or personal task contracts, and to introduce disincentives for the premature termination of commercial agency arrangements, and so on and so forth.

We need to emphasize that our notion of stability targets applies predominantly to work relations, and is not seen as an accessory of successful labour market mobility or transitions. We aspire to a notion of stability that is built into personal work contracts and relations, rather than to one emerging from successful transitions between different work relations, though we do not regard the two as

[82] *The Economist* (2009) 'Pay for Delay – Economic Focus' (7 November 2009).
[83] OECD (2009) *Employment Outlook 2009 – Tackling the Job Crisis* Paris: OECD, 55.

mutually exclusive. We see this as the best way to guarantee dignity at work and a commitment to the enhancement of workers' capabilities on the part of the state and employers alike. Finally we acknowledge that both the set of rights pertaining to the concept of stability, and the ones that we attach to the ideas of dignity and capability will inevitably require setting up a new process for the progressive mutualization, between employers and workers, as well as within society at large, of the risks attendant upon the making and execution of arrangements for the doing of work. This is a point which we explore further in the Conclusion of this work.

In the course of this chapter, we have argued for a certain way of thinking about the conceptual activity which is normally understood as the taxonomy of labour law or the establishing of the personal scope of labour law in general or particular labour laws. We have tried to reconceive that activity as a more complex one involving elements both of classification and regulation, and we have used the terminology of legal characterization to identify that more ambitious conception. We have suggested ways in which that activity might be undertaken, suggestions which have led us to articulate the notion of the 'personal work profile' and more fully to identify a process of emergence of new, often innominate, types of personal work relation or profile. These arguments have pointed towards the need for some quite fundamental stocktaking of the ways in which normative characterization is being done. In the next and final chapter of this work, we consider the possibility that some such stocktaking might usefully take place, so far as the European region is concerned, within the compass of EU labour or employment law by which we mean primarily EU labour or employment law, as will shortly appear.

# PART IV

# THE PERSONAL WORK RELATION
# IN EUROPEAN LAW

# 10

# The Legal Construction of Personal Work Relations and the Role of European Law

## Introduction

In this chapter, we seek to draw together and to bring to a culmination the arguments which have been put forward and developed in the course of the present work. In order to do so, we diverge from the path of English-law-based comparison between European national legal systems which we have hitherto pursued. We move instead onto a somewhat different track, on which we follow out and seek to elucidate the role of European law in the legal construction of personal work relations in European national legal systems in general and in national labour law systems in particular. It may be useful to clarify from the outset what we mean by 'European law' in the context of the present chapter. In this context, we use that term to refer primarily to the law of the European Union[1] while acknowledging the growing interdependence between this particular stream of European law and the rules and principles that originate from, or are produced by, legal sources and regulatory and judicial bodies that are associated with the Council of Europe, first and foremost the European Convention for the Protection of Human Rights and Fundamental Freedoms, the European Social Charter, and the European Court of Human Rights, an interdependence which is likely to further intensify with the entry into force of the Lisbon Treaty in December 2009.

This diversion from our previous track is, however, a tactical rather than a strategic one. That is because, although we regard an excursus into European law in that sense as being of real intrinsic interest in and of itself, we also see it – indeed, we see it primarily – as a way of obtaining both a particular external perspective and an especially sharp focus upon the recent and current development of the legal construction of personal work relations in the national legal systems of the Member States of the EU. In order to develop this analysis from a European law perspective, we first identify the set of problems which beset the legal construction of personal work relations in European national labour law systems which have emerged through the successive stages of the present work, and we suggest that European law, and EU law in particular, has itself become deeply implicated in that complex

[1] On the semantics surrounding the idea of 'European labour law' in particular, cf. N. Countouris (2009) 'European Social Law as an Autonomous Legal Discipline', *Yearbook of European* Law, 95.

set of issues (Section 1). We then proceed to suggest ways in which EU law could begin to provide solutions to these analytical problems for national labour law systems, to which EU law itself is, to a certain extent, a contributor (Section 2). In particular, we advance the notion of a 'European Legal Framework for Personal Work Relations', which would be in certain respects analogous to the Common Frame of Reference currently being advanced for European private law,[2] but which would be, in contrast to that experiment, more taxonomical than prescriptive in its character. This notion is heavily reliant on a particular variant of the layers of regulation theory, which we develop in relation to European law and discuss in Section 3. Finally, (in Section 4) we link these reflections to our earlier discussion of the concept of the normative characterization on personal work relations in European law and the 'personality in work' concept, which was explored in the concluding section of the previous chapter.

## Section 1:  European Law and the Fragmentation of Personal Work Regulation

We shall proceed to identify, by way of conclusion from earlier chapters, the key issues or problems which beset the legal construction of personal work relations in European national labour law systems, and to suggest that EU law has itself become deeply implicated in that complex set of issues. The first subsection (A) identifies what we describe as the underlying and problematical phenomenon of the denormalization of personal work arrangements, and the second (B) points out how this has given rise to a taxonomical confusion both in European national labour or employment law systems and in the labour or employment law of the EU itself. We argue in a third subsection (C) that this confusion is deepened by a set of normative uncertainties in EU labour or employment law, an idea which we express as that of the 'normative patchiness of EU employment law'.

### A.  The Denormalization of Personal Work Arrangements

There is a real sense in which the subject-matter and essential concerns of the present work have clarified themselves in the course of the writing of it – to the authors, at least, and we hope to the readers also. That is to say, our European comparative inquiry into the legal construction of personal work relations has

---

[2] Cf. C. Von Bar, E. Clive, H. Schulte-Nölke, H. Beale, J. Herre, P. Schlechtriem, M. Storme, S. Swann, P. Varul, A. Veneziano, F. Zoll, (eds.) (2008) *Principles, Definitions and Model Rules of European Private Law, Draft Common Frame of Reference (DCFR), Interim Outline Edition*, Munich: Sellier. It should be noted that, since the European Commission published on 1.7.2010 its *Green Paper on policy options for progress towards a European Contract Law for consumers and businesses* (COM (2010) 348 final), the initiatives for a Common Frame of Reference on European Contract Law are being pursued in the form of arguably rather more limited proposals for an 'Optional Instrument on European Contract Law'.

revealed not only very significant divergences in that process of legal construction at quite a basic level as between European national labour law systems, but also a transnationally shared sense of uncertainty and anxiety about how that process of legal construction is developing and whether it is fulfilling its social and economic function in an appropriate way. At the heart of that uncertainty and anxiety is a perception that there is a particular phenomenon, essentially deregulatory in character and effect, which is in varying degrees affecting the practice of personal work relations throughout Europe, and with which national labour law systems are having difficulty in keeping pace. We identify that phenomenon as one of 'denormalization'; we argue that it presents basic structural or definitional challenges to labour law systems; and we suggest that EU law has become quite deeply implicated in it.

So we make the observation, on the basis of the analyses conducted in earlier chapters, that there is a very prominent, though nationally variable, phenomenon of what we may style the 'denormalization' of personal work relations in most if not all European countries. This phenomenon is brought about by a series of interactions between the practice and conventions of personal work relations and the legal systems which shape and regulate those relations. We advance this notion as one which has affinities with the ideas of 'deregulation of the labour market' and 'the growth of atypical forms of employment', but as one which in certain important ways both combines and transcends those more familiar notions.

We can best explain the phenomenon of denormalization as a departure from or reversal of a process of 'normalization' which had preceded it. That earlier 'normalization' of personal work relations was the process by which, broadly speaking during the period from 1945 to 1975, there was an accumulation of normative factors which served to 'normalize' personal work relations in the sense of moving them into various 'normal states' characterized by quite high levels of protection of workers against the various economic and social risks of unemployment and fluctuations in demand for their work, and incapacity for work by reason of ill-health, parenthood, old age, and so on. The normative factors which produced this movement consisted primarily (in varying degrees) of collective bargaining and labour legislation and of various combinations between them, and also, more broadly speaking, the changing nature and role of the state, and its involvement in labour market regulation and the provision of welfare.[3]

This movement is often regarded as having given rise to a 'standard' form or model of employment relations. We believe that to be rather an over-simplification, especially if it is regarded as a description of something occurring uniformly across Europe. We find it more instructive to think about there being a considerable variety of personal work relations, but which were subject to a general 'normalizing' tendency or discipline which was worker-protective and risk-reductive in the way that we have identified. As Lyon-Caen put it in respect of France – but a similar

---

[3] Cf. S. Deakin and F. Wilkinson (2005) *The Law of the Labour Market*, Oxford: OUP; also, from a comparative perspective, B. Hepple and B. Veneziani (2009) *The Transformation of Labour Law in Europe: A Comparative Study of 15 Countries 1945–2004*, Oxford: Hart esp. chs. 2–4.

reasoning could apply to other European experiences – 'whatever one may say, there has never been a unique legal model. But the diversity did not receive any public encouragement, and encountered some limits.'[4] All employment relations were by no means homogenized, still less were all personal work relations homogenized; but they were generally affected by this normalizing tendency, and did seem to be converging upon each other, for example in the form of an erosion of various kinds of differentiations between the work relations of 'white collar' and 'blue collar' workers.

It should not be thought, however, that we are overly idealizing that 'normalized' state of affairs in the sphere of employment relations or personal work relations which had been reached by the later 1970s. We should emphasize that this 'normalization' was in certain ways patchy and incomplete, most especially but not solely in the way that it failed to recognize or cater for the situation of women within or as entrants into the labour market. Moreover, though this is a reflection rather beyond the scope of the present work, it could scarcely be maintained that this 'normalized' state of affairs in the sphere of personal work relations had given rise to a sustainable equilibrium in collective labour relations or in the politics of the labour economy; in the UK in particular, there was significant disarray at those levels.

Perceptions of disarray and dysfunctionality in the labour economy must have contributed to the tendency towards 'denormalization' of personal work relations which, we suggest, became more and pronounced through the 1980s and 1990s and persisted into the subsequent decade. This is a phenomenon that has received a considerable degree of attention in academic literature, most recently by Hepple and Veneziani (2009) through the concept of 'path departure' from the earlier regulatory trajectories and approaches that we briefly discussed in the previous paragraphs.[5] The authors identify a number of factors 'influencing the transformation of labour laws',[6] many of which have an evident EU dimension. Although it would be fair to say that English employment law has still, on balance, benefitted from the process of European integration, there is an extensive and continuing scholarly analysis of the deregulatory impact that certain aspects of EU law have had on national systems of labour law and labour market regulation,[7] including the British one.[8]

---

[4] A. Lyon-Caen (1988) 'Actualité du contrat de travail', *Droit Social*, 541. Our translation from the original French.
   [5] B. Hepple and B. Veneziani (2009) *The Transformation of Labour Law in Europe*, Oxford: Hart, 21.
   [6] Ibid.
   [7] Cf. S. Sciarra (ed.) (2001), *Labour Law in the Courts: National Judges and the ECJ*, Oxford: S Sciarra *et al.* (eds.) (2004) *Employment Policy and the Regulation of Part-Time work in the European Union: A Comparative Analysis*, Cambridge: CUP; D. Ashiagbor (2005) *The European Employment Strategy: Labour Market Regulation and New Governance*, Oxford: OUP; P. Syrpis (2007) *EU Intervention in Domestic Labour Law*, Oxford: OUP; M. Freedland *et al.* (2007) *Public Employment Services and European Law*, Oxford: OUP.
   [8] C. Barnard (2009) 'Chapter 3: *Viking* and *Laval*: A Single Market Perspective' in K. D. Ewing and J. Hendy QC (eds.), *The New Spectre Haunting Europe – The ECJ, Trade Union Rights, and the British Government*, London: IER, 19; N. Countouris and R. Horton (2009) 'The Temporary Agency Work Directive: Another Broken Promise?' *ILJ*, 329.

However, the role of EU law in the process of 'denormalization' of personal work relations is arguably more complex than the antithesis or tension between regulation and deregulation may help suggest. Arguably, the complex interaction between the two dynamics of European integration and denormalization of personal work relations has at least two other equally interesting and important aspects.

The first one, with which we are mostly concerned in this section of the chapter, amounts to the extent to which EU law engages and interacts with national processes of 'denormalization' of personal work relations. Here our inquiry is into the extent to which EU law, and more precisely the various branches composing EU social law, has the ability, competence, and the motivation to control national processes of 'denormalization' by defining and enforcing autonomous EU level, normative characterizations of work relationships for the purpose of the application of the instruments of EU law in the social sphere. For instance a number of EU directives in the area of labour law shape their personal scope of application by reference to the formula of the 'contract of employment or employment relation-ship',[9] a formula that, as confirmed by the ECJ,[10] does not have a Community meaning, but is to be determined by reference to the law, collective agreement, or practice in force in each Member State. This is not the case for all areas of European social and labour law. For instance, as we will briefly explore in the following subsection, there are areas such as equal treatment or free movement of workers that are more consistently claimed by EU law, and where the scope for national variants of 'denormalization' is minimal. Unsurprisingly these are the areas where the ECJ has been unequivocal in claiming a Community meaning for the concepts of 'employment relationship'[11] and 'worker',[12] shaping their respective personal scope of application. This regulatory approach has attracted a considerable degree of academic interest in the past[13] which has concentrated upon the fact that it has led to a taxonomical quagmire, a point which we analyse later.

The second important aspect concerns the ways in which this quagmire can be resolved and rationalized, and the extent to which EU law is adequately equipped to address the regulatory idiosyncrasies emerging from it. Much has been written in

---

[9] Cf., for instance, Clause 2(1) of both Council Directive 97/81/EC of 15 December 1997 concerning the Framework Agreement on part-time work concluded by UNICE, CEEP and the ETUC as amended by Directive 98/23/EC (OJ 1998 L131/10) consolidated [1998] OJ L131/13; and Council Directive 99/70/EC of 28 June 1999 concerning the Framework Agreement on Fixed-term Work concluded by UNICE, CEEP and the ETUC [1999] OJ L175/43 corrigendum OJ 1999 L244/64.

[10] Case 105/84, *A/S Danmols Inventar* [1985] ECR 2639 [25]–[26].

[11] Cf. Case C-256/01, *Allonby v. Accrington & Rossendale College and Others* [2004] ECR I-873.

[12] Case 66/85, *Lawrie-Blum* [1986] ECR 2121.

[13] G. Cavalier and R. Upex (2006) 'The concept of Employment Contract in European Private Law', *IJCLLIR*, 608; N. Countouris (2007), *The Changing Law of the Employment Relationship* Aldershot: Ashgate, Chapter 5; J. Kenner (2009) 'New Frontiers in EU Labour Law: From Flexicurity to Flex-Security', in M. Dougan and S. Currie, *50 Years of the European Treaties: Looking Back and Thinking Forward*, Oxford: Hart, 279.

the past on the possible rationales behind these complexities.[14] Our view on this point has evolved in a direction suggesting that this quagmire is actually determined and deepened by a set of uncertainties about the normative and taxonomical imperativeness of EU labour or employment law vis-à-vis the national labour law systems of the EU Member States.

Before turning to explore that hypothesis, we feel the need to acknowledge that other explanations may well be advanced as plausible alternatives. The instinctive reaction for any EU lawyer would be that of approaching and understanding these idiosyncrasies as emerging from different types of competences in harmonizing specific sectors of EU social and labour law. Another alternative would be that of attempting to justify them from a subsidiarity perspective as something that is appropriately left to the national systems of labour regulation, which often manifest similarly incoherent taxonomies and normative characterizations. Our own understanding is that these idiosyncrasies and uncertainties can be better understood, though not necessarily better explained, if seen as a peculiar manifestation of a range of regulatory options falling within the spectrum from *jus cogens* to *jus dispositivum*, and the interaction between national and EU layers of regulation. While these uncertainties do, to some extent, mirror the uncertainties underlying some of the national debates on the scope of application of employment and labour law, it appears to us that the manifestation of the problem in EU law is the consequence of a lack of autonomous internal elaboration which, as we will further discuss, leads to a number of regulatory deficiencies.

## B. The Fragmentation of EU Employment Law With Regard to Taxonomy

There is hardly any doubt that, over the years, EU law-making institutions have progressively built up a complex and articulate body of law regulating important aspects of the working lives of the peoples of Europe. Continental academics have been speaking of 'European Social Law'[15] since the 1960s. But a striking feature of this body of law is its inconclusiveness and incoherence in respect of the personal scope of its application. Some of the rights directly afforded by EU law to European working people apply to 'workers', for instance those rights deriving from EU law provisions on 'free movement of workers' as deriving from Article 45 of the Treaty on the Functioning of the EU. This is a very broad definition, which was originally construed on the continental notions of 'subordination' and 'dependence',[16] but has since extended to a wider range of work relationships. Over the years it has been

---

[14] Ibid.; see in particular G. Cavalier and R. Upex (2006) 'The Concept of Employment Contract in European Private Law', IJCLLIR, 587, 606; N. Countouris (2007) *The Changing Law of the Employment Relationship*, Aldershot: Ashgate, ch. 5.

[15] Cf. G. Lyon-Caen (1969) *Droit Social Européen*, Paris: Dalloz. For an exceptionally comprehensive review of the various terminologies used in this context see Chapter 1 in B. Bercusson (1996) *European Labour Law*, London: Butterworths.

[16] For an interesting perspective cf. S. Giubboni (2010) 'La Nozione Europea di Subordinazione' in S. Sciarra (ed.), *Manuale di Diritto Sociale Europeo*, Torino: Giappichelli, Chapter 2.

interpreted by the ECJ as including, under some conditions, job-seekers, on-call-workers, remunerated trainees, and workers on workfare-like schemes.[17] However, this broad personal scope must be read in the context of the core substantive rights that EU law accords to 'workers': essentially free movement and access to the labour market and employment on non-discriminatory terms.

At the opposite end of the spectrum, as noted previously, there is a significant number of EU instruments that simply do not seek to clarify to which set of workers they ought to apply. Member States retain the ability to use their own definitions when implementing Directives providing for 'partial harmonization', which paradoxically includes several Directives on working conditions. A keystone for understanding this part of the *acquis* of EU law is *Danmols Inventar*, a case where the Luxembourg Court was explicitly asked whether the 'employee' notion contained in the Acquired Rights Directive was capable of an autonomous meaning, along the lines of the 'worker' notion in the context of free movement. The Court was adamant that that was not the case, as that measure was 'intended to achieve only partial harmonization'. According to the Court, its aim was therefore 'to ensure, as far as possible, that the contract of employment or the employment relationship continues unchanged with the transferee', and it was 'not . . . intended to establish a uniform level of protection throughout the Community on the basis of common criteria'.[18]

The *Danmols* approach has resisted the test of time, and has been reaffirmed by the Court on numerous occasions.[19] In *Collino and Chiappero v. Telecom Italia Spa*,[20] the question was whether the Acquired Rights Directive could apply in the context of a transfer in the form of an administrative concession between a public telecoms operator and its private – but still publicly owned – successor, Telecom Italia Spa. The Court was inclined to accept that these particular processes of privatization did constitute a transfer for the purposes of the Directive. But when confronted with the question of whether workers with a 'public-law status', and thus not included in the domestic 'employee' notion, qualified under the personal scope of the Directive, it was less open to a progressive reinterpretation of its earlier jurisprudence. Though it was submitted by the Commission that the Directive should apply if the tasks performed by the employees of the public company were 'substantially the same as those performed by the employees of a private-law company governed by national labour law', and while it was noted 'that Article 3 of the Directive refers not only to contracts of employment but also more generally to employment relationships',[21] the Court confirmed in *Collino* that 'the Directive

---

[17] For an overview Cf. C. Barnard (2006) *EC Employment Law*, 3rd ed., Oxford: OUP, Chapter 4; also cf. N. Countouris (2007) *The Changing Law of the Employment Relationship*, Aldershot: Ashgate, pp. 173–7.

[18] Case 105/84, *Foreningen af Arbejdsledere i Danmark v. A/S Danmols Inventar* [1985] ECR 2639, [26].

[19] Cf. Case C-29/91, *Redmond Stichting* [1992] ECR I-3189, para. 18, and Case C-173/96, *Sánchez Hidalgo*, [1998] ECR I-8237, para. 24.

[20] Case C-343/98, *Collino and Chiappero v. Telecom Italia Spa* [2000] ECR I-6659.

[21] Ibid., [29].

does not apply to persons who are not protected as employees under national employment law, regardless of the nature of the tasks those persons perform'.[22]

This approach, which still remains the orthodox view adopted by the ECJ, may well need to be qualified by reference to the more progressive suggestions advanced by A.G. Kokott in her Opinion in *Wippel*,[23] seeking to bring the concepts of 'contract or employment relationship', contained in provisions such as Clause 2(1) of the Framework Agreement on part-time work, within a broad Community dimension, albeit *de minimis*. While recognizing that this was a domestic, rather than a Community concept, the Advocate General noted that national systems encountered some limits, albeit 'only the very broadest limits', in the exercise of their discretion. For instance, 'It could ... constitute a breach of the duty of co-operation (Article 10 EC) if a Member State were to define the term "worker" so narrowly under its national law that the Framework Agreement on part-time work were deprived of any validity in practice and achievement of its purpose.'[24] However the Court paid little attention to this analysis in its final judgment. While it has no doubt that casual part-timers such as Ms Wippel were covered by EC equal pay legislation, it repeated that their inclusion within the scope of Clause 2(1) of the Framework Agreement on part-time work depended on the national definition of 'contract or employment relationship', and on whether the Member State had or had not excluded them pursuant to Clause 2(2).

*Wippel* provides a good pointer to the fact that, between the two extremes of the Article 45 TFEU 'worker' definition and the narrow 'contract or employment relationship' *Danmols* notion, lay a range of other areas of EU social law with their own specific normative characterizations and personal scopes. EU instruments on equal pay, for instance, have been interpreted by the ECJ as having a very broad scope of application. In *Preston* the Court introduced a notion of 'stable employment relationship'[25] that was far less reliant on national definitions and, equally importantly, far more relational and less contractual in character. This contributed to bringing within the scope of EU equal pay rules a number of part-time and intermittent contracts, otherwise excluded by national equal pay frameworks. In *Allonby*, the ECJ noted that the 'formal classification of a self-employed person under national law does not exclude the possibility that a person must be classified as a worker within the meaning of Article 141(1) EC if his independence is merely notional, thereby disguising an employment relationship within the meaning of that article'.[26]

In addition, the Court firmly established that the term 'worker' used in what was then Article 141(1) has a Community meaning, and that 'For the purposes of that provision, there must be considered as a worker a person who, for a certain period of time, performs services for and under the direction of another person in return for which he receives

[22]  Ibid., [38].
[23]  Opinion of the AG in Case C-313/02, *Nicole Wippel v. Peek & Cloppenburg GmbH & Co KG*, ECR [2004], I-9483.
[24]  Ibid., [45].
[25]  Case C-78/98, *Preston* [2000] ECR I 3201, para. [70].
[26]  C-256/01, *Allonby v. Accrington and Rossendale Community College* [2004] ECR I-873 [70].

remuneration'[27] making explicit reference to its jurisprudence on free movement of workers. The absence of strict mutuality of obligation, or in the Court's words, 'the fact that no obligation is imposed on [the worker] to accept an assignment' was held to be of no consequence in that context'.[28] This was an extremely important decision, though its impact was ultimately overshadowed by the fact that the absence of a sufficiently strong link between the final employer or end-user and the intermediary business meant that 'the differences identified in the pay conditions of workers performing equal work or work of equal value cannot be attributed to a single source'.[29]

Recent judgments by the Luxembourg Court have effectively suggested that other areas of EU social law may also have a personal scope of application essentially as broad as the one informing free movement of workers. In *Kiiski*,[30] the Court commented that the notion of 'pregnant worker' under Directive 92/85 was based on the 'worker' definition derived from the case-law on free movement.[31] This decision is consistent with earlier judgments of the Court casting a broad scope for EU health and safety law.[32] Anti-discrimination legislation similarly relies on a broad personal scope of application, certainly broader than the one deriving from the *Danmols* doctrine. The Court in *Wippel* affirmed that 'a worker with a contract of employment... under which hours of work and the organization of working time are dependent upon the quantity of available work and are determined only on a case-by-case basis by agreement between the parties, comes within the scope of Directive 76/207'.[33] What emerges from this, perhaps inevitably, cursory review is the considerable fragmentation of the normative characterizations, and underlying personal scopes, employed by EU legislators involved in the drafting of labour law instruments. This is problematic in and of itself. It becomes even more so, when it is coupled with what we shall style as the 'normative patchiness of EU employment law', a notion which we explore in the next section.

However, before doing so, we should refer to one further important taxonomical development, namely that the new EU anti-discrimination instruments rely on a personal scope definition that applies to 'persons' 'in employment or occupation', something that has not gone unnoticed by the European Court.[34] These formulations of EU employment law are bound to have a considerable impact in respect of the scope of application of national rules governing discriminatory dismissal, effectively prohibiting the termination of a variety of personal work relations on a number of substantive grounds including gender[35] and race.[36] The Commission has already made clear that the personal and material scope of application of these Directives is

---

[27] Ibid., [67].

[28] Ibid., [72].

[29] Ibid., para. [46].

[30] Case C-116/06, *Sari Kiiski v. Tampereen kaupunki* [2007] ECR I-7643.

[31] Ibid., para. [25].

[32] Case C-173/99, *BECTU v. Secretary of State for Trade and Industry* [2001] ECR I-4881.

[33] C-313/02, *Nicole Wippel v. Peek & Cloppenburg GmbH & Co KG* [2004] ECR I-9483, [40].

[34] Case C-88/08, *David Hütter* [2009] ECR I-0000 [33].

[35] Cf. Article 14(1)(c) of Directive 2006/54.

[36] Article 3(1)(c) of Directive 2000/43. Similar provisions are contained in Article 3(1)(c) of Directive 2000/78 in respect of other grounds of discrimination.

such that Member States ought to 'ban . . . discrimination as regards civil servants, self-employment, and membership of or participation in a professional organisation', and 'cover access to self-employment or occupation', as well as 'cover[ing] dismissal'.[37] This should hardly be a surprise given the breadth of the concept of 'occupation'. ILO Convention C-111, which also seeks to combat discrimination 'in employment and occupation' and is expressly recalled in the preliminary considerations of the new anti-discrimination Directives, is well known for embodying a broad concept of 'occupation'. According to the ILO, employment 'refers to work performed under an employment relationship with an employer', whereas '"Occupation" means the trade, profession or type of work performed by an individual, irrespective of the branch of economic activity or the professional status of the worker'.[38]

The adoption of the Charter of Fundamental Rights of the EU, and its coming into force after the ratification of the Lisbon Treaty, adds a further layer of complexity to this already intricate normative panorama. The Charter recognizes a number of important labour rights to 'workers', including the right to be protected in case of 'unjustified dismissal,'[39] and the right to 'fair and just working conditions',[40] posing the question of 'who is a worker' for the purposes of the application of its provisions. In light of the arguments advance in the previous paragraphs, the bone of contention is likely to be twofold. A first question is whether, in this specific context, the 'worker' concept should receive an EU meaning, or should instead be defined by reference to the national laws of the Member States. A second one concerns the relative breadth of this particular notion of the 'worker', particularly if this were to emerge as an EU-wide concept. A textual analysis of the relevant Charter provisions offers no help in answering either question. The formula 'in accordance with Union law and national laws and practices', is equally unhelpful in clarifying this important conundrum.

Neither the general provisions contained in Title VII of the Charter, nor the sibylline wording of Protocol No 30,[41] appear to shed any light on this notion of the 'worker'. On the other hand we know from the Charter's *travaux preparatoires*, and more precisely from the 'Explanations' produced by the Convention in 2000,[42] that some of the labour rights contained in the Charter are derived from similar provisions contained in the European Social Charter and in the Community

---

[37] EC Commission (2008) '"Employment" Directive (2000/78/EC): list of Member States to which a reasoned opinion or letter of formal notice will be sent', MEMO 08/68 of 31 January 2008.
[38] ILO (2007) *Eliminating Discrimination Against Indigenous and Tribal Peoples in Employment and Occupation – A Guide to ILO Convention No.11*, Geneva: ILO, at 13. At the time of writing it remains to be seen if this corresponds to the concept of 'class or category of jobs' as deployed by Elias LJ in *X v. Mid Sussex Citizens Advice Bureau* [2011] EWCA Civ 28, para. 62.
[39] Charter of Fundamental Rights of the European Union [2010] OJ C 83/389, Article 30.
[40] Ibid., Article 31.
[41] Protocol (No. 30) on the Application of the Charter of Fundamental Rights of the European Union to Poland and to the United Kingdom [2010] OJ C 83/313.
[42] Convention Praesidium (2000) 'Draft Charter of Fundamental Rights of the European Union – Text of the explanations relating to the complete text of the Charter as set out in CHARTE 4487/00 CONVENT 50', CHARTE 4473/00 CONVENT 49 (Brussels, 11 October 2000).

Charter of the Fundamental Rights of Workers.[43] In *Wippel* the Advocate General noted that 'the concept of "worker" in ... the Community Charter of the Fundamental Social Rights of Workers, is to be considered a Community concept and afforded a wide interpretation. The definition that the Court of Justice has developed in the context of freedom of movement for workers ... can be taken as the guideline for this purpose.'[44] This would appear to suggest that at least some of the Charter's labour rights should be based on an autonomous and broad definition of 'worker'. So, for instance, to the extent that Article 31 of the EU Charter 'draws on Article 3 of the Social Charter',[45] there should be little doubt that 'for the purposes of Article 3§1 of the Charter, all workers, including non-employees, must be covered by health and safety at work regulations.... [The European Committee on Social Rights] has consistently maintained this interpretation, on the grounds that employed and non-employed workers are normally exposed to the same risks in this area.'[46]

Similarly, the degree of deference that the European Social Charter accords to Member States in respect of the definition of a contract of employment is undoubtedly smaller than the one implicit in the *Danmols* jurisprudence. Article 24 of the Social Charter – the provision that inspired Article 30 of the EU Charter of Fundamental Rights – does clarify in its Appendix that, in the first instance: 'It is understood that this article covers all workers', even if 'a Party may exclude ... workers engaged under a contract of employment for a specified period of time or a specified task; workers undergoing a period of probation or a qualifying period of employment, provided that this is determined in advance and is of a reasonable duration; workers engaged on a casual basis for a short period'. The European Committee on Social Rights has been quite stringent in enforcing this provision, for instance by stating that 'the non-application in Italian law of the protection against redundancy for household employees, professional athletes and employees over the age of 60 obviously goes beyond the provisions of the Appendix'.[47] It also considered that 'the exclusion of employees from protection against redundancy during a probationary period violates Article 24'.[48]

At the time of writing, the personal and material scope of application of the EU Charter have yet to be tested before the ECJ. What is clear to us, however, is that a contextual reading of its provisions ought to suggest a shift towards a broader and increasingly autonomous and EU notion of 'worker' for the purposes of the application of EU social and labour fundamental rights. For the time being however we feel we ought to confine ourselves to analysing the consequences and

---

[43] Ibid., 26–9.

[44] Opinion of the AG in Case C-313/02, *Wippel v. Peek & Cloppenburg GmbH & Co KG*, ECR [2004] I-9483 [49]; cf. above p. 392.

[45] Convention Praesidium (2000) 'Draft Charter of Fundamental Rights of the European Union – Text of the explanations relating to the complete text of the Charter as set out in CHARTE 4487/00 CONVENT 50', CHARTE 4473/00 CONVENT 49 (Brussels, 11 October 2000), 29.

[46] European Committee of Social Rights, Conclusions XVI-2 (Austria), (Strasbourg, 2005), 11.

[47] Council of Europe (2008) *Digest of the Case Law of the European Committee of Social Rights* (1 September 2008), 333.

[48] Ibid.

possible root causes of the rather unsatisfactory status quo described in this subsection, a status quo which we identify as the main manifestation of the underlying normative patchiness of EU employment law, a notion which we now proceed to expound more fully.

## C. The Normative Patchiness of EU Employment Law

In this section we advance the argument that the taxonomical incoherences and deficiencies discussed in the previous paragraphs lead, perhaps inevitably, to a set of rather evident regulatory deficiencies, emerging as the primary consequence of what we describe as the normative patchiness of EU labour law. This is something that we do primarily by reference to a number of distinct, but in our view interlinked, regulatory dynamics that exemplify both the taxonomical and normative deficiencies we are referring to. We begin by considering a selection of judgments produced in recent years by the ECJ, in which the Court's reasoning has shown the limitations of having a piecemeal approach to the normative characterizations of work relationships for the purpose of the application of EU instruments in the social sphere, as well as a willingness to depart from some of its strictest applications.

An important set of limitations emerges from the arguably self-evident observation that, in reality, work relations display a complexity of normative profiles to which the rigid and self-contained matrix of personal scopes of EU social law discussed in the previous section is often unable to adapt. Put simply, while different areas of EU social law apply to different types of 'worker', in reality workers are likely to be the object of infractions involving multiple dimensions of labour and social rights. For instance a worker may be discriminated against both due to her gender and due to her status as an atypical and casual worker, or as a part-timer – with the obvious implications in terms of discrimination on grounds of sex – but also as an on-call worker providing her services through an intermediary. In many such cases, EU social law has displayed a disappointing and unsatisfactory level of protection, or alternatively has had to readjust its personal scopes of application.

To illustrate this, we may revert to the decision of the ECJ in *Wippel*. At a fundamental level the Court was called to decide whether Ms Wippel, a part-time on-call worker, had been the victim of discriminatory practices and statutory provisions, effectively because of the type of contractual relationship linking her to her employer. Ever since *Jenkins*,[49] the Court has developed a solid jurisprudence on indirect discriminatory practices afflicting part-time female workers, founded on the provisions of the equality Directives and on what was originally Article 119 EC, now Article 157 TFEU. But in *Wippel* the Luxembourg judges were being called to assess the existence of indirect discrimination against a part-time female worker also by reference to the Part-time Work Directive 97/81. The legal quagmire that could potentially derive from this set of circumstances is fairly evident. In theory it was conceivable that an atypical worker such as Ms Wippel could have derived some

---

[49] C-96/80, *Jenkins v. Kingsgate* [1981] ECR 911.

redress from the more generous jurisprudence and scope of application of EU gender discrimination legislation, while missing out in terms of legal protection if subjected to the scope of the Part-time Work Directive. In practice the Court was forced partly to abandon the *Danmols* doctrine and applied a strong presumption in favour of casual workers such as Ms Wippel falling 'within the scope of the Framework Agreement annexed to Directive 97/81'.[50] Ultimately the ECJ concluded that no discrimination emerged due to the impossibility of identifying any of the suitable comparators under either Directive 76/207 or Directive 97/81.[51]

More recent cases have shown a growing willingness on the part of the ECJ progressively to retreat from the *Danmols* orthodoxy and reduce the margin of discretion recognized to national legal systems in the context of discriminatory practices against some atypical workers. This has most evidently occurred in respect of fixed-term workers, where the Court has substantially limited the leeway granted to national legal systems in concretely defining the scope of application of Directive 99/70.[52] In *Del Cerro Alonso* the Court forcefully maintained that 'Directive 1999/70 and the Framework agreement are applicable to all workers providing remunerated services in the context of a fixed-term employment relationship linking them to their employer', arguably a significant departure from the *Danmols* orthodoxy.[53] In *Angelidaki*, the Court asserted that 'it is clear...that...the scope of the Framework Agreement is not limited solely to workers who have entered into successive fixed-term employment contracts; on the contrary, the agreement is applicable to all workers providing remunerated services in the context of a fixed-term employment relationship linking them to their employer'.[54]

Similar, albeit perhaps more limited, retreats from *Danmols* have occurred in other contexts too. For instance in *Ruben Andersen*, the Court noted that the concept of 'temporary contract or employment relationship' imposed by Directive 91/533 was left to the determination of national authorities and courts, but also that it had to 'be fixed so as not to prejudice the effectiveness of the second subparagraph of Article 8(2) of Directive 91/533', whose object 'is to permit workers in a precarious situation to enforce directly, by judicial process, the rights conferred on them by the Directive'.[55]

In our view, these decisions display a visible anxiety on the part of the ECJ and an attempt to reduce the margins of discretion which the EU regulatory instruments it is called upon to interpret have left to implementing Member States. In other words the Court restates the elements of cogency of EU legislation, by retuning the personal scope of application of, in this case, Directive 99/70. This

---

[50] Case C-313/02, *Nicole Wippel v. Peek & Cloppenburg GmbH & Co KG* [2004] ECR I-9483, [40].

[51] Ibid., paras. [62] and [65] of the judgment.

[52] Cf. cases such as Case C-212/04, *Adeneler and Others* [2006] ECR I-6057, paras. 54–57 and Case C-53/04, *Marrosu and Sardino* [2006] ECR I-7213, paras. 40–43.

[53] Case C-307/05, *Yolanda Del Cerro Alonso v. Osakidetza-Servicio Vasco de Salud* [2007] ECR I-7109, para. [28].

[54] Ibid., [116].

[55] Case C-306/07, *Ruben Andersen v. Kommunernes Landsforening* [2008] ECR I-10279, para. [53].

undoubtedly progressive jurisprudential approach does come, however, with its limitations, and merely tinkering with the degree of fragmentation of the normative characterizations underpinning EU labour law may not protect sufficiently broad categories of workers. The Court is inevitably constrained by the textual and normative restrictiveness of some of these instruments.

More recently, the Court was asked to pronounce upon the case of a male employee seeking to obtain a particular type of parental leave granted to Spanish female employees for the purposes of early childcare or, if the female worker does not claim it for herself, to the child's father, provided he is also an employee.[56] Mr. Roca Álvarez applied to his employer for such time off work. His request was refused on the ground that the child's mother was self-employed and consequently was not personally entitled to time off work. Underlying this application are two fundamental questions about the nature of EU anti-discrimination law, but also about the overlaps, or rather the protective *lacunae*, created by gender and employment status. The Court agreed with A.G. Kokott and noted that to refuse entitlement to this particular type of leave to fathers whose status is that of an employee, on the sole ground that the child's mother is self-employed, could have the effect 'that a woman [ ... ] who is self-employed would have to limit her self-employed activity and bear the burden resulting from the birth of her child alone, without the child's father being able to ease that burden'.[57]

The adoption of the Temporary Agency Work Directive[58] provides further fertile ground for possible clashes between the different normative characterizations of the various areas of EU social law, and their corresponding protective scopes. It remains to be seen whether the Court will acknowledge that this Directive provides a statutory solution to the absence of the *Allonby* 'single source' of discrimination typical of multilateral work relations. But undoubtedly the very narrow personal and substantive scope of the Directive, perfectly exemplified by the various definitions contained in its Article 3, means that some atypical workers employed through intermediary entities will most likely fall outside this particular 'equal treatment' instrument.

As a provisional conclusion to this first section of the chapter, we would like to suggest that, when it comes to identifying a consistent central organizing idea for the purposes of shaping its scope of application, EU labour law is still in limbo. The Court's jurisprudence is arguably seeking to strike a balance between rules that are mandatory and rules that may be derogable, by adopting different scopes of application for different areas of EU law, and often by abstaining from any involvement in the choices made by implementing Member States. But this approach of the Court is not without its shortcomings, as very often the enjoyment of those rights that it sees as verging towards the *jus cogens* end of the regulatory spectrum, for instance those that are connected to the general principle of equality

---

[56] Case C-104/09, *Pedro Manuel Roca Álvarez v. Sesa Start España ETT SA*, judgment of 30 September 2010 (unreported at the time of writing).
[57] Ibid., para. [37].
[58] Directive 2008/104/EC on Temporary Agency Work [2008] OJ L 327/9.

and equal treatment, are inevitably connected with areas of regulation that are relinquished to *jus dispositivum*. The following section seeks to suggest ways of addressing this inherent contradiction affecting EU social law.

## Section 2: A European Legal Framework
## For Personal Work Relations

In the previous section we considered the various ways in which EU law, and in particular EU social law, has added its own layers to the depths of confusion and uncertainty in which the legal construction of personal work relations seems to be buried so far as the labour law systems of its Members States are concerned. However, in this section we now seek to find, at the heart of this body of analytical difficulty and normative complexity, an opportunity for the positive development of a fresh understanding of the legal construction of personal work relations. We argue that this positive development might be achieved by means of the articulation of a European Legal Framework for Personal Work Relations. We seek to show that this provides a way of drawing together the strands of analysis which have been woven in the earlier chapters of this work.

Initially, we outline the objectives and the components of our suggested European Legal Framework, comparing and relating these objectives and components to those of the Draft Common Frame of Reference for European Private Law (subsection A). We then set out the methodology of our suggested European Legal Framework, indicating that there will be both a relational dimension turning upon the notion of 'the personal work relation' and a dimension in which we are concerned with the notion of 'multi-layered regulation' (subsection B). We then go on to develop the relational dimension, arguing that a significant proportion of the modern development of the legal construction of personal work relations in EU Member States can be attributed to the influence of EU law, which therefore provides a number of relational templates for our suggested European Legal Framework (subsection C).

We then argue (in subsection D) that the impact and significance of these relational templates has to be understood within another dimension, consisting of elaborate variations in the rigour with which those templates are imposed; we deploy for this purpose the notion of 'layered regulation' which was developed earlier in this work. It is suggested that these variations on the spectrum from *ius cogens* to *ius dispositivum*, which we refer to as 'cogency rules', have themselves been much elaborated by and as a result of EU law, and that the understanding of their significance forms a very important element in the articulation of our suggested European Legal Framework; and concludingly we seek to show how both these dimensions can be combined into our suggested European Legal Framework.

## A. The Objectives and Main Components of a European Legal Framework For Personal Work Relations

In this subsection we present an outline of the nature and main components of our suggested European Legal Framework for Personal Work Relations, and of the purposes which might be served by articulating an instrument of that kind. We should begin by considering the purposes of such an exercise, because they should and do determine its nature and its methodology. Both the purposes and the methodology of our suggested European Legal Framework can usefully be identified by comparison and contrast with the purposes and methodology of the currently developing exercise in articulating a Draft Common Frame of Reference for European Private Law (DCFR).[59]

As we have observed earlier in this work, the purposes and methodology of such exercises are crucially intertwined and can be identified at various different levels; this is true both of the DCFR and our own suggested European Legal Framework. At one level, the DCFR seems to be essentially codificatory in its purposes and methodology; it seems to be an exercise in distilling and codifying a set of principles for European Private Law – though there is considerable uncertainty and ambiguity about the status and normative effect of those codified principles. By contrast with the apparent alternative narratives for the nature and intended effect of the DCFR, we disclaim any particular codificatory ambitions for our suggested European Legal Framework. Our idea is that it would provide a cognitive map of the legal constructions of personal work relations both in EU law and in the legal systems of the Member States – a guide through the complexities and diversities of those legal constructions rather than an attempt to hammer them into a single set of rules or principles.

This might appear to suggest that our suggested European Legal Framework would be steered on such a different course from that of the DCFR as to make comparison between them impossible. However, at a deeper level their purposes and methodologies could be seen as more convergent ones. That is to say, the DCFR seems to have, at a fundamental level, an objective and methodology of delineating and analytically organizing a certain legal domain within European law – that of 'private law'; our suggested European Legal Framework would have, at that level, a parallel ambition for a different legal domain within European law, namely that of the law of personal work relations. Those objectives and that methodology are, in essence, the very ones which we have identified for the present work itself. So in what sense do we contend that these objectives and this methodology can be carried forward into our suggested European Legal Framework? And what might be the utility of such an exercise if we disclaim a codificatory rationale for it?

---

[59] Cf. C. Von Bar, E. Clive, H. Schulte-Nölke, H. Beale, J. Herre, P. Schlechtriem, M. Storme, S. Swann, P. Varul, A Veneziano, F Zoll, (eds.) (2008) *Principles, Definitions and Model Rules of European Private Law, Draft Common Frame of Reference (DCFR), Interim Outline Edition*, Munich: Sellier.

Our suggested answer to those questions is that the development of EU law generally and EU employment law in particular has presented a special set both of needs and of opportunities for the articulation of the kind of European Legal Framework which we are proposing. By identifying and considering those needs and opportunities, we can draw together the discussions about the objectives and the methodology of our suggested European Legal Framework. We will argue that, in a sense, these needs and these opportunities are the two faces of a single coin – which consists of the quite intense and intimate involvement of EU law in the legal construction of personal work relations in the Member States. We proceed to consider that involvement first as presenting needs and then as presenting opportunities for the articulation of a European Legal Framework for Personal Work Relations such as we have in mind.

These factors pointing to the need for a European Legal Framework for Personal Work Relations may be identified as follows. One such factor consists of the taxonomical confusion which, as we saw in the previous section, has been brought about by the partial renormalization of personal work relations both at EU and Member State levels. EU law has been a significant contributor both to that partial renormalization and that confusion, for example by reason of the elaborately crafted and compromised formulations of the three Directives which addressed the increasing resort to marginal or precarious forms of work, that is to say the Part-time Work Directive, the Fixed-term Work Directive, and the Temporary Agency Work Directive.[60]

Another such factor pointing to the need for a European Legal Framework for Personal Work Relations arises from the Draft Common Frame of Reference itself. That is because, although those engaged in the formulation of the DCFR consistently locate the law of the contract of employment as being in a different domain from the one with which they are concerned, they seem equally consistently to assume that other contractual personal work relations may lie within their private law domain. A clear example is provided by the DCFR's concern with what it refers to, without ever defining them, as 'service contracts'.[61] One of the central arguments of the present work has been that contractual personal work relations should all be regarded as falling within a domain of personal work relations which is distinct and distinctively regulated from that of the contractual relations of private law in general. The generic use of the term 'service contract' belies the fact that a number of such service contracts will inevitably regulate the provision of personal work either directly, for instance in the form of franchising or subcontracting arrangements,[62] or indirectly, for instance in the case of a contract between an

[60] Council Directive 97/81/EC of 15 December 1997 Concerning the Framework Agreement on Part-Time Work Concluded by UNICE, CEEP and the ETUC, [1998] OJ L 14/9; Council Directive 1999/70/EC of 28 June 1999 Concerning the Framework Agreement on Fixed-Term Work Concluded by ETUC, UNICE and CEEP [1999] L 75/43; Directive 2008/104/EC of the European Parliament and of the Council of 19 November 2008 on Temporary Agency Work [2008] OJ L327/9.

[61] Cf. 'Draft Common Frame', IV. C.–2.

[62] Cf. Chapter 8.

employment agency and a user company.[63] At the level of EU law, this encroachment of the DCFR upon the domain of personal work relations explored by our work seems to us to point strongly to the need for a European Legal Framework for Personal Work Relations to maintain an appropriately distinctive kind of conceptualization of that set of contractual personal work relations beyond the contract of employment which are being tacitly colonized by the architects of the DCFR.

On the other hand, we would argue that those factors of need could also be regarded as factors of opportunity for the kind of European Legal Framework which we have in mind. Thus, the existence of the DCFR in a certain sense legitimizes, even in a sense demands, the articulation of a European Legal Framework for Personal Work Relations, especially if, as we strongly suggest, the latter could be designed to avoid censure for being too prescriptive. Moreover, if the DCFR is regarded – as we think it should be – as an invitation or provocation to a policy discussion about the desirability of an enveloping conception of European private law, then it provides a real opportunity, or even a kind of obligation, to think about whether and how far that conception should extend or intrude into the sphere of personal work relations. The opportunity – and indeed the need – for such a debate is further heightened by the fact that the European Commission has in recent years been at pains to open up a distinctive discussion about the 'modernising of labour law'[64] – a discussion in which the delineation of the appropriate interface between labour law and general private law plays a significant part.

The other factor which we adduced as indicating the need for a European Legal Framework for Personal Work Relations – namely the taxonomical confusion into which European employment has descended, not least by reason of the involvement of EU employment law – can also be regarded as equally presenting an opportunity for the articulation of that framework to be regarded as a productive and worthwhile undertaking. By identifying that opportunity more precisely, we can also delineate more precisely the shape which we think that framework could most usefully take. It is an opportunity which we can encapsulate in the idea of an emerging new architecture for the legal construction of personal work relations, to which we believe that EU law is making a significant, though in many ways incomplete and imperfectly articulated, contribution. There is as we have said a real need to tackle the taxonomical confusion in which that new architecture is enmeshed; the outlines of the new building are obscured by very untidy scaffolding. On the other hand, there is a real opportunity to articulate a European Legal Framework for Personal Work Relations precisely in order to mark the fact that a new structure does seem to be emerging. We proceed to elaborate upon that idea.

Our suggestion is that this 'new architecture' has emerged – in a difficult and contested way – from the denormalization of personal work relations, and the

---

[63] Unsurprisingly Articles L. 1251-42, and following of the French *Code du Travail* specifically regulate the *Contrat de mise à disposition*, which is the legal vehicle for such arrangements.

[64] Most notably with its Green Paper (2006) 'Modernising Labour Law to Meet the Challenges of the 21st Century', COM 708 final.

partial renormalization of them to which EU law has significantly contributed. The normative constraints, whether imposed by legislation, or by collective bargaining, or by other institutional mechanisms such as the conventions of trade associations, which had ensured the prevalence of stable and 'standard' employment relationships during the post-war welfare-state period in Europe began to recede as from, let us say, the mid-1970s onwards. Those normative constraints have not on the whole been reinstituted in anything like their original form; but they have been succeeded by more partial or weaker constraints which seek to control the more extreme manifestations of precarity or inequality which occur within an increasingly denormalized labour market.

As we have previously indicated, EU employment law has been significantly involved in these evolutions. It has been somewhat implicated in the denormalization of personal work relations, and indeed in recent years has taken something of a lurch in that direction, in the view of many commentators, in its approach to collective bargaining and industrial action in defence of national labour standards.[65] But it has, on the other hand, been at the centre of contested initiatives for partial renormalization in various forms. The Part-time Work Directive, the Fixed-term Work Directive and the Temporary Agency Work Directive are the conspicuous manifestations of that involvement;[66] but the tendency has other manifestations too, as we shall hope to show.

The crucial point here, for the purposes of our present argument, is that these measures of partial renormalization frequently amount to or involve the introduction of particular legal constructions of personal work relations – and particular processes of the kind which we have identified in the course of this work as the normative characterization of personal work relations. Thus we can see that each of those three Directives concerning atypical work patterns has introduced its own particular template for a particular kind of personal work relation – the part-time work relation with an inbuilt claim to parity of treatment with the full-time work relation, the fixed-term work relation with an inbuilt claim to parity of treatment with the permanent work relation, and the temporary agency work relation with an inbuilt claim to parity of treatment with the directly employed work relation. And we can also see that each of those three Directives instituted its own processes of normative characterization, on the basis of those templates, within the Member States, while at the same time granting considerable and – in light of our earlier discussion we might say excessive – leeway to national legal orders.

We can further observe that where, as in the instance of the atypical work Directives, these measures of partial renormalization are taken or initiated at the EU level itself, their transposition into the legal systems of the Member States is often an especially intricate matter, both as to the legal patterns or templates which they represent, and as to the processes of normative characterization which they institute. Moreover, and perhaps most notably, such measures take up or give rise

---

[65] Cf. K. Ewing and J. Hendy QC (2009) *The New Spectre Haunting Europe – The ECJ, Trade Union Rights and the British Government*, London: IER.

[66] See above p. 233.

to very complex and refined positions on the spectrum from *ius cogens* to *ius dispositivum*. We might describe this by saying that the 'cogency rules', that is to say the rules or doctrines of law which determine how rigorously the templates are imposed, are very complicated ones and that the full extent of that dimension of complexity is often not sufficiently examined or understood.

We suggest that it is precisely in the mapping of those evolutions and those complexities that the important role for our suggested European Legal Framework for Personal Work Relations is to be found. This role would, in our suggestion, consist in the first instance of establishing the category of the personal work relation as a distinctive one within EU law, with its own identity and coherence. It is firstly in that sense that there would be a 'European legal framework' for the legal construction of personal work relations in European law. The role of our suggested European Legal Framework would in the second instance consist of identifying and tracking the development of particular types of personal work relation within that outline frame of reference, and within or under the influence of EU employment law. We now consider the methodology for achieving these objectives or playing these roles.

## B. The Methodology of a European Legal Framework for Personal Work Relations

In order to show how our suggested European Legal Framework for Personal Work Relations might achieve the objectives which we have identified for it, and in order to indicate what shape and form that instrument might take, we will seek to make further use of some of the analytical tools which have been developed in the course of this work. First and foremost, we will make use of the idea of the personal work relation itself as a legal category, but we will also reinvoke the notions of multilayered regulation, of the personal work nexus, of the personal work profile, and of the normative idea of personality in work. We will also for this purpose develop further the notion of there being a wide variety of different cogency rules which apply in the various different regulatory contexts with which we are concerned.

The first two of those concepts upon which it will be helpful to concentrate are those of the personal work relation itself, and of multilayered regulation. Our suggested methodology for a European Legal Framework for Personal Work Relations would deploy and develop those two concepts in a way which would mirror their deployment and development in this work itself; but there would be the great difference that, for the reasons we have given, the starting points would be those of EU employment law rather than those of European national labour law systems which have been the focus of this work.

Each of those two key concepts would be deployed and developed in its own way in the creation and elaboration of our suggested European Legal Framework, as they have been in the course of this work. As in this work, each of those two key concepts would have an analytical function; but whereas the function of the concept of multilayered regulation would be primarily one of descriptive analysis, the function of the concept of the personal work relation would be more in the nature of prescriptive analysis. We shall explain that contrast, concentrating first on the prescriptive function of the concept of the personal work relation.

The prescriptive function of the concept of the personal work relation in our suggested European Legal Framework would be, as it has been in this work, that of establishing an outline definitional category for the domain of labour or employment law – in this case, an outline definitional category for European employment law in the sense in which we have identified that body of law at the beginning of this chapter. That function is a prescriptive one both in a negative and a positive sense. It is prescriptive in the negative sense that the concept is not a recognized or established one within European employment law, that is to say it does not have a current descriptive existence within European employment law. It is also prescriptive in the positive sense that we are arguing for its development and deployment as something which should or ought in our view to happen in the context of European employment law, in much the same way as we have prescriptively advanced the same notion throughout this work in the context of European national labour law systems.

Having deployed the concept of the personal work relation in a prescriptive way in order to create an outline definitional category for our suggested European Legal Framework for Personal Work Relations, we would propose to accord a more descriptive function to the other foundational concept which we intend to use in its construction, that of multilayered regulation. That is to say, whereas we do not think that the personal work relation has a current existence as a definitional category in European law, we think that EU employment law does make its own contribution to an already multilayered body of legal regulation of those relations in European legal systems. In other words, by invoking the notion of multilayered regulation, and by focusing on the layers which have been introduced by or in response to EU employment law measures, we are describing something which already exists, rather than inventing and imposing a category of our own.

We will now seek to show how this particular combination of prescriptive and descriptive analysis of the legal construction of personal work relations, taking the measures and constructs of EU employment law as its starting point, could be the means of creating our suggested European Legal Framework, and how it could play a useful part in the development of European employment law. As the next two steps in that argument, we shall now elaborate our key concepts of, firstly, the personal work relation as the framing category for our suggested European Legal Framework for Personal Work Relations, and, secondly, the notion of multi-layered regulation as providing the descriptive content of that instrument.

## C. The Personal Work Relation as the Framing Concept for a European Legal Framework for Personal Work Relations

In this section we specify what we see as the significance of adopting the personal work relation as the framing concept or definitional category of our suggested

European Legal Framework for Personal Work Relations, and we secondly consider how, as a taxonomical category, the personal work relation maps on to the categories which are currently used in EU employment law measures. The significance of adopting the personal work relation as the framing concept for our suggested European Legal Framework is, we think, not inconsiderable; but alternative views are possible as to the extent of that significance. It could be viewed as a very radical proposal or as a relatively uncontroversial one. We proceed to consider those alternative views.

Jeffrey Kenner, himself the proposer of quite radical ideas of a similar kind, correctly perceived that the first author of this work had been tending towards a fairly revolutionary notion of eliminating the binary division between contracts of employment and contracts for services by imposing the overarching and unifying category of the personal employment contract.[67] He regarded that as more of a challenge to the legal and policy structures of EU employment law than it would be wise or even feasible to mount in the short term. Such a view might be taken even more strongly of our present proposal with regard to the personal work relation, a category even more novel and transgressive than that of the personal employment contract in the face of the traditional taxonomies of European employment law.

We might, however, argue that in one sense our adoption of the personal work relation as the framing category for our suggested European Legal Framework for Personal Work Relations is a less radical or transgressive one than it might appear to be. This might be argued on two grounds. Firstly, we propose the adoption of the personal work relation as a framing category for the domain of European employment law as a whole, rather than as a category designed to supersede or eliminate the existing categories within that domain. Secondly, we take the view that, whereas EU employment law does not use the category of the personal work relation as such, and whereas it quite often uses narrower categories such as that of 'the employment contract or relationship', nevertheless there are, as we shall see, various instances in which EU employment law does make use of categories which are as wide as, or even wider than, that of 'the personal work relation' – so that the adoption of that category would not take EU employment law into territory where it had never before ventured.

As one might expect, given that both these points of view are perfectly tenable ones, the best view would seem to lie between these two extremes. The adoption of the personal work relation as the framing category for our suggested European Framework does not override or suppress the existing taxonomy of EU employment law in a disruptive way, or take it into a whole new area of virgin territory. It does involve some reinforcement and sharpening of outer boundaries, and the locating of those boundaries in moderately ambitious positions. This brings us to the technicalities of adopting the personal work relation as the framing category for

---

[67] J. Kenner (2009) 'New Frontiers in EU Labour Law: From Flexicurity to Flex-Security', in M. Dougan and S. Currie (eds.), *50 Years of the European Treaties: Looking Back and Thinking Forward*, Oxford: Hart, 304.

our suggested European Legal Framework for Personal Work Relations, which we consider in the ensuing paragraphs.

Most of the groundwork for adopting the personal work relation as the framing category for our suggested European Legal Framework has been carried out earlier in this work. We have sought to show why we think it is an appropriate framing category for labour or employment law in the context of European national legal systems. The question which remains is that of how it fits into the categories which are used in EU law in the regulation of work relations.

The problems of locating the category of the personal work relation with regard to the existing categories of EU law are, we suggest, rather unexpected ones. They do not consist of the well-worn debates about what EU law measures mean when they speak of 'the employment contract' or 'the employment relationship' or even of the relation between 'worker' and employer. That is because all those categories, slippery and elusive as they are, nevertheless, as we have seen in the context of European national legal systems, all fall squarely and comfortably within our conception of the personal work relation. The crucially defining boundary of our category of the personal work relation has to be drawn, in EU law much as in national legal systems, not as between 'the contract of employment' and 'the contract for services', nor between 'the employee' and 'the worker', but at the much less familiar and well-understood interface between 'personal' work relations and other work relations which are not 'personal' in the sense that the work provider does not undertake to provide the work in person.

Indeed, we would go further and suggest that the creation and application of a definitional outline category for European employment law at this particular interface – our proposal being for the personal work relation as that category – represents a significant present need which has not been sufficiently recognized. That need arises, we believe, from the use of a number of definitional categories in EU law which are deployed either on the margins of or even beyond the perceived boundaries of EU employment law, but where some at least of the work relations which fall within those categories should be regarded as within the domain of employment law. We can think of these categories as the employment-law-ambivalent categories of EU law (which of course have many counterparts in European national legal systems).

There are some examples of these ambivalent categories which are quite general across the whole spheres of work relations and economic activity, and others which are more sector-specific. Instances of a general kind are those of 'occupation', 'self-employment', as found for example in various anti-discrimination Directives discussed in the earlier parts of this chapter, and 'professional activity', as found in the main general Directive on the recognition of professional qualifications within the EU.[68] Instances of a more sector-specific kind are those of 'commercial agents' and 'persons performing mobile road transport activities' as found respectively in

---

[68] Directive 2005/36/EC of 7 September 2005 on the recognition of professional qualifications [2005] L 255/22.

Directives 86/653/EEC and 2002/15/EC. Each of these categories could be construed as extending to non-personal as well as to personal work relations.

The ambivalence of these categories presents an existential conundrum for EU employment law, of both a theoretical and a practical kind, the extent of which has, as we have said, by no means been fully recognized. There are those who doubt whether it is ever appropriate for labour law to be extended beyond the sphere of dependent employment contracts or relationships and thus into the sphere of self-employment among others. But even for those who are prepared for some extension of labour or employment law beyond the sphere of dependent employment, or who acknowledge the present reality of such extensions, there is still a real and in our view fully warranted concern about extensions of the categories of labour or employment law into what might be regarded as entirely commercial work relations. The use in EU law of equivocal categories such as those cited above presents that dilemma in an acute form. Are the EU measures which extend to those ambivalent categories to be regarded and construed as part of EU employment law? If so, can EU employment law claim to maintain a coherence and integrity as a distinctive body of regulation with its own appropriate sphere of operation?

We believe that the development of a European Legal Framework with the personal work relation as its outline definitional category provides the path to a solution to this essential dilemma. We argue that it would be strongly appropriate for these ambivalent categories to be located in relation to the definitional category of the personal work relation so that our suggested European Legal Framework for Personal Work Relations, bounded by that category, would provide a clearer outline framework than currently exists for determining the scope of the domain of European employment law. We proceed to indicate the ways in which we think these ambivalent categories might be located or construed by reference to the idea of the personal work relation.

We would argue that the idea of the personal work relation as the appropriate outline definitional category for European employment law is sufficiently persuasive and robust to justify its being used as an aid or instrument in the construction of the ambivalent categories which we have identified. We suggest that the definitional category of the personal work relation could be used as an instrument of construction in the following way: a distinction could be drawn between three different types of EU law measure, presenting three differing interpretative contexts for the construction of ambivalent relational categories. The distinction which we think may be useful, even if it does not always yield totally decisive outcomes, is between, firstly, measures of EU law which are primarily within the domain and normal personal scope of EU employment law, secondly those which are more or less equally within and outside the domain and normal personal scope of EU employment law, and thirdly those which are primarily outside the domain and normal personal scope of EU employment law. For this purpose, we identify the domain of EU employment law as that of the regulation of relations between working persons and the persons or enterprises for whom they work; and we identify the normal personal scope of EU employment law as extending to 'employees' and 'workers'.

We suggest that, when the outline definitional concept for our suggested European Legal Framework for Personal Work Relations, that of the personal work relation, is applied to the ambivalent categories of EU law, different canons of construction might appropriately apply according to the type of EU law measure which is in issue. If an EU law measure, which makes use of an ambivalent category, is deemed to be of the first type, that is to say primarily within the domain and normal personal scope of EU employment law, then the ambivalent category should be construed according to a very strong presumption that the ambivalent category is intended to apply only to personal work relations, as befits a measure which is primarily one of EU employment law. If an EU law measure, which makes use of an ambivalent category, is deemed to be of the second type, that is to say more or less equally within and outside the domain and normal personal scope of EU employment law, then the ambivalent category should be construed according to a presumption that it is intended to apply partly to personal work relations, but partly to non-personal work relations, as befits a measure which is partly one of EU employment law. If, on the other hand, an EU law measure which makes use of an ambivalent category is deemed to be of the third type, that is to say primarily outside the domain and normal personal scope of EU employment law, then the ambivalent category should be construed according to a presumption that the ambivalent category is primarily intended to apply to non-personal work relations, but with a readiness to recognize that it may marginally intersect with the domain and personal scope of EU employment law.

The application of and differentiation between these canons of construction would of course involve judgments which might be controversial, but would nevertheless, we suggest, be useful and constructive in the development of European employment. It will be helpful to offer illustrations from among the examples of ambivalent categories which were cited earlier. The category of 'occupation' has often been deployed in EU law measures which are primarily concerned with controlling various kinds of discrimination in the employment field. It would seem appropriate to regard those measures as being of the first type, and accordingly to construe that category in that context as intended to apply only to personal work relations. A similar argument could we think be made out for the ambivalent category of 'persons performing mobile road transport activities' as found in the Directive with that title.[69]

On the other hand, the ambivalent category of 'professional activity' is found in the context of measures concerning the recognition of professional qualifications within the EU. Those measures should probably be regarded as being of the second type, that is to say more or less equally within and outside the domain and normal personal scope of EU employment law. That would mean that this ambivalent category should be construed, in that context, according to a presumption that it is intended to apply partly to personal work relations, but partly to non-personal work

---

[69] Directive 2002/15/EC of the European Parliament and of the Council of 11 March 2002 on the organization of the working time of persons performing mobile road transport activities [2002] OJ L 80/35; see also above pp. 407–8.

relations. That is to say, the category should be construed in the context of those measures as applying partly to personal professional activity, but partly to non-personal professional activity in the sense of professional activity conducted by firms or professional enterprises. Such a measure would be regarded as falling within the domain of European employment law, and within the ambit of our suggested European Legal Framework for Personal Work Relations, so far as it referred to the former kind of professional activity but not the latter. Of course, this recognizes the fact that the relationships and nexuses established *within* a given firm or professional enterprise, may well themselves constitute personal work relations squarely within the ambit of the European Legal Framework for Personal Work Relations.

Two further illustrations will be useful. As an example of an EU law measure making use of an ambivalent category, which should be deemed to be of the third type, that is to say primarily outside the domain and normal personal scope of EU employment law, we would suggest that of the Commercial Agents Directive.[70] So we would argue that the ambivalent category of 'commercial agent' should be construed as being intended to apply primarily to non-personal work relations, but with a readiness to recognize that some commercial agents may be engaged in personal work relations, so that there is some intersection with the domain and personal scope of EU employment law. And finally, as an example of the difficulty and controversiality, but also we hope the utility, of this system of construction, we offer the use of the category of 'self-employment' in the various EU regulatory contexts. Its use in the context of the so-called Directive on Equal Treatment of the Self-employed (86/613/EEC, to be replaced in 2012 by 2010/41/EU) should be regarded as a case of the first type, while its use in the context of freedom of establishment should probably be regarded as a case of the second type but possibly of the third type.

Having thus elaborated the first of the two key concepts which are foundational for our suggested European Legal Framework, namely that of the personal work relation as the framing category, we are in a position to move on to the second one, namely the notion of multilayered regulation as providing the descriptive content of that instrument.

## D. Multilayered Regulation and the Idea of EU Regulatory Layers

Having we hope established the outline or definitional category for our suggested European Legal Framework for Personal Work Relations, we now revert to the notion of multilayered regulation as the key to articulating its content within that overall category. As we have argued earlier, in Chapter 3 of this work, it is useful to think of each of the many kinds of legal regulation of the personal work relation as constituting or forming part of a layer of regulation, and therefore to think of the legal construction of the personal work relation as having a multilayered composi-

---

[70] Council Directive 86/653/EEC of 18 December 1986 on the coordination of the laws of the Member States relating to self-employed commercial agents [1986] OJ L 382/17; see also above pp. 407–8.

tion consisting of many such strata. As we have previously argued, each such layer is the subject of its own particular normative characterization, which accords it a particular relational definition and place in the taxonomy of personal work relations. And we would add in the further notion that each such layer is the subject of its own set of cogency rules, which determine how rigorously that normative characterization is imposed.

So, to recapitulate, our idea of multilayered regulation is the following one. The legal construction of each personal work relation is composed of a number of layers of regulation, each derived from its own source of regulation, which may consist of legislation or case-law or interpretative doctrine, or a combination of them, and might also draw on wider sources of regulation such as collective bargaining. Each such layer of regulation can be regarded as involving an act or process of normative characterization of the personal work relation to which it applies. Each such layer of regulation thus consists of the following elements: firstly, a relational element whereby a particular normative character is assigned to a particular category of personal work relations, and, secondly, a cogency rule or set of rules which prescribes how rigorously that character is assigned; we revert shortly to further explanation of that latter element.

We would suggest that it might be very useful to think of EU employment law as having on a number of occasions contributed its own set of layers of regulation to the legal construction of personal work relations in the Member States. We would not wish to go to the lengths of arguing that each and every measure of EU employment law should be regarded as having that effect, but we would firmly assert that some of them do so. Many measures forming part of EU employment law can be said to involve their own normative characterizations of personal work relations; they create their own particular templates or patterns for certain kinds of personal work relation; and they form the basis of new layers of regulation of personal work relations, adding further strata to an already multilayered legal construction of those relations.

Let us give two key examples from among two possible ones. The Acquired Rights Directive[71] involves a normative characterization of a relatively large set of employment contracts or relationships, as having a continuity which survives the transfer of the employing undertaking from one owner or employer to another. This amounts to the normative characterization of that set of employment contracts or relationships as being in a special sense multilateral ones as between the employee, the transferor employer, and the transferee employer at least for a transitional period around the time of transfer. This is in our view tantamount to the creation of a particular kind of template or pattern for a particular set of personal work relations. To give our other example, the age discrimination provisions of the Equal Treatment Framework Directive[72] also involve a normative

---

[71] Directive 77/187 EEC on the approximation of the laws of the Member States relating to the safeguard of employees' rights in the event of transfer of undertakings, businesses or parts of businesses, [1977] OJ L 61/26; amended by Council Directive 98/50 of 29 June 1998, [1998] OJ L 201/98. The two now consolidated with Council Directive 2001/23/EC of 12 March 2001, [2001] OJ L 82/16.

[72] Council Directive 2000/78/EC of 27 November 2000 establishing a general framework for equal treatment in employment and occupation [2000] OJ L 303/16.

characterization of a large set of employment relationships, for they in a sense create a template which expresses the conditions in which such contracts or relationships may be terminated by retirement, that is to say on the ground that the worker in question has reached a certain age.

The understanding of the meaning and importance of these new regulatory layers contributed by EU employment law therefore turns very much upon their capacity to effect new kinds of normative characterizations of personal work relations, and thereby to lead to the creation of new kinds of personal work nexus and personal work relation. Another analytical concept which we think is crucial to the understanding of the role and significance of EU regulatory layers is that of cogency rules and the spectrum from *ius cogens* to *ius dispositivum*. Continuing with the idea of taking EU employment law as the starting point for our suggested European Legal Framework for Personal Work Relations, we argue that each of the various normative characterizations of personal work relations which are effected by EU employment law measures, and each of the new kinds or variants of personal work relations which are thereby created, has its own particular set of cogency rules associated with it, dictating the rigorousness with which the template in question is applied. We have observed in the course of this work that the cogency rules associated with particular templates are apt to be complicated ones, representing many nuanced positions on the spectrum from *ius cogens* to *ius dispositivum*. In the case of the measures of EU employment law which create and impose such templates, the associated cogency rules are apt to be especially complex ones by reason of the interactions between EU law and national laws which are involved.

That is a complexity which we will seek to explain and unravel in due course, but it will be useful to give an illustration of it at this juncture. A vivid instance of it may be found by reverting to our earlier example of the age discrimination provisions of the Equal Treatment Framework Directive 2000/78/EC. As we have said, those provisions create a template which outlines a quite restrictive set of conditions in which such contracts or relationships may be terminated on the ground that the worker in question has reached a certain age. In the few years since the date on which those provisions were required to be implemented in and by the Member States, an extensive body of legislation at Member State level, and of interpretative doctrine in the ECJ and in national courts, has developed in order to determine how rigorously those conditions will be imposed.[73]

We will revert to the explanation of these complexities of the cogency rules which form part of or result from the implementation of EU employment law measures. At this juncture, it suffices that we have identified in outline the way in which some EU employment law measures constitute or give rise to new regulatory layers in the legal construction of personal work relations. So we have identified the notion of regulatory layers derived from EU employment law and playing a part in the legal construction of personal work relations in Member States – a notion

---

[73] Cf. C. O'Cinneide (2005) *Age Discrimination and European Law*, Luxembourg, Office for Official Publications of the European Communities.

which we can abbreviate as European Union regulatory layers, and upon which we can confer the acronym of EU regulatory layers.

It follows from the arguments which we have so far advanced that the articulation of our suggested European Legal Framework depends crucially upon these EU regulatory layers; they form the starting point of the analysis of what takes place within the domain of the personal work relation, which we have argued should be regarded as the defining category for that European Legal Framework. In the next section of this chapter, we seek further to develop our understanding of these EU regulatory layers and of their role as that starting point for the European Legal Framework we suggest, distinguishing more fully between two dimensions or aspects which we have indentified – the relational dimension or aspect and the cogency dimension or aspect – and then seeking to create some degree of synthesis between them.

## Section 3: EU Regulatory Layers as the Basis of a European Legal Framework for Personal Work Relations

In the previous sections we set out our proposals for the articulation of a European Legal Framework for European employment law, constructed around the two ideas of the personal work relation as an outline definitional category and of multilayered regulation as a way of analysing the legal construction of personal work relations in and by European employment law. The idea of the personal work relation as an outline definitional category was developed in detail, and the idea of multilayered regulation as an analytical key was developed to the point where we singled out and focused upon a notion of EU regulatory layers as the basis or starting point for spelling out the content of our suggested European Legal Framework for Personal Work Relations. In this section, the notion of the EU regulatory layers is developed in more detail. That development consists, firstly, of arguing that the notion should itself be regarded as normally consisting of two sublayers, one constituted an EU employment law measure which gives rise to the EU regulatory layer, and the other constituted by the response to that measure at the national or Member State level (subsection A). We then proceed to consider in more detail the relational aspect of EU regulatory layers, that is to say the particular kinds of personal work nexus and personal work profile which are created or envisaged by or as the result of EU employment law measures, making the link between the relational aspect of this notion we are investigating and the no less important aspect of them which concerns the cogency rules that apply to them (subsection B). Finally, we seek to show through some key examples how the content of our suggested European Legal Framework might be constructed on the basis of and from the starting point of an analysis of EU regulatory layers (subsection C).

## A. The Complex Nature of EU Regulatory Layers

We embark upon the detailed analysis of the nature of EU regulatory layers, with a view to showing in due course how and why they can appropriately form the basis and starting point for elaborating the content of our suggested European Legal Framework. It will be argued that EU regulatory layers are of an essentially complex nature. We have argued that this complexity consists especially in the way that they combine complex normative characterizations of personal work relations with no less complex cogency rules. It will now further be suggested that both the normative characterizations and the cogency rules, of which EU regulatory layers are essentially composed, are endowed with an especial complexity because they function on two distinct though inter-related levels, that is to say an EU law level and a national or Member State level. It will be argued from this that EU regulatory layers should be understood as layers of regulation which themselves can be broken down into two sublayers, an EU-level one and a national one.

We begin this argument with a recapitulation of the ideas of normative characterization and of the cogency rule or regime, and by an initial consideration of the way in which those two ideas are crucially connected with each other in the formation of layers of regulation in general and of EU regulatory layers in particular. It will be recalled that our notion of 'normative characterization' depicts the way in which legal measures or processes of legal regulation may impose a certain normative character upon a certain category or set of personal work relations, thus linking legal category with legal character. Such acts or processes of normative or relational characterization form a central part, arguably the central part, of the whole business of the legal construction of personal work relations. They offer to characterize the personal work relations to which they apply as consisting of a certain kind of personal work nexus and as forming part of a certain personal work profile for the working person or work provider concerned.

We have said that acts or processes of normative characterization offer to characterize personal work relations in a certain way, rather than that they actually characterize personal work relations in a certain way. It will also be recalled that we have invoked the notion of the cogency rule or cogency regime to identify the set of rules or principles which apply to determine how rigorously a normative characterization will in fact be imposed. It is this cogency rule or cogency regime which locates a particular normative characterization of a particular kind of personal work relation on a spectrum between *jus cogens* and *jus dispositivum*. The ways in which cogency rules or cogency regimes may apply to normative characterizations of personal work relations are very intricate and complex. But it is those intricate combinations between normative characterizations and cogency regimes which form the very essence of the legal construction of personal work relations; it is the cogency regime which gives three-dimensional reality to normative characterizations which would otherwise simply be theoretical models or ideal-types of the personal work relation.

Since the analysis and exegesis of layers of regulation in general, and of EU regulatory layers in particular, would form the essential content of our suggested European Legal Framework, we now attempt to develop our understanding of the complex nature of EU regulatory layers to a further stage. Our explanation of this concept, and indeed of regulatory layers in general, as being composed of combinations of normative characterizations with cogency rules, gives rise to the question of whether EU employment law measures should be regarded as creating a single layer of regulation composed of both the measure itself and the response to that measure in each Member State, or whether on the other hand the EU measure and the national response should be regarded as two separate layers of regulation. That question, although apparently rather theoretical, is important because the consideration of it enables us to understand better how layers of regulation function and interact.

The question thus posed may be refined into the issue of whether, in the case of a given measure of EU employment law, the responses at the national level to that measure are sufficiently distinctive from the original measure as to be regarded as constituting a separate regulatory layer. And it follows from our previous arguments that the distinctiveness of the national responses, from the original EU law measure itself, may be found either in their normative characterizations or in their cogency rules or both. In fact we will argue that the national responses are, for reasons which we shall give, systemically distinctive from the original EU employment law measures which gave rise to them, both as to the normative characterizations which they effect and as to the cogency rules or regimes which apply to them.

Our reasons for regarding national responses to EU employment law measures as systemically distinct from the original measures themselves are the following ones. With regard to the normative characterizations which they effect, the national responses are distinctive from the corresponding EU employment law measures in that those measures represent norms which stand above and outside the national systems, and which have to be applied within and through those national systems. In the course of that application, the norms of EU employment law are moulded into a distinctive shape and form by the inevitable imprint of each national legal system, each with its own singular mode of legal construction of personal work relations. Equally, EU employment law measures each have their own set of cogency rules, but which are then supplemented by and filtered through a further set of cogency rules operated by each national legal system. The result is that the national response to an EU employment law measure is distinctive from it in both the normative aspect and the cogency aspect.

It may be helpful at this stage to provide a couple of illustrations, from previously cited examples, of the distinctiveness of the national responses from the EU employment law measures to which they correspond. We will take as one example a rather tightly drawn and highly cogent Directive, and as the other a set of provisions in another Directive which are more loosely drawn and of lower cogency. Our example of the former kind is that of the Acquired Rights Directive. The normative propositions of that Directive are relatively specific and concrete, so much so that they could be regarded as capable of very direct implementation in national legal systems. Moreover, its provisions are framed in such a way as to suggest that it is intended to require Member States to recognize and give effect to concrete rights of employees in the transfer of the undertakings for which they work, rights moreover which are not to be subject to derogations at the national level or on the part of the employing enterprises involved.

We can better appreciate the intention of the EU law-making bodies to strengthen the cogency of this particular instrument by examining its personal scope of application from a historical and evolutionary perspective. In this respect it is important to notice that the original scope of Directive 77/187/EC was amended by Directive 98/50/EC, to strengthen the traditional 'contract or employment relationship with a set of provisions seeking to restrict the ability of implementing Member States tempted by the option of excluding from the material scope of the Directive contracts or relationships because of the number of working hours performed, their fixed-term or temporary nature'.[74] No less importantly, the two latter concepts are not left to national law definitions but are prescribed by reference to the definition contained in Article 1(1) and 1(2) of Directive 91/383 which, as observed earlier in this chapter, is best seen as a health and safety measure,[75] and as such appropriate for a broader and more cogently imposed personal scope.[76]

Nevertheless, despite the relatively high specificity and cogency of this measure, it is very evident that its transposition into national legal systems has been the subject of an enormously complex and varied set of national responses in a continuing process of iteration and reiteration between the EU legislators and courts and their national counterparts. That complexity is especially attributable to the variety, as between Member States, of mechanisms for corporate restructuring, for the transfer of undertakings or their assets, and for the contracting-out of business activities. Thus the TUPE regime of English law is quite a distinctive one both in relation to the Acquired Rights Directive itself and by comparison with responses to that Directive in other Member States.[77]

Our other illustration, this time of a European employment law measure of much lower specificity and cogency, makes the point about the distinctiveness of national responses even more forcefully. This is the case of the provisions of the Equal Treatment Framework Directive (2000/78/EC) concerning age discrimination, and their bearing upon the whole question of the termination of personal

---

[74] Article 2(2) of Council Directive 2001/23/EC of 12 March 2001 on the approximation of the laws of Member States relating to the safeguard of employees' rights in the event of transfer of undertakings, businesses or parts of undertakings or businesses, [2001] OJ 82/16.

[75] On this see N. Countouris (2007) *The Changing Law of the Employment Relationship*, Aldershot: Ashgate, pp. 189–90.

[76] In this specific sense cf. also Case C-458/05, *Jouini v. Princess Personal Service GmbH (PPS)* [2007] ECR I-07301, para. 36.

[77] The variety of implementations transpires from European Commission, Report on Council Directive 2001/23/EC of 12 March 2001 on the approximation of the laws of the Member States relating to the safeguarding of employees' rights in the event of transfers of undertakings, businesses or parts of undertakings or businesses COM (2007) 334 final. See also C. Marzo and F. Lecomte (2010) 'Le Refus d'être Transféré: Droit Comparé', *Droit Social*, 698.

work relations by retirement, and in particular the question of how much freedom may be accorded to the employing enterprise to impose retirement upon the worker by reason of having reached a certain age. Both because the requirements of the Directive are not very precise in this respect, and because the Directive itself provides various justifications for derogation from those require-ments, the national responses to these provisions of EU employment law, have been very heterogeneous between the Member States, and sometimes very dis-tinctive by comparison with the Directive itself. For instance, the Regulations which were first enacted in English law by way of response to the requirements of the Directive revolved around a notion of 'default retirement age' which, al-though it has been found to be compliant with the Directive, is so specific to the context of English employment law that it has to be regarded as quite distinctive from the Directive itself.[78]

In the course of this section we amplify these points about the distinctiveness of national-level normative characterizations and national level cogency rules or regimes. But we should first conclude the discussion about whether that distinc-tiveness is such that the national responses to EU employment law measures should be regarded as representing their own layer of regulation, separate as such from the corresponding EU layer of regulation. The arguments thus far developed might be thought to demonstrate such high levels of distinctiveness as to point inevitably towards the dual-level analysis.

However, we are of the view that an outright dual-level analysis would be a misleading one, to the extent that it would understate the crucial connectedness and interdependency which exists between the EU employment law measures and the national responses to them. We therefore suggest that the EU measures and national responses should be regarded as constituting a single composite layer of regulation – the EU regulatory layer itself – but one which is internally split or perforated as between the EU level and the national level of regulation. With that construct in mind, we proceed to consider more fully the ways in which EU regulatory layers have evolved, firstly with regard to normative or relational charac-terization and secondly with regard to cogency rules. In the course of those discussions, it will emerge more fully that it is the interplay between its two internal levels which makes the EU regulatory layer such a complex conception, but also means that it is crucial to an understanding of the legal construction of personal work relations in and by European employment law.

## B. The Relational Aspect of EU Regulatory Layers

In this subsection we seek further to develop our understanding of the construc-tion and working of EU regulatory layers, concentrating our attention on the regulatory regimes which are created by or in response to EU employment law

---

[78] Cf. M. Connolly (2009) 'Forced Retirement, Age Discrimination and the *Heyday* Case' 38(2) *ILJ*, 233. See now, however; the Employment Equality (Repeal of Retirement Age Provisions) Regulations 2011, SI 2011/1069.

measures. We shall aim to show in some detail the ways in which EU regulatory layers engage in novel kinds of relational or normative characterization of personal work relations, thus creating or giving rise to new models or patterns of personal work nexus and personal work profile. The analytical focus of this discussion will be on the way that these relational characterizations take place on two levels, the EU level and the national one, and on the distinctiveness of the outcomes of these processes at the national level, that is to say in the legal system of each Member State.

To recapitulate for a moment, we may recall our earlier propositions that relational or normative characterizations consist of the imposing of normative consequences or effects upon a selected category of personal work relations in such a way as to re-characterize that category or to create a new subcategory with its own special normative character. We have argued that it is useful to regard EU employment law measures as in many instances effecting or giving rise to these kinds of relational or normative characterizations; and that when such characterizations result from an EU employment law measure, they do so as the outcomes of a split-level process with takes place partly at the EU level itself and partly, by way of response, at the national or Member State level. We proceed to anatomize these split-level processes in greater detail, concentrating particularly upon the reasons for which the national-level responses are apt to be very distinctive ones.

Our argument about the distinctiveness of the national-level responses to EU employment law measures is the following one. Although the processes of formation of EU regulatory layers are mutually interactive and mutually reflexive as between the two levels – EU and national or Member State – on which they take place, nevertheless we take the view that the effective normative outcomes of those processes necessarily occur at the national level and are inevitably distinctive or specific to each Member State in their fine texture, even if they all conform to a general norm which has been formulated at the EU level. There is nothing really surprising about that view; it would only be an illusionary understanding of the way in which EU employment law operates which could suggest otherwise. However, since the contrary understanding of EU employment law measures as universal and virtually self-executing norms throughout the Member States is quite a widespread one, we shall need to substantiate our argument about national distinctiveness quite carefully. Our contention in this regard is that the national-level implementation of, or response to, any given EU employment law measure is necessarily path-dependent upon and system-specific to the pre-existing legal construction of personal work relations in and by the legal system of each individual Member State.

The path-dependency and system-specificity of national responses to EU employment law measures is in some aspects obvious but in other respects much less so. Reminding ourselves that the processes of relational characterization, with which we are concerned, consist of attaching normative characters and outcomes to specified categories of personal work relation, we can observe that national distinctiveness has been more obvious with regard to the categories than with regard to the normative outcomes – though in fact the normative outcomes are at least as specific to each Member State as the categories are. Thus the EU legislators have generally been very conscious that, when they evoke general categories on which to impose new characteristics – such as the category of 'employment contracts or relationships' – those general categories will have to be moderated through quite distinctive national understandings of those general categories. Indeed, the EU legislators have been so quick to refer the definition of those categories down to national systems that they have sometimes been regarded as fighting shy of producing their own European-wide conceptions of those categories. There has however been much less readiness to acknowledge that the national responses to EU employment law measures are equally distinctive with regard to the normative outcomes which those EU measures are designed to achieve.

A rather neglected or understated part of the explanation for this phenomenon consists in the fact that Member States find themselves in very distinctively different starting positions with regard to EU employment law measures. This is true in two particular senses. It is true firstly in the sense that the legal system of each Member State has its own set of legal constructions of personal work relations, so that an EU employment law measure will fall to be implemented within a distinctive legal context in each Member State. It is secondly true in the sense that, by reason of the somewhat reflexive and reiterative character of the process of enactment and interpretation of EU employment law measures at the EU level itself, any given EU employment law measure is likely, if not in its inception then at least in its ultimate form, to reflect or coincide with the existing law of some Member States more than with that of others. So the challenges which are presented by EU employment law measures to existing national employment law systems will vary considerably as between the different Member States.

For this among other reasons, we should not be at all surprised to find that the responses of Member States to EU employment law measures – the measures which they take and the interpretations which their courts adopt – are in their turn very varied and distinctive as between the different Member States. In order to refine our understanding of this diversity and national distinctiveness, it is useful to distinguish, in a broad and relative sense, between active and passive responses on the part of Member States to EU employment law measures. We might regard a Member State as making a passive response to an EU employment law measure where its legislators and/or courts decide (whether with or without the agreement of their EU counterparts) that the law and practice of the Member State is in compliance with the EU requirements so that no local action needs to be taken. Because, as we have remarked, the starting position of each Member State in relation to any given EU employment law measure is a distinctive one, a passive response may be more appropriate for one Member State than for another, though of course it may be locally subjective or political factors which determine such choices. This is a potentially risky approach, as it can expose a Member State to various kinds of liabilities occurring from the practice of non-implementation,[79] but it still remains a distinct possibility.[80]

The same thing may be said of the contrasting kind of response, which is also the most common, namely the response of an active kind, whereby the legislators or the courts of the Member State deem it appropriate to engage actively in changing the law of the Member State in order to comply with the requirements of the EU employment law measure. We may further distinguish between two main types of active response, namely the response by incorporation of the EU measure, and the response by adaptation to the EU measure. The former type of active response occurs where the Member State simply replicates the EU measure directly in its own national legal system.[81] The latter type of active response occurs where the Member State devises an adapted or specially tailored version of the EU measure in order to arrive at an accommodation between that EU measure and the existing provisions of the national legal system.[82]

We might be able to discern generic reasons why a particular Member State might tend towards one of these kinds of response rather than another. A particular Member State might tend to regard itself as a source of or exemplar for EU employment law measures, and hence might incline towards passive responses to those measures. A Member State which had recently acceded to the EU might incline towards active responses by incorporation in order to deal as swiftly and simply as possible with a backlog of compliance requirements. Another Member State might find itself seriously out of step with EU employment law measures and might be disposed towards elaborate adaptations in order to resolve the compliance issues with which it is faced. However, rather than attempting to classify such differences of response more elaborately,[83] we might do better to regard them simply as further indicators of path-dependent national distinctiveness, and to move on, in the next subsection, to consider a range of examples of different kinds of EU employment law measures and national responses to them.

---

[79] First and foremost state liability for failure to implement an EU Directive as in Case C-178–9/94, *Dillenkofer v. Germany* [1996] ECR I-4845, paras. 21–3.

[80] According to Schömann, Caluwert, and Düvel, for instance, in Luxembourg the Fixed-term Work Directive/Agreement 'was never transposed for the reason that the national legislation was already in compliance with the Directive, as confirmed by the Commission', cf. I. Schömann, S. Clauwaert, W. Düvel (2003) *Legal Analysis of the Implementation of the Fixed-Term Work Directive*, Brussels: ETUI, 16.

[81] This has been a long-established practice in the implementation of EU social policy instruments in the UK, and is now officially sanctioned by government since 'EU directives will normally be directly copied into UK law ('copy-out'), except where it would adversely affect UK interests', cf. V. Miller (2011) 'EU Legislation: Government action on "goldplating"' (SN/IA/5943 of 19 April 2011).

[82] An interesting example is provided by the way the UK has chosen to implement Article 1(a) of Council Directive 98/59/EC of 20 July 1998 on the approximation of the laws of the Member States relating to collective redundancies [1998] OJ L225/16, so as to minimize the burden for businesses.

[83] For a thought-provoking review of the 'transposition styles' of a number of 'new' and 'old' Member States cf. G. Falkner and O. Treib (2008) 'Three Worlds of Compliance or Four? The EU-15 Compared to New Member States', 46(2) *JCMS*, 293.

## C.  EU Regulatory Layers – Some Key Examples

In this subsection we therefore evoke some key examples of EU regulatory layers in the field of labour or employment law. As we have previously said, our aim in doing so will be to demonstrate the ways in which EU employment law measures may involve new kinds of relational characterization, issuing forth in new patterns of personal work nexus or personal work profile. It follows from the argument which we have now developed, about the distinctiveness of national responses, that, where EU employment law measures do issue forth in these new legal constructions of personal work relations, those new legal constructions will not, however, be directly or universally imposed by the measures themselves. It is rather that new patterns of personal work nexus or personal work profile will evolve in different ways as between the Member States as each Member State responds in its own distinctive and path-dependent way to the original EU-level measure. It is a process of composition in which the theme tunes or *leitmotifs* are articulated at the EU level, and the variations are written and played at the Member State level.

What follows is necessarily no more than an illustrative selection of EU regulatory layers, the purpose of which is to point to some occasions on which EU employment law measures have given rise to novel relational characterizations, creating possibilities which have been realized in distinctive ways in the different Member States. In considering this selection of EU regulatory layers, our attention will be focused on the capacities which the EU employment law measures in question have shown, by requiring certain normative effects to be imposed upon certain categories of personal work relation, to bring about the development of particular patterns of personal work nexus and personal work profile – albeit in quite distinctive ways as between different national legal systems. Two preliminary points should be made to explain how we select certain EU regulatory layers to achieve that focus.

Firstly, it is important to make the point that certain EU regulatory layers are much more transformative of the legal construction of personal work relations than others, and that our selection will concentrate on the most transformative ones. The arguments which we have developed in this and the immediately preceding chapters have conceptualized or crystallized such transformations as the evolution of new forms of personal work nexus or personal work profile. In one sense, each and every EU regulatory layer could be regarded as effecting some degree of transformation in personal work nexuses or personal work profiles; and it would not be profitable to become enmeshed in debates about the precise point at which such transformations amount to a change in kind, so that a new kind or pattern of personal work nexus or personal work profile should be deemed to have arisen. Nevertheless, some EU regulatory layers do present themselves as having such transformative effects much more clearly and obviously than others, and our selection will be concentrated on those obviously transformative ones.

The second preliminary point concerns the presentation of EU regulatory layers in a set of loosely defined groups. It follows from the arguments which we have

previously advanced that each EU regulatory layer operates on a certain category or
set of categories of personal work relations, and has certain normative effects upon
that category or set of categories. Each layer has its own history, in terms both of
law and policy, which determines or explains the normative effects which it achieves
and the categories upon which it operates. Provided that it is not regarded as a
dogmatic classification, we think it is useful to present our illustrative EU regulatory layers as falling into a set of four groupings, organized according to their subject
matter, but also reflecting similarities of chronology and personal scope. These four
groups are:

1. EU regulatory layers concerned with the regulation of the termination and
   transfer of employment;
2. EU regulatory layers concerned with the health and safety of workers and
   with their family life and responsibilities;
3. EU regulatory layers concerned with the control of discrimination in employment and occupation; and
4. EU regulatory layers concerned with the regulation of atypical forms of work.

We proceed to examine and take examples from each of those groupings in turn.

Our first suggested grouping is that of EU regulatory layers concerned with the
regulation of the termination and transfer of the standard employment contract or
relationship. That description groups together a set of regulatory layers mainly
originating in the reorganizations of the structures of industry and commerce
occurring in the 1970s; the Collective Dismissals Directive, the Acquired Rights
Directive, and the Employers Insolvency Directive.[84] This group of measures, and
indeed the national responses to them and therefore the EU regulatory layers of
which they form part, is the most traditional and least innovative of the four groups
with regard to the categories of personal work relations to which the measures
apply: these measure are more or less tightly confined to the contractual employment relationship. This group of EU regulatory layers is also the least productive
one so far as new patterns of personal work nexus or profile are concerned, though
in some Member States such as the UK the Acquired Rights Directive, as we have
remarked previously in this work, has been dramatically transformative of the
'standard' employment contract or relationship. That transformation consists, as
illustrated in Chapter 5, in some jurisdictions such as that of English law, in
converting employment contracts or relationships, which were previously very
tightly specific to the original employment enterprise, into ones which are continuous between employing enterprises in a range of situations of corporate or business

---

[84] Originally, Council Directive 75/129/EEC of 17 February 1975 on the approximation of the
laws of the Member States relating to collective redundancies [1975] OJ L48/29; Council Directive
77/187/EEC of 14 February 1977 on the approximation of the laws of the Member States relating to
the safeguarding of employees' rights in the event of transfers of undertakings, businesses or parts of
businesses [1977] OJ L 61/26; Council Directive 80/987/EEC of 20 October 1980 on the approximation of the laws of the Member States relating to the protection of employees in the event of the
insolvency of their employer [1980] OJ L 283/23.

restructuring, thus significantly changing the nature of the personal work nexus for those contracts or relationships and the personal work profile of the employees concerned. This is also an example of the potential for variation in national responses; in some Members States, as we have remarked, the kind of continuities between employing enterprises which were envisaged by the Acquired Rights Directive were already partially or fully provided.

In identifying our second grouping of EU regulatory layers as being concerned with the health and safety of workers and with their family life and responsibilities, we intend to bracket together a number of Directives of the later 1980s and early 1990s which have in common that kind of subject-matter or driving concern; we have in mind especially the Framework Directive on Health and Safety of 1989, the Directive on Pregnant Workers of 1992, and the Working Time Directive of 1993.[85] These measures, as noted above, extended to a somewhat broader range of personal work relations than those in the previous group, being directed towards the category of 'workers' (as variously formulated in detail). Each of those measures initiates transformations of the personal work nexus within that broad category. The Framework Directive on Health and Safety moves towards heightening the mutual responsibilities of workers for the health and safety of others at work, thus strengthening the inter-worker links within the personal work nexus of those concerned. The Directive on Pregnant Workers tends not only to transform the personal work nexus of workers in general by stipulating for maternity leave and for security against dismissal by reason of pregnancy, but also to usher in the increasingly significant personal work nexus and personal work profile of the worker temporarily replacing a pregnant worker during the latter's maternity absence or maternity leave.

However, of all the measures in this second grouping, it is probably the Working Time Directive which has had and continues to have the most transformative impact upon the legal construction of personal work relations. In aspiration at least, it represents a very significant heightening of the regulation of the whole category of 'worker' relations, though the outcomes of that enhancement of regulation are quite various as between the different Member States, especially by reason of the large scope for derogation, an aspect which we shall consider more fully in the next subsection. Moreover, even if the impact of the Directive is a variable one, it does have the further transformative effect of stimulating a considered articulation of the sub-categories of the 'worker' relation according to the ways in which working time is structured and arranged – in particular by requiring differentiation between situations of measured and of unmeasured working time and of 'on-call' working – a set of developments becoming tantamount to the evolution of new kinds of personal work nexus or profile characterized in those particular ways.

---

[85] Directive 89/391/EEC of 12 June 1989 on the introduction of measures to encourage improvements in the safety and health of workers at work [1989] OJ L183/1; Council Directive 92/85/EEC of 19 October 1992 on the introduction of measures to encourage improvements in the safety and health at work of pregnant workers and workers who have recently given birth or are breastfeeding [1992] OJ L348/1; Council Directive 93/104/EEC of 23 November 1993 concerning certain aspects of the organization of working time [1993] OJ L307/18.

Our third grouping of EU regulatory layers, that is to say those concerned with the control of discrimination in employment and occupation, is no less rich than the previous two in its transformative implications for and effects upon the legal construction of personal work relations in the Member States, or in the novel relational characterizations to which it has given rise. This grouping is based upon a long series of EU measures which form part of EU employment law but which merge into an even larger body of EU law concerned with the control of discrimination of many types across a broad range of locations of economic and social activity. They consist essentially of what are now Articles 19 and 157 of the Treaty on the Functioning of the European Union (TFEU), and the Directives eventually gathered together into the Consolidated Equality Directive of 2006.[86] We draw attention to three respects in which this very large segment of EU employment law has been productive or transformative of a wide range of personal work nexuses and profiles.

The first of those three dimensions of transformativeness is that of personal scope. As we have previously observed, the law concerning discrimination in employment is much more apt than other aspects of employment law to be regarded as continuous with the regulation of other areas of economic and social activity. This can mean that the law of employment discrimination loses its distinctiveness within the larger body of discrimination or equality law. However, although that diffuseness is sometimes encountered in EU equality law, nevertheless EU anti-discrimination measures have had the effect of creating a large definitional space which can satisfactorily be regarded as the law of equality in personal work relations. That is especially due to the evolution of the composite category of 'employment and occupation' in EU discrimination law, although, as we have previously argued, the capacity of that composite category to represent a large domain for employment equality law does depend upon its being construed to remain within the bounds of personal as opposed to non-personal work relations – as to which there could easily be a lack of consistency at the national level as well as at the EU level itself.

If EU employment equality law is a transformative part of EU employment law in respect of the definitional categories which it involves, it is no less transformative in two other respects, both of which are concerned with the shape and character of the personal work nexus, and with the strengthening and supplementing of the cross-links between workers within the personal work nexus. Firstly, EU employment discrimination law has made a number of significant contributions to the whole notion of fellow-workers as comparators,[87] in respect not only of pay but also of treatment at work more generally,[88] a notion which is the very touchstone of the law of equality in employment. Secondly, EU employment discrimination law has

---

[86] Directive 2006/54/EC of the European Parliament and of the Council of 5 July 2006 on the implementation of the principle of equal opportunities and equal treatment of men and women in matters of employment and occupation (recast) [2006] OJ L204/23.

[87] Cf. the combined effect of Articles 1(b) and 2(1)(a) of the recast Directive 2006/54/EC.

[88] Cf. Case C-54/07, *Firma Feryn NV* [2008] ECR I-5187.

also enormously reinforced the links of legal responsibility between workers, both vertically and horizontally across organizational hierarchies, by making the idea of discriminatory harassment into a major plank of the platform of protection which it provides. If it is appropriate, as we believe, to ascribe to EU employment equality measures such a transformative role with regard to personal work nexuses and the personal work profiles, it is nevertheless important not to lose sight of the split-level character of EU regulatory layers, that is to say their evolution by interaction between EU law measures and national level starting points and responses. Without wanting to detract from the innovative and progressive impact that EU equality law has had in respect of each EU Member State, it is possible to argue that EU employment equality law measures are usually generalizing the law and practice of some Member States rather than making innovations for all Member States, and the responses at national level may serve to open up new diversities between Members States while reducing previously existing ones. Keeping that in view is particularly important when considering the development of the fourth and last of the groupings of EU regulatory layers which we have singled out, that concerned with the regulation of atypical forms of work.

This fourth and final set of EU regulatory layers essentially consists of the Directives of 1997, 1999, and 2008 respectively concerning Part-time Work, Fixed-term Work, and Temporary Agency Work,[89] and the national-level re-sponses to those measures, though it should be mentioned that there is an interesting precursor of a certain kind in the Proof of Employment Directive of 1992,[90] and that there are proposals for a further Directive on Seasonal Work.[91] The three Directives of 1997–2008, and indeed the national responses to them, represent a new genre of partial renormalization of personal work relations which is of considerable novelty and interest so far as the relational aspects of EU regulatory layers are concerned. The singular feature of this new genre of regulation is that the forms or patterns of work in question – regarded as atypical ones – are regulated relatively to the corresponding 'typical' or 'standard' work pattern, rather than in a freestanding way. So certain entitlements are conferred on those working in the atypical work pattern to parity of treatment with those working in the corresponding typical pattern; and there is also regulation of transfer between the atypical work pattern and the corresponding typical one, for example by limiting

---

[89] Council Directive 97/81/EC of 15 December 1997 concerning the Framework Agreement on part-time work concluded by UNICE, CEEP and the ETUC [1998] OJ L 14/9; Council Directive 1999/70/EC of 28 June 1999 concerning the framework agreement on fixed-term work concluded by ETUC, UNICE and CEEP [1999] OJ L 175/43; Directive 2008/104/EC on Temporary Agency Work [2008] OJ L 327/9.

[90] Council Directive 91/533/EC of 14 October 1991 on an employer's obligation to inform employees of the conditions applicable to the contract or employment relationship [1991] OJ L 288/32.

[91] European Commission, 'Proposal for a directive of the European Parliament and of the Council on the conditions of entry and residence of third-country nationals for the purposes of seasonal employment', COM (2010) 379 final.

transfer into the atypical form of work, or by imposing transfer into the typical form of work, in certain circumstances.[92]

This kind of regulation is in various ways particularly productive of new kinds or patterns of personal work nexus and personal work profile. Firstly, it requires the articulation of new subsets of the personal work nexus in order to recognize and give effect to the antithesis between each respective typical and atypical work pattern. So a 'part-time personal work nexus' and a 'full-time personal work nexus' have to be identified in contrast with each other, a 'fixed-term personal work nexus' and a contrasting 'permanent personal work nexus', and a 'temporary agency personal work nexus' and a contrasting 'directly employed personal work nexus'; in many national systems there may well have been no such clearly identified antitheses. Secondly, this kind of regulation in effect gives rise to personal work nexuses which include links to comparators in the contrasting work pattern, on the basis of which parity claims may be made. Moreover, in the case of the parity claims between temporary agency workers and directly employed workers, the links to comparators widen the personal nexus so that it extends to workers for different employers. Thirdly, this kind of regulation may involve the attaching of new significance to new kinds of personal work profile – as where a personal work profile composed of several successive fixed-term contractual personal work relations triggers conversion to a 'permanent' contractual personal work relation.

For these various reasons, this grouping of EU regulatory layers provides the appropriate conclusion to our survey of key examples of EU regulatory layers. We have seen how this new genre of regulation presents in their most acute and interesting form the complexities of EU regulatory layers – the ambivalence of the definitional categories which they invoke both at EU and national levels, the diversity of national regulatory starting points from which each Member State makes its response to the EU employment law measure, and, most especially, the diversity and distinctiveness of those national responses themselves. We have also seen how those complexities are further heightened by variations between different EU regulatory layers in their other aspect, that is to say in the cogency rules or regimes which attach to them both at the EU level and the national level.

However, if the four groupings of EU regulatory layers, which we have thus considered, do constitute key examples of those layers, they do not, as we have previously emphasized, represent a comprehensive catalogue of all the species of regulation which could be regarded as forming part of what we might please to regard as 'EU labour or employment law'. These four groupings were put forward as a selection of EU regulatory layers which would illustrate the idea of those layers and give a sense of how they worked and interrelated with each other. In order to complete that comprehensive catalogue, we would on any view need to include a further grouping of regulatory layers consisting of measures, additional to those within existing groupings, requiring employing enterprises to engage in consultation with workers' representatives – most conspicuously the original European

---

[92] These points are further discussed in N. Countouris (2007) *The Changing Law of the Employment Relationship*, Aldershot: Ashgate, Chapters 3 and 6.

Works Council Directive 94/45[93] and the National Information and Consultation Directive.[94]

Moreover, we should also arguably include three further groupings of regulatory layers which, although they do not come within the traditional perceptions of labour or employment law systems at the national level, nevertheless figure quite significantly in accounts of EU employment law. The first of these consists of the 'European Employment Strategy' as revitalized by the Europe 2020 Agenda,[95] and the partial co-ordination of its implementation at national level by means of the process known as the 'Open Method of Co-ordination'.[96] This would seem to fall outside the traditional perceptions of labour or employment law systems at the national level both in the sense that it is more concerned with market regulation than with the regulation of relations between employers and workers, and in the sense that it conspicuously represents a form of 'soft law' in its lack of coerciveness towards the Member States.

The second such grouping of regulatory layers consists of the relevant provisions, of greater or lesser cogency and generality, of the EU Charter of Fundamental Rights. This would seem to fall outside the traditional perceptions of labour or employment law systems at the national level, in that, whereas in national systems such charters or declarations would normally be endowed with a fully constitutional status, and would as such provide a constitutional backdrop or underpinning for labour or employment law, the provisions of the Charter, although identified as legally 'binding' by the Lisbon Treaty, do not have a fully fledged prior constitutional status but instead stand in a complex and sometimes fraught relationship with other principles or norms of EU law – most obviously with the economic freedoms as deployed by the ECJ in the body of doctrine instituted by the *Viking* and *Laval* cases.[97]

The third grouping of regulatory layers which we would need to include, in order to lay claim to any degree of comprehensiveness in our accounting for EU labour or employment law, consists of the large and growing body of EU law which concerns the economic migration of workers – whether in the very general form of the law of freedom of movement of persons between Member States,[98] or in the more specific

---

[93] [1994] OJ L 254/64; currently Directive 2009/38/EC of the European Parliament and of the Council of 6 May 2009 on the establishment of a European Works Council or a procedure in Community-scale undertakings and Community-scale groups of undertakings for the purposes of informing and consulting employees (Recast) [2009] OJ L 122/28.

[94] Directive 2002/14/EC of the European Parliament and of the Council of 11 March 2002 establishing a general framework for informing and consulting employees in the European Community – Joint declaration of the European Parliament, the Council and the Commission on employee representation [2002] OJ L 80/29.

[95] European Commission 'EUROPE 2020 A strategy for smart, sustainable and inclusive growth', COM (2010) 2020 final.

[96] Cf. D. Ashiagbor (2005) *The European Employment Strategy: Labour Market Regulation and New Governance*, Oxford: OUP; S. Velluti (2010) *New Governance and the European Employment Strategy*, London: Routledge.

[97] Case C-438/05 *ITF v. Viking Line ABP* [2007] ECR I-10779; Case C-341/05 *Laval v. Svenska Byggnadsarbetareförbundet* [2007] ECR I-11767.

[98] Cf. in particular Directive 2004/38/EC on the right of citizens of the Union and their family members to move and reside freely within the territory of the Member States [2004] L 158/77.

form of law concerning the 'posting' of workers between Member States,[99] or in the increasingly prominent form of legal controls upon immigration for work from states outside the EU.[100] Measures and regulatory layers of this kind fall outside the traditional purview of national labour or employment law systems not by reason of any lack of coerciveness – they are fully or highly coercive 'hard law' – but in that their subject-matter or preoccupation is not concerned with the regulation of relations between employers and workers in the conventional sense.

By extending our survey of EU regulatory layers in that way, we have brought ourselves to the point where we can offer a summary and an assessment of our proposals for a European Legal Framework for Personal Work Relations. That will be the task of the final section of this chapter.

## Section 4:  A European Legal Framework for Personal Work Relations: Prospects and Problems

Our discussion has now reached the stage where we can make an assessment of the prospects for and problems with establishing a European Legal Framework for Personal Work Relations. It will be useful firstly to specify, largely as we have said by way of recapitulation, what the structure and content of this legal framework would be (subsection A). It will then be important to consider whether this legal framework can be regarded as a normatively coherent one; suggestions will be advanced as to how that assessment might be made and what its outcome might be (subsection B).

### A.  Prospects

The structure of the suggested European Legal Framework for Personal Work Relations will be largely evident from what has gone before. It would be an analysis framed by the concept of the personal work relation; it would deploy the notion of the personal work nexus as a way of understanding the internal patterns of personal work relations; it would be conducted from the perspective of the personal work profile; and it would bring to bear upon its subject-matter the values of dignity, capability, and stability.

Implied, but less fully articulated, in what has gone before is the content and subject-matter of our suggested legal framework for personal work relations. Two

---

[99] Directive 96/71/EC of the European Parliament and of the Council of 16 December 1996 concerning the posting of workers in the framework of the provision of services [1997] OJ L 18/01.

[100] Council Directive 2009/50/EC of 25 May 2009 on the conditions of entry and residence of third-country nationals for the purposes of highly qualified employment [2009] OJ L155/17; Directive 2009/52/EC of 18 June 2009 providing for minimum standards on sanctions and measures against employers of illegally staying third-country nationals [2009] OJ L168/24; European Commission, 'Proposal for a directive of the European Parliament and of the Council on the conditions of entry and residence of third-country nationals for the purposes of seasonal employment', COM(2010) 379 final; European Commission, 'Proposal for a Directive of the European Parliament and of the Council on conditions of entry and residence of third-country nationals in the framework of an intra-corporate transfer', COM (2010) 378 final.

points remain to be more fully spelt out than they have hitherto been. The first concerns the analytical rather than codificatory nature of the content of our suggested framework. The second concerns the way in which we put forward EU regulatory layers as the starting point for, though not the entirety or end point of, the subject-matter of that legal framework. These points will be successively considered.

So far as the content of our suggested legal framework is concerned, our main idea is that it would be more in the nature of a treatise than of a codification. It would, in effect be a more comprehensive or encyclopaedic elaboration of the analysis which we have sought to conduct in the present work. Unlike the Draft Common Frame of Reference or for that matter the American Restatements,[101] it would not primarily seek to distil out a set of principles and rules, but rather to create the basis for lawmakers to do so, whether by way of legislation or by way of judicial pronouncement.

The substance of our suggested legal framework for personal work relations would therefore consist for the most part of an elaborate exercise in comparative law, in which the tools of comparison were the organizing concepts of the personal work relation, nexus, and profile, and the normative notion of personality in work. This exercise would not, as we have said, be codificatory in its nature, and would not aspire to a homogeneity in its substance; on the contrary, its main effect would be to point up the differences between national labour law systems which are revealed when they are viewed through those conceptual lenses.

There would be, however, one particular element in the substance of our suggested legal framework which was partially unificatory in character: as we have explained in the preceding sections, its substance would be constructed from the starting points of EU regulatory layers. That is to say, the points of departure for the substance of the analysis would be the regulatory layers which have their basis in EU labour or employment law. There would be other regulatory layers to be added, representing those kinds of labour law interventions which are excluded from or have not been brought within the scope of EU law or the competences of its law-makers; but the stage would be initially set by the scenery of EU law, and would therefore display the various kinds and degrees of commonality which EU law has imparted to the labour or employment law systems of the Member States.

This unificatory effect would, it must be emphasized, be a limited one. Our portrayal of EU regulatory layers has focused upon the way that these layers operate upon two levels – the supranational or EU level and the national or Member-State level – and it has highlighted the diversity which sets in when the EU measures enacted or taken at the first level are implemented at the second level. So the taking of the starting points for the substance of our suggested legal framework in EU regulatory layers does not in and of itself belie the non-codifcatory and non-unificatory character of that framework. It does, however, introduce some problems about the normative coherence of our suggested legal framework which we should identify and consider.

---

[101] Cf. in particular American Law Institute (2009) *Restatements of the Law – Employment Law – Tentative Draft No. 2*, Philadelphia: ALI.

## B. Problems

The problems which we perceive to arise about the normative coherence of our suggested European Legal Framework for Personal Work Relations are of the following kind. It has emerged in the course of this work as a whole, but more especially in the course of this chapter, that the arguments which we have advanced in favour of that suggested framework, when taken to their logical conclusion, constitute a proposition for a new way of writing about labour law as a whole. The problem of normative coherence amounts to nothing less than the question of whether such a new account or rendering of labour law remains faithful to the original purposes and commitments which have previously animated the development of labour law as a theoretical and practical legal discipline.

That question is of course a very large one, to the entirety of which we shall shortly revert in the Conclusion to this work as a whole. At this point, we concentrate upon one particular aspect of that larger problem – an aspect which is however of central importance to this particular chapter. That specific aspect of the more general problem is the question of whether, in the sense in which we have just articulated it, our criterion of normative coherence for our suggested legal framework for personal work relations is satisfied by taking EU labour or employment law as a major starting point or focal point for that legal framework.

Much of the ground of this discussion has been covered earlier in this chapter. In the first section of the chapter, we considered at length a set of problems which were identified as those of fragmentation of personal work regulation and the denormalization of personal work arrangements. We concerned ourselves with what could be regarded as the normative deficiencies of EU employment law in responding to those challenges. Those normative deficiencies were acknowledged or argued to be in certain respects extensive and significant ones. That discussion focused upon various shortcomings in dealing with the evolutions within the EU Member States towards increasingly precarious personal work relations or arrangements, which could be regarded as having brought about the emergence of an increasingly vulnerable or disadvantaged workforce in many sectors and pockets of the European labour economy.

However, in sections 2 and 3, our argument then took a very different turn. It was firstly argued that it would be useful to envisage and try to establish a European Legal Framework for Personal Work Relations; and it was secondly suggested that a good starting point for composing the content or substance of that legal framework would be found in the analysis of a set of regulatory layers which could be derived from the various measures and interventions of EU employment law. This presents an apparent tension or inconsistency: how can it be contended that EU employment law provides a good starting point for a European legal framework for personal work if it is itself subject to such normative deficiencies? We shall argue that this apparent tension or inconsistency is explicable or resoluble, but in a way which leads on to the consideration of a yet larger set of normative issues or problems concerning our suggested legal framework.

We suggest that the explanation or resolution of that apparent tension or inconsistency consists in the recognition of the fact that EU employment law is developing in an intensely fraught economic and social environment, and is at the centre of many regulatory debates and conflicts. Therefore EU employment law embodies many difficult regulatory outcomes and contested compromises which may be perceived as giving rise to normative deficiencies. On the other hand, the evolution of EU employment law is, in this respect and indeed in many respects, quite representative and reflexive of the evolution of labour law in the several Member States themselves. The development of EU employment law is both a mirror and, at times at least, a harbinger of the development of labour or employment law in the Member States themselves.

That is why the regulatory layers which derive from EU employment law form such an obvious starting point for our suggested European Framework for Personal Work Relations. These EU regulatory layers instantiate the very locations in which are played out the central modern conflicts of labour or employment law in Europe. It is in exactly those locations that we argue for the relevance and utility of our suggested legal framework. It is at those points that we most need the enlargement and refinement of the analysis of the legal construction of personal work relations which we hope that our suggested legal framework might ultimately be able to provide.

But this approach is not at all unproblematic. It amounts to the proposition that one new way of thinking about European labour law deserves another. That is to say, we seem to be claiming that a novel way of constructing the substance and content of the labour law of European countries – from and around EU regulatory layers – is complemented and reinforced by an equally novel methodology for doing so – namely framing and analysing that substance and content through the lens of the personal work relation, with all the ideas which we have articulated as flowing from that central organizing notion. On this view, the regulatory layers of EU employment law identify themselves as an appropriate set of starting points for our suggested legal framework, even if they do give rise to concerns about their normative deficiencies.

So by this course of argument, we have claimed that much of the methodology and critique of the legal construction of personal work relations, which we have sought to build up in the successive parts and chapters of this work, can itself be linked to and associated with a set of analytical starting points consisting of the regulatory layers which derive from EU employment law. That does seem to present a rather novel way of thinking about labour or employment law in European countries. It is a way of thinking which is implicit in much contemporary theorizing about European employment law; but it cannot be assumed, from this, that the large problems of normative coherence will have been resolved by the open articulation of this implicit position.

On the contrary, the argument which we have developed in the course of this chapter has ended up by confronting us with a set of issues about the normative coherence, not just of our particular proposal to regard EU employment law as providing the starting points for our suggested European Legal Framework for

Personal Work, but of our general proposal for that European Legal Framework itself. That is to say, it has become apparent that this legal framework, indeed much of the whole thesis about the legal construction of personal work relations as we have developed it in the course of this book, is intimately bound up with certain shifts, which have taken place in recent years, in the directions and preoccupations of labour or employment law, in the European region at least.

We might point particularly at the shift in preoccupation or focus towards the promotion of various kinds of equalities and the controlling of various kinds of discrimination, as between certain groups of workers delineated for example by gender or race or age, and as between certain kinds of patterns of work, in particular between full-time and part-time work, permanent and fixed-term work, and between agency work and work arranged on a directly employed basis. It is useful to focus on those examples, because they represent areas in which the personal scope or relational framing of labour law's interventions are very obviously brought into question. So these examples point up and re-emphasize how closely the analytical and taxonomical concerns which are at the heart of the present work are bound up with changes in the contemporary preoccupations or agendas of labour law.

So we have to regard our proposals for a European Legal Framework for Personal Work Relations as touching upon some very general issues about the normative coherence of labour law systems which are going through these shifts in their concerns and pre-occupations. These are issues which have been immanent to and have been hovering in the air through much of the present work. They have been thrown into sharp relief in the course of this final chapter. We seek to address those issues more directly in the ensuing Conclusion to this work.

# Conclusion: Mutualization and Demutualization in the Legal Construction of Personal Work Relations

Having in the preceding chapters completed our suggested analysis of the legal construction of personal work relations, we shall attempt in this Conclusion to address some issues and problems concerning the implications of this analysis for labour or employment law as a whole. They are issues and problems which have been touched upon in the course of this work but whose resolution we have deferred until this point. The issues are primarily normative ones; they concern the central question of whether our suggested analysis makes a positive and constructive contribution to the development of labour or employment law as a whole. Our method of approaching those issues will be first to recapitulate briefly upon the main lines of the analysis which we have put forward in the preceding chapters, and then to try to locate that analysis within the conceptions, which have been and are currently entertained by the makers and theorists of labour or employment law, as to the appropriate agenda or agendas for that discipline.

The recapitulation consists of a reminder of how we have in the course of this work taken a new category, that of 'the personal work relation' as the framing concept for individual employment law, and ultimately for labour law at large, and of how we have tried to devise some new methods of analysis of the content of the law of personal work relations within that frame of reference. The location of these analyses within the changing agendas of labour law will be an exercise of a more normative character. It will involve the canvassing and exploration of an idea of mutualization of risk[1] as being central to those changing agendas.

So we can begin the recapitulation by recalling how the essential point of departure for this work consists in its adoption of the category of 'the personal work relation' as the framing concept or boundary of the analysis which the work undertakes. As we have explained in the course of the work,[2] this represents a confirmation of and a further advance upon moves which we have each of us made in earlier writings away from 'the contract of employment' as a framing category or boundary concept for the analysis of the legal construction of those relations of

---

[1] First introduced earlier at p. 382.     [2] Cf. Chapter 1, pp. 19–34.

personal work with which we believe that individual employment law and indeed labour law as a whole are and properly should be concerned.

This further move to the category of 'the personal work relation' is a radical one in two respects. Firstly, it confirms the inclusion of 'personal work' rather than 'employment' within the framing concept – thus making a decisive rather than tentative move into the sphere of 'the personal contract for services' and of relations of 'personal self-employment'. Thus we are deliberately straddling the binary divide between those two spheres, only the first of which has traditionally or classically been regarded as the proper sphere of employment law.

The second respect in which the move to the category of 'the personal work relation' is a radical one is in confirming the extension of the framing concept from 'contract' to 'relation'. This is a notion which includes contractual relations but extends beyond them. This means that the framing concept includes relations of personal work which may be regarded as entirely non-contractual in character – as, in certain legal systems, the work relations of public employment or public office-holding are regarded. It also means there are included within the framing concept those personal work relations which may be regarded as partly contractual and partly non-contractual in character – and that the non-contractual aspects or elements of such personal work relations will not be excluded from view in the way they are apt to be by traditional contractual canons of analysis.

We have also sought to argue that this move to the category of 'the personal work relation' is a radical one in a further sense. For, far from representing the abandonment of a concrete framing concept for individual employment law, it actually amounts to the adoption of a framing concept which, although much more inclusive than that of 'the contract of employment', is nevertheless still a quite specific and hard-edged one. That is by reason of its confinement to those work relations which are 'personal' in the sense of being contracts or relations by which or in which the worker is engaged on or in work to be performed by himself or herself in person rather than by others. This we think serves, paradoxically in a sense, to make our framing concept more challenging to a traditional orthodoxy which tends to regard the contract of employment as the only hard-edged framing concept, beyond which lies only an amorphous zone of contracts or relations of self-employment.

We have also sought to effect some changes, from the traditional approaches to the contract of employment, in the methods of analysis of the legal constructions which take place within this enlarged domain or sphere of personal work relations. It will be useful briefly to remind ourselves of several novel approaches which we have introduced:

1. mapping the domain of personal work relations as a 'family of relations' (rather than as a set of concentric circles expanding outwards from a core consisting of the contract of employment);[3]

---

[3] Cf. Chapter 3, at pp. 120–8, and Chapter 7, at pp. 284–90.

2. establishing similarities and differences between legal constructions of personal work relations on the one hand within and on the other hand beyond the contract of employment;[4]

3. focusing attention upon the way in which the legal construction of personal work relations is composed of many 'layers of regulation', differently constituted as between different national legal systems;[5]

4. establishing a comparative methodology suited to the task of comparing the way in which personal work contracts and relations in general, and employment contracts and relations in particular, are constructed and regulated as between different national legal systems;[6]

5. identifying, in particular, an 'integration variable' in order to compare and contrast the differing ways in which those layers of regulation are combined with each other in different legal systems; and

6. deploying the ideas of the 'personal work nexus' and the 'personal work profile' to deepen our analysis of the legal construction of personal work relations.[7]

Our perception has been that the combination of this new framing concept with these novel methods of analysis requires its own normative or critical concept to underpin it; for that purpose, we have advanced the notion of 'personality in work', itself embodying a trilogy of values, those of 'dignity, capability and stability'.[8] We have suggested that this concatenation of analytical and normative concepts might form the basis of a 'European Legal Framework for Personal Work',[9] which could be constructed around those regulatory layers which have been created or introduced by the legal system of the EU itself and by other elements of European supranational law such as the European Convention on Human Rights.

At this point, having briefly recapitulated upon what we have sought to do in the course of this work, we should acknowledge the deficiencies of which we are aware and then try to address what we perceive as the unresolved problem of locating our project within the current agendas of labour or employment law as a whole. The deficiencies of which we are conscious are significant ones, but they can be succinctly identified. Some of them are inherent in the nature of the project upon which we are embarked, while others amount to shortcomings in what we have been able to achieve in the realization of our project.

An inherent limitation of the project consists in the fact that, being predominantly concerned with de-constructing an existing framework of analysis of personal work relations still very largely centered upon the contract of employment, it provides less by way of positive exegesis of existing analyses of the legal construction of personal work relations than some readers of this work might regard as feasible and desirable. In particular the work will disappoint those who hope to come nearer

---

[4] This has been the main objective of Chapters 4, 5, 6, 7, and 8.
[5] Cf. Chapter 3, section 1.C in particular.      [6] Chapters 2 and 3.
[7] Cf. Chapter 8.      [8] Chapter 9, section 4.B.      [9] Chapter 10, section 2.

to finding that philosopher's stone of individual employment law which consists of a robust and satisfactory way of distinguishing between the contract of employment and the contract for services, or between the relations of employment and of self-employment. We have been especially unwilling to engage in that specific pursuit, even as 'devil's advocates' because we are so sceptical of the feasibility or utility of those distinctions.

A more contingent or accidental deficiency consists in the fact that we should like to have been able to conduct a more comprehensive and detailed comparative survey than was in fact possible given the constraints of time and resources. Most of our energy was devoted to theoretical speculation and development. Our comparative arguments have to be regarded as being to a certain degree in the nature of only partly, and often selectively, tested hypotheses. We hope that our work might stimulate or give rise to further comparative inquiry, ideally on the part of those with truly internal perspectives upon each European national labour or employment law system.

Beyond those limitations, moreover, lies a set of less tangible but nevertheless significant issues about the implications of our project for the evolution of labour or employment law as a whole. In short there is a real question to be considered as to whether our suggested changes in the scope and methodology of the analysis of personal work relations have a destabilizing effect upon the conceptual foundations of the theory and practice of labour or employment law. We have touched upon these concerns at various points in the course of this work but are now at the point where they need to be addressed as directly and fully as possible.

The issues at stake in this discussion can be encapsulated in the following question. The contract of employment is often regarded as the foundation or 'cornerstone' of labour or employment law; by displacing it in favour of 'the personal work relation', do we risk shaking in a dangerous way the conceptual foundations of labour or employment law itself? We shall suggest that this is not a major risk, if only because the contract of employment has quite long since ceased to be the foundation or cornerstone of labour or employment law in the sense in which it once could be so regarded. Moreover the agendas of labour or employment law have themselves changed quite considerably in recent decades and continue to do so. There are on the other hand underlying continuities of agenda; and those are, we shall suggest, well served rather than badly served by the shift from 'the contract of employment' to that of 'the personal work relation' as a foundational concept.

These arguments can best be explored by concentrating upon two particular aspects of our general problem. The general problem can be identified as that of the legal construction of personal work relations as possibly undermining of the rationale for labour or employment law. We can usefully focus upon the particular problems of, firstly, the arguable expansion to an unduly wide interest-group and secondly, the arguable severing of the link between individual employment law and collective labour law. We shall expand upon and seek to address these two issues in turn.

These two particular problems have it in common with each other that they both concern the ways in which our analysis of the legal construction of personal work relations seems to be incompatible with the classical rationale for labour or employment law as the redressing of the inequality of bargaining power which is inherent in the contract for subordinate or dependent employment between the employer and the individual employee. The first particular problem focuses upon the way that this rationale appears to be negated if the field of application of labour or employment law is extended significantly beyond that of the contract of employment. It may appear in other words that the original rationale for labour or employment law cannot satisfactorily be sustained if it is attempted to apply it in favour of an interest-group which has been extended to workers who cannot be regarded as among those whom labour or employment law is designed or conceived of to protect. On this view, labour or employment law is normatively diluted by its purported extension to undeserving clients; and the problem is only worsened by admitting that its regulations need not apply uniformly throughout the enlarged interest-group which our analysis embraces.

Of the two particular problems which we have set out to address, this first one is in our view much the easier one to resolve. The classical idea, that the mission of labour law is to redress the inequality of bargaining power inherent in individual contract employment, has at its heart the assumption that the workers who need and deserve the protection of labour law can be exhaustively identified by reference to the notion of subordinate or dependent employment. We believe that this is an equation which is no longer a valid one. On the one hand, the domain of the contract of employment itself is no longer inhabited exclusively or even predominantly by workers who are needy and vulnerable in the way that was imagined according to the traditional stereotype.[10] On the other hand, we equally believe that, in order fully to encompass the whole group of workers who do require and deserve the protection of some at least of the regulation of labour or employment law, it is necessary to adopt the more inclusive category of the personal work relation, and appropriate to invoke the broader normative notion of 'personality in work'. The status quo, premised on a number of false dualisms that we discussed in the course of this work, is only likely to accelerate the 'flight from labour law' lamented by several of our continental European colleagues,[11] but also, and no less worryingly, is likely to encourage the various calls for further labour law deregulation as the panacea for remedying those labour market dualisms for which deregulation should largely be blamed in the first place.[12]

However, if that line of argument provides a satisfactory way of addressing the first of our two particular problems, it still leaves the second one conspicuously unresolved. The second and more difficult problem is that the classical notion of redressing the inequality of bargaining power inherent in the individual contract for

[10] Arguably legal scholars have long been aware of this; cf. M. G. Garofalo (1989) 'Complessità del Modo di Produzione e Possibilità di Governo Attraverso il Diritto del Lavoro', in M. Pedrazzoli (ed.), *Lavoro Subirdinato e Dintorni*, Bologna: Il Mulino, 195.

[11] See in particular the Italian notion of the '*fuga dal diritto del lavoro*', as discussed in P. Ichino (1990) 'La Fuga dal Diritto del Lavoro', *Dem. Dir*, 69; and F. Liso (1992) 'La Fuga dal Diritto del Lavoro', *Industria e Sindacato*, 1.

[12] As discussed in Chapter 8, at p. 336, we very much see the various calls for a 'single contract' as representing this type of deregulatory dynamic.

subordinate employment represented, consciously and intentionally, a particular way of forging a link between the individual and the collective in labour law and indeed of placing the whole weight of labour law upon that essential linkage. The very idea was that the injustices which would result from unregulated individual contracting for personal work or labour could be satisfactorily averted only by regulation of collective bargaining as reinforced by collectively agreed and imposed labour legislation. The analytical shift from the contract of employment to the personal work relation, and the normative shift from the redressing of inequality of bargaining power to the vindicating of personality in work, might seem to weaken or even to sever that crucial connection.

One response to that important difficulty – though in our view a rather incomplete response – is to recognize that the agenda or mission of labour or employment law has in any event moved on in various ways in the course of time. On this view, the original notion, of the redressing of the inequality of bargaining power inherent in the individual contract for subordinate employment, has receded to being a largely symbolical or totemic ideal rather than a comprehensive state-ment of the practical purpose of labour law. It would follow that our proposed substitution of that notion by the ideas of the personal work relation and of personality in work would be merely recognizing and confirming a change of agenda which had previously and independently taken place, rather than under-mining a still current organizing ideal.

There is much that can be said in support of that argument. It does not, we hope, involve any undue concession to the neo-liberal viewpoint from which the norma-tive primacy of unregulated individual contracting for personal work is reasserted. Those other makers and theorists of labour or employment law for whom worker-protective regulation has retained its central necessity, and who still articulate that necessity in the classical form of the need to redress the inequality of bargaining power inherent in the contract for subordinate employment, might nevertheless agree that their more immediate agendas for labour or employment law are now rather differently formulated from the way in which they once were.

There are at least two strongly recurring strands in these changing agendas – strands which are distinct but not incompatible with each other. There is a line of thought or set of ideas according to which the protection of workers is, to a greater extent than it formerly was, conceptually organized around variously defined catalogues of the fundamental human rights and social rights of workers, in which there is crucially included a set of rights against various kinds of discrimina-tion between groups of workers and in favour of various degrees of equality or parity between the situations of workers in those groups. The other such strand of ideas is one in which the agenda of labour law is formulated as or within various notions of 'the regulation of the labour market'.[13] Such formulations tend to bring into play, more evidently than was previously the case, considerations of employ-

---

[13] The now classical exposition of this approach is that of S. Deakin and F. Wilkinson (2005) *The Law of the Labour Market – Industrialization, Employment and Legal Evolution*; Oxford: OUP; cf. also H. Collins (2001) 'Regulating the Employment Relation for Competitiveness', 30 *ILJ* 17.

ment policy, that is to say elements of public policy especially concerned with the creation and maintenance of high levels of employment and their reconciliation with considerations of preservation or enhancement of the quality of employment.

We could in a sense content ourselves with that reflection as a way of quieting our anxiety about the supplanting, which is implicit in our present work, of the classical rationale for labour or employment law and the corresponding weakening of the bond between the individual and the collective in labour law. We could say that to analyse the legal construction of personal work relations, both descriptively and prescriptively, in a way which ceases to emphasize the central tension between individual employment contracts and the collective regulation of terms and conditions of employment, is simply to walk through a conceptual door which has already been thrown wide open by these existing transformations in the agendas of labour or employment law. However, we think that this might be an unduly complacent way of claiming to have tackled the underlying problem.

We advance the following suggestion as providing a possibly more rigorous basis for addressing our second set of concerns, that is to say our concerns with the undermining of the link between individual contracting and collective regulation in the sphere of labour or employment law. We have been careful not to claim that the legal construction of personal work relations is co-extensive with the whole field of labour or employment law itself, or that the normative idea of personality in work could function as a rationale for labour or employment law as a whole. We take the view that the legal construction of personal work relations should be seen as a theme or aspect of labour or employment law itself, and that the idea of personality in work should be seen as a rationale for that theme or aspect rather than for labour or employment law as a whole. We suggest that it is accordingly important, and might be helpful in addressing our outstanding problem, to attempt particularly to locate the legal construction of personal work relations, and its attendant rationale of personality in work, within or in relation to these changing agendas for labour or employment law as a whole.

For that purpose, we think it may be useful to consider a factor or aspect of those changing agendas which goes quite some way towards unifying them. We suggest that these changing agendas of labour or employment law could be regarded as having the common element that they are to some extent and in some sense concerned with the mutualization, between employers and workers (and work-seekers), of the risks attendant upon the making and execution of arrangements for the doing of work. The worker-protective functions of labour law could be regarded as being centrally concerned with the fair mutualization of those risks which bear especially upon the situation of the workers themselves. We might be able to deploy this analytical idea of mutualization, and this normative idea of fair mutualization of the risks to workers, in order to locate the ideas of the legal construction of personal work relations and of personality in work more precisely within the original and changing agendas of labour or employment law, and moreover to safeguard the essential link between the individual and the collective aspects of labour law.

For this purpose it may be useful somewhat to elaborate the notion of mutualization of risks to workers. We can do this by advancing some propositions which will define or explain that basic idea of mutualization of risks to workers. Firstly, we suggest that many aspects of the arrangements which are made for the creation and conduct of personal work relations are concerned with the allocation of risks affecting workers. These risks may be of many kinds – risks to their health and safety, to their welfare and wellbeing in various senses, to the continuity or security of their income or their employment. Secondly, we suggest that the allocation of such risks to workers may consist of sharing or dispersing them so that they do not fall on each particular worker alone – such allocations can be regarded as the mutualization of risks to workers; but the allocation of such risks may be in the contrary direction, consisting of imposing or concentrating those risks upon particular workers alone, in which case such allocations can be regarded as being in the nature of demutualization of those risks.

It should be noted that the logical extreme of mutualization consists in the dispersal of risk entirely away from the individual worker, just as the logical extreme of demutualization consists in the concentration of risk entirely upon the individual worker. It follows that normative perceptions of 'fair mutualization' might include either of those two extremes. We do not seek to present here a detailed view of 'fair mutualization', but we do go as far as to say that our normative notion of 'personality in work', and in particular its 'dignity' aspect, points firmly away from the concentration of any risks entirely and solely upon the individual worker, and suggests that some risks, for example those to health and safety, should be entirely dispersed away from the individual worker.

If those foundational propositions are simple ones, we must nevertheless acknowledge that processes of mutualization and demutualization of risks to workers have many complex dimensions. They may vary greatly as to how far particular kinds of risks are mutualized or demutualized, and, so far as the sharing of risks is between workers, as to the width of the groups between whom these distributions are made. Moreover, a wide variety of actors and participants may be involved in these processes of mutualization or demutualization – as actors in the sense of effecting the distributions in question, or as participants in the sense of being or becoming the bearers of the risks in question. We revert shortly to the consideration of the actors in these processes and concentrate first on the variety of participants. The primary or immediate participants in such processes are workers and the enterprises in which they are employed or the persons for whom they engage to work; but in this discussion we need constantly to remind ourselves of the presence of many secondary or proximate participants, foremost among them trade unions, organizations of employers, and agencies of government and the public state. There is also of course a real sense in which all kinds of groupings of people in society at large are or may become tertiary participants in the mutualization or demutualization of risks to workers, whether doing so as, for example, members of voluntary associations which provide insurance or support for workers, or, in a very different sense, as providers of unpaid work in families or households.

With those important caveats about the significance of secondary and tertiary participants, we suggest that our analysis of acts or processes of mutualization and demutualization can usefully be refined by some further elaboration of their working as between the primary participants, that is to say workers and the enterprises or persons for whom they work. We think that within that context it is useful to distinguish between different directions or trajectories along which mutualization or demutualization may occur. We believe in particular that it is meaningful and informative to distinguish between vertical, horizontal, and diagonal mutualization or demutualization. The first two of those typologies are quite easily understood and explained, so that vertical mutualization or demutualization consists of the allocation or reallocation of risks between workers on the one hand and their employer or employing enterprise on the other, while horizontal mutualization consists of allocation or reallocation of risks between workers. The third typology represents a more complex but no less real form of mutualization or demutualization in which the bearing of risks to workers is reorganized by the introduction of intermediary or associated employing organizations or enterprises, so that risks to workers are multilateralized and thereby reallocated in a whole variety of different ways.

A further refinement of our notions of mutualization and demutualization can be achieved by identifying the variety of actors who or which are involved in its processes. Thus far, we have concentrated upon employers and workers themselves, and most especially upon employers, as the actors in processes of mutualization and demutualization; but no less prominent as actors in those processes are the agencies, both governmental and non-governmental, of regulation of the arrangements by which employers and workers mutualize or demutualize risks to workers. It follows that the ideas of mutualization and de-mutualization, as thus elaborated, might be applied to various aspects of labour or employment law, and moreover might be applied in such a way as to bring out the continuities between its individual and its collective dimensions. We could take as an illustrative example the various ways in which labour or employment law may regulate the laying-off of workers or the effecting of redundancies by employing enterprises by reason, for instance, of lack of demand for their products or services.

There may be regulation of the permissibility of such actions and/or of the compensation payable to workers in respect of such actions; such regulation would represent a primarily vertical distribution or mutualization of the risk of such actions as between the employer and the workers in question. There may be regulation, by legislation or by or through collective agreements, of the relative entitlements of individuals or groups of workers not to be selected for lay-off or redundancy – such regulation brings in elements of horizontal distribution or mutualization of these risks as between workers. There will be regulation of the freedom which workers have to take industrial action to oppose lay-offs or redundancies. Such regulation could be seen as controlling, in an extended sense, both the vertical and horizontal mutualization of the risks for workers of lay-off or redundancy. There may be regulation to limit the various and increasingly prominent processes of diagonal demutualization by which arrangements for employment and other personal work may be triangulated between employing enterprises so as to fragment the protections of workers against lay-off or redundancy, though the view might well be taken that such processes have tended to outstrip the regulation of them.

From this set of examples, we might advance towards a useful understanding of the changing agendas of labour law as being very often concerned with the mutualization of risks to workers, and as being, in recent times as at least, equally often concerned with the demutualization of those risks. As we have previously stressed, we have to be very careful not to seek to pour all aspects of labour law into the mould of mutualization or demutualization. That said, we do suggest that the ideas of mutualization and demutualization may provide a more discriminating way of understanding some aspects of the modern evolution of the agendas of labour law than is provided by the fashionable contrast between changes to labour law as 'regulation' or 're-regulation' on the one hand or 'deregulation' on the other. The analysis of some at least of those changes in terms of mutualization and demutualization may help to avoid the apparent paradox that many exercises in 'deregulation' of employment and other personal work relations seem to involve more 'regulation' than previously existed. As the statute books and codifications of labour law become ever heavier, it is easier to understand the constant additions to them as movements between mutualization and demutualization of risks to workers than as shifts between regulation and deregulation.

If and to the extent that these notions of mutualization and demutualization of the risks to workers are found to be useful in the understanding of the changing agendas of labour or employment law, they suggest a possible basis for locating our key ideas of the legal construction of personal work relations and of personality in work within these changing agendas. That is to say, we suggest that these ideas have a useful contribution to make to discussion about mutualization and fair mutualization, and moreover a fuller and more significant contribution than the corresponding but narrower notions of the contract of employment and the redressing of the inequality of bargaining power inherent in the individual contract of employment. We continue by briefly signalling some particular respects in which we believe this to be the case.

Firstly, we suggest that analysis of the legal construction of personal work relations can enable and help us to understand the many different ways in which labour or employment law does and might concern itself with the mutualization of risks which affect and bear upon workers. This analysis tends to enrich such a discussion by ensuring that it extends across the full range of personal work relations and is not confined to contractual employment relations. That extension to the full range of personal work relations serves to bring into play, as we hope this work has demonstrated, the width of variety of patterns and degrees of mutualization which are created or revealed in the course of the legal construction of personal work relations by the legal systems of Europe. Understanding the default models which are assumed and the outline models which are imposed by or in the course of the legal constructions of personal work relations does not in and of itself provide a complete account of labour law as the mutualization of risks affecting workers, but it can make a significant contribution towards doing so.

The second kind of contribution which we believe that our analysis of the legal construction of personal work relations might make to the better understanding of labour law, in many of its aspects, as the mutualization or demutualization of the risks affecting workers, stems from its capacity to display the full complexity and multilaterality of personal work relations, breaking through the opaque carapace of single contractual bilaterality which they normally present according to traditional methods of analysis. This displaying of the complexity and multilaterality of personal work relations operates, among other things, to reveal the many ways in which a large set of actors, a cast of characters much bigger that the duo of employer and 'worker', may be engaged in the formation and conduct of personal work relations, and may therefore be involved in the mutualization of risks affecting workers. This set of actors involved in the mutualization of risks may in particular, include collective actors such as trade unions or employers' associations, and may also, in another sense, include agencies of the state as providers of employment services or as social-security or fiscal authorities. The adoption of the 'personal work relation' as the central organizing concept for this new way of thinking about the scope and purpose of labour law may require the inclusion of professional bodies and associations as emerging key actors in this new collective discourse.[14]

We have thus suggested some ways in which the theory of the legal construction of personal work relations which we have sought to develop in the course of this book might contribute to an understanding of the changing agendas of labour law in terms of the idea of mutualization and demutualization of risks affecting workers. However, this contribution is not a one-way process but a reciprocal one – we now revert to the major argument of this Conclusion, which is that the understanding of the changing agendas of labour law in terms of the idea of mutualization and demutualization of risks affecting workers itself provides a path towards the further development in the future of our theory of the legal construction of personal work relations. In the last chapter, we were bold enough to suggest that such a theory might one day form the basis of a European Legal Framework for Personal Work Relations. If such a development were ever to occur, its realization would depend upon being able convincingly to locate this theory of the legal construction of personal work relations within a larger body of thinking about the regulation of employment and other personal work relations more generally. We now suggest some further ways in which the idea of mutualization and demutualization of risks affecting workers might help to do this.

We in fact suggest two particular ways in which we might use the idea of mutualization and demutualization of risks affecting workers to develop the theory of the legal construction of personal work relations. The idea of mutualization and demutualization of risks affecting workers provides a critical theory for better understanding, firstly, evolutions in the practice of personal work relations and in the regulation of those relations, and, secondly, the particular role of the legal construction of personal work relations in those evolutions of practice and of

---

[14] In that sense, cf. G. Lyon-Caen (1990) *Le droit du travail non salarié*, edns. Paris: Sirey, pp. 133–136.

regulation. In each of those two aspects, the idea of mutualization and demutualization of risks affecting workers might help us to relate our own theory of the legal construction of personal work relations to wider genres of social and legal theoretical writing. We proceed to expand briefly upon these possibilities.

Firstly, therefore, we proceed to flesh out our suggestion that the idea of mutualization and demutualization of risks affecting workers can help to understand evolutions in the practice of personal work relations and in the regulation of those relations, in particular by providing a path into relevant discourses concerning the theory and sociology of employment relations. Thus deploying the idea of mutualization and demutualization of risks affecting workers, we can identify a significant set of trends towards such demutualization in the practice of personal work relations and in the regulation of those relations, and a growing body of literature which identifies and analyses those trends.

We can identify these trends towards demutualization, and can source that identification in recent literature, in each of the three directions or trajectories of mutualization or demutualization which we have previously specified. Thus from one stream of recent literature we can identify a generic trend towards shift of various risks to workers downwards from employing enterprises to their workers,[15] and we can instantiate that trend especially by charting a general retreat from defined benefit occupational pension provision[16] – a retreat which, within the European region, is especially prominent in the United Kingdom.

Another such stream or genre of writing begins to identify a systemic trend towards horizontal demutualization of risks to workers between those workers, consisting of a general individualization of terms and conditions of employment, a decline in collective standard-setting, and an associated growth in pay inequalities between groups of workers.[17] Horizontal demutualization between workers may consist not only of increasing inequalities and competition between workers with regard to pay and terms and conditions of employment – as we have already recognized – but also of increasing insecurity and competition for security between workers. So horizontal demutulization creates or increases something which we might identify as 'individualized precarity' or 'personal precarity' in employment and other personal work relations, and it is useful to connect our thesis

---

[15] See especially, with primary reference to the USA, Jacob S. Hacker (2008) *The Great Risk Shift – The New Economic Insecurity and the Decline of the American Dream*, New York: OUP, (2006 revised and expanded 2008).

[16] An illuminating analysis is provided by Kendra Strauss (2011) 'Flexible Work, Flexible Pensions: Labor Market Change and the Evolution of Retirement Savings' a chapter in H. Arthurs and K. Stone (eds.) *Employment Regulation After the Standard Employment Contract: Innovations in Regulatory Design*, New York: Russell Sage, forthcoming in 2011.

[17] The starkest picture is that presented for the USA by Jacob S. Hacker and Paul Pierson (2010) *Winner-Take-All Politics: How Washington Made the Rich Richer – and Turned Its Back on the Middle Class*, New York: Simon & Schuster; strong accounts of similar evolutions in the UK are provided by W. Brown, and others (2000) 'The Future of Collectivism in Employment', *The Future of Work Bulletin*, Issue 2(2), and, more specifically, V. Antcliff, R. Saundry, and M. Stuart (2005) 'Individualisation, Collectivism and the Management of Risk in a Freelance Labour Market: The Case of the UK Television Industry' (Paper Presented at the British Sociological Association Conference 2005). Available online at: www.britsoc.co.uk/user_doc/05BSAAntcliffValerie.pdf.

about horizontal demutualization to existing literature which is documenting such evolutions.[18]

A third such discourse charts the spread of the phenomenon which our theory identifies as diagonal demutualization, in the form of various kinds of transfer of those risks from employing enterprises to intermediary enterprises and to workers working in or for intermediary enterprises. This phenomenon is assuming myriad forms such as agency employment, labour-only subcontracting, franchising of service provision, and, in another sense, ownership and control of employing enterprises by private equity corporations so that the owned and controlled employing enterprises tend to assume the role of intermediary employers; such developments are graphically but appropriately identified as creating situations of 'fragmented' or 'fissured' employment.[19]

Our further suggestion which requires elaboration was that our theory of mutualization and demutualization might assist in the understanding of the role of the legal construction of personal work relations in the regulation of those relations. Our argument is that the theory of mutualization and demutualization helps to analyse the consequences or implications of the various different approaches to the legal construction of personal work relations which we have identified in the course of this work. In particular this theory may serve to illuminate the role of the idea of the contract of employment and of different approaches to the idea of the contract of employment as a way of constructing employment relations and classifying personal work relations more generally. Moreover, we think that the theory of mutualization and demutualization could inform the development and use of the theory of legal construction of personal work relations itself.

The advancing of that argument brings us to another point at which we have to confront the fact that the comparative theory of the legal construction of personal work relations which we have advanced in this work is probably only the beginning and certainly not the end of a project of understanding and criticizing the architecture of regulation of personal work relations in European labour law systems and labour law systems more generally. The taking further of that project would

---

[18] We particularly direct attention towards D. Gallie, M. White, Y. Cheng, and M. Tomlinson (1998) *Re-structuring the Employment Relationship*, Oxford: OUP, the symposium volume N. De Cuyper, K. Iasksson, and H. De Witte (2005) *Employment Contracts and Well-Being among European Workers*, Aldershot: Ashgate; cf. also D. Marsden (1999) *A Theory of Employment Systems – Micro Foundations of Societal Diversity*, Oxford: OUP and L.F. Vosko (2010) *'Managing the Margins – Gender, Citizenship, and the International Regulation of Precarious Employment*, Oxford: OUP and, for the corresponding evolutions in French employment relations and employment law, P. Adam (2005) *L'Individualisation du Droit du Travail – Essai sur la Réhabilitation Juridique du Salarié Individu*, Paris: LGDJ.

[19] Powerful evidence of such a trend is provided by the symposium volume, M. Marchington, D. Grimshaw, J. Rubery, and H. Willmott (2005) *Fragmenting Work – Blurring Organisational Boundaries and Disordering Hierarchies*, Oxford: OUP; and cf. D. Weil (2011) 'Fissured employment', (Paper to 2011 ISA Meetings, Pittsburgh, PA). Available online at: www.industrystudies.pitt.edu/pittsburgh11/documents/Presentations/PDF Presentations/1-5 Weil.pdf. Cf. also W. Njoya (2007) *Property in Work – The Employment Relationship in the Anglo-American Firm*, Aldershot: Ashgate, especially chapter 2 'Ownership of the Firm'.

essentially involve much more detailed comparative and empirical work about the effects of different approaches to the legal construction of personal work relations than we have been able to accomplish. That work would involve the fuller connecting of our theory about the legal construction of personal work relations into a body of ideas and literature about the theory and practice of regulation of employment relations which in European labour law systems are regarded as being essentially contractual ones.[20]

This would represent an effort to understand not just the difficulties and short-comings of the practice of the legal construction of personal work relations at a doctrinal level but also how the regulatory impacts and effects of different approaches to the legal construction of personal work relations might be optimized. That effort is increasingly required of those who engage in the theory and practice of labour law, in a context in which the idea of 'the contract of employment' in general and the idea of 'the standard contract of employment' in particular[21] have ceased in and of themselves to provide an adequate theoretical and structural basis for that engagement. The main purpose of this Conclusion has been to suggest that the theory of mutualization and demutualization may be of assistance in that endeavour.

We hope that these reflections around the themes of mutualization and demu-tualization may have further assisted us in locating the analysis of the legal construction of personal work relations within an understanding of the changing agendas of labour law itself. We hope that they indicate ways in which the analysis of the legal construction of personal work relations can, so far from undermining the foundations of labour law, actually reinforce those foundations. In particular we hope it might serve to enhance the continuity between 'individual' and 'collective' labour or employment law, and also the different kinds of continuity between labour or employment law and the other topics or disciplines which form or contribute to the whole body of 'social law' in the broadest sense. This is the point at which we have to leave it to the judgment of our readers whether that aspiration is a realistic one and whether we have succeeded in setting in train its achievement.

---

[20] Reference may be made to S. Vittori (2007) *The Employment Contract and the Changed World of Work*, Aldershot: Ashgate and more generally to a number of symposium volumes of the past decade, in particular H. Collins, P. Davies, and R. Rideout (eds.) (2000) *Legal Regulation of the Employment Relation*, London: Kluwer Law International, J. Conaghan, R.M. Fischl, and K. Klare (eds.) (2002) *Labour Law in an Era of Globalisation – Transformative Practices and Possibilities*, Oxford: OUP, J. Conaghan and K. Rittich (eds.) (2005) *Labour Law, Work, and Family*, Oxford: OUP, G. Davidov and B. Langille (eds.) (2006) *Boundaries and Frontiers of Labour Law – Goals and Means in the Regulation of Work*, Oxford: Hart Publishing, G. Davidov and B. Langille (eds.) (2011) *The Idea of Labour Law*, Oxford: OUP, and S. Lee and D. McCann (eds.) (2011) *Regulating for Decent Work – New Directions in Labour Market Regulation*, London and Geneva: Palgrave Macmillan and ILO.

[21] For recent thinking about this notion in particular, compare H. Arthurs and K. Stone (eds.) (2011) *Employment Regulation After the Standard Employment Contract: Innovations in Regulatory Design*, New York, Russell Sage, (forthcoming in 2011).

# Bibliography

Abelleira, F. G. (2004) 'Valides y Efectos del Contrato de Trabajo del trabajador Extranjer sin Autorización para Trabajar' *Relaciones Laborales* 523

Aiginger, K., 'Labour Market Reforms and Economic Growth – The European Experience in the Nineties' (WIFO Working Paper 232/2004)

Alleva, P. (2006) 'Nuove Norme per il Superamento del Precariato e per la Dignità del Lavoro' XXX Quale Stato 219

American Law Institute (2009) *Restatements of the Law – Employment Law – Tentative Draft No. 2*, Philadelphia: ALI

Anderman, S. D. (2000) 'The Interpretation of Protective Statutes and the Contract of Employment' 29 *ILJ* 223

Antonmattei P. H. and Sciberras, J.-C. (2008) *Le travailleur économiquement dépendant: quelle protection Rapport à M. le Ministre du Travail, des Relations sociales, de la Famille et de la Solidarité.*

Antonmattei, P. H. and Sciberras, J. C. (2009) 'Le travailleur économiquement dépendant, quelle protection?' *Droit Social* 221.

Ashiagbor, D. (2005) *The European Employment Strategy: Labour Market Regulation and New Governance*, Oxford: OUP

Bar, C. von, and Clive, E. (eds) (2009) *Principles, Definitions and Model Rules of European Private Law – Draft Common Frame of Reference*, Munich: Sellier

Bar, C. von, Clive, E., Schulte-Nölke, H., Beale, H., Herre, J., Schlechtriem, P., Storme, M., Swann, S., Varul, P., Veneziano, A., and Zoll, F. (eds) (2008) *Principles, Definitions and Model Rules of European Private Law, Draft Common Frame of Reference (DCFR), Interim Outline Edition*, Munich: Sellier

Barendrecht, M. *et al.* (2007) *Principles of European Law – Service Contracts ('PEL SC')*, Oxford: OUP

Barassi, L. (1901) *Il Contratto di Lavoro nel Diritto Positivo Italiano*, Milano: Società Editrice Libraria

Barassi, L. (1949) *Diritto del Lavoro – Vol. I*, Milano: Giuffrè

Barmes, L. (2004) 'The Continuing Conceptual Crisis in the Common Law of the Contract of Employment' 67 MLR 435

Barnard, C. (2003) *EC Employment Law*, 3rd ed., Oxford: OUP

Barnard, C. (2009) '*Viking* and *Laval*: A Single Market Perspective', Chapter 3 of Ewing, K. D. and Hendy, J., QC, (eds), *The New Spectre Haunting Europe – The ECJ, Trade Union Rights, and the British Government*, London: IER

Barnard, C., Deakin, S., and Hobbs, R. (2001) 'Capabilities and Rights: An Emerging Agenda for Social Policy?' 32 *IRJ* 464

Bavaro, V. (2009) 'Tesi sullo Statuto Giuridico del Tempo nel Rapporto di Lavoro Subrdinato', Chapter 1 of Bavaro, V. and Veneziani, B. (eds), *Le Dimensioni Giuridiche dei tempi del Lavoro*, Bari: Cacucci

Benedict XVI (2009) *Encyclical Letter 'Caritas in Veritate'*

Bercusson, B. (1996) *European Labour Law*, London: Butterworths

Bernier, M. J. *et al.* (2003) *Les Besoins de Protection Sociale des Personnes en Situation de Travail non Traditionnelle*, Gouvernement du Québec

Bianca, M. (2000) *Diritto Civile Vol. 3, Il Contratto*, 2nd ed., Milano: Giuffrè

Billotte, I., Kenel, P., and Steinmann, T. (2005) *Le Contrat d'Agence Commerciale en Europe*, Bruylant/LGDJ/Schulthess

BIS (2009) *Employment Rights on the Transfer of an Undertaking*

Blanc-Jouvan, X. (1981) 'Initiative et imputabilité: un eclatement de la notion de licenciement' *Droit Social* 207

Boeri, T. and Garibaldi, P. (2008) *Un Nuovo Contratto per Tutti*, Milano: Chiarelettere

Borenfreund, G. (2001) 'Les syndicats bénéficiaires d'un accord collectif' 9/11 *Droit Social* 821

Brown, W. (ed) (1981) *The Changing Countours of British Industrial Relations*, Oxford: Blackwell

Browne, J., Deakin, S., and Wilkinson, F. (2002) 'Capabilities, Social Rights and European Market Integration, ESRC Centre for Business Research Working Paper No. 253.

Brun A. and Galland, H. (1958) *Droit du Travail*, Paris: Sirey

Busby, N. (2011) *A Right to Care? – Unpaid Care Work in European Employment Law*, Oxford: OUP

Cabeza Pereiro, J. (2008) 'The Status of Self-employed Workers in Spain' *ILR* 91

Cabrelli, D. (2005) 'Comparing the Implied Covenant of Good Faith and Fair Dealing with the Implied Term of Mutual Trust and Confidence in the US and UK Employment Contexts', 21 *IJCLLIR* 445

Cahuc, P. and Kramarz, F. (2004) *De la précarité à la mobilité: vers une Sécurité sociale professionnelle*, Paris: La Documentation française

Camerlynck, G. H. (1982) *Droit du Travail – Le Contrat de Travail – Tome I*, 2nd ed., Paris: Dalloz

Camerlynck, G.H. (1986) *Traité de Droit du Travail – Contrat de Travail*, Paris: Dalloz

Carinci, F. (2008) 'Attività professionali, rappresentanza collettiva, strumenti di autotutela' WP C.S.D.L.E. "Massimo D'Antona".IT – 69/2008

Carinci, F. (2009) 'Una dichiarazione d'intenti: l'Accordo quadro 22 gennaio 2009 sulla riforma degli assetti contrattuali' *Rivista Italiana di Diritto del Lavoro* 177

Carinci, F. (2009) 'Una Dichiarazione d'Intenti: l'Accordo Quadro 22 Gennaio 2009 sulla Riforma degli Assetti Contrattuali', D'Antona Working Paper No. 86/2009

Carinci, F. (2010) 'Se quarant'anni vi sembran pochi: dallo Statuto dei lavoratori all'Accordo di Pomigliano' WP C.S.D.L.E. "Massimo D'Antona".IT – 108/2010

Caruso, B. (2004) 'The Concept Of Flexibility In Labour Law. The Italian Case in the European Context' WP CSDLE "Massimo D'Antona" N. 39/2004

Caruso, B. (2010) 'Il Contratto di Lavoro come Istituzione Europea', WP CSDLE "Massimo D'Antona" INT – 84/2010

Casale, G. (ed) (2011) *The Employment Relationship – A Comparative Overview*, Oxford: Hart

Casillo, R. (2008) 'La Dignità nel Rapporto di Lavoro' Working Paper "Massimo D'Antona" 71/2008

Castelvetri, L. (2001) 'Correttezza e Buona Fede nella Giurisprudenza del Lavoro. Diffidenza e Proposte Dottrinali', *Diritto delle Relazioni Industriali* 238

Cavalier, G. and Upex, R. (2006) 'The Concept of the Employment Contract In European Union Private Law' 55 *ICLQ* 587

Cavalier, G. and Upex, R. (2006) 'The Concept of Employment Contract in European Private Law', *IJCLLIR* 608

Cendon, P. (ed) (1997) *Commentario al Codice Civile, vol 4 artt. 1173–1645*, Torino: UTET

Cester, C. (ed) (2007) *Il Rapporto di Lavoro Subordinato: Costituzione e Svolgimento – II*, Milano: Wolters Kluwer Italia Giuridica, 150

*Chitty on Contracts* (2008) 30th ed.

Clark, J. and Lord Wedderburn, in Lord Wedderburn, Lewis, R., and Clark, J. (eds) (1983) *Labour Law and Industrial Relations: Building on Kahn-Freund*, Oxford: Clarendon

Cohen, G. A. (1995) *Self-ownership, Freedom, and Equality*, Cambridge: CUP

Cohen, G. A. (1998) 'Freedom and Money – In Grateful Memory of Isaiah Berlin' (1998), 7, available online at www.howardism.org/appendix/Cohen.pdf

Cohen, G. A. (2003) 'Facts and Principles' 31 *Philosophy & Public Affairs* 211

Cohen, G. A. (2005) 'Are Freedom and Equality Compatible?', Chapter 27 in Goodin, E. and Pettit, P. (eds), *Contemporary Political Philosophy – An Anthology*, Oxford: Blackwell

Cohen, G. A. (2009) *Why not Socialism?*, Princeton: Princeton University Press, 2009

Collins, H. (1989) 'Labour Law as a Vocation' 105 *LQR* 468

Collins, H. (1990) 'Independent Contractors and the Challenge of Vertical Disintegration to Employment Protection Laws', 10 *OJLS* 353

Collins, H. (2000) 'The Employment Rights of Casual Workers', 29 *ILJ* 73

Collins, H. (2007) 'Legal Responses to the Standard Form Contract of Employment', 36 *ILJ* 2

Collins, H. (2010) *Employment Law*, 2nd ed., Oxford: OUP

Connolly, M. (2009) 'Forced Retirement, Age Discrimination and the *Heyday* Case' 38 *ILJ* 233

Convention Praesidium (2000) 'Draft Charter of Fundamental Rights of the European Union – Text of the explanations relating to the complete text of the Charter as set out in CHARTE 4487/00 CONVENT 50', CHARTE 4473/00 CONVENT 49 (Brussels, 11 October 2000)

Corazza, L. (2004) *"Contractual integration" e rapporti di Lavoro – Uno studio sulle tecniche di tutela del lavoratore*, Padova: Cedam

Corazza, L. (2009) 'La nuova nozione di appalto nel sistema delle tecniche di tutela del lavoratore' WP C.S.D.L.E. "Massimo D'Antona" .IT – 93/2009

Cotis, J. P. (2003) 'Reforming European Labour Markets: the Unfinished Agenda', address made to the Vienna Economics Conference 'Fostering Economic Growth in Europe', 12–13 June 2003, The crisis, the "cost" of job security, and a new role for public policy'

Council of Europe (2008) *Digest of the Case Law of the European Committee of Social Rights* (1 September 2008)

Countouris, N. (2007) *The Changing Law of the Employment Relationship: Comparative Analyses in the European Context*, Aldershot: Ashgate

Countouris, N. and Horton, R. (2009) 'The Temporary Agency Work Directive: Another Broken Promise?' 38 *ILJ* 329

Countouris, N. (2010) 'European Social Law as an Autonomous Legal Discipline' 28 *Yearbook of European Law 2009*, 95

Cour de Cassation, *Bulletin d'information* no. 485 du 15/01/1999

Cour de Cassation, *Rapport du Oxford University Presse de travail de la Cour de cassation Sur l'avant-projet de réforme du droit des obligations et de la prescription* (15 juin 2007)

Court de Cassation (2009) *Les Discriminations dans la Jurisprudence de la Cour de Cassation – Rapport Annuel 2008*, Paris: La Documentation française

Couret, A. *et al.* (1996) *Les Frontières du salariat – actes du colloque org. les 26 et 27 oct. 1996 à l'Université de Cergy-Pontoise*, Paris: Dalloz

Crouch, C. (2005) *Capitalist Diversity and Change – Recombinant Governance and Institutional Entrepreneurs*, Oxford: OUP

Dalmasso, R. (2009) 'Salariés, travailleurs indépendants et travailleurs économiquement dépendants: vers une troisième catégorie juridique régissant la relation de travail?'. Available online at http://gree.univ-nancy2.fr/digitalAssets/51826_DALMASSO.pdf

Dannemann, G. (2006) 'Comparative Law; Study of Similarities or Differences?', ch 11 of Reimann, M. and Zimmermann, R., *The Oxford Handbook of Comparative Law*, Oxford: OUP

Dardalhon, L. (2005) 'La liberté du travail devant le Conseil constitutionnel et la Cour de Cassation' 64 *Revue française de droit constitutionnel* 755

Däubler, W. (1999) 'Working People in Germany' 21 *CLLPJ* 80

Davidov, G. (2005) 'Who is a Worker?' 34 *ILJ* 57

Davidov, G. (2009) 'A Purposive Interpretation of the National Minimum Wage Act' (2009) 72 *MLR* 581

Davidov, G. and Langille, B. (eds) (2011) *The Idea of Labour Law*, Oxford: OUP

Davies, A. C. L. (2007) 'The Contract of Intermittent Employment' 36 *ILJ* 102

Davies, A. C. L. (2009) *Perspectives on Labour Law*, 2nd ed., Cambridge: CUP

Davies, A. C. L. (2009) 'Sensible Thinking About Sham Transactions: *Protectacoat Firthglow v Szilagyi*' (2009) 38 *ILJ* 318

Davies P. and Freedland, M. (2000) 'Employers, Workers and the Autonomy of Labour Law' in Collins, H., Davies, P. L., and Rideout, R., (eds), *Legal Regulation of the Employment Relation*, London: Kluwer

Davies P. and Freedland, M. (2004) 'Changing Perspectives on the Employment Relationship in British Labour Law' Chapter 6 of Barnard, C., Deakin, S. W., and Morris, G. S. (eds), *The Future of Labour Law: Liber Amicorum Sir Bob Hepple QC*, Oxford: Hart Publishing

Deakin, S. (2001) 'The Contract of Employment: a Study in Legal Evolution' ESCR Working Paper No. 203

Deakin, S. (2001) 'The Many Futures of the Contract of Employment', Chapter 9 of Conaghan, J., Fischl, M., and Klare, K. (eds), *Labour Law in an Era of Globalisation; Transformative Practices and Possibilities*, Oxford: OUP

Deakin, S. (2005) 'The Capability Concept and the Evolution of European Social Policy' ESRC Centre for Business Research Working Paper No. 303

Deakin, S. (2005) 'The Comparative Evolution of the Employment Relationship' ESCR Working Paper No. 317

Deakin, S. (2009) 'Capacitas: Contract Law, Capabilities and the Legal Foundation of the Market', Chapter 1 of Deakin, S. and Supiot, A. (eds), *Capacitas – Contract Law and the Institutional Preconditions of a Market Economy*, Oxford: Hart

Deakin, S., Lele, P., and Siems, M. (2007) 'The Evolution of Labour Law: Calibrating and Comparing Regulatory Regimes', Centre for Business Research, University of Cambridge Working Paper No. 352

Deakin, S. and Morris, G. (2001) *Labour Law*, 3rd ed., London: Butterworths

Deakin, S. and Morris, G. (2009) *Labour Law*, 5th ed., Oxford: Hart

Deakin, S. and Supiot, A. (eds) (2009) *Capacitas – Contract Law and the Institutional Preconditions of a Market Economy*, Oxford: Hart

Deakin, S. and Wilkinson, F. (2005) *The Law of the Labour Market*, Oxford: OUP

de Sande Pérez-Bedmar, M. (2007) 'El Estatuto Básico del Empleado Público: Comentario al Contenido en Espera de su Desarollo' 18 *Relaciones Laborales* 58

Dockès, E. (2004) 'De la supériorité du contrat de travail sur le pouvoir de l'employeur', Chapter 1 of Arsequel, A. *et al.* (eds), *Analyse juridique et valeurs en droit social: Mélanges en l'honneur de Jean Pélissier*, Paris: Dalloz

D'Onghia, M. (2005) *La Forma Vincolata nel Diritto del Lavoro*, Milano: Giuffrè

Drouin, R.-C. (2009) 'Capacitas and Capabilities in International Labour Law', Chapter 8 of Deakin, S. and Supiot, A. (eds), *Capacitas – Contract Law and the Institutional Preconditions of a Market Economy*, Oxford: Hart

DTI (2005) 'TUPE Draft Revised Regulations Public Consultation Document' (March 2005)

DTI (2007) 'National Minimum Wage and Voluntary Workers – Consultation Document' (June 2007)

Durand, P. (1945) 'Le Particularisme du Droit du Travail', *Droit Social* 301

Dworkin, R. (1986) *Law's Empire*, Harvard: Harvard University Press

EC Commission (2008) '"Employment" Directive (2000/78/EC): list of Member States to which a reasoned opinion or letter of formal notice will be sent' MEMO 08/68 of 31 January 2008.

European Committee of Social Rights (2005) 'Conclusions XVI-2 (Austria)', Strasbourg

European Commission (2006) Green Paper 'Modernising Labour Law to Meet the Challenges of the 21st Century' COM (2006) 708 final

European Commission (2006) 'Commission Staff Working Document – National implementation measures of Directive 1999/70/EC (EU-15)' SEC 1074

European Commission (2007) 'Implementation Report on Directive 1999/70/EC concerning the Framework Agreement on fixed-term work concluded by UNICE, CEEP and ETUC (Czech Republic, Estonia, Cyprus, Latvia, Lithuania, Hungary, Malta, Poland, Slovenia and Slovakia)' (March 2007)

European Commission (2008) 'Commission Staff Working Document – National implementation measures of Directive 1999/70/EC (EU-10)' SEC 2485

European Commission (2010) 'EUROPE 2020 A strategy for smart, sustainable and inclusive growth' COM (2010) 2020 final

European Commission (2010) 'Proposal for a directive of the European Parliament and of the Council on the conditions of entry and residence of third-country nationals for the purposes of seasonal employment' COM (2010) 379 final

European Commission (2010) 'Proposal for a Directive of the European Parliament and of the Council on conditions of entry and residence of third-country nationals in the framework of an intra-corporate transfer' COM (2010) 378 final

European Commission (2010) 'Report on the application of Article 17 of Directive 86/653/EEC on the co-ordination of the laws of the Member States relating to self-employed commercial agents' COM (1996) 364

European Commission (2010) 'Report on Council Directive 2001/23/EC of 12 March 2001 on the approximation of the laws of the Member States relating to the safeguarding of employees' rights in the event of transfers of undertakings, businesses or parts of undertakings or businesses' COM (2007) 334 final.

European Commission (2010) 'Commission Staff Working Paper – Detailed report on the implementation by Member States of Directive 2003/88/EC concerning certain aspects of the organization of working time ("The Working Time Directive")', SEC 1611/2

European Expert Group on Flexicurity (2007) *Flexicurity Pathways – Turning Hurdles into Stepping Stones*

European Foundation for the Improvement of Living and Working Conditions (2009) *Report on Self-employed workers: industrial relations and working conditions*, Dublin

EuSoCo Group (2011) 'Public Consultation on the Green Paper from the Commission on policy options for progress towards a European Contract Law for consumers and businesses' (January 2011)

Ewing K. and Hendy, J. QC. (2009) *The New Spectre Haunting Europe – The ECJ, Trade Union Rights and the British Government*, London: IER

*Fairness at Work* (1998) White Paper Cm 3968, HMSO May 1998.

Falkner, G. and Treib, O. (2008) 'Three Worlds of Compliance or Four? The EU-15 Compared to New Member States' 46 *JCMS* 293

Forshaw, S. and Pilgerstorfer, M. (2003) 'Illegally formed contracts of employment and equal treatment at work' 34 *ILJ* 158

Fredman, S. (2004) 'The Ideology of New Labour Law', Chapter 1 of C. Barnard, S. Deakin, and G. Morris (eds.), *The Future of Labour Law – Liber Amicorum Sir Bob Hepple*, Oxford: Hart

Freedland, M. (1976) *The Contract of Employment*, Oxford: Clarendon Press

Freedland, M. R. (2002) 'Jus Cogens, Jus Dispositivum, and the Law of Personal Work Contracts', Chapter 12 of Birks, P. and Pretto, A. (eds), *Themes in Comparative Law in Honour of Bernard Rudden*, Oxford: OUP

Freedland, M. (2003) *The Personal Employment Contract*, Oxford: OUP

Freedland, M. (2006) 'Re-thinking the Personal Work Contract' in 2005 *Current Legal Problems*, Vol. 58, Oxford: OUP, 517.

Freedland, M. R. (2006) 'The Evolving Approach to the Public/Private Distinction in English Law', in Freedland, M.R. and Auby, J.-B. (eds), *The Public-Private Divide – Une Entente Assez Cordiale?*, Oxford: Hart, 93.

Freedland, M. (2008) 'Private Law, Regulation and Governance Design and the Personal Work Contract', Chapter 9 of Cafaggi, F. and Muir-Watt, H. (eds), *Making European Private Law – Governance Design*, Cheltenham: Edward Elgar

Freedland, M., (due early 2012), in Arthurs, H, and Stone, K., (eds), *Employment Regulation after the Demise of the Standard Employment Contract*, Russell Sage: forthcoming)

Freedland, M., Craig, P., Jacqueson, C., and Kountouris, N. (2007) *Public Employment Services and European Law*, Oxford: OUP

Freedman, J. (2001) *Employed or Self-Employed? Tax Classification and the Changing Labour Market*, London: Institute of Fiscal Studies

Fudge, J. (2010) 'A Canadian Perspective on the Scope of Employment Standards, Labor Rights, and Social Protection: The Good, the Bad, and the Ugly' 31 *CLLPJ* 253

Gaeta, L. (2001) 'Lodovico Barassi, Philipp Lotmar e la Cultura Giuridica Tedesca' 90 *Giornale di Diritto del Lavoro e di Relazioni Industriali* 179

Garofalo, D. (2004) 'Mobbing e Tutela del Lavoratore tra Fondamento Normativo e Tecnica Risarcitoria', Chapter XXX of Various Authors, *Scritti in Memoria di Massimo D'Antona*, Milano: Giuffrè

Garofalo, D. (2004) 'Statuto Protettivo del Lavoro Parasubordinato e Tutela della Concorrenza', in Rusciano, M., and Zoppoli, L., (eds), *Mercato del Lavoro. Riforma e Vincoli di Sistema della Legge 14 Febbraio 2003 n. 30 al Decreto Legislativo 10 2003 n. 276*, Napoli: Editoriale Scientifica, 231.

Garofalo, M. G. (1989) 'Complessità del Modo di Produzione e Possibilità di Governo Attraverso il Diritto del Lavoro', Chapter XXX of Pedrazzoli, M., (ed), *Lavoro Subordinato e Dintorni*, Bologna: Il Mulino

Garofalo, M. G. (2003) 'La legge delega sul mercato del lavoro: prime osservazioni', XXX RGL 362

Garofalo, M. G. (2008) 'Unità e pluralità del lavoro nel sistema costituzionale' 117 *Giornale di Diritto del Lavoro e di Relazioni Industriali* 22

Gaymer, J. (2001) *The Employment Relationship*, London: Sweet & Maxwell

Ghai, D., (ed) (2006) *Decent Work: Objectives and Strategies*, Geneva: ILO

Ghera, E. (2005) 'Sul Lavoro a Progetto', XXX *Rivista Italiana di Diritto del Lavoro* 208

Ghera, E.(2006) 'Subordinazione, Statuto Protettivo e Qualificazione del Rapporto di Lavoro', 109 *Giornale di Diritto del Lavoro e di Relazioni Industriali* 29

Ghera, E. (2007) *Diritto del Lavoro – il rapporto di lavoro*, 16th ed., Bari: Cacucci

Giubboni, S. (2010) 'La Nozione Europea di Subordinazione', Chapter 2 of Sciarra, S. (ed), *Manuale di Diritto Sociale Europeo*, Torino: Giappichelli

Giugni, G. (1953) 'Verso il tramonto del recesso ad nutum dell'imprenditore. La disciplina interconfederale dei licenziamenti nell'industria', XXX *RDL* 201

Giugni, G. (2007) *Diritto Sindacale*, XXX ed., Bari: Cacucci

Goodin E. and Pettit, P. (eds.) (2005) *Contemporary Political Philosophy – An Anthology*, Oxford: Blackwell

Gorelli Hernández, J. (2003) 'El contrato de trabajo fijo discontinuo', in Ojeda Avilés (eds.), *Modalidades de Contrato de Trabajo*, Madrid: Tecnos Editorial

Gottardi, G. (2004) 'Lavoro intermittente. Commento agli artt. 33–40', in Gragnoli, E. and Perulli, A. (eds), *La Riforma del Mercato del Lavoro e i Nuovi Modelli Contrattuali*, Padova: Cedam, 496

Gouvernement du Grand-Duché de Luxembourg, Contribution du Gouvernement du Grand-Duché de Luxembourg au LIVRE VERT 'Moderniser le droit du travail pour relever les défis du XXIe siècle' (30 March 2007)

Graziadei, M. (2006) 'Comparative Law as the Study of Transplants and Receptions', Chapter 11 of Reimann, M. and Zimmermann, R. (eds.), *The Oxford Handbook of Comparative Law*, Oxford: OUP

Griffin, J. (2008) *On Human Rights*, Oxford: OUP

Hall, P. A. and Soskice, D. (eds), (2001) *Varieties of Capitalism – The Institutional Foundations of Comparative Advantage*, Oxford: OUP

*Halsbury's Laws of England* (1995) 4th edn. reissue, London: Butterworths, Vol. 44(I) 'Solicitors', para 99, 'meaning of "retainer"'

Hancké, B. (ed), (2009) *Debating Varieties of Capitalism – A Reader*, Oxford: OUP

Hansard HC Deb, 14 February 1963, vol. 671 cc1555–618

Hart, H. L. A. (1973) 'Rawls on Liberty and Its Priority', 40 *University of Chicago Law Review* 534

Hascöet, M. (2007) 'Le contrat de projet: le nouveau visage de la parasubordination en Italie', XXX *Droit Social* 879

Hepple, B. (1986) 'Restructuring Employment Rights' (1986) 15 *ILJ* 69

Hepple, B., (ed) (1986) *The Making of Labour Law in Europe*, London: Mansell

Hepple, B. (2009) 'The Aims of Equality Law', in O'Cinneide, C. and Holder, J. (eds), *Current Legal Problems 2008*, Oxford: OUP

Hepple, B. and Veneziani, B. (eds), (2009) *The Transformation of Labour Law in Europe: A Comparative Study of 15 Countries 1945–2004*, Oxford: Hart

Ichino, P. (1990) 'La Fuga dal Diritto del Lavoro', XXX DemDir 69

ILO (1997) *Contract labour – Fifth item on the agenda Report V (1) to the International Labour Conference 86th Session 1998*, Geneva

ILO (2003) *International Labour Conference Report V – The Scope of the Employment Relationship – Fifth Item on the Agenda*, Geneva

ILO (2007) *Eliminating Discrimination Against Indigenous and Tribal Peoples in Employment and Occupation – A Guide to ILO Convention No.11*, Geneva: ILO

ILO (2010) *Decent Work for Domestic Workers – Report IV(1)* to the International Labour Conference, 99th Session, Geneva

Jeammaud, A. (2002) 'L'assimilation de franchisés aux salaries', XXX *Droit Social* 158

Kahn-Freund, O. (1954) 'Legal Framework', in Flanders, A., and Clegg, H. (eds) *The System of Industrial Relations in Great Britain*, Oxford: Blackwell

Kahn-Freund, O. (1967) 'A Note on Status and Contract in Modern Labour Law' (1967) 30 *MLR* 635

Kahn-Freund, O. (1972) *Labour and the Law*, London: Stevens & Sons

Kahn-Freund, O. (1977) 'Blackstone's Neglected Child: The Contract of Employment' 93 *LQR* 508

Kahn-Freund, O. (1977) *Labour and the Law*, 2nd ed., London: Stevens & Sons

Kenner, J. (2009) 'New Frontiers in EU Labour Law: From Flexicurity to Flex-Security', in Dougan, M., and Currie, S., (eds) *50 Years of the European Treaties: Looking Back and Thinking Forward*, Oxford: Hart

Knegt, R. (ed), (2008) *The Employment Contract as an Exclusionary Device – An Analysis on the Basis of 25 Years of Developments in The Netherlands*, Antwerp: Intersentia.

Koukiadaki, A. (2009) 'Case-law Developments in the Area of Fixed-term Work' 38 *ILJ* 89.

Labour Asociados (2008) *The Impact of New Forms of Labour on Industrial Relations and the Evolution of Labour Law in the European Union* (Brussels: IP/A/EMPL/ST/2007–019 9, 2008)

Lando, O. (2007) 'Is Good Faith an Over-arching General Clause in the Principles of European Contract Law', in Andenas, M., *et al.* (eds.), *Liber Amicorum Guido Alpa – Private Law Beyond the National Systems*, London: British Institute of International and Comparative Law

Langille, B. (2009) 'What is International Labor Law for?' (2009) 3 *Law & Ethics of Human Rights* 47

Leighton, P. and Wynn, M. (2011) 'Classifying Employment Relationships – More Sliding Doors or a Better Regulatory Framework?' 40 *ILJ* 5

Lindsay J. (2001) 'The Implied Term of Trust and Confidence' 30 *ILJ* 1

Lingemann, S., von Steinau-Steinrück, R., and Mengel, A. (2008) *Employment & Labor Law in Germany*, München: Verlag C. H. Beck

Liso, F. (1992) 'La Fuga dal Diritto del Lavoro', XXX *Industria e Sindacato* 1

Lokiec, P. and Robin-Olivier, S. (2008) 'La période d'essai' (2008) XXX *Revue de Droit du Travail* 258

Lord Wedderburn (1966) *The Worker and the Law*, Harmondsworth: Penguin

Lord Wedderburn (1987) 'Labour Law: From Here to Autonomy?' 16 *ILJ* 1

Lord Wedderburn (1992) 'Inderogability, Collective Agreements, and Community Law' 21 *ILJ* 245

Lyon-Caen, G. (1969) *Droit Social Européen*, Paris: Dalloz

Lyon-Caen, G. (1973) 'Négociation Collective et Législation d'Ordre Public', XXX *Droit Social* 89

Lyon-Caen, A. (1988) 'Actualité du contrat de travail', XXX *Droit Social* 541

Lyon-Caen, G. (1990) *Le Droit du Travail non Salarié*, Paris: Sirey

Martín Valverde, A., Rodríguez-Sañudo Gutiérrez, F., and García Murcia, J. (1996) *Derecho del Trabajo*, 5th ed., Madrid: Tecnos

Marx, K. (1978) *Wage Labour and Capital*, Peking: Foreign Languages Press, pp. 18–19

Marzo, C., and Lecomte, C. (2010) 'Le Refus d'être Transféré: Droit Comparé', XXX *Droit Social* 698

McCallum, R. (1989) 'Exploring the Common Law: Lay-off, Suspension and the Contract of Employment' 2 *Australian Journal of Labour Law* 211

McKendrick, E. (2007) 'The Meaning of 'Good Faith'', in M. Andenas *et al.* (eds), *Liber Amicorum Guido Alpa – Private Law Beyond National Systems*, London: British Institute of International and Comparative Law

Mégnin, S. (2003) *Le Contrat d'Agence Commerciale en Droit Français et Allemand*, Paris: Litec

Mercader Uguina, J. R. and de la Puebla Pinilla, A. (2007) 'Comentario a la Ley 20/2007, de 11 de julio, del Estatuto del Trabajo Autónomo', 20 *Relacione Laborales* 99

Michaels, R. (2006) 'The Functional Method of Comparative Law', Chapter 10 of Reimann, M. and Zimmermann, R. (eds.), *The Oxford Handbook of Comparative Law*, Oxford: OUP

Middlemiss, S. (2004) 'The Truth and Nothing but the Truth: the Legal Liability of Employers for Employees' References', 33 *ILJ* 59

Miller, V. (2011) 'EU Legislation: Government action on "goldplating"' (SN/IA/5943 of 19 April 2011)

*Model Rules of European Private Law – Draft Common Frame of Reference (DCFR) Outline Edition*, München: Sellier, 2009

Morgado Panadero, P. (ed.) (2010) *Empleo, trabajo autonomo y economia social*, Madrid: Comares

Mouly, J. (2008) *Droit du Travail*, Paris: Bréal

Mückenberger, U. and Deakin, S. (1989) 'From Deregulation to a European Floor of Rights: Law, Flexibilisation and the European Single Market', *Zeitschrift für Ausländisches und Internationales Arbeits und Sozialrecht* 153

Nicholas, B. (1992) *The French law of Contract*, 2nd ed., Oxford: Clarendon Press

Njoya, W. (2007) *Property in Work – The Employment Relationship in the Anglo-American Firm*, Aldershot: Ashgate

Nogler L. and Refiner, U. (2010) 'Social Contracts in the Light of the Draft Common Frame of Reference for a Future EU Contract Law', WP C.S.D.L.E. "Massimo D'Antona" INT – 80/2010.

Nogler L. and U. Reifner (2010) 'Social Contracts in the Light of the Draft Common Frame of Reference for a Future EU Contract Code', in Antoniolli, L. and Fiorentini, F. (eds), *A Factual Assessment of the Draft Common Frame of Reference*, Munich: Sellier, 365

Nogler, L. (2008) 'Why do Labour Lawyers Ignore the Question of Social Justice in European Contract Law?' 14 *ELJ* 483

Nussbaum, M. (2000) 'Women and Equality: the Capabilities Approach' 138 *ILR* 227

Nussbaum, M. C. and Sen, A. K. (1993) *The Quality of Life*, Oxford: Clarendon

O'Cinneide, C. (2005) *Age Discrimination and European Law*, Luxembourg: Office for Official Publications of the European Communities

Oats, L. and Sadler, P. (2008) 'Tax and the Labour Market: Taxing Personal Services Income in the UK' 1 *Journal of Applied Law and Policy* 59

OECD (1993) *Employment Outlook 1993*, Paris: OECD

OECD (1994) *Employment Outlook 1994*, Paris: OECD

OECD (1999) *Employment Outlook 1999*, Paris: OECD

OECD (2004) *Employment Outlook 2004*, Paris: OECD

OECD (2009) *Employment Outlook 2009 – Tackling the Job Crisis*, Paris: OECD

OECD (2010) *Greece at a Glance: Policies for a Sustainable Recovery*, Paris: OECD

Ojeda Avilés, A. (2010) *La Deconsrtucción del Derecho del Trabajo*, Madrid: La Ley

Pedrazzoli, M. (2006) 'Le complicazioni dell'inutilità: note critiche sul lavoro a progetto', in L. Mariucci (ed.), *Dopo la flessibilità, cosa? Le nuove politiche del lavoro*, Bologna: Il Mulino

Pélissier, J., Supiot, J., and Jeammaud, A. (2000) *Droit du Travail*, 20th ed., Paris: Dalloz

Pélissier, J., Supiot, J., and Jeammaud, A. (2006) *Droit du Travail*, 23rd ed., Paris: Dalloz

Pélissier, J., Supiot, J., and Jeammaud, A. (2008) *Droit du Travail*, 24th ed., Paris: Dalloz

Perulli, A. (2002) 'La Buona Fede nel Diritto del Lavoro' 53 *Rivista Giuridica del Lavoro* 3

Perulli, A. (2003) *Economically dependent/quasi-subordinate (parasubordinate) employment: legal, social and economic aspects.* Available online at: www.ec.europa.eu/employment_social/labour_law/docs/parasubordination_report_en.pdf

Perulli, A. (2011) 'Subordinate, Autonomous and Economically Dependent Work: A Comparative Analysis of Selected European Countries', Chapter 5 of Casale, G. (ed), *The Employment Relationship – A Comparative Overview*, Oxford: Hart

Pilgerstorfer, M. and Forshaw, S. (2008) 'A Dog's Dinner? Reconsidering Contractual Illegality in the Employment Sphere' 37 *ILJ* 279

Pinto, V. (2006) 'La Categoria Giuridica delle Collaborazioni Coordinate e Continuative e il Lavoro a Progetto', in Curzio, P. (ed), *Lavoro e Diritti a Tre Anni dalla Legge 30/2003*, Bari: Cacucci, 431.

Raimondi, E. (2008) 'Rifiuto di Svolgere Mansioni Inferiori e Licenziamento per Giusta Causa: un Revirement nella Giurisprudenza della Cassazione?' 27 *Rivista Italiana di Diritto del Lavoro* 597

Ratti, L. (2009) 'Agency Work and the Idea of Dual Employership: A Comparative Perspective' 30 *CLLPJ* 835

Rawls, J. (1971) *A Theory of Justice*, Cambridge: Harvard University Press

Ray, J.-E. (1991) 'Fidélité et Exécution du Contrat de Travail' XXX *Droit Social* 376

Razzolini, O. (2010) 'The Need to Go Beyond the Contract: "Economic" and "Bureaucratic" Dependence in Personal Work Relations' 31 *CLLPJ* 267

Rideout, R. (1976) *Principles of Labour Law*, London: Sweet & Maxwell

Roman, D. (2005) 'Le Principe de Dignité dans la Doctrine de Droit Social', in Hennette-Vauchez, S. and Girard, Ch. (eds), *La Dignité de la Personne Humaine, Recherche sur un Processus de Juridicisation*, Paris: PUF

Ruiter, D. W. P. (2001) *Legal Institutions*, Dordrecht: Kluwer

Sabbath, E. (1964) 'Effects of Mistake in Contracts: A Study in Comparative Law' 13 *The International and Comparative Law Quarterly* 803

Sánchez Torres, E. (2010) 'The Spanish Law on Dependent Self-employed Workers: A New Evolution in Labour Law' 31 *CLLPJ* 231

Santoro-Passarelli, G. (1952) *Nozioni di Diritto del Lavoro*, 6th ed., Napoli: Jovene

Savatier, J. (2000) 'Entre bénévolat et salariat: le statut des volontaires pour le dévelopement', XXX *Droit Social* 146

Schömann, I., Clauwaert, S., and Düvel, W. (2003) *Legal analysis of the implementation of the fixed-term work directive*, Brussels: ETUI

Sciarra, S. (ed), (2001) *Labour Law in the Courts: National Judges and the ECJ*, Oxford: Hart

Sciarra, S. (2005) *The Evolution of Labour Law 1992–2003 – Vol.1 General Report*, Luxembourg: Office for Official Publications of the European Communities

Sciarra, S., Davies, P., and Freedland, M. (eds) (2004) *Employment Policy and the Regulation of Part-Time work in the European Union: A Comparative Analysis*, Cambridge: CUP

Seifert, A. and Funken-Hötzel, E. (2004) 'Wrongful Dismissal in the Federal Republic of Germany', 25 *CLLPJ* 489

Sen, A. (1979) 'Equality of What?', The Tanner Lecture on Human Values, Stanford

Sen, A. (1985) *Commodities and Capabilities*, Deventer: North Holland

Sen, A. (1999) 'Address by Mr. Amartya Sen, Nobel Laureate in Economics' (87th International Labour Conference, Geneva, 15 June 1999)

Sen, A. (1999) *Development as Freedom*, Oxford: OUP

Sen, A. K. (2000) 'Social Justice and Distribution of Income', Chapter 1 of Atkinson, A. B. and Bourguignon, F. (eds), *Handbook of Income Distribution*, vol. 1, Amsterdam: North Holland

Silcani, J.-L. (2008) *Livre Blanc sur l'Avenir de la Fonction Publique*, Paris: La documentation Francaise

Social Justice in European Contract Law (2004) 'Social Justice in European Contract Law: a Manifesto' 10 *ELJ* 653

Sorge, S. (2010) 'German Law on Dependant Self-employed: A Comparison to the Current Situation under Spanish Law' 31 *CLLPJ* 249

Souriac-Rotschild, M.-A. (1996) 'Le Contrôle de la Légalité Interne des Conventions et Accords Collectifs' XXX *Droit Social* 395

Spadafora, M. T. (2004) *Diritto del Lavoro Sportivo*, Torino: Giappichelli

Speziale, V. (2006) 'Il trasferimento d'azienda tra disciplina nazionale ed interpretazioni "vincolanti" della Corte di Giustizia Europea' (2006) WP C.S.D.L.E. "Massimo D'Antona".IT - 46/2006

Speziale, V. (2007) 'Il Lavoro Subordinato tra Rapporti Speciali, Contratti "Atipici" e Possibili Riforme', WP C.S.D.L.E. "Massimo D'Antona".IT – 51/2007

Speziale, V. (2010) 'Il datore di lavoro nell'impresa integrata', WP C.S.D.L.E. "Massimo D'Antona".IT – 94/2010

Starck, B., Roland, H., and Boyer, L. (1998) *Droit Civil – Les Obligations 2. Contrat*, 6th ed., Paris: Litec

Stiglitz, J. (2009) 'The Global Crisis, Social Protection and Jobs' 148 *ILR* 11

Stone, K. (2008) 'The Future of Labor and Employment Law in the United States', UCLA School of Law – Law-Econ Research Paper No. 08–11

Supiot, A. (1994) *Critique du Droit du Travail*, Paris: PUF

Supiot, A. (2000) 'Les nouveaux visages de la subordination', XXX *Droit Social* 131

Supiot, A (2006) 'Les salariés ne sont pas à vendre. En finir avec l'envers de l'article L.122–12, alinéa 2' *XXX Droit Social* 264

Supiot, A. (2007) 'Le Statut des Travailleurs Migrants Extracommunautaires en Droit Français', in Various Authors, *Lavoratore Extracomunitario ed Integrazione Europea – Profili Giuridici*, Bari: Cacucci

Supiot, A. (2009) 'En Guise de Conclusion: La Capacité, Une Notion à Haut Potentiel', Chapter 9 of Deakin, S., and Supiot, A., (eds), *Capacitas – Contract Law and the Institutional Preconditions of a Market Economy*, Oxford: Hart

Supiot, A., Casas, M. E., De Munck, J., Hanau, P., Johansson, A., Meadows, P., Mingione, E., Salais, R., and van der Heijden, P. (1998) *Transformation of labour and future of labour law in Europe – Final Report* (June 1998)

Supiot, A. *et al.* (1999) *Au-delà de l'emploi: transformations du travail et devenir du droit du travail en Europe: rapport pour la Commission des Communautés européennes*, Paris: Flammarion

Supiot, A. *et al.* (2001) *Beyond Employment – Changes in Work and the Future of Labour Law in Europe*, Oxford: OUP

Syrpis, P. (2007) *EU Intervention in Domestic Labour Law*, Oxford: OUP

Teubner, G. (2000) 'Legal irritants: Good faith in British Law, or How Unifying Law Ends Up in New Differences', Chapter 14 of Snyder, F. (ed), *The Europeanisation of law: The Legal Effects of European integration*, Oxford: Hart

*The Economist*, 'Pay for Delay – Economic Focus' (7 November 2009)

The Law Commission (2010) 'The Illegality Defence' (March 2010)

Torrente, A. and Schlesinger, P. (2007) *Manuale di Diritto Privato*, 18th ed. Milano: Giuffrè

Treu, T. (2007) *Labour Law and Industrial Relations in Italy*, Alphen aan den Rijn: Kluwer Law International

Tucker, E. (2010) 'Renorming Labour Law: Can We Escape Labour Law's Recurring Regulatory Dilemmas?' 39 *ILJ* 119

UK Department for Business, Innovation and Skills, 'Phasing Out the Default Retirement Age: Government Response to Consultation' (January 2011)

Uricchio, A. (2006) *I Redditi dei Lavori tra Autonomia e Dipendenza*, Bari: Cacucci

Valdès Dal-Ré, F. and Leclerc, O. (2008) 'Les nouvelles frontières du travail indépendant. A propos du statut du travail autonome espagnol', XXX *RDT* 296

Vallauri, M. L. (2010) 'L'argomentazione della "Dignità Umana" nella Giurisprudenza in Materia di Danno alla Persona del Lavoratore' 128 *Giornale di Diritto del Lavoro e di Relazioni Industriali* 659

Vatinet, R. (2002) 'Les conditions de validité des clauses de non-concurrence: l'imbroglio' XXX *Droit Social* 949

Velluti, S. (2010) *New Governance and the European Employment Strategy*, London: Routledge

Veneziani, B. (1986) 'The Evolution of the Contract of Employment', in Hepple, B., (ed) *The Making of Labour Law in Europe: A Comparative Study of Nine Countries up to 1945*, London: Mansell

Veneziani, B. (2002) 'Contratto di Lavoro, Potere di Controllo e Subordinazione nell'Opera di Lodovico Barassi', XXX *Giornale di Diritto del Lavoro e di Relazioni Industriali* 43

Veneziani, B. (2003) 'Contratto di lavoro, potere di controllo e subordinazione nell'opera di Ludovico Barassi', in Napoli, M., (ed), *La Nascita del Diritto del Lavoro – Il "contratto di Lavoro" di Lodovico Barassi cent'anni dopo*, Milano: Vita e Pensiero

Veneziani, B. (2007) 'Il Popolo degli Immigrati e il Diritto al Lavoro: una Partita Incompiuta', in Various Authors, *Lavoratore Extracomunitario ed Integrazione Europea – Profili Giuridici*, Bari: Cacucci

Veneziani, B. (2010) 'Il Lavoro tra l'ethos del Diritto ed il Pathos della Dignità' 126 *Giornale di Diritto del Lavoro e di Relazioni Industriali* 257

Vettori, S. (2007) *The Employment Contract and the Changed World of Work*, Aldershot: Ashgate

Viala, Y. (2005) 'Le maintien des contrats de travail en cas de transfert d'entreprise en droit allemand' XXX *Droit Social* 200

Vigneau, C. (2004) 'L'Impératif de Bonne Foi dans l'Exécution du Contrat de Travail' XXX *Droit Social* 706

Vimercati, A. (2009) 'Capacité et l'evolution du Droit du Travail Italien', Chapter 6 of Deakin, S. and Supiot, A. (eds), *Capacitas – Contract Law and the Institutional Preconditions of a Market Economy*, Oxford: Hart, 102

Vroussalis, N. (2010) 'G. A. Cohen on Socialism', available online at www.theorein.org/vrousalis-cohen.pdf

Walker, R. and M. Wiseman (2003) 'Making Welfare Work: UK Activation Policies Under New Labour' 56 *Iss. Rev* 3

Wank, R. (1999) 'Workers Protection – National Study for Germany for the ILO', ILO

Weiss, M. (2005) 'The Interface between Constitution and Labor Law in Germany' 26 *CLLPJ* 182

Weiss, M. and Schmidt, M. (2008) *Labour Law and Industrial Relations in Germany*, Alphen aan den Rijn: Kluwer Law International

Whittaker, S. and Zimmermann, R. (2000) 'Good Faith in European Contract Law: Surveying the Legal Landscape', Chapter 1 of Zimmermann, R. and Whittaker, S. (eds), *Good Faith in European Contract Law*, Cambridge: CUP

Zimmerman, R. (1996) *The Law of Obligations – Roman Foundations of the Civilian Tradition*, Johannesburg: Juta & Co., reissued Oxford: OUP

Zimmerman, R. (2005) *The New German Law of Obligations – Historical and Comparative Perspectives*, Oxford: OUP

Zwanziger, B. (2005) 'Collective Labour Law in a Changing Environment: Aspects of the German Experience' 29 *CLLPJ* 309

# Index

head word in semi-bold, cross references not in bold.

academic tenure 142
accidents and injuries at work
  incapacity 213–14, 217, 235, 387
  injury caused by fault 191
  injury to a person's feelings 250
  and suspension of employment 206
  mental injury 194
  *see also* health and safety at work; sick pay
Acquired Rights Directives 77, 166, 255–8, 270,
  335, 361, 391, 411, 415, 422
advocates 42
agency, law of 274–6, 286, 334
agency work
  agency temps/ workers 123, 349, 426
  Agency Workers Regulations (2010) 334–5
  employment agencies 35
  Employment Agencies Act (1973)
  Italian regulation of 155
  Private Employment Agencies
    Convention 334 n. 20
  temporary agency work 77 n. 91, 115, 165–7,
    294–5, 334, 354, 367, 432, 445
  temporary agency contract 157, 165
  Temporary Agency Work Directive
    (2008) 165, 335, 361, 388 n. 8, 398,
    401–3, 425
American Law
  labor and employment law 13–14
  Law Institute 429 n. 101
  Restatements 429
annual leave 215
anomie 22, 71
*Antonmattei-Sciberras Report* 115, 345
appellate courts 93, 108, 208
appointees 140–4
apprenticeships 125, 137–40, 277–8, 302
  n. 70, 317, 355
  apprentices 137–40
  Modern Apprenticeship 138–9, 295
  *see also* Internship; traineeship; job training
ARD 416
asylum seekers 152
  *see also* immigration
at-will contract of employment 172, 366
atypical workers 77, 154–6, 204, 348–9, 354,
  363, 368, 379, 396–8, 403, 422, 425–6
  *see also* casual employment; temporary work;
    part-time work
Austria 276 n. 21, 395 n. 46
automatic insertion 66, 68
autonomous work 61, 115, 156, 269, 279, 283,
  289 n. 48, 346, 348, 367

Statute on Autonomous Work 345
  *see also* Spanish labour law, TRADES
autopoiesis 107, 348

bargaining power, inequality of 20, 117–18,
  183–4, 287, 370–2, 437–8, 442
barristers 42
  pupil 123
Belgium 144 n. 47, 276 nn. 21, 22
best-fit analysis 328–9
Beveridge Report (1943) 114
Big Society policy 347
  *see also* United Kingdom
bilaterality 34, 158–61, 164, 166, 196, 443
binary divide, the
  as an analytical concept or tool 38, 129
  comparative assessment of 78, 85, 112–20,
    126–7, 154, 269–71, 292, 309–11,
    343–5, 360, 434
  and English Law 42–3
  independent institutional view of 106
  pros and cons of 43, 104–12, 177, 271, 273,
    312, 339
'blue collar' workers 110, 114, 190, 388
  *see also* 'white collar' workers; work,
    types of
'boss' *see* employer
boundary conception 30, 32, 34, 41
BPCC 283
bureaucratic control 126
business(es)
  activities, contracting out 416
  and 'agency' business-to-business contract
    270, 275
  business-to-consumer contract 275, 282,
    293
  Centre for Business Research 133 n. 9, 270
    n. 4, 377 nn. 58, 63, 378 n. 68
  commercial 354, 357
  corporate 163
  employer's 211
  entrepreneurs 56
  European Contract Law for 287 n. 43, 386
    n. 2
  formation of 160
  goodwill of 306
  as a labour intermediary 35
  and personal work contracts 275, 277
  and redundancy 420
  restructuring 423
  small 163, 230
  transfer of 77 n. 89, 255, 361 n. 20

**business(es)** *(cont.)*
    undertaking 277–8, 282, 411 n. 71, 416
        nn. 74, 77, 422 n. 84
    *see also* companies; enterprises; self-
        employment; transfer of undertaking

**Canadian labor and employment law** 14, 345
        n. 10
**capability** 10, 22, 32, 45, 74, 246–7, 303, 340,
        370–2, 375, 377–9, 381–2, 428, 435
**capitalism**
    market 55, 57
    and Marxism 376
    varieties of 51, 55–6
**care, duty of** 192–3
    *see also* health and safety
**career** 144, 236–7, 342–4, 364–9
    *see also* working life
**carer, disabled** 339–41
    *see also* disability
**casual employment**
    as atypical work 348, 396
    casual work(ers) 123
    manual work 286
    marginalization of 154, 355
    occasional 174
    part-timers 392
    as precarious 172
    regular 122, 124
    regulation of 168, 170
    rights of 299 n. 67, 381, 397
    short-term 395
    temporary 35, 351, 353
    *see also* atypical workers; 'blue collar' workers;
        part-time work; temporary work
**casuistry** 148
**CEEP** 77 n. 91, 233 nn. 15, 16, 361 n. 21, 389
        n. 9, 401 n. 60, 425 n. 89
**charity work** 35
    *see also* voluntary work
**childcare** 25, 398
**Civil Codes**
    19th Century 188
    and English law 119
    a 'European' 275 n. 20
    and 'special' laws
    various national 105, 116, 119, 159, 290–1
    *see also* French Civil Code; German Civil
        Code; Italian Civil Procedure Code
**civil servants,** *see* public sector employment
**class power** 379
**co-working** 325–6
**Code of Civil Procedure** 63
**cogency rules** 225, 399, 404, 411–17, 426
**collective action** 78, 378
**collective agreements**
    Act on Collective Agreements 39 n. 27
    and common labour law 144
    and the *Conseil d'État* 65

    and continental European employment law
        94
    and the 'contract of employment' 67, 160–1,
        211
    and English Law 70, 94, 100
    in France, '*effet normatif*' 70–1, 140, 160
    in Germany 71, 122 n. 60
    guarantee arrangements under 204, 210–11
    in Italy 73, 95
    national level 65
    and regulating personal work relations 62, 64,
        100, 441
    and remuneration 206
    and the Scandinavian legal system 66
    and sickness absence 215, 220
    and statutory regulation 68, 70, 88, 102, 153,
        180
    relevance of 60
    standards derived from 92
    and termination of employment 229–30, 236
    and transformations 251
    and unfair dismissal 68
    *see also sui generis*
**collective bargaining**
    across European legal systems 51, 70–1, 200
    arrangements for 160, 326
    and employment protection 216–17, 270
    function of 183
    impact of 161
    in English Law 71–3, 161
    establishment of 69
    and normalisation 387
    norms derived from 94–102, 225, 403
    in the post-World War II era 64
    and personality in work 379
    presence or absence of 7
    and regulation 91, 171, 179, 214–15, 286,
        411, 438
    and remuneration 176
    rights for unionized workers 14
    role for 67–8
    and standardization 92, 243
    substitutes for 21
    various levels of 65, 71
    worker-protective effects of 69
**collective labour law** 15, 89, 378–9, 436
**collective** *laissez-faire* 72
**collegiality** 352
**commercial agents** 157, 273–4, 288–9, 303,
        407, 410
    Commercial Agents Directive (1986) 410
    Commercial Agents (Council Directive)
        Regulations (1993) 157
**commercial law** 39, 190
**commercial relations** 34–6
**common law**
    vs. civil law 51–5, 59–60, 179, 193, 273
    and collective bargaining 69
    concept of contractual consideration 8

of the contract of employment 198, 200,
    207–8, 213, 216–21, 243–6, 253–4,
    311
of contract and tort 244
courts of 72, 94, 153, 244
doctrine of restraint of trade 152
in Germany 102
historical inadequacy of 70
judges 217, 296
and the 'law of contract' 101
norms and doctrines of 99, 151, 184, 201–6,
    245
notion of 'implying' 187
regulation 303
rights and obligations of civil servants 142
statute, supremacy of 67, 290, 311–12
*see also* Contract of Employment; doctrine of
    entire contracts; English Law; dismissal
community
    Community Law 67, 76, 151 n. 76, 153 n. 95
    community-scale undertakings 427 n. 93
    sector organizations 145 n. 54
    *see also* European Community Law
companies
    amalgamated 254
    'associated' 255
    broadcasting 54
    director/ senior manager 35, 273, 307
    duties owed to 190
    equity in 254
    law 163
    mining 253–4
    one-person 306
    private-law 391
    public 391
    shareholders of 190
    *see also* business(es); principle of effectiveness
Comparative Law, European
    difference-focused 50
    English vs. European law 5–10
    functional methodology of 48–58, 92, 179,
        182
    as a legal science 5
    role of language in 57
    similarity-seeking 50
    *see also* English Law; French labour law;
        German labour law; Italian labour law;
        Spanish labour law
compensation
    for denial of the opportunity to work 217
    pecuniary 248, 261
    aand redundancy 441
    and voluntary workers 146
    and wrongful termination of contract 241
    *see also* remuneration
competence 7, 73, 353, 389–90, 429
competition law 95
conditionality mode 326–7, 330

conditions of formation 129–46, 176–7
confidentiality of information 261
consciousness/ self-consciousness 365
consultants 122, 285, 348–9
consumer contracts 96, 197, 275
consumption 380
continuity of employment 170, 173, 175,
    255–6
contract of employment
    analytical approach to 127
    applying labour laws beyond 34
    central paradigm of 49
    concept of 33
    content and performance of 177–221
    as the 'cornerstone' of employment law 87
    and the definitional category of the Personal
        Work Contract 104–19
    as a distinctive legal sphere 85
    formation and structure of 129–76
    'global'/ 'umbrella' 126
    as an institution 51
    institutionalisation of 47
    integrated vs. dis-integrated visions of 178,
        199–201
    the law of 9, 83–5
    performance of 199–206
    personal and organizational structure of
        157–76
    and personality 158–61
    post-employment phase 260 n. 89
    private law relationship 16–17
    public law relationship 16–17
    psychological 366
    social autonomisation of 117–18
    standardization of/ 'standard' 61, 154, 156,
        227 n. 3, 237, 242–3, 366, 446
    *see also* at-will; collective agreements;
        common law; regulatory context;
        transformation; Personal Work
        Contract
Contracts of Employment Act (1963) 69, 119,
    154, 242–3
contract labour 24, 27
Contract Labour Draft Convention (1998) 334
contract law
    commercial 287, 350
    doctrines of 132–3, 135, 147, 151, 181, 203,
        205, 220, 303, 311
    English 112, 197, 296, 300, 302
    European 78, 186 n. 8, 195 n. 37, 196, 287
        n. 43, 386 n. 2
    French 149
    general private 62, 66, 102, 150, 184–5, 191,
        214, 272, 296–7, 299, 311
    influence of 203
    Italian 149, 180
    remedies 250 n. 61
    role of 222–41

contract law (*cont.*)
 vs. statute law 101, 311
 *tout court* 188, 278 n. 25
 *see also* gross misconduct; dismissal; Italian
  labour law; *pacta sunt servanda*
contract for services
 categorization of 271
 and the contract of employment 34, 75,
  104–7, 111, 269, 285, 294, 407, 436
 and employees 302 n. 70
 independent 126
 non-personal
 personal 105–7, 109, 111–12, 121, 127–8,
  134, 136, 227, 272–6, 281, 289, 291–6,
  310, 343, 350–1, 353, 357, 434
 for personal performance 291
 with the public authority 142
 sphere of the 76, 118
 *see also* self-employment
'contract workers', concept of 23–4, 42, 122,
  320–1, 329–30, 334, 349
contractual
 co-operation 182, 300
 intention 134–46, 296
 invalidity 148–9
 perspective, narrowness of 303–8
contractualism 89–90, 207
contractuality 84–104
constructive dismissal
 *see* dismissal
co-operatives 347
corporate enterprise 163 n. 127
corporate law 252
corporate veil 163
corporatist solidarity 196
Court of Appeal 54, 138, 145, 152, 198, 295,
  321–2
'creditor' 196
criminal law 151
 *see also* homicide, law of
crisis of fundamental concepts 19–20, 38
customs, *see* HM Revenue & Customs
Cyprus 233 n. 16
Czech Republic 233 n. 16

*Danmols* doctrine 389 n. 10, 391–3, 395,
  397
DCFR (Draft Common Frame of Reference)
  78, 275, 276 nn. 21, 23, 287 n. 43, 386
  n. 2, 400–2, 429
 *see also* European Union (EU)
'debtor' 192, 196
decentralisation 73
Denmark 271, 69 n. 72
denormalisation 386–9, 401–3, 425, 430
dependency
 dependent employment 25–6, 34, 39, 95,
  109, 113, 117, 133, 189, 343, 346, 353,
  408, 437

economic 38–9
 partial 39
 *see also* subordination
deregulation 73, 96, 183, 379–81, 387, 389
derogable legislation 64
 non-derogable legislation 64
 *see also* inderogability; Italian labour law
  determinative roles/ functions 325–6
difference principle 375
dignity 10, 21–2, 32, 45, 49, 74, 181, 250, 340,
  370–8, 381–2, 428, 435
Directives (EC) *see* EC Directives
directorship 35, 190, 273, 307
disability
 anti-discriminatory legislation 145
 disabled workers 135–6
 discrimination 41
 *see also* carer, disabled; discrimination
disciplinary sanctions 254
discrimination
 age 411–12, 416–17
  Employment Equality (Age) Regulations
   (2006) 362
 anti-discrimination legislation, EU 22, 42,
  289, 330–1, 398, 424, 393, 397
 anti-semitism 196
 in employment 22, 144, 289, 302, 320–1,
  422, 424
 Employment Discrimination
  Framework Directive (2000) 362
 non-discrimination principle 69
 protection against 41, 289, 333
 race 331
 religion and belief 41
 sexual orientation 41
 *see also* disability; equal pay; Race Relations Act
  (1976)
disguised employment 40, 360
dismissal
 at will 141
 collective 225
 Collective Dismissals Directive 422
 concept of 244
 control of 257
 constructive 9, 198, 249
 and disciplinary suspension 218
 discriminatory 393–4
 formal procedure of 228, 233–4, 238
 general discipline of 102
 for personal or economic reasons 235
 just cause for 211, 213, 228, 247
 Protection Against Dismissal Act
  (*Kündigungsschutzgesetz*) 212–13
 by reason of bankruptcy 211
 by reason of pregnancy 423
 for redundancy 235
 regulation of 199
 and retirement 237
 summary 303

unfair 6–7, 9–10, 22, 68, 72, 93, 101–2,
172–3, 180, 198–9, 212, 219–20,
229–31, 235–6, 238 nn. 35, 36,
240–50, 256, 258, 302–3, 317–18,
327–30, 358, 369, 378
wrongful 101, 163, 229 n. 7, 230–1, 242–50,
303
*see also* discrimination; redundancy;
retirement; termination of employment;
unfair dismissal law
diversifying elements 60–2
Divisional Court 141
doctrine of entire contracts 202–5
domestic work 25, 102, 230, 334, 341
household work 25, 35, 440
Dual Employership 165 n. 133
Dual Regulation 241–50
*see* regulation; termination of employment
contract

EC Directives
Acquired Rights Directives 77, 166, 255–8,
270, 335, 361, 391, 411, 415, 422
Collective Dismissals Directive (1975) 422
Commercial Agents Directive (1986) 410
Commercial Agents (Council Directive)
Regulations (1993) 157
Consolidated Equality Directive (2006) 424
Directive on Pregnant Workers (1992) 423
Directive on Seasonal Work (2010) 425
EC Directive (1991) 154
Employers Insolvency Directive (1980) 422
Employment Discrimination Framework
Directive (2000) 362
Employment Equality (Age) Regulations
(2006) 362
Equal Treatment Framework Directive
(2000) 411–12, 416
European Works Council Directive (2009)
427 n. 93
Fixed Term Work Directive (1999) 232, 335,
361, 401, 403, 420 n. 80
Framework Directive on Health and Safety
(1989) 423
National Information and Consultation
Directive (2002) 427
Part-Time Work Directive (1997) 396–7,
401, 403, 425
Proof of Employment Directive (1992) 425
Temporary Agency Work Directive
(2008) 165, 335, 361, 388 n. 8, 398,
401–3, 425
Working Time Directive (1993) 77, 93, 319
n. 8, 341 n. 3, 423
economic efficiency 45
economic reality test 108
economic structures, terminology of 130–1,
167, 176

economics
Coasean 163 n. 127
and law 45
perspective 45
education
education contracts 139, 286
Education Reform Act (1988) 142 n. 41
and training 139
and volunteering 146
*eiusdem generis* contract 294
'employee'
definition of 15, 45, 57, 122–3, 125, 278–9,
302 n. 70, 342, 365, 391
'employer'
notion of 123, 162–4, 166, 324–5, 329
*see also* 'worker'
'employment'
concept of 31, 33–4, 289
and 'personal work' vs. self-employment 36,
343–4, 348
employment agency
*see* agency work
Employment Appeal Tribunal (EAT) 99 n. 25,
139, 145, 218 n. 101, 247 n. 50, 281 n.
34, 294
*see also* tribunals
employment contract
*see* contract of employment
Employment Relations Act (1996) 172 n. 143
Employment Rights Act (ERA) (1996) 15 n. 9,
39 n. 27, 87, 137 n. 16, 218 n. 102, 234,
277, 299 n. 67
engagement 22, 30–3, 43, 137
English Law
in the 1950s, 60s and 70s 67
in the 20th Century 69
and the binary divide 42–3
and Civil Codes 119
and collective agreements 70, 94, 100
collective bargaining in 71–3, 161
comparison with different legal systems
12–13, 19
concept of mutual trust 180
contract law 112, 197, 296, 300, 302
and contracts of employment 9
definition 3 n. 1
vs. European law 5–10
job security in 244–50
jurisprudence 70, 101
law of employment contracts 244–50
and termination of employment contracts
241–50
variation in employment law 207–8
'worker' concept in 115, 122, 277–8, 289
*see also* anomie; common law; United
Kingdom
enterprise
joint 305–8

enterprise *(cont.)*
  medium-sized 233
  networks 336
  small 230, 354
  protection 96
entry conditions, contractual 165, 169
EPL (Employment protection legislation) 380–1
ETUC 77 n. 91, 233 nn. 15, 16, 361 n. 21, 389
    n. 9, 401 n. 60, 425 n. 89
equality
  Employment Equality (Age Regulations
      (2006) 362
  Equal Pay Act 68 n. 65
  Equality Act (2010) 42, 68 n. 65, 72 n. 84,
      145, 362 n. 23
  Equality and Human Rights Commission
      (EHRC) 145
  principle of equal opportunities 424 n. 86
  *see also* Discrimination; EC Directives;
      Employment Rights Act (ERA)
equity 63–4, 195, 202, 206, 254, 445
*erga omnes* 70, 94, 100
Estonia 233 n. 16
Europe 2020 Agenda 427
European Commission 24, 27, 233 n. 16, 274
    n. 17, 386 n. 2, 402, 416 n. 77, 425 n.
    91, 427 n. 95, 428 n. 100
  *see also* EC Directives
European Convention on Human Rights
    (ECHR) 399, 435
European Court of Human Rights 399
European Court of Justice (ECJ) 40, 140,
    193, 215, 237, 257–8, 271, 275, 388 n. 7,
    8, 389, 391–2, 395–7, 403 n. 65, 412, 427
European Employment Strategy 388 n. 7, 427
European Labour Law
  20th Century patterns 37–43
  definition 3 n. 2
  of personal work contracts 3–4
  and Personal Work Regulation 385–99
European legal framework
  for Personal Work 428–32
  for Personal Work Relations 399–413
  *see also* European Union, regulatory layers
European Social Charter 385, 394–5
European social law 390
European social policy 377–8
European Union (EU)
  27 EU Member States 390
  anti-discrimination instruments 393
  Charter of Fundamental Rights and
      Freedoms of the EU 373
  Community Charter of the Fundamental
      Rights of Workers 395
  free movement of enterprise 78
  policy making and theoretical
      development 24
  regulatory layers 410–428
  social directives 66

social and labour law 389–90
social regulation 8, 66
Treaty on the Functioning of the European
    Union (TFEU) 392, 396, 424
*see also under individual Member States*;
    *see* DCFR (Draft Common Frame of
    Reference); EC Directives; European
    legal framework

fair dealing 185, 194–9, 210
fairness 197, 241, 278 n. 25, 374
  *see also* dismissal, Unfair; fair dealing; Unfair
      Terms in Consumer Contracts
      Regulation
false dichotomy argument 107–10, 112
'false friend' 334
false opposites 107, 109–12, 312 n. 3
false symmetries 107, 109–10, 112, 312 n. 3
false unities 107, 109, 112, 272, 312 n. 3
family-friendly work 368
  *see also* flexibility of employment
family law 39, 62
*favor* 150–1, 187
fellow-workers 191, 424
*fictio juris* 376
fidelity 185, 188–91, 195–5, 198
fiscal systems 127
fissured employment 445
fixed-term work
  fixed-term contract 54, 126, 140, 154–5,
      165, 172–3, 232, 236 n. 28, 237–8, 246,
      295, 331, 335, 361, 380, 426
  Fixed-term Employee Regulations 331
  Fixed Term Work Directive (1999) 232, 335,
      361, 401, 403, 420 n. 80
Fordist era 54
  post-Fordist era 114, 355
formality and information 153–7
formation and structure 290–300
  intention, formality and legality in 296–300
  paradigm and variety in 290–6
flexibility of employment
  flexible-firm 123
  flexible working 336, 341, 362
  numerical flexibility 381
  *see also* family-friendly work
flexicurity 77, 362–3, 369
  *Flexicurity Pathways Report* 363
  spectrum
floor of rights 52 n. 9, 65, 68, 71, 236 n. 25,
    379
floor of wages 68
framing concept 16, 23, 30, 44, 405–6,
    433–5
France
  as a coordinated market economy 55
  legal system in 60, 69–71, 144 n. 47, 271,
      345, 387–8
  *see also* French; French labour law

**franchising** 320–1, 329, 401, 445
  franchise contracts 286
**fraud** 145, 148
**free movement**
  of enterprise and service provision 78
  EU legislation 140
  of workers 40 n. 30, 389–91, 393
**freedom of association** 69, 205, 378–9
**freelancers** 285, 349
**freestanding work** 346
  *see also* autonomous work
**French**
  Civil Code 116, 195
    *louage d'ouvrage (contrat d'entreprise)* 116, 270, 276
    *louage de services* 116
    *obligation de loyauté* 189
  Commercial Code 157
  *Court de Cassation* 54
  legal discourse/ language 57
  reality television 54
    *l'Ile de la tentation* 54
**French labour law**
  *Au delà de l'emploi* 24, 27, 377 n. 57
  *bonne foi* 180, 186, 196–8
  *clauses guillotine/ couperet* 240
  *clientele, la* 306
  *Code du Travail* 70, 87, 139 n. 31, 140 n. 33, 154–5, 157 n. 118, 165 n. 130, 187 n. 10, 192, 198, 203, 219–20, 230, 235–6, 240, 255, 270, 272, 280, 296 n. 61, 318 n. 4, 334 n. 19, 355 n. 14, 402 n. 63
  *Dispositions Particulières à Certaines Professions et Activités* 280, 334 n. 19
  *exceptio non adimplenti contractus* 203, 205
  *faute lourde* 219
  *cause réelle et sérieuse de licenciement* 220
  *médecin du travail* 220
  *présomptions de salariat* 280
  *Conseil d'Etat* 65
  *contract unique* 336
  *contrat d'adhésio*n 96
  *contrat d'apprentissage* 139 n. 31, 296
  *contrat d'avenir* 140
  *contrat d'insertion Revenue Minimum d'Activité* 296
  *contrat de mission* 165 n. 131
  *contrat de professionnalisation* 140 n. 33, 296
  *Contrat de travail* 57, 90, 132, 270, 273
    *à durée determinée* 295
    *interimaire* 295
  *contrat jeune en enterprise* 296
  *contrat première embauche* 356
  *contrat unique* 363
    *d'insertion* 355
  *contrats aides* 140
  *contrepartie pécuniaire* 261
  *devoir de fidélité* 196

*Doctrine de Droit Social* 373 n. 34
*droit du travail* 13–14, 65, 66 n. 52, 283 n. 40
  *non salarié* 304–8, 334 n. 19, 443 n. 14
  *Traite du Droit du Travail* 64
*droits de tirage sociaux* 25
*effet impératif* 160
*faveur* 71
*fonds de commerce, le* 306
*licenciement* 220, 235
*Loi Fillon* 71, 73
*mandat social* 190, 308 n. 93
*nullité partielle* 149
*nullité totale* 149
*obligation de sécurité* 192
*offices ministériels* 306
*ordre public absolu* 61, 65
*ordre public économique et social* 150
*ordre public general* 151
*ordre public social* 65, 69, 94, 132, 250
*patrimoine et revenu professionnels* 306
*période d'essai* 236
*personnalité morale* 307
*préavis non travaillé* 235
*présomption de salariat* 360 n. 16
*principe du droit de résiliation unilatérale* 228
*rapports collectifs de travail* 305
*sociétés civiles professionnels* 307
*société unipersonelle* 306
*travail associé, le* 307
*travail de gestion, le* 307–8
*travail salarié* 283 n. 40, 305
*voyageur, représentant ou placier* 157
*see also* France
**French work, types of**
  *artisan* 285
  *contrat d'éducation* 139
  *dirigeant mandataire* 307 n. 91
  *dirigeants* 190
  *domestiques* 116
  *gens de travail* 117
  *dirigeants de sociétés anonyms* 273
  *journaliers* 116
  *mandataires* 273
  *particularisme* 63–4, 273
  *relations professionelles* 88
  *statut professionnel* 25–6, 102, 341–2
  *travailleur indépendant* 88, 305
  *voyageur représentant placier* 285
**full-time work** 155, 236, 301, 367, 403, 426, 432
  *see also* part-time work
**functionality** 20, 49, 78

**gang workers** 122–3
**gangmaster** 35, 335
**garden leave** 214
**gateway function** 131
**gender analysis** 377

468 *Index*

**German**
 Civil Code *(Bürgerliches Gesetzbuch (BGB))*
  195, 198, 205, 234, 255, 270–1
  *Dienstvertrag* 270, 276
  *Werkwertrag* 270
 Federal Labour Court 257
 *Grundgesetz* (Federal Constitution) 257
 jurisprudence on transfers of 257
 legal language 57
**German labour law**
 *arbeitgeber* 88
 *arbeitnehmer* 61, 88, 115, 122, 278
 *Arbeitnehmerähnliche*
  *Personen* 39 n. 27
 *Arbeitnehmerüberlassungsgesetz* 167
 *Arbeitsplatzteilung* 160
 *Arbeitsrecht* 13–14
 *Arbeitsverhältnis* 270
 *arbeitsvertrag* 88
 *Aufhebungsvertrag* 240
 *Berufsbildungsgesetz* (Vocational
  Training Act (2005)) 140
 *Betriebsrätegesetz* (Works Council Act) 228
 *Betriebsrisikolehre* 205
 *Betriebsverfassungsgesetz* (Works
  Constitution Law) 164, 230
 *Freier Mitarbeiter* 88
 *Günstigkeitsprinzip* 71
 *Handelsgesetzbuch* 88, 157, 270
 *Kündigungsschutzgesetz* 212, 230
 *persönenlich abhängig* 88
 *selbständiger* 88
 *Sozialrecht* 26, 52 n. 9
 *Tarifvertragsgesetz* 270, 278 n. 26
 *Tarifvertragsverordnung* 70
 *Teilzeit und Befristungsgesetz* 155
 *Treu und Glauben* 180, 186, 195–6
**Germany**
 as a coordinated market economy 55
 Weimar Period in 205
 *see also* German labour law; Third Reich, the
  good faith 9, 50, 111, 180–2, 185–6,
  188–9, 191, 194–9, 210–11, 250,
  300–1
**goods**, suppliers of 110, 197, 321
**Greece**, bail-out of 336 n. 28
**gross misconduct** 247
**guarantors** 326

**'hard' vs. 'soft' law** 427–8
**harassment** 289 n. 48, 351, 425
**Harrods Ltd** 329–32
**health and safety**
 of the employee 42, 194, 373, 440
  mental 187, 194
  physical 187, 194
  well-being
 Framework Directive on Health and Safety
  (1989) 423

Health and safety at Work Act (HSWA),
  (1973) 42 n. 40, 193
 as a legal right 374
 legislation 42, 191–3, 297, 393, 395, 416,
  422–3
 regulation of 333
 *see also* accidents and injuries at work; illness at
  work; sickness
**hierarchy of norms** 58–79
 *see also* regulation, sources of
**hiring** 102, 117, 130, 135, 167
**HM Revenue & Customs** 64, 138 n. 20, 139
  nn. 23, 27, 28
**holiday pay** 174
**homeworkers** 122, 124, 285
**homicide, law of** 106
 manslaughter 106
 murder 106
 *see also* criminal law
**House of Lords (UK)** 248–9, 253, 257, 299 n.
  67
**human rights legislation** 59
**Hungary** 233 n. 16

**illegality** 147–52
**illicitness** 149, 151
**illness at work** 206, 219, 378
 *see also* sick pay
**ILO (International Labour Organization)**
 Conference of 23–4
 on the Contract Labour Draft Convention
  (1998) 334
 Decent Work Agenda 373
 Declaration of Philadelphia 373
 on employment 394
 ILO labour standard-setting 23–4, 97
 Recommendation 198, 26–8
**IMF (International Monetary Fund)** 379
**immigration** 148, 428
 *see also* asylum seekers
**'implied terms' of contracts of employment**
  180–99
**'imposition'** 167–9
**incentives** 107, 165, 297–8, 351, 381
**independent contracting** 109, 343
**inderogability** 53, 68–9, 71, 151, 153, 187,
  378–9
 *see also* derogable legislation
**incapacity** 213–14, 217, 235, 387
**income security** 171, 173, 175–6, 262
**independent work**
 contracts 39
 vs. dependent work 39, 113, 344–5
 independent worker 88, 305–6
 *see also* self-employment
*inderogabilità in pejus* 71, 153
**indexation of wage increases** 64
**individualism** 89–90
**individuality** 85–104, 158–61

industrial action 204–5, 213, 217, 219, 254, 403, 441
  *see also* strike action
industrial law 67
industrial relations 67, 73, 95, 195–6, 293
Industrial Relations Act (1971) 243, 245
Industrial Revolution 343 n. 6
inequality
  *see* discrimination; equality
inflation
  *see* wage-adjustment
insolvency 422 n. 84
  *see* EC Directives, Employers Insolvency Directive
institutional
  adaptability 56
  embeddedness 44
  entrepreneurs 56, 77
  hypothesis 59
  perspective 46–50, 74
institutions, definition of 46–7
insurers 326
integration variable 73, 92 n. 14, 226–7, 435
intermittent work 170, 174, 318, 334 n. 22, 361, 392
International Labour Conference (1998) 23 n. 11, 24 nn. 12, 13; 27, 334 nn. 15, 17, 373 n. 38 nn. 15, 16, 373 n. 38
  *see also* ILO
Internship
  interns 348, 355
  *see also* apprenticeship; traineeship; work experience
intervention formula 91
Italian Civil Procedure Code 39 n. 27, 53, 63, 95, 102, 110 n. 35, 117, 122 n. 61, 151, 181 n. 2, 186, 187 n. 9, 189–92, 195–6, 205–6, 209–10, 228–30, 236 n. 27, 246 n. 27, 246–7, 256, 269, 272
  *exceptio non adimplenti contractus* 203, 205
  dismissal for *giusta causa* 246–7
  *obbligo di fedeltà* 189
  *parasubordinati* 39 n. 27, 115, 122 n. 61, 278
Italian courts
  Constitutional Court *(Corte Costituzionale)* 53, 64, 155, 363 n. 30
  Court of Cassation 73, 190
Italian Framework Agreement (2009) 73
Italian industrial relations 73, 95
Italian labour law
  *annullabilità* 149
  *autonomia negoziale* 153
  Biagi Law 122 n. 61, 156, 165 n. 131, 289 n. 48, 318 n. 4
  *buona fede* 180–1, 186, 195–6
  *certificazione* 363
  *contratti di lavoro a progetto* 156

*contratto a progetto* 293
*contratto unico* 336, 363
*decreto delega legislative* 363
*diritto del lavoro* 13–14, 63
  *il concetto del diritto del lavoro* 63
  *Nozioni di diritto del Lavoro* 63
*diritto sindacale* 14–15
*dovere di buona fede* 196
*dovere di correttezza* 196
*indennità di disponibilità* 176
*inderogabilità in pejus della disciplina legale* 153
*forma vincolata* 153
*giustificato motivo* 229
*Il rapporto di lavoro* 88
*indisponibilità del tipo contrattuale* 153
*inserzione automatica* 66
*La legge* 63
*lavoro a progetto* 39 n. 27, 122 n. 61, 156, 278 n. 27
  *Parasubordinazione* 122 n. 61
*lavoro autonomo* 269, 276 n. 22
  *contratto d'opera* 276 nn. 21, 22, 23
*lavoro intermittente* 318 n. 4
*lavoro ripartito* 160
*lavoro subordinato* 269
*leggi categoriche* 64
*leggi dispositive* 64
*locator operarum* 117
*norme inderogabili* 66
*nullità* 149
*parallelismo delle tutele* 231
*parasubordinati* 39 n. 27
*patto di prova* 236
*preavviso* 235
*pretore del lavoro* 363
*probiviri* 195
*rapporto di lavoro* 88
*recesso ad nutum* 228–9
*regolamento concordatario* 63
*rescindibilità* 149
*sistema delle fonti* 63
  *gerarchia delle fonti* 64
  *le fonti* 63
*scala mobile* 64
*sostituzione legale* 66
  *delle clausole difformi* 153
*Statuto Albertino* 63
*Statuto dei Lavoratori* 163, 192, 203, 209–10, 229–30
Italian Ministry of Welfare 156
Italian post office 210
Italian Republic, Constitution of the 63
Italian work, types of
  *dirigenti* (managers) 190
  *lavoratori a domicilio* (home-workers) 285
  *lavoratori domestici* (domestic workers) 230
*ius variandi* 211

job security 62, 171–4, 223, 228, 232, 242,
336, 380–1
in the English law of employment contracts
244–50
job-seekers 340, 391
*see also* unemployment
job-sharing 160, 326
job-training, *see* training
jobs, types of, *see* work, types of
Jurisprudence
English 70, 101
of the European Court 98, 187, 256–8, 391
French 53, 189, 237
Italian 64, 234
and legal scholarship 247
*jus cogens* 60, 92, 94, 101, 182, 337, 340, 362,
390, 398, 414
*jus dispositivum* 92, 101, 182, 337, 340, 362,
390, 399, 414
*jus variandi* 210–12

Labour Code 59, 181
French 54 n. 17, 63, 70 n. 76, 140, 154, 360
n. 16
German 70
*see also* French labour law, German labour law
labour courts 47
*see also* tribunals
Labour Law
central paradigm function 16–17
collective vs. individual 15, 89, 378–9, 436
crisis of fundamental concepts 19–20
vs. employment law 11–12, 14–15
history of 252
as a legal science/ discipline 22, 31, 62–3, 67,
153, 180, 430
meaning differences across systems 13
purpose vs. scope 20–1
relational definition of 13, 15–17, 19, 22, 47
relational scope of 11–19
relational and structural analysis of 10
and 'social law' 26
terminology 11–15
theorists, designers and practitioners of 8
translation to other languages 13
*see also* American Law; Canadian labor and
employment law; English labour law;
French labour law; German labour law;
Italian labour law; Spanish labour law
labour market
flexibility in 91
functioning of 38, 356
structures 46, 55, 57
systems 51
Latvia 233 n. 16
lay-off, economic 175, 204, 213, 217–18, 381,
441
layered regulation 85–104
contractual vs. statutory 131, 301, 337

layers of regulation theory 120, 386
and national assemblages of regulation 202
national vs. EU 390, 414–15
and the personal work relation 411, 435
self-regulation 97, 305
terminology of 52–3, 58, 73, 84
unfair vs. wrongful dismissal and 249
*see also* regulation
Learning and Skills Council 139
leave *see under* annual leave; garden leave;
maternity leave; sickness absence
liability mode 326–7, 330
liberal professions 285, 348, 352
accountancy 352
architecture 352
law 352
medicine 286, 352
*see also* work, types of
liberalisation 352, 379
Limited Liability Partnerships Act (2000) 307
n. 89
Lisbon Treaty 385, 394, 427
Lithuania 233 n. 16
Luxembourg
Court 391, 393, 396
Government 283 n. 40, 420

Malta 233 n. 16
marginal workers 356
market economies
coordinated 55
liberal 55
Marxism 376–7
master and servant relations 116, 158–60, 228,
253, 365
law of master of servant 184
maternity leave 214, 423
*see also* parenthood leave; pregnancy leave
military service 206, 214
minimum labour standards 21, 242
minimum wage
legislation 45, 138, 146, 295, 301
National Minimum Wage Act (1998) 122 n.
62, 138, 146
misconduct 235, 237, 246–7, 303
*see also* gross misconduct
modality
of autonomy 125
of subordination 125
modernity 338 n. 1
moral philosophy, Christian 375
moulds and matrices 54
multidimensional analysis 120–8
multilateralisation 166
mutable diversity hypothesis 57
mutual obligation
continuing 34, 169, 171, 175
contractual 54
doctrine of 172

from French restrictive covenants 261
mutuality of obligation test 108
notion of 'mutuality of obligation' 111–12,
    125, 145, 169–70, 174, 175 n. 151,
    281–3, 293, 393
performance of 209
of trust and confidence 9, 199, 301
**mutual trust**
English concept of 180
and good faith 186, 194–9
implied obligation of 9, 111–12, 163, 186,
    194–9, 213, 219, 244, 249–50, 301, 303
**mutualization/ de-mutualization** 433–46

**National Insurance System** 204
**Netherlands, the** 118, 144 n. 47, 276 n. 21
Contracts of Employment Statute (1908) 118
*opdracht* 276 n. 21
**New Deal** 138
*see also* job-training; United Kingdom,
    government of the normative
    characterization
cross-European comparison 10, 319, 323,
    386, 389, 392–3, 398, 417
in English labour law 43
notion of 6, 8, 313, 317–18, 321–2
of personal work relations 6–7, 313–14, 328,
    396, 403, 411–12, 414, 418
process of 331, 337
*see also* regulatory context
**notice period** 228, 234
*see also* **termination of employment**

**obedience** 188–91, 194
**occasional work** 35, 174
*see also* casual work
**OECD** (Organisation for Economic
    Co- operation and Development) 336 n.
    28, 379–81
**office-holding** 140–4
**on-call work** 122–4, 176, 318–19, 334, 391,
    396, 423
**on-demand work** 318
**open-ended contract** 155, 172, 222, 228,
    232–4, 236–40, 247, 334 n. 22
**outworkers** 122, 124
*ordre public absolu* 61, 65
*ordre public relatif, dit "social"* 132
*ordre public social* 65, 69, 94, 132, 250

*pacta sunt servanda* 210
**parenthood leave** 213, 217, 387
*see also* maternity leave; **pregnancy leave**
**Parliamentary supremacy** 67
**part-time work**
as 'atypical' work 348, 396
Framework Agreement on 77 n. 91,
    389 n. 9, 392
French regulation of 155

in Italy and Spain 156
Law on Part-Time Work and Temporary
    Employment Contracts 155
Part-Time Work Directive (1997) 396–7,
    401, 403, 425
and patterns of work 432
personal work nexus 426
social acceptance of 155
temporary agency 367
and 'standard' employment 351
**partnership** 307, 352
partners 42, 95, 160, 275
*see also* Limited Liability Partnerships Act
**paternalism** 196
**path departure** 388
**path-dependency** 9–10, 418
*see also* system-specificity
**payment reference period** 202
**PEL SC** 275 n. 20, 276 n. 21
**pensions**
entitlement to 224
flexible 444 n. 16
occupational pension arrangements
    261–2, 444
pension benefits 326
pension entitlement 224
pension fund 326
pension providers 262
pensionable age 224
pensioners 262
*see also* retirement
**performance**
and content 300–2
integration and dis-integration 199–201
and remuneration, continuity of 203–6
and termination 300–3
and the wage-work bargain 201–3
'**personal,' terminology of** 32–3, 84, 407, 434
**Personal Task Contract** 290–6, 381
'**personal work,' terminology of** 31, 33,
    43, 434
**Personal Work Arrangements**
de-normalisation of 386–90
**Personal Work Contract**
as a definitional category 104–19, 267–8
economic structure of 167–76
individual contractuality 84, 95
the law of
    individuality and contractuality 89–96
    as regulatory modelling 86
    as layered regulation 96–104
medium-term and long-term 127
other than the Contract of
    Employment 267–96
system-specific notion of 99
*see also* contract of employment; layered
    regulation
**Personal Work Nexus**
complex varieties of 355–7, 412–14, 424

**Personal Work Nexus** (*cont.*)
  concept/ notion of the 4, 28, 30, 399, 404,
    428
  contract and relationship within 322–3
  directly employed 426
  evolution of 353
  fixed-term 426
  full-time 426
  legal connections of 323–30
  part-time 426
  patterns of 418, 421–2, 426
  and the Personal Work Profile 423, 435
  and the Personal Work Relation 74–6, 83,
    309–22, 330–40, 349, 350–2
  temporary agency 426
  transformative role 425
**Personal Work Profile**
  idea of 340–4
  and legal characterization 358–64
  and the Personal Work Nexus 423, 435
  and Personal Work Relations 358–69
  and the personal work situation 340–2
  and personality in work 338–82
  as a regulatory framework 364–9
  and working life/ career 342–4
**Personal Work Regulation**
  and European Law 385–99
  fragmentation of 430
**Personal Work Relation(s)**
  alignment with existing categories 36–43
  as a Complex Network/ Nexus 315–23
  conceptual definition of 29, 315
  as a contract 83–264
  critical taxonomy of 344–69
  as the domain of labour law 19–28
  European Common Legal Framework for
    399–413
    methodology 404–5
    objectives and components 400–4
  in European Law 385–432, 405–10
  a functional definition of 18–36
  legal analysis of 3, 79
    boundaries, paradigms and legal
      formats 11–43
    contractual construction of 120–8
    European comparative approach to 44–79
  legal construction of
    as contracts 83–128
    Contract, Relation and Nexus 309–37
    defining the notion 5–6
    and the role of European Law 385–432
    evolution and reformulation in 3–10
    path-dependency 9–10
    mutualization and demutualization in
      433–46
  *see also* Comparative Law, European
  as a legal nexus 267–308
  notion of 5, 21

  and the Personal Work Nexus 310–22,
    330–7
  and the Personal Work Profile 358–69
  as a 'soft' boundary for labour law 29
  values in the legal handling of 10
**'personality'**
  of contracts of employment 158–61
  of the employee 124–5, 191, 213, 281–2
  legal 307
**Personality in Work** 10
  concept of 10, 21, 30, 74, 162, 324, 339–82,
    386, 404, 429, 435, 437, 439–40
  and dignity 21
  functional critique of 10
  and the Personal Work Profile 338–82
  as a set of values 370–82
    Capability 377–9
    Dignity 372–6
    Stability 379–82
  vindicating of 438
**'personalness'** 124
**'personhood'** 375
**placements, work** 35
**Poland** 233 n. 16, 394 n. 41
**political philosophy** 374
**political science** 46
**Portugal** 271
**Portuguese labour law** 293
  *contrato de trabalho come regime especial* 293
**post-traumatic stress disorder (PTSD)** 194
  *see also* health and safety at work
**precarious employment** 170, 172
**pregnancy in employment**
  dismissal by reason of 206, 217, 423
  Directive on Pregnant Workers (1992) 423
  pregnancy leave 368
  *see also* parenthood leave; maternity leave
**preliminary contract** 262
**principle of effectiveness** 155
**priority of liberty principle** 375
**private law**
  employment relationship 16–17, 140
  European 78, 197, 275, 386, 400, 402
  general 52
  of contract 34, 52, 116–18, 289
  vs. public law 16, 142, 311–12
  *see also* Civil Codes; companies; DCFR (Draft
    Common Frame of Reference); fair
    dealing; good faith; public law
**private sector employment** 100, 294
  *see also* work, types of
**privatisation** 352
**probationary period** 234, 236–8, 248, 336, 395
  *see also* termination of employment
**professional bodies** 305, 352, 443
**professions, range of,** *see* work, types of
**pseudo-contracts** 115
**public authorities** 142, 352, 355

public functionary 35, 352
public law
  employment relationships 17, 62
  in France 143, 262
  general 67
  obligations of 78 n. 94
  vs. private law 16, 142, 311–12
  status 352, 391
  *see also* private law; public sector employment
public office holders 42, 140–3
  *see also* public sector employment
public sector employment
  and 'Big Society' 347
  civil servants 141–2, 144, 394
  classes of workers in 144
  police officers 42
  prison officers 142
  *see also* Spanish labour law, Basic
    Statute for Public Servants
public subsidies 381
punitive deductions 202
pupillage 138
  *see also* apprenticeship; barristers, pupil;
    traineeship
purpose/relational scope equation 24, 28,
    36, 44–5, 49, 74

quasi-dependence
  in Germany 289 n. 48
  notion of 283
  regulating 115
  worker's contract 289

race discrimination law 331
  Race Relations Act (1976) 321
  *see also* discrimination
*ratione materiae* 72
recession 381
recombinant governance 56
Recommendation on the Employment
    Relationship 24
redundancy
  collective 236 n. 23, 420 n. 82, 422 n. 84
  dismissal for 235
  and grounds for termination 235, 237
  imposition of 225, 441
  payments
    legislation 207–8, 243
    norms on 68, 208
  proposed 224
  protection against 395
  Redundancy Payments Act (1965) 69,
    207 n. 73, 243
  *see also* dismissal; termination of employment
regulation
  of agency work 334–5
  of casual employment 168, 170
  of collective agreements 68, 70, 88, 102,
    153, 180
  of collective bargaining 91, 171, 179,
    214–15, 286, 411, 438
  common law 303
  Dual 241–50
  and European Law 385–99
  external sources of 200, 205, 207–8, 251
  of health and safety 333
  multilayered 410–13
  of Personal Work Relations 358–69
  regulatory context 6–9
  sources of 58–79
  of the suspension of employment 213–21
  of the termination of employment 222–64
  of the welfare state 68
  of working time 22, 139
  *see also* deregulation; dismissal; EC Directives;
    layered regulation
'relation,' concept of 31–2, 43, 434
religious employment
  ministers of religion 143
  religious office-holding 143
remuneration
  and collective agreements 206
  and collective bargaining 176
  continuity of 203–6
  provision of remunerated work 171–6
  and working time 168, 170
  *see also* compensation; pensions; redundancy
    payments; salaried employee; wage
    earner
re-qualification 130
restitution 205, 261
resumption of employment 261–2
retirement
  arrangements concerning 234, 236, 362
  default age of 237, 362
    in France and the UK 237
  early 326
  mandatory 239–40, 417
  notion of 224
  Repeal of Retirement Age Provisions 417 n. 78
  savings 444
  and termination of employment 238, 412,
    416–17
  *see also* pensions; termination of employment
risk
  and bureaucratic control 126
  and employer liability 191, 205, 372
  mutualization of 433, 439–45
  risk transfer/ legal exclusion paradox 206, 294
  risks to workers 333, 352, 395, 439–45
  of unemployment 387
  *see also* health and safety at work; job security;
    termination of employment
rogue's charter 93
Roman Law, classical 52, 113, 116, 205, 291
  *exceptio non adimplenti contractus* 203, 205
  *locatio conductio operarum* 52, 113, 116–17,
    159, 291

Roman Law, classical (*cont.*)
  *locatio conductio operis* 52, 113, 116–17, 272,
    276, 291
  *see also* Italian labour law

'salaried employee' 204
salary, deferred 261
savings rates 380
Scandinavian legal system 66
  *see also* Swedish Employment Protection Act
seasonal work
  Directive on Seasonal Work (2010) 425
security
  income, *see* income security
  job, *see* job security
self-employment
  category of 51, 156, 410
  and discrimination 41–3, 394
  vs. employment 36, 40, 113–17, 276 nn. 21,
    22, 295, 311, 343–4, 348, 361
  independent/ autonomous worker 39, 289 n.
    48
  in Italy 53, 289 n. 48
  and tax evasion 148
  and transformation 261, 263
  *see also* contract for services
self-ownership 373–4
servants
  *see* master-servant relations
'service' 201
  *see also* 'willingness to work'
service contracts 275–6, 401
  *see also* contract for services
Shaeffer Pens (UK) Ltd 321–2, 330
sham contract 152, 298–9, 360
short-term work 127, 168, 379
sickness
  sick pay 204, 218
  sickness absence 204, 218, 340, 368
  *see also* accidents and injury at work;
    illness at work
single contract 173, 224, 272, 285, 289,
    366, 443, 437 n. 12
Slovakia 233 n. 16
Slovenia 233 n. 16
social drawing rights 25–6, 342
social insurance law 378
social justice
  and distribution of income 374 n. 48, 375 n. 50
  in European Contract Law 186 n. 8, 287 n. 43
  for workers 45
social security law
  and the binary divide 108
  broad sense of 26 n. 20
  Social Security Contributions and Benefits Act
    (1992) 218 n. 103
  and pensions 224
  and the personal work profile 342
  post-war 119

regulatory context of 296–7
  and tax 48, 297–8
socio-economics 86, 347, 349, 351
sociology of employment relations 444
solicitor-client relations 292
solidarity
  and good faith 186, 196, 374
  international 146
Spanish
  labour law
    Basic Statute for Public Servants 144
    *contrato de obra* 276 nn. 21, 22, 23
    *contrato de servicio* 276 n. 21
    *contrato único* 363
    *derecho del trabajo* 13
    *Trabajadores autónomos económicamente
      dependientes (TRADES)* 39 n. 27, 61,
      115, 279 n. 29
  legal language 57
  workers
    *functionarios de carrera* (career civil
      servants) 144
    *personal laboral* (working personnel) 144
  Workers' Statute 133
sponsors 326
stability 379–82
stable employment relationship 392
strike action 204, 218, 379
  *see also* industrial action
sub-contracting 115, 165 n. 131, 333
subordination, notion of 34, 38–9, 117–18,
    125–6, 159, 170, 188, 190, 228 n. 4,
    283, 316, 370–1, 390
  quasi-subordination 38–9
  *see also* dependency; Italian labour law
*sui generis* 61–2, 140
Supiot Commission 25
Supiot Report, The 24–8
suspension of employment
  disciplinary 217–18, 220 n. 108
  investigatory 213–14, 217
  precautionary 213–14, 217
  regulation of 213–21
  and termination of employment 213–17
Swedish Employment Protection Act 66
  *see also* Scandanavian legal system
*synallagma, causa* 170
system-specificity 10, 418
  *see also* path-dependency

tax
  and social security law 48, 151, 297–8
  tax cases 122 n. 63, 124 n. 79
  tax evasion 148
  tax fraud 148
  tax law 108
Telecom Italia Spa 391
temporary work 155, 353, 380
  *see also* agency work; part-time work

termination, of employment contracts
Dual regulation 241–50
duration of 231–8
grounds and procedures for 239–41
integrated vs. disintegrated paradigm 223–4
and performance 300–3
procedure for 234
regulation of 222–64
regulation and integration 224–31
and the role of contract law 222–31
and transformation 222–64, 302–3
wrongful 102, 112, 218, 239, 241
*see also* dismissal; notice; probation;
retirement
**thick vs. thin stratum approach** 102–3
**Third Reich**, the 196
**tort**
common law of 72, 219, 244
liability 205, 327
of negligence 193–4
**trade associations** 305, 403
**trade, restraint of** 112, 134, 147–8, 152–3,
157
**trade unions** 24, 63, 70, 73, 440, 443
**training**
job-training 138–9
trainees 35, 123, 137–40, 348, 355–6, 391
*see also* apprenticeships; internship; New Deal;
work experience
**transfer of employment** 254–5, 422
**transfer of undertakings** 77 n. 89, 255 n. 67,
256, 302 n. 70, 335 n. 24, 361 n. 20,
411 n. 71, 416
Transfer of Undertakings (Protection of
Employment)) Regulations (TUPE)
256–8, 302–3, 335, 361, 416
**transformation**
of the contract of employment 199, 262
and termination 222–64, 259–64, 302–3
**triangulation** 166
triangular work relations 23
**tribunals, employment** 47, 72, 99 n. 25, 108,
132, 148, 150, 166, 174–6, 208, 244
*see also* EAT
**Truck Acts** 202
**Turkish nationals** 140

**UMP** 336 n. 28, 363 n. 25
**unemployment** 355, 378, 380–1, 387
*see also* job-seekers
**unfair dismissal law** 7, 22, 230, 378
**Unfair Terms in Consumer Contracts
Regulation** (1999) 197
**UNICE** 77 n. 91, 233 nn. 15, 16, 361 n. 21,
389 n. 9, 401 n. 60, 425 n. 89
**United Kingdom**, the
and the Charter of Fundamental Rights 394
n. 41
collective bargaining in 161

Department for Business, Innovation and
Skills 362 n. 23
Department of Trade and Industry, UK
(DTI) 146
government of Coalition government 347,
362
*see also* Big Society policy
New Labour government 122, 139 n. 23,
377 n. 66
*see also* New Deal
Secretary of State 68
laws of the 3 n. 1, 144
and pension provision 444
regulatory frameworks in 144 n. 47
*see also* House of Lords
**Universal Declaration of Human Rights**
(UDHR) 373
**universalist argument** 113
**unpaid work** 25, 340, 440
*see also* carer, disabled; childcare; domestic
work; job-seeker
**unreliability problem** 57–8
**upward harmonisation** 49

**values**
*see* dignity; capability; stability
**variation** 206–13
from a comparative perspective 208–13
contractual 208–9, 213, 258
in English employment law 207–8
**varieties of capitalism thesis** 51, 55–6
*see also* capitalism
**vicarious liability, law of** 108, 163
**voidability** 149
**voluntarism** 67
voluntarist approach 183
**voluntary work** 35, 144–7, 356
youth volunteering 146
*see also* charity work

**wage-adjustment** 64
*see also* inflation; Italian labour law, *scala
mobile*
**'wage-earner'** 204
**wage-work bargain**
and maximum hours of work 378
and performance 201–3
regulation of 178
**Wages Act** (1986) 202
**welfare state**
post-war 114, 403
regulation of the 68
**'white collar' workers** 110, 190, 388
*see also* 'blue collar' workers; work,
types of
**White Paper on the Future of the Public Service**
(2008) 143
**'willingness to work'** 201, 203–5
*see also* 'service'

**work experience** 137, 139, 144
 *see also* apprenticeship; internship; traineeship;
  work experience
**work, types of**
 agents 274
 'blue collar' 110, 114, 190, 388
  factory worker 190
  day labourers 116
  domestic servants 116
  manual worker 236 n. 28
  plumbing trade 353
  workmen 15, 343
 commercial
  agent 157, 273–4, 285, 288–9, 303,
   407, 410
  traveller 285, 289
 domestic workers 102, 230, 334
 entertainment industry 120, 275, 285
 home-workers 285, 334
 media industry 120, 285
  journalists 334
 medical practice 286
  doctor 273, 352
  pharmacist 273
 professional activity/ services 275, 305–6,
  407, 409–10
  consultancy services 120, 263, 286
 sportsperson 120, 273, 275, 285, 334
  professional athlete 102, 230, 395
  sports contracts 275
 travel and tourism
  mobile transport activities 407, 409
  tour guides 124
  travelling salesperson 203, 334
 'white collar' 110, 190, 388
  bank director 190
  clerical worker 117
  company director 273, 307
  corporate executive 273
  executive/ senior manager 190, 307 n. 91
  managers 102, 164, 190, 230, 351
 *see also* liberal professions; public sector
  employment
**'worker'**
 definition of 122–3, 125, 138, 140, 145,
  277–8, 280–1, 389, 391–6

 and pupil barristers 138, 295
 relation with 'employer' 407, 423
 relational category of 39 n. 27, 41, 45, 342
  in English employment law 115, 122,
   277–8, 289
  typology of 15
  and voluntary work 123
 *see also* 'employee'; 'employer'; 'worker's
  contract' concept
**worker-protectiveness** 51, 147–8
 worker-protective legislation 93–4, 96,
  184–5, 195, 200, 208, 213, 217, 279
**'worker's contract' concept** 42
**working conditions**
 changes to 209–10, 212–13
 directives on 391
 fair and just 394
 improvement of 293 n. 54
 of the salaried worker 65
 and working environment 13, 16
**working life** 237, 340, 342–4, 364–7, 367, 374,
  378
 *see also* career
**working person**, terminology of the 107–8
 *see also* employees
**working time**
 conception of 77
 legislation controlling 45, 66 n. 56, 77 n. 90,
  393
 and mobile road transport 40 n. 30, 409 n. 69
 regulation of 22, 301, 341
  Working Time Regulations (1998) 139
 and remuneration 168, 170
 and self-employment 88
 Working Time Directive (1993) 77, 93, 319
  n. 8, 341 n. 3, 423
 working week 93, 175
**works council**
 European 427 n. 93
 in Germany 71, 212
 involvement in dismissal procedures 228
 jurisdiction of 71
 *see also* EC Directives
**World War II** 183, 196, 229, 254

**zero-hours contracts** 175, 318